NORTH AMERICAN
EXPLORATION

MICHAEL GOLAY
JOHN S. BOWMAN

CASTLE BOOKS

This edition published in 2006 by
CASTLE BOOKS ®
A division of Book Sales, Inc.
114 Northfield Avenue
Edison, NJ 08837

This edition published by arrangement with and permission of
John Wiley & Sons, Inc.
111 River Street
Hoboken, New Jersey 07030

Originally published by John Wiley & Sons, Inc., Hoboken, New Jersey.
Published simultaneously in Canada.

Photo credits: Courtesy John S. Bowman: 4, 63, 71, 73, 104, 354, 468; Courtesy Library of Congress: 11, 34, 46, 70, 82, 100, 107, 119, 138, 141, 145, 147, 178, 185, 202, 208, 223, 224, 240, 249, 254, 257, 262, 263, 282, 287, 291, 297, 307, 314, 355, 392, 400, 412, 418, 434, 436, 442, 444, 474, 492; Courtesy National Archives: 54, 112, 218, 220, 232, 331, 338, 340, 345, 349, 351, 360, 370, 375, 380, 388, 393; © Philip Baird/www.anthroarcheart.org: 7; Courtesy Dawn Ferreira, Mystery Hill, America's Stonehenge: 14; Courtesy Winterville Mounds, Mississippi Department of Archives and History, photo taken by John Sullivan: 18; Photo Parks Canada/Andre Cornellier: 23; Courtesy Library of Congress, Geography and Map Division: 29, 481; Courtesy Idaho State Historical Society: 37; Runestone Museum Foundation: 45; Adapted from map © RMC, R. L. 02-8-61, www.randmcnally.com: 57, 124, 395; University of Toronto: 140; Courtesy U.S. Navy: 464

Design and production by Navta Associates, Inc.

Library of Congress Cataloging-in-Publication Data

Golay, Michael, date.
   North American Exploration / Michael Golay, John S. Bowman.
        p.   cm.
   Includes bibliographical references and index.
      1. North America—Discovery and exploration—Encyclopedias. I. Bowman, John
   Stewart, 1931-   II. Title

E101.G63 2003
917.04—dc21   2002027434

ISBN-13: 978-0-7858-2258-5
ISBN-10: 0-7858-2258-5

Printed in the United States of America

Contents

Acknowledgments   x

Introduction   1

PART I   **North America before Columbus**   **5**

Africans	6	Libyans	26
Antilia	7	maps	26
Asians	8	Markland	32
Bjarni Herjolfsson	10	Muslims	32
Brendan, Saint	11	Native Americans	33
Bristol, England	12	navigation	37
Celts	14	Newfoundland	44
Day, John	15	Norse	45
disputed claims for		Phoenicians	46
pre-Columbian contacts	16	Pining and Pothorst	46
Egyptians	18	Piri Reis map	47
Erik the Red	18	Scolvus, Johannes	48
Greeks	19	Sinclair, Henry	48
Greenland	20	skraelings	49
Helluland	21	Vinland	49
Henry the Navigator	21	Vinland Map	52
Irish	22	Welsh	53
L'Anse aux Meadows	22	Zeno brothers	54
Leif Eriksson	24		

PART II   **The Spanish Enter the New World,**
               1492–1635   **56**

Alarcón, Hernando de	58	Alvarado, Pedro de	59
Alvarado, Hernando de	58	Anian, Strait of	61

Balboa, Vasco Núñez de 61
Bolaños, Francisco de 62
Bosque and Larios
　expedition 62
Cabeza de Vaca, Álvar
　Núñez 62
Cabrillo, Juan Rodríguez 64
Carvajal y de la Cueva,
　Luís de 66
Castaño de Sosa, Gaspar 66
Cermeño, Sebastián
　Rodríguez 66
Columbus, Christopher 68
Coronado, Francisco
　Vásquez de 73
Cortés, Hernán 76
Cosa, Juan de la 78
Cuba 79
Diaz, Melchior 80
disease 80
Drake, Sir Francis 84
Espejo and Beltrán
　expedition 86
Estevánico 87
Fuca, Juan de 88
Gali, Francisco 90
Grijalva, Juan de 90
Gutiérrez de Humaña and
　Leyva de Bonilla
　expedition 91
Hernández de Córdoba,
　Francisco de (1) 92

Hernández de Córdoba,
　Francisco de (2) 93
Hispaniola 94
Jiménez, Fortún 95
Lavazares, Guido de 95
legendary destinations 96
López de Cárdenas, García 99
Marcos de Niza 99
Montejo, Francisco 101
Moscoso Alvarado,
　Luís de 102
Narváez, Pánfilo de 103
New Spain 104
Ocampo, Sebastián 105
Ojeda, Alonso de 106
Oñate, Juan de 107
papal bulls 109
Pizarro, Francisco 110
Possession, Spanish
　Act of 110
Pueblo Indians 112
Puerto Rico 114
Rodríguez, Agustín 115
Salas-López expedition 116
Tordesillas, Treaty of 116
Ulloa, Francisco de 118
Unamuno, Pedro de 118
Vespucci, Amerigo 119
Vizcaíno, Sebastián 120
Zaldívar, Vicente de 122

PART III **The Atlantic Seaboard, 1497–1680** **123**

Abenaki 125
Acadia 126
Alaminos, Antonio de 126
Algonquin 127
Alvarez de Pineda, Alonso 128
Amadas-Barlowe expedition 128
Ayllón, Lucas Vásquez de 129
Batts-Fallam expedition 130

Beothuk 131
Bland-Wood expedition 132
Blue Ridge Mountains 132
Boston 133
Brûlé, Étienne 133
Bry, Théodore de 134
Byrd, William II 135
Cabot, John 135

Cabot, Sebastian	138	Lederer, John	167
Cape Cod	138	Luna y Arellano, Tristán de	167
Cartier, Jacques	139	Martyr, Peter	168
Champlain, Samuel de	145	Menéndez de Avilés,	
Chesapeake Bay	148	Pedro	168
Chozas and Salas		Needham and Arthur	
expedition	149	expedition	170
Corte-Réal expeditions	150	Newfoundland	171
Fagundes, João Alvarez	150	New France	172
Fernandes, João	151	Norumbega	172
Fernández de Écija,		Oldham, John	173
Francisco	151	Pardo, Juan	173
Florida	152	Ponce de León, Juan	174
François I	153	Quejo, Pedro de	175
Funk Island	153	Raleigh, Sir Walter	176
Gilbert, Sir Humphrey	154	Ribaut and Laudonnière	
Gómes, Estevåo	155	expeditions	177
González, Vicente	156	Roanoke Colony	178
Gosnold, Bartholomew	157	Roberval, Sieur de	180
Grenville expeditions	158	Rut, John	181
Hakluyt, Richard	160	Saguenay	181
Hariot, Thomas	161	St. Lawrence River	182
Hochelaga	162	Sandford, Robert	182
Hore, Richard	162	Smith, John	183
Huron	162	Soto, Hernando de	184
Ingram, David	163	Velázquez, Antonio	187
Jamestown	164	Verrazano, Giovanni da	187
Jerome and Rocque		Villafañe, Ángel de	191
expedition	164	Waymouth, George	192
Labrador	165	Wood, Abraham	193
Lane, Ralph	166	Woodward, Henry	194

PART IV **Exploring West of the Mississippi, 1635–1800** **195**

Agreda, María de Jesus	197	Barroto, Juan Enríquez	203
Aguayo, Marqués de		Bodega y Quadra, Juan	
San Miguel de	198	Francisco de la	205
Aguirre, Pedro de	199	Casa Calvo, Sebastián Calvo	
Alarcón, Martín de	199	de la Puerta y O'Farril,	
Anza, Juan Bautista de	200	Marqués de	207
Aranda, Miguel de	202	Cook, James	207
Barreiro, Francisco Alvarez	203	Del Río, Domingo	209

Escalante and Domínguez
  expedition   210
Escandón, José de   211
Espinosa, Isidro Félix de   212
Espinosa-Olivares-Aguirre
  expedition   212
Evia, José Antonio de   213
Fagés, Pedro   214
Finiels, Nicolas de   215
Garcés, Francisco Tomás   216
Grenier, Chevalier   217
Guadalajara, Diego de   217
Hezeta, Bruno de   218
Kino, Eusebio Francisco   220
La Pérouse, Jean-François
  Galaup, Comte de   221
León, Alonso de   222
Malaspina, Alejandro   224
Martín-Castillo expedition   225
Martínez, Esteban José   225
Mendoza-López
  expedition   227
Olivares, Antonio de San
  Buenaventura y   228
Ortiz Parrilla, Diego   228

Pérez, Juan José Pérez
  Hernández   229
Pez and López de Gamarra
  expedition   230
Portolá, Gaspar de   231
Posada, Alonso de   233
Quimper, Manuel   234
Rivas and Iriarte
  expedition   235
Rivera, Juan María de   235
Rivera, Pedro de   236
Rivera y Moncada,
  Fernando de   237
Rubí, María Pignatelli
  Rubí Corbera y San
  Climent, Marqués de   238
Serra, Father Junípero   239
Sútil and Mexicana
  expedition   242
Terán de los Ríos,
  Domingo de   243
Uribarri, Juan de   244
Valverde y Cosio, Antonio   245
Vargas, Diego José de   246
Villasur, Pedro de   247

PART V   From the Appalachians to the
           Mississippi, 1540–1840   **248**

Albanel, Charles   250
Allouez, Claude Jean   251
Appalachian Mountains   251
Bartram, John   252
Béranger, Jean   253
Bienville, Jean-Baptiste Le
  Moyne, Sieur de   254
Blanpain, Joseph   255
Bond, William   255
Boone, Daniel   256
Brébeuf, Jean de   258

Cadillac, Antoine
  de La Mothe   258
Cahokia   259
Carver, Jonathan   260
Catesby, Mark   261
Céloron de Blainville,
  Pierre-Joseph   262
Charlevoix, Pierre
  François Xavier de   263
Chaussegros de Léry,
  Gaspard-Joseph   263
Cherokee   264

Chickasaw	264	Lahontan, Louis-Armand de Lom d'Arce, Baron de	290
Choctaw	265		
Collot, Georges Henri Victor	265		
Couture, Jean	267	La Salle, René Robert Cavelier, Sieur de	291
Creek Confederacy	267	Le Sueur, Pierre-Charles	293
Cumberland Gap	268	Louisiana	294
Dablon, Claude	269	Mézières, Athanase de	294
Daumont de Saint-Lusson, Simon François	270	Miami	295
Delaware	270	Michaux, André	296
Derbanne, François Guyon Des Prés	271	Mississippi River	297
		Montreal	298
Dollier and Galinée expedition	272	Nicolet, Jean	298
		Nicollet, Joseph Nicolas	299
Druillettes, Gabriel	273	Nolan, Philip	300
Dulhut, Daniel Greysolon	274	Noyon, Jacques de	301
Dunbar, William	275	Ohio River	301
Dutisné, Claude-Charles	276	Peré, Jean	302
Fort Michilimackinac	277	Robutel de la Noue, Zacharie	303
Freeman, Thomas	277		
Gist, Christopher	279	Rogers, Robert	303
Grosseilliers and Radisson expeditions	280	Roseboom, Johannes	304
		Sagean, Mathieu	305
Hennepin, Louis	282	Saint-Denis, Louis Juchereau de	306
Iberville, Pierre Le Moyne, Sieur d'	283	Schoolcraft, Henry Rowe	307
Illinois	284	Sioux	307
Jesuit missionaries	285	Spotswood, Alexander	309
Jogues, Isaac	286	Tonty, Henri	309
Jolliet and Marquette expedition	287	Viele, Arnold	310
		Walker, Thomas	311
Kelsey, Henry	289	Welch, Thomas	312

PART VI Across the North American Continent, 1720–1880 313

American Fur Company	315	Bent's Fort	318
Ashley, William Henry	316	Bidwell, John	318
Astor, John Jacob	317	Blackfoot	319
Bannock	317	Bonneville, Benjamin Louis Eulalie de	319
Benton, Thomas Hart	318		

Bourgmond, Etienne Venard de	320
Bridger, James	322
Broughton, Henry	322
California Trail	323
Carson, Kit	324
Chouteau, Auguste Pierre	324
Clark, William	325
Colter, John	325
Columbia River	326
Continental Divide	327
Corps of Topographical Engineers	328
Davis, Jefferson	328
De Voto, Bernard Augustine	329
Dutton, Clarence	329
Emory, William H.	330
Fidler, Peter	331
Fitzpatrick, Thomas	332
Fort Astoria	332
Fort Hall	333
Fort Laramie	333
Fort Vancouver	334
Fraser, Simon	334
Frémont, Jessie Benton	335
Frémont, John Charles	336
Grand Canyon	340
Grand Teton Mountains	340
Gray, Robert	341
Great American Desert	341
Gros Ventre	342
Hayden, Ferdinand Vandeveer	343
Henday, Anthony	343
Henry, Andrew	344
Holmes, William H.	344
Hudson's Bay Company	345
Humboldt River	347
Hunt, Wilson Price	348
Irving, Washington	348
Ives and Macomb surveys	349
Jefferson, Thomas	350
King, Clarence	351
La Harpe, Jean-Baptiste Bénard, Sieur de	352
La Vérendrye, Pierre Gaultier Varenne, Sieur de	353
Lewis, Meriwether	353
Lewis and Clark expedition	354
Lisa, Manuel	358
Long, Stephen H.	359
Louisiana Purchase	360
Mackay-Evans expedition	361
Mackenzie, Alexander	361
Mackenzie, Donald	365
Mallet expeditions	365
Manifest Destiny	366
Marcy, Randolph Barnes	367
Missouri River	367
Muir, John	368
North West Company	369
Ogden, Peter Skene	369
Oregon Trail	370
Pacific Railroad surveys	371
Palliser and Hind surveys	372
Parker, Samuel	373
Pattie, James Ohio	374
Pike, Zebulon	375
Platte River	376
Pond, Peter	377
Powell, John Wesley	378
Rocky Mountains	380
St. Louis	381
Sierra Nevada	382
Smith, Jedediah	382
Stuart, Robert	384
Sublette, William	386
Thompson, David	386
U.S. Geological Survey	388
Vancouver, George	389
Warren, Gouverneur Kemble	389
Wheeler, George M.	390
Wilkes exploring expedition	392
Yellowstone expeditions	393

PART VII The Arctic and Northernmost Regions, 1576–1992 394

Amundsen, Roald	396	Hudson, Henry	444
Anderson, William	399	James, Thomas	445
Back, George	401	Kane, Elisha Kent	446
Baffin, William	401	Kashevarov, Alexander	
Baffin Island	402	Filippovich	448
Baranov, Alexander		Kellett, Sir Henry	448
Andreevich	403	Knight, James	449
Bartlett, Robert A.	404	Kotzebue, Otto von	450
Bering, Vitus	405	MacMillan, Donald B.	450
Bernier, Joseph-Elzéar	407	McClintock, Francis Leopold	452
Boyd, Louise Arner	409	McClure, Robert John Le	
Button, Thomas	410	Mesurier	454
Bylot, Robert	410	Middleton, Christopher	455
Byrd, Richard Evelyn	410	Moor, William	456
Campbell, Robert	413	Nansen, Fridtjof	457
Coats, William	414	Nares, George Strong	459
Collinson, Richard	416	North Pole	460
Cook, Frederick Albert	417	Northwest Passage	464
Davis, John	418	Parry, Sir William Edward	469
Dease, Peter Warren	420	Peary, Robert Edwin	471
DeLong, George Washington	422	Rae, John	474
Dezhnev, Semen Ivanovich	423	Rasmussen, Knud Johan	
Ellesmere Island	424	Victor	476
Foxe, Luke	424	Roque, Marguerite de la	477
Franklin, Lady Jane	425	Ross, Sir James Clark	477
Franklin, John	425	Ross, Sir John	478
Frobisher, Sir Martin	431	Russians in North America	480
Glazunov, Andrei	432	Schwatka, Frederick	483
Greely, Adolphus		Scoresby, William, Jr.	484
Washington	432	Simpson, Thomas	485
Hall, Charles Francis	433	Stefansson, Vilhjalmur	486
Harriman expedition	435	Sverdrup, Otto	490
Hayes, Isaac	437	Teben'kov, Mikhail	
Hearne, Samuel	438	Dimitrivich	490
Henson, Matthew	440	Vasil'ev, Ivan Yakovlevich	491
Herbert, Sir (Walter William)		Vasil'ev, Mikhail Nikolaevich	491
Wally	443	Wilkins, Hubert	492

Bibliography 493

Index 498

Acknowledgments

No work of this scope would be possible without assistance from many sources. We especially thank Harry Anderson for his major contribution to the Arctic section and Eva Weber for her significant contributions to material on the early Southwest and West; we also thank Stephen Soitos for his contributions. We also would like to thank the scholars who have come before us (key works are cited in the Bibliography), pathfinders without whose labors such a book as this would be impossible to assemble. We thank, too, the librarians at Phillips Exeter Academy in Exeter, New Hampshire, Smith College in Northampton, Massachusetts, and the University of Massachusetts at Amherst. Finally, we gratefully acknowledge the encouragement and understanding we have received from our literary agent, Edward M. Knappman of Chester, Connecticut, and our editor at John Wiley and Sons, Chip Rossetti.

Introduction

The narrative of North American discovery and exploration reads like a novel—a postmodern novel at that, in which definitions are elusive; claims are relative and subject to revision; and obscure, offstage characters are as vital to the outcome as those with documentable identities, personal histories, and catalogues of achievement. Any attempt to engage the history of North American exploration and discovery has to begin with some understanding of terms. For example, what constitutes "North America"? What do we mean by "discovery"? How does one define an "explorer"?

For the purposes of this work, we use the conventional geographers' definition of North America, which includes Mexico, Central America, and the islands of the Caribbean. The geographers' definition also encompasses Greenland as well as the Arctic regions up to the North Pole, the destination of a generation of obsessive twentieth-century adventurer/explorers. We have divided the book into seven parts organized geographically as well as chronologically:

Part I: North America before Columbus
Part II: The Spanish Enter the New World, 1492–1635
Part III: The Atlantic Seaboard, 1497–1680
Part IV: Exploring West of the Mississippi, 1635–1800
Part V: From the Appalachians to the Mississippi, 1540–1840
Part VI: Across the North American Continent, 1720–1880
Part VII: The Arctic and Northernmost Regions, 1576–1992

Within each chapter, entries are arranged in alphabetical order.

The bands of prehistoric people who drifted over the Bering land bridge that once joined Asia and North America thousands of years ago might properly claim credit as "discoverers" of the continent that extends from the eternal chill of the Bering Sea to the rain forests of the Isthmus of Darien in eastern Panama. Neither the ancient Asians nor their Native American descendants who peopled the continent from time immemorial left a conclusive written account. The first people to provide evidence of setting foot in North America were the Norse who came ashore in Newfoundland almost five centuries before Columbus made landfall off the Bahama Islands in October 1492. They left a tangible record of their visitation in saga form and in the archaeological remains at L'Anse aux Meadows.

Columbus believed he had discovered the geographical outworks of Asia, not a new continent. But it would not be long before the Italians, the Spanish, the Portuguese, the English, and the French were establishing that this was indeed a vast New World. They would eventually be joined by the Dutch, the Russians, the Scandinavians, and finally American conqueror/colonists from the sixteenth century down to the twentieth to explore, map, exploit, and subdue the vast North American landmass. The stories of these explorers—heirs of the first arrivals from Asia, of Leif Eriksson, of Columbus—contain elements of heroism, willpower, fortitude in the face of extreme hardship, and physical endurance all but inconceivable to the comfort-loving world of the twenty-first century. They contain elements, too, of lust, greed, meanness, betrayal, rapacious exploitation, armor-plated cultural arrogance, and unimaginable, sometimes genocidal, cruelty.

We define the category of "explorer" broadly. De Soto sailed to the New World for gold and conquest, but he traversed three thousand miles of unknown territory in what is now the southeastern United States and became the first European to cross the Mississippi. Scores of missionaries set forth primarily to convert the natives to Christianity, but in the course of their journeys they blazed trails through all manner of remote territories. The men and women of the Roanoke Expeditions came to plant a colony, but expedition leaders carried out important explorations of the North Carolina sounds and the tidewater interior. It would be more strictly accurate to treat Daniel Boone as a market hunter and pioneer colonist, but he did blaze trails into trackless places. So too is the term "discovery" problematic. We try to use qualifiers such as "the first documented crossing of South Pass" or "the first European known to sight the coast of California," knowing only too well that these "empty" or "virgin" lands, these "howling wildernesses," were in fact familiar landscapes to the natives who peopled them. Apropos of which, we follow the practice of most contemporary scholars and generally use modern place names rather than the Native American original names. Likewise, we generally use the modern names of geographic features such as lakes, bays, and other bodies of water, as well as islands, peninsulas, and other landmasses, even though these may have been named many years, or even decades, after our explorers encountered them.

One authority goes so far as to suggest that Alexander Mackenzie, who in 1789 traveled the river that now bears his name, went along as hardly more than a passenger on an Indian "conducted tour" of the Canadian Northwest. The point is arguable, and we recognize the crucial, often decisive role Native Americans played in what after all *were* discoveries to Europeans glimpsing the marvels as well as the terrors of North America for the first time. Many of the journeys here described would have been impossible without Indians as guides, interpreters, and providers of transportation, food, shelter, and guarantees of safe conduct. All the same, Mackenzie conceived the expedition out of his own rich and restless imagination, managed it with skill, survived hardships and danger, and bequeathed his knowledge of mysterious places to an eager world.

Entries on individual explorers make no attempt to be complete biographies of their lives, still less of their times. They focus on what, after all, is the theme of this book, the exploration and opening of the North American continent. We do, however, make an effort to present these pathfinders as personalities. We try to let the explorers speak for themselves, to let their voices be heard down through the centuries whenever possible, both in the entries and in companion extracts from letters, diaries, and official reports.

A note on format: For the reader's convenience, cross-referenced entries will appear in bold italics the first time they appear in the text of an entry. If the boldface cross-reference points the way to an entry from another part of the book, its location will be identified with the part number in brackets; otherwise, the cross-reference will simply appear in bold italics.

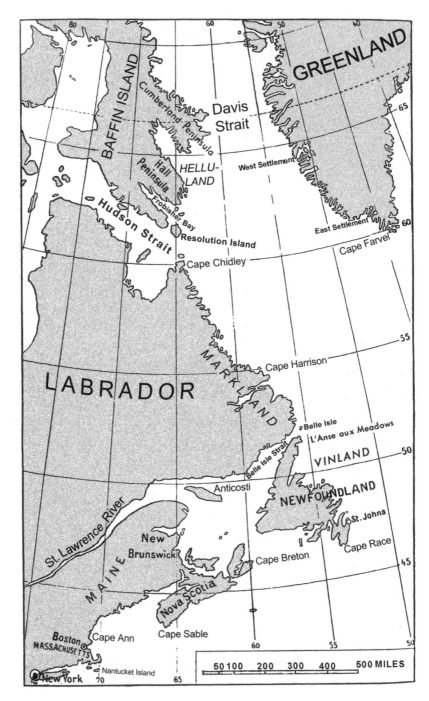

This map shows the lands from Greenland to New England that are associated with the Vikings' voyages circa A.D. 1000. There is no disputing their settlements in Greenland, nor that they reached Baffin Island, Labrador, and at least New-foundland. What is in dispute is just how far down the Atlantic coast of North America they may have traveled.

PART I

North America before Columbus

There was a time, not all that long ago for many Americans, when the history of the exploration of North America began simply and abruptly with the first voyage of Christopher Columbus. (It was no coincidence that generations of American schoolchildren all knew by heart the "beginning" of their history: "In fourteen hundred and ninety-two / Columbus sailed the ocean blue." Today it is widely recognized that this history is more complicated—and certainly more exciting. Indeed, the history of pre-Columbian exploration of North America has become so "exciting" that it is sometimes in danger of becoming disorienting—literally as well as figuratively. To put it bluntly: Widely circulated accounts often make it hard for the general public to distinguish possibilities from probabilities, the claimed from the proven, fiction from fact.

One of the unfortunate results of this confusion is that many people focus more on the allegations and ignore the more interesting realities. More North Americans probably know of the claims about finding Atlantis in North America than of the actual finding of the Norse site at L'Anse aux Meadows, Newfoundland. And for every American who is aware of the French and Portuguese fishermen who were coming ashore on the coast of Canada by 1505, there are probably ten who believe that people from all over the Old World had been visiting North America long before then.

There is nothing wrong with considering the many unproven claims made for pre-Columbian events, expeditions, explorers, and evidence. In fact, this work has gone out of its way to recognize them all (including some that probably few except the more dedicated "alternative theory" buffs are aware of). We are as beguiled as the next person by the mysteries, the great unanswerables, of history. But we insist on examining these many claims with objective standards of proof: Merely asserting that something "might well have" happened does not prove that it did. When doubts remain, when there are still those "possibilities," we readily admit as much. But people should not confuse serious scholars' doubts and disagreements about certain details—such as exact landfalls made by early explorers—with the positive assertions made by proponents of various fanciful scenarios.

It does seem a shame that so many people are willing to believe the various questionable, and even spurious, stories when the proven history is at least as exciting. What is more interesting than knowing about those Norse up there in Newfoundland? They have left more than enough evidence to provoke speculation about their time in the far corner of the Northeast without making additional claims about their being present all over North America. Meanwhile, there are some genuine mysteries regarding other possible pre-Columbian contacts with the Western Hemisphere, mysteries that will be examined here with neutrality.

There exists an annotated bibliography of writings about these pre-Columbian contacts; it runs to some 5,000 books and articles, yet still the editors explain: "We realize that the bibliography is incomplete, but so large a topic could never be exhausted." Here, too, we cannot claim to be exhaustive, but we have tried to include all the most relevant topics.

Africans

One of the least-known claims is that Africoid people (that is, Negroid Africans as opposed to North Africans, Egyptians, Arabic Africans, etc.) made contact with the Americas at several points in history before *Columbus [II]* "discovered" the New World he believed to be Asia. Yet even the primary proponent of this claim, Ivan Van Sertima, admits that this is a "highly controversial thesis." He sees two main contact periods—one sometime between about 1200 and 700 B.C., and the other in the fourteenth and fifteenth centuries A.D.—and cites abundant specific evidence involving physical anthropology (burials of skeletons); cultural artifacts (from boats to sculptural depictions of Africoid types); textual references (including statements by Columbus himself); religious, ritual, and ceremonial parallels; and botanical specimens (including corn, cotton, and maize). The arguments are suggestive—and sometimes convincing. Thus, there is the claim that in 1312, Bakari II, the Malinke Emperor of Mali, led two hundred large pirogues on an expedition westward across the Atlantic, where he is said to have reached Brazil. The investigations into this broad topic will presumably continue, but for now, not even the main proponents claim that these Africoid people added to the geographic knowledge of North America.

Large heads of this type (this one is nine feet high), found in the Mexican states of Tabasco and Veracruz, were made by the Olmec Indians (circa 1200–100 B.C.). Those who claim that Africans must have been present in the Americas before Columbus often cite these heads, with their alleged Negroid features, as evidence to support their theory.

Antil(l)ia

Of the several legendary islands long believed by Europeans to be located in the Atlantic, Antilia is arguably the one that had the greatest impact on voyages of exploration that led to the real islands and mainland of the Americas. Although there have been countless explanations for the source of the name itself, it is most likely derived from two Portuguese words *ante* and *illa,* meaning "opposite island." Its first appearance on a map seems to be that of the so-called Pizzi (or Pizzigano) Nautical Chart of 1424. From that date on, Antilia—in various spellings, shapes, orientations, and locations—appears on maps and globes for several centuries. Meanwhile, by about 1450 Antilia was also combined by some with another legendary island off in the Atlantic, the Island of the Seven Cities (which in turn often becomes combined with another legendary Atlantic island, Brazil, or Hy-Brasil). There are several authentic accounts of pre-Columbian voyages into the Atlantic in search of Antilia, but the one that matters most is that *Columbus [II]* himself believed in its existence and expected to find it en route to Asia. (In fact, he had been convinced by the letter of Paolo Toscanelli that he would find Antilia on the twenty-eighth parallel; had he held to that course, he would have made his first landfall in Florida.) Some of Columbus's contemporaries believed that one of the islands he did discover was, in fact, Antilia, while some serious modern scholars believe that Antilia was inspired by pre-Columbian discoveries of actual islands such as *Cuba [II]*. In any case, the Portuguese and the French quickly applied the name "Antilles" to the newly discovered West Indies, and this name preserves the allure of the various imaginary islands in Europeans' discovery of the Americas.

Asians

There is a long-standing and respectable school of scholarship that contends that peoples from relatively advanced cultures of Asia made a number of contacts with the Americas in the centuries before *Columbus [II]*. This thesis, usually summed up as "trans-Pacific contacts," is extremely complicated because there are so many different claims made by so many different scholars. For example, one claim asserts that on various occasions rafts or small boats involuntarily drifted or were blown by storms across the Pacific, and the sailors aboard found themselves stranded in the Americas. At the other extreme are the claims that the Chinese deliberately sent forth maritime expeditions to explore the farthest reaches of the Pacific: Two periods—300–100 B.C. and the early 1400s A.D.—are usually cited. (The most recent claim is that the Chinese admiral Zheng He, on one of his seven famous voyages between 1405 and 1433, circumnavigated the globe, and some Chinese settled North America.) But once again, virtually all the pre-Columbian contacts advanced by serious scholars involve Middle or South America, not North America, and cultural influences, not geographical knowledge. Then there are those who claim that two classic Chinese texts refer to ancient Chinese visiting North America. One of these, dated to about 200 B.C., is the *Shan Hai Ching (Classic of the Mountains and Rivers)*; scholars of Chinese literature insist its subject matter is mythological, not geographical. The other text, found in the *Liang-shu (Records of the Liang Dynasty)*, allegedly describes the travels of a Buddhist monk, Hwui Shan, to a place called Fu-Sang around A.D. 500. Proponents of Fu-Sang as a place in the Americas locate it anywhere from Oregon to Guatemala and find American equivalents for all the most exotic elements in Fu-Sang: The La Brea tar pits are the "sea of varnish"; men with dogs' heads are the Hopi Indians' Kachina ceremonial masks; while the fu-sang plant that gave the country its name was anything from the prickly pear to maize. Once again, professional scholars reject all such claims.

IN THEIR OWN *Words*   Pre-Columbian Chinese in North America?

Have walked about three hundred li since Bald Mountain. Here, Bamboo Mountain is near the river which looks like a boundary. There is no grass, or trees, but some jasper and jade stones. The river is impeded in its course here by rocks, but flows on southeast to the great body of water . . . to the south, Lone Mountain is found. Upon this there are many gems and much gold, and below it many beautiful stones. Muddy River is found here, a stream flowing southeasterly into a mighty flood, in which there are many T'iao-Yung. These look like yellow serpents with fish's fins . . . three hundred li to the south, Bald Mountain is found . . . wild animals are found here which look like suckling pigs, but they have pearls. They are called Tung-Tung, their name being given to them in imitation of their cry. The Hwan River is found here, a stream flowing easterly into a river . . . one authority says that it flows into the sea. In this there are many water-gems. . . . Three hundred li farther south, Bamboo Mountain is found, bordering on a river. . . . There is no grass, or trees, but there are many green-jasper and green-jade stones. The Kih River [water impeded in its course by rocks] is found here, a stream flowing into T'su-Tan [larger water of some sort]. In this place there is a great abundance of dye plants.

—SHAN HAI CHING (*CLASSIC OF THE MOUNTAINS AND RIVERS*), CIRCA 200 B.C.

Bjarni Herjolfsson (?–?)

This Norwegian merchant-sailor would be unknown to history except for the one reference to him in *The Saga of the Greenlanders* (written down sometime before A.D. 1263). According to this saga, Bjarni operated a trading ship that made annual trips between Iceland and Norway. He settled down every winter in Iceland with his father, but when he got there in A.D. 986 he learned that his father had sailed off to Greenland with *Erik the Red.* Bjarni decided to sail there, but due to conditions at sea he missed Greenland; continuing northwest, he spotted a land "level and covered with woods"—presumably Labrador; sailing on northward, he spotted another similar land—presumably *Baffin Island [VII].* He did not go ashore but turned back and, sailing eastward this time, found Greenland. There he is said to have told Erik the Red of his sightings, suggested further exploration, and even to have lent his ship to *Leif Eriksson* to retrace his voyage. Except for the claim that he continued to make trading voyages to Greenland for the next fourteen years before settling in Norway, nothing more is known of Bjarni. But if there is any truth to this story, Bjarni Herjolfsson deserves to be known as the first European to

IN THEIR OWN

Words

The First European to Sight North America?

*T*hey [Bjarni Herjolfsson and his crew] put out [from Iceland for Greenland] and sailed for three days before losing sight of land. Then their following wind died down and north wind and fogs overtook them so that they had no idea which way they were going. This continued over many days but eventually they saw the sun and could get their bearings. They now hoisted sail and sailed that day before sighting land and debated among themselves what this land could be. To his way of thinking, said Bjarni, this could not be Greenland. . . . After this they sailed for two days before sighting another land. . . . In his opinion, this was no more Greenland than the first place . . . they turned their prow from the land and sailed out to sea three days . . . and then they saw the third land, and this land was high, mountainous and glaciered . . . they held on along the land and came to see that it was an island.

—*THE SAGA OF THE GREENLANDERS*, WRITTEN DOWN CIRCA A.D. 1200 report a sighting of continental North America—making him, in effect, the European discoverer of the New World.

Brendan, Saint (484–577)

Brendan was a historic figure, an Irish Catholic priest known as Saint Brendan of Ardfert and Clonfert. Born near Tralee, County Kerry, he was ordained a priest in 512, and during his life he traveled around Ireland, Wales, and Iona and founded several monasteries and churches. He enters the story of North America by way of a fifteenth-century Irish book, *The*

Book of Lismore (in turn said to draw on much earlier works), which claims to contain a true account of Brendan's voyages to lands far to the west and north. Most authorities are content to accept that he may have traveled around the coast of Ireland, to islands off Scotland, or even as far as Iceland, but there have always been some people who insist that he made his way to North America—in some versions alone in a small hide-covered boat, in other versions in a large wooden ship with a crew that numbered anywhere from 18 to 150. In the several versions that survive, Brendan reaches an island or island group that is warm

There are no contemporary illustrations of Saint Brendan, but this 1621 woodcut captures the fanciful and exaggerated notions that surrounded the story of his sailing across the Atlantic to North America.

IN THEIR OWN *Words* — Saint Brendan Arrives in North America?

Then getting down from the boat they saw a spacious land with apple trees bearing fruit. While they were there it was never night. They took as many of the apples as they wanted and they drank from springs, and then for forty days they wandered over the land but they could not find an end to it. A certain day they came to a great river flowing through the middle of the island. Then Saint Brendan told his companions, "We cannot cross this river, and we will never know how big this island is."

—*VOYAGE OF ST. BRENDAN*, WRITTEN DOWN IN THE NINTH CENTURY

and lush, and since this would not describe the islands of the northeastern Atlantic, some people have concluded from this that Brendan had reached some point along the coast of North America. Even earlier than the written accounts is a map of 1275 associating Brendan's name with the so-called Fortunate Isles, generally agreed to be the Canary Islands off the coast of northwest Africa. A 1339 map then assigns his name to the Madeira Islands, also off northwest Africa, and in the next few centuries Brendan's name is linked to various islands, real and imagined, all over the Atlantic. By the 1500s "San Brandan Island" is being located off the coast of northern Newfoundland. This led to modern claims that Brendan went ashore in North America and traveled well into the interior as a missionary. It hardly seems necessary to say that serious scholars reject all such claims.

Bristol, England

A port city in southwestern England at the confluence of the Avon and Frome Rivers, founded in the eleventh century and chartered in 1155, Bristol was already a flourishing seaport and trading center in 1245, when engineers improved the harbor by diverting the Frome and building a stone quay, known for centuries as "the key," for seagoing vessels.

The original name, Brygstowe, means "place of the bridge." The city lay eight miles from the estuary of the Severn up the narrow, difficult-to-navigate Avon. The river flowed through a rocky gorge; the tides, with a rise and fall of twenty-one feet, were among the world's greatest in range, and tidal currents in the Avon moved with powerful, potentially destructive force.

Yet by 1400 Bristol had become England's second-most-important seaport; in time, the phrase "shipshape and Bristol fashion" became a byword for maritime quality and attention to detail. Voyages to Iceland probably commenced before 1425. *Columbus [II]* may have sailed in Bristol ships in an alleged voyage to Iceland in 1477.

Bristol developed into an outlet for the export of Cotswold wool; an importer of dried fish, wine, olive oil, salt, and fruit; and the center of a triangular trade between England, Iceland, and the Iberian peninsula. By 1450 Bristol mariners were regularly involved in trade with the Portuguese cities of Oporto, Lisbon, and Faro. As the fifteenth century advanced, conflict with Icelanders and competition with Denmark prompted Bristol merchants and fishermen to begin looking elsewhere for trade. Although the city, with a population approaching ten thousand, prospered in the 1480s and 1490s, the Iceland trade entered a period of steep decline. Bristol sought new routes and opportunities, among them a shorter ocean passage connecting Europe to the spice markets of Asia.

Circumstantial evidence suggests the possibility that a voyage underwritten by Bristol investor Thomas Croft sighted Newfoundland in 1481, eleven years before Columbus reached America. In this account, sailors from Bristol then told some Spaniards about this new land, and they in turn passed on the word to Columbus; all of this is based on a misreading of the letter ascribed to *John Day.* Very likely Day's remark was based on another questionable claim, namely that a Bristol shipmaster, Thomas Lloyd, had discovered Newfoundland while sailing the Atlantic in 1480 in search of the "Isle of Brasil," or one of the other reputed but imaginary islands off to the west. Most serious scholars reject all such claims, but Bristol merchants and mariners would still play a significant role in the early explorations of North America.

The industrious, ambitious citizens of Bristol were open to investing in anything that promised a profit and—already heavily involved in commerce with various European countries—they would be quick to see the opportunities for trade in the newly discovered Americas. The object of *John Cabot's [III]* voyage of 1497, however, was to discover a better route to the "Indies." Sailing from Bristol, he mistook cold, remote, sparsely populated *Newfoundland* for Cathay at first, but his error led to the first English presence in the New World, and his disappearance (he perished on his second voyage in 1498) did nothing to discourage the search for the *Northwest Passage [VII].* The Bristol-based Anglo-Azorean Syndicate, initially comprised of two Bristol merchants and three Portuguese Azores Islanders, evidently sponsored several voyages, probably in search of a passage through North America, in the early years of the sixteenth century. According to historian David B. Quinn, King Henry VII partly financed at least one of the ventures, the voyage of 1504.

Little evidence of these explorations survives. Historian Samuel Eliot Morison speculates that the controversial Oliveriana Map, probably produced in Florence between 1504 and 1510, contains evidence of a voyage toward Newfoundland in 1501 or 1502. He cites place names on the map that appear nowhere else. Morison also cites Henry VII's household records—one of which, dated January 2, 1502, shows that the king gave five pounds to "men of bristoll that found th' isle," presumably New-foundland. Other documentary evidence records gifts from "the merchaunts of Bristoll that have been in the newe founde lande," including hawks and an "Egle," among other items.

Bristol's interest in discovery waned later in the sixteenth century. The city's Society of Merchant Venturers, established in 1552, vigorously pursued trade and profits but proved less aggressive in seeking out new lands.

Celts

Among the many candidates proposed as the earliest visitors to North America, perhaps none have been more strongly promoted than the Celtic peoples. According to the proponents—the most prominent being Barry Fell, a Harvard marine biologist who published several books arguing that numerous peoples had visited North America before *Columbus [II]*—about 1000 B.C. Celtic mariners sailed across the Atlantic and made their way to New England. There these Celts established a kingdom they called Iargalon, "Land Beyond the Sunset" in Celtic. They built villages and temples, raised Druids' circles of standing stones, and buried their dead in marked graves. Beyond such remains that Fell and others find at scores of sites throughout New England, other parts of the Northeast, and as far west as Oklahoma and Colorado, they find inscriptions using Ogam, the ancient Celtic alphabet. These Celts, according to the proponents, although related to the Celts of Ireland, were more closely tied to the Celts of the Iberian Peninsula (modern Spain and Portugal); based on this connection, the proponents then contend that the Iberian Celts in the New World had also welcomed their *Phoenician* and Basque neighbors from the Mediterranean. These Celts and Phoenicians are claimed to have made frequent trips to and from the New World, carrying furs, metals, and other valuables back to the Old World. But although the proponents of the Celtic presence produce

Located near Salem, New Hampshire, is a complex of freestanding stones and stone structures—the one pictured is called the "Oracle Chamber"—that the owners call "Mystery Hill" and "America's Stonehenge." Although their exact nationality is left somewhat open, the original builders of the site were allegedly pre-Columbian visitors to North America.

scores of Celtic and Iberian-Punic inscriptions in the New World, they have never demonstrated the presence of any artifacts of Old World derivation in the New World, nor vice versa. On the other hand, they claim that scores of free-standing stones and stone structures found in the Northeast (e.g., Mystery Hill, New Hampshire) were placed there by Celtic peoples.

Day, John   (?–?)

John Day was a late-fifteenth- and early-sixteenth-century English merchant with a somewhat shadowy, even dubious, reputation. He is known to have been in *Bristol* during at least part of the early 1490s, but by about 1500 he was in Spain, where he had long been conducting trade. In 1956, there was discovered in the archives of Simancas, Spain, an authentic letter from John Day, addressed to "El Señor Almirante Mayor," almost certainly *Christopher Columbus [II].* This letter from Day, composed apparently during the winter of 1497–1498, describes in considerable detail *John Cabot*'s first voyage to North America. But in the course of it, Day claims that "this same point of land [found by Cabot] at another time was found and discovered by those of Bristol . . . and is presumed and believed to be the tierra firma which those of Bristol discovered." Although some scholars have been willing to believe that Bristolmen got to North America before Columbus, few accept this. The Day letter, however, remains a valuable document regarding the early voyages to the New World. Incidentally, a map he refers to as accompanying his letter has never been found.

IN THEIR OWN *Words*

A Bristolman Writes of a Pre-Columbian Visit to North America

You will note that he [John Cabot] did not go ashore save at one place of tierra firma, *which is close to where they made the first landfall . . . and they found big trees from which masts of ships are made . . . and the land was very rich in pasturage . . . and along the coast they found many fish of the kind that in Iceland are cured . . . and it seemed to them that there were cultivated lands where they thought there might be villages, and they saw vegetation whose leaves appeared fair to them. . . . It is considered certain that this same point of land at an earlier time had been found and discovered by those of Bristol.*

—LETTER FROM JOHN DAY TO COLUMBUS, 1497

disputed claims for pre-Columbian contacts

Ever since Europeans first came to the Americas, there have been claims that others from outside the Western Hemisphere (aside from the *Norse* of circa A.D. 1000, that is) made contacts with this region before the voyages of *Columbus [II]*. (For the moment, we shall not even impose the strict boundaries of North America on this discussion, although in fact many of the claims do not directly involve this continent.) If it is all too easy to accept such claims, it is equally all too easy to reject them out of hand. It is better to be willing to at least look at such claims objectively and apply the same rules of evidence that are required for all historical events.

In their appropriate alphabetical locations elsewhere in this section, the claims made for the following peoples are examined: *Africans, Asians, Celts, Egyptians, Greeks, Irish, Libyans, Muslims, Norse, Phoenicians,* and *Welsh.*

But before considering any such claims, it seems necessary to establish a few ground rules for inclusion in an encyclopedia of exploration of North America. To rate entrance here, some link, some relatively tangible contribution, to geographic discoveries and knowledge is required. This link should be traceable in one of two regions: back in the region where the individuals originated (thereby contributing to geographical knowledge there of this New World) or in the region of North America where they made contact (and thus advancing knowledge of and in the New World itself). And no matter what the soundness of the claims for pre-Columbian contacts, such links are essentially always missing. Seldom do the proponents of the various pre-Columbian peoples argue that their discoveries were known to, let alone

---

IN THEIR OWN *Words*

The Jaredites Come to America circa 3000 B.C.

Which Jared came forth with his brother and their families . . . from the great tower [of Babel] at the time the Lord confounded the languages of the people, and swore in his wrath that they should be scattered upon all the face of the earth, and according to the word of the Lord the people were scattered . . . and it came to pass that they did travel in the wilderness and did build barges in which they did come across many waters being directed continually by the hand of the Lord, and the Lord would not suffer that they should stop beyond the sea in the wilderness but he would that they should come forth even unto the land of promise, which was choice above all other lands which the Lord God had preserved for a righteous people.

—THE BOOK OF MORMON

recorded by, their home cultures. And seldom do they propose that these pre-Columbian peoples contributed to, or advanced geographic knowledge, within the Western Hemisphere. In fact, almost all claims for contributions made by these pre-Columbian peoples fall under the rubric of cultural influences (such as religion, arts, and crafts), linguistics and alphabets, technology and science, and biological (that is, physical characteristics or botanical species). Perhaps the major exception to this would be any *maps* that are believed to incorporate knowledge from pre-Columbian visitors; in a few such instances, proponents contend that these maps contributed to the body of knowledge about the New World (although here again, it is seldom North America that is involved). (See *Piri Reis map.*)

Another distinction should be made. In addition to those who claim that various individuals or groups arrived in the Western Hemisphere before Columbus, there are others who insist that the Amerindians themselves are (at least to some degree) descendants of peoples other than the Asians accepted as their forebears by most authorities. Most reputable authorities consider these latter claims to be so totally unsubstantiated as to be essentially pseudoscience.

For the record, some of the groups that have been proposed by serious individuals as settlers before and alongside those recognized today as Native Americans are Atlanteans (i.e., from the Lost Continent of Atlantis), Assyrians, Basques, Canaanites, Catalans, Celts, Chinese, Cro-Magnons, Etruscans, French, Gauls, Greeks, Hindus, Huns, Irish, Israelites (i.e., The Lost Tribes), Jaredites, Nephites, Lamanites (the Mormons' candidates, originally from ancient Israel or Palestine), Koreans, Lemurians (survivors of the lost continent of Mu), Madagascans, Malinke (Mandingoes), Portuguese, Romans, Scythians, Spanish, Tartars, Trojans, and Welsh. Although all these peoples have been promoted—some as contributing to the ancestry and culture of Amerindians, some as living apart and becoming extinct—in virtually no instance has it been claimed that they contributed anything to the geographic knowledge of North America.

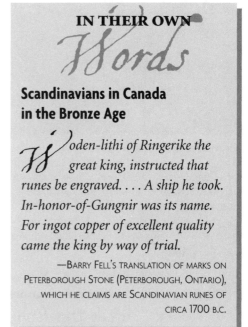

IN THEIR OWN *Words*

Scandinavians in Canada in the Bronze Age

Woden-lithi of Ringerike the great king, instructed that runes be engraved. . . . A ship he took. In-honor-of-Gungnir was its name. For ingot copper of excellent quality came the king by way of trial.

—BARRY FELL'S TRANSLATION OF MARKS ON PETERBOROUGH STONE (PETERBOROUGH, ONTARIO), WHICH HE CLAIMS ARE SCANDINAVIAN RUNES OF CIRCA 1700 B.C.

Egyptians

The claim that ancient Egyptians visited the New World is largely based on alleged similarities between Egyptian pyramids and Mesoamerican temple mounds. But there are a few individuals who claim that a script used by the Micmac and other Algonquian Indians of southeastern Canada and northern New England is derived from Egyptian hieroglyphics. One of the chief proponents of this claim was Barry Fell, a Harvard marine biologist who devoted many years and several books to his linguistic analyses of alleged pre-Columbian scripts found throughout North America. To account for what he insisted were Egyptian hieroglyphics, Fell claims that Egyptian astronomer-priests visited North America about 800 B.C. and traveled about introducing Egyptian rituals and other aspects of Egyptian culture. In particular, Fell insists that a "calendar stele" found in Davenport, Iowa, in 1874 has Egyptian writing on it (along with writing in the Ibero-Punic and Libyan scripts). Fell's claims are not accepted by most authorities in this field of study.

The Mississippian Mound culture phase, which existed throughout the Mississippi Valley all the way from the gulf to Minnesota between about A.D. 1000 and 1700, was distinguished by its large earthen "pyramid" mounds such as this one at Winterville, Mississippi. Some people insist that such mounds attest to the presence of ancient Egyptians.

Erik the Red   (950?–1003?)

His real name was Eirik Thorvaldsson, but he gained the nickname from his red hair, which was said to be matched by the proverbial hot temper. He was born in southwestern Norway about A.D. 950, and while he was still a youth his father took him and his family off to Iceland "because of some killings," according to the sagas. On Iceland, Erik had only poor land until he married the daughter of a prosperous landowner; again, more quarrels and killings led to his being declared an outlaw, and he was banished for three years. Instead of returning to Norway, he decided to seek out islands that previous *Norse* voyagers had reported lying to the west. About 982 he took his ship, family, and crew and set out; whatever those islands were, Erik sailed on to make landfall at an unknown landmass. He continued to explore along the coast of this land until he came to its southwestern shores and found some relatively hospitable land. He returned to Iceland to organize a colonizing expedition, and in order to encourage people to accompany him, he named this new place "*Greenland.*"

About 985 he led an expedition of some twenty-five ships and several score of people back to Greenland (although only fourteen ships made it all the way). Once ashore near the tip of southwestern Greenland, Erik chose a prime locale as his property; the Norse colony quickly took hold and even spread to a second locale about three hundred miles up the coast to the north. Erik presumably served as the chief "lawspeaker" of the colony—what we might think of as the premier—and although he seems to have resisted Christianity, his wife did convert and had a small church built near their farmstead. Erik remained the colony's leader until his death about A.D. 1003. Although he was most likely a difficult man, Erik the Red probably deserves credit for being the first identifiable European who deliberately sailed to, and colonized, the Western Hemisphere. He was also the father of the *Leif Eriksson,* who, it is now generally accepted, led the first landing of Europeans on the mainland of North America.

Greeks

Apparently the first serious proposal for the ancient Greeks as pre-Columbian visitors came from American Harold S. Gladwin, who, in his superficially reasonable *Men Out of Asia* (1947), claimed that after the death of Alexander the Great (323 B.C.), members of his fleet commanded by Admiral Nearchus sailed eastward and, gradually picking up scores of people from India and Southeast Asia, arrived on the shores of Central America. From there they dispersed north and south, and they and their descendants allegedly introduced most of the advanced cultural elements (e.g., metallurgy, textiles, pottery) to the primitive Mongoloid Paleoindians in North America. These people from the Mediterranean have been proposed as the "bearded white men" found in the legends and myths of Middle and South American Indians. Meanwhile, at least one amateur student of pre-Columbian North America claims to have found evidence of an ancient Greek presence in the languages of New England Indians. Serious scholars do not accept any claims about ancient Greeks having been present in the New World.

Greenland

Although most North Americans probably do not think of it as part of their history or environment, Greenland, the largest island in the world, belongs to North America by virtue of its geological connection to the tectonic plate known as the Canadian Shield (whereas its close neighbor, Iceland, belongs to the Mid-Atlantic Ridge). Most of Greenland is covered by an ice sheet, ice caps, or glaciers; there are no forests; prevailing cold winds and ocean currents make it even more inhospitable. However, Paleoeskimos had been living there since as early as 2500 B.C.; they came over from the Arctic lands to the west in a series of migrations. Scholars cannot be sure which group of Eskimos was present when the first Europeans settled there, some believing they were Dorset Culture, others arguing they were the later Thule Culture. Whoever these first visitors and settlers were, they stayed close to the coasts and did not contribute to later knowledge of the island.

Although it is believed that the *Norse* had sighted Greenland by about A.D. 875, the first Europeans to come ashore were Norse from Iceland, led by *Erik the Red,* about the year 982; it was he who is said to have named it "Greenland" so as to attract fellow Norse colonists to this rugged land. In any case, Norse from Iceland and Norway soon settled there, and by about A.D. 1100 there were possibly as many as 6,500 Norse living in Greenland. They clustered in two regions: The one known as the Eastern Settlement was located at what we today regard as the southwestern tip of the island; the Western Settlement was located about three hundred miles to the north of that, along the western coast (and only some five hundred miles from the mainland of North America). There is no evidence that these early Norse explored Greenland much beyond their coastal settlements; indeed, they never knew exactly what the land's actual dimensions or boundaries were as they never sailed around it; in fact, for several centuries, maps would depict Greenland as an extension of the continent of Asia.

The Norse had enough to do just to survive: They set up farms to grow grain; They tried to maintain cattle, sheep, goats, and pigs; they hunted—seals, polar bears, caribou, foxes; but surprisingly, there is little or no evidence that they fished. In the end, some combination of factors caused the decline, and then the closing out, of this phase of Norse settlement during the late 1400s; some evidence suggests that their attempts to impose their familiar crops and animals onto the land led to its devastation and so they were driven to starvation. Although European mariners occasionally put in to Greenland during the 1500s and 1600s, it would be 1721 before a Norwegian Christian missionary, Hans Egede, established a mission and trading center on Greenland. This next phase of the island's history belongs to the story of Arctic exploration. It can be argued that the first settlement links Greenland more to Europe than to North America, but the first Norse of Greenland have a special place in history because it was they who set off to explore the unknown sea and land to their west and in so doing were probably the first Europeans to reach the North American mainland.

Helluland

According to "The Saga of the Greenlanders," the medieval *Norse* account of *Leif Eriksson*'s first trip to what came to be known as *Vinland,* the first land he sighted west of Greenland was nothing more than rock and glaciers. Leif and his crew named it Helluland, Norse for "slab-land." It is believed that this is what we today know as *Baffin Island [VII]*. Scholars feel virtually certain that the Greenland Norse continued to visit Helluland in the centuries after the end of the Vinland colony; the name Helluland survived on some maps until well into modern times, although the English renamed it after the Englishman who explored that region between 1612 and 1616, *William Baffin [VII]*.

Henry the Navigator   (1394–1460)

Any account of pre-Columbian exploration by Western Europeans must recognize the role of this Portuguese prince, even though he himself never sailed on any expedition. Henry—to the Portuguese, Infante D. Henrique—was the third son of King John I of Portugal; his mother, Philippa, was the daughter of the English Duke of Lancaster, John of Gaunt. Henry was not drawn to court life so he moved to Sagres, on the coast of Cape Vincent, the southwesternmost point of Portugal. There, about 1420, he set up a research institute that drew scholars, mariners, and mapmakers, mostly from Portugal but also from other European nations. Here some worked on developing better ships and navigational instruments, compiling all that was known of the new discoveries beyond Europe and incorporating this information in *maps.* Others set forth on exploratory voyages, and Henry's expeditions deserve credit for revealing much of the coast of west Africa and for reaching the Madeiras, the Azores, and the Cape Verde islands. At least one of Henry's expeditions—that of Diego de Tieve and Pedro de Velasco, in 1452—set off in search of islands reputed to be far off across the Atlantic, but they ended up finding only the westernmost of the Azores. Although there are claims that some Portuguese reached the Caribbean during Henry's lifetime, there is no hard evidence that any of his expeditions sailed to, let alone returned from, the Western Hemisphere. There is no denying, however, that the support Henry the Navigator gave to explorers would greatly contribute to the eventual opening up of the New World to Europeans.

IN THEIR OWN

Words

The Portuguese in New England

M iguel Cortereal by Will of God, here Chief of the Indians, 1511

—ALLEGED INSCRIPTION IN PORTUGUESE ON DIGHTON ROCK, MASSACHUSETTS, ACCORDING TO EDMUND DELABARRE (1936)

Irish

Although presumably descendants of the ancient *Celts* described earlier, the medieval Irish referred to here differ in their time frame and in the nature of their alleged contacts with the New World. The claims of the Irish monk *Saint Brendan* have also been examined. But there are claims for still other Irish in North America. Starting in the late seventh century, hundreds of Irish clerics and laypeople sought refuge in Iceland, the former from the controls of their Roman Catholic superiors, the latter from Viking raids. By the late ninth century, however, when the Vikings showed up in Iceland, the Irish fled, and according to several of the *Norse* sagas, many of them made their way to *Greenland* or *Vinland* (and even to the Carolinas, according to one scholar). No Irish artifact of this era, however, has ever been found in North America.

L'Anse aux Meadows

This is the one site in North America that has been accepted by virtually all scholars as evidence that the *Norse* reached North America (beyond

Greenland, that is) before 1492. It is located on the northern tip of a region of *Newfoundland* known as the Great Northern Peninsula. As the French word *anse* ("bay") indicates, the site is on a small bay (today known as Épaves Bay). The English word *meadows* might seem to refer to the relatively flat and grassy terrain adjacent to the water, but this does not seem to be the case: Most authorities claim it is merely the anglicization of the French word *méduse* (jellyfish); a more recent claim is that although it is a French word, it refers to an actual French ship, *Medée,* that put in to the bay some centuries ago.

In any case, local residents of this part of Newfoundland had long known that there were buried remains on this site, but they assumed they belonged to an Eskimo people. As early as 1837, the Danish scholar Carl Rafn was alleging that the Norse had in fact landed on the shores of North America, as stated by the sagas, but he could not provide any specific evidence. Then in 1914, William A. Munn, a Newfoundland businessman and amateur antiquarian, published a booklet claiming that the Vikings had landed at, or near, the site of L'Anse aux Meadows. In 1956, Danish archaeologist Jørgen Meldgaard did some excavating about twenty miles from L'Anse aux Meadows but found nothing.

Then in 1960, Norwegian explorer/researcher Helge Ingstad and his wife, Anne Stine, a trained archaeologist, came to Newfoundland seeking remains of Norse settlers; they were directed to this particular site by a local man, George Decker. Ingstad and Stine began to excavate here in 1961 and almost immediately uncovered what they realized were remains of a Norse settlement. In the years that followed, they and other archaeologists uncovered the foundations of structures and various other artifacts (a soapstone spindle-whorl, a bronze pin, etc.) that establish the Norse presence. Based on the old Norse accounts, the site is regarded as probably the one established by *Leif Eriksson* about the year A.D. 1000 in the land he called *Vinland.* If this was the site

It is now firmly established that the Norse spent about ten years circa A.D. 1000 at L'Anse aux Meadows on the northern tip of Newfoundland. Based on the foundation remains and other evidence of construction materials and methods, the Canadian government has reconstructed the largest of the sod communal houses and one of the smaller houses.

described in the sagas, it is known that the Norse made at least two more serious efforts to settle here, and it is assumed that the Norse did not erect all the structures the first time; in any case, only the foundations survive. The main buildings are two great houses similar to Norse dwellings in

Greenland; the larger is seventy by fifty-five feet. The walls were turf and stone fill, a total of six feet thick; the roofs were of timber covered with sod; inside the great halls were hearths and benches, and around the central hall were small rooms. There were also smaller houses outside the two larger structures, and each of these had a central hearth. There is also evidence that they had crude ironworks, with a forge, to make items such as nails from the bog iron, a crude metal that precipitates from minerals in water and collects in the roots of the bog vegetation.

Other finds excavated over the years suggest that this site may have served as something of a trading station, possibly a collection point for goods acquired by Norse farther south to be trans-shipped to Greenland and other Norse settlements to the east. According to the accounts in the sagas, the Norse traded, but also fought, with the natives, whom the Norse called *skraelings,* a term of contempt meaning something like "barbarians" or "weaklings" or even "pygmies"; they may have been Amerindians or possibly ancestors of today's Inuit people. Exactly when and why the Norse abandoned this site is not known, but it would appear to fit into the sagas' story of Vinland, which means that it was abandoned after only some ten to twenty years. In 1978, the site, with its excavated remains, was designated a UNESCO World Heritage Site.

Leif Eriksson (980?–1025?)

As his name indicates, Leif was the son of an Erik—*Erik the Red.* He was born in Iceland only a few years before his father took the whole family off to *Greenland.* According to two of the *Norse* sagas, Leif visited Norway in A.D. 999 and was charged by King Olaf Tryggvason with introducing Christianity to Greenland; sailing back, he was blown off course and ended up discovering new lands to the west; he landed and brought back timber, grapes, and other valued produce. This is almost certainly an apocryphal story, designed to enhance Leif's image and Christianity's role. In the other main saga, Leif was inspired by the tale of *Bjarni Herjolfsson*'s chance sightings of lands to the west; in this account, Leif actually sailed in Bjarni's ship and retraced his route west. Considering that his father was a restless, intemperate, and acquisitive man, however, we need not look far to understand why Leif may have been quick to want to seek new lands. It would have been about the year A.D. 1000 when he took one ship with its crew off to the west. Exactly where they landed and how long they

Words

Leif Eriksson Lands on Newfoundland and Names It Vinland

They sailed toward this land and came to an island which lay to the northward off the land. There they went ashore and looked about them, the weather being fine, and they observed that there was dew upon the grass, and it so happened that they touched the dew with their hands and touched their hands to their mouths. And it seemed to them that they had never before tasted anything so sweet. . . . They afterwards determined to establish themselves there for the winter, and they accordingly built a large house. There was no lack of salmon there either in the river or in the lakes, and larger salmon than they had ever seen before. . . . They slept the night through and on the morrow Leif said to his shipmates: "We will now divide our labors, and each day will either gather grass or cut vines and fell trees, so as to obtain a cargo of these for my ship." They acted upon his advice, and it is said that a second boat was filled with grapes . . . and when the spring came they made their ship ready and sailed away; and from its products Leif gave the land a name, Vinland.

—THE SAGA OF THE GREENLANDERS, WRITTEN DOWN CIRCA A.D. 1200

stayed ashore cannot be proven for sure, but the strongest candidate for at least his base camp remains *L'Anse aux Meadows.*

Almost certainly Leif sailed along the coast to the south, either to the eastern coast of Newfoundland and Nova Scotia or the eastern coast of the continental mainland—possibly even some way up the *St. Lawrence River [II].* How long they stayed is also uncertain, but on his return, Leif told about such natural resources—meadows for grazing animals, great trees for ships and housing, and above all, grapes for making wine—that he named it *Vinland.* For whatever reason, Leif never returned there, but instead left it to his two brothers, first Thorvald, then Thorstein, to return. Leif would have been a prosperous landowner and had family obligations, even political power (as his father died about 1003 and he became the chief "lawspeaker"). It was enough for Leif to give his support to the subsequent voyages. (In fact, Thorstein failed to reach Vinland, and it was his widow, Gudrid, and her second husband, Thorfinn Karlsveni, who conducted the third, and most ambitious, expedition there.) If his father deserves to be known as the first European to have colonized the Western Hemisphere (that is, Greenland), then Leif Eriksson deserves to be known as the first European to have explored continental North America.

Libyans

Claims have been made that ancient Libyan inscriptions have been found in isolated locales throughout the United States. This Libyan language is said to be derived from the Coptic Egyptian, Middle Egyptian, and Nubian languages. Some even go so far as to claim that the Zuni Indians' language and some elements of their culture are derived from the Libyans who settled in that region. Barry Fell tends to combine the presence of Libyans with Egyptians, dating both to about 800 B.C. Most authorities in this field reject such claims by Fell and others.

maps

The history of exploration is essentially inseparable from the history of maps. Certainly this seems true when it comes to the Europeans' explorations and discoveries in North America.

When the first Europeans set off across the Atlantic—whatever their goals—they would have had no maps with correct distances or geographic features. This holds true no matter which Europeans one prefers to believe were the first. Even if one accepts the *Vinland Map* as authentic, the people responsible for providing its details could not have had such a map when they first discovered those details. But aside from the disputed Vinland Map, it has been generally accepted that there is no evidence that the early Norsemen who sailed back and forth between Scandinavia and *Greenland*—and at least three times to *Vinland*—contributed anything other than verbal accounts to early European mapmakers. This view has been challenged, however, by James Robert Enterline, a serious student of cartography, who makes a case for pre-Columbian *Norse* having gained knowledge of at least northeastern North America's terrain through their contacts with the Inuit and then having passed this on to medieval mapmakers. Enterline argues that details in the coastline of what these pre-Columbian mapmakers depicted as Arctic Asia actually correspond to features on the Arctic coast of North America. It remains to be seen how widely accepted Enterline's claims become.

What the fifteenth-century Europeans who set off across the Atlantic did have were maps often filled with mythical islands and lands, as well as outright errors in distances and details. Above all, they had maps that showed no great landmass between Western Europe and Eastern Asia: Although they did believe that the earth was a sphere, they continued to believe that there was essentially one great landmass surrounded by the one Ocean Sea. If you set off from the one coast (Europe) of that great landmass, you would cross that ocean to reach the other coast (Asia) of the same landmass. At least since Ptolemy in the second century A.D., this had been the view of most people in the Western world.

Accepting for the moment that *Columbus [II]* was the first from the Old World (since the first Norse, that is) to complete a round-trip to the Western Hemisphere, he had available a certain amount of information. There were several of the *mappamundi* ("world maps") and many portolan charts (coastal navigational charts) he would have known, but none that depicted the New World he would reach. There were also maps that Columbus did not know about, specifically the 1427 map by the Dane Claudius Clavus, which depicted Greenland as a large promontory of Asia extending into the ocean. There are stories about Columbus's having different maps to guide his voyage—one from Spanish or Portuguese sailors who had been blown ashore in the Caribbean about 1483–1484 and returned, or a map sent to Columbus (about 1474) from the Florentine cosmographer Paolo Toscanelli. Serious scholars, however, do not accept either of these claims. What is known is that Columbus essentially accepted the representation of the world as drawn from Ptolemy.

By coincidence, the oldest globe still extant was also made in 1492, by Martin Behaim, a German who had long lived in the Azores and for a time was keeper of the Portuguese king's map room. Behaim knew about many maps and charts then available to the Portuguese, and he incorporated this information on his globe. It is possible that Columbus knew Behaim, but Columbus had gone off to Spain by 1488, and there is no evidence that he was in touch with Behaim by 1492. In any case, Behaim's globe simply represented the conventional version of the world before Columbus's voyage—namely, one landmass in one Ocean Sea: anyone who sailed west would arrive at Japan or other islands off Asia and/or the edge of the great continent itself.

When Columbus returned from his first voyage in March 1493, his discoveries were almost immediately publicized in the letter he wrote to his friend and sponsor Luís de Santangel, and would soon be incorporated into maps. Columbus himself had only his own rough drawings of the new lands he had come across, but among his crew on the second voyage was *Juan de la Cosa [II],* an experienced navigator. After returning to Spain, de la Cosa began work in 1500 on what is generally regarded as the first authentic map showing the New World. By then, too, Columbus himself had apparently made a detailed map showing the islands and coastlines he had sailed by, but all that survives is a small sketch of the northwest coast of the island of *Hispaniola [II]* (see *Piri Reis map*). De la Cosa's map also seems to include data based on *John Cabot*'s *[III]* voyage to North America in 1497. Although greatly limited in his details and audience, de la Cosa is credited with being the first to literally and figuratively put the Western Hemisphere on the map.

From then on, maps of the New World began to appear with some regularity. The second that is recognized as authentic is known as the Cantino Map of 1502. It is named after an Italian, Alberto Cantino, who acquired it from an anonymous Portuguese mapmaker; it includes a suggestion of land that might be Florida or the Yucatan, but most scholars believe that this land was intended to represent some part of China. Although the Cantino Map remained hidden in Italy for close to a century, it appears that a copy remained in Portugal because many of its details would appear on maps made during the next eighteen years.

A more problematic map is the so-called King-Hamy chart, dated to around 1502–1503 and attributed to either an Italian or a Portuguese source. Although its rendering of Greenland, *Labrador [III],* and *Newfoundland* is hardly correct, it does appear to incorporate knowledge gained by the voyage of *João Fernandes [III].* Another problematic map is the Oliveriana Map, held at Pesaro, Italy, usually dated to 1503, and possibly made for Lorenzo de' Medici of Florence, Italy, to accompany *Amerigo Vespucci*'s *[II]* account of his voyages to the New World. It is fairly accurate in its depiction of the northeast coast of South America and some Caribbean islands, but it is shaky in its depiction of lands to the north.

Among those was the first printed map (as opposed to a handmade copy) to show any part of the New World. It was made by Giovanni Matteo Contarini and engraved in 1506 in Florence; it incorporated much of what Europeans had reported up till then but still showed the new land as a peninsula off Asia. Then in 1507 the German Martin Waldseemuller published the first map of the world that applied the name America to the New World; he based this on Amerigo Vespucci's claims to have sailed there in 1497.

In 1508 German geographer Johann Ruysch published a world map in an edition of Ptolemy's *Geographia*. Its relatively detailed depiction of the northwestern Atlantic region, including Greenland and Labrador, suggests that Ruysch drew on information from John Cabot's voyage or possibly even his own voyage to the region in the company of experienced sailors, most likely fishermen from **Bristol, England.** In any case, Greenland and Newfoundland were still regarded as promontories of Asia.

Although it may be assumed that none of these early maps circulated widely among the general public, the men who were preparing to sail off to this New World would have found ways to learn about the details. Undoubtedly many of the early maps existed in only the one copy made by the original explorer and were thus not known to many others. Then, too, the first maps to be printed in multiples, up to about the year 1550, were usually made from woodcuts and so did not have very precise details; even when intaglio printing came into use after 1550, it would be another 150 years before maps could reproduce really good details.

Furthermore, all the early maps inevitably lacked complete information and were filled with misconceptions, which were often based on Europeans' secondhand knowledge gained from their Native American informants. Giacomo Gastaldi, for example, issued his map, Terra Nueva, in 1547–1548, based on *Jacques Cartier*'s *[III]* account, which in turn was based on information given to him by Amerindians. But the role of *Native Americans* in the early mapping of North America deserves to be more widely recognized. Again, specialists who are familiar with the firsthand accounts of the early Europeans know of numerous references to the Native Americans' role—not only in providing verbal descriptions but

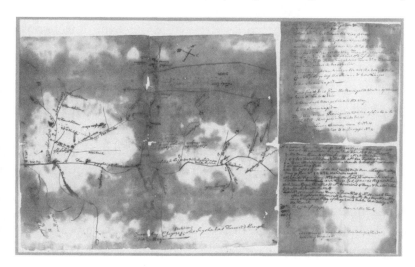

The rivers and settlements on this map were drawn by an Indian named Chegeree–probably a Miami–about 1755; an Englishman added the names, distances, and various notations. Showing essentially the Ohio Valley from the Mississippi (left) all the way to western Pennsylvania, it reveals how Native Americans' intimate knowledge of geography aided Europeans.

also in drawing crude maps on the ground or making models with sticks or pebbles. The oldest extant map made by a North American Indian dates to 1602; it was drawn for the Spanish by an Indian they called Miguel and shows many details of the area that is now eastern Texas and northern Mexico. But long before that, Native Americans were providing vital details to the early Europeans. One of the earliest recorded examples of this involved the Spanish explorer *Hernando de Alarcón [II],* who in 1540 had an elderly Indian draw a "charte" showing his knowledge of the lower Colorado River. And in 1605, Indians using charcoal provided by *Samuel de Champlain [III]* and pebbles of their own made a relatively detailed model map of what is now Massachusetts Bay.

For the first decades of the 1500s, maps of the New World tended to vary in the way they represented the newly discovered lands, some showing them as an appendage to Asia, some recognizing them as separate islands. And when the maps did suggest that the New World was a continent, the land was shown as relatively narrow. One misconception was mainly promoted by the map made in 1529 by Girolamo Verrazano, brother and shipmate of *Giovanni da Verrazano [III];* it showed the Atlantic and Pacific Oceans separated at one point by a narrow isthmus, near the coast of present-day North Carolina; Verrazano's map otherwise depicted the coast of northeastern America fairly accurately. A map made by a Portuguese, Diogo Ribeiro, that same year, but based on the voyages of *Estevåo Gómes [III]* and *Lucas Vásquez de Ayllón [III],* provided slightly more accurate details of the coast from *Florida [III]* to the Gulf of St. Lawrence.

By the 1540s mapmakers in Portugal, France, and other European lands were producing reliable maps of the New World's northeastern coasts that the mariners were charting. Meanwhile, the Spanish were busy mapping the west coast of Mexico and gradually charting the details of the coast of California. There had also emerged by this time the question of whether there was a sea route across the top of the North American landmass that would lead relatively easily to the Pacific—what became known as the *Northwest Passage [VII];* this was shown quite clearly on one of the most famous and influential maps of that era, the one issued in 1537 by Gemma Frisius and his pupil, Gerardus Mercator. Numerous other maps continued to depict all manner of imaginary islands in the waters off North America, maps that in turn are said to be based on spurious voyages.

By the 1560s ambitious maps of the New World were appearing. In 1564 a Dutch mapmaker, Abraham Ortelius, issued a world map, and in

1569, Mercator published a world map that was almost immediately accepted as showing the most reliable representation of the world (although it depicted at least ten Atlantic islands that were purely imaginary). Mercator also introduced the so-called projection that made it easier for navigators to plot their positions on the straight lines of his map. Drawing on European accounts from many sources, these and subsequent maps were surprisingly realistic, at least when it came to the well-explored eastern coasts of North America, much of Central America, and the west coast of Mexico, but they inevitably perpetuated many errors—misunderstandings about the exact locations and sizes of islands, rivers, lakes, and other geographic features. One such major error was introduced by a respected Spanish priest-geographer, Fray Antonio de la Ascension, who after sailing on the *Vizcaíno [II]* expedition of 1602–1603, submitted a report in 1608 that described the Gulf of California as a strait that went along the entire eastern "coast" of California—that is, made California an island. This error would be perpetuated by some maps for over a hundred years.

Despite these many errors, Europeans' maps of the New World were becoming increasingly more detailed and reliable by the 1600s. In 1611 a Spanish map, known as the Velasco map, was published; it was based on a map made by an unknown Englishman sent by King James I to map the English holdings in North America; this Englishman's map included even more territory by drawing on other maps and writings from explorers such as Samuel de Champlain, *John Smith [III],* and *Henry Hudson [VII].* (The map depicts in blue those features that were based on "relations of the Indians.") In 1612 John Smith published a famous map of "Virginia": it depicts the *Chesapeake Bay [III]* area—between the Atlantic coast of the Delmarva Peninsula and the Allegheny Mountains. Distinctive symbols indicate "what beyond is by relation"—that is, dependent on Indians' accounts.

That same year, 1612, Samuel de Champlain published one of the most important early maps, "Carte geographique de la Nouvelle Franse en son vray meridiein." Among its mixture of real and mistaken features, it depicts six waterways between the *St. Lawrence [III]* and Ottawa Rivers above their confluence. In fact, these did not exist, and it is believed that what Champlain was showing were routes known to his Indian informants and that involved some water and some overland traveling. In 1616 a Dutchman, Cornelius Hendricks, published a detailed map of the Hudson River; this was based on his own surveys but also drew on the work of other Dutchmen, who in turn had drawn on Indians' knowledge. In 1677 an Englishman, John Foster, published "A Map of New-England" that shows an unnamed lake dominating central New Hampshire; clearly based on the Indians' perspective of this lake, it would turn out to be what is now known as Lake Winnipesaukee.

By the 1700s maps of North America were becoming increasingly more reliable with the passage of each decade, as Europeans pushed farther and farther into the uncharted regions. Even so, many errors persisted. Guillaume De l'Isle's "Carte De L'Amérique Septentrionale" of 1743, for example, included among its many errors a river flowing westward from the Mississippi across the continent and emptying into the Pacific. It was just such misconceptions that would inspire *Thomas Jefferson [VI]* to commission the *Lewis and Clark expedition [VI]* and ultimately lead to the most accurate mapping of North America up to that time.

Markland

According to the "Saga of the Greenlanders," the medieval *Norse* account of *Leif Eriksson*'s first trip to what came to be known as *Vinland,* the second land he sighted west of *Greenland* (after *Helluland*) was seen to have forests, so Leif and his crew named it Markland, Norse for "forest-land." It is believed that this was a southerly stretch of the coast of what we today know as *Labrador [III]*. Scholars have for some time agreed that the Greenland Norse probably made occasional visits to Markland in the centuries after the end of the Vinland colony, in particular to cut highly valued large trees. But it was not until the year 2000 that some tangible evidence was found there, a strand of Norse yarn dated to about 1200. The name Markland survived on many maps until well into the sixteenth century, after which it was assigned the name Labrador, after the Portuguese word for "farmer," to honor *João Fernandes [III],* the Portuguese explorer who claimed to have discovered this land.

Muslims

Unknown except to a few specialists are the claims that medieval Muslims from Spain and West Africa got to the New World by the tenth century A.D. Many of the claims are based on Muslim texts. One suggests that Muslim navigator Khashkhash Ibn Saeed Ibn Aswad of Córdoba, Spain, crossed the Atlantic in A.D. 889 and returned with fabulous treasures. Another claim involves another Muslim navigator, Ibn Farrukh of Granada, Spain, who sailed westward in A.D. 999 and found two islands, presumably off the coast of the Americas. Another text describes a voyage by Shaikh Zayn-eddine Ali ben Fadhel Al-Mazandarani sometime between A.D. 1286 and 1307; setting out from Morocco, he supposedly reached a Green Island in the Caribbean.

Supporters of Muslims' early contributions to opening up the New World claim that two of *Columbus*'s *[II]* ship captains, the brothers Martin and Vincente Pinzon, were from a Muslim family. Meanwhile, these supporters go on to claim that when Columbus first arrived in the New World, he heard natives speaking Arabic words, saw them using spears and colorful handkerchiefs of African Muslim origin, and even reported seeing a mosque. Some supporters go still further, claiming that pre-Columbian Muslims conducted Muslim schools in North America, left inscriptions on rocks all over the Southwest, became ancestors of numerous North American Indian tribes, and provided Arabic words for hundreds of tribal and place names in North America. The major students of the pre-Columbian Americas dismiss all these claims as isolated and arbitrary similarities to Native American languages and writing systems.

Native Americans

The basic question of just what constitutes an "explorer" arises immediately with the first human inhabitants of the Western Hemisphere. Aside from the questions of when, from where, and how, they came over, there is the question of what motivated the first people to come to this hemisphere. It is assumed that these first "Americans" came in search of food, specifically, big game animals, but this cannot be proven. Considering the relatively sparse population of Asia at the time and what must have been relatively plentiful food sources, it might seem strange that anyone would go all the way to North America. But students of this subject suggest that real or imagined pressures from neighboring populations prompted these people to move in the one direction where there was no competition.

Even then, it seems plausible that at least some of the first humans to make their way into the Western Hemisphere were motivated by the sheer desire to see what lay farther on. And to the extent that with each step they

This map shows where the land designated as Beringia (the white area) protruded above sea level about 12,500 B.C. and also where great glaciers isolated Beringia from Alaska and the rest of North America. After the glaciers melted and the sea rose, Paleolithic people began to move forward into and past the sites indicated.

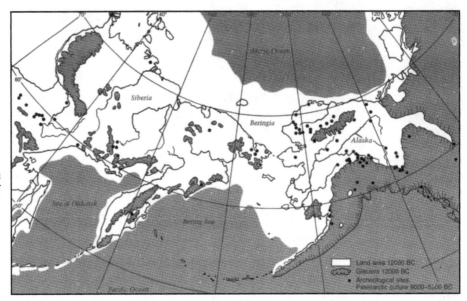

took, with each yard of water and ground they advanced across, they were opening up North America to human knowledge, they deserve to be regarded as explorers.

Exactly when these first humans came to the Western Hemisphere is still being debated. There is a small school of serious archaeologists and anthropologists who believe that they came very early—anywhere from 250,000 B.C. to 100,000 B.C. Then there is a slightly larger school that believes they came between 100,000 B.C. and, say, 35,000 B.C. But undoubtedly the majority of authorities believe the first humans did not come until sometime between 35,000 and 12,000 B.C. (It should also be noted that most authorities in this field now accept that there were at least two major waves of migrants, whether during this time frame or later.) Even this represents an adjustment from the long-held belief that they did not come until perhaps 20,000 B.C. to 10,000 B.C. This last claim was based largely on the earliest accepted finds of human-made stone tools in the hemisphere—particularly the Clovis and Folsom projectile points found at those sites in New Mexico and dated respectively to about 10,000 B.C. and 8000 B.C. But in the late decades of the twentieth century, other sites and finds were proposed by their excavators as being considerably older: Pedra Furada, in Northeastern Brazil, is dated to 46,000 B.C.; Orogrande in New Mexico has been dated by some to 28,000 B.C. Even though not all archaeologists accept those finds as evidence of human occupation at such early dates, sites in other remote regions suggest that the Paleo-Indians, as the first inhabitants of the hemisphere are often called by archaeologists, must have come over fairly early to be able to make their way to such distant points. Among such sites are Meadowcroft rock shelter in western Pennsylvania (at least 12,000 B.C.); Cactus Hill in southeastern Virginia (possibly 14,000–13,000 B.C.); Monte Verde in southern Chile (at least 10,500 B.C.); and Fell's Cave in southern Argentina (about 9000 B.C.).

Exactly who these first Americans were and where they originated are not questions essential to this work, but they are certainly of interest. Again, there have been several "schools," but the most widely accepted theory is that they were inhabitants of Asia, most likely long resident in northeastern Siberia by the time they first set off. Most anthropologists believe they were primarily of the same physical stock as the so-called Mongoloid peoples of Asia; within this school there are some who trace these people's ancestry to the same stock who inhabited Mongolia, China, and Japan; some trace them more directly to the inhabitants of Southeast Asia or even Tibet. But it should be recognized that some anthropologists strongly reject this model, contending that far more diverse groups, including people of the Caucasoid type, contributed to the ancestry of modern American Indians. In particular, the 1996 discovery in eastern Washington of a skull and other skeletal remains of a man—dubbed Kennewick Man, from the locale where he was found—and interpreted by some anthropologists as having Caucasoid features, has raised even more controversy about the origins of North American Indians.

How the first Americans made their way to the Western Hemisphere is also a matter of some disagreement. Again, most authorities believe they made their way by foot across the land bridge that joined present-day Siberia and Alaska. Known as Beringia (after the Bering Sea that now exists there), it was simply the exposed ocean floor created by the long period of glaciation that "locked up" so much ocean water during the period roughly 21,000–11,000 B.C. In this scenario, the first immigrants made their way south through a corridor along the edge of the Canadian Rockies; once south of the glaciers, they spread overland relatively quickly southward and eastward. (A subsection of this school holds that some at least, once on the North American mainland, made their way southward and eastward in small boats across and down the waterways of the north.) A second school now challenges that view and suggests that the first people ashore may have originated in Siberia and come by small boats down along the coasts of Alaska, Canada, and northwestern America. There are still more controversial "schools," but none generally accepted by major scholars. (The first arrival of the ancestors of the Inuit and Aleut people of the Arctic regions is another issue, dealt with in Part VII.)

Whatever the mode of travel or first points of entry, there is no question that by about 12,000 B.C. human beings had made their way to many distant points throughout the Western Hemisphere. Along the way, they discovered many of the natural features of the land—streams and rivers, mountains and valleys, lakes and ponds, forests and grasslands, inlets and islands. They were certainly aware of much of the wild flora and fauna, for they depended on them for their nourishment and shelter and clothing. They also discovered many of the mineral resources (although it would not be until about five thousand years ago that they began to extract metals—first copper and, centuries later, gold).

It cannot be proven that these first Americans set out systematically or self-consciously to explore new places, nor did they discover every single feature of the land. But they were the first to explore the Western Hemisphere. This became more than apparent when the first European explorers arrived and drew on the Native Americans' knowledge to make their "discoveries." Beyond the several recognized and named Indian "guides" and "pilots"—*Coronado*'s *[II]* "The Turk," the New England Pilgrims' Squanto, *Lewis and Clark*'s *[VI]* Sacagawea—there were countless unnamed Native Americans who led the Europeans to otherwise unknown destinations. From Columbus's first expedition on, Indians were taken captive or otherwise persuaded to go with Europeans, and many learned at least some European language. Meanwhile, various Europeans—shipwrecked, captured, runaways—would live among Indians and learn their language. By the seventeenth century, increasing contacts between the natives and Europeans led to the transfer of crucial geographic information.

Some of the information drawn from Native Americans was in error or at least misunderstood by the Europeans. Native Americans, for one thing, made little distinction between the real world and the mythical; in addition, both their experiences and belief systems embraced a relatively

IN THEIR OWN *Words*

American Indians as Tartars

The north-east people of America, that is, N. England, etc, are judged to be Tartars, called Samoades, being alike in complexion, shape, habit, and manners. The Mohawks are about 500; their speech is a dialect of the Tartars (as also is the Turkish tongue).

—JOHN JOSSELYN, *NEW ENGLAND RARITIES* (1672) AND *AN ACCOUNT OF TWO VOYAGES IN NEW ENGLAND* (1674)

small world, so that their accounts of distant geographic features might be highly fanciful. Sometimes Indian informants deliberately misled Europeans by providing false information; these false reports were not lies but simply the Native Americans' different perceptions of distances or features.

On the other hand, early Europeans noted the Indians' fine sense of direction, their ability to read the stars, and their navigational skills on land and water. And this was not just the occasional observation; the Native Americans passed on detailed knowledge of the land around them from generation to generation.

Europeans' dependence on Native Americans' geographic knowledge is particularly clear when it comes to the history of *maps* of North America. But one need not turn to the past or to books to find confirmation of this. Naming a new place has always been the traditional prerogative of explorers. It is estimated that to this day, about half of the natural features of North America have Native American names, a living testament to their role in exploring the continent.

Thousands of years ago, Native Americans traveled about North America as hunters and food-gatherers, and some etched records of their travels on rocks—petroglyphs. Map Rock is a basalt boulder located near the Snake River near Givens Hot Springs, Idaho, at a spot easily seen by travelers along the river. Approximately 10 feet by 9 feet by 5 feet, it has been interpreted as a map of the upper Snake River and surrounding environment. It is believed to have been made by Shoshone Indians who entered the region in the fifteenth century.

navigation

With few exceptions, those who sailed to and around North America depended on virtually the same navigational instruments and methods from the earliest times until the twentieth century. And many of these had been devised centuries earlier. Only a few crucial navigational instruments and methods were developed during the years between 1492 and 1922. To this day, when we "log on" to our computers, we are using an expression derived from one of the ancient navigators' basic devices.

As long as ships stayed in familiar waters and close to shore, mariners needed little more than a directional compass, a pair of dividers (the geometric compass), and what have been called "the three L's": a lookout to watch for obstacles or familiar landmarks; lead for dropping a line to measure depths to the bottom or to warn of hard submerged objects; and a log to measure speeds.

The lookout relied on his eyesight until the seventeenth century and the invention of the telescope. This is usually assigned to the year 1608 and credited to a Dutchman, Hans Lippershey; Galileo then quickly took it on and improved it. Although it aided mariners looking for distant objects or an approaching landfall, the telescope did not aid navigation on the open seas, where there was nothing to be seen.

The more sophisticated lead weights had a socket filled with a sticky tallow (animal fat) that, on making contact with the bottom, picked up a sample that told an experienced navigator where the ship was. Meanwhile, centuries of sailing along the coasts of the Old World had produced pilot books, or portolans—charts showing in considerable detail the features of the coastlines and coastal waters, including shallows and obstacles that navigators would want to avoid. The Vikings, by the way, took depth soundings with a lead weight on a line; as they pulled it up, they measured it by the length of their outstretched arms, known as a *fathmr*, the root of the English word "fathom," still the standard unit for measuring marine depths (about 6 feet, or 1.83 meters).

Finally, mariners sometimes wanted to measure the speed at which they were traveling. The standard method for doing this had been around for many centuries; the device was known as a log, and the unit of measurement was known as a knot. (Both these terms have remained in use.) Originally the log was nothing more than just that—a piece of wood attached to a line that was thrown overboard by a sailor who counted the number of equally spaced knots that he released into the water during a fixed period of time, usually thirty seconds; these were either counted off by a seaman or measured by a half-minute sandglass timer. Experienced mariners, of course, were good at estimating their speed without resorting to such measurements. This log, by the way, gave its name to the "logbook," a record of the ship's daily proceedings, and this in turn was adopted by the computer industry as "log on" (or in or out), to enter the command to start each day's session.

The first Europeans generally accepted to have traveled to and from the New World, the Norsemen, apparently had only the most basic navigational devices and systems. They did not have a magnetic compass but simply tried to maintain a route along a given latitude. They took the latitude by measuring the angular height of the North Star at night and the sun's azimuth during the day. During thick weather, when they couldn't see sun or stars, they had to sail on as best they could; then when the weather cleared, they would use a "sun-shadow board": a wooden disc on which concentric circles were marked; in the center was a pin that could be raised or lowered to account for the angle of the sun above the horizon. The disc might be floated in water to keep it level in relation to the earth as the ship tossed and turned; the shadow cast by the sun at the meridional gave a rough indication of how far off the desired latitude the ship was, and they would then adjust their direction to get back onto the desired latitude.

So long as ships plied the long-familiar routes, navigators could afford to be fairly relaxed about using these devices and methods. It was enough to know that it usually took two or three days to get from Point A to Point B; in any case, ships would seldom be that far from land—in the Mediterranean, two hundred miles at most. But once European mariners set off to explore unknown waters and distances and destinations, it became important to use all means available. There were essentially four elements that the long-distance navigators needed to be able to keep track of: the speed at which they were traveling, the distance being traveled, the direction in which they were traveling, and their location on the globe at any given moment.

The means for measuring speed remained the log, but by about 1600, this device began to be improved in several ways. For one, a lead weight was attached to one edge of the log so that it remained upright in the sea and resisted towing. This log was tied to a line of cord or heavy string that was wound up on a reel; when the line was thrown into the sea as the ship sailed along, the log remained more or less stationary and caused the line to unreel. Meanwhile, starting at 60 feet from the log, the line was knotted at intervals of 42 feet (later corrected to 47 feet, 3 inches); one knot at the first point, two knots at the second, three at the third, and so on. The line was allowed to unreel for 30 seconds as timed by a half-minute sand glass (later to be timed at 28 seconds), and the number of knots unreeled was then counted. That was the speed per hour—5 knots meant 5 nautical miles. The reason for 30 seconds was that that time period was in proportion to one hour what 42 feet was to the then definition of a nautical mile—namely, 1/120th. (The 28 seconds and 47 feet 3 inches are in the same proportion to the corrected nautical mile of 6,076.1 feet, or 1,852 meters.) Again, though, experienced navigators probably relied on their own estimations of speed much of the time.

The goal of the earliest maritime navigators traveling to distant lands was to keep track of distances and locations so that they could report back with these and the voyages could be repeated. Units of measurement for distances at sea—as on land—differed from country to country (as they still do, affecting scholars' calculations). The basic unit for measuring distance on land in Europe was the mile, derived from the Roman *mille passuum*, "thousand steps"; although its actual distance differed from country to country, by about A.D. 1500 the English converted it to the 5,280 feet we know today. (The metric system was created by French scientists in the 1790s.) The nautical mile, however, is intended to reflect the actual area of the earth; it is arrived at by dividing the circumference of the earth into 360 degrees, and then dividing each degree into 60 minutes. One nautical mile then equals one minute, or 1/21,600 of the earth's circumference.

Another unit commonly used during the early centuries of exploration for measuring distances at sea and on land was a "league" (a term derived from the ancient Gauls). Again, its actual distance varied considerably from country to country and over time. A nautical league today equals 3 nautical miles, or 5.5556 kilometers. Columbus used a "league" that was the equivalent of about 3.8 English nautical miles. The French tended to use a *petit mille marin* ("small nautical mile"), three of which made the *petite lieue marine* ("small nautical league"); until about 1633, the French league was the equivalent of between 2.2 and 2.31 English nautical miles; in 1633, the French nautical mile was made the exact equivalent of the English nautical mile (or 1,852 meters). Most Italians used a mile that was the equivalent of 4 French leagues. As for the league as a unit of distance on land, this varied greatly from the 1400s to at least the early 1800s—anywhere from 2 to 3.6 modern U.S. miles. Given this wide variation, this work avoids giving distances in terms of leagues.

For most of the early exploration of North America, the exact circumference of the earth was not known, so the unit used to measure distances at sea differed over time. The result of all these variations was that reports of distances were inevitably inconsistent. In general, though, mariners knew how to calculate and adjust for the differences. Once ashore in the New World, of course, Europeans encountered Amerindians who had their own systems for keeping track of distances along their coasts, lakes, and rivers.

As for finding directions, experienced mariners knew how to navigate based on the position of the sun and stars. But this was not adequate for sailing day after day on open and unknown seas. For this, the magnetic compass came into use. The Chinese had known of the application of the magnetic lodestones for many centuries and had almost certainly developed some type of magnetic direction indicator by at least the third century A.D., although it is believed that the Chinese did not employ a magnetic compass for navigation until about A.D. 1050–1090. Mediterranean navigators were using magnetic compasses about a century later. These first magnetic compasses were nothing more than magnetized needles placed on a straw or cork that floated in water; soon the needle itself was fixed to pivot on a pin attached to a base. During the 1200s came the compass card, on which the directions were divided into thirty-two equal units and painted with colorful symbols. The compass was often enclosed under a waterproof "binnacle," a wooden box that had a small whale-oil lamp so that the compass could be read in the darkness. On smaller ships, the officer on duty watched the compass and called out directions to the helmsman; on larger ships, the helmsman had his own compass.

As magnetic compasses came into wider use, navigators realized that the needle did not point to geographic north but to magnetic north; the angle between these two points as measured from a particular location is known as magnetic declination. Navigators began to learn how to use these compasses with increasing accuracy as they learned about the declination of magnetic needles in different parts of the world. Eventually, too, they learned that the declination varies at different times of a year and in different years, so that navigators must have a declination chart to calculate these variations.

In order to make full use of the various measurements, some device to keep track of time was also required. Clocks that worked well on land were not reliable at sea, and most ships carried a half-hour sand glass; a cabin boy was expected to turn it precisely every half hour (the basis of the sounding of bells adopted later). Simple sundials were also used. Coordinating the measurements of distance traversed and direction with the passage of time was the basis for allowing experienced navigators to proceed by dead reckoning—that is, simply plotting a ship's course on a chart. No matter how many instruments and aids the early navigators had, they relied heavily on their experience in dead reckoning. One other thing should be kept in mind when reading about the early centuries of explorations: Virtually all reports of latitude must be taken with some allowance for the fact that the readings were based on inaccurate tables of the declination of the sun (not to be confused with magnetic declination). This could result in an error of from $\frac{1}{2}$ degree close to the equator to 2 degrees farther to the north.

All this was sufficient to get back and forth on a given voyage—but the goal of serious navigators and explorers was to be able to report where they had been, record it fairly precisely on a map, and then to be able to repeat the voyage and return to these same destinations. For this, more exact measurements were required. This had long been accomplished by what is known as "celestial navigation"—calculating a ship's latitude by sightings made on the sun, stars, moon, or planets. By the time *Columbus [II]* and his immediate successors were traversing the Atlantic, experienced navigators had two basic instruments for celestial navigation—one known as the astrolabe, the other called a quadrant.

Astrolabes had been in use at least since the time of the ancient Greeks, but they were usually quite bulky and were used mainly on land. The more portable mariner's astrolabe came into general use only in the 1400s. It was a metal disc with graduations and a center-pivoted bar with sights. The quadrant was a simpler device—Columbus's was nothing but a wooden triangle with a plumb bob on a thread.

Both astrolabe and quadrant performed much the same function. They were used to determine the angle of elevation of the sun or other heavenly bodies above the horizon. Using one of these, navigators based their calculations on the positions of two celestial bodies—the sun and the North Star (also known as Polaris). If they were relying on the sun, navigators had declination tables that allowed them to make noontime observations of the position of the sun and then adjust to calculate the approximate latitude. If they were reading Polaris at night, they had sailing directions known as rutters (from the French word *routiers*) that allowed them to make their adjustments depending on the positions of two stars of the Little Bear (or the Little Dipper). In addition to rutters, ships carried various almanacs, tables, and other publications that showed the positions of various celestial bodies at different times of the year, different times of day, and different points of the earth.

There was yet another device that some navigators preferred for taking the altitudes of heavenly bodies and thereby determining latitude. To continental Europeans, it was known as the *balestilas;* the English called it the cross staff (or Jacob's staff). A short cross piece, or cross vane, could be slid up and down the long piece of wood, the staff; the bottom tip of the cross vane was aligned with the horizon, and the vane was then moved along the staff piece until its top edge was aligned with the viewer's line of sight up to the North Star or the sun. This simple device proved to be easier to use and in some ways at least as efficient as the quadrant and astrolabe. And it became even more valued when *John Davis [VII]*, the noted English navigator, improved this with his "backstaff," which allowed the user to keep his back to the sun.

All these devices were fine so long as the wind was favorable and skies were clear enough to see the heavenly bodies. But there were many times when these conditions did not prevail, and ships deliberately sailed, or were blown, well off course; this was called traversing, what modern sailors know as tacking. For such situations, navigators had developed a device known as a traverse board, a board with small holes, into which the seaman on watch stuck a peg for every half hour or hour that the ship was sailing off course; pegs in other holes indicated the estimated speed during each course. The data were then transferred to a chart known as a "carde"—basically a sheet of paper that was ruled for latitude and longitude; the navigator pricked the card for each known period of time to reveal their position along a continuous line. When conditions were right, ships could then readjust their course.

Although the astrolabe and the quadrant would be improved somewhat over the centuries, they remained relatively the same until they were replaced by the sextant (or reflecting quadrant). This was invented independently by two men about 1730, John Hadley in England and Thomas Godfrey in America. The sextant, incorporating mirrors, was a far more sophisticated and accurate device for determining the angle of elevation of these heavenly bodies. Refinements of the sextant would produce the instrument still used by many navigators today (the U.S. Naval Academy stopped teaching its use only in the year 2000).

All these instruments and methods proved adequate for determining latitude, but longitude proved to be more difficult. Experienced mariners had their own methods, but there was no reliable device or method for doing so until the eighteenth century. In 1713 the British government offered a prize of £20,000 for the invention of an accurate means of determining longitude; it was eventually awarded to John Harrison, who in 1726 produced the first of his chronometers, which allowed for accurate timekeeping in moving ships. Once this device was invented, nothing much changed to improve navigation for another two hundred years.

Of course many of these devices and techniques were not even available when the first ships set off to explore the New World. Many sailors did not possess the equipment or knowledge—they simply relied on taking "eye altitudes" of the sun and the North Star. Even when they had astrolabes and quadrants, these did not always guarantee exact measurements, and it would be some time before all ships could afford to carry the chronometer. But master navigators such as *Verrazano [III], Cartier [III],* Davis, and many others were amazingly accurate when it came to assigning latitudes to now-known places. At the same time the earliest explorers were usually far off in their estimates of the distances they had traveled across the sea: They usually overestimated their speed and underestimated the length of a degree of longitude, so that Verrazano, for instance, reported he had sailed some 4,800 miles across the Atlantic (when the distance was probably not more than 4,000).

George Best, an Englishman, wrote of *Martin Frobisher*'s *[VII]* voyages in his *True Discourse* of 1578: "The making and pricking of Cardes, the shifting of Sunne and Moone, the use of the compasse, the houre glass for observing time, instruments of Astronomie to take Longitudes and Latitudes of Countleys, and many other helps, are so commonly knowen of every Mariner now adayes, that he that hathe bin twice at Sea, is ashamed to come home, if he be not able to render accompte of all these particularities." Although somewhat exaggerated, this confirms that the early explorers of the New World could—and did—make reasonably accurate records of their trips and discoveries.

Newfoundland

It is now generally accepted that the *Norse* remains at *L'Anse aux Meadows* on the northern tip of Newfoundland attest to the earliest known settlement of Europeans in the Americas. After they abandoned this site—probably around A.D. 1015—Newfoundland pretty much vanished from the consciousness of Europeans, although scholars suspect that some Norse from *Greenland* may well have put ashore for occasional brief visits. It was not until the late 1490s that Newfoundland reemerged in the pages of recorded European history.

Norse

In addition to the Norse contacts generally accepted by all serious scholars—specifically, those discussed under *Vinland, Helluland, Markland*—claims are made for all kinds of evidence of the presence of Norsemen in North America. The most controversial of these involves the Kensington Stone, allegedly dug up near Kensington, Minnesota, in 1898; its supporters insist that the inscription in the medieval Norse script known as runes is authentic and denotes the presence of Norse this far west in the year 1362; most serious scholars reject the Kensington Stone as a hoax. A claim of a much earlier (Bronze Age!) Norse presence in this region is based on petroglyphs, or rock carvings, found on a stone at Peterboro, Ontario.

The famous Kensington Runestone, found in Minnesota in 1898, is alleged to have an inscription in an old Norse rune script indicating that Norse were present in 1362, but many scholars dispute this.

Another equally controversial claim of widespread Norse presence is based on a tower in Newport, Rhode Island, long called the Viking Fort; it has been proven (at least to scholars' satisfaction) to have been erected by colonists in the 1600s. Beyond these two major artifacts, there are many others cited by proponents of the wide presence of Norse in North America. These include alleged runic inscriptions at Spirit Pond, Maine; No Man's Island, Massachusetts; Le Flore County, Oklahoma; and Dighton Rock at Berkley, Massachusetts. (It should also be noted that the inscriptions on this

IN THEIR OWN *Words* Medieval Norse in Minnesota

*G*oths [Swedes] and 22 Norwegians on a voyage of discovery from Vinland westward. *We made our camp by 2 skerries [rocky inlets] one day's journey north of this stone. We were out fishing one day. When we cam home we found 10 men red with blood and dead. AVM save us from evil. We have 10 men by the sea to look after our ships, 14 days' journey from their island. Year 1362.*

—KENSINGTON STONE INSCRIPTION IN NORSE RUNES, ALLEGEDLY EXCAVATED NEAR KENSINGTON, MINNESOTA, IN 1898

Dighton Rock, which scholars believe are of Algonkin Indian origin, have been attributed to countless others aside from Norse—Chinese, Japanese, Mongolians, *Phoenicians,* Portuguese; someone even claimed that Jesus Christ inscribed his initials there on a visit in A.D. 15.) Another favored type of "evidence" of Norse presence are so-called mooring stones, found at various shore sites along the Atlantic and as far west as Minnesota. The plain fact is that almost all academically trained authorities in the appropriate disciplines reject both the "evidence" and the proposition that the Norse ever traveled so widely in North America.

Because of its unusual design, the stone tower at Newport, Rhode Island, has long intrigued people, and many insist that it was built by pre-Columbian visitors—Vikings being the chief contenders—but archaeologists have established that it was built in colonial times as a mill.

Phoenicians

Since the ancient Phoenicians were undeniably a great seafaring people who sailed far to establish their colonies and trade, it is inevitable that there should be claims that some made their way to the New World. The major claim involves the alleged discovery in 1872 of a stone tablet in Brazil with a Phoenician inscription, translated as an explicit statement by Phoenicians from Sidon; all serious scholars dismiss it as a hoax (especially since the stone itself has never been produced). As indicated elsewhere, Barry Fell finds Punic, or Phoenician, inscriptions all over North America, but he traces these to Phoenicians based in Iberia. Others have also claimed that sites from New Hampshire to Pennsylvania confirm a Phoenician presence, but most authorities reject such claims.

Pining and Pothorst   (*fl.* late 1400s)

Among the more dubious candidates as predecessors of Columbus in discovering the New World are these two individuals. Didrik Pining and

Hans Pothorst were described as "notorious pirates" in Olaus Magnus's *History of the Northern Peoples* (1555), but elsewhere they are said to have served as valued privateers in the service of King Christian I of Denmark in the late 1400s. Not much is known about Pothorst except that he was probably a German. Didrik Pining is also believed to have been a German, but he may have been a Norwegian nobleman; most significantly, he served the Danish king as governor of part of Iceland for several years beginning in 1478. Probably the closest Pining and Pothorst got to North America is the small island of Hvitsark, halfway between Iceland and Greenland, but some have tried to link them to a 1476 exploratory voyage attributed to *Johannes Scolvus,* or Skolp. (In some sources, the Portuguese João Vaz *Corte-Réal [III]* is also said to have been on this voyage.)

Piri Reis map

Along with the *Vinland Map,* this is one of the most suggestive, if controversial, documents relevant to early knowledge of the Western Hemisphere. Unlike the Vinland Map, though, the authenticity of this map is not questioned; what is debated is the source and nature of its information, dated to 1513. Piri Reis (1465?–1554) was an Ottoman-Turkish admiral (*reis* in Turkish) who displayed an interest in making *maps* based on whatever sources he could tap. In 1513, he had drawn the first of two world maps (the second was made in 1528), both of which he presented to the great Sultan Suleiman the Magnificent. The maps were eventually lost among the rich treasures of the Sultan's Topkapi Serai Palace in Istanbul, but in 1929 the 1513 map was found when the palace was being converted into a museum. Although the only part found is the left section, it does depict the newly discovered territories of the Western Hemisphere, and an inscription on the map states that among the sources for the New World are four contemporary Portuguese maps and a map by none other than *Columbus [II].* Scholars do agree that the map's depiction of several islands in the West Indies, most especially *Hispaniola [II]* and *Cuba [II],* seem to rely on Columbus's reports from his second voyage. But they reject the more outlandish claims made by some (e.g., that Antarctica is accurately depicted, or that this is based on maps left by extraterrestrials or people from Atlantis). In any case, the Piri Reis map reveals knowledge of only the portion of North America around the Caribbean.

Scolvus (Skolp), Johannes (*fl*. late 1400s)

Johannes Scolvus, or Skolp, seems to have been a historical personage, but little is known of him. In one sixteenth-century text, he is said to have been a Polish seaman, in another, English, in another, Norwegian, and in still another, Danish. In any case, he is referred to in several sixteenth-century texts as a mariner who made his way to *Greenland* and other Arctic lands, and in at least two sources this voyage is dated to 1476 (or 1477 or 1474). Although there is really not much more to go on than the sixteenth-century texts—which may simply be repeating the same misinformation—there is a slim possibility that at least Johannes Scolvus made his way to Greenland and possibly even around its southwesternmost point, Cape Farewell. But just as the Portuguese claim that João Vaz Corte-Réal, father of *Gaspar Corte-Réal [III]* discovered the New World in 1472 (or 1473), some Poles insist that Scolvus's real name was Jan of Kolvo (or Kovno), Poland, and thus he deserves to be recognized as having discovered the New World in 1476. (A Catalan, meanwhile, claims that Scolvus's real last name was Colom, and that the voyage in question was that of *Christopher Columbus [II]* in 1477.)

Sinclair, Henry (circa 1345–circa 1400)

Alleged by some to have been a visitor to North America a century before Columbus, Henry Sinclair was born near Edinburgh, Scotland, and inherited the title and responsibilities of the Earl of Orkney. The Orkney Islands, lying between Scotland and Norway, were then held by Norway's king, so Sinclair is said to have played a role in Norway's history. Little is known for certain about Sinclair—he is said to have made a pilgrimage to the Holy Land, to have fought in a crusade, to have been a Knight Templar—but more relevant, he is said to have been a great mariner. In this role, he is said to have known the *Zeno* family of Venice, and drawing on their knowledge and his own skills, he set sail for the land to the west. It is then claimed that he landed on Nova Scotia in 1398 and in Massachusetts in 1399. Some even claim he built the Newport Tower. (See *Norse.*) After this he vanished from history, but his grandson memorialized this alleged voyage in a stone at Rosslyn Castle, near Edinburgh, and his descendants actively promote Sinclair's pre-Columbian feat to this day.

skraelings

Skraelings is the name used in the *Norse* sagas for the natives encountered in *Vinland.* It is a Norse word that meant something like "barbarians" or "wretches"—inferior beings; one scholar has translated it as "scruffy wimps." Whatever its exact meaning, the word expresses contempt. The skraelings were evidently not encountered on the first visit to Vinland by *Leif Eriksson,* but they did attack the second expedition led by Leif's brother Thorvald; eight of the skraelings were killed, but others mortally wounded Thorvald. By the time the next Norse expedition tried to settle in Vinland, the skraelings were so aggressive that they evidently discouraged the Norse from staying. Indeed, it is generally agreed that the hostility of the skraelings was a major factor in convincing the Norse to abandon all plans to settle in this New World.

Just who the skraelings were has long been a matter of scholarly debate. Some authorities believe they may have been paleoeskimos of the Dorset Culture phase, and there is little dispute over the fact that these Dorset people were on Newfoundland by the year A.D. 1000. But the broader consensus now is that these skraelings were ancestors of the *Beothuk [III]* Indians encountered by the Europeans who arrived on Newfoundland in the early 1500s.

Vinland

This is the name the medieval *Norse* gave to the land they discovered and settled to the west of *Greenland.* Although most scholars accept that it refers to *Newfoundland,* they admit that this leaves some problems. The principal sources for the account of the Norse in this new land are known as "sagas," in particular, the *Graenlendiga saga* ("Saga of the Greenlanders") and *Eiriks saga rauoa* ("The Saga of Erik the Red," sometimes referred to as "The Saga of Thorfinn Karlsevni"). Exactly when they originated as oral histories is not known, but it was probably the thirteenth century before either was written down—and there remain many inconsistencies between them. The sagas describe the first visit to this new land as the expedition led by *Leif Eriksson,* assumed to have occurred about A.D. 1000. ("The Saga of the Greenlanders" tells of a *Bjarni Herjolfsson* who sighted an unknown land to the west of Greenland when his ship was blown off course; this was several years before Leif led the first group ashore, but even if true, it can never be proven that he sighted the same landmass soon to become known as Vinland. He might have sighted any number of other islands or extensions of North America.) According to "The Saga of the Greenlanders," Leif Eriksson named the land Vinland because he and his people discovered grapevines and grapes growing there. The saga recounts that they loaded a small boat with these grapes to bring back to Greenland.

Even Adam of Bremen, an eleventh-century German Catholic canon and chronicler who was the earliest known person to write about the Norse discoveries, reported about A.D. 1075 that the king of Denmark "spoke of an island in that [northern] ocean . . . which is called *Winland,* for the reason that vines yielding the best of wine grow there wild." Yet botanists agree that wild grapes could not have grown as far north as Newfoundland, especially at the location of ***L'Anse aux Meadows,*** the one proven Norse site in the New World, even if we accept that the climate may have been somewhat warmer at that time. However, since 1910 some botanists have proposed that the word in the sagas translated as "grapes," *vinber,* actually means "wineberrry" and might well have been the mountain cranberry, wild red currant, or gooseberry. This does not satisfy those who insist that the Norse would never have confused matters by invoking wine. On the other side, some people suggest that the name *Vinland* should not be taken literally, that it may have been an attempt to make this distant and forbidding land a more desirable destination for colonists. One group of scholars argues that the name derives from the Norse word *vin* with a short vowel (as opposed to the long vowel) and that it refers to "green meadow"; this possibility seems highly appealing, but most scholars reject this. Still another argument is that the Leif and his people most likely "imported" grapes from a region to the south, just as they apparently brought other produce (specifically butternuts, *Juglans cinerea*) from that same southern region to this tip of Newfoundland. "The Saga of Erik" also claims that the first Norse found "self-sown wheat" in Vinland; again it is a fact that the species known today as wheat has never grown there, but many scholars believe that the *hveiti* translated as "wheat" is most likely lyme grass, a wild grass with a wheatlike head that grows along shores from Iceland to New England; even up to modern times it has been used by Icelanders to make flour for bread.

The sagas explicitly describe three more expeditions to Vinland over the next thirteen years or so. The second was led by Leif's brother Thorvald; he spent about two years exploring the new land, but after his men killed several natives, the *skraelings,* they retaliated in great numbers. Thorvald was killed and buried in the New World, and his party returned to Greenland. Another of Leif's brothers, Thorstein, led an expedition westward, but he apparently never made it to the land. Thorstein's widow, Gudrid, then married a prosperous Icelandic merchant, Thorfinn Thordsson Karlsveni, and they led another colonizing party over to Vinland; there Gudrid gave birth to a boy, Snorri, who may have been the first white child born in the New World. This group spent perhaps two or three years in Vinland but seems to have been discouraged eventually by some combination of the extreme environment and the hostile skraelings. (In one of their fights with the skraelings, a Viking woman bared her breasts, slapped them with a sword, and screamed, so terrifying the skraelings that they fled.)

After Gudrid and her family left Vinland, there are no specific or clear-cut accounts of Norse settlers in Vinland, although there is some evidence to suggest that some Norse may have returned there off and on in search of trees or other natural resources. There is even one claim that an Icelandic Roman Catholic bishop, Eirik Gnupsson, visited Vinland in the twelfth century. Gudrid, incidentally, converted to Christianity on returning to Iceland and became a nun; she is then said to have walked all the way to Rome, where she met with the pope and reported on the state of Christianity in Greenland and Iceland. Her epic journeys have earned Gudrid the sobriquet of "the most traveled woman of the Middle Ages."

But if the Norse abandoned the settlement of Vinland, there is growing evidence that the Norse continued to make contact with Dorset or Thule Eskimo peoples in the late eleventh through the fifteenth centuries. This evidence includes various items such as chess pieces, iron ship rivets, woven cloth, bits of chain mail, and wooden barrel staves found on the edges and islands of Arctic North America. Especially suggestive are several small wooden carvings, found at Inuit sites dated from about A.D. 1100 to 1300, and almost certainly depicting Europeans. On the island of Kingittorsuaq off the west coast of Greenland, three Norsemen inscribed runes on a stone indicating they had been there in about A.D. 1250. Perhaps the most suggestive of all is the so-called Maine Penny: a Norwegian coin from the reign of Olaf Kyrre (1065–1080) excavated at a twelfth-century Indian site on the Maine coast. However, as it was found with objects indicating trade with Dorset Eskimos of northern Labrador, most serious scholars believe that this coin was carried there by the indigenous peoples, not by Norse.

It is tempting to assert for certain that the site at L'Anse aux Meadows is the very Vinland of Leif Eriksson, and the odds are that it was at least its base camp; but the fact is that the exact location of the Vinland of the Norse sagas remains undetermined, and this has been one of the reasons that some people for many years have continued to argue that the Norse made their way much farther down the coast of North America—some arguing for landings as far south as Chesapeake Bay. (See also *Norse.*)

Vinland Map

In 1965, the Yale University Press published a book called *The Vinland Map and the Tartar Relation,* edited by three reputable scholars, R. A. Skelton, Thomas A. Marston, and George D. Painter. Its centerpiece was a map showing much of the known world around the year 1440, and for the most part this map conforms with other known maps of that era. What distinguished this map, however—and produced an instant sensation and ongoing controversy—was that it included two elements never before depicted: It showed *Greenland* as an island (whereas all other maps up until then had depicted it as a peninsula of Asia) and assigned the name "Vinlanda" to what we know as *Baffin Island [VII].* If authentic, it strongly suggested that Norsemen had gathered and mapped an amazing amount of accurate detail about Greenland and Baffin Island well before *Columbus's [II]* voyage. The claim of the scholars was that the complete map was intended to illustrate a manuscript copy of *The Tartar Relation,* attributed to an Italian Franciscan friar, John of Plano Carpini, or possibly to Benedict the Pole, who accompanied Carpini on his trip to Mongolia in the 1240s. Both the map and the manuscript were brought to the Yale scholars by Laurence C. Witten, a book dealer in New Haven, Connecticut, who would say only that he acquired them in Europe in the 1950s. Later, when Yale acquired a manuscript of the *Speculum historiale,* part of an encyclopedia compiled in the thirteenth century by Vincent de Beauvais, Witten claimed that it had the same bookworm holes as his *Tartar Relation* and so the texts must have once been bound together; since the *Speculum* was genuine, the map must also be genuine.

Most scholars, however, regard the Vinland Map as a forgery. Their rejection centers on two main points: the chemical composition of the ink, which many experts feel could only be of modern origin; and the fact that Iceland, Greenland, and Baffin Island are drawn with a realism and precision totally inconsistent with the knowledge or maps of this time. Indeed, the rejectors point out, somehow this map depicts Iceland and Greenland with far greater accuracy than it depicts Scandinavia and the rest of the world. The final word on the chemical analysis of the ink remains to be pronounced, especially since some experts claim that the chemicals found in the ink could be present in medieval ink. Although the rejectors accept that the parchment is of medieval origin, they contend that some modern forger obtained an old piece of parchment, copied one or another genuine map of the late fifteenth or early sixteenth century onto it, and then added the three islands to make it appear that the Norse had considerable knowledge of North America well before the voyages of Columbus and the other southern Europeans. In 2002 Kirsten Seaver, a recognized scholar in the field of Norse/Vinland studies, proposed that the map was a forgery by a German Jesuit, the Reverend Josef Fischer, a noted expert on old maps. Seaver believes he made it in the 1930s to embarrass the Nazis by inscribing on the map that a Roman Catholic bishop of Greenland got to Vinland, too, so that if the Germans wanted to claim "Aryan" Norse priority in America, they would also have to accept an early Catholic presence there. Even if the map was proven to have been drawn in the 1200s, a single copy like this would not have had much, if any, influence on the main thrust of exploration in the centuries that followed.

Welsh

The claim for the presence in North America of medieval Welsh—who are regarded as *Celts* because of their language and heritage—is based on nothing more than perceived similarities with certain Native American Indian languages, physical characteristics, or cultural artifacts. But the most enduring claim is that Prince Madoc of Wales sailed west alone in a small boat around A.D. 1170 and arrived near Mobile, Alabama. He went back to Wales and this time set forth with a fleet of ten ships. Madoc and his men sailed up the Alabama River and then vanished in the wilderness. By the late seventeenth century, a Welsh clergyman traveling in the

The Mandan Indians have lived in North Dakota for almost two thousand years. When the American artist George Catlin visited them in the 1830s, he claimed that many of them had blond hair and blue eyes, and so he linked them to stories of pre-Columbian Welsh visitors to North America. Although this reproduction of one of Catlin's portraits of a Mandan female does not show either blond hair or blue eyes, he does seem to go out of his way to depict Caucasian features.

Carolinas reported that he came upon a Tuscaroran tribe with whom he could communicate in Welsh. In the decades that followed, accounts surfaced of tribe after tribe, usually fair-skinned, that spoke Welsh. Others saw Indians on the Missouri River using small skin-covered boats and claimed they were derived from the Welsh coracle. George Catlin, the famous nineteenth-century portrayer of Indians, was among those who decided that the Mandans of North Dakota were of Welsh descent. Over the years individuals have attributed everything from the Indian mounds of central United States to the entire Aztec culture to Welshmen. None of these stories can be seriously considered, although Queen Elizabeth I is said to have employed the Welsh tales of Madoc to assert English priority to North America over Spain's claims.

Zeno brothers

In Venice, Italy, in 1558, a book was published: *The Discovery of the Islands of Frislanda, Eslanda, Engroneland, Estotiland, . . . and Icaria made by two brothers of the Zeno family, Messire Nicolo the Chevalier and Missire Antioni.* Almost certainly its author was Nicolo Zeno, a descendant of the Zeno brothers' Venetian family, although he claimed that it was a true account based on letters written by the brothers. The story says that the two brothers were shipwrecked about 1380 on the island of Frislanda, far to the west in the Atlantic; hearing tales of other islands still farther west, they sailed to explore them and had all sorts of fabulous experiences. The 1558 volume included a map showing the location of these islands, scattered around the North Atlantic; the one farthest west seems to be Estotiland; its location and the description of its features suggests that it is *Newfoundland.* In fact, the conclusion of all serious scholars is that the book (and thus its map) is a total fabrication, based on accounts and maps of the discoveries of the New World since 1492. Although the story of the Zeno brothers belongs in a history of science fiction, not in a history of exploration, the tale was believed by many contemporaries and misled navigators and mapmakers for over a century.

IN THEIR OWN *Words*

Zeno Brothers Land in North America, circa 1475

Six and twenty years ago four fishing boats put out to sea and, encountering a heavy storm, were driven over the sea in utter helplessness for many days; when at length, the tempest abating, they discovered an island called Estotiland, lying westward over one thousand miles from Frislanda [Faroes or Iceland]. One of the boats was wrecked, and six men that were in it were taken by the inhabitants and brought into a fair and populous city. . . . The king sent them with twelve boats to the southwards to a country that they call Drogio . . . they were taken into the country and the greater number of them were eaten by savages. . . . He says that it is a very great country and, as it were, a new world; the people are very rude and uncultivated, for they all go naked and suffer cruelly from the cold. . . . They have no kind of metal. They live by hunting and carry lances of wood, sharpened at the point. They have bows, the strings of which are made of beasts' skins. . . . The farther you go southwards, however, the more refinement you meet with, because the climate is more temperate; and accordingly there they have cities and temples dedicated to their idols, in which they sacrifice men and afterwards eat them.

—NICOLO ZENO, *THE DISCOVERY OF THE ISLANDS OF FRISLANDA, ESLANDA, ENGRONELAND, ESTOTILAND . . . ,* 1588

PART II

The Spanish Enter the New World, 1492–1635

This part—covering the period from 1492 to 1635, and focusing primarily on the Spanish explorers who entered the New World through the Caribbean and Middle America and then moved northward—is the opening chapter of the grand epic that is the exploration of North America. On the one hand it is the part that includes some of the best-known figures in that epic—Columbus being only the most obvious. But it is also a chapter that includes feats little known to most Americans—the incredible journey of Cabeza de Vaca and Estevánico, for one. And although most of the individuals in this part are, as indicated, Spanish, one of the contributions of this work is that it not only identifies the international nature of the opening up of the New World but also recognizes the ongoing contributions of the Native Americans to this great venture.

If the title of this section were "the golden age of exploration" of North America, it would express the underlying ambivalence of the story. Many of these explorers are, in fact, the same men known in other contexts as "the conquistadors"—the conquerors—and there can be no denying that for many, the main motive was to enrich themselves, if not by actual gold and other rare minerals, then by land and other resources. Nor

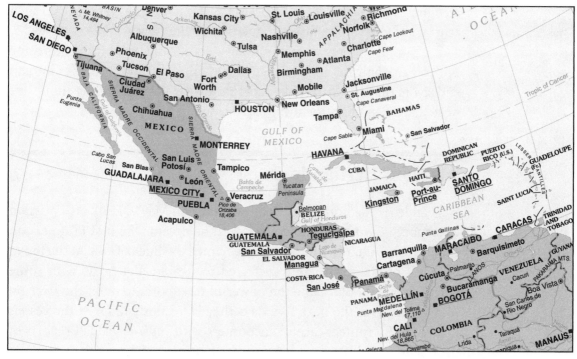

The regions now commonly known as Middle America (which also includes Mexico and Central America) are in fact regarded by geographers as part of North America.

can it be denied that they could be ruthless in pursuit of these goals. They killed and conquered the natives who stood in their way; they abused and enslaved the survivors, raped the women, stole their land and resources, and above all disrupted and dislocated their societies.

But it is hard not to acknowledge that the story of these early venturers into unknown regions of North America, whether by sea or land, is one of incredible daring and courage. The hardships they endured, the obstacles they overcame, are almost beyond modern comprehension.

While admitting, then, that one of the themes this part sounds is that exploration was by no means always a disinterested pursuit, it should also be recognized that there were many early explorers who were indeed motivated by the sheer desire to open up and understand this vast new continent. Mariners, navigators, mapmakers, scientists, naturalists, physicians, scholars, linguists, even sociologists and anthropologists before such terms existed—many were genuine seekers after knowledge. And although we today may not approve of those who try to impose their own religious beliefs on others—especially when it involves coercion—we may recognize the many dedicated priests and missionaries who played such crucial and demanding roles in opening up the New World.

Again, if there is a certain ambivalence to this concept of "opening up," it is arguably the ambivalence underlying the whole history of human endeavors on this earth. That is perhaps what most strikes us about this next chapter in the story of the exploration of North America.

Alarcón, Hernando de   (1466?–1541?)

Hernando de Alarcón sailed from Acapulco on May 9, 1540, on a mission to resupply *Coronado*'s expedition, and he became the first European to explore the Colorado River, which he named the Buena Guía. At the top of the Gulf of California he transferred to two smaller boats with some twenty men and overcame the powerful tidal bores to enter the river on August 26. Over the next 15½ days they laboriously dragged the vessels upstream. En route, peaceful encounters with Indians yielded reports of the legendary Cibola (see *legendary destinations*), of *Estevánico*'s death, of bison to the east, and of armed European men. Failing to contact Coronado, they floated back downstream. On September 14 he set out on a second ascent, this time pushing as far as the vicinity of Fort Yuma above the junction with the Gila River (near present-day Yuma, Arizona). There he erected a cross and secreted letters later found by Coronado's men. He returned south still looking for signs of Coronado, and planned a second expedition to the river. Instead he became involved in the Mixton War, a revolt of the Indians in western Mexico in 1541. His exploration added to evidence that Baja California was a peninsula and not an island.

Alvarado, Hernando de   (?–?)

As part of the *Coronado* expedition, on September 8, 1540, Hernando de Alvarado discovered the Río Grande, which he named Río de Nuestra Señora. In late August he had marched eastward from expedition headquarters at Hawikuh pueblo (now known as Zuni pueblo, in western New Mexico) and on the way became the first European to see Acoma, a pueblo atop a mesa that is one of the oldest continuously inhabited towns in the United States. In the Upper Río Grande Valley he found the main group of pueblo adobe villages of Tiguex, surrounded by fertile cultivated lands. He continued east to the Pecos River, the boundary between the Pueblo and the Plains Indians. Heading toward Texas, he descended the Pecos and proceeded east along the Canadian River, viewing immense herds of bison. His report to Coronado, which included Indian tales of Quivira, a city of gold to the northeast (possibly at Wichita, Kansas) (see *legendary destinations*), led Coronado to move his headquarters to Tiguex and set out in the spring of 1541 for Quivira.

Alvarado, Pedro de (1486–1541)

Named Tonatiuh ("sun") by the Aztecs for his red hair, Spanish conquistador Pedro de Alvarado was considered impetuous as well as courageous and brutal. In 1510, along with his three brothers, Alvarado arrived in *Hispaniola.* The next year he joined Diego Velázquez in the exploration and conquest of *Cuba.* In 1518 he sailed as captain of one of *Juan de Grijalva's* four ships to explore Mexico's Yucatán coastline and westward beyond the Isthmus of Tehuantepec. Against orders, he forced his ship into the Río de Papaloapán, which the Spaniards named Río de Alvarado and where nearby Indians related tales of inland gold. On June 24, after receiving gifts from the Aztec emperor Moctezuma, Grijalva formally took possession of the site of what is today Veracruz. The same day Grijalva sent Alvarado in his damaged ship back to Cuba, bearing Mexican gold and a report to Velázquez.

Near the end of the year, Alvarado joined the *Cortés* expedition as a ship's captain. In February 1519, he arrived in Mexico two days ahead of Cortés, at the island of Cozumel, and there proceeded to loot a village; he was forced to return the booty. Later, during the occupation of the Aztec capital, Cortés left him in charge when he marched off to deal with *Narváez.* Alvarado apparently provoked the Aztecs into a rebellion that ended in a massacre of Spaniards. Following the final conquest of the Aztecs, Cortés sent him south from Mexico City to subdue Aztec allies and subjects in the coastal region of Oaxaca. In 1522, he sent him back to Oaxaca to explore for the source of Aztec gold and to seek a waterway to the Pacific. Alvarado was also instructed to survey other natural resources such as soil fertility, flora, and fauna. He found no waterway but reported various bays on the Pacific coast as ideal for development as ports.

In December 1523 Cortés sent Alvarado, along with some 450 Spaniards and thousands of Indian allies, to explore the Pacific coast to Guatemala. Over the next six months, he marched through Central America, including Guatemala, most of Honduras, all of El Salvador, and northwestern Nicaragua. Back in Guatemala, Alvarado crisscrossed the region, extorting gold, enslaving Indians to work the mines, exploring, and conquering and reconquering. In 1530 he returned from Spain with the title of governor and captain general (thus removing him from the control of Cortés), along with the right to build ships at his own expense for expeditions to the Spice Islands and to explore and settle north along the Pacific Coast. In 1534, in violation of his contract with the Spanish crown, he sailed his fleet of discovery to Ecuador, where he planned to partake of *Pizarro*'s Incan booty. Instead he was forced to sell his ships to Pizarro, whom most of his men joined, and to return in 1536 to Spain to explain his actions.

While there, the news of *Cabeza de Vaca*'s transcontinental journey aroused great interest in the lands north of Mexico. Alvarado was able to renew his contract, and he returned in 1539 with ship-fitting supplies and a large contingent of Spanish volunteers to find that *Juan Rodríguez Cabrillo* had almost completed construction of a new fleet. He persuaded Cabrillo to serve as admiral, and in late summer 1540, thirteen ships carrying over a thousand men—one of the largest such fleets of the era—set sail up the Pacific coast. Twice Cabrillo was forbidden by the new viceroy's agents to take on supplies, a situation that was alleviated after Alvarado met with Viceroy Antonio de Mendoza in November 1540 to conclude a twenty-year partnership in which the viceroy received a half share of Alvarado's enterprise, and Alvarado received a similar share in the future discoveries of Mendoza's Coronado and *Alarcón* expeditions, already in progress. Alvarado's plan to return to Guatemala was curtailed by his accidental death in early July 1541, in the Indian revolt in western Mexico known as the Mixton War, and his ships were taken over by Mendoza.

In the end the Alvarado-Mendoza partnership, competing with Cortés's exploration of the Pacific coast, was responsible for sending out the major expeditions of the era: those of *Marcos de Niza* and of Coronado into the American Southwest, and those of Alarcón, *Bolaños,* and Cabrillo up the Pacific coast, as well as that of Villalobos across the Pacific, through which Spain claimed possession of the Philippines.

Anian, Strait of

This body of water first appeared in 1566 on the Spaniard Zaltierri's map, where it is shown as passing through a narrow isthmus that connected the northern reaches of North America and Asia. Since no European had the slightest notion of what that part of the world was really like, anyone who trusted this map could locate this strait almost anyplace, and for almost 230 years, many people did just that. Some mariners regarded it as the exit point of the *Northwest Passage [VII]* (or the entrance if one was coming from the Pacific). Some believed it to be located well down into North America so that it promised a link from the Great Lakes (or even the Hudson River!). The closest thing to such a strait was the one found by *Vitus Bering [VII]* in 1728 and named after him. The origin of the name *Anian,* by the way, remains in dispute, but some scholars believe it comes from a Chinese province that Marco Polo called Ania.

Balboa, Vasco Núñez de   (1475?–1519)

Growing up in Moguer, a port in southwest Spain that was visited by ships sailing to and from the recently discovered New World, Vasco Núñez de Balboa was attracted by the possibilities of making his fame and fortune there. In 1501 Balboa sailed with Rodrigo de Bastidas to Colombia to discover the mouths of the Magdalena River. Returning to *Hispaniola,* Balboa became a planter and a pig raiser. In 1510 fleeing creditors, he stowed away on a ship to Panama, then known as Tierra Firme. There he led a coup and installed himself as interim governor. Hearing Indian reports of another sea and of gold, he led an epic twenty-five-day march through the jungles of the isthmus. On September 25, 1513, standing on a mountain ridge, he became the first European to sight the Pacific Ocean. Four days later he reached the water and took possession of the South Sea and all lands surrounding it for Spain. He returned to find himself replaced as governor. He began to construct ships to explore the South Sea but was arrested by the new governor, convicted of treason, and beheaded. Balboa's exploration opened the way to the conquest of Peru and to the discovery of Baja and Alta California.

Bolaños, Francisco de (?–?)

Under orders from the viceroy of *New Spain,* Francisco de Bolaños sailed with three ships from La Navidad, Mexico, on September 8, 1541, to explore Baja California's Pacific coast. In search of the illusory *Strait of Anian* (allegedly a waterway from the Pacific to the Atlantic), he surveyed and named suitable harbors from the tip of Baja possibly as far north as Isla de Cedros. Some historians believe he was the first to use the name California in referring to the region.

At the end of the sixteenth century, another Francisco de Bolaños served as chief pilot on the 1595 voyage of *Sebastián Cermeño* up the California coast. After his ship foundered in Drake's Bay, he returned as pilot of a second expedition led by *Sebastián Vizcaíno* in 1602–1603.

Bosque and Larios expedition (1675)

On April 30, 1675, a small party from Mexico's Coahuila province led by Fernando del Bosque and accompanied by Franciscan Friar Juan Larios set out northward from the Guadalupe area. On May 11 they arrived at the Río Grande, which they named Río del San Buena Ventura del Norte, and crossed it on a raft, probably near Paso de Francia. They followed the river upstream through south-central Texas, taking possession by erecting wooden crosses along the way. They reported seeing bison and baptized fifty-five Indian infants before turning back on May 29. Reaching home in mid-June, Bosque wrote a detailed report enumerating the differences between the tribes and recommending three main settlements in the region. No action was taken on his recommendation for decades.

Cabeza de Vaca, Álvar Núñez (1490?–1557)

Álvar Núñez Cabeza de Vaca, whose 2,500-mile trek across part of North America is one of the most astounding feats of any of the early explorers, was born near Cádiz to a distinguished Andalusian family. With military experience in European wars, he was appointed royal treasurer on February 15, 1527, of the expedition of *Pánfilo de Narváez* and sailed with it to the New World. Cabeza de Vaca's own adventure began on November 6,

1528, when he and other starving expedition survivors washed up on an island—Galveston Island by many accounts, though possibly Follet's Island or San Luis Island—off the Texas coast. By the time the bitter winter had passed, most of the eighty castaways were dead.

Cabeza de Vaca spent a year of slavery among the Karankawan islanders before escaping to join the mainland Charrucos Indians for nearly three years. They allowed him to operate as an independent trader inland, exchanging shell knives and ornaments for flint, red ocher, arrow shafts, canes, and hides. Wanting to reach Pánuco (at Tampico, Mexico), he escaped to the Matagorda Bay area and then to the Guadalupe River, where he was enslaved by the Mariames Indians. While there, he plotted escape with three other Narváez castaways—Alonso del Castillo Maldonado, Andrés Dorantes de Carranza, and Dorantes' African slave *Estevánico.* They were able to slip away in September 1534 but were pressed into service as healers by the coastal Avavares Indians, with whom they remained through the winter. The next spring they moved on westward to other tribes between the Nueces River and the Río Grande.

In August 1535 the four set out across the continent (to avoid the hostile Indians of the Gulf coast), passing with escort parties from one tribe to another and earning their meals by healing the sick. Their seven-month route is a matter of conjecture, but they probably traveled along

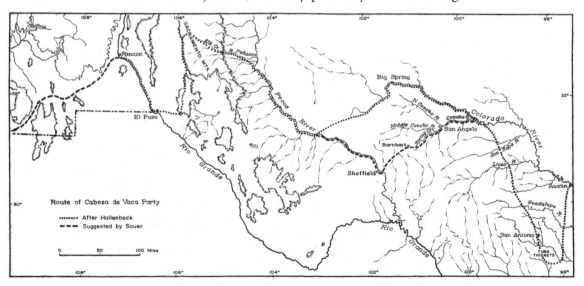

This map shows two scholars' attempts at reconstructing the route taken by Cabeza de Vaca and his three companions between 1528 and 1536. Basing their claims on the account published by Cabeza and their knowledge of the actual terrain, the scholars differ at several points along the way.

Indian trails southwest through Texas, crossing the Río Grande thirty-four miles from the sea at Falcon Reservoir, then crossing back into Texas near Presidio, and finally crossing to the south bank again some seventy-five miles south of El Paso. From there they set off westward toward the Pacific through Mexico's northwestern Chihuahua to southwestern Sonora, where they came upon Spanish slave hunters on the Río Yaqui in late December 1535. By way of Culiacán and Compostela, the four survivors—Cabeza de Vaca, Estevánico, Dorantes de Carranza, and del Castillo Maldonado—arrived in Mexico City on July 24, 1536, to meet with Viceroy Mendoza.

By 1537 Cabeza de Vaca was back in Spain, possibly to seek a royal patent to the lands he had crossed; the grant had already gone to *de Soto [III]*. Instead, his reward was the governorship of South America's Río de la Plata province. There political difficulties resulted in his 1543 arrest and eventual return to Spain, where in 1551 he was sentenced to eight years of African exile (evidently not enforced). After a royal pardon, he died in Seville in 1557.

Cabeza de Vaca's tale (published in 1542), which alluded to Indian reports of a prosperous Pueblo culture in the American Southwest, helped motivate the expeditions of *Coronado,* de Soto, and others. His achievements, aside from his epic journey, include sympathetic ethnographic observations of the numerous native peoples he encountered (twenty-three tribes in Texas alone), along with the first descriptions of the terrain, flora, and fauna (including bison) of the region.

IN THEIR OWN *Words*

Cabeza de Vaca's Account of His Travels

The people gave us innumerable deerhide and cotton blankets, the latter being better than those of New Spain, beads made of coral from the South Sea, fine turquoise from the north—in fact, everything they had including a special gift to Dorantes of five emerald arrowheads such as they use in their singing and dancing. These looked quite valuable. I asked where they came from. They said from lofty mountains to the north, where there were towns of great population and great houses, and that the arrowheads had been purchased with feather brushes and parrot plumes.

—Álvar Núñez Cabeza de Vaca, *Relación*, 1542

Cabrillo, Juan Rodríguez   (?–1543)

Spanish conquistador Juan Rodríguez Cabrillo (he was probably not Portuguese as has often been noted) arrived in Mexico with *Pánfilo de*

Narváez on a mission to arrest *Cortés.* Instead he joined Cortés in his 1521 conquest of the Aztecs and in 1523 accompanied *Pedro de Alvarado* in his exploration and conquest of Guatemala. By the 1530s he was one of Guatemala's wealthiest men. Alvarado assigned him to construct a flotilla of ships to explore the Pacific coast. After Alvarado's death, Viceroy Antonio de Mendoza delegated Cabrillo to carry out Alvarado's contract: to explore the coast of Baja California and northward in search of new lands and of the *Strait of Anian,* a legendary waterway to the Atlantic. Cabrillo may have even been ordered to sail on to China by way of the Moluccas. On June 27, 1542, he set sail from La Navidad, Mexico, with three small ships and made slow progress up the coast, reaching central Baja at Isla de Cedros on August 10. On September 28 he arrived at San Diego Bay and stopped there during a three-day storm. The first known European visitor to the Alta California coast, he landed near San Diego at Point Loma, now the site of the Cabrillo National Monument. Farther north, he stopped at Santa Catalina Island and San Pedro (the port of Los Angeles) and sailed beyond Santa Barbara to Point Conception (October 18). Some accounts place this as his northernmost point reached, while others have him reaching either Monterey Bay or Drake's Bay at a latitude of 38° before being driven by storms back to San Miguel Island off Santa Barbara. There he died on January 3, 1543, from a broken bone. (Some scholars believe he died on Santa Catalina Island.) The expedition was taken over by his chief pilot, Bartolomé Ferrelo (also Ferrel or Ferrer), who sailed north again to the California-Oregon border at a latitude of 41° or 42°. On April 14, 1543, Ferrelo arrived back at La Navidad.

Some of the uncertainty about the expedition's discoveries is probably due to latitude readings based on inaccurate tables of the declination of the sun in use at the time. (This could result in an error of from ½° close to the equator to 2° farther north.) Cabrillo's were the earliest observations of the California coastal peoples and terrain. This survey of some 1,200 miles along the coast helped establish Spanish claims to California, but there was no immediate follow-up to the expedition; generally Cabrillo ignored the fertile coastal areas and sheltered harbors suitable for settlement. His navigational notes were apparently used by Andrés de Urdaneta in his 1564–1565 voyage to establish the Manila galleon route between Acapulco and the Philippines. Spanish exploration of the coast finally resumed in 1584 with *Gali,* followed by *Unamuno, Cermeño,* and *Vizcaíno.*

Carvajal (Carabajal) y de la Cueva, Luís de (?–1590)

In 1572 the Spanish viceroy in Mexico City ordered Luís de Carvajal, the mayor of Tampico, Mexico, to find a route from the gulf coast to the rich silver mining district southwest of Saltillo. Then he was to head east to the mouth of the Río Grande and veer south, punishing coastal Indians hostile to wrecked Spanish ships, as he returned to Tampico. Starting out in late May or early June 1572 on his ten-month journey, Carvajal eventually became the first European since *Cabeza de Vaca* to cross the Río Grande into Texas. In 1580, after receiving a vast land grant for Nuevo Reyno de León, which extended north nearly to Austin, Texas, he was seen as challenging the authorities, and he eventually died in a Mexico City prison. His exploration and settlement of Mexico's northeastern frontier set the stage for the first Spanish colonizing expeditions into the American Southwest.

Castaño de Sosa, Gaspar (?–?)

On July 27, 1590, lieutenant governor of Nuevo León province Gaspar Castaño de Sosa led a group of 170 colonists on an unauthorized expedition from the failed northeastern Mexican mining town of Almadén into the American Southwest. Leading the first wagon train (of two-wheeled carts) to cross the plains, he pioneered a new route across the Río Grande near Del Rio, Texas, and up the Pecos River to the area of Albuquerque, New Mexico. After capturing Pecos, he continued his conquest (and atrocities toward recalcitrant Indians) through Tehua, Queres, and Tiguas pueblos, ascending as far as Taos. There he was arrested on the viceroy's orders the following spring and returned in chains, along with his colonists, to Mexico, where he was found guilty of invading the lands of peaceable Indians. Exiled to the Philippines for six years, he was killed on the voyage out by rebellious slaves.

Cermeño, Sebastián Rodríguez (Cermenho, Sebastião Rodrigues) (?–?)

A half century after *Cabrillo*'s exploration of the Pacific coastline (1542–1543), Sebastián Cermeño was ordered by the viceroy to survey this shore from near the California-Oregon border down to Mexico on the return leg of his trip from the Philippines. An experienced pilot of Portuguese origin, he was the third Manila galleon captain to do so: *Gali*'s and *Unamuno*'s attempts to locate a suitable port for the galleon on the coast had been unsuccessful. The use of this major merchant vessel for exploration served two purposes: It saved the royal treasury the expense of sending out an actual expedition, and by approaching North America on its voyage from the Philippines it could take advantage of favorable winds and oceanic currents.

He left the Philippines to set out across the Pacific on July 14, 1595, as captain of the *San Agustín* with **Francisco de Bolaños** as pilot. On October 29 he neared land at 42° and on November 4 sighted the California coast. Proceeding south, he named Cape Mendocino and took possession for Spain of Drake's Bay, some sixteen years after **Drake** had taken possession for England. (In fact, Cermeño named this San Francisco Bay, which for some time caused confusion among accounts claiming priority of discovery of present-day San Francisco Bay.) He traded with the local Indians, possibly some of the same Miwok described by Drake. While anchored off Point Reyes there, his galleon was wrecked in a storm, and its cargo of beeswax, silk, and porcelain lost.

Cermeño either built, or had brought along on board, a bark *(viroco)* named *Santa Buenaventura*. From this small vessel, carrying seventy seamen and passengers, he charted the shoreline and landed parties to make brief explorations inland as he worked his way southward, briefly investigating islands and various bays as possible harbors. This survey was hampered by the urgency of getting his ill, injured, and starving companions back to Mexico. After passing Monterey Bay, through the Santa Barbara Channel, Catalina and San Clemente Islands, and San Diego Bay, he reached San Miguel Island off northern Baja in late December. At the tip of the Baja peninsula, he set some of his more desperate passengers ashore and officially ended his exploration, reaching La Navidad, Mexico, in January 1596. The loss of the ship and its valuable cargo ended the practice of using the Manila galleons to explore the Alta California coast. Despite his disaster, Cermeño was able to gather useful information about the shore and about fertile sites capable of supporting colonists, but he found no **Strait of Anian** (the legendary waterway to the Atlantic), and no harbor was selected for the galleon route. No other action was taken until the 1602 *Vizcaíno* expedition.

Columbus, Christopher (1451–1506)

The life and achievements of Christopher Columbus are too long and too well documented in other sources to require recounting in a work focused on the exploration of North America. In fact, Columbus would not be expected to be found in such a work, were it not that this volume treats North America as formal geographers do—that is, as including the West Indies and Central America, which he was the first European to explore. In other ways, he had a direct impact on the early landings and movements of Europeans on the mainland of America to the north. It is these various connections with North America that will be treated here.

Long before 1492, Columbus may have had a near miss with North America. In 1476, Columbus was a crew member on a Genoese ship that was part of a convoy sailing from Genoa, Italy, to England. Off Portugal, the convoy was attacked by a Franco-Portuguese fleet, and Columbus was wounded as his ship was sinking. He was able to reach shore and make his way to Lisbon, where his brother Bartholomew was working as a cartographer. It is claimed that young Christopher learned a considerable amount about *maps [I]* and distant lands from this brother.

Before long he sailed again, this time on a Portuguese ship bound for England and Flanders. From there it appears that the ship sailed to Galway, Ireland, and then, in February 1477 to Iceland. The story of Columbus's visit to Iceland is based entirely on the biography of Columbus by his son, Ferdinand, who in turn said he was quoting from a now lost document of his father. There, Ferdinand says, Columbus wrote: "In the month of February 1477, I sailed 100 leagues beyond the island of Tile whose southern part is in latitude 73° north . . . and at the time when I was there the sea was not frozen, but there were vast tides." Although the latitude reading would not be correct, it is generally agreed that "Tile" is in fact "Thule," a name applied to Iceland in those days. It is tempting to speculate what might have happened had Columbus sailed several hundred more leagues to the west—and reached *Greenland [I].* By this time the *Norse [I]* colony there had been abandoned, but at least it could be said that Columbus reached North America.

Not content with such speculations, some amateur students of Columbus like to speculate that in Iceland Columbus heard tales of lands to the west—not only of the former Viking settlements on Greenland but even of the *Vinland [I]* visited by *Leif Eriksson [I]* and his followers. Professional scholars reject such stories.

In fact, some professional historians question whether Columbus ever got near Iceland. It is accepted, though, that while Columbus was living in the Madeira islands off Africa during the late 1470s and early 1480s, he would have heard tales of lands to the west. Driftwood and other materials that washed up on shore in the Madeiras and the Azores suggested to the inhabitants that there was land across the Atlantic—the only questions were which land and how far away. There were even reports of "Oriental"-appearing individuals who appeared—dead and alive—on the Atlantic coast of Europe: Presumably they were Inuit or Native Americans. Columbus was by no means the only man of his time who believed there were unknown lands to the west. What distinguished him was that he persisted in acting on his belief.

It is not known exactly what stimulated Columbus to begin thinking about sailing west across the Atlantic to reach Asia and the East Indies. But sometime about 1475 he was corresponding with Paolo dal Pozzo Toscanelli, a physician in Florence, Italy, who was convinced that there was a short route to China and Japan across the Atlantic. Columbus believed that Toscanelli's calculations were too large, that the distance was even shorter. About 1482, he took his proposal for such a voyage to King John II of Portugal, but Columbus made so many demands that the king turned him down.

In 1485 Columbus moved to Spain, where almost at once he began trying to convince the royal couple Ferdinand and Isabella to support what he later called "the enterprise of the Indies." For many years they refused his demands, but finally, having driven the Moors out of Spain in January 1492, Queen Isabella guaranteed the financial backing as well as meeting his various other demands.

On his first voyage, Columbus sailed from Spain on August 3, 1492, and made his first landfall on October 12. It is generally thought that this was the island of San Salvador in the Bahamas, although not all scholars

IN THEIR OWN *Words*

A Letter That Influenced Columbus

From the island Antillia, which you call Seven Cities, and whereof you have some knowledge, there are ten spaces, which make 2,000 miles to the most noble island of Cipango [Japan] ... most fertile in gold, pearls and precious stones, and they cover temples and the royal residences with solid gold. ... Thus by the unknown ways there are no great spaces of the sea to be passed.

—PAOLO TOSCANELLI, LETTER TO CANON MARTINS, JUNE 25, 1474

accept this. (The island has also been known as Watlings Island.) Whichever island it was, he met his first Native Americans, the Arawak, but he called them the name they would be known by in the future, Indians. After several days there, Columbus sailed on to arrive off the northeastern coast of *Cuba;* he sent an exploring party ashore, but aside from seeing men smoking tobacco, they did not gain much knowledge of this New World. Columbus sailed on to the island he named *Hispaniola;* at Cap-Haitien, his ship, the *Santa Maria,* was wrecked; he left about forty of his men there to seek gold, and with several captive Indians, he sailed back to Spain in the *Nina.*

In this highly fanciful late-nineteenth-century lithograph by a French artist, Columbus is shown being virtually worshipped by the Indians as their deliverer—an image that many were long willing to believe.

On his second voyage, he reached the West Indies on November 3, 1493. He sailed among the islands of Domenica, Guadeloupe, Antigua, Nevis, St. Croix, Puerto Rico, and others before reaching Cap-Haitien. There he discovered that the Indians had killed all of his men because they had mistreated the natives. Columbus sailed on to the north coast of Hispaniola, where he founded the first European colony in the Americas, Isabela (in the present-day Dominican Republic). During the summer of 1494, still searching for Japan, he explored the coast and island of Cuba and discovered the island of Jamaica.

On his third voyage, he departed on May 30, 1498, and took a more southerly route. He discovered the island of Trinidad and then sailed on to the mouth of the Orinoco River and the coast of Venezuela—and there his crew, if not Columbus himself, became almost certainly the first Europeans to set foot on the mainland of the Americas. Despite his reputation for never having realized he was not in Asia, Columbus wrote in his journal "I believe that this is a very great continent which until now has been unknown." He even called it the "Other World."

On May 5, 1502, Columbus sailed on his fourth voyage. This time he made landfall at Martinique, then sailed on to Hispaniola. From there he sailed on past Jamaica to southern Cuba, then crossed the Caribbean to land at the Bay Islands off Honduras. Again, it is tempting to speculate what might have happened had Columbus sailed north, but instead for the next few months he sailed east and south along the coast of Central

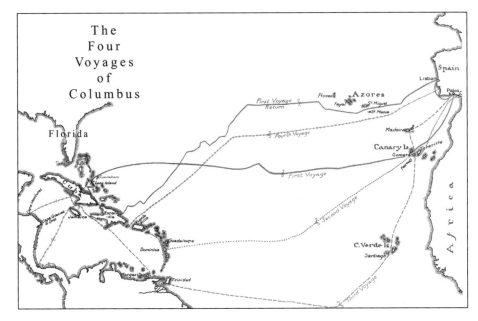

The
Four
Voyages
of
Columbus

The routes taken by
Columbus on his
four voyages to
the New World are
indicated here.
Although scholars
differ on certain
details, these are the
generally accepted
routes.

America. Passing along the coast of Nicaragua and Costa Rica, he put into
Almirante Bay in Panama. In Panama he was informed by the natives that
here was indeed another large ocean only a few days' walk over the mountains, but Columbus chose not to make this journey because he was interested only in a sea passage to Asia. He continued his explorations along the
coast of Panama and even tried to establish a settlement there, but con-
flicts with the local Indians drove the Spaniards away. Leaving Central
America, Columbus's ship became waterlogged, and he had to beach it on
Jamaica, where he was marooned for a year before finally being rescued
and sailing for Spain.

What did Columbus contribute to the knowledge of North America—aside, obviously, from the fundamental confirmation of the existence of this New World to Europeans? To begin with, there were the
many new lands he discovered—the West Indies islands, the landmass of
Central America, and even Venezuela. Beyond reports of these new lands,
however, he provided a mixture of valuable information and misinformation. Few of his original writings survive. The journal, or logbook, that he
kept on his first voyage he presented to Ferdinand and Isabella; they in
turn had a copy made for him; both these disappeared, and what is known
as "The Journal of Christopher Columbus" is in fact an abstract made by
the noted Dominican historian of that time, Bartolomé de las Casas. It is
believed he had access to the copy kept by Columbus's family. The las

Casas version of the journal, however, went unknown until it was discovered in a private Spanish library in 1791; even then it was not published until 1825. Columbus also wrote at least six letters addressed to the rulers of Spain and other officials providing a condensed account of his voyage; at least one of these was published and widely distributed throughout Europe. This letter, not the journal, was what made the greatest and most immediate impact on Europeans of that day.

Aside from his writings, Columbus also had some influence on the maps of his day. The noted historian and biographer of Columbus, Samuel Eliot Morison, is one of many who believe that Columbus was a skilled chartmaker, as seen in his sketch of northern Haiti. Although no other original charts or maps of Columbus survive, it is certain that some were passed around in his lifetime; elements at least appear to have been used in compiling the famous *Piri Reis map [I]*.

There are now some who denigrate Columbus because of his harsh treatment of the Native Americans, his promotion of the New World as a source for material enrichment, and his general failure to respect the cultures, possessions, and priorities of its inhabitants. There is nothing much that can be said in his defense except that in all this he was but a man of his era. It is also agreed that sooner or later some other European mariner would have sailed to the Americas. The fact remains that Columbus was the individual who persisted and became the first European to make known the possibilities offered by further exploration of the Western Hemisphere.

IN THEIR OWN *Words*   ## Columbus Plans to Visit Japan

I was anxious to fill all the ships' casks with water here; accordingly if the weather permit, I shall presently set out to go round the island, until I have had speech with this king and have seen whether I can obtain from him the gold which I hear that he wears. After that I wish to leave for another very large island, which I believe must be Cipangu [Japan], according to the signs made by these Indians I have with me; they call it "Colba" [Cuba]. They say that there are many ships and many very good sailors there. Beyond that island there is another which they call "Bofio" [Santo Domingo], which they say is also very large.

—*JOURNAL OF COLUMBUS*, OCTOBER 21, 1492, AS PUBLISHED BY HIS SON, FERNANDO

Coronado, Francisco Vásquez de   (1510?–1554)

The younger son in a wealthy Spanish family, Francisco Vásquez de Coronado decided to make a fortune and a name for himself in the New World. He first arrived in Mexico in 1535 as part of the entourage of Antonio de Mendoza, New Spain's first viceroy, who appointed Coronado provisional governor of Nueva Galicia in 1538. Spurred by *Cabeza de Vaca*'s allusions to a prosperous *Pueblo* kingdom in the American Southwest, Mendoza organized a major expedition for which he chose as captain-general Coronado. Before it set out, *Marcos de Niza* returned from a preliminary 1539 reconnaissance with an exciting report of the legendary Cibola. That November, Mendoza sent *Melchior Diaz* out to verify the account of Marcos, as well as to explore the route from Culiacán to southwest Arizona's Gila River valley. Diaz made a negative report, but it had little effect on Coronado's expedition, which had become an ambitious military enterprise of over three hundred soldiers, more than a thousand Mexican Indians, and over fifteen hundred animals, including horses.

On April 22, 1540, Coronado, guided by Marcos, led an advance party of two hundred soldiers from Culiacán. Traveling along old Indian trails, they probably passed into Arizona at the San Pedro River and pushed northward to Hawikuh, just over the New Mexico border. The Cibola (see *legendary destinations*) evoked by Marcos as a metropolis turned out to be an unimpressive pueblo village, and Marcos was sent home in humiliation. After capturing Hawikuh on July 7, 1540, Coronado made it his temporary headquarters and dispatched his

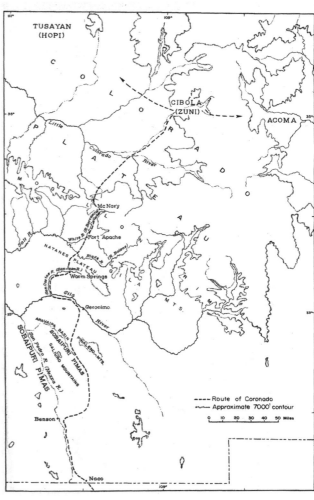

This map shows the route taken in 1540 by Coronado on his famous expedition to seek out the "golden cities" of Cibola.

officers on various reconnaissances while he awaited the arrival of the main group led by *Tristán de Luna y Arellano [III]*. Toward the northwest he sent Pedro de Továr across the Painted Desert to the land of the Hopi; Továr returned with Indian reports of a great river beyond, thus gaining the distinction of being the first European to hear about the Grand Canyon. On a second foray, *García López de Cárdenas* marched twenty days west of the Hopi and in September reached the edge of the Grand Canyon, from which he viewed the Colorado River far below; he thus has the distinction of being the first European to see the Grand Canyon. Concurrently, *Hernando de Alarcón,* sent by sea to resupply the expedition, ascended the Colorado River from the Gulf of Mexico but failed to make contact (Melchior Diaz later found a message left there by Alarcón). At the end of August, another party under *Hernando de Alvarado* set out eastward, visiting Acoma, entering the Tiguex pueblo country near Bernalillo and continuing on to Pecos pueblo on the edge of the Great Plains. After Alvarado discovered the Pecos River, he traveled east along the Canadian River into the Texas panhandle, encountering vast herds of bison along the way and hearing Indian tales of Quivira, a fabulously wealthy realm to the northeast (see *legendary destinations*). On his return he told Coronado about Quivira and also advised him to move headquarters to Tiguex, east of the Río Grande and north of Albuquerque. During the bitter winter of 1540–1541, the Spaniards seized food and clothing from the Pueblo people, inciting them to rebellion.

On April 23, 1541, Coronado started out along a meandering route toward Quivira. By this time, he had engaged an Indian the Spanish called El Turco ("the Turk"—because something about his appearance or clothing reminded them of Turks), who said that he could lead them to Quivira. Food and water shortages at the end of May in the Texas panhandle forced Coronado to send most of his army back to Tiguex. With the remaining thirty-six soldiers he then turned north, advancing through western Oklahoma, with the Turk supposedly leading the way. On June 29 he crossed the Arkansas River near Ford, Kansas, and followed the river downstream to the first Quivira settlement (July 6), probably east of Great Bend around Lyons, Kansas. It was a disappointing village of thatch-roofed round lodges set in a pleasant, fertile countryside. At this point, Coronado had the Turk executed; in one version, it was because he confessed that he had been lying all along, hoping to weaken the Spanish by leading them so far and thus making it easier for his fellow Indians to wipe them out; more likely Coronado was simply furious at his exaggerated tales of a wealthy community. After several weeks in the region (outside modern Wichita) seeking information about more distant lands, he headed back to New Mexico by way of a new, relatively direct route that may have approximated the later Santa Fe Trail and reached Tiguex in late summer. Meanwhile, Luna y Arellano had sent Francisco de Barrio Nuevo north on an expedition to procure provisions for the coming winter. After visiting the Jemez, he proceeded north along the Río Grande to Chamita, where the northern Tehuas fled into the hills. He continued on to the impressive pueblo of Taos before returning. At the same time, another officer explored the Río Grande some two hundred miles downstream to the southern limit of Pueblo country before turning back. Following the difficult winter of 1541–1542, Coronado was accidentally injured, causing him to put aside his plans to explore beyond Quivira.

In April 1542 he began a humiliating retreat to Mexico with a starving, quarrelsome band of men, including some who had wanted to settle in the region. The Franciscans who stayed behind were soon slain by the Indians. He had found no gold, and the Pueblo peoples were averse to pacification. The dismayed viceroy soon removed Coronado from his governorship as well, and after he was found innocent of cruel treatment of Indians, he faded into obscurity. The achievements of the expedition—an accumulation of valuable geographic and ethnographic knowledge about the southwest—resulted in no further Spanish exploration or exploitation of New Mexico for four decades.

Cortés, Hernán (Valle de Oaxaca, Marqués del) (1485–1547)

Conquistador Hernán Cortés, of noble Spanish lineage, arrived in the New World at age nineteen. In 1511 he moved on from *Hispaniola* to serve Diego Velázquez during the conquest of *Cuba* and there accumulated considerable wealth from a trading partnership as well. As Cuba's governor, Velázquez planned the fourth and major expedition to Mexico, which had been discovered and coastally explored on three earlier voyages: that of *Hernández de Córdoba* to the Yucatan in 1517, followed by the voyage of *Juan de Grijalva* in 1518 and that of Cristóbal de Olid later in 1518 in search of Grijalva. Excited by the Mayan and Aztec gold artifacts sent back by the first two explorers, Velázquez moved ahead with the enterprise, appointing Cortés its leader. When Olid and Grijalva finally reported back to him, Velázquez became suspicious of Cortés's ambition and tried to remove him from command, but he was too late. The canny Cortés had already sailed from Santiago, stopping along the Cuban coast to pick up most of Grijalva's men, along with some from the first voyage.

It was February 18, 1519, by the time the eleven-ship fleet—carrying nearly six hundred Spaniards, some two hundred native Cubans, several Africans, and sixteen horses—set out from westernmost Cuba's Cabo San Antón. After reaching the island of Cozumel, the expedition followed the Yucatan coast into the Gulf of Mexico, defeated the natives at Tabasco, and in May reached Veracruz. To thwart Velázquez supporters among his ranks, Cortés scuttled all his ships except the one he sent on July 16, 1519, bearing Aztec gold to Spain, thus seeking direct royal authority for his venture. On August 16 he began a march on the Aztec capital of Tenochtitlán (Mexico City), located on an island in Lake Texcoco. On November 18 he occupied the city, aided by alliances with various Indian groups opposed to Aztec ruler Moctezuma.

From there he sent out four small expeditions to explore rivers and search for gold up to three hundred miles from the capital. Gold was found at Tutupec in Oaxaca, not far from the Pacific, and he sent soldiers there to build a settlement. In search of a better port, he also ordered a land party to examine the coast southeast of Veracruz. They surveyed and sounded the promising Río Coatzacoalcos, and Cortés sent 150 men there to build a fort. Cortés made his conquest final only after defeating

Narváez, sent by Velázquez to arrest him, and then the forces of Francisco de Garay, who had obtained a patent, or royal commission, to the northern gulf coast in the Pánuco (Tampico) region. Men from both forces ended up joining him. After an Aztec rebellion and a massacre of the Spanish, he also had to recapture Mexico City.

Once he was secure, he sent out more exploratory parties, ordering them to document the terrain and natural resources (including minerals, fertile soils, building materials, and flora and fauna), as well as search for a transcontinental water passage to the South Sea, as the Pacific Ocean was then known. Juan de Valle's 1521 exploration of the Isthmus of Tehuantepec was followed in 1522 by Olid's survey of Michoacán, *Pedro de Alvarado*'s survey of Oaxaca, and Pedro Alvarez Chico's survey of the Guerrero coast. No one located the water route, but they all found promising bays along the Pacific. There, in 1523–1524, Gonzalo de Sandoval conquered the coast of Guerrero and Colima, nephew Francisco Cortés explored the coast of Jalisco and Nayarit to the north, and Alvarado led 450 men along the Pacific coast to Honduras. In October 1524, Cortés himself set out from Mexico City to lead a large force to Honduras (under attack by Olid, now a Velázquez ally again), forging a new and extremely difficult land route toward the Gulf coast and across the lower Yucatan. His absence resulted in political turmoil, and he returned nearly two years later to be stripped of his authority as governor.

His final decade in the New World was devoted to explorations of the Pacific region. In July 1527, under royal orders, he sent a four-ship expedition under his cousin Alvaro Saavedra Ceron to explore the ocean to the East Indies and China, and to search for Jofre García de Loaysa, who, along with Andrés de Urdaneta, had set out in July 1525 from Spain to circumnavigate the globe. Both Loaysa and Saavedra were lost, but survivors of the voyages later related tales of the rich islands and pearls of the Moluccas, south of the Philippines.

On a 1528 trip to Spain, Cortés obtained a royal contract to discover, explore, and settle the Pacific coast, the nearby islands, and the west-central part of the mainland named Nueva Galicia, governed by Nuño de Guzmán. He was also granted various concessions and titles, including that of Marqués del Valle de Oaxaca, of captain general of New Spain and of the provinces and coasts of the South Sea, and of governor of the new territories. (The only changes from previous grants were the stipulations of the Royal Order Regulating Conquest and Settlement of November 17,

1527, requiring just treatment of the Indians, as well as their religious conversion and instruction, and a ban on their enslavement other than in warfare.) At the same time, Cortés was relieved of his leadership of New Spain, as Mexico was then known.

In 1530 he returned from Spain to build more ships at Tehuantepec. The first two expeditions he sent out under the new contract ended in disaster. On June 13, 1532, his cousin Diego Hurtado de Mendoza sailed with two ships from Acapulco to explore the Pacific coast northwest of New Spain: The venture ended in mutiny, a massacre by Nuño de Guzmán, governor of the northwest province of Mexico, and the disappearance of Hurtado on one ship. On the second expedition in 1533, while Hernando de Grijalva sailed out to sea and came upon the uninhabited Islas Revilla Gigedo, the men of Diego Becerra's ship mutinied under pilot *Fortún Jiménez,* who, after killing Becerra, crossed the Gulf of California (then named the Sea of Cortés) to discover Baja California, where he and twenty others were killed by Indians at Bahía de la Paz. In 1534 Cortés himself led the third expedition along the Pacific coast to found Santa Cruz (La Paz) on Baja California, to exploit its reputed pearls; it was abandoned in 1536. In 1539, Cortés sent *Francisco de Ulloa* to explore the outer Baja coast.

In 1540 he returned to Spain to seek justice, including redress against Guzmán, to press for the crown's share of his expedition expenses, and, most important, to defend his contractual rights, which had been usurped by new viceroy Antonio de Mendoza in partnership with Pedro de Alvarado. Cortés never returned to the New World in which he and his officers had explored lands from Central America through a large part of Mexico to Baja California.

Cosa, Juan de la (1460?–1510)

A Spanish navigator, mapmaker, and shipowner, Juan de la Cosa (also known as Juan Biscayno) chartered his *Santa Maria* to *Columbus* for the 1492 voyage and was also hired as master and second in command of the ship. For his second voyage, Columbus engaged Cosa as master of chart-making. In 1499 Cosa sailed with *Alonso de Ojeda* and *Vespucci* to verify the discoveries of Columbus, surveying the coast of, and islands off, northern South America. In 1501 he sailed with Rodrigo de Bastidas and *Balboa* along the Panama-Colombia coast and was present at the discov-

ery of the mouths of the Magdalena River. In 1509–1510 he sailed with
Ojeda and *Pizarro* to Colombia, where he died of arrow poison while on
a slave raid up the Magdalena River. Cosa's controversial 1500 map, which
incorporated Ojeda's discoveries, challenged the identification of the New
World with Asia; it was also the first important record of North American
exploration, as it included information from the 1497 *John Cabot [III]*
voyage and showed that Cabot had penetrated farther south along the
Atlantic coast than other documents had indicated.

Cuba

Shortly after arriving in the New World on his first voyage, *Christopher
Columbus* sighted the island of Cuba on October 27, 1492, and claimed it
for Spain. (He named it Juana, but it eventually became known by the
European pronunciation of its Indian name, *Colba.*) He sailed in and out
of harbors along the northern coast and even sent an exploratory
party into the island (to present-day Holguin), but then he sailed on eastward to *Hispaniola,* where the Spanish conquest of the Americas began. In
1509 *Sebastián Ocampo* circumnavigated Cuba and made a favorable
report of the island. In 1511 Diego Velázquez, who had arrived in Hispaniola in 1493 on the second voyage of Columbus, was appointed by Diego
Columbus, Christopher's son, to lead an expedition to Cuba. He landed
near the island's eastern end and there established its first permanent European settlement, Baracoa. By 1514 Velázquez had completed the conquest
of Cuba with the help of *Pedro de Alvarado* and *Pánfilo de Narváez* (who
in 1509 had explored Jamaica with Juan de Esquivel, and in 1526 was to
lead an expedition to Florida). As governor, Velázquez went on to found a
number of other towns, which soon attracted Spanish settlers.

As the largest and westernmost of the West Indies, and with its strategic location at the entrance to the Gulf of Mexico close to the Yucatan and
Florida, Cuba became a major staging area for expeditions to the mainland. Havana, initially founded in 1515 on the southern coast and relocated in 1519 to its present site on the north coast, became a port of
resupply for conquistadors and colonists, and a meeting place for galleons
sailing in convoy back to Spain. From 1517 to 1520, Velázquez supported
the explorations of the Yucatan and Mexico by *Francisco Hernández de
Córdoba, Juan de Grijalva,* and *Hernán Cortés.* The conquest of Aztec

Mexico initially siphoned many Spaniards off to the mainland, putting Cuba into a temporary economic decline. Havana and other towns fell prey to pirates and privateers in pursuit of Spanish riches. Yet after the introduction of African slaves (1517), Cuba eventually became one of New Spain's most prosperous New World provinces through the cultivation of sugar and tobacco. Meanwhile, Havana was a port of assembly and support for numerous Spanish expeditions to Florida, up the Atlantic seaboard as far as Virginia, and to the Gulf coast region through the eighteenth century: Cuba was essential to the ventures of *Juan Ponce de León [III]*, *Hernando de Soto [III]*, and *Pedro Menéndez de Avilés [III]*, among many others.

Diaz, Melchior (?–1541?)

In November 1539 Mexican viceroy Mendoza sent Melchior Diaz and Juan de Saldivar north to check on *Marcos de Niza*'s tales of Cibola. They probably entered southern Arizona, where they wintered with the *Pueblo* people. Diaz's report verified Marcos's geographical discoveries but disputed claims for great potential wealth. In spring 1540, Diaz joined the main *Coronado* expeditionary force, for which he served as an advance scout. In mid-October, Diaz and his party relieved *Luna y Arellano*'s Sonora outpost. From there Diaz set out with twenty-five men, following the coast to meet *Alarcón*'s supply ships. These he missed by some two months, but he did find Alarcón's letters buried along the Colorado River, which Diaz named Río de Tízon ("Firebrand River") after the firebrands carried by the Yuma people. He then traveled back upstream to find a ford but had to construct rafts to carry his men and horses across. Marching out from the Colorado, he found an inhospitable desert terrain. Returning eastward to Coronado, Diaz was fatally wounded by his own lance.

disease

No one questions that the Europeans, starting with the very first explorers, introduced new pathogens—bacteria, viruses, parasites, and others—to the Native American inhabitants of the New World. The diseases in question were several. It is usually claimed that the most devastating was smallpox, followed by yellow fever and malaria, but measles, scarlet fever, diphtheria, typhus, typhoid fever, tuberculosis, cholera, dysentery, influenza, and the bubonic plague were also introduced at one time or another.

The explanation for why peoples in the Western Hemisphere had never experienced these diseases is also now generally accepted to be that most of the pathogens originated long before in animal populations in the Old World, and because the inhabitants there domesticated so many animals and lived closely with them, the bacteria and viruses that cause these diseases eventually "jumped" over to human populations. That was one difference: Native Americans did not domesticate animals, other than dogs (and, in the Andes, the llama). But there was another factor: Old World populations began to live in settled communities from an early stage in history, and as the years went by, they congregated in ever larger and larger numbers. These large concentrated communities provided hospitable breeding grounds for these pathogens, whatever their origins. Native Americans, meanwhile, with some notable exceptions, did not live in large settlements—and certainly not in close proximity with cattle, sheep, chickens, pigs, and rabbits.

As for the effect on the size of the Indian population at the time *Columbus* first set foot in the New World, this is where controversy now arises. It is generally agreed that a disproportionate percentage of the pre-Columbian inhabitants of the Western Hemisphere lived in Mexico and Central America, then in the Caribbean and Peru; the others were spread about from the southern tip of South America to the farthest reaches of the Arctic North. But the debate starts with estimates of the total population of the Western Hemisphere, which range from 10 million to 110 million and even more. And it is precisely the disparity in estimates of the actual populations that has led some scholars to question the impact of disease on their numbers. Thus, if the lower range of estimates is accepted, then the decline in population would not be so severe; if the higher range of estimates is true, then the decline would be extremely drastic.

Just as estimates of the total population vary considerably, so, too, do estimates of the percentage who died in the first hundred years: 50 percent would be a reasonable compromise. After that first century, however, the fate of Native Americans seems to go in two different directions. In the Americas from Mexico south, although large numbers of Indians undoubtedly continued to die from these imported diseases, many other Indians also began to be absorbed into the general population—this may be seen to this day in many parts of Middle and South America. In North America from the Río Grande to the edge of the Arctic, however, the Indians were increasingly isolated and they continued to be prey to diseases and warfare. As a result, where the population of this part of North America has been estimated at least about 1,000,000 (and as much as 18,000,000) in 1492, it had declined to some 250,000 by 1892. Again, the largest proportion of that decline has for some time now been attributed to the various diseases mentioned.

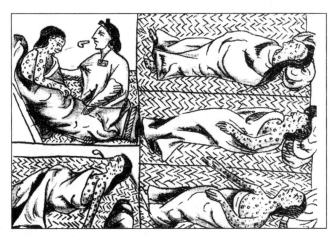

These Aztec Indians, as depicted in the *Codex Florentino* (1577), a manuscript by Fray Bernardino de Sahagun, are shown sick and dying during one of the first of the devastating smallpox epidemics that came with the Spanish explorers.

The impact of these diseases began to appear from early on, with smallpox the prime villain. It has been estimated that smallpox, introduced by African slaves brought to the Caribbean islands of Santo Domingo and Puerto Rico, wiped out anywhere from 55 to 80 percent of the native Indians. Ten years after *Cortés* set foot in Mexico (1519), some scholars believe that smallpox alone had wiped out almost 75 percent of the native population. Again, other scholars are now questioning this scenario; they do not deny that large numbers of Indians in these locales died off during those early "contact" years, but they question whether the native population was that large in the first place. Furthermore, some of these skeptics argue, smallpox could not have spread all that fast. And in any case, these scholars argue that there were multiple factors in the sharp decline and that the basic difficulties of their way of life, more so than diseases, led to a pervasive demoralization and declining birth rates.

As for the impact of diseases in America north of the Río Grande, it is generally agreed that many of them spread northward even before the first European explorers began to move among the Indians. Smallpox had certainly entered the United States by 1600—the first major outbreak among Indians on the northeastern Atlantic coast was sometime in 1616–1619; so devastating was this epidemic that it is believed to be the reason for the relative weakness of the Indians when the first English colonies began to settle in New England. By the end of the 1600s, smallpox had spread as far west as the Great Lakes and all along the Atlantic seaboard; during the 1800s, of course, smallpox spread throughout the lands west of the Mississippi. One of the most famous outbreaks was that of 1837–1840 among the Mandan, *Blackfoot [VI]*, and Assiniboine Indians of the northern plains, which killed almost 98 percent of those infected.

As stated, not all these diseases or epidemics can be laid on the doorstep of explorers. Europeans of every kind, including the best-intentioned missionaries, carried these pathogens—hunters, trappers, traders, trailblazers, soldiers, government officials, and settlers from all parts of Europe who moved into the Americas. It should be observed that many of these people also suffered from diseases that they brought with them: Given their poor diets, weather and environments to which they were not acclimated, and isolated from proper medical help, they, too, died in great numbers. But the fact remains that the Europeans introduced diseases that contributed to decimating the Native American peoples, and the very individuals who are honored as pathbreaking explorers must also accept responsibility for spreading many of these diseases.

This still leaves the disease that has inspired so much controversy over whether it was originally transmitted to the Europeans from Native

IN THEIR OWN *Words*

The Coming of the Spanish as Viewed by the Aztecs

While the Spaniards were in Tlaxcala [Mexican region], great plague broke out here in Tenochtitlán [the Aztec capital]. It began to spread during the thirteenth month and lasted for seventy days, striking everywhere in the city and killing a vast number of our people. Sores erupted on our faces, our breasts, our bellies; we were covered with agonizing sores from head to foot. The illness was so dreadful that no one could walk or move. The sick were so utterly helpless that they could only lie on their beds like corpses, unable to move their limbs or even their head. . . . If they did move their bodies, they screamed with pain. A great many died from this plague, and many others died from hunger. They could not get up to search for food, so they starved to death in their beds.

—AZTEC ACCOUNT, RECORDED BY FRAY BERNARDINO SAHAGUN, IN *CODEX FLORENTINO*, 1528

Americans or vice versa: syphilis. It was only a few years after Columbus and his men returned from their first voyage to the New World that the disease eventually to be called syphilis began to be diagnosed and described in Europe—at least by 1495. And although it cannot be claimed that any direct trail leads from the ports of Spain or Portugal, or for that matter, from any nation's ports, the disease did begin to spread rather quickly throughout Western Europe after 1492. Given the type of male who might be expected to visit the New World—sailors, soldiers, adventurers, explorers, entrepreneurs—the spread of syphilis was not unreasonably associated with them and blamed on their New World contacts. Then, whether they had carried it from the Americas or not, early European visitors to the New World were soon spreading it around via Native American females, who in turn would transmit it to their menfolk.

Whatever is ultimately proved about syphilis, this is not really the major concern of those who examine the impact of Europeans on Native Americans. Serious students of the subject take a far broader view of the links between disease and the Europeans, an association sometimes referred to as part of "the Columbus exchange"—the animals, crops, and diseases, that is, which Europeans and Native Americans exchanged with each other's cultures. Syphilis is often singled out as one that Native Americans gave Europeans, but even if this proves to be the case, there can be no denying that the Native Americans got the worst in the exchange of disease. Although explorers, even as defined most broadly, cannot be blamed for all these disease and mortality rates, they have to be recognized as the initial, if inadvertent, bearers and transmitters of many of these deadly diseases.

Drake, Sir Francis

(1540?–1596)

As an explorer, buccaneer, and English naval hero, Sir Francis Drake did more than anyone else to challenge Spanish dominance in the New World and on the seas in the sixteenth century. In 1567 he first sailed to the Americas as captain in a slave-trading fleet headed by his relative, John Hawkins. In 1572 he sailed on the first of his own privateering expeditions to attack the Spanish in Cartagena, Colombia, and Panama, where he seized a rich booty of silver.

On his second voyage (1577–1580), intending to circumnavigate the globe, he worked his way up the western coast of South America, plundering Valparaíso, Chile, and other ports. In March 1579 off Costa Rica, he captured a Spanish ship with two Manila galleon pilots aboard. From their navigation charts and sailing directions, Drake apparently learned the details of the hitherto secret Spanish trade route between Acapulco and the Philippines. This knowledge enabled him to reach northern California in a remarkably short time by sailing out to sea to catch favorable trade winds northeast back to the California coast. His northernmost point reached—some historians put it at 48° latitude (at Washington State's Olympic Peninsula), but a more likely area is 42° (at the California-Oregon border)—remains a subject of controversy, as is the California landing site to which he returned. Drake's Bay (at 38°, just north of San Francisco) is almost certainly a misnomer, as most historians place his landing site further north at Bodega Bay. From June 17 to July 23, 1579, in this bay, Drake repaired his booty-laden ship and took on fresh water and wood, for which he conducted short treks to the interior, where he found abundant game and friendly Indians (possibly Miwok). He also took possession in the name of Elizabeth I of the territory he named New Albion, thus establishing England's claim to the Pacific Northwest north of the lands occupied by Spain. (It was later reported that he left behind a metal plaque engraved with his claim; in 1934, a man produced such a plaque, but it has been dismissed as a hoax by all serious scholars.)

As this trip's log either was lost or was suppressed by the queen, it is not clear whether Drake's mandate included, in addition to a survey of the lands and islands of the Pacific region, a search for Spain's legendary *Strait of Anian* (a legendary passage to the Atlantic Ocean). At any rate, Drake's ideas about North American geography—that America and Asia drew close to each other in the north, and

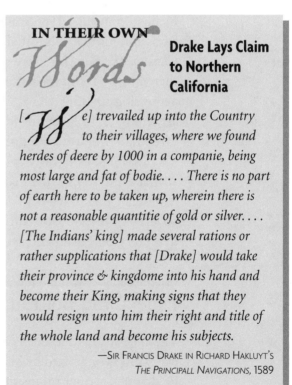

IN THEIR OWN Words

Drake Lays Claim to Northern California

[W]e trevailed up into the Country to their villages, where we found herdes of deere by 1000 in a companie, being most large and fat of bodie. . . . There is no part of earth here to be taken up, wherein there is not a reasonable quantitie of gold or silver. . . . [The Indians' king] made several rations or rather supplications that [Drake] would take their province & kingdome into his hand and become their King, making signs that they would resign unto him their right and title of the whole land and become his subjects.

—SIR FRANCIS DRAKE IN RICHARD HAKLUYT'S *THE PRINCIPALL NAVIGATIONS,* 1589

that no navigable northwest passage existed—would be proven correct. On July 25, 1579, after a day of hunting seals on the Farallon Islands and after again missing the entrance to San Francisco Bay, Drake set sail across the Pacific, arriving back in Plymouth, England, on September 26, 1580. The relative speed of his final leg led the Spanish to wonder whether he had returned by way of the Strait of Anian. Today there is some debate over whether Drake's California incursion and the danger this posed to their Manila trade route spurred the Spanish to renew exploration of the California coast.

A large part of Drake's third voyage of 1585–1586 focused on attacking and plundering Spanish ports in the New World, including Santo Domingo and Cartagena. Motivated perhaps by a rumor that the Spanish at Santa Elena (off South Carolina's Port Royal Sound) planned to attack the English of *Roanoke Colony [III]* (off North Carolina's Albemarle Sound), he bypassed Havana and headed north to attack Santa Elena. Almost by accident he came upon the Spanish settlement at St. Augustine, Florida, which he partially destroyed after stripping it of useful items to pass on to those at Roanoke. Continuing up the coast, he missed Santa Elena and in June 1586 reached Roanoke, which he found low on provisions and morale. His initial plans to lend a shallow-draft vessel to explore *Chesapeake Bay [III]* were set aside when a storm destroyed the boat. He then returned with most of the colonists to England. As a result of Drake's aggression, in 1587 the Spanish abandoned Santa Elena and moved the settlers back to a rebuilt St. Augustine; they also set aside any plans to extend their Florida dominion north to Chesapeake Bay.

In 1588, as naval vice admiral, Drake helped to defeat the Spanish Armada and to shift the mastery of the oceans and the initiative in North American exploration to England. On his disastrous last privateering voyage of 1595–1596 with Hawkins to the West Indies, Drake died of dysentery off Portobello, Panama, and was buried in the Caribbean Sea.

Espejo and Beltrán expedition (1582–1583)

The expedition to rescue Fray *Agustín Rodríguez* from the Indians in New Mexico was organized by his fellow Franciscans. Antonio Espejo, a wealthy landowner, former Inquisition official, and fugitive from justice, offered to equip and lead fourteen soldiers as an escort and to pay Fray Bernaldino Beltrán's expenses. Espejo hoped this noble deed might earn him a pardon and that he could also investigate rumors of gold and silver in the *Pueblo*

Indian country. On November 10, 1582, the party left San Bartolomé (Allende, Mexico) and followed the Río Conchos up to the Río Grande, finally reaching the southernmost Piros pueblos in late December. They then marched upstream to Puaray, above what is now Albuquerque, and there on February 17, 1583, learned of the death of Rodríguez and his fellow friar. After punishing the Indians, Espejo visited the Acoma and Zuni pueblos and marched north to Taos and then southwest to Hopi lands, where he received four thousand cotton blankets and witnessed the Hopi snake dance. He continued on, crossing the Little Colorado River to the Flagstaff, Arizona, area, seeking an elusive lake of gold. Further west, near the Prescott area, he discovered what he reported as rich veins of copper and silver. (Diego Pérez de Luxán, a more reliable chronicler, reported the veins as worthless.) He searched for minerals until mid-July before turning back east. From Zuni pueblo, where Beltrán and half the party had remained (and from where they set out early to return home), Espejo headed toward Texas by way of the Buffalo Plains and passed near Pecos before reaching the Río Grande and turning homeward. He arrived some days after Beltrán on September 10.

Narratives of Espejo's journey, which was essentially a rediscovery of New Mexico some forty years after *Coronado,* inventoried the region's agriculture, trade goods, natural resources, and pueblos, overestimating their population and describing their ethnographic features. His enthusiastic report on New Mexico garnered wide publicity in Mexico and Spain, where it was published in 1586, yet he was unable to procure for himself the royal commission for its conquest. En route to Spain to pursue his case, he died in *Cuba.* Not until fifteen years later, with the official expedition headed by *Juan de Oñate,* was the Spanish settlement of the Southwest finally initiated.

Estevánico (Esteban) (?–1539)

Estevánico, by some accounts an Arab from Morocco and by others a black African, probably walked a longer distance across the wilderness of North America than any other Spanish explorer. He did so first with *Cabeza de Vaca* from the Texas coast to northwestern Mexico near the Pacific coast, and then as a forward scout for a 1539 expedition from northwestern Mexico into the Pueblo country of the American Southwest. As slave to Andrés

Dorantes, he accompanied his master on the ill-fated 1528 *Narváez* expedition to conquer *Florida [III].* Beset by hostile Indians and starvation, most of the four hundred men led by Narváez perished, except for a group that eventually washed up off the Texas coast. Enslaved by Indians for years, most of the survivors died, and the remaining four castaways finally escaped in 1534. The group, led by Cabeza de Vaca and including Alonso del Castillo, as well as Dorantes and Estevánico, took some twenty-two months to make its way across southeast Texas and northern Mexico to the west coast. Escorted by tribal parties along old Indian trails, the castaways earned food by performing cures on the diseased.

In March 1539 Mexican viceroy Antonio de Mendoza sent out an exploring party preliminary to Coronado's expedition of 1540–1542. He acquired the services of Estevánico from Dorantes and placed him under the leadership of the Franciscan *Marcos de Niza.* After leaving Culiacán, Marcos sent him on ahead to scout and report back. Together with a group of some three hundred Sonoran Indians, he headed north either up the Sonora or Yaqui valley, made the long Arizona desert crossing northeast of the Gila River, and traversed a pass between Sierra Mogoyon and Sierra Blanca. Dressed in full medicine-man regalia and traveling with pomp, he received gifts of turquoise, woven blankets, and buffalo skins from the Indian groups he encountered. After entering New Mexico, he reached Hawikuh pueblo, where he was slain by the Zuni; they apparently perceived him as threatening or arrogant. The fleeing Indians of his retinue informed Marcos, who then dared view the pueblo only from a distance before turning back to Mexico with enticing tales of a treasure city. Estevánico is considered among the earliest explorers of the Southwest, and the tale of his death lives on in Zuni legend.

Fuca, Juan de (Valerianos, Apóstolos)   (1536?–1602?)

Most historians reject the claim that in 1592 Juan de Fuca, a Greek pilot (his true name was Apóstolos Valerianos) with forty years in Spanish service, discovered the strait between Washington State's Olympic Peninsula and Vancouver Island, a strait later named after him. His claim, documented in seventeenth- and eighteenth-century maps, was accepted until 1792, when the legendary *Strait of Anian* (a reputed water passage from the Pacific to the Atlantic) was definitively proven not to exist. Since Fuca had claimed in his narrative that he had found the outlet to Anian, his discovery of the Juan de Fuca Strait was also rejected outright. His fanciful report of ample gold, silver, and pearls was a common feature of tales told by explorers seeking funds for further expeditions. The absence of other documentary support may be due to the Spanish policy of secrecy about explorations; reports were buried in archives in Spain and Mexico, and some of them have since been lost to fire and other disasters.

But some scholars are willing to consider that Fuca's tale, as told to English merchant-venturer Michael Lok, was not necessarily fictional. It yields geographical details that indeed support his claim of discovering the Juan de Fuca Strait, from which he sailed some twenty days north up the inland waterway between Vancouver Island and mainland British Columbia, finally turning back at Queen Charlotte Sound, which he called the North Sea and which he may have mistaken for the entrance to Anian. His purported discovery of Anian stimulated various expeditions to the Northwest, until a 1792 joint survey by Spaniard *Alejandro Malaspina [IV]* and English captain *George Vancouver [VI]* disproved the Anian story. The discovery of the Juan de Fuca Strait then came to be attributed to Charles William Barkley, captain of an English fur-trading vessel, in 1787.

IN THEIR OWN Words — Support for Juan de Fuca's Claim

When I was in Venice in April 1596, happily arrived there an old man, about three score years of age, called commonly Juan de Fuca but named properly Apóstolos Valerianos, of Nation a Greek . . . and he said that the Viceroy of Mexico sent him out again Anno 1592 with a small Caravela and a Pinnace, armed with Mariners only to follow the said Voyage for discovery of the same Straits of Anian and the passage thereof into the Sea, which they call the north Sea, which is our Northwest Sea. And that he . . . entered thereinto, staying therein more than twenty dayes and found . . very much broader Sea than was at said entrance and that hee passed by divers Ilands. . . . And he also said that he went on Land in divers places and that he saw some people on Land, clad in Beasts skins; and that the Land is very fruitful, and rich of Gold, Silver, Pearle and other things, like Nova Spania.

—MICHAEL LOK'S ACCOUNT OF JUAN DE FUCA'S 1592 VOYAGE, 1625

Gali, Francisco (also Galli or Gualle)   (?–?)

In 1584, under orders from the Mexican viceroy, Francisco Gali surveyed the Alta California coast while sailing his galleon on the return leg of the recently established Spanish galleon trade route from Acapulco, Mexico, to the Philippines and back. After crossing the Pacific Ocean, he sighted land between San Francisco and Santa Cruz. Sailing south, he conducted a superficial inspection of the shoreline down to the tip of Baja California. He planned a second survey on his next return from Manila, but died before the ship was made ready. *Pedro de Unamuno* took over his mission.

Grijalva, Juan de   (1490?–1526)

Shortly after the 1517 return of the *Hernández de Córdoba* expedition that discovered the Yucatan, *Cuba*'s governor Diego Velázquez began organizing a second expedition under a *Hispaniola* license to "trade for gold, pearls, and precious stones," at the same time applying for Spanish royal permission to explore, conquer, and colonize this new territory. His nephew Juan de Grijalva, who had helped to conquer Cuba, led the exploratory force of two hundred, which included survivors of the Hernández expedition. His four ships set out across the Yucatan strait on May 1, 1518, and two days later landed at Cozumel Island. Soon after crossing to the mainland on May 7, the Spaniards viewed from the sea the impressive ruins of Tulum, an ancient Mayan city, before they followed the coast south to Bahía de Ascensión, which they believed to be the end of the island of Yucatan, but found it too shallow to sail through westward to the Gulf of Mexico. After turning back, they passed and named Isla Mujeres ("Island of Women") for the many women they saw there at a Mayan temple. They reached Cabo Catoche and followed Hernández's route along the west coast. On May 26, desperate for fresh water, they landed at Campeche despite Mayan hostility and chased their warriors from the field in a fierce battle. Further south at Champotón, the ships' artillery repulsed canoes filled with irate warriors.

On May 31 they finally reached a haven at Laguna de Términos, a large sheltered bay where they repaired their ships and gathered water, fish, and wood while the wounded recovered. Believing the bay to be a water passage to the Yucatan's east coast, chief pilot *Antonio de Alaminos [III]* still considered the peninsula an island. From this point, which Alaminos declared the limit of the lands discovered by Hernández, the expedition sailed on June 5 onward to the unknown territory, which Grijalva was the first European to explore—the Mexican mainland, soon to be called New Spain. Passing a mouth of the Usumacinta, they entered Río de Tabasco and traded for gold items with the curious Tabascoans, from whom they heard of great mountains inland, a river rich with gold, and another ocean two months' march away. They arrived at the site of present-day Veracruz, where on June 24 Grijalva took possession for the Spanish crown. The same day he sent *Pedro de Alvarado,* one of his captains, back to Cuba with a report for Velázquez: Messengers from Moctezuma had greeted the voyagers with gifts from the Aztec monarch, including gold, which Alvarado brought back with him.

Ignoring his men's pleas to begin colonization (and thus missing out on the spectacular inland discoveries that would be made by *Cortés*), Grijalva continued on north to Cabo Rojo, south of Tampico, before turning back on June 28 and setting sail on July 27 for Cuba. Adverse winds and currents drove his ships back to Laguna de Términos. From there they retraced their route up the Yucatan, fighting off a Mayan ambush at Campeche, and finally returned to Cuba on September 30. Meanwhile an impatient Velázquez had sent out a search party led by Cristóbal de Olid, who also explored the Yucatan coast from Cozumel to Laguna de Términos. By then anxious for the return of both Grijalva and Olid, Velázquez assigned Cortés to head an expedition to hunt for them, explore the new lands, and establish trade. Velázquez unsuccessfully tried to recall Cortés when Grijalva and Olid returned.

Attention turned back to the Yucatan after Mexico's conquest by Cortés. In 1523 Grijalva had returned to Mexico at the head of the Garay expedition, only to be arrested by Cortés's men. In 1526 he died in a Cuban Indian uprising.

Gutiérrez de Humaña and Leyva de Bonilla expedition (1593–1594)

Motivated by dreams of wealth, Antonio Gutiérrez de Humaña and Francisco Leyva de Bonilla led an unauthorized expedition from Nueva Vizcaya in Mexico north into the American Southwest in 1593. After the adventurers spent nearly a year in *Pueblo* country at Bove (near San Ildefonso, New Mexico), they set out in a northeasterly direction toward a rumored settlement at the Arkansas River, traveling either by way of the Purgatory River in southeastern Colorado or by way of the Texas panhandle. From the Arkansas they marched twelve days north toward a still larger river, possibly the Platte in Nebraska. Somewhere on the plains, probably between the Arkansas and Smoky Hill rivers in eastern Kansas, Humaña fatally stabbed Bonilla during a dispute. The rest of the party was massacred by Indians. Their Indian guide Jusephe escaped to New Mexico. After a year of captivity by the Apache, he returned to Pecos and later met up with the *Oñate* expedition in 1598.

Hernández (Fernández) de Córdoba, Francisco de (1) (?–1517)

Francisco Hernández de Córdoba, a wealthy Cuban planter, is credited with the 1517 discovery of Mexico's Yucatan peninsula, although Spanish slave raiders had visited the region previously. Around February 8, 1517, the three ships set sail from Santiago de Cuba piloted by *Antonio de Alaminos [III],* who had navigated *Ponce de León*'s *[III]* 1513 trip to Florida. The Hernández expedition's route through the Caribbean's unexplored western waters may have been suggested by Alaminos, who in 1502 had noticed that *Columbus* had restrained himself, because of inadequate ships, from sailing toward what he thought might be a potentially rich land. Around February 20, they passed *Cuba*'s westernmost point, Cabo San Antón, and entered the Yucatan Channel.

Around February 28, after a two-day storm, they neared Cabo Catoche on a narrow island off the northeast point of the Yucatan, which Alaminos believed to be a large island. From their anchorage, they viewed a large town, which they named Gran Cairo, probably for its impressive pyramidal temple. Several days later the flagship was approached by some thirty Mayans in long dugout canoes with oars and sails. They boarded the ship and lured the Spanish into a land ambush by brightly plumed warriors protected by shields and quilted cotton armor, and wielding lances, bows and arrows, and slings. The Spanish crossbowmen and musketeers won the day and seized two young Mayans as potential interpreters, along with clay idol figurines and gold ornaments as evidence of their discovery of the sophisticated thousand-year-old Mayan civilization, in decline since the ninth century. The Spaniards then followed the Yucatan coast west and then south for fifteen days, anchoring on March 29 off Campeche to take on fresh water. Invited to visit by people clad in colorful cotton mantles, they observed a town of paved streets with squares and marketplaces bordered by brick and mortar houses with towers and elevated courts accessible by long stairways, along with monumental temples. They were then warned off by priests with an ominous human sacrifice and by a threatening cadre of armed soldiers. After sailing south, around April 10 they were attacked again at Champotón while seeking water. In the desperate hour-long battle, over half the Spanish were killed and nearly all the others were wounded, including Hernández, who was pierced by ten arrows. They retreated back north and from Río Lagartos reached the Florida Gulf coast on April 18. At the site visited by Ponce de León between Cape Roman and Cape Sable, they were again attacked while fetching water. The now seriously wounded Alaminos found a shortcut back to Cuba between the Marquesas and Key West. Hernández died ten days after their return.

News of this wealthy Mayan culture rapidly spread throughout the Caribbean and reached Spain. The two captives also reported, misleadingly, that there was much gold in the Yucatan, named by the Spanish after the Mayan words for *yuca tlati,* the manioc plant and source of cassava, an essential regional food staple. Velázquez claimed the discovery as his own and the voyage's immediate result was the 1518 *Juan de Grijalva* expedition, closely followed by that of *Cortés,* which ended in the conquest of Mexico's Aztec empire.

Hernández (Fernández) de Córdoba, Francisco de (2) (?–1524)

Not to be confused with the Spaniard of the same name credited with discovering the Yucatan peninsula, little is known of this Hernández de Córdoba until he was sent in 1523 by Pedro Arias de Ávila (Pedrarias), governor of the Darien region of Panama, to take control of Nicaragua. It had been conquered by Gil González de Ávila in 1522, but he fled to *Hispaniola* rather than tangle with the brutal Arias de Ávila. Hernández de Córdoba moved down into Nicaragua, explored the territory, and founded two cities,

León and Granada. When he decided to claim Nicaragua for himself, he was killed by an officer in his army on orders of Arias de Ávila, but he lives on in the name of modern Nicaragua's unit of coinage, the córdoba.

Hispaniola

This second-largest island in the West Indies was first seen by a European when in December 1492 *Columbus* sailed along the north coast and, impressed by its vegetation, called it *La Isla Española* ("the Spanish Island"). This was eventually anglicized as Hispaniola. On December 24 his ship, the *Santa Maria,* was wrecked on a reef near Cap Haitien in the present Republic of Haiti. A local Arawak Indian chief helped the sailors save their cargo. Columbus built a fort from the remains of his ship and named it *La Navidad;* he left forty men behind when he returned to Spain in January 1493. When he returned to Hispaniola on his second voyage in 1493, all the men had been killed because of their mistreatment of the Indians. Columbus decided to abandon this site but sailed east along the northern coast and there founded what arguably deserves to be known as the first European colony in the New World, Isabela. Thousands of Spanish settled on Hispaniola, conquering the Indians, and in 1496 they established a capital on the south coast; they named it La Nueva Isabela, and it would later become Santo Domingo. By the time Columbus returned on his third voyage, in 1498, many of the colonists had become angry because they were not discovering the gold that Columbus had said awaited them. Word of this discontent reached Spain, and Francisco de Bobadilla was sent out to Hispaniola; he arrested Columbus and his two brothers and sent them back to Spain in chains. Ferdinand and Isabella released them, and in 1502 Columbus sailed on his fourth and final voyage, once again visiting Hispaniola and its new capital, Santo Domingo. That was his last visit there, but Hispaniola remained an important part of Spain's empire in the Caribbean.

By the mid-1500s, however, more Spanish were attracted to Cuba, Mexico, and other parts of their New World empire, and gradually other European nationalities were moving onto Hispaniola. By this time, too, the Spanish, having killed off most of the Indians, had imported thousands of African slaves. Then in 1697, under the Treaty of Ryswick, which ended the War of the League of Augsburg, Spain ceded the western third of the island to France. The French named their new colony Saint

Domingue and imported even more thousands of slaves, but after the revolt of these slaves succeeded in establishing an independent country in 1803, its new leaders named it Haiti, apparently an Arawak Indian word meaning "high ground" (although Indians also called the whole island Quisqueya). Today, the eastern two-thirds is the nation of the Dominican Republic; the other third, to the west, is the nation of Haiti, but the old name, Hispaniola, is still used to refer to the island as a whole.

Jiménez, Fortún (Ximénes de Bertandoña, Ortuño) (?–?)

Fortún Jiménez, a Basque pilot, is credited with the 1533 discovery of Baja California, making him the first European to reach the southernmost limits of California. He sailed on a voyage of discovery with Diego Becerra, who was sent north from Acapulco by **Hernán Cortés.** Jiménez led a mutiny against the detested Becerra, who was murdered; other wounded officials and three Franciscans were set ashore on the Colima coast. Described by Bernal Diaz as a "great cosmographer," Jiménez sailed on north past the tip of Baja and into the Gulf of California (Sea of Cortés). On the peninsula's eastern shore, he entered the Bahía de la Paz ("Bay of Peace"), reportedly named for its calm waters. Jiménez, who believed Baja California to be an island, is the earliest of the candidates suggested as the person who named the area California. On a shore trip to get fresh water, he and others were killed by hostile Indians. The survivors sailed back south, where their ship was seized by Nuño de Guzmán, conqueror of Nueva Galicia and a bitter rival of Cortés. All that reached Cortés was the "good news" of pearl beds and illusory gold. This led him to found in 1535 the short-lived settlement of Santa Cruz at La Paz.

Lavazares (Bazares, Labazares), Guido de (?–?)

An experienced mariner and Seville native, Guido de Lavazares arrived in Mexico in the 1530s. After the viceroy ordered him to survey the coast of the Gulf of Mexico from Río de las Palmas to the tip of the Florida peninsula as a preliminary to colonization, he set out with three ships on September 3, 1558, from San Juan de Ulúa at Veracruz. After stopping briefly at Río Pánuco, he sailed for Kingsville on the Texas coast. From there the ships hugged the shore, reaching a large body of water, probably Matagorda Bay, which he named San Francisco Bay and claimed for the Spanish king (127 years before *La Salle*'s *[V]* arrival). Contrary winds forced him to sail back toward the Yucatan in order to set a course for the Florida peninsula. Next reaching an island on the east side of the Mississippi Delta blocking the river's sound, he went ashore to complete the act of possession and to name the Bahía de los Bajos ("Bay of Shoals"). Further exploration revealed a coast bordered by shallow, often submerged, land and thus unsuitable for settlement.

He then continued east to Alabama's Mobile Bay, which he named Bahía Filipina and again claimed for the king. Exploring it, he noted the mouth of a large river. Terming the bay the "largest and most commodious in all that coast," he documented impressive stands of timber, good grazing lands, plentiful game and fish, red banks as a source of building stone, and deposits of clay suitable for making bricks and pottery. Twice trying to advance onward from Mobile Bay in the face of strong headwinds and bad weather, he reached just east of Choctawhatchee Bay before ending the expedition to return to Mexico, arriving on December 14. Six years later Lavazares was treasurer of an expedition to discover a route across the Pacific and to conquer the Philippines, of which he was named governor in 1572.

legendary destinations

Many of the early Spanish explorers were primarily motivated by the possibility of finding fabulous troves of gold and riches, and luring them on were often tales of places of fantastic wealth. These tales were sometimes based on sheer fantasies, sometimes on misunderstandings, and sometimes even on certain realities, but in any case they assumed legendary status and played a major role in early explorations.

In the American Southwest, the most famous legendary place was found in the myth of the Seven Cities of Cibola, which were believed to be cities of gold. The name *Cibola* is believed to come from the name of a Zuni pueblo *(Shivola),* while the notion of the Seven Cities is linked to an eighth-century Portuguese legend in which seven bishops fled the conquering Moors to find refuge across the Atlantic Ocean in a land called

Antilia (the source of the name Antilles for the Caribbean islands). After *Cabeza de Vaca* journeyed across the continent, he passed on tales he had heard of wealthy Indian communities to the north. This led the Mexican viceroy to send *Marcos de Niza* and *Estevánico* north into New Mexico to find these sites. After Estevánico was slain by Pueblo Indians, Marcos observed Hawikuh, the southernmost Zuni pueblo, from a distance before turning back. His report, compiled from the tales told him by Indian informants, was interpreted to mean that he had indeed found the first of the Seven Cities. This resulted in the 1540 expedition led by *Francisco de Coronado* into the Southwest. On reaching Hawikuh, Coronado was disappointed to see only subsistence-level pueblo villages and nothing resembling the grandeur of Aztec Mexico or Incan Peru.

Coronado was then told of Quivira, another Indian culture still farther north and also reputed to possess quantities of gold. (The name *Quivira* is apparently the Spanish transliteration of these Indians' name for themselves and their region.) This tale was related by the Turk (so called by the Spanish for his unique headdress), a Pawnee slave at Pecos pueblo. So, in 1541, Coronado and a large force set out for Quivira, guided by the Turk and Ysopete, another Indian. After reaching the west Texas plains, Coronado suspected Turk of trickery and placed him in chains. Sending most of his men back to the pueblos of the upper Río Grande, Coronado continued northward to Kansas. There he was again disappointed, this time to find the grass huts of the Quivirans. The Quivira myth was probably created either by the Pecos in an attempt to rid themselves of their unwelcome visitors, or by the Turk, who wanted an escort back to his homeland. Today's historians agree that the Quivira Indians of the Great Bend area of the Arkansas River in south central Kansas were in fact the Wichita, the southernmost of the Plains village tribes.

During the Coronado expedition, yet another southwestern legend that emerged was that of Teguayo, a wealthy kingdom to the north where the people lived along the shore of a lake called Copala. Again, Coronado's men found no Teguayo in their exploration of the land of the Utahs. The 1776 *Escalante and Domínguez expedition [IV]* into the region placed Teguayo in Utah's Great Salt Lake area. In some versions, Copala was the origination site of the Aztecs, who later journeyed south to Mexico. Francisco de Ibarra, who set out from Zacatecas, Mexico, to find Copala, explored to the north and west, possibly traveling as far as southern Arizona in the mid-sixteenth century.

Still another southwestern legend was that of Sierra Azul (Blue Mountain), apparently a mountain of silver. After *Diego José de Vargas [IV]* reconquered New Mexico after the 1680 *Pueblo* revolt, he used (and perhaps fabricated) the Sierra Azul tale to keep the Spanish administration focused on New Mexico's colonization. This myth lingered into the nineteenth century. And despite Coronado's disillusionment, the legends of the Seven Cities, of Quivira (variously placed in Kansas, Texas, and even Nebraska), and of Teguayo lived on to lure such later explorers as Antonio *Espejo* and *Juan de Oñate.* Both of them did find some southwestern mineral deposits but certainly not in the amounts reported by legend or approaching the quality of the great Mexican silver mines at Zacatecas.

The legend of La Gran Copala also spurred on the sixteenth-century Spanish explorers of Greater Florida, which extended from the lower Mississippi River northeastward through Virginia. For these adventurers, it was a wealthy Indian city with a trove of gold, rubies, and diamonds located somewhere in the mountains of the Carolinas, Georgia, Alabama, or Tennessee. But La Gran Copala was only one of several mythic sites that attracted sixteenth-century Spanish and French explorers and colonists to venture into the American Southeast and to the Atlantic seaboard region. (It should also be noted that early explorers in the Northeast were also influenced by certain legendary locales, such as *Norumbega [III]* and *Saguenay [III].*) The legend of Chicora, named after the original Indian inhabitants of the South Carolina coastal area, is linked to the explorations of *Hernando de Soto [III]* and *Lucas Vásquez de Ayllón [III].* Originally, the Chicora myth was associated with the Spanish site of Santa Elena (in the Port Royal Sound area of South Carolina), which reputedly was a gateway to a region rich in pearls and silver. Also part of the Chicora legend was Xapira, an inland area rich in gemstones. Later, the expeditions of *Juan Pardo [III]* and his men inland to the Carolina mountains and beyond into Tennessee gave rise to the myth of Los Diamantes, a fabulous mountain of diamonds. In fact, these "diamonds" were the mica, corundum, and quartz crystals dug up by Indians. Although the Spanish were apparently unable to track down these legendary places, such myths had some basis in fact. The British colonists of the region later discovered gold mines in western North Carolina and northern Georgia, also the site of gemstone deposits. Archaeologists found evidence of ancient Indian mines in the region as well. Yet if the tales of fabulously rich places generally proved illusory, they did serve to spur on many of the early explorers of North America.

López de Cárdenas, García   (?–?)

In 1540, while on the *Coronado* expedition into the American southwest, García López de Cárdenas was the first European to view the *Grand Canyon [VI]*. The second son of a Spanish nobleman and a valued lieutenant of Coronado, he had saved Coronado's life when he was wounded during the Spanish attack on Hawikuh, or Cibola, which then became the expedition's temporary headquarters. When expedition member Pedro de Továr returned from a scouting mission to the northwest to investigate Hopi settlements, he repeated stories of a great river flowing between mountain walls farther to the west. Coronado sent Cárdenas with a small party to find this river. Following Továr's route, he climbed the Colorado Plateau, crossed the Painted Desert, and reached the land of the Hopi. Their guides led him on a twenty-day trek to the edge of the Grand Canyon, near Moran Point, in September 1540. They stayed for three days while two Spaniards tried to climb down to the Colorado River, but they were able to descend only one-third of the way. The Spaniards were more impressed by the canyon as an immense obstacle rather than by its spectacular beauty. On his return, Cárdenas reported nothing else of interest (i.e., gold) in the region, to Coronado's disappointment.

He then ordered Cárdenas to prepare a new expedition headquarters in the Tigues pueblo country north of Albuquerque, New Mexico. During the severe winter of 1540–1541, the Spanish forcibly took clothing and food from the Pueblo people, inciting them to a lengthy armed rebellion. Cárdenas made an example of the pueblo of Arenal, burning its surrendering warriors alive at the stake. After the Coronado expedition, Cárdenas traveled to Spain to claim an inheritance. There he was convicted of acts of cruelty toward the Indians and died in prison.

Marcos de Niza   (1495?–1558)

A French Franciscan from Nice, accomplished in theology and reputedly in cosmography and navigation, Marcos de Niza arrived in the Americas in 1531. He traveled with *Pizarro* to Peru and trekked from Guatemala to Mexico in 1537. To test the ideas of *Cortés* about the lands north of the Gulf of California, he made a little-known first expedition in 1538 to the

Pacific coastal region. He erroneously assumed the eastern shore of the Gulf to be the ocean coast; he also mistakenly reported that the coast turned sharply west at 35°, a claim documented on the 1541–1542 Battista Agnese map. Leaving the coast, he stopped at La Junta de los Ríos and other native villages, finding Indians with permanent dwellings who grew beans, corn, and pumpkins, and who used cotton blankets. Some of them traded for turquoise and buffalo robes with people farther north, who reportedly lived in a fertile valley along a great river (the upper Río Grande).

This is believed to have been one of several pueblos around Zuni, New Mexico. These villages convinced the early Spanish that they had reached the site of the legendary Seven Cities of Cibola. Viewed from some distance, glistening in the sunlight, these pueblos initially seemed to promise "cities of gold."

In 1539, under the orders of Mexican viceroy Antonio de Mendoza, Marcos de Niza made a reconnaissance into the American Southwest preliminary to the *Coronado* expedition, in which he also participated. On this expedition, Marcos left Culiacán, Mexico, on March 7, 1539, with another friar who soon turned back, a group of Indians, and *Estevánico,* a black veteran of *Cabeza de Vaca*'s transcontinental trek, who was to operate as his forward scout. Planting crosses along the way as acts of possession, Marcos pushed north toward the legendary Seven Cities of Cibola, proceeding by way of either the Sonora or Yaqui valley, through Arizona's San Pedro valley, veering northeast to the Gila River, and passing between the Sierra Mogoyon and Sierra Blanca. On July 7 he cautiously approached Hawikuh (Cibola) (see *legendary destinations*) near Zuni, New Mexico. He had been informed of Estevánico's murder by its inhabitants, so he viewed the pueblo only from a distance. Taking possession of Cibola and all towns beyond for the Spanish king, he named the region the New Kingdom of San Francisco. On his return home, he offered fantastic tales of a wealthy city even larger than Mexico City.

This accelerated the organization of the Coronado expedition, which moved with pomp out of Composeta on February 22, 1540, with Marcos along. Some five months later, the travelers first viewed at close hand Hawikuh (Cibola), a small crowded village so disappointing that Marcos was branded a liar and sent back in disgrace. His health broken, he died in Jalapa, Mexico, in 1558.

Controversy clouds the extent of Marcos's misrepresentation: viewed from afar through a dry atmosphere, Hawikuh could seem much larger than it actually is because of an optical illusion. The details he heard about its wealth were reported by Indians whose powers of imagination may have exceeded their skills of translation. In any case, in his report Marcos had tried to be careful about distinguishing what he actually observed from what was hearsay or rumor. The tendency of its readers was probably to put the most optimistic spin on the report.

Mendoza's instructions to Marcos—to observe the various peoples and carefully inventory the fertile lands, climate, flora, fauna, terrain, rivers, and minerals, collecting samples whenever possible—have gained this expedition the honor of being the first scientific one by the Spanish in North America, as opposed to a purely military one. It was also the first instance of a missionary taking possession of new territories for the Spanish crown, a policy later pursued in colonizing California.

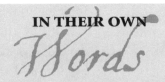

IN THEIR OWN Words

Marcos Promotes Cibola, the Fabled Seven Cities of Gold

When I showed the natives the sample of gold I had, they said there were vessels of it among their people. They wore ornaments of it hanging from their noses and ears, and also they have blades of gold to scrape the sweat from their bodies. Many of the people I saw wore silk clothing down to their feet. Of the richness of that country I cannot write, because it is so great it does not seem possible. They have temples of metal covered with precious stones—emeralds, I think. They use vessels of gold and silver for they have no other metal.

—Fray Marcos de Niza, *Relación*, 1540

Montejo, Francisco (1479–1553)

Born in Salamanca, Spain, into a noble family, Montejo traveled to the New World in 1514 with the expedition of Pedro Arias de Ávila (Pedrarias). On *Cuba,* he was assigned one of the richest estates. After the death of *Juan de Grijalva* in 1526, Francisco de Montejo, one of his captains, obtained the royal contract to explore, conquer, and settle the Yucatan peninsula, with himself as governor. Having first returned to Spain, in June 1527 he set sail with a fleet of four vessels and with Alonso de Ávila as second in command. By October he had established the first Spanish town of Salamanca near Tulum on the Yucatan. He and Ávila spent the next seven years fruitlessly crisscrossing the Yucatan and fighting the fiercely rebellious population. At the end of 1534 no Spaniards were left in the Yucatan: Exploration had revealed it as a peninsula and its interior as arid, rocky, or swampy, seemingly infertile, and, worst of all, devoid of gold. After Montejo withdrew to govern Chiapas and Honduras, his son and nephew, both named Francisco de Montejo, began a new phase of conquest. In January 1542 his son established Mérida as capital near the ruins of the Mayan city of T-hó, and on May 24, 1543, his nephew founded Valladolid. Following the 1546–1547 Mayan rebellion, the Yucatan finally became a Spanish dominion. Montejo, meanwhile, had returned to Spain, where he died in 1553.

Moscoso Alvarado, Luís de (?–?)

Just before he died on May 21, 1542, during a three-year journey into the wilderness of the American Southeast, *Hernando de Soto [III]* appointed as his successor Luís de Moscoso Alvarado, nephew of *Pedro de Alvarado.* On June 5 Moscoso's stranded party set off from the Mississippi near its junction in southeastern Arkansas with the Arkansas River, in search of a land route to Mexico. Traveling southwest, they crossed the Sabine, Angelina, and Neches Rivers, probably penetrating as far as the Trinity River in southwest Houston County in East Texas; some accounts place their end point at the Middle Brazos River or even in the Austin area. In October, starvation and impending harsh weather forced them to retrace their steps. In January 1543, after many hardships, they were encamped by the Mississippi near their starting point.

The plan now became to reach Mexico by sea, and over the next six months, in a remarkable feat, they built seven brigantine vessels by using available materials and forging slave chains into nails. On July 2, 1543, after releasing some 500 Indian slaves, Moscoso's 322 Spaniards (of the 600 who arrived with Soto) set sail downstream. The first Europeans to voyage along the Mississippi, they reached its mouth after seventeen days of constant Indian harassment. After first trying the open sea, they decided to follow the shore. During their fifty-three-day trip from the Mississippi to Tampico, Mexico, thirty days were spent in transit and the rest on necessary stops and brief explorations. Beset by mosquitoes, they found crude oil in a Texas cove, which they used to caulk their leaky vessels. They probably also entered Matagorda and Corpus Christi Bays. Moscoso safely returned to civilization 310 of the Spaniards for whom he had assumed responsibility. The Mexican viceroy welcomed the Soto survivors and offered Moscoso leadership of another expedition to the Alabama area. This Moscoso declined, but he did enter the viceroy's service, accompanying him to Peru in 1550.

Narváez, Pánfilo de (1470?–1528)

After Spanish conquistador Pánfilo Narváez arrived in the New World on the 1493 voyage of *Columbus,* he assisted in the conquests of Jamaica and *Cuba.* In 1520 Cuban governor Diego Velázquez sent him to Mexico to arrest *Cortés,* who captured and imprisoned him. In 1525 he returned to Spain to obtain a royal contract to explore, conquer, and colonize *Florida [III].* In June 1527 he left Spain with five ships, and after stops at *Hispaniola* and Cuba, he anchored off the Florida gulf coast on April 9, 1528.

His landing site is controversial: Probably it was south of Tampa Bay, although some historians place it at Sarasota Bay or at Charlotte Harbor. Several days later Narváez, *Cabeza de Vaca,* and forty-six men made a short foray northward and discovered what was probably Tampa Bay proper (by some accounts, Old Tampa Bay). On a second exploration of the bay's shore, Narváez found a Timucuan village, where he treated the Indians brutally (a tendency that persisted through his expedition), ensuring continuing Indian hostility. In a fateful decision, he sent away his ships to search for a certain bay: The ships and the main expedition group never found each other again.

They marched for fifty-six days through difficult terrain, harassed by Indians, and arrived in late June at Ivitachuco near Tallahassee. They occupied the village for some twenty-five days, conducting three small expeditions to the northeast, a countryside of forests and lakes with abundant game. After crossing the Ochlockonee River into the Apalachicola National Forest, they headed southeast toward the Gulf coast, arriving on July 29 at Acute, probably near Saint Marks. From there Narváez sent Cabeza de Vaca to find the sea.

Narváez moved his sick, starving, and mutinous men to a camp on the bay. After a council decided to build ships with which to reach Pánuco, Mexico, the Spanish constructed five shallow boats from the materials at hand. After their last horse had been killed for food, they spent a week dragging the vessels through the marshes to the sea, and in late September the

This map shows the probable route taken by the ill-fated 1528 expedition led by Pànfilo Narváez. He would disappear at the end, and Cabeza de Vaca's epic adventure would then commence.

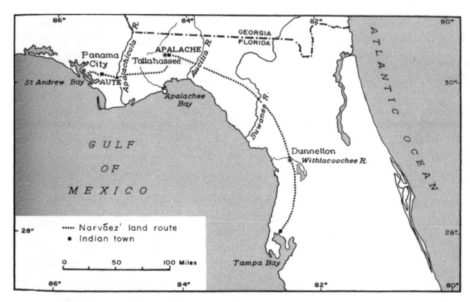

248 survivors voyaged westward, with stops for water, food, and shelter from storms, all the while losing still more men to illness and Indian attacks. They passed along the coasts of Alabama, Louisiana, and Texas, stopping at Pensacola and Mobile Bays. After being scattered by the strong Mississippi current, two of the boats washed up on or near Galveston Island on November 6. That of Narváez drifted out to sea off Matagorda Bay, and he was never seen again. Of his expeditionary force of some four hundred men, only four returned to civilization in April 1536 after Cabeza de Vaca's transcontinental trek.

New Spain *(Nueva España)*

Nueva España, New Spain, was the name *Hernán Cortés* gave to the New World territories gained with his 1521 conquest of Mexico, and *Nueva España* long continued to play a major role in the exploration of North America. In 1535 New Spain began operation with the arrival of the first Spanish viceroy, Antonio de Mendoza. The viceroy held administrative authority over all lands north of the Isthmus of Panama, including the four Spanish islands of the Greater Antilles—*Cuba,* Jamaica, *Hispaniola,* and *Puerto Rico*—as well as the Philippines (until 1589).

In practical terms, the New Spain viceroyalty, centered in Mexico City, exercised political control over the area north from the Isthmus of Tehuantepec, encompassing the present nation of Mexico and extending farther northward well into the present United States. Here the territory originally explored and claimed by New Spain included the Pacific coastal region up through California, Oregon, and Washington; the Southwest, encompassing Arizona and New Mexico, and including parts of Colorado, Nevada, Utah, Kansas, Oklahoma, and even Wyoming; Texas; the Gulf of Mexico coastal region, including Louisiana and parts of Arkansas; and Greater *Florida [III]*, which, in addition to peninsular Florida, encompassed parts of Mississippi, Alabama, Tennessee, Georgia, the Carolinas, and Virginia.

Once Cortés consolidated control over Mexico, New Spain became the source of, and staging area for, numerous exploratory expeditions. Notably active in organizing these ventures was Cortés himself, followed by the early viceroys, particularly Mendoza (ruled 1535–1549), Luís de Velasco (ruled 1550–1564) and his son, also named Luís de Velasco (ruled 1590–1595, 1607–1611). Early expeditions to explore and conquer Honduras, Guatemala, and the Yucatan were followed by journeys to Baja California and sixteenth-century maritime surveys of the California coast by *Juan Cabrillo, Sebastián Cermeño, Francisco Gali, Francisco de Ulloa, Pedro de Unamuno,* and *Sebastián Vizcaíno.* Mendoza sent *Marcos de Niza* and *Francisco de Coronado* into the American Southwest, later followed there by *Agustín Rodríguez,* Antonio *Espejo, Juan de Oñate,* and *Eusebio Kino [IV].*

Explorers of the gulf coast and Greater Florida included *Angel de Villafañe [III], Guido de Lavazares,* and *Alonso de León [IV],* who was sent to find *La Salle*'s *[V]* elusive colony on the Texas coast. This French "trespass" into New Spain led to renewed Spanish exploration of the region and to an attempt to colonize Texas beginning in the late seventeenth century. The Russian incursion of the late 1740s into northern California finally motivated New Spain to start an active program of exploration and colonization of California. Among this era's explorers were *Gaspar de Portolá [IV]* and *Juan Bautista de Anza [IV].* By the end of the eighteenth century, however, the Spanish New World empire began to disintegrate, effectively limiting New Spain's exploratory initiatives into the western territories, and in 1821 Mexican independence finally put an end to the New Spain viceroyalty.

Ocampo, Sebastián   (?–?)

Sebastián Ocampo arrived in the New World as an exile on the second voyage of *Columbus.* After making numerous trading voyages across the

Caribbean, he was assigned by Santo Domingo governor Nicolás de Ovando to circumnavigate *Cuba,* proving it an island rather than a continent, and to investigate its suitability for colonization. In late 1508 he set out on an eight-month voyage with two ships to follow Cuba's northern coast, where he found Havana harbor. Ocampo is considered the discoverer of the Gulf of Mexico, which he encountered after reaching Cuba's westernmost point, Cabo San Antón. He continued back along the southern shore, where he discovered Cienfuegos Bay, which he judged a superior harbor. After Ocampo returned in the spring or summer of 1509, no action was taken until Diego Columbus, Christopher's son, took over as Santo Domingo governor and launched the 1511–1514 conquest of Cuba. Ocampo returned to Spain in 1514.

Ojeda (Hajeda), Alonso de   (1466?–1515?)

A Spanish explorer and conquistador, Alonso de Ojeda sailed on the second voyage of *Columbus* (1493–1496). Commissioned by the Spanish court to verify Columbus's discoveries, in 1499 Ojeda set sail for the New World with two other veterans of Columbus voyages, *Amerigo Vespucci* and *Juan de la Cosa.* Just before reaching land, Ojeda and Vespucci decided to separate. Together with Cosa, Ojeda explored the northeast coast of South America, sailing as far as Cabo de la Vela near the present Colombia-Venezuela border. En route they found rich pearl fisheries and new islands, including Aruba and Curaçao. On his controversial new world map of 1500, Cosa depicted Ojeda's discoveries. Cosa obtained permission for Ojeda to colonize and further explore the northern coastal area of South America.

In 1498 Ojeda became the governor of "Tierra Firme of the Ocean Sea," the mainland of Central and South America. When his colony on the Gulf of Urabá, near the Panama-Colombia border, encountered problems with Indians and starvation, Ojeda left to seek help, leaving *Pizarro* in charge; the colony was later abandoned. In 1509–1510, Ojeda, together with Cosa and Pizarro, made an expedition to Colombia. In his voyages, Ojeda helped to reveal the continental aspect of the Americas. Furthermore, his rich discovery of pearls far surpassed Columbus's frustrating search for gold.

Oñate, Juan de (1552?–1626)

Sometimes called "the last conquistador," Juan de Oñate led the final major Spanish expedition into the American Southwest. A member of a wealthy and aristocratic Spanish family in Mexico—his wife was both a granddaughter of *Cortés* and a great-granddaughter of Moctezuma—and an experienced Indian fighter, he won the coveted license to explore, conquer, and settle New Mexico because of his political connections to the viceroy. (His father, Cristóbal Oñate, one-time Nueva Galicia governor, had founded the rich Zacatecas silver mines in north central Mexico.) After expensive delays caused by his rivals, he finally set out on January 26, 1598, from San Gerónimo, near Santa Bárbara, with a 130-man army and 10 Franciscans, with wives, children, servants, and slaves bringing the total to over 500 persons. The two-mile-long column included eighty wagons and carts and seven thousand head of livestock. He sent his nephew *Vicente de Zaldívar* on ahead to blaze a more direct route through the Chihuahua Desert west of the Conchos to the Río Grande. On May 4 the expedition crossed the Río Grande at El Paso.

After riding on ahead with a smaller party up the Río Grande valley, Oñate reached his destination of San Juan pueblo (Okhe) north of Santa Fé. Here he planned to build the capital of his new kingdom (in early 1599 he moved it across the river to San Gabriel pueblo). Before the rest of the wagon train arrived on August 18, he conducted a series of forays from San Juan to explore the *Pueblo Indian* country and to search for minerals. A first reconnaissance north to Taos was followed by a second one east to Pecos pueblo and a swing southwest through the Tano villages of the Galisteo Basin, and by a third westward one southwest of the Jemez Mountains to the Towa pueblos. On September 15 he sent Vicente Zaldívar out with sixty men to bring in a winter's supply of buffalo meat. With Jusephe

The so-called Inscription Rock is in the El Morro National Monument in northwestern New Mexico. People have cut inscriptions here for thousands of years, but perhaps the most notable is the one left by the explorer Juan de Oñate (in Spanish): "Passed by here, the Adelantado Don Juan de Oñate, from the discovery of the Sea of the South, the sixteenth day of April 1605."

(a survivor of the Humaña expedition) as guide, Zaldívar pushed east beyond Pecos through the plains, where he met the Apache, and close to the Texas border, where he found vast herds of buffalo.

On October 6 Oñate started westward by way of Acoma and Zuni pueblos toward the Pacific, where he planned to locate a port for his supply ships. From Zuni he sent Marcos Farfán south, where he found an exceptional salt lake. Later, from Arizona's Hopi country, Oñate sent Farfán southwest to explore and collect mineral samples in the Verde Valley of the Cruzados people. Farfán returned with news that the Pacific was thirty days distant and offered rich pearl beds. In mid-1600, when Oñate sent Zaldívar back there, he reached Arizona's southwest corner, reportedly three days from the sea, before returning.

On June 23, 1601, Oñate set out with seventy soldiers and an eight-cart baggage train to find Quivira, the same legendary rich kingdom that had lured **Coronado** eastward in 1541. (See **legendary destinations.**) After following the Canadian River across the Texas panhandle to the Oklahoma border, he turned northeast to cross the Cimarron River into south central Kansas and reached the Arkansas River near Quivira, a large Indian village of round lodges thatched with grass and surrounded by fertile agricultural fields. He came back to San Gabriel to find that most of his settlers had fled to Mexico. From the outset, his followers had become mutinous when it became evident that New Mexico was an arid land of food shortages and bitter winters, with no spectacular mineral deposits. The Franciscans had been upset by Oñate's callous treatment of the Indians, including his brutal suppression of rebellions at Acoma, and later at Taos, thus blocking their effort to convert the Pueblo peoples. After another expedition toward the Pacific in early 1604 by Fray Francisco de Velasco, Oñate himself set out in late 1604 through central Arizona to the Bill Williams River, which took him to the Colorado River. By late January 1605, he reached the river's mouth, declaring it an excellent harbor. As conditions in the colony continued to disintegrate, the viceroy accepted Oñate's resignation, and he returned to Mexico in 1609. From 1610 on, in Mexico City Oñate defended himself against legal charges and then sailed to Spain in 1621 to pursue further appeals. In 1624 the king appointed him Spain's mining inspector and he died there while on the job.

Despite Oñate's failures, his wide-ranging explorations contributed much to the knowledge of the American Southwest. He helped to launch the Franciscan missionary program on the northern frontier from Texas to California, eventually leading to further exploration. By some accounts, he was responsible for the founding of Santa Fe, one of the oldest cities in the United States. As a trailblazer, he extended the Camino Real ("royal highway"), originally connecting Mexico City to Santa Bárbara, by some six hundred miles into northern New Mexico, and he selected the official campsites along this new stretch of what was to be North America's longest road (two thousand miles) for several centuries.

papal bulls

Shortly after *Columbus* returned from his first voyage, Spanish monarchs Ferdinand and Isabella sought to validate their claim to the New World by insisting on an official pronouncement from Alexander VI, a Spanish-born and notably corrupt pope. In a 1493 series of four papal bulls (or "donations") culminating in *Inter caetera* and *Dudum siquidem,* he established a north-south demarcation line 100 leagues (318 miles) west of the Azores in the Atlantic Ocean. To Spain went the lands west of the line and to Portugal the non-Christian lands, including Africa and India, to the east. Portugal's outrage—Pope Alexander VI had clearly favored his homeland—led to the 1494 *Treaty of Tordesillas,* which shifted the line

---

IN THEIR OWN Words   **The Pope Divides Up the World**

We have indeed learned that you [Ferdinand and Isabella] . . . have chosen our beloved son, Christopher Columbus . . . to make diligent quest for these remote and unknown mainlands and islands through the sea where hitherto no one had sailed . . . wherein dwell many peoples living in peace and, as reported, going unclothed and not eating flesh . . . by the authority of Almighty God conferred upon us . . . give, grant, and assign . . . all islands and mainlands found and to be discovered toward the west and south by drawing and establishing a line from the Arctic pole, namely the north, and to the Antarctic pole, namely the south . . . said line to be distant one hundred leagues toward the west and south of any of the islands commonly known as the Azores and Cape Verde.

—ALEXANDER VI, *INTER CAETERA . . .*, MAY 4, 1493

westward so that Portugal was able to claim the right to Brazil. (In fact the exact longitude was never clearly defined or measured.)

In a 1501 bull Alexander granted the "tithes and first fruits" of the New World to the Spanish crown to help finance the conquest and religious conversion of the native peoples called for in the earlier bulls. This extraordinary power of the Spanish crown as administrator of the Catholic church in the Americas was broadened by the 1508 *Universalis ecclesiae* bull of Julius II; the church thus became a vital agent of Spanish exploration and colonization. In response to queries from French monarch Francis I, later popes less favorably disposed toward Spain disputed its rights: According to Pope Leo X the Alexandrine bulls did not apply to lands not under actual Spanish occupation, and Pope Clement VII rejected Spain's exclusive claim on the basis that North America had not actually yet been discovered in 1493, and that Columbus had simply sailed among some Atlantic islands.

Pizarro, Francisco   (1476?–1541)

Francisco Pizarro, a cousin of *Cortés,* first came to notice in 1510 when *Alonso de Ojeda* left him in charge of his starving Tierra Firme colony on the Panama-Colombia border. Several years later, Pizarro was along when *Balboa* crossed the Panama isthmus and first sighted the Pacific Ocean in 1513. This led Pizarro to begin exploration of the Pacific coast of the Americas, first on an expedition to the San Juan River on the border between Colombia and Ecuador, and in 1526–1528 further south. After a 1528 return to Spain to obtain a license for Peru, he began the conquest of the Incas in 1532 with the help of his brothers Gonzalo, Juan, and Hernando. News of their fabulous booty of Inca gold motivated other adventurers to spread out in explorations of Baja California and the Pacific coast, and the Southwest of the United States. Pizarro was assassinated in Peru after making enemies among other Spaniards.

Possession, Spanish Act of

Among the cliché images of the early Spanish explorers are paintings depicting them "planting" their flag and a Christian cross on some newly "discovered" land while the natives look on in awe. In fact, many such events did take place, and not only involving the Spanish—the French and

Words

God our Lord created the heaven and earth, and one man and one woman of whom we and you [the Native Americans] and all men in the world have come . . . but because of the infinity of offspring that followed in the five thousand years and more since the world was created, it has become necessary that some men should go in one direction and others in another. . . . All these nations God our Lord gave in charge to one person, called Saint Peter, that he might be Master and Superior over mankind. . . . And He commanded him to place his seat in Rome . . . him they call Pope. . . . One of the popes who succeeded him [Peter] to that seat . . . made a gift of these islands and main of the Ocean Sea to the said Emperor and Queen [named at the outset]. . . . Wherefore, as best you can, I entreat and require you to understand this well . . . that you recognize the church as Mistress and Superior of the Universe . . . and [the Spanish monarch] as sovereign. . . . If you shall do so you will do well in what you are held and obliged; and their Majesties and I, in their royal name, will receive you with love and charity.

If you do not do this, and of malice you be dilatory, I protest to you that, with the help of Our Lord, I will enter with force, making war upon you from all directions and in every manner that I may be able, when I will subject you to obedience to the Church and the yoke of their Majesties; and I will take the persons of yourselves, your wives and your children to make slaves, sell and dispose of you, as their majesties shall think fit, and I will take your goods, doing you all the evil and injury that I may be able . . . and I declare to you that the deaths and damages that arise therefrom, will be your fault and not that of his Majesty, nor mine, nor of these cavaliers who came with me. And so I proclaim and require this, I ask of the Notary here that he give a certificate, and those present I beseech that they will hereof be the witnesses.

—Spanish *Requerimiento*, or Ceremony of Possession, circa 1512

English would often conduct some formal ceremony as they came ashore to declare possession for their monarch and their faith. But the Spanish went further in that very early on they had a standard text known as a "summons." Early in the 1500s, a group of learned men—jurists and others—associated with the Council of the Indies drew up this statement, which was read by an expedition's leader at the first opportunity. Because it was couched in legal language and the ceremony of the reading was attended by both Spanish government officials and Catholic priests, the Spanish regarded it as a binding document.

The opening section would naturally vary, depending on the specific date, the reigning monarch, and the expedition's leader, but the rest of the text was standard. With the completion of the ceremony, the Spanish felt free to take on their new land. No record exists of what the Native Americans made of this ceremony or text, but the fact that any Native Americans in attendance could not have understood a word being said did not deter the Spanish.

Pueblo Indians

The Pueblo Indians of the American Southwest played both a prominent and a problematic role in the early exploration of their region. To begin with, the very name *Pueblo* had nothing to do with their own identity; this word, meaning "village" or "town" in Spanish, was assigned to them by the first Spaniards, who were impressed by the large multistoried stone-and-

Although taken by Ansel Adams in 1941, this photograph of the Taos, New Mexico, pueblo conveys what the pueblos must have looked like to the first Europeans who viewed them. In the twentieth century, Taos became a magnet for many prominent artists, writers, and phtographers, including Georgia O'Keeffe and D. H. Lawrence.

adobe buildings that many of these Indians lived in. Although most of the so-called Pueblo Indians shared many cultural elements—descent from the earlier Anasazi Indians, related (but not the same) languages, religious traditions, and such—they identified more closely with their own village groups such as the Acoma, the Taos, and the Zuni. The Spaniards who first encountered these Indians, however, were not sensitive to such differences. Rather, they viewed the Pueblos with their own prejudices—namely, the belief that these Indians inhabited fabulous cities, rich in gold and silver and precious jewels: the legendary Kingdom of Cibola (see **legendary destinations**). This legend had been passed on to the Spanish in northern Mexico by local Indians and perpetuated by *Estevánico,* the African who had accompanied *Cabeza de Vaca* on his epic journey across the American South (1528–1536). Estevánico's tales inspired the expedition in 1539 led by Fray **Marcos de Niza** up into the American Southwest; there they came across products of the Pueblo Indians such as turquoise and blankets. It was Estevánico, acting as the expedition's advance man, who was probably the first non-native to approach a pueblo, the Hawikuh pueblo of the Zuni. The Indians distrusted him and killed him; the Spaniards fled, but Marcos insisted he had glimpsed Hawikuh pueblo and that it appeared wealthy. (It is now generally agreed that the "golden cities" legend was probably inspired by the glow of the pueblos' adobe surface in the sunlight.)

The next year, 1540, **Coronado** led an expedition in search of the Kingdom of Cibola; he found six Zuni pueblos in the area around Gallup, New Mexico, conquered them, and named them Cibola. Members of his expedition, meanwhile, went off and visited other pueblos such as those at Acoma, Pecos, and Taos. Over the winter of 1540–1541, relations among the Spaniards and Indians deteriorated, as Coronado forced the Indians to accommodate and feed the several thousand men in his party. In 1541 Coronado set out for Quivira, another fabulous land also said to be rich in gold and silver. He got as far as present-day Kansas but, failing to find such a city, went back to the Pueblo Indian territory. During his absence, some of the Spaniards had committed various atrocities against the Indians of the Tiguex Pueblo—stealing their food and clothes, raping their women, and burning captives alive. When Coronado returned to spend the winter of 1541–1542 there, he joined in attacking the Tiguex settlements; after destroying the pueblos, he enslaved the survivors, effectively wiping out the Tiguex as a people. It would be forty years before any Europeans moved into this region of New Mexico again; this time it was a relatively small expedition in 1581 led by a Franciscan friar, **Agustín Rodríguez,** and a Spanish soldier, Francisco Chamuscado. They traveled to the fringes of the Pueblo country, where Rodríguez and another friar chose to stay to await a larger party. Chamuscado died on his way back to Mexico; when a new expedition under the command of Antonio de **Espejo** arrived back in the Pueblo country in December 1582, the two friars had been killed by Indians of the Tigua tribe. Espejo spent some months exploring the region around the Zuni pueblo, then returned to Mexico in September 1583; he reported valuable agricultural land and the prospects of mineral wealth in the valley of the upper Río Grande. This effectively marked the end of the Spaniards' exploratory expeditions into Pueblo Indian territory.

It by no means marked the end of Spanish intrusions—and aggression—in the Pueblo Indians' settlements and lives. The Spaniards continued to come as conquerors, colonizers, and converters—the most notable of these being *Juan de Oñate,* who moved into New Mexico in 1598 and, before he returned to Mexico in 1609, treated several of the pueblos brutally. Such actions, plus the tactics used to destroy the Pueblo Indians' religion and convert them to Christianity, guaranteed that they would continue to be adversaries of the Spaniards during the ensuing decades. The climax came in the Pueblo Revolt—also known after its leader's name as Popé's Revolt—which lasted from 1680 to 1696. With its suppression, the Pueblo Indians effectively lost their land and their independence.

Puerto Rico

The Caribbean island of Puerto Rico was discovered by *Christopher Columbus* on his second voyage to the New World. Sailing with a fleet of seventeen ships, Columbus arrived on November 19, 1493, in a bay (the port of Aguada) on the west coast. Taking possession of the island in the name of the Spanish royal crown, he named it San Juan Bautista (Saint John the Baptist). To its some 30,000 Taino Indian inhabitants, the island was known as Boriquén (land of the valiant one); the Spanish changed this original pronunciation to Borínquén. After a two-day exploration, Columbus continued on west to *Hispaniola* to establish the first New World settlement, Isabela. For the next fifteen years, the Spanish showed little interest in Puerto Rico. Finally, motivated by tales of gold, *Juan Ponce de León [III]* (who had arrived on Columbus's second voyage) sought permission to explore and colonize the island. In December 1508 he landed on the north shore to establish the settlement of Caparra near one of the best natural harbors in the Caribbean. This bay he named Puerto Rico (rich port) for its economic potential. In 1511 Caparra was renamed Ciudad de Puerto Rico, and in 1521 the town was moved across the bay to the present site of San Juan. Puerto Rico later became the name of the whole island.

Ponce de León served only for a short while as the island's governor. In 1511 he was replaced by a new governor chosen by Diego Columbus, the son of Christopher Columbus. Ponce de León then sailed on a voyage of exploration that ended in his discovery of *Florida [III].* From this time onward, Puerto Rico's role in exploration was minimal—although *Hernán Cortés* reportedly used horses raised in Puerto Rico in his conquest of Mexico. The Puerto Rican gold resources were exhausted by the 1530s. Despite the introduction of sugarcane cultivation in 1515 and of African slaves in 1518, Puerto Rico suffered economically from disease, emigration, and pirate raids, beginning around 1528. The massive fortification of San Juan harbor served to protect Spanish convoys from pirates and from English and Dutch privateers. During a 1595 English attack on San Juan, the Spanish fought off Sir *Francis Drake* in a battle that left Sir John Hawkins mortally wounded. Following its defeat in the Spanish-American War, Spain ceded Puerto Rico to the United States in 1898.

Rodríguez, Agustín   (?–?)

Some four decades after the almost forgotten *Coronado* expedition, New Mexico was rediscovered by Franciscan missionary Agustín Rodríguez, who was spurred on by the possibility of many Indian souls to convert, as well as by rumors of wealth in the *Pueblo Indian* country. He was sponsored in this by the Mexican viceroy. As the Spanish 1573 New Law of the Indies strictly forbade territorial conquest, including military operations against Indians, without royal permission, expeditions now required a missionary guise. On June 5, 1581, Rodríguez, two other friars, and seventy-year-old veteran Francisco Sánchez Chamuscado leading nine soldiers—a party of some twenty-eight persons in all—carrying trade goods and leading a large herd of cattle, sheep, goats, and hogs (for food en route) set out from Santa Bárbara, Mexico. They headed north along the Río Conchos and upstream along the Río Grande into the heart of New Mexico. Rodríguez took possession for the king of this region, which he named San Felipe del Nuevo México. There his party traded with the various Pueblo peoples, observed large herds of bison ("humpbacked cows"), took samples of silver ores and salts, and carefully noted down the number of houses in, and populations of, the sixty-one pueblos that they visited and renamed after Catholic saints. Ranging north as far as Taos and west toward the Colorado River, they found three survivors of the Coronado expedition at Zuni. From Santa Fe one Franciscan set off to report to the viceroy, but was killed after three days by Tanos.

Over Chamuscado's strong objections, Rodríguez and Fray Francisco López stayed to found a mission at Puaray, a Tigua town north of Albuquerque. As they tried to convert the Indians, the friars also achieved martyrdom. In April 1582 the rest of the expeditionary party (without the ill Chamuscado, who died close to home) returned to Santa Bárbara, bearing exciting and exaggerated news of a fabulous new kingdom. Three months later, fleeing mission servants arrived to report the death of López back in New Mexico. In November the *Espejo and Beltrán expedition* set out in a futile attempt to rescue Rodríguez. The eventual result of the Rodríguez expedition was *Oñate*'s 1598 expedition to conquer and settle New Mexico.

Salas-López expedition (1629)

In July 1629 a group of some fifty Jumano Indians arrived at New Mexico's Isleta Franciscan mission south of Albuquerque to request that religious teachers be sent to their lands. Soon after, Franciscans Juan de Salas and Diego López, along with three soldiers, set out from Santa Fe and followed the Jumano representatives to their tribal homeland along the Conchos River near the Colorado River in the plains of southwest Texas. Exploring the region east of the Pecos River along the way, they tried to encourage the nomadic tribes there to settle down in permanent homes. After several days among the Jumanos, they returned with some Indian converts to their New Mexico mission. In 1632 Franciscans Ascencio de Zárate and Pedro de Ortega led a second expedition to the Jumanos. These expeditions helped open up trade between New Mexico and the Jumanos, which was probably their original intent in requesting missionaries.

Tordesillas, Treaty of

Pope Alexander VI was determined to avoid a conflict between Spain and Portugal, two of his valued Catholic lands, over the recently discovered "new world," so in 1493 he proposed a north-south line of demarcation some 100 leagues (about 375 miles) west of the Cape Verde islands— allowing Spain to lay claim to all lands to the west of that line. Portugal naturally objected, and after negotiations, the line was set at 375 leagues (about 1,400 miles) west of the Cape Verde Islands in the Atlantic Ocean. In June 1494 representatives of the two nations signed the Treaty of Tordesillas (named for the town in north-central Spain where it was signed), but it was 1506 before the pope gave his formal approval of this agreement. Spain claimed most of the New World west of the line, although the

IN THEIR OWN *Words* — Spain and Portugal Draw a Line

Whereas a certain controversy exists between [Portugal and Spain], as to what lands, of all those discovered in the ocean up to the present day pertain to each one of the said parts, respectively therefore, for the sake of peace and concord . . . it being the pleasure of their Highnesses, their said representatives acting in their name and by virtue of their powers herein described, covenanted and agreed that a boundary or straight line be determined and drawn north and south, from pole to pole, on the said ocean sea, from the Arctic to the Antarctic pole . . . a distance of three hundred and seventy leagues west of the Cape Verde Islands. . . . And all the lands both islands and mainlands, found and discovered already or to be found and discovered hereafter by the said King of Portugal and by his vessels on this side of said line . . . shall belong to and remain in the possession of, and pertain forever to, the said King of Portugal and his succcessors. And all other lands, both islands and mainlands, found or to be found hereafter, discovered or to be discovered hereafter, which have been discovered or shall be discovered by the said King and Queen of Castile, Aragon, etc. by their vessels on the western side of said bound . . . shall belong to and remain in the possession of, and pertain forever to, the said King and Queen of Castile, Aragon, etc, and to their successors.

—TREATY OF TORDESILLAS, JUNE 7, 1494

redrawn line allowed Portugal to claim Brazil and *Newfoundland [III]*, along with Africa, India, and other areas east of the line.

After *Balboa*'s 1513 discovery of the Pacific Ocean, followed by Spain's grandiose claim to all islands within it and lands bordering it, the demarcation line was continued around to the other side of the globe, thus giving Spain title to the Philippines and—mistakenly, since it fell within Portugal's assigned sector—to the Moluccas. Declaring the demarcation line in a document was quite another matter from finding it geographically, as longitude could be calculated by only the crudest methods with the era's primitive navigational technology. Spain and Portugal disputed the line's actual location in both the Pacific and Atlantic throughout the sixteenth century. Meanwhile, other major European maritime powers (such as England and the Netherlands) were Protestant countries and did not consider the papal bull binding. They contended that physical occupancy followed by economic development, rather than prior discovery and exploration together with rituals of possession, was the necessary basis of a claim to North American and other territories.

Ulloa, Francisco de   (?–1540?)

Sailing out with a fleet of three small ships from Acapulco, Mexico, on July 8, 1539, under the orders of *Cortés,* Francisco de Ulloa circumnavigated the Gulf of California. Along the way he periodically stopped to take official possession for the Spanish crown. He investigated the coastal terrain, the islands, and the good ports, along with the availability of pearls. His report documented wary encounters with Indians—skirmishes with some while getting fresh water, and trade with others—enlivened by ethnographic observations. Ulloa then continued the difficult journey up Baja California's western coast as far as Cabo del Engaño (Cape Disappointment, today's Punta Baja), about three-quarters of the way up the peninsula. On April 5, 1540, from Isla de Cedros, he sent back one of the ships with his report; whether Ulloa himself ever returned is unknown. Ulloa's trip was significant for its preliminary charting of the coastline and for effectively establishing that Baja California was a peninsula, not an island. His discoveries and place names were soon incorporated into New World maps.

Unamuno, Pedro de   (?–?)

Following the establishment of the Manila galleon Spanish trade route across the Pacific between Acapulco, Mexico, and the Philippines, the Mexican viceroy assigned Pedro de Unamuno to explore the California coastline on the return leg of his voyage back to Acapulco. On October 17, 1587, he sighted land through a thick fog at above 35° N. The next day he anchored in a bay he named Puerto de San Lucas (Morro Bay) in the vicinity of San Luis Obispo and led ashore an exploring party of twelve soldiers and some Filipinos. After taking possession for the Spanish crown, they followed a river upstream, looking for minerals, and found a deserted native village. They went out again on October 19 and 20, finding another larger deserted village. Returning to their ship, they were attacked by Indians, who killed one of the party and wounded four. Gunfire from the Spanish killed some of the attackers. On October 21 Unamuno sailed southward, still searching for suitable harbors, but didn't stop again as the coast remained foggy and medical help was needed for the wounded. He reached Acapulco on November 22. His brief expedition inland from the California coast was largely forgotten.

Vespucci, Amerigo (1454–1512)

In 1492 Italian-born Amerigo Vespucci moved to Seville to manage the Medici commercial agency in Spain. As a ship chandler, he helped prepare the vessels for *Columbus*'s second and third voyages to the New World. Later he would claim that he made a voyage in 1497, during which he discovered the new land that would later be known as South America. Most scholars today reject this claim, but they do accept that in 1499, he sailed with *Alonso de Ojeda* to the Caribbean, where the two separated by mutual agreement. Vespucci sailed south to reach the Guiana coast and possibly as far as the mouth of the Amazon River. During his 1501–1502 voyage for Portugal, he explored Brazil's coastline down to Río de Plata at Buenos Aires; that he went as far as 50° S, to Argentina's southernmost tip, as claimed, is unlikely. On a voyage in 1503–1504 he sailed along the southern coast of Brazil.

Sometime around 1502–1503 he wrote a letter to Lorenzo de' Medici of Florence in which he claimed to have discovered a new continent; he described the land and its inhabitants in some detail. The letter was published in 1503–1504 under the title *Mundus Novus* (New World), and it circulated widely throughout Europe. In 1507 Martin Waldseemüller, a German mapmaker, published a map depicting what was then known of the discoveries in the Western Hemisphere, and it was he who applied the name *America* (the Latinized version of "Amerigo") to the southern continent. (See *maps [I].*) Because he also published an account of Vespucci's voyages along with this map, he further promoted Vespucci's claims to priority. (A small group of people, mostly English-

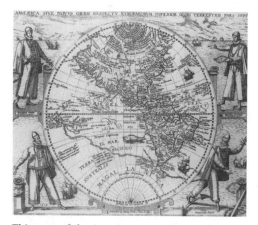

This map of the Americas, an engraving by Theodore de Bry, was first published in 1600 in Munich, Germany. Around its borders (clockwise) are Columbus, Vespucci, Pizarro, and Magellan—then hailed as the four great explorers of the New World.

men, persist in claiming that America was named after a citizen of Bristol, England, Richard Ameryk, [or Amerike], evidently a financial backer of *John Cabot*'s *[III]* 1497 voyage to *Newfoundland [III],* but no scholars take this seriously.)

After Vespucci became a citizen of Castille and León in 1506, he was appointed Spain's pilot major to oversee the official mapping of new lands. He also developed a relatively accurate system for calculating longitude. In 1512 he died from malaria contracted during his explorations. Today, few scholars accept the claim that Vespucci even made a voyage in 1497, and they are inclined to credit Columbus with being the first European (since the Vikings, circa 1000) to discover the mainland of the Western Hemisphere, when he set foot on Venezuela in 1498. But Vespucci does get credit for making Europeans aware that the lands to the west were not part of Asia but a New World.

Vizcaíno, Sebastián   (1548–1628)

In 1583 veteran Spanish soldier Sebastián Vizcaíno arrived in Mexico, where he eventually became a prosperous merchant-investor. A decade later he procured a royal license for Pacific coastal fishing and mining rights, and in 1596 he led an expedition to start a short-lived settlement at La Paz, in Baja California. To carry out a 1599 royal order calling for a thorough exploration of the California coast, the viceroy named Vizcaíno to head the expedition, with *Francisco de Bolaños* as chief pilot. The three ships sailed from La Navidad on May 22, 1602, to chart the shore from the tip of Baja to Cape Mendocino and beyond if conditions permitted. Progress was slowed by the meticulous mapping required, as well as by contrary winds, fogs, and stops for fresh water, wood, and provisions, and by periodic bartering sessions with various native groups.

Vizcaíno spent November 10–20 at San Diego Bay, which he recognized as an excellent harbor. He passed November 24–December 1 at Santa Catalina Island, from which he crossed to the mainland and landed at a bay he named San Pedro (near Los Angeles). On December 13 the ships reached Monterey Bay, which he deemed a fine port for Manila galleons. A party sent to the interior documented plentiful fresh water, wood, and wild game; they also made contact with the Costanoan Indians of the region. From here, on December 29, he sent back to Mexico the *Santo Tomás* with expedition records, letters, and the sick (during the voyage many became seriously ill with scurvy). On January 4, 1603, the other two ships reached Point Reyes, and the next day a storm separated them, blowing Vizcaíno's *San Diego* north of the California-Oregon border to Cabo Blanco on January 21, at about 43° N. The *Tres Reyes,* blown north of Cabo Blanco, on the way back, reportedly at about 39° N, sighted a large river, a possible candidate for the *Strait of Anian.* Sailing southward separately, neither ship entered *Drake*'s Bay to try to recover the cargo from *Cermeño*'s wrecked galleon, and both missed discovering San Francisco Bay as well. Vizcaíno's *San Diego,* beset by scurvy and by food and water

> ## IN THEIR OWN *Words*
>
> **The Spanish Explore the California Coast**
>
> *I have discovered many harbors, bays, and islands, as far as the port of Monterey, a harbor which is 37 degrees of latitude, surveying all & sounding, & noting the sailing directions . . . and noting what the land and the numerous peoples dwelling therein seemingly promise. . . . I advise His Majesty concerning the great extent of this land and its numerous population and what promise it holds forth, and what the Indians have given me to understand concerning the people of the interior, and of how gentle & affable the people are, so that they will receive readily, as I think, the holy gospel and will come into subjection to the royal crown.*
>
> —SEBASTIÁN VIZCAÍNO, LETTER TO THE VICEROY IN MEXICO, DECEMBER 28, 1602

shortages, reached Acapulco on March 21, 1603. The *Tres Reyes* also made it back to Mexico, but its captain, Martín de Aguilar, was among those who died due to the terrible conditions at sea.

Critics of the voyage point out various inaccuracies in the Vizcaíno charts and accuse him of deliberately renaming places previously named by *Cabrillo.* It is possible, though, that he had little or no access to Cabrillo's documents and thus was, to some degree, unaware of the names Cabrillo had chosen. Only confusion about the geography north of California ensued from the report of a possible *Strait of Anian,* which was placed further north with each retelling. Also, a certain Fray Ascension who accompanied the expedition published his account in 1620 and claimed that the large river sighted connected with "the Gulf of California," thus perpetuating the idea that all of California was an island.

Another negative effect arising from this venture was that the Spanish now considered their knowledge of the Pacific coast of North America complete and thus stopped sending out expeditions to make surveys: San Francisco Bay would not be discovered until 1769. Vizcaíno enthusiastically promoted Monterey Bay as a settlement site, apparently to no avail, although an archival manuscript reports a brief 1606 settlement there.

Zaldívar, Vicente de (circa 1573–?)

Vicente de Zaldívar was born in northern Mexico to a family related by marriage to *Juan de Oñate,* and so in 1595 when Oñate began to organize his expedition to colonize what would become New Mexico he selected Vicente (and his brother Juan) for officers' positions. The expedition did not get under way until 1598, and Vicente was the one who found a crossing point on the Río Grande, what became known as El Paso. Once in New Mexico, Vicente was also sent on a side expedition to eastern New Mexico and may have even crossed into Texas. Either during his absence or shortly after returning, his brother Juan was killed during an Indian revolt of the Acoma pueblo. Vicente was given the charge of subduing the revolt, which he crushed in January 1599; he also took a major hand in the trial and harsh punishment of many Acoma Indians. In mid-1600, while based in Arizona's Hopi country, Vicente was sent by Oñate to Arizona's southwest corner; he returned claiming he had come within three days' journey from the Pacific Ocean. He then returned to Mexico, married a daughter of Juan de Oñate, and at least temporarily prospered with the silver mining at Zacatecas.

PART III

The Atlantic Seaboard, 1497–1680

The search for a sea route to Asia and the attraction of codfish as a source of food led the early European merchant-adventurers to the Atlantic shores of North America. John Cabot's voyage of 1497 touched off a century of exploration and exploitation of his "new founde lands." By the turn of the seventeenth century the English, the French, and the Spanish had established the beginnings of permanent settlements along the Atlantic littoral.

Indirect evidence suggests that two ships sailing from Bristol, England, in quest of the "isle of Brasile" may have sighted Newfoundland as early as 1481. What is known for certain is that Cabot, with the patronage of King Henry VII of England, cruised the chilly coasts of Newfoundland and Nova Scotia in the caravel *Mathew* in the early summer of 1497. Sailing from Bristol in May, he caught a first glimpse of land through the mists after a month-long voyage: probably Cape Breton, Nova Scotia.

So it began, a century of discovery, report, follow-up, conflict. Cabot's first voyage foreshadowed fateful consequences for the native peoples of the Atlantic seaboard. Europeans would be in full control of the Atlantic coast by 1650; traders, planters, and missionaries were determined to extend the European domain inland up the great rivers to the eastern slopes of the Appalachians and beyond.

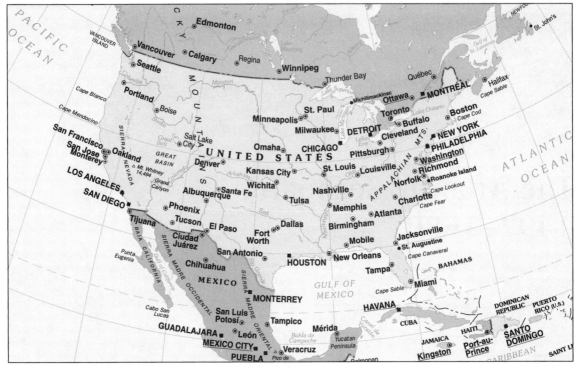

It would take four hundred years for the forty-eight contiguous states that make up
part of the continent of North America to be completely explored.

Cabot thought he had reached Asia. Though it soon became clear
that he had not, the search for a route to the fabled East intensified. Then,
too, his report of the riches of the offshore fishery supplied motive enough
for continued European interest. The seas were "swarming with fish," he
wrote, "which could be taken not only with the net, but with baskets let
down by a stone." So Portuguese and Bretons followed the ill-fated Cabot.
Gaspar Corte-Réal may have sighted Labrador in 1501; like Cabot in 1498,
he ended up on the bottom of the sea. His brother Miguel Corte-Réal
reached home safely, however, with a cargo of fifty captive Micmac or
Beothuk Indians whom he sold as slaves in the Lisbon markets.

In a 1524 voyage Giovanni da Verrazano revealed the outline of the
Atlantic coast. Making landfall at Cape Fear in early March, he glided to
anchor in Pamlico Sound a few weeks later and, from the masthead, espied
what he took to be the eastern seas washing "India, China and Cathay." The
1529 map his explorations yielded proved more accurate than his masthead
forecast; it showed an unbroken coastline from Florida to Nova Scotia.

Jacques Cartier became the first European to penetrate deep into the eastern third of the continent. His voyages of 1534–1536 carried him up the St. Lawrence River beyond the site of Montreal. Soon the lands he explored were given the name Canada, possibly deriving from the Iroquois-Huron word *cannatta,* meaning settlement. The French inflated the term to connote a region—the St. Lawrence lowlands, primarily— and, eventually, a country of enormous expanse.

Far to the south, the bold, tough, and homicidal Hernando de Soto crossed three thousand miles of what is today the southeastern United States from 1539 to 1543, demonstrating to the natives in uncompromising terms the meaning of the European visitation. In a fiery encounter near present Montgomery, Alabama, in 1540, de Soto's soldiers slaughtered 2,500 Choctaw Indians. A few months later, his expedition reached the Mississippi River.

The Spanish in Florida and the French along the St. Lawrence were permanently, if precariously, in residence by 1600. Within a few years, Samuel de Champlain would build the foundations of New France, and Captain John Smith would help establish Jamestown and explore inland from the Virginia tidewater. From their numerous footholds on the littoral, the Europeans were beginning to open up the vast interior of the North American continent.

Abenaki

A collective name for Algonquian-speaking tribes inhabiting northern New England and eastern Canada, Abenaki translates as "people of the dawn"—the East. Abenaki homelands stretched from the Atlantic coast of Maine to Lake Champlain, and from the St. Lawrence Valley of Quebec to northern Massachusetts.

Tribal groups include the Sokokis of the upper Connecticut River, the Pennacooks of New Hampshire's Merrimack Valley, and the Penobscots and Passamaquoddys of eastern Maine.

Abenakis were hunters and gatherers primarily, though communities in southern New England raised corn (maize) long before the Europeans arrived. Most Abenaki communities combined hunting, gathering, fishing, and the cultivation of corn.

The first European encounter with Abenakis to be recorded in detail occurred in 1524 with the arrival on the Maine coast of the Italian navigator *Giovanni da Verrazano,* whose French-sponsored voyage explored the

Atlantic coast from North Carolina to Nova Scotia. Comparing the Abenaki invidiously to the Wampanoags of Massachusetts, Verrazano found them "of such crudity and evil manners, so barbarous, that despite all the signs we could make, we could never converse with them." Abenaki bands shot volleys of arrows at Verrazano's shore parties and fled into the woods on the sailors' approach. Samuel Eliot Morison suggests that native hostility to Verrazano indicates the likelihood of earlier European visits along the Maine coast, in which Abenakis were perhaps carried away as slaves.

The Indians, however, could not resist offers to trade. Early contacts led to exchanges of beaver pelts for steel knives and axes, woolen blankets, and other manufactured goods. But events would prove the Abenakis had been shrewd in resisting the earliest Europeans. The aliens brought *disease [II]*. A plague introduced from Europe along the Maine coast in 1617 and smallpox epidemics in the Connecticut and Merrimack valleys in 1633–1634 killed thousands of Abenakis. A population estimated at 25,000 at first contact had dwindled to about 2,500 by the early eighteenth century.

Acadia (l'Acadie)

France's North American Atlantic seaboard claim, centered on present Nova Scotia and stretching south into New Brunswick and along the coast of Maine, Acadia became a focal point of Anglo-French territorial rivalry in the seventeenth and eighteenth centuries. The name, lifted from Virgil's *Eclogues,* connotes an ideal pastoral landscape. *John Cabot* may have landed in Nova Scotia in 1497, and European fishermen were familiar with the island's east coast in the sixteenth century.

Samuel de Champlain explored the Bay of Fundy in 1604 and established a post on the Ste. Croix River in Maine. He and his crew passed a difficult winter there before helping to found what would become the first permanent European settlement in Canada at Port Royal (later Annapolis Royal) in 1605. In 1607 Champlain explored the east coast of Acadia, today's Nova Scotia.

Alaminos, Antonio de $\hspace{2cm}$ (1482?–?)

Considered the most experienced pilot in the West Indies, Antonio de Alaminos first arrived in the New World with *Columbus [II]* on his last voyage. His own four voyages, the first to *Florida* and along the Gulf of Mexico from 1513 to 1519, surveyed the coastline and studied water currents.

In 1513 Alaminos sailed as chief pilot to *Ponce de León* on his expedition to Florida. Setting out from *Puerto Rico [II]*, de León's three vessels followed Florida's Atlantic coast perhaps as far north as the present Daytona Beach area and then sailed south through the Florida Keys and up Florida's west coast, possibly as far as Charlotte Harbor. On the return home, Alaminos discovered the Bahama Channel and identified the Gulf Stream.

Alaminos in 1517 was chief pilot for *Hernández de Córdoba's [II]* voyage exploring the Yucatan coast. When storms blew his ship back across the gulf, he again landed at Ponce de León's Florida bay. In 1518 he was chief pilot for *Juan de Grijalva's [II]* voyage of exploration around the Yucatan and up Mexico's gulf coast, and in February 1519 he piloted the expedition of *Cortés [II]* that ended in the conquest of Mexico.

In July 1519 Alaminos set out with the first shipment of Aztec gold to Spain, pioneering a new route through the Straits of Florida and the Bahama Channel. He returned to Spain permanently in 1522.

Algonquin

This band of Algonquian-speaking Indians inhabited a region on both sides of the Ottawa River in what is today the Canadian province of Ontario. Primarily hunters, though they did cultivate small patches of maize, they were never a large tribe. Iroquois raids and the spread of European diseases decimated the Algonquins in the seventeenth century.

The French explorer *Samuel de Champlain* encountered Algonquin bands in June 1613 as he followed an Indian trade route westward up the Ottawa toward Lake Huron, the "freshwater sea" he designated *La Mer Douce*. He reached Allumette Lake before a war party of Algonquins, reluctant to permit French fur traders to push on to the west, barred his progress. Champlain completed the journey to Lake Huron in 1615.

In 1616 Champlain allied with the Algonquins and their southern neighbors the *Hurons* in a campaign against the Iroquois. Unlike other tribes, the Algonquins remained in the region of their homeland after colonists arrived in significant numbers.

Alvarez de Pineda, Alonso (?–1520)

Jamaica governor Francisco de Garay sent Pineda out in early 1519 with four armed vessels to challenge the landing of *Cortés [II]* in Mexico. Approaching Mexico by a new route from the northeast, which he charted in detail, Pineda sailed along western *Florida* and circled around, passing the coasts of Alabama, Mississippi, Louisiana, and Texas.

En route, he noted what was probably Mobile Bay; named the *Mississippi River [V]* the Río de Espíritu Santo ("River of the Holy Ghost"); marked down the Las Palmas, which was probably the Río Grande; and stopped periodically to take possession in the king's name.

In late July or early August, after Cortés seized some of his men and refused to cooperate in setting boundaries between his lands and those claimed by Garay, Pineda started back north. To repair his ships he sailed some twenty miles up what probably was the Río Pánuco (at Tampico) and started a settlement to enforce Garay's claim. Pineda may have sent ships back to Jamaica with his report and maps. Returning with supplies in early 1520, the Spanish found the Hiastecs had attacked the settlement and killed Pineda.

Pineda was the first European to survey the entire gulf coast from the Florida Keys to just above Veracruz, demonstrating that Florida is a peninsula and confirming the non-existence of a strait to the Pacific Ocean in that region, which he named Amichel. His first independent map of Florida still exists.

Amadas–Barlowe expedition (1584)

With *Humphrey Gilbert*'s death at sea in 1583, his half-brother *Sir Walter Raleigh* inherited his North American colonization project. Raleigh obtained a patent from Queen Elizabeth on March 15, 1584, and chose Philip Amadas and Arthur Barlowe to cross the Atlantic and scout for a site.

Amadas and Barlowe sailed from Plymouth, England, in two small barks on April 27. Amadas commanded the flagship, which carried the Portuguese navigator Simão Fernandes, who had sailed to Maine for Gilbert a few years previously, as pilot. Following the transatlantic paths of *Columbus [II]* and *Verrazano* to catch the trade winds, they reached the West Indies in June and probably called at *Puerto Rico [II]* before sailing north along the *Florida* coast. By early July the Englishmen were in shoal water off the coast of Georgia, "which smelt so sweetely," Barlowe wrote later, "as if we had been in the midst of some delicate garden." They sighted land on July 4, probably at a point on the Outer Banks of North Carolina between Cape Fear and Cape Lookout.

Following the coast north, Fernandes discovered a breach in the banks near present Oregon Inlet on July 13. The ships came to anchor after a difficult entry just inside Pamlico Sound. Amadas named the anchorage Port Ferdinado, for Fernandes, who may have been there before in Spanish service, claimed the country all around for Elizabeth I, and named it "Virginia" in honor of the virgin queen. The land was flat, heavily forested, and densely peopled with Algonquian-speaking Indians. On the sixteenth, the Englishmen made first contact with the local people, three men in a dugout canoe. They were Roanokes—"very handsome, and goodly people, and in their behavior as mannerly, and civill, as any in Europe," Barlowe reported. The country was fertile too, and thick with game, "Deere, Hares and Fowle, even in the middest of Summer." Barlowe learned that the Indians made three crops of corn (maize) in one growing season.

With seven men, Barlowe took the longboat north up Pamlico Sound as far as Albemarle Sound and the Albemarle River. He counted nine cedar houses in the Indian village on Roanoke Island, with a stockade of sharpened trees for defense. On his return, the barks made preparations for the homeward voyage. Two natives, Manteo, a Hatteras Indian, and Wanchese, a Roanoke, volunteered to sail to England with the expedition.

Amadas and Barlowe took their departure on August 23 and, according to Barlowe, arrived in England on September 15. Historian David Quinn speculates that Fernandes led the expedition north into *Chesapeake Bay* to scout other potential sites for settlement before they shaped their course for home. He also mentions evidence that the vessels encountered storms and other delays on the way home and did not reach England until December. The expedition represents the first serious English attempt to explore and settle the east coast of America.

Ayllón, Lucas Vásquez de (1475–1526)

A high court justice of Santo Domingo in the Spanish Caribbean colony of *Hispaniola [II]*, Ayllón in 1521 commissioned a ship to explore the coast north of Florida and report on prospects for colonization. The expedition commander, Francisco Gordillo, returned with a cargo of seventy Indian slaves taken along the Carolina coast and little else. Ayllón freed the slaves and determined to lead an expedition of discovery and settlement himself.

In 1523 Ayllón obtained a royal patent to explore 2,500 miles up the coast of North America, seek out any possible straits leading to the Pacific, and plant a colony. He sailed with five hundred men, women, and children in command of five ships and auxiliaries.

The expedition met with one misfortune after another. The flagship ran aground and had to be abandoned. The remainder of the fleet touched on the coast of North Carolina, possibly at Cape Fear, and established a colony that Ayllón named San Miguel. The natives, perhaps in retaliation for Gordillo's depredations, were hostile and refused to provision the colonists. Only 150 managed to return safely to Santo Domingo. Ayllón was not among them. He died of fever at San Miguel in October 1526.

Ayllón's enterprise had a mostly negative effect. Along with that of *Estevåo Gómes* in 1525, his voyage lessened Spain's interest in North America, leaving the gains of exploration and colonization there to France and England.

Batts-Fallam expedition (1671)

Thomas Batts led a 1671 expedition from Fort Henry near present Petersburg, Virginia, in search of passes through the *Blue Ridge Mountains* into western Virginia. *Abraham Wood,* commanding at Fort Henry, instructed Batts and Robert Fallam to blaze a trade route to the Indians of the interior and discover whether the waters beyond the mountains flowed into the Pacific Ocean.

Following the line of the Staunton River through the Blue Ridge, Batts and Fallam reached the New River on the western flank of the mountains and claimed the region for England. Mistaking the current of the New River for a tidal flow, they returned to Fort Henry to report, erroneously, that Fallam had found a way to the Pacific. Batts determined that the river in fact emptied into the Ohio, a discovery that formed the basis for England's claim to the Ohio Valley.

The travels of *John Lederer* (1669–1670) and the *Needham and Arthur expedition* (1673) were related efforts to establish trade connections with Indian tribes beyond the Blue Ridge.

Beothuk

Little is known about this native people of *Newfoundland.* The Beothuk are regarded as being closely related to other Indians of Algonkian origin such as the Micmac, the Montagnais, and the Naskaupi of historical times. It is also now believed that the first ancestors of the Beothuk, possibly the people known as *skraelings [I],* appeared in Newfoundland around 50 B.C., by which time Paleoeskimos had long been resident there. The Beothuk probably spoke an Algonquian language variant and followed a seasonal cycle of the winter caribou hunt and the summertime exploitation of sea and river fish and shellfish. Early Europeans in Newfoundland called the Beothuk "red Indians" because they rubbed red ochre onto their skin and clothes.

First contact occurred with the arrival of the *Norse [I]* about A.D. 1000. The Beothuk nation numbered an estimated five hundred when *John Cabot* reached Newfoundland in 1497. They were shy of Europeans; Cabot did not encounter any on his first voyage, though evidence of European items later in Beothuk possession suggests the possibility that he met them on his ill-fated second journey to the Newfoundland coast.

The Beothuk were in conflict with Europeans from the outset. The expedition of Portuguese explorer Gaspar Corte-Réal (see *Corte-Réal expeditions*) abducted fifty-seven Beothuk or Micmac Indians in 1501 and brought them to Lisbon as slaves. The Portuguese found them an appealing people. "Their manners and gestures are most gentle; they laugh considerably and manifest the greatest pleasure," one observer wrote. The Beothuk were uninterested in trade, though, and they tended to harass the land-based fishing operations of Europeans. The French and English soon became their implacable enemies. One of *Jacques Cartier*'s officers remarked that the Beothuk "had no more God than beasts, and are bad people."

As increasing numbers of Europeans moved onto Newfoundland in the 1700s, they not only began to compete with the Beothuk for caribou, seals, and bird eggs, but they threatened the very existence of the Beothuk with their firearms. In 1769 the British authorities issued a proclamation (reissued over the years) making it a capital crime to murder a Beothuk. But in the early 1800s a new threat appeared—the Beothuks' relatives, the Micmac, began to move into Newfoundland, and they were a more assertive people. They dealt more freely with the Europeans, they used firearms, and they intermarried with the Beothuk. The last known full-blooded Beothuk, a woman named Shanawdithit, died of tuberculosis in

1829. But if the theory of the ancestors of the Beothuk is correct, other descendants of the skraelings still live on in eastern Canada.

Bland-Wood expedition (1650)

Trader/colonist *Abraham Wood* built and garrisoned Fort Henry, part of a Virginia frontier defense line of four forts, near present-day Petersburg in 1645–1646. In 1650, Wood and Edward Bland led seven men on an exploring expedition into the then-wilderness between Fort Henry and present Weldon, North Carolina.

The expedition covered 180 miles over nine days. Wood would later organize expeditions into the Appalachians in search of a route to the Pacific and in pursuit of trade with the Indians.

Blue Ridge Mountains

A heavily forested eastern range of the Appalachians, the chain extends from near present-day Carlisle in southeastern Pennsylvania through parts of Maryland, Virginia, North Carolina, and South Carolina to Fort Oglethorpe, Georgia.

The Blue Ridge broadens from north to south, reaching a maximum width of 70 miles in North Carolina; the average elevation is 2,000 to 4,000 feet. Mount Mitchell, North Carolina, at 6,684 feet, is the highest peak east of the Mississippi River. The highest points in Virginia, South Carolina, and Georgia are in the Blue Ridge.

The Blue Ridge probably first came to the attention of Europeans in 1607, when Christopher Newport returned from an expedition up the James River with an Indian-drawn map showing "certaine huge mountains called Quirank." In the spring of 1670, the German physician/explorer *John Lederer* ascended the eastern slopes of the range on one of his three journeys into the interior of Virginia. Two years later Occaneechee Indians killed James Needham as he explored near the base of the Blue Ridge in southwestern Virginia.

Although many gaps pierce the Blue Ridge, it long remained an obstacle to westward movement from the English seaboard colonies. In 1716 Virginia governor *Alexander Spotswood [V]* led an expedition of the "Knights of the Golden Horseshoe" through the James River gap in the range and north down the Shenandoah Valley as far as present Staunton, Virginia. In 1750 Dr. *Thomas Walker [V]* of the Loyal Land Company of Virginia crossed the Blue Ridge, followed the line of the Holston River, and in April, cleared the *Cumberland Gap [V],* which eventually became the route through which thousands of migrants streamed into Kentucky and Tennessee.

Boston

The Puritan elder John Winthrop founded Boston on the Shawmut peninsula in 1630, and his "city upon a hill" became the chief settlement of England's Massachusetts Bay Colony.

As the political, cultural, and commercial capital of New England, Boston became the staging point for important exploratory expeditions into the region's interior. *John Oldham* blazed an overland route from Boston to the Connecticut River in 1633. In the 1640s, trader Simon Willard explored the lower reaches of the Merrimack River north of Boston.

Boston played a key role in later exploration as well. *Robert Gray*'s *[VI] Columbia* sailed from Boston to the Pacific Northwest in 1790 and claimed the discovery of the mouth of the "Great River of the West," which he named for his ship, in May 1792. Soon Boston-based sailors became so commonplace in the Pacific Northwest that the Indians there referred to whites as "Bostons." Nathaniel Wyeth's overland Oregon expeditions of 1832 and 1834 were planned and outfitted from Cambridge, Massachusetts, across the Charles River from Boston.

Brûlé, Étienne   (1592?–1633?)

Brûlé arrived in *New France* with *Samuel de Champlain* in 1608 and received permission in 1610 to live among the *Huron* to learn their language. As Brûlé's travels are not well documented, most of his explorations are presumed rather than certain. He may have blazed the main westward fur trade canoe route from the *St. Lawrence River* up the Ottawa River and west along the Mattawan to Lake Nipissing, and down the French River to Lake Huron's Georgian Bay, thus becoming the first white man to enter Huron country.

In 1615 Champlain sent him to seek an alliance with the Susquehanna Indians against the Iroquois. He voyaged south from Lake Simcoe to cross Lake Erie's west end to travel, with portages, by way of the Niagara and Genessee rivers to the Susquehanna headquarters at Carantouan (between present Elmira and Binghamton, New York). From there he accompanied a group of southern Susquehannas to their homeland, exploring the Susquehanna River to its mouth. Along the way he was probably the first white man to enter Pennsylvania. While south, he probably explored *Chesapeake Bay*'s shore and islands. On his 1618 return north, he was captured, tortured, and later befriended by the Senecas.

In his wide travels to advance the fur trade, he was probably the first European to see four of the five Great Lakes, missing only Lake Michigan. In 1622 or 1623, while exploring Lake Huron's north shore to Lake Superior, he may have continued on to reach Duluth. Intrigued by Indian life, he spent his last years with the Bear clan of the Hurons, who killed and cannibalized him. The tribe attributed its later misfortunes to his avenging spirit.

Bry, Théodore de (1528–1598)

A native of Flanders who worked in Frankfurt-am-Main, Théodore de Bry issued the finest visual images of the great age of exploration. He based his elegant mannerist-style engravings on the drawings, watercolors, and woodcuts brought back by expedition artists, who recorded whatever was found, including plants, animals, terrain, and indigenous peoples.

From 1590 to 1634 de Bry (and after his death, his family) issued the thirteen-volume series, *Historiae Americanae,* also known as the *Grands Voyages,* which surveyed the discoveries in North America, the Caribbean, Central America, and South America in over 250 engravings accompanying the accounts of thirty-five explorers. Only three volumes were devoted to North America: The first was based on John White's drawings of the 1584–88 English settlement of *Roanoke Colony* in Virginia; the second covered the 1562–1565 *Ribaut and Laudonnière expeditions* to the Carolina coast, then considered part of *Florida,* as depicted by Jacques le Moyne de Morgues. The final volume included material on the 1607 English colony at *Jamestown,* Virginia.

The English placed a high value on these images as propaganda to attract investors and settlers. The prints portrayed, for the most part, an arcadian America ripe for exploitation with abundant game and fish, lush forests and fields, and probable mineral riches in a country of navigable waterways and mild climate, peopled with idealized Indians in orderly settlements.

From 1594 to 1596 de Bry issued three volumes devoted to Girolamo Benzoni's *La Historia del Mondo Nuovo,* which described Spanish cruelty toward African slaves in *Hispaniola [II]* and the Indians of the Americas. This cruelty served as powerful anti-Spanish propaganda and became known as the "Black Legend," which was promoted by Spain's rivals to their own advantage.

Byrd, William II (1674–1744)

A native of Henrico County, Virginia, Byrd spent most of his youth in England and won admission to the bar and, by age twenty-two, to England's leading scientific institution, the Royal Society. He inherited his father's estate, Westover, on the James River, in 1704. He laid out the city of Richmond, later Virginia's capital, on part of his land in 1737.

In the late winter of 1728, Byrd joined six other members of a Virginia–North Carolina boundary survey at Carrituck Inlet on the Atlantic. The expedition, consisting of seven commissioners, four surveyors, forty laborers, and a chaplain, set out on March 5 and pushed steadily westward through the Great Dismal Swamp. The party reached the Meherrin River in six weeks. There the North Carolina commissioners dropped out; the Virginians pressed on to Peters Creek in present Patrick County, Virginia, more than 240 miles from the ocean.

Byrd wrote two accounts of the expedition. His lively *Secret History of the Dividing Line,* written in code, lay unpublished until 1929. A tamer *History of the Dividing Line,* a satirical account that describes flora and fauna as well as commissioners, back-country settlers, and other characters, first appeared in print in 1841.

Cabot, John (1450?–1498?)

Little is known of John Cabot's early life. No likeness, and no letters, documents, or maps in his hand, survive. He was probably born in Genoa, Italy, and may have been bred to the sea; in Italian, his name *Caboto* means "coaster," or coastal sailor. Cabot became a citizen of the Venetian Republic in 1476 and lived there for about fifteen years. Spain and Portugal rejected his early proposals for voyages of discovery.

Reaching England in about 1495, Cabot settled his family in the west country seaport of *Bristol [I]* and persuaded King Henry VII to approve his proposal for a sea expedition in search of a northern route to China. The king's patent, dated March 5, 1496, gave Cabot broad license "to sail to all parts, regions and coasts of the eastern, western and northern sea . . . to find, discover and investigate whatsoever islands, countries, regions or provinces of heathens and infidels, in whatsoever part of the world placed, which before this time were unknown to all Christians."

Cabot sailed from Bristol about May 15, 1497, with a crew of eighteen in a small vessel, roughly the size of *Columbus*'s *[II] Niña,* whose name seems to have been *Mathew.* Few details of the Atlantic crossing are extant. *Mathew* must have been a fast ship, for Cabot would make the round-trip in eleven weeks—a transatlantic record that stood for a century. According to his son *Sebastian Cabot*'s map inscription of 1544, he made his New World landfall on the morning of June 24, probably, historian Samuel Eliot Morison speculates, off Cape Degrat near the northern tip of *Newfoundland.*

Cabot may have landed at present Griquet Harbor four miles south of Cape Degrat. He and his crew encountered no one, though *Beothuk* Indians and Micmacs from Nova Scotia frequented the shore in the warmer months to fish and dig for clams. They did, however, report seeing snares, fishnets, and other signs of human habitation. A combination of cold, fog, and mosquitoes prompted Cabot to push southward. A contemporary source says he coasted 300 leagues (more than 950 miles) to the south, but Morison calculates he reached no further than Cape Race in southeastern Newfoundland. There Cabot doubled back to Cape Degrat and took his departure for England about July 20.

A fast fifteen-day passage brought *Mathew* to the coast of Brittany and a couple of days later to Bristol. Landing on August 6, 1497, Cabot at once traveled to London to inform Henry VII of his discovery—"the new founde land," which Cabot evidently mistook for part of the European landmass. The king must have been pleased with the

IN THEIR OWN *Words*

That Venetian of ours . . . says he has discovered mainland 700 leagues away . . . and that he coasted it for 300 leagues. . . . The discoverer of these things planted on the land which he has found a large cross with a banner of England and one of St. Mark, as he is a Venetian, so that our flag has been hoisted very far afield.

—LORENZO PASQUALIGO IN LONDON TO HIS
BROTHERS IN VENICE, AUGUST 23, 1497

result, a bargain as Cabot's voyage cost his treasury only fifty pounds. He ordered a reward for "hym that founde the new Isle," and in December 1497 he granted the explorer a royal pension.

What had Cabot discovered? Sebastian Cabot's 1544 map annotations describe a *Prima Terra Vista* whose denizens dressed in animal skins and hunted with bows and arrows, lances and darts, slings, and wooden clubs. The younger Cabot went on: "It is a very sterile land. There are in it many white bears, and very large stags like horses, and many other animals; and likewise there is infinite fish, sturgeons, salmon, very large soles a yard in length, and many other kinds of fish; and the greatest of them are called Baccallaos [codfish]; and likewise there are in the same land hawks black as crows, eagles, partridges, linnets, and many other kinds of birds of different species."

Three contemporary letters detailing Cabot's voyage survive. In August 1497 Lorenzo Pasqualigo wrote from England to his brothers in Venice that Cabot had discovered "the country of the Grand Khan." Raimondo de Soncino in December wrote the Duke of Milan that Cabot sailed from Bristol, passed Ireland, then "bore to the north, in order to sail to the east"—to Asia. He had, Soncino added, raised the royal standard and claimed a new country for the English monarch. The undated "John Day letter," an English merchant's account addressed to the "Grand Admiral"—possibly Columbus—reports that Cabot needed thirty-five days to make landfall and spent thirty days exploring the coasts of Newfoundland and Nova Scotia.

Henry VII issued patent letters for Cabot's second voyage on February 3, 1498. Soncino informed the Duke of Milan that Cabot and his flotilla would seek Cipango (Japan), reputed to be the source of the world's jewels and spices, and that he intended to establish a trading factory there. "By means of this," Soncino reported, "they hope to make London a more important mart for spices than Alexandria." Cabot sailed from Bristol in command of a fleet of five ships in early May 1498. One of the vessels met trouble early and put into a port in Ireland. The others vanished, their fate unknown.

"In the event, he is believed to have found the new lands nowhere but the very bottom of the ocean," an early sixteenth-century chronicler wrote rather cruelly, "to which he is thought to have descended together with his boat, the victim himself of that self-same ocean; since after that voyage he was never seen again anywhere."

Cabot, Sebastian

(1474–1557)

Born probably in Venice, the son of the explorer *John Cabot,* he claimed to have accompanied his father on his 1497 voyage of discovery to *Newfoundland.* There is, however, no documentary evidence to support this.

Historians generally accept Cabot's claim that he attempted a northwest passage to China in a 1508 voyage. *Peter Martyr,* the Italian who wrote the first history of the New World, says that Cabot outfitted two ships at his own expense, sailed with a crew of three hundred, and reached as far south as the latitude of *Cuba [II].* Cabot may have approached the entrance to Hudson's Bay before turning southward; Cabot himself reported that he explored the North American coast from *Labrador* to the Delaware Bay and beyond.

With English interest in North American exploration on the decline, Cabot entered Spanish service in 1512. He sailed in a Spanish expedition of 1526 charged with following Magellan around the world. Cabot abandoned the expedition after discovering the estuary of the River Plate on the east coast of South America in 1528 and returned to Spain.

Cabot reentered English service in 1547 and helped found the Company of Merchant Venturers, which pursued a northeast passage and developed trading relations with Russia. Cabot's reputation rests on his claim to have sailed with his father in 1497 and on his 1508 voyage. He was also important as a chartmaker and trainer of ships' pilots.

The historian Samuel Eliot Morison is skeptical of many of Sebastian Cabot's claims. He calls him "a genial and cheerful liar."

In this half-length portrait of 1903 after the original attributed to Holbein, Sebastian Cabot poses with compass and globe. Cabot's importance as an explorer rests on his claim that he sailed with his father to Newfoundland in 1497 and on his 1508 voyage in search of the Northwest Passage.

Cape Cod

A sandy, low-lying peninsula with a distinctive hook shape, Cape Cod extends sixty-five miles into the Atlantic Ocean and ranges in width from one to twenty miles. The English mariner *Bartholomew Gosnold* explored Cape Cod in the spring of 1602. He gave the peninsula its name after taking "a great store of codfish" into his ship, the bark *Concord.*

English Pilgrims seeking a New World haven landed at the site of Provincetown at the tip of Cape Cod in 1620 before moving on to Plymouth. It is today contiguous with Barnstable County, Massachusetts.

Cartier, Jacques (1491–1557)

One of the most important of early North American explorers, Cartier was the discoverer of the *St. Lawrence River,* and his three voyages in the 1530s and 1540s opened the Canadian interior to European trade, conquest, and settlement.

A kinsman of the abbot of Mont-Saint-Michel on the coast of Normandy, Cartier exploited the connection to gain an audience with King *François I,* a patron of *Giovanni da Verrazano* and an advocate of French maritime power. The abbot suggested Cartier, a master pilot with voyages to *Newfoundland* and Brazil on his résumé, as commander of an exploring expedition, and offered to help defray the cost. The king himself advanced six thousand livres to fund Cartier's commission to search out a *Northwest Passage [VII]* to Asia.

Cartier sailed from Saint-Malo on April 20, 1534, in two ships carrying sixty-one men. There is no record of the names of the ships, but it is known that Cartier made a fast twenty-day voyage, sighting land off Cape Bonavista, Newfoundland, on May 10. He put in to the harbor of present Catalina southwest of Bonavista to refit and, after a 10-day respite there, upped anchor and shaped a northerly course. At *Funk Island,* the crew slaughtered a sufficient quantity of flightless great auk to fill two ships' boats ("These birds are so fat that it is marvelous," Cartier wrote), salting the meat down for later consumption. Leaving the island, they sighted a swimming bear "as big as a cow and white as a swan," killed and ate the creature, and pronounced its flesh as flavorful as that of a two-year-old heifer.

Cartier cruised along the south shore of *Labrador* on the Canadian main and in early June reached Chateau Bay, so named for castle-like rock formations and already by the 1530s a meeting place for European fishing vessels. He continued southwest up the strait of Belle Isle, studded with islands "so numerous that it is impossible to count them," and went ashore from time to time. The waters were difficult to navigate, the country barren.

Cartier sailed south toward the largely unexamined west coast of Newfoundland on June 15. He judged Brion Island, a mile wide by five miles long and named for one of his supporters, "the best land we have seen; for two acres of it is worth more than the whole of Newfoundland." After two days of exploration among the Magdalen Islands, he struck west on June 29 and at dawn on the thirtieth sighted Prince Edward Island. "All this coast is low and flat but the finest land one can see, and full of beautiful trees and meadows," he wrote. Cartier failed to realize Prince Edward was an island, nor did he know that *Estevåo Gómes* and possibly *João Alvarez Fagundes* had seen it before him.

The French vessels crossed Northumberland Strait on July 2. Cartier entered and named Chaleur Bay on the third, and briefly held out hope it might be a strait that led to China. It was a pleasant and temperate anchorage, he found, with a rich soil, and so the ships lay in the harbor of present Port Daniel for a week and a day. A fleet of forty or fifty Micmac Indian canoes laden with pelts turned up on July 6—a clear indication Europeans had appeared here before. "We made signs that we wished them no harm," Cartier wrote, "and sent two men on shore, to offer them knives and other iron goods, and a red cap to give to their chief." He then pushed up Chaleur Bay in search of the passage to Asia, reaching its head after a hard and ultimately disappointing row of eighty miles.

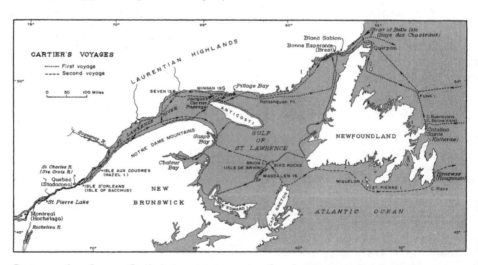

Breton mariner Jacques Cartier's two great voyages of exploration revealed the St. Lawrence estuary and river valley to Europeans. On the second voyage, Cartier entered the St. Lawrence River west of Anticosti Island and penetrated a thousand miles into the North American interior. This map was first published in H. P. Biggar, *The Voyages of Jacques Cartier*, Ottawa, 1924.

The explorers resumed the circumnavigation of the Gulf of St. Lawrence on July 12. Cartier sent out small boats to explore Gaspé Bay and, while at anchor in Gaspé Harbor from July 16 to July 25, met a party of three hundred *Huron* men, women, and children on a mackerel-fishing expedition. "They are the sorriest folk that can be in the world," he thought; "and the whole lot of them had not anything above the value of five sous, their canoes and fishing nets excepted." Cartier raised a thirty-foot-tall cross and claimed the country for France on July 24, overcoming the doubts of the Hurons' chief—"he made us a long harangue . . . and then he pointed to the land all around about as if he wished to say it belonged to him"—with a gift of hatchets and knives.

In a council of war aboard the flagship on August 1, Cartier queried his officers: Sail for home or reconnoiter for a winter anchorage? The vote was overwhelmingly for a return to France. Cartier took his departure for home from Blanc Sablon on August 15 and reached Saint-Malo on September 5 after an uneventful crossing.

On this first voyage, Cartier had thoroughly and painstakingly reconnoitered the Gulf of St. Lawrence—the beginning, in historian Samuel Eliot Morison's phrase, "of the great axis of penetration of the North American continent."

Cartier's patron, Philippe Chabot de Brion, granted him a patent for a second voyage on October 30, 1534. His orders bade him to explore beyond Newfoundland and discover new places. He had

Jacques Cartier's flagship on the 1535 voyage, the twelve-gun galleon *Grande Hermine*. In the margins are cameos of Cartier and his patron, François I, king of France.

three vessels this time, and their names are known: *La Grande Hermine* (weasel), a ship of twelve guns; *La Petite Hermine,* four guns; and *L'Emerillon,* a pinnace, a small craft handy for inshore exploration.

The flotilla left Saint-Malo on May 19, 1535, with a crew of 112 officers and men. Cartier's *Brief recit,* published in 1545, records that he encountered stormy weather beginning on May 26 that delayed the expedition a month. The vessels became separated; the flagship made landfall off Funk Island on July 7, salted down two boatloads of bird meat, and reached Blanc Sablon eight days later. The smaller vessels joined Cartier there on July 26. After three days of refit, the exploration got under way in earnest on July 29.

An east wind carried the flotilla swiftly up the Strait of Belle Isle. Cartier did not linger this time. He doubled West Point on Anticosti Island on August 13, turned southwest, and sailed along the Gaspé coast before turning north for the Bay of Seven Islands (in fact there are eight) on August 17. Cartier consulted two Hurons, who informed him he had just crossed an estuary of sixty miles in width and that this was the way to the mouth of the great river of Hochelaga—the stream he would soon christen St. Lawrence.

Here the French had reached the entrance to the great waterway, *le chemin de Canada.* Ahead lay the Indian kingdom of *Saguenay,* soon to grow in Cartier's imagination into a rival of sumptuous Peru. At the mouth of the Moisie River the French encountered walruses for the first time, "fish in appearance like horses," wrote Cartier, "which go on land at night but in the day-time remain in the water." He had now advanced well beyond the farthest reach of his 1534 voyage. On August 24, he led the flotilla up the St. Lawrence River itself.

On the first day of September Cartier entered the Saguenay River where it flows into the St. Lawrence. "This river issues from between lofty mountains of bare rock with but little soil on them," he observed, though trees flourished there all the same. "We saw a tree suitable for masting a ship of 30 tuns, and as green as it could be, growing out of a rock without a trace of earth." There were more aquatic wonders too—beluga whales "very similar to a greyhound about the body and head." Upstream progress was slow against the strong St. Lawrence current, though. All the same, Cartier reached the present Île d'Orléans on September 7 and sent the ship's boats upstream to the Huron town of Stadacona.

The settlement lay at the base of a high promontory called the Rock of Quebec, the site of Quebec City. Cartier ordered the ships up from the Île d'Orléans on September 14 and decided to moor the *Hermines* in the St. Charles River for the winter.

With a small crew, Cartier pushed upstream in *L'Emerillon* and two longboats on September 19. They made thirty-two miles that day, and in the evening an Indian approached with a warning of rapids ahead. He also made Cartier a gift of two children, an infant boy and a girl of eight or nine; the Frenchman refused the boy and accepted the girl. Beginning next day, the going became labored, and the expedition covered only seventy-three miles over the next nine days. The river widened out to twenty miles at Lac St. Pierre, and five channels led westward on the far side. Indians pointed out the main channel and told Cartier *Hochelaga,* their capital, lay three days distant. He moored the pinnace on September 29 and struck westward in the longboats, taking thirty-four officers and men.

They reached the neighborhood of Hochelaga—present *Montreal [V]*—on October 2 and went up to the village along a well-worn path the next day. Cartier dubbed a nearby hill Mont Royal and, climbing it, caught a distant view of a violent rapids he named Lachine, thinking wishfully that they were on the route to China. But they were impassable, he judged, to anything larger than a canoe. And the Hurons stigmatized Saguenay, beyond the Ottawa River to the west, as a country of "bad people, who were armed to the teeth."

Thus Cartier reached his point of maximum penetration, a thousand miles from the sea. He retraced his route downstream and regained the pinnace on October 4. On the eleventh he reached the *Hermines* moored in the St. Charles. In his absence, the sailors had built a log fort armed with ships' guns. Cartier decided to pass the winter there.

The French hunkered down in quarters from mid-November 1535 to mid-April 1536. Ice formed twelve feet thick on the St. Charles, and the snow piled four feet deep. Scurvy broke out in December among the Hurons and then the French; some fifty Hurons died, as did several Europeans. By February perhaps only 10 of Cartier's 110 men were fit for duty. Doubtless many more would have perished had not the Indians produced the ground leaves and bark of the arborvitae, which, when boiled, produced a curative tea. The Europeans learned to soothe themselves with tobacco over the winter; Cartier makes the first recorded mention of it. The Hurons sun-dried the plant and smoked it in clay pipes. "They say it keeps them warm and in good health," Cartier wrote.

With the coming of spring, Cartier decided to abandon the smaller *Hermine* and sail for home in the flagship with the pinnace as escort. Strictly against orders, he also carried off the kidnapped Huron chief Donnaconna, who had regaled him with tales of the fabulous riches of Saguenay. He took his departure from Renewse Harbor, Newfoundland, on June 19. The expedition reached Saint-Malo on July 16, 1536, concluding the second voyage, the most productive of Cartier's New World explorations.

Saguenay would prove to be a mythical kingdom. Cartier believed in it though, and he and the abducted Huron chief persuaded François I of its existence. So on October 17, 1540, the king issued a new commission to Cartier to return to Canada so that he "might discover more than was done before in the former voyages," wrote **Richard Hakluyt,** "and attain (if it were possible) unto the knowledge of the Countrey of Saguenay." In early 1541 François put Jean-François de la Roque, *Sieur de Roberval,* in overall command of the expedition, with instructions to establish a settlement and convert the Indians of the St. Lawrence to Christianity.

Cartier sailed from Saint-Malo in *La Hermine* with four other ships on May 23, 1541. Roberval, unready to leave, remained behind. After a difficult crossing, the flotilla made landfall at Cape Degrat and reached Stadacona on August 23. The Hurons there proved friendly in spite of the kidnapping of Donnaconna; they may have helped Cartier select a settlement site at Cap Rouge nine miles upstream of the Indian town. Two of the ships turned back for France in early September. Cartier and the colonists, meanwhile, built a settlement behind palisades and named it Charlesbourg-Royal after a son of the king.

Cartier then took the longboats up to Montreal/Hochelaga. He advanced to the head of the Lachine rapids, then turned back after being warned of more rough water ahead. This was the extent of Cartier's penetration. He returned to Charlesbourg-Royal to find that the Hurons, suspicious and resentful of the French decision to colonize the area, had turned hostile.

Intermittent Indian attacks claimed the lives of thirty-five colonists over the winter of 1541–1542. Cartier broke camp early in June 1542 and sailed downriver with the surviving colonists in the remaining three ships, reaching St. John harbor, Newfoundland, by month's end. He found Roberval with three ships at anchor there. Roberval ordered Cartier to return to Canada, but the veteran explorer refused and set sail for France, arriving in Saint-Malo in mid-October.

So ended Cartier's career of discovery. Maps of North America now showed the Gulf of St. Lawrence and the river of the same name stretching westward to the Lachine Rapids. Roberval had been an ineffectual commander, and the king never punished Cartier for flouting his senior's

IN THEIR OWN

Words

We went along, and about a league and a halfe farther, we beganne to find goodly and large fieldes, full of suche Corne as the Countrey yieldeth. In the midst of those fields is the Citie of Hochelaga, *placed heere, and as it were joyned to a great mountaine that is tilled round aboute, very fertile, on the top of whiche, you may see verye farre, we named it Mount Royall.*

—JACQUES CARTIER, *NAVIGATIONS TO NEWE FRAUNCE* (1580)

orders. He divided his time between his home in Saint-Malo and a farm on the outskirts in the years that remained to him. He died on September 1, 1557, during an epidemic. Cartier was sixty-six.

Champlain, Samuel de   (circa 1567–1635)

The first explorer to map the Atlantic coast from the Bay of Fundy to *Cape Cod,* Samuel de Champlain came to North America with a colonial and christianizing vision and an ambition to establish a powerful French influence on the continent. Over the course of three decades, he laid the foundations for French settlement in Canada; historians would dub him the "father of *New France.*"

Details of Champlain's early life are sketchy. He was born in Brouage, France; his father may have been a naval officer. Little is known about his schooling, other than the fact that he somehow learned the skills of draftsmanship and mapmaking. Toward the end of his life he claimed to have fought in the French Wars of Religion of the 1590s, with the forces of Henri IV against the Catholic League. He sailed to the West Indies and to Mexico in a Spanish expedition of 1599–1601. On his return to France, Henri appointed him royal geographer.

Champlain first came to Canada in 1603 with the fur-trading expedition of François Gravé du Pont. The traders pushed up the *St. Lawrence River* to Tadoussac, a meeting place of traders and Indians. There Montagnais Indians told him of a tribe that lived along a saltwater sea to the north—Hudson Bay. Champlain then explored Saguenay River forty miles above Tadoussac. With Gravé, he advanced as far as the Lachine Rapids above present *Montreal [V],* where Indians told him of a great river to the south that eventually flowed into the Atlantic (the Hudson) and of three great lakes lying to the west, the third of which,

In armor, holding a sword and helmet, French explorer Samuel de Champlain strikes a heroic pose overlooking a lake. The full-length portrait by William Haskell Coffin was published in 1924.

Huron, he took to be the Pacific. Champlain reasoned that this chain of lakes offered a water route to the Pacific and thence to China. Returning to France, he argued at the royal court for government-sponsored exploration and control of this supposed route to the western ocean.

On his second voyage in 1604, Champlain, with Pierre du Gua de Monts, who had obtained a royal monopoly on the new country's trade, established a trade and settlement base on an island at the mouth of the Sainte-Croix River, which flows into the Bay of Fundy and forms the border of present-day Maine and New Brunswick. Snow fell early in October and lay thick upon the ground through the following April. Scurvy spread through the camp over the winter, claiming nearly half the garrison of seventy-nine men. In the spring, de Monts and Champlain moved the post across the bay to Port-Royal in Nova Scotia; the little settlement survived until 1607.

Champlain set out that summer on the first of his three *Acadia* voyages, exploring the Maine coast (he discovered and named Mount Desert Island in present Acadia National Park) and penetrating some fifty miles up the Penobscot River. Successive explorations led him as far south as Martha's Vineyard. Taken together, the cruises yielded a more accurate rendering of the island-studded Maine coast and added the Bay of Fundy and the peninsula of Nova Scotia to maps of North America.

Abandoning Port-Royal, Champlain returned to the St. Lawrence in 1608, pausing in early July at a narrows near the abandoned Indian village of Stadacona to establish an outpost on the site of Quebec. Only eight men of the garrison of twenty-eight survived the first winter there, and cold, snow, and ice took a toll on the natives too—"they looked like skeletons," Champlain remarked. Still, Quebec proved to be a permanent settlement and would survive to become the seat of French power in the New World.

Champlain looked to the fur trade to fund his exploration and empire-building schemes. His alliances with the *Algonquin, Huron,* and other northern tribes against the warlike Iroquois Confederacy to the south were designed to further these aims. Traveling with a Huron war party in June 1609, Champlain ascended the Richelieu River to a long, narrow lake that—in an understandable fit of narcissism—he named for himself.

IN THEIR OWN Words

*A*fter returning in 31 days from the land of Acadia in New-France, Monsieur de Monts showed us a live female moose, at the most six months old and yet as high as a medium-sized horse, with legs, like those of the doe, very small in proportion to its body. The head was very long for its size, and the ears very broad. . . . It was, however, the horseshoe crab that seemed to me more wondrous than anything on account of the great shell that covers its head and entire body: It is more than a span in diameter and as thick as a finger.

—NICOLAS-CLAUDE DE FABRI, *NOTES ON SPECIMENS FROM ACADIA, 1605–1606*

In 1610 Champlain assigned the young French trader *Étienne Brûlé* to live among the western Indians, learn their languages, and reconnoiter for furs. In his travels, Brûlé saw four of the five Great Lakes and may have been the first European to reach Lake Superior. Champlain traveled between France and Canada during the years 1610–1613, raising money and building interest in his New World ventures. With the post at Quebec now secure, he recruited missionaries for service among the Indian tribes. He also married (his bride was twelve years old, and he promised not to consummate the marriage for two years), and thus secured a substantial dowry to fund his colonization efforts.

Champlain mapped 175 miles of the Ottawa River in 1613 before skeptical Algonquin Indians barred his progress. This turned out to be a prelude to a more extensive reconnaissance of the forested west in 1615–1616. Setting out from the Lachine Rapids with a small party, he pushed on west along the Ottawa and French Rivers beyond his farthest advance of 1613, reaching the *Mer Douce* (or freshwater sea)—Georgian Bay, Lake Huron—in August.

Ranging southeast along the shore of the lake and then cross-country to the north shore of Lake Ontario, he fell in with a Huron-Algonquin war party in September. Wounded in the leg and knee in an attack on an Iroquois fortified town, he was carried off in "hellish torment" in a basket strapped to the back of one of his Indian allies. In his farthest westward penetration, Champlain in January 1616 reached the southeast shore of Lake Huron in the country of the Ottawa Indians.

Meanwhile, Champlain kept the printing presses clanking with accounts of his explorations, illustrated with maps and drawings. Editions of his *Voyages*—journals, travel accounts, and histories—appeared in 1613, 1619, and 1632. He also acceler-

In this Native American ceremony in the St. Lawrence Valley of Canada, a procession follows a medicine man carrying a turtle on a pole, as seated Indians observe. The engraving was first published in Paris in 1619 in explorer Samuel de Champlain's *Voyages et descouvertures faîtes en la Nouvelle France.*

ated his efforts at court, lobbying for colonists and a military garrison for the outpost at Quebec and for reinforcements for the four Récollet missionaries who had come to Canada in 1615. And he continued to believe that "the South Sea passage to China and the East Indies" lay through Canada.

Champlain saw a major advance of his colonial dream in 1627 with the establishment of the Compagnie de La Nouvelle France under the patronage of the powerful Cardinal Richelieu, Louis XIII's chief minister. The greatest of the early explorers of Canada, the "father of New France" wholly concerned himself with the affairs of the company until his death in 1635.

Chesapeake Bay

An inlet of the Atlantic Ocean, the 3,237-square-mile Chesapeake Bay separates what is today the Delmarva Peninsula from the Maryland-Virginia mainland. The Susquehanna River flows into the northern end; the entrance 325 miles to the south is a 12-mile-wide passage between Capes Henry and Charles. The bay ranges in width from 3 miles to about 30 miles.

Spanish explorer **Pedro de Quejo** briefly entered Chesapeake Bay in 1525. *Antonio Velázquez* effectively "rediscovered" it for Spain in 1561. The Spanish Jesuit missionaries Luís de Quirós and Juan Baptista de Segura reached the southwestern shore in 1570. Pedro **Menéndez de Avilés** and his nephew Pedro Menéndez Marquez explored and surveyed the bay in separate expeditions in the 1570s. An English exploring party under **Ralph Lane** pushed northeast from the **Roanoke Colony** to the southern shore in the winter of 1585–1586. *Vicente González*, seeking evidence of English penetration, sailed as far north as the mouth of the Susquehanna in 1585. On his return to Spain, he lauded the Chesapeake region's commercial and agricultural potential.

The English colonist **John Smith,** in search of a route to the Pacific, explored and surveyed the bay from *Jamestown* in the summer of 1608. Smith's efforts yielded an accurate map. Though the Jamestown venture failed, the Chesapeake region became the first important seat of English settlement in North America.

IN THEIR OWN Words

From some Indians we have had some information about the region farther inland. Three or four days' journey lie the mountains. For two of these days one travels on a river. After crossing the mountains by another days' journey or two, one can see another sea. If any new information can be had with more certainty and clarity, we will get it.

—LUÍS DE QUIRÓS AND JUAN DE SEGURA FROM CHESAPEAKE BAY, SEPTEMBER 12, 1570

Chozas and Salas expedition (1597)

Shortly after his arrival in Saint Augustine, the new *Florida* governor Gonzalo Méndez de Canzo heard reports of Tama (known as the chiefdom of Altamaha in *Hernando de Soto*'s time, and later explored by *Juan Pardo*), an inland region of present-day Georgia believed to have potential as a Spanish agricultural settlement.

The governor dispatched an expedition of some thirty Indians accompanying three Spaniards—Gaspar de Salas, a veteran soldier with linguistic ability, and two Franciscans, Pedro Fernández de Chozas and Francisco de Verascola. The party set out in a north-northwesterly direction, trekking across infertile and apparently uninhabited plains, hills, and swamplands. On the eighth day they reached Tama (most likely in central Georgia around Milledgeville), and investigation revealed abundant game and plentiful fruits, maize, and beans. The Spaniards also gathered specimens of sparkling stones (perhaps rock crystal), minerals, and a medical herb valued by the Indians.

They marched on for an additional day to Ochute, apparently farther up the Oconee River, and after the chief warned them of the dangers of proceeding further inland, they turned back to Tama. There Chozas, who had preached there earlier, was saved by Salas from being scalped.

Their favorable report led Canzo to recommend a new colony at Tama, as well as another expedition to the interior to establish contact with New Mexico (assumed to be far closer than it was) and the opening of an overland route to *New Spain [II]* (Nueva Galicia and Guadalajara) to transport supplies more expeditiously than along the relatively hazardous sea lanes. The financially pressed Spanish crown failed to respond to Canzo's grandiose proposals. In 1602 Canzo sent Juan de Lara to investigate whether Spanish soldiers from New Mexico had reached the Tama-Ochute area; it is unclear whether he actually reached Tama.

Meanwhile, other Franciscans continued to study the territory. The friar Baltasar López examined the Potano region of the Timucua Indians, west of the St. John's River in present northeast Florida, reporting that he had followed the river forty leagues upstream but was unable to locate a predicted water passage to the Gulf coast. The investigations of Francisco Pareja were ethnographic and linguistic rather than geographic. He completed a bilingual Castilian-Timucuan catechism and confessional, the earliest surviving text in a North American Indian language. These texts represent a legacy of Franciscan endeavors in Florida more enduring than Canzo's attempts to prove the validity of Spain's confused geographical concepts.

Corte-Réal expeditions (1500–1502)

With a patent from King Manoel I of Portugal, Gaspar Corte-Réal sailed in the summer of 1500 to "a land that was very cool and with big trees"— *Newfoundland.* Landing three years after *John Cabot,* he found European relics ashore that probably came from Cabot's ship.

He returned to Lisbon in the autumn of 1500 and the next year made preparations for a second voyage with three caravels outfitted at his own expense. Two of the vessels returned to Portugal in October 1501 to report the expedition had reached Newfoundland, which Corte-Réal called *Terra Verde.* The returning captains also delivered fifty-seven captive Indians, probably *Beothuks,* to be sold as slaves. As for the expedition commander, he was last seen sailing to the southward.

Nothing more is known of Corte-Réal's fate. His elder brother Miguel Corte-Réal obtained half his brother's royal patent in January 1502 and left for the North Atlantic in two ships to go in search of the missing caravel. Miguel Corte-Réal's ship was lost with all hands; the second vessel returned with nothing new to report.

A 1502 map erroneously claims for Gaspar Corte-Réal the discovery of Newfoundland, which he believed to be part of Asia. "Those who discovered it did not disembark," the map legend reads, "but saw on it jagged mountains. This is the reason, in the opinion of the cosmographers, it is believed to be the Point of Asia."

Fagundes, João Alvarez (?–?)

A shipowner of Viana do Castelo, Portugal, Fagundes sailed no later than 1520 to *Newfoundland* and the Gulf of St. Lawrence, discovering St. Pierre, Miquelon, and other islands off the south coast of Newfoundland.

Returning to Portugal, Fagundes obtained a royal patent, returned to the Canadian coast, and set up a shore station for curing fish on Cape Breton Island, probably near today's Ingonish. Samuel Eliot Morison calls this venture the earliest European colonial enterprise in North America, except for that of the *Norse [I]*.

The Indians turned hostile, however, and competing Breton Grand Banks fishermen sabotaged his gear. Packing up, Fagundes sailed south in search of a more secure site, discovering the Bay of Fundy and possibly reaching as far south as the Penobscot River of Maine.

Fernandes, João (?–?)

A small landowner of Terceira, an island in the Portuguese Azores, Fernandes obtained a patent from King Manoel I in 1499 for a voyage "to go in search of and discover certain islands in our sphere of influence." Another Azorean, Pedro Maria de Barcelos, may have financed the voyage.

Fernandes sailed from Terceira on an unknown date in 1500 and sighted Cape Farewell, at the southern tip of *Greenland [I]*, in the summer. A farmer ashore, he decided to call the cape *Tera del Lavrador*—land of the husbandman. (Geographers later claimed the name for the eastern part of mainland Canada.) From there he may have sailed on to *Newfoundland.*

Returning to Terceira, he learned that the king had issued a similar patent to Gaspar Corte-Réal (see *Corte-Réal expeditions*). He struck out for England and, with others, in March 1501 obtained from Henry VII a patent for the Anglo-Azorean Syndicate to explore anywhere in the world. Almost nothing is known of the syndicate's voyages, however.

Fernández de Écija, Francisco (?–?)

A veteran of the Spanish *Florida* garrison at St. Augustine, Francisco Fernández de Écija in 1598 made a series of voyages to Georgia and the Carolinas to negotiate the release of a Franciscan held captive by Indians after the 1597 revolt against the Guale (Georgia coastal) missions. Over the next eleven years he completed four key explorations of the Gulf and Atlantic coasts.

In 1604 Florida governor Ibarra sent Fernández out to find Spaniards held captive by Indians near Bahía de Carlos, probably present Charlotte Harbor, Florida. Finding none, his party explored inland eastward to Lake Okeechobee (Laguna de Maymi) with the idea they might find an east-west strait. They later found the headwaters of the San Mateo River not in the lake but in a swamp. This ended Spanish hopes for an inland route to the gulf that avoided the Straits of Florida and the hazardous Florida Keys.

In early 1605 the governor dispatched him to investigate an Anglo-French exploring and trading expedition. In Saint Helena Sound on the Carolina coast, he captured the expedition's two ships, including the *Castor and Pollux,* captained by Bertrand Rocque (see *Jerome and Rocque expedition*).

In August 1606 Fernández led an expedition to find the English settlers at Croatoan along the North Carolina coast. He investigated the Carolina coast between Santa Elena (off Port Royal Sound) and Cape Fear. Finding no one and hearing nothing of the English at *Jamestown,* he turned back south in September.

In a 1609 follow-up expedition up the Atlantic coast, Fernández investigated the coastal Indian groups, noting their linguistic differences. By mid-July he was sailing north along the Carolina Outer Banks and observing smoke signals but no Europeans. On July 24 at Cape Henry (the entrance to *Chesapeake Bay*), an English ship barred his way. Back in Saint Augustine by September 24, he finally reported that he had identified the location of the English settlement at Jamestown; he also noted the strategic importance of Chesapeake to the English as a base from which to begin the takeover of Spanish lands in North America.

The next Spanish voyage, the Molina-Pérez Expedition to Jamestown in 1611, resulted in the English capture of its leaders and forced Spanish acceptance of the English presence in Virginia.

Florida

A long, low semitropical peninsula of southeastern North America, Florida stretches from the St. Mary's River along the border of present Georgia to the Straits of Florida ninety miles from *Cuba [II].* The peninsula's southeastern projection appeared on Spanish maps as early as 1502. Sailing from *Puerto Rico [II], Juan Ponce de León* landed on Florida's east coast during Easter Week (*Pasqua Florida*) 1513 and claimed the country for Spain.

The Gulf Stream carried Ponce de León southward to the tip of the peninsula, which he mistook for a large island. He then sailed past the Florida Keys before turning to the north and landing on the gulf coast at a place he named San Carlos Bay (present Charlotte Harbor). Ponce de León met fierce resistance from the natives when he returned in 1521 with a colonizing expedition. Wounded in an assault on his beachhead, he withdrew to Cuba and died of complications some months later.

Fending off French forays in the 1560s, Spain retained an interest in Florida for its strategic value as flank protection for treasure ships sailing for home via the straits. *Pedro Menéndez de Avilés* founded the Spanish colony of St. Augustine in 1565.

François I   (1494–1547)

François d'Angoulême, a cousin of Henry VII of England, assumed the French throne in 1515. Although mainly occupied with waging war on land, he pursued maritime ambitions for France from the beginning of his thirty-two-year reign, ordering the reconstruction and fortification of the port of Le Havre at the mouth of the Seine in 1516. Le Havre replaced the harbor at Harfleur, which had silted up.

A patron of the Florentine navigator *Giovanni da Verrazano,* he charged Verrazano in 1523 with exploring the coast of the New World from *Florida* to *Newfoundland* and from *Labrador* to *Greenland [I]* in search of a strait leading to Asia. The French navy supplied Verrazano's flagship, *La Dauphine.*

François also commissioned *Jacques Cartier*'s first voyage of exploration (1534), supplying Cartier with six thousand livres to find a passage to Asia. His patronage contributed significantly to French exploration and colonization of North America.

Funk Island

An islet in the North Atlantic at latitude 49°45'N, thirty-two miles northeast of the tip of *Newfoundland,* Funk Island was a provisioning place for early transatlantic mariners. It was also one of the last breeding grounds for the now-extinct great auk, a diving bird of the north seas. European fishermen and explorers slaughtered thousands of auk and salted down their meat for subsistence on long voyages.

Jacques Cartier dubbed the rock "Isle of Birds" on his 1534 voyage. "The numbers are so great as to be incredible unless one has seen them," the explorer wrote, "for although the island is about a league in circumference, it is so exceedingly full of birds that one would think they had been stowed there."

Gilbert, Sir Humphrey (1539–1583)

Born into a noble family, a half-brother of the famous *Sir Walter Raleigh,* Gilbert was a close friend of the lord deputy Sir Henry Sidney, under whom he served in Ireland in 1566, putting down an insurrection. He was on friendly terms with Queen Elizabeth and was assisted by her at a number of crucial points in his career.

From early in his life, Gilbert devoted himself to the study of navigation and to the art of war. At first it seemed that he would follow a soldier's career; he was wounded in a campaign in France in 1563 fighting against the French Catholics. During the early part of his life he also took part in a number of military ventures, mainly against the Irish. In 1569 he became governor of the province of Munster, Ireland, having defeated the famed Irish rebels O'Neil and McCarthy.

But Gilbert's real interests lay elsewhere. In 1566, he had delivered to the Queen a petition for privileges "concerning the discovery of a passage by the northwest to go to Cathaia." (Cathay was a name for China.) His interest in a *Northwest Passage [VII]* to the East was timely. The Spanish controlled the long and arduous route to the East around the tip of South America; if England were to share in the riches of Cathay, then an alternate route would have to be found. Queen Elizabeth was well aware of the importance of finding a new route. But it may have been that she considered Gilbert more useful as a soldier than as an explorer, because she did not respond to the petition but, rather, sent him on another military assignment.

In 1574 Gilbert wrote his treatise "Discourse of a Discovery for a New Passage to Cathaia." This was submitted to Queen Elizabeth in support of the original petition of 1566. Appended to it was a further proposal to colonize *Newfoundland* in the New World and disrupt the Spanish influence there and in the West Indies. Because of intricate court politics, the privilege of the search for the passage was given to *Martin Frobisher [VII],* but Gilbert did obtain in 1578 a charter to plant a colony in Newfoundland. On September 26, 1578, he sailed with a fleet of seven ships, but they never got further than Ireland because he had started so late. He then had to raise the funds for a second expedition, and it was June 11, 1583, before Gilbert sailed from England with five vessels. On August 5, 1583, Gilbert landed at St. John's harbor in Newfoundland and took possession in the name of the queen, thereby planting the first English colony in North America.

The company, however, was composed of raw adventurers and opportunists, lazy landsmen and useless sailors, and felons released from prison to be the servants of the colonists. Gilbert could not cope with the chaos and the lawlessness and within a month decided to return to England. He set sail with the only three surviving ships and sailed south to Cape Breton, where one of the ships was lost. Setting sail across the Atlantic, Gilbert, in the small *Squirrel* and accompanied by the *Golden Hinde,* got as far as the Azores, where he and his men found themselves in a fierce storm. Gilbert called out to the men, "We are as near to heaven by sea as by land." Shortly thereafter, the lights of the *Squirrel* disappeared, and the sea swallowed up the ship.

Gilbert's fame was based on his firm belief in the possibility of a Northwest Passage and establishing a stable colony in the New World; political circumstances of the time and his own poor seamanship prevented him from ever putting those beliefs to the test.

Gómes, Estevåo (Esteban Gómez)   (?–?)

A native of Oporto, Portugal, Gómes was considered for command of Spain's round-the-world expedition of 1519 before King Charles V settled on Ferdinand Magellan instead.

Gómes sailed with the fleet as pilot of the ship *San Antonio.* He mutinied in the Strait of Magellan on the southern tip of South America, seized the vessel, and sailed for Spain. In his defense, he argued that the strait was a dangerous and impractical passage to the Pacific Ocean and offered to discover a better one. Charles forgave the mutiny, freed Gómes from prison, commissioned him in March 1523 to find a North American passage leading to the Philippines and the Moluccas, and ordered a ship to be built for the voyage.

The expedition fitted out rapidly, possibly because Spain had received intelligence of **Giovanni da Verrazano**'s voyage for France.

Accounts of the voyage of Gómes's ship, *La Annunciada,* are brief and contradictory. Gómes sailed, probably from Corunna in northwestern Spain, in September 1524. (By then, Verrazano had returned to Dieppe.) He reached the coast of Nova Scotia after a stormy crossing in February 1525, making a landfall near Cape Breton, and entered the Gulf of St. Lawrence, sighting Prince Edward Island before standing southward along the coasts of Nova Scotia and Maine.

Gómes entered the Penobscot River of Maine, probably in June, naming it *Rop de las Gamas* on account of the large herds of deer he saw there. He met bands of **Abenaki** Indians and sailed as far inland as present Bangor before concluding the Penobscot was not the passage to Asia.

La Annunciada cruised southward in late June and July. Gómes assigned Spanish names to Pemaquid Point, the Kennebec and Merrimack Rivers, Cape Ann, and **Cape Cod.** He departed for home in early August, carrying a number of Indians—possibly Wampanoags—to Spain as slaves. The chronicler **Peter Martyr** concluded Gómes had discovered nothing exotic, only places with products similar to Europe's. "It is to the southward, not the icy north, that everyone in search of a fortune should turn, for below the equator everything is rich," Peter Martyr advised.

Gómes, however, had a substantial influence on North American *maps [I]* until the expeditions of **Samuel de Champlain** and Captain **John Smith** yielded more accurate information early in the seventeenth century.

González, Vicente   (?–?)

In the late 1500s Vicente González, a Portuguese mariner in Spanish service, sailed on a series of voyages along the Atlantic coast in search of European settlements and of the legendary **Strait of Anian [I]** (a water passage to the Pacific). In 1570 he sailed from Havana by way of Santa Elena (off South Carolina's Port Royal Sound) to deliver Spanish Jesuit missionaries to **Chesapeake Bay.** *Florida* governor **Menéndez de Avilés** had asked the Jesuits to investigate the possibility of a route to the mountains and to China. González sailed three times to try to resupply the Jesuits, who fell victim to Indian attacks in the meantime.

Hearing that the French had been seen in South Carolina's Charleston harbor, Florida governor Pedro Menéndez Marquez in 1582 dispatched González with fifty soldiers in two ships. González surveyed all possible harbors along the coast but found no French presence. Following a 1585 expedition to search for English at Chesapeake Bay, in 1588 he set out on a coastal survey to latitude 39° (off present New Jersey), taking careful sightings and soundings.

During his detailed reconnaissance of the Chesapeake, beginning at the bay's west end, he investigated the estuaries; noted a large river, possibly the Potomac; documented the mouth of the Susquehanna River; and described the terrain around to the eastern shore. Querying the few Indians he met, he heard of precious metals in the *Appalachian Mountains [V],* and he also found freshwater mussel pearls. Indian reports apparently led him to consider the James and Susquehanna Rivers as possibilities for a passageway to the Pacific.

Leaving on June 24, 1588, to return to Saint Augustine, González sailed along the western shore of the Outer Banks and found debris from English colonists but failed to find evidence of the English *Roanoke Colony* on Roanoke Island; he reported that the English had disappeared. The next year found him in Spain to report on Chesapeake Bay, which he praised as an excellent agricultural and trade site, but the crown lacked the will and finances to pursue Spanish colonization of the region, thus leaving it open to the English.

Gosnold, Bartholomew (circa 1572–1607)

The son of a squire of Suffolk County, England, Gosnold commanded an exploring expedition in 1602 along the coast of New England from southern Maine to Narragansett Bay. Gosnold's voyage, the first direct transatlantic crossing between England and New England, alerted his countrymen to the possibilities for trade and settlement along the New England coast.

Gosnold left Falmouth in the bark *Concord* with a crew of thirty-one on March 26 and made landfall near Cape Porpoise in southern Maine. He then stood southward to a point of land he named *Cape Cod.* Rounding the cape, he explored Nantucket Sound and named an islet there, probably today's Chappaquiddick, Martha's Vineyard in honor of his mother-in-law. (The English later transferred the name to the larger island that still bears it.) He then built a fort on Elizabeth's Isle, now Cuttyhunk, and examined the north shore of Buzzard's Bay.

IN THEIR OWN

Words

We returned to our ship, where, in fiue or six houres absence, we had pestered our ship so with Cod fish, that we threw numbers of them ouer-boord againe: and surely, I am persuaded that in the moneths of March, April, and May, there is vpon this coast, better fishing, and in as great plentie, as in Newfoundland: *for the sculles of Mackerell, herrings, Cod, and other fish, that we dayly saw as we went and came from the shore, were wonderfull.*

—JOHN BRERETON, *A BRIEF AND TRUE RELATION* OF GOSNOLD'S VOYAGE, 1602

Reaching to the south, Gosnold cruised the mainland coast from West Island to Narragansett Bay, covering an area *Giovanni da Verrazano* had explored in 1525. He set sail for home on June 17 and arrived safely on July 23. One of the *Concord*'s crewmen, John Brereton, published a narrative of the voyage later in 1602. Gosnold encountered some political trouble in England. Gosnold's patron was the Earl of Essex, *Sir Walter Raleigh*'s enemy, and Raleigh accused Gosnold of encroaching on his royal patent.

Commanding the ship *God Speed,* Gosnold carried fifty-two of the original *Jamestown* colonists to the Virginia coast in 1607. He died of malaria in Jamestown on August 22, 1607.

Grenville expeditions (1585, 1586)

A kinsman of *Sir Walter Raleigh,* Richard Grenville (1542–1591) led the second of the *Roanoke Colony* voyages, a follow-up to the *Amadas-Barlowe expedition* to the Outer Banks of North Carolina of 1584. Raleigh aimed to establish a colony in the region he called Virginia to serve as an English foothold in the New World, a base of exploration, and a haven for privateers preying on the Spanish in the Caribbean. With government assistance, he organized a fleet of seven vessels to sail in the spring of 1585. The Royal Navy loaned *Tiger* to the expedition as flagship. Of the 600 men in Grenville's charge, 108 were colonists.

A soldier with little experience at sea, Grenville sailed with the Portuguese navigator Simão Fernandes as fleet pilot in *Tiger.* Raleigh named *Ralph Lane,* like Grenville a veteran of the Irish campaigns, as governor of the colony. He also appointed *Thomas Hariot* as expedition scientist/surveyor and John White as artist-naturalist. Hariot's *A Briefe and True Report of the New Founde Land of Virginia,* published in 1588, would remain an important source of information about North America for a century.

On the strength of the voyages of *Gómes* and *Ayllón,* Spain had established claims to the American coast as far north as the Hudson River. With England and Spain now at war, Grenville's expedition took on elements of a military operation. He would harass Spanish shipping in the Caribbean and challenge Spanish influence north of *Florida.* The fleet sailed from Plymouth on April 9, 1585. Fernandes followed a southerly route, but before the expedition could reach the trade winds, a storm off Portugal scattered the ships and sank one of the pinnaces. *Tiger* pushed on to the Canary Islands and then to the West Indies, raising Dominica in early May. Grenville landed on *Puerto Rico [II],* threw up a temporary fort on shore, and set his shipwrights to building a new pinnace to replace the one lost at sea.

The English cruised the Caribbean in late May in search of Spanish prizes, practicing what in times of peace is known as piracy. *Tiger* and her consorts "fell in with the mayne of Florida" around June 20. Fernandes guided the ship into Pamlico Sound on June 29 and promptly ran it aground. On July 3 Grenville informed the Indians on Roanoke Island that his colonists intended to settle there.

With three small craft, Grenville explored Pamlico Sound. Ranging twenty-five miles to the north, he marched inland as far as the Indian village of Secoton. Doubling back, he ordered the village of Aquascogoc burned and the inhabitants' corn destroyed on suspicion that someone there had stolen a silver cup from him. Grenville's fit of temper would have grim consequences for the colony later on. For now, he returned safely to the ship and sailed for the Port Ferdinando anchorage. One of the Indian chiefs there invited him to plant the colony on nearby Roanoke Island.

Grenville sailed for England in the refloated and repaired *Tiger* in late August and reached Plymouth on October 18. Lane, meantime, established a settlement on Roanoke Island. At first, anyway, he waxed enthusiastic about the place. "If Virginia had but Horses and Kine in some reasonable proportion, I dare assure my selfe, being inhabited with English, no realme in Christendome were comparable to it," Lane wrote. But the ten-mile-long, two-mile-wide island, though fertile and thickly forested, proved to be a poor choice for a colony, as the surrounding waters were shallow and inaccessible to large vessels. Besides, like Grenville, Lane soon managed to alienate the natives. The Roanoke chief Pemisapan and his allies refused to supply the English with food. As the winter advanced, "The famine grewe extreem among us," Lane wrote. He learned, too, that Pemisapan meant to attack and destroy the colony when opportunity presented.

Outnumbered and hungry, Lane decided to launch a preemptive attack on the Indians. He landed with twenty-five men near Pemisapan's village on the night of June 1, 1586, killed and beheaded the chief, then retreated to the colony to await the counterattack. A week later, Lane's lookouts on Croatoan Island reported sighting "a great Fleete of 23 sails" on the horizon. A relief expedition under *Sir Francis Drake [II]* had arrived before the Indians could launch a reprisal. At Lane's request, he and the surviving colonists, 103 in number, were taken aboard Drake's vessels, which sailed for England on June 18, 1586.

When a supply ship from Raleigh arrived two days later, embers of the colonists' fires must have been still warm. Grenville himself reached the Outer Banks with his relief expedition of several ships in mid-July, a few days before Drake's fleet landed the colonists safely in England. Grenville scouted around but found no trace of Lane and his people; he finally learned that they had abandoned the settlement. "Unwilling to loose possession of the countrey," wrote *Richard Hakluyt,* "hee determined to leave some men behind to reteine posession." He landed eighteen men on Roanoke Island with two years' provisions and shaped a course for home, patriotically attacking Spanish shipping and despoiling towns in the Portuguese Azores along the way.

When the next Raleigh colony arrived in 1587, the Roanoke Island garrison had vanished.

Hakluyt, Richard (circa 1551–1616)

A scholar, cleric, and publicist for what he regarded as England's mission to Christianize the natives of North America and develop colonies and markets there, Hakluyt, in works beginning with *Divers Voyages, touching the discoverie of America* (1582), recounted the exploring expeditions of *John Cabot, Verrazano, Ribaut,* and others. His purpose, as he put it, was to shake the insular English out of their "sluggish security."

At *Sir Walter Raleigh's* request, Hakluyt addressed to Queen Elizabeth I a spirited plea for English colonization of North America titled *A*

Discourse on Westerne Planting. America, he argued, would provide a base for explorations for the *Northwest Passage [VII]* and for raids on Spanish possessions in *Florida* and the Caribbean. Settlement there would also create new markets for English goods and supply new products for the home country. The queen obliged in 1584 with a broad colonizing patent for Raleigh; Sir Philip Sidney later called Hakluyt "a very good Trumpet" for the courtier.

In 1589 Hakluyt began publishing *The Principall Navigations, Voyages, Traffiques and Discoveries of the English Nation,* a "prose epic" that presents firsthand narratives of exploration and colonization in America, including the voyages of John Cabot, *Sir Humphrey Gilbert,* and *Martin Frobisher [VII].* The work, published in an expanded three-volume edition in 1598–1600, was of major importance in touching off and sustaining English interest in the New World.

Hakluyt campaigned for the search for a Northwest Passage and, in 1600, became an adviser to the newly established East India Company. He declined (or was unable) to accept an appointment as rector of the *Jamestown,* Virginia, colony in 1607. Hakluyt is buried in Westminster Abbey, London.

Samuel Purchas in 1625 saw some of Hakluyt's unpublished material into print as *Hakluytus Posthumous, or Purchas his Pilgrimes, contayning a History of the World in Sea Voyages and Land trevell by Englishmen and others.*

Hariot, Thomas   (1560–1621)

Born in Oxford, England, and a graduate of the university there, Hariot tutored *Sir Walter Raleigh* in math. Raleigh rewarded his labors with an appointment as surveyor on the first of the *Grenville expeditions* to the Outer Banks of North Carolina in 1585.

The assignment yielded Hariot's *Briefe and True Report of the New Founde Land of Virginia,* published in 1588. The British *Dictionary of National Biography* calls it "one of the earliest examples of a statistical survey on a large scale," and it remained an important source of information about North America for more than a century.

Richard Hakluyt included Hariot's *Report* in the third edition of his *Voyages,* published in 1600.

Hochelaga

Jacques Cartier reached this *Huron* Indian capital on the site of present *Montreal [V]*, Quebec, on October 3, 1534, during the second of his three voyages of discovery. Cartier found a wooden citadel protecting a circular village of roughly fifty bark and wood longhouses with a population of 1,500. Open fields planted in maize (corn) surrounded the town, and the inhabitants cultivated the slopes of an eminence Cartier named Mont Royal.

Hore, Richard   (?–?)

A London leather merchant, Hore chartered two ships in 1536 and sailed from Gravesend for *Newfoundland* on April 19. Hore's purposes were to exploit the Grand Banks codfishery and to carry a group of Londoners on a tourist cruise. Historian D. B. Quinn suggests the voyage had some political purpose as a follow-up to French discoveries in Canada.

Hore reached the south coast of Newfoundland after a difficult two-month voyage. Provisions soon ran short, starvation claimed several lives, and there were a number of incidents of cannibalism. The chronicler *Richard Hakluyt* interviewed the last survivor of Hore's voyage and provided vivid details. "Here and there the fellow killed his mate while he stopped to take up a root for his relief," Hakluyt wrote, "and cutting out pieces of his body who he had murdered broiled the same on the coals and greedily devoured them."

The English were saved by the arrival of a French vessel, which they promptly boarded, captured, and ransacked. The survivors reached England in their ship, *William*, and the pirated French ship in late October. Hore had probably carried out an examination of part of the Newfoundland coast in July and August, but he returned home with little new information.

Huron

The Huron Indians, numbering from 16,000 to 30,000 at the beginning of the eighteenth century, occupied some eighteen often palisaded villages in the *St. Lawrence River* valley and in Huronia, between Georgian Bay and

Lake Ontario. As the region's most important traders, they also monopolized corn and tobacco exchanges and charged tolls for the use of their trails.

The Huron Confederacy consisted of four or five Northern Iroquoian-speaking tribes, most of whom probably came originally from the Mississippi Valley. European contact occurred in 1534 with *Cartier* and in 1609 with *Champlain,* for whom the Hurons acted as guides and as intermediaries to other tribes. Their longtime enmity with the *Iroquois,* who used Dutch firearms and were allied with the English, reached its climax in 1648 and ended with their total defeat two years later.

Fleeing in all directions, some Hurons joined other bands, including the Eries and even the Iroquois. Those reaching Green Bay remained active in the fur trade, and around 1700 they moved to the Detroit area. Around 1750 the group that claimed the lands north of the *Ohio River [V]* in Ohio and Michigan became known as the Wyandot. By the mid-nineteenth century, most Wyandots had ceded these lands and departed for the Kansas Indian Territory. Of them, a large group relocated in 1867 to the new Indian Territory of Oklahoma.

Ingram, David (?–?)

With two others, the castaway Englishman David Ingram in 1568–1569 performed the extraordinary feat of walking from the Gulf of Mexico to Nova Scotia. On October 8, 1568, English privateer John Hawkins marooned 114 sailors just north of Tampico, Mexico, following a disastrous battle with Spanish ships near Veracruz. The men, starving and unarmed, split into two groups, with half heading south toward Tampico.

IN THEIR OWN *Words*

He hathe travayled in those Countryes from beyonde terra florida extendinge towardes the Cape Britton about eleaven moneths in the whole. . . . In which tyme as the said Ingram thincketh he travayled by land 2000 myles at the leaste, and never contynued in any one place above 3 or 4. daies savinge onlye at the Cittie of Balma where he stayed VI or VII daies.

—DAVID INGRAM, ON HIS TREK ALONG THE ATLANTIC COAST, 1569

Those who survived devastating Indian attacks were eventually imprisoned by the Spanish in Mexico; some of these later lost their lives to the Inquisition in 1575. Of the group heading north, Ingram and his companions Richard Twide and Richard Browne survived to reach safety and freedom eventually.

Using Indian trails, they probably followed the gulf coast to the Río Grande and then trekked inland through Alabama and Georgia, passing near *Florida*'s St. John's River. The descriptions in Ingram's narrative are difficult to tie to a definitive itinerary, but they then apparently followed the Atlantic coast, for the most part, north to New Brunswick, Canada. There they traded pearls they had gathered along the way for passage on a French ship and reached England by the end of 1569.

Ingram wrote a fanciful and confusing account of their journey that *Richard Hakluyt* published in *Principall Navigations* but omitted from the second edition because of its incredible nature. Yet for all his embroideries and exaggerations, Ingram is generally credited with having made the journey he recounted.

Jamestown

The first permanent English settlement on the North American mainland, established in 1607 on the James River in southeastern Virginia, Jamestown served as a base for explorations west into the interior of Virginia and north into *Chesapeake Bay.*

In May 1607 Captain *John Smith* and Christopher Newport pushed up the James as far as the falls above present-day Richmond. Smith led a small exploring party up the Chickahominy River in December, the occasion of his famous capture and three-month imprisonment in the country of Powhatan.

Smith extensively explored the Chesapeake in 1608 and produced a detailed and accurate map of the bay and its estuaries. The Jamestown colony, however, failed to prosper and was eventually abandoned.

Jerome and Rocque expedition (1604–1605)

In January 1604 King Henry IV of France issued to Guillaume de la Mothe and Bertrand Rocque, mariners from Saint-Malo, a patent to trade along the Atlantic coast of the Americas between the Amazon River and Cape Breton in defiance of Spain's claims. This unusual Anglo-French exploring and trading expedition, financed in part by the London-based Channel Islander Pierre Beauvoir, sailed from Plymouth, England, with John Jerome as captain of the *Castor and Pollux* and Rocque as captain of the *Pollux and Castor.*

In the Caribbean, they substituted a small Spanish ship for Jerome's *Castor and Pollux.* While there, they loaded tobacco and maize to trade along the Carolina coast in the Santa Elena region. They also had with them weapons and tools for barter with the Indians. Aboard was a French herbal expert to lead their search for medicinal plants. They were to search as well for other trade resources and for minerals, in particular for mines on Maine's Penobscot River and a reported copper mine in *Acadia* (Nova Scotia).

While sailing up the *Florida* coast, Jerome and Roque were spotted by the Spanish on February 3, 1605, near St. Augustine. Continuing north, they collected china root, sassafras, and pelts and looked for milkweed, the pod of which was believed to be a valuable new source of textile fiber. Their orders included a stop at Croatoan off Virginia to contact the lost members of the *Roanoke Colony* before proceeding to Penobscot Bay and the Bay of Fundy.

The expedition as planned was never completed. Near Cumberland Island off southern Georgia, Indians attacked and killed Jerome and his pilot; some of his men continued north in the small vessel. By March 5, 1605, three Spanish ships under *Francisco Fernández de Écija* captured the *Castor and Pollux* and the rest of the expedition in St. Helena Sound. He turned most of the prisoners over to the Indians for slaves or sacrifice and returned Rocque and a few others to St. Augustine for interrogation. Spain used the incident to discourage further French and English exploration of the Atlantic region.

Labrador

A harsh, forbidding peninsula of eastern Canada lying across the Strait of Belle Isle from *Newfoundland,* Labrador long remained unexplored and unmapped except for its long and deeply indented Atlantic coastline. Bands of native peoples occupied its rugged terrain as long ago as 5000

B.C. The Vikings may have landed along the coast of Labrador about A.D. 1000, and it may be the *Markland [I]* of the *Norse [I]* sagas.

English mariner *John Rut* sailed as far north along Labrador's coast as 53°, present Hawke Bay, in 1527. Basque whalers established a station at Red Bay before *Jacques Cartier* explored the south coast in 1535–1536. Unimpressed, Cartier called Labrador "the land God gave to Cain." Portuguese explorers and fishermen followed Cartier. One, *João Fernandes,* a *lavrador* or landowner at home, gave Labrador its name.

Later explorers neglected Labrador for more promising country. Finally, in 1828, *Hudson's Bay Company [VI]* agent William Hentry penetrated the interior of the Labrador peninsula. The journeys of Eland Erlandson in 1834 and John McLean in 1839 further examined the hinterland. Following the course of the Grand River, McLean came upon a "stupendous fall" greater in height than Niagara— present Churchill Falls.

> ## IN THEIR OWN *Words*
>
> *There we found many great Ilands of Ice and deepe water, we found no sounding, and then we durst go no further to the Northward for feare of more ice.*
>
> —JOHN RUT ON LABRADOR, LETTER OF 1527

Lane, Ralph

(1530?–1603)

A protégé of *Sir Walter Raleigh,* Lane commanded the first large-scale colonial expedition to the Outer Banks of North Carolina, landing on Roanoke Island with more than a hundred settlers in August 1585. (See *Grenville expeditions.*)

Lane oversaw the building of a fort and established trading and supply links with the Indians. Over the winter of 1585–1586, he led parties that explored north and west into Pamlico and Albemarle Sounds and penetrated mainland estuaries. One expedition pushed as far north as the southern end of *Chesapeake Bay.*

A clumsy diplomat, Lane managed to arouse Indian hostility. Trouble with the natives and internal discord doomed the colony, and Lane and 103 survivors took ship for home in the spring of 1586. A second attempt to settle in 1587 ended in the destruction of the colony; the fate of the settlers is unknown to this day. (See *Roanoke Colony.*)

Lederer, John

A German physician, Lederer explored inland Virginia as far as the *Blue Ridge Mountains* in 1670. In March he pushed west from the headwaters of the York River toward the distant Blue Ridge, which he glimpsed from an "Eminent Hill." In August, in search of the South Sea (the Pacific Ocean), Lederer ascended the Blue Ridge. Looking across the Shenandoah Valley, he saw not the glint of a broad ocean but rather the distant peaks of the *Appalachian Mountains [V]*.

Lederer speculated that beyond the mountain barrier "we may imagine some great arm of the Indian Ocean or Bay [stretching] into the Continent towards the Apalataen Mountains into the nature of a mid-land sea." He published an account of his travels, *Discoveries,* in 1672.

Luna y Arellano, Tristán de   (?–?)

Second in command to *Coronado [II]* in the Spanish expedition into the American Southwest of 1540–1542, in the late 1550s Luna y Arellano won appointment as *Florida* governor with orders to start a settlement on the gulf coast and to travel overland through Coosa (a prosperous chiefdom stretching from central Alabama to eastern Tennessee) to establish a second Spanish base at Punta Santa Elena at Tybee Island near the site of Savannah, Georgia.

Luna sailed from Veracruz, Mexico, on June 11, 1559, with eleven ships carrying some 1,500 people. After a stop at Cape San Blas (south of Panama City, Florida), the fleet landed at Mobile Bay before finally finding Pensacola Bay. After selecting a town site, Luna sent an expedition north to explore the Escambia River. On September 19 a hurricane destroyed seven ships with most of the provisions aboard and killed many colonists. A second expedition north found the deserted Indian village of Nanicapana (in Monroe County, Alabama, near *de Soto*'s 1540 battle site) and recommended it as a settlement site.

By mid-February 1560 Luna began to relocate most of his group inland by way of Mobile Bay to Santa María de Nanicapana. From there Luna sent two expeditions north to Coosa for food supplies. While the second was still in progress, the starving and increasingly mutinous colonists returned to Pensacola, and from there moved on to Mobile Bay. On August 10 Luna sent three ships to Punta Santa Elena by way of Havana; another hurricane aborted this mission. By November the Coosa expedition was back at Pensacola for the difficult winter of 1560–1561.

After the appointment of *Ángel de Villafañe* to replace Luna as Florida governor and expedition leader, Luna sailed to Havana en route to Spain to answer charges about his performance. Villafañe, as it happened, had no better success than Luna in establishing a Spanish presence in the Carolinas.

Luna's failure, a costly one for the crown, resulted from bad luck, weak leadership, inadequate resupply efforts, and internal dissent fueled by disease and starvation. The failure also derived from mistaken Spanish ideas about the region's geography, particularly in underestimating the distances to northern Mexico and to the Georgia coast.

Martyr, Peter (Pietro Martire d'Anghiera) (1457–1526)

A Milanese official at the Spanish court of Ferdinand and Isabella, Peter Martyr wrote a history of the early Spanish explorations in the New World, with an account of the discovery of America, *De Orbe Novo,* published beginning in 1511.

Richard Eden translated the work into English as *The Decades of the Newe Worlde or West India* in 1555. Chronicler **Richard Hakluyt** prepared a new version of Eden's work in 1587. Peter Martyr's history inspired English explorers of the Elizabethan Age and augmented their knowledge of navigation. He also provided details of **Sebastian Cabot**'s little-understood North Atlantic voyage of 1508—details he had gotten from Cabot himself, whom he knew well in Spain in 1512–1515.

Menéndez de Avilés, Pedro (1519–1574)

A Spanish naval commander and sometime privateer, Pedro Menéndez de Avilés obtained a royal contract for the exploration and settlement of La *Florida,* a vast territory extending from the northern gulf coast to the upper Atlantic coast.

After sailing from Spain by way of **Puerto Rico [II]**, Menéndez arrived off Florida's Atlantic shore on August 28, 1565, with five ships carrying some eight hundred persons. There he founded St. Augustine, while at the same time brutally killing, capturing, and driving out the French under Philip II's orders. (See **Ribaut and Laudonnière expeditions.**) He seized their Fort Caroline, forty miles to the north on the St. John's River, and renamed it San Mateo; it became his second settlement.

Next he began to explore the region while forging alliances with various Indian leaders and establishing a chain of coastal forts and missions from Tampa Bay to South Carolina's Port Royal Sound. He also searched for a water passage across peninsular Florida and a passage from **Chesapeake Bay** to the Pacific Ocean and sought to open a route to northern Mexico's mining district—plans based on mistaken Spanish concepts of North American geography.

In November 1565 Menéndez surveyed southward along Florida's Atlantic coast before sailing to Havana for the winter. In February 1566 he located a passage between the Tortugas and the Marquesas and sailed on to explore Florida's lower gulf shore. After dealing with mutinies caused by food shortages at St. Augustine and San Mateo, he examined the Georgia coast and Sea Islands, marking St. Catherines Island with its Guale Indian villages as a future colonization site, and continued on to Punta Santa Elena and Port Royal Sound, where by April 1566 he founded on Parris Island the settlement of Santa Elena.

After returning south, in early August he sent an expedition under Pedro de Coronas from San Mateo to Chesapeake Bay. By August 14 Coronas reached Maryland's Chincoteague Bay, and after a storm caused him to again miss the opening of the Chesapeake to the south, he explored the Outer Banks, probably at North Carolina's Currituck Sound.

At Santa Elena, Menéndez ordered **Juan Pardo** to explore inland; his two treks from 1566 to 1568 would penetrate central South Carolina, southwestern North Carolina, and eastern Tennessee in an attempt to reach Coosa, a prosperous chiefdom extending into central Alabama.

IN THEIR OWN *Words*

It is just a waste of time in a place like this to think of establishing the Holy Gospels here with soldiers alone. Your honor should be sure that, unless I am much mistaken, the Word of Our Lord will spread in these areas. For most of the ceremonies of [the Florida Indian tribes] involve worshipping the sun and the moon, and they use dead game animals as idols, and other animals too.

—PEDRO MENÉNDEZ DE AVILÉS TO A JESUIT FRIEND, OCTOBER 15, 1566

During the summer of 1566, Menéndez also ascended the St. John's River, crossing Lake George before turning back when the river narrowed and the Indians became hostile.

Menéndez returned to Spain in 1567–1568 to seek support for his faltering enterprise. Indians rose in rebellion during that time against most of his forts and missions, and the colonists continued to suffer starvation. Diminished exploration efforts accompanied a short-lived Jesuit mission at Chesapeake in 1570. In 1572, on his way to Spain again, Menéndez sailed to Chesapeake to punish the Indians responsible for the Jesuits' deaths. He assigned Diego de Velasco to make a survey of the area, probably limited to the York Peninsula.

Menéndez never returned; he died in Spain a poor man. Before his demise, he ordered his nephew and successor Pedro Menéndez Marquez on an extensive 1573 survey of the Florida coast from the keys north to Chesapeake: This venture called for the meticulous recording of depths, distances, shoals, bars, bays, rivers, and sailing directions, capped by an exploration of Chesapeake Bay. In the end, the grand enterprise disintegrated. Only St. Augustine survived the depredations of starvation and hostile Indians.

Needham and Arthur expedition   (1673)

This expedition, one of three in the 1670s that sought to open trade routes with the Indians beyond the Appalachians, set out from Fort Henry at the falls of the Appomattox near present Petersburg, Virginia, in May 1673. Traveling southwest, James Needham, with a young illiterate named Gabriel Arthur and eight Indian guides, reached the Yadkin River after a journey of nine days. Beyond the Yadkin, the party struck due west and through the *Blue Ridge Mountains.* A fifteen-day march brought Needham and company to a Cherokee village near the headwaters of the Tennessee River.

Needham here turned back for Virginia, leaving Arthur with the Indians. After a refit at Fort Henry, Needham set out in September with an Indian guide hired for him by the expedition sponsor, Colonel *Abraham Wood.* The guide murdered Needham en route.

"Soe died this heroick English man whose fame shall never die if my penn were able to eternize it, which had adventured where never any English man had dared to atempt before," wrote Wood.

Arthur ranged with Indian raiding parties from the Ohio River as far south as *Florida* before returning safely to Fort Henry in June 1674.

Newfoundland

Scholars now generally accept that the *Norse [I]* remains at *L'Anse aux Meadows [I]* on the northern tip of Newfoundland attest to the earliest known settlement of Europeans in the Americas. After they abandoned this site—probably around A.D. 1015—Newfoundland pretty much vanished from the consciousness of Europeans, although scholars suspect that some Norse from *Greenland [I]* may well have put ashore for occasional and brief visits.

It is not until the 1490s that Newfoundland reemerges in the pages of recorded European history. In 1497 *John Cabot* made his first landfall in the New World, possibly near Cape Degrat at the northern tip of Newfoundland. (If so, this was only about five miles overland from L'Anse aux Meadows.) Alternatively, his first landfall may have been on the coast of Cape Breton, Nova Scotia. In any case, for the next twenty-five days, Cabot sailed down and then back up the eastern coast of Newfoundland (or Nova Scotia), but he did not go ashore again during that entire time; he may have been afraid of confronting hostile natives, the *Beothuks* (although he makes no mention of them). In any case, Cabot reported the plentiful cod and tall trees that "New Island" offered.

Rewarded on his return by King Henry VII, Cabot set off on his second voyage in May 1498 with five ships; only one returned, and John Cabot vanished at sea. But Cabot's "New Island" became known to Europeans and began to appear on maps as early as 1506, although at first it was depicted as an extension of the continent of Asia. (In 1502, Henry VII first referred to the island as "the new founde lande," which before long became "Newfoundland.") Almost immediately after word of Cabot's discovery spread across Europe, French and Portuguese fishermen began to appear off the coast of Newfoundland as well as Nova Scotia. One historian has claimed that English fishermen were fishing off Newfoundland as early as 1498, but 1502 for Portuguese fishermen and 1504 for French fishermen are the more accepted early dates.

Although the French navigator *Jacques Cartier* explored the coast in 1534, *Sir Humphrey Gilbert* claimed Newfoundland for England in 1583, and the first English settlers arrived in 1610. From that point on, Newfoundland gradually revealed its terrain and resources to the spreading inhabitants.

New France

France designated its possessions in Canada—*Acadia,* Quebec, and the interior of the west—New France. *Jacques Cartier* claimed all of Canada for France during his voyage of exploration in 1534.

The explorer *Samuel de Champlain* founded a fortress-settlement at Quebec in 1608 with a view to colonization of the *St. Lawrence River* valley. He and his supporters pressed for a formal French presence to promote trade and settlement of the region. New France duly became a royal province in 1663.

Britain obtained title to France's holdings in Canada at the close of the Seven Years' War in 1763.

Norumbega (Oranbega, Norembèque)

Giovanni da Verrazano in 1524 appropriated Norumbega, a word of *Abenaki* origin translated as "a stretch of still water between rapids," to describe a place on the Penobscot River of Maine. His cartographer brother Girolamo da Verrazano showed "Oranbega" on his map of 1529.

Later writers magnified the Verrazanos' Norumbega to encompass a vast region between the Hudson and *St. Lawrence Rivers.* They imagined a sumptuous city on the Penobscot, also called Norumbega, as capital of the empire. "The inhabitants of this country are docile people, friendly and peaceful," a French chronicler wrote in 1545. "The land overflows with every kind of fruit; there grow the wholesome orange and the almond, and many sweet smelling trees." Another writer said the inhabitants were tall and fair, spoke words that sounded like Latin, and worshipped the sun.

Simão Fernandes, a Portuguese in English service, and John Walker scouted the Penobscot in separate voyages for *Sir Humphrey Gilbert* in 1579–1580. They returned with a description of the Penobscot estuary but made no mention of a city filled with gold, silver, and pearls. In any event, Gilbert chose not to sail in search of Norumbega.

Samuel de Champlain finally debunked the Norumbega myth. He sailed up the Penobscot as far as the site of Bangor in 1604 and reported that he found no city or town at all, much less a rich and sophisticated native capital.

Oldham, John   (1600?–1636)

The English-born colonist and trader John Oldham arrived in July 1623 in Plymouth, from which he was expelled the following year. After trading at Nantasket and Cape Ann with New England's coastal Indians, he later moved to Watertown in the Massachusetts Bay Colony.

Responding to a 1631 Indian delegation, Oldham and three others made the first overland journey in 1633 to the Connecticut River. On this trading expedition, he stayed at Indian villages and noted sites suitable for settlement. In 1632 Plymouth's Edward Winslow had sent Lieutenant William Holmes to ascend the Connecticut River, resulting in the September 1633 founding of a Plymouth trading post at Windsor, just north of the Dutch Fort Good Hope (at Hartford) founded in June 1633.

Oldham's 1636 murder by Indians, as he returned from a trading trip to Block Island, was one of the causes of the Pequot War of 1637.

Pardo, Juan   (?–?)

Juan Pardo arrived from Spain in mid-July 1566, landing with a company of 250 men at Santa Elena off Port Royal Sound, South Carolina. *Menéndez de Avilés,* who had recently founded the settlement, instructed Pardo to explore the interior, pacify and evangelize the Indians, and find a route to the silver mines at Zacatecas in northern Mexico.

Pardo struck out in a northeasterly direction on December 1, 1566, along an Indian trail between the Coosawatchie and Salkehatchie Rivers. He entered North Carolina just west of Charlotte and eventually reached the Marion area in the foothills of the *Blue Ridge Mountains.* There at the Indian town of Joara he built Fort San Juan and left Hernando Moyano (Boyano) in charge. Pardo then followed the Catawba River to near Salisbury, North Carolina, before turning back to Santa Elena, which he reached on March 7, 1567.

On a mission against Chiaco warriors, Moyano left San Juan in early April along a trail that led into northeastern Tennessee. His route may have taken him to the upper Nolichucky River near present Embreeville, and on to Olamico, the Chiaha chiefdom's main town on an island (now under Douglas Lake) in the French Broad River near Dandridge, Tennessee.

On September 1, 1567, Pardo set out on a second expedition, generally following the route of his first one and keeping detailed records of the terrain, hydrology, flora, fauna, and other natural resources, along with sites suitable for future towns. From San Juan he continued to Olamico, and from there set out on October 13 on a southwesterly course for Coosa (a prosperous chiefdom extending from eastern Tennessee to central Alabama). After following the Little Tennessee River to Satapo, he returned by a different trail ("The Great Indian Warpath"), reaching Olamico on October 20. He continued back, erecting five forts along the way and surveying for mineral and gemstone deposits, and arrived at Santa Elena on March 2, 1568.

Although Pardo failed to reach Zacatecas, he gathered useful knowledge about eastern Tennessee, western North Carolina, and central South Carolina. There was no follow-up to his explorations, and his forts soon fell to Indian attacks.

IN THEIR OWN *Words*

I set off toward Zacatecas and the silver mines of San Martín. I went three days through open country, and after three days I arrived at a town whose name I do not remember, and I assembled the chiefs and Indians and gave them the usual talk, and they replied to me that they were ready to do what His Holiness and His Majesty ordered and that they were willing to be Christian; this land is very good, and I think there are metals in it of gold and silver.

—JUAN PARDO ON HIS EXPEDITIONS INTO THE SOUTH CAROLINA INTERIOR, 1566–1567

Ponce de León, Juan   (1474–1521)

Of noble Spanish birth and a veteran of the Moorish wars, de León arrived in the New World on the second voyage of *Christopher Columbus [II]*. Between 1502 and 1504 he led the Spanish to victory over the Indians in the Higuey, the eastern province of *Hispaniola [II]*, and was rewarded with an appointment as governor. He shifted to *Puerto Rico [II]* in 1508 and, after conquering it, was appointed governor (1509–1512) there; during these years he became wealthy from dealing in gold and slaves.

Hearing reports of a rich island known as Bimini, de León in 1512 obtained a crown license to discover, conquer, and settle the island. Whether he sought the fabled "Fountain of Youth" there is a matter of debate. On March 4, 1513, he set out from Puerto Rico with three ships and *Antonio de Alaminos* as pilot and sailed northwest following the outer Bahamas, then known as the Lucayos. Instead of Bimini, he found a larger landmass that he took to be an island, where he landed on April 2, naming it La *Florida* after the Easter holiday the Spanish called "Pascua Florida."

Owing to latitude errors, his landing site is a matter of controversy: It may have been near Ponce de León Inlet at what is today New Smyrna Beach. He sailed north on April 8 but soon turned back to follow the coast south. The first natives he encountered near Cape Canaveral attacked; they may have heard tales of Spanish slave raiders. On May 13 he sighted what was probably Biscayne Bay and continued along the Florida Keys, or Los Mártires.

Ponce de León probably passed the Marquesas Keys around May 23 and turned north to approach Florida's gulf coast. Again, his May 27 landing site there remains uncertain. Charlotte Harbor is a popular choice, while other historians place it at Tampa Bay, Apalachee Bay, and even Pensacola Bay; recently a good case has been made for the area between Cape Sable and Cape Romano, perhaps even at Ponce de León Bay. After an Indian attack there, he sailed on June 14 for the Dry Tortugas Islands. After a side trip to western *Cuba [II]* (not to the Yucatan, as some believe), he sailed back along the Keys to Miami Beach and from there toward the Bahamas, where he surveyed Grand Bahama Island. Before he returned to Puerto Rico on February 20, 1514, he sent one ship to search for the elusive Bimini.

Ponce de León soon obtained a royal license to settle and govern the new Florida territory, but was unable to return until early 1521. Seriously wounded in an Indian attack along the gulf coast, he retreated to Cuba to die in July, unaware that Florida was not an island but the tip of a new continent. His voyages were responsible for moving Spanish exploration into the gulf's northern coastal regions. The discovery of the Gulf Stream and other hydrological observations are credited to his pilot Alaminos.

Quejo (Quexos), Pedro de   (?–?)

While on a fruitless hunt in 1521 to seize Indians as slaves in the Bahamas, Pedro de Quejo met up with Francisco Gordillo, who was on the same mission for *Lucas Vásquez de Ayllón* and his Santo Domingo partners.

Agreeing to search together, Quejo and Gordillo set out from Andros Island on June 15, 1521, and sailed north for eight days, arriving on the South Carolina coast and anchoring in the South Santee River. Moving their ships to adjacent Winyah Bay on June 28, first Gordillo and then Quejo took possession of the land for their respective employers. For two weeks they explored, visited villages of proto-Cherokee Indians, traded for freshwater pearls, and possibly visited Charleston Harbor.

After luring aboard some sixty Indians, they set sail on July 15 south from the region, which they named Chicora. During the voyage back, a disagreement with his pilot led Gordillo to move over to Quejo's ship; his own ship never made it back.

Their joint discovery led Ayllón to obtain, in 1523, a crown grant to colonize the area between latitude 35° and 37° within three years. In 1525 Ayllón sent Quejo, now in his employ, on a reconnaissance of the Atlantic coast, from approximately 30°40' to 39°40'. On May 3, Quejo landed at the Savannah River and on May 9 reached his 1521 landing site of Chicora. He then sailed to the Cape Fear River, which he named Río de Arrecifes (river of reefs). Returning to the Savannah River, he sailed south until May 22, when he reached the tip of Amelia Island off *Florida*'s northern border.

There Quejo turned back north to seek Ayllón's upper limit, and by June 24 he reached Delaware Bay, which he entered. Turning back south, he briefly entered *Chesapeake Bay,* passed Cape Hatteras, and completed his survey on July 10 midway between Cape Lookout and Wilmington, North Carolina. Erecting stone markers of possession at various sites, he completed a meticulous record of coastal soundings and bearings, surveyed the natural resources, and tried to encourage Chicora natives to cultivate European seeds. Though the mostly sandy coastal pine barrens seemed less than promising, he had assembled vital information for Ayllón's next step—Spanish settlement of the Carolinas.

Raleigh, Sir Walter (circa 1552–1618)

A favorite of Queen Elizabeth I, Raleigh exploited the royal connection to launch a series of attempts to plant an English colony on the east coast of North America in present North Carolina. Raleigh named the vast region he hoped to settle Virginia, in honor of England's virgin queen.

Elizabeth's preferment carried a price: Raleigh had to remain in England to play the courtier, entrusting his ample domain—in effect, the Atlantic coast from the Carolinas to Nova Scotia—to surrogates. He organized expeditions that explored the coast from *Florida* to North Carolina, established a colony on Roanoke Island, North Carolina, that failed in 1587 or 1588, and made equally unsuccessful attempts to colonize what is today Virginia. He never managed to visit his American "holdings."

Though his settlement efforts failed, Raleigh did succeed in introducing potatoes and tobacco to the British Isles. In his later career he fell into disfavor with Elizabeth's successor, James I. Stripped of his estates and charged with conspiring against the king, Raleigh suffered confinement in the Tower of London, where he wrote the first (and only) volume of his *History of the World* (1614). James released him in 1616 to search for gold along the Orinoco River of South America. The expedition proved little short of a disaster—storms and shipwreck, desertions, disease—and he returned with virtually nothing to show for his efforts.

Raleigh was beheaded at Westminster under his original sentence on October 29, 1618.

Ribaut and Laudonnière expeditions   (1562–1565)

With discouraging reports of settlement prospects along the *St. Lawrence River* of Canada, French explorer-colonists turned their attention to the south toward Spanish *Florida.* Jean Ribaut sailed from Dieppe with 150 Huguenot colonists in 1562 and, after exploring the coast north from St. Augustine, found "one of the greatest and fairest havens" at Port Royal, South Carolina. But the settlers of Charlesfort returned to France discouraged two years later.

IN THEIR OWN
Words

We discovered and clearly perceaved a faire cost, stretching of a gret length, covered with an infenite number of highe and fayre trees . . . the country seming to us playn, without any shewe of hills.
—JEAN RIBAUT, TO GASPARD DE COLIGNY FROM THE FLORIDA COAST, APRIL 1563

In 1564 René de Laudonnière led a second exploring/colonizing expedition, also Protestant, to Florida, building Fort Caroline at the mouth of the St. John's River. He dispatched exploring parties into the interior in search of precious metals and a route to the fabled Cibola pueblos in present Arizona. (See *legendary destinations [II]*.)

Jealous of their claims, the Spanish sent a fleet under *Pedro Menéndez de Avilés* to destroy the French. He attacked the fort and massacred the "heretical" French defenders, among them Ribaut himself, who had turned up to rescue Laudonnière's colonists.

Gallorum ad Maij flumen navigatio. II.

In this Théodore de Bry engraving, the expedition of French explorer/colonizer Jean Ribaut enters the River of May (St. John's River) in Florida in 1562. Ribaut built a stone column at the site of his Florida landing, claiming the area for France. René de Laudonnière's larger expedition of 1563, made up of French Protestants fleeing persecution at home, found Ribaut's marker and established an outpost there. Spanish forces destroyed the French settlement in 1565.

Roanoke Colony

With the return to England of the first contingent of Roanoke Island colonists in 1586, *Sir Walter Raleigh* immediately began to plan for a second attempt to establish a settlement on the east coast of North America. Raleigh named John White, the artist on the 1585 expedition, governor of the new venture and directed him to find a site on *Chesapeake Bay.*

The second effort involved women and children—counting unattached people, there were eighty-nine men, seventeen women, and eleven children. Among the colonists were Ananias Dare and his pregnant wife, Eleanor White Dare, the governor's daughter. Assembled at Plymouth, the flotilla consisted of the *Lion* of Richard *Grenville*'s 1585 voyage as flagship and two smaller vessels, a flyboat and a pinnace. The expedition weighed anchor on May 8, 1587, and raised Dominica in the Windward Islands on June 19. After stops at St. Croix, Virgin Islands, and *Puerto Rico [II]* and a few weeks' privateering in the Caribbean, the flotilla reached Roanoke Island on July 22.

Here the fleet pilot Simão Fernandes ordered a change in Raleigh's plan, which called for White to make his "seate and forte in the Baye of Chesapiok." He put the colonists ashore at Roanoke with instructions to build on the remains of *Ralph Lane*'s settlement, where several cottages still stood. The fort had been demolished, though, and White discovered within a week that relations with the natives had not improved with the passage of time. Indians murdered one of the colonists on July 28 as he fished for crabs.

The governor sailed to Croatoan Island off Cape Hatteras to try to "renew our old freindshippe" with the Indians. The Croatoans fled at first, but White explained through the Hatteras Indian Manteo that the English had come "to live with them as brethren, and friendes." He set a date a week hence for a parley, and when the Indians failed to turn up, he decided he had waited long enough to avenge the murder of one of his colonists. White's attack on a mainland village misfired, however, as it turned out to harbor Indians friendly to the English.

On August 18 Eleanor Dare delivered a daughter, Virginia, the first European on record as being born in America. A second child was born at Roanoke a few days later. Meantime, White, at the colonists' urging, prepared to return home to act as agent for the nascent settlement. He sailed on August 27 and reached England after a difficult voyage via the Dingle Peninsula, Ireland, in early November to find the island in a state of alarm over an expected Spanish invasion. With the Spanish threat looming, Raleigh had little choice but to leave the colonists to their own devices.

Raleigh eventually organized two expeditions to relieve what came to be known as the "Lost Colony." Despite the threat of the Spanish Armada, he managed to outfit the bark *Brave* and the pinnace *Roe* and see them off with supplies and Governor White aboard on April 22, 1588.

Two more powerful French ships attacked and plundered the English vessels and forced them to return to England. There matters stood until the spring of 1590, when Raleigh organized a flotilla under the command of John Watts for the last of the Roanoke Voyages. Two ships and a pinnace sailed from Plymouth on March 20, with a bark and a pinnace to follow.

With bad weather, the combined fleet did not raise Cape Hatteras until August 9. Watts finally reached Roanoke Island on the seventeenth.

Wrote White, "We let fall our Grapnel neere the shore, & sounded with a trumpet a Call, & afterwardes many familiar english tunes of songs, and called to them friendly; but we had no answere."

The fort and houses were deserted and ruined; contents of chests lay littered about, including three of White's own; the word *Croatoan* was carved on a post near the entrance to the settlement. There were no human remains. White proposed going to Croatoan Island, hoping the colonists had found refuge with friendly Hatteras Indians there, but a storm blew up and forced Watts to take the fleet to sea. The expedition reached Plymouth on October 24 with no word of the Lost Colony.

The fate of the colonists is a mystery to this day. They may have all been killed; a legend persists that they fled the coast and eventually assimilated with an inland tribe, possibly the Lumbees.

Roberval, Sieur de (1500?–1560)

In January 1541 King *François I* of France gave Jean-François de la Roque, Sieur de Roberval, authority over Canadian lands that *Jacques Cartier* had explored during his first two voyages to the *St. Lawrence River.* The king made Roberval the overall commander of Cartier's third expedition and ordered him to establish a settlement on the St. Lawrence and to make a priority of converting the Indians.

Cartier had sailed a year before Roberval, and the latter never managed to exert any authority over the former. In fact, when the homeward-bound Cartier encountered Roberval with three ships at anchor in St. John harbor, *Newfoundland,* in June 1543, he, Cartier, refused Roberval's order to return to Canada.

Roberval proceeded up the St. Lawrence on his own to pursue the search for the mythical kingdom of *Saguenay.* The flotilla dropped anchor in late July off Cartier's abandoned Charlesbourg-Royal. He renamed the place France-Roy and built a fortified camp near the Charlesbourg site.

In mid-September Roberval sent two of his vessels home and prepared to winter over at France-Roy. An estimated fifty colonists died of scurvy during the winter, perhaps a third of his total complement. Roberval began his search for Saguenay in early June 1544, advancing upstream with seventy men in eight boats. One boat was lost with eight men drowned. Roberval decided not to advance beyond the Rapids of Lachine above *Montreal [V]* and turned back for France-Roy.

Roberval decided later in the summer to abandon the France-Roy settlement and return home. With his return to Europe, the dream of fabled Saguenay died.

Rut, John   (?–?)

Bristol [I] merchants may have inspired John Rut's 1527 voyage in search of the *Northwest Passage [VII]*. Whatever the initial impulse, King Henry VIII ordered two ships to make the voyage, and they set out from London on May 20, 1527. The two ships, Rut's *Mary of Guilford* and *Sampson* under an unknown commander, were separated in a storm; *Sampson* vanished with all hands.

Rut pressed on, reaching what he took to be *Newfoundland* on July 21. It was more likely Battle Harbour or St. Lewis Inlet, *Labrador.* He sailed as far north as Hawke Bay before turning south. Entering the harbor of St. John, Newfoundland, on August 3, he found no fewer than fourteen fishing vessels there.

Continuing south, Rut cruised past Nova Scotia and New England and ultimately followed the Atlantic coast to the tip of *Florida.* He then called at the Spanish colonies of Santo Domingo and *Puerto Rico [II]* before returning in the spring of 1528 to England, where the *Mary of Guilford* resumed her role in the Bordeaux wine trade.

Historian Samuel Eliot Morison calls Rut's voyage a "pleasure cruise" and notes that he missed two opportunities to enter the Gulf of St. Lawrence ahead of *Jacques Cartier.* All the same, Rut confirmed *Verrazano*'s report that the continental landmass lay athwart the route to the Pacific. D. B. Quinn regards the expedition as "a planned reconnaissance of the new empire," and the most important English foray on the North American coast during the reign of Henry VIII.

Saguenay

A mythical kingdom north of the "Great River of Canada," the *St. Lawrence,* Saguenay's reputed riches lured *Jacques Cartier* to set sail from France on his third voyage of exploration in 1541. The *Huron* chief

Donnaconna had beguiled Cartier with tales of Saguenay spices, oranges, pomegranates, and uniped inhabitants.

Cartier visited the Saguenay River where it enters the St. Lawrence from the north in 1535. *Samuel de Champlain* explored the lower reaches of the 125-mile-long Saguenay in 1603. Explorers, missionaries, and traders used it as a highway to the northern interior from the early seventeenth century on.

St. Lawrence River

Jacques Cartier's "Great River of Canada," the St. Lawrence flows from the east end of Lake Ontario 744 miles to the Gulf of St. Lawrence north of Cape Gaspé, where it widens to 90 miles at its mouth. From the earliest European penetration, the St. Lawrence was a major route for the exploration of the North American interior and an important trading thoroughfare for *New France.*

With Indian guides, Cartier made the European discovery of the river in 1535. Explorer *Samuel de Champlain* established the settlement of Quebec near a deserted Indian village at the St. Lawrence narrows in 1608. Champlain used the St. Lawrence, Ottawa, and French Rivers as a highway for his great 1615 journey west to Georgian Bay of Lake Huron.

Sandford, Robert   (?–?)

In 1666 Robert Sandford made the most extensive English exploration to date of the South Carolina coast, from Cape Roman down to the Savannah River, in search of a settlement site as ordered by the Carolina colony's Lords Proprietors in London. In 1664 the company had established at the mouth of the Cape Fear River the settlement of Charles Town. Following a failed 1665 attempt to explore the region to its south by new Carolina governor John Yeamans, the task fell to Sandford, who had previously assisted in the colonization of Surinam and the Barbados.

Arriving from the Caribbean, Sandford sailed southward on June 16, 1666, from Cape Fear. Four days later he had advanced some five miles up the North Edisto River. While exploring Bohicket Creek on June 23, he landed to take formal possession, in the name of King Charles II, of all Carolina between latitudes 36° and 29° extending south and west to the

South Sea (the Pacific). Making careful notes, Sandford reported rich soils, well-cultivated fields of Indian corn, excellent pastures, a variety of trees suitable for building lumber, and dense clay useful for making bricks. He continued up the North Edisto, reaching Ladinwah Creek before returning downstream and sending out small parties to explore inland from the river's west bank. On June 27 he passed, apparently by way of the Dawhoo River, to the South Edisto River.

After exploring this region, Sandford sailed back down to the Atlantic and, following Hilton's directions, headed southward to explore St. Helena and Port Royal Sounds. On Parris Island gift-bearing Indians met him, and he viewed a Spanish cross at the century-old site of the Santa Elena colony of *Menéndez de Avilés*. After surveying the Savannah River up its western branch to the hill country and then visiting various Sea Islands, he turned back northward on July 7, leaving behind *Henry Woodward* to learn the Indian language. Three days later he reached first Kiawah Island and then the site of the future Charles Town (Charleston, South Carolina), where he named the Ashley River. On July 12 he ended his voyage back at Cape Fear's Charles Town.

Smith, John   (1579–1631)

The son of a Lincolnshire, England, yeoman farmer, John Smith helped found the *Jamestown* colony in Virginia in 1607. Powhatan's Indians took him captive on a James River exploring expedition in 1608; the story of the chief's daughter Pocahontas's intervention on his behalf has become an indelible chapter of American popular history.

IN THEIR OWN *Words*

New England is that part of America in the Ocean Sea opposite to [California] in the South Sea. . . . And here are no hard Landlords to racke us with high rents, or extorted fines to consume us, no tedious pleas in law to consume us. . . . So freely hath God and his Majesty bestowed those blessings on them that will attempt to obtaine them, as here every man may be master and owner of his owne labour and land, or the greatest part in a small time.

—JOHN SMITH, *A DESCRIPTION OF NEW ENGLAND* (1616)

Smith's exploration of the *Chesapeake Bay* in 1608 produced an accurate map. In 1614 he explored the Atlantic coast from *Cape Cod* north to the Penobscot River of Maine. With a view to promoting colonization, he named the region New England.

Smith's firsthand account of the New World, *Generall History of Virginia, New-England and the Summer Isles* (1624), stimulated early migration from England to North America.

Soto, Hernando de (1500?–1542)

A veteran of Spanish expeditions to the New World, de Soto campaigned in Central America in the 1520s and served as governor of Nicaragua before marching with *Francisco Pizarro [II]* in the conquest of Peru from 1531 to 1536. He returned to Spain rich with Inca plunder, but he wanted the glory of independent command too. De Soto's expedition of 1539–1543, the first European venture to penetrate southeastern North America, would become a byword for cruelty and bloodlust.

De Soto began preparing for a major foray into *Florida* in 1537. Riches as well as exploration and conquest were his objective; a royal commission as governor gave him license to rob and kill such natives as he encountered. He sailed from Havana, *Cuba [II],* in May 1539 with six hundred men, two hundred horses, and a pack of war hounds trained to tear an adversary apart, landing at Tampa Bay on May 30. Destroying the native town of Uzita, the Spanish encamped on the ruins and remained in the Tampa region until mid-July. The governor then pushed north into the Florida interior, looting Indian villages along the route and provoking a series of running fights with the tribes.

In a pitched battle with Seminoles near present Ocala, the Spanish took three hundred prisoners at slight loss to themselves. Moving north after this Battle of the Lakes, de Soto decided to go into winter camp at the Apalachee Indian village of Anhaica, near present Tallahassee, with its plentiful stocks of maize, pumpkins, beans, and dried plums. The Spanish remained in Anhaica, with mounted parties stripping the countryside of provisions and valuables, from October until March 1540.

Doubtless wanting to draw him out of their country, the Apalachees told de Soto of a great golden kingdom to the north with a capital town "of wonderful size" and a female chief who "collected tribute from many of her neighboring chiefs, some of whom gave her clothing and others gold in abundance." Fired by a vision of treasure, the governor set out on March 3, 1540, in search of this rich land.

Crossing the Savannah River on April 30, the Spanish pressed on into the interior of present South Carolina, reaching the Catawba villages of Cofachiqui and Talomeco by mid-May. Looting yielded some mussel pearls but little else of permanent value, and with provisions increasingly scarce and the ravages of epidemic evident, the governor decided not to linger. Soldiers, priests, and slaves pressed on, trailed by a large drove of pigs (several hundred of which were de Soto's personal property), striking as far north as the vicinity of present Charlotte, North Carolina, before turning west into *Cherokee [V]* country. In June 1540 de Soto's men, following the line of the French Broad River from western North Carolina into Tennessee, became the first Europeans to cross the *Appalachian Mountains [V]*.

The Lady of Cofachiqui (Cofitachequi), chief of her Native American village, shows Hernando de Soto and his soldiers the contents of a treasure chest. Artist George Gibbs's idealized rendering of a de Soto encounter with Indians was published in 1898 as the frontispiece to *De Soto and his men in the land of Florida* by Grace Elizabeth King. Indian traditions locate Cofitachequi village at modern Silver Bluff on the east bank of the Savannah River in Barnwell County, South Carolina.

During the following two years, the expedition tracked a wide meandering course west, southwest, north, and west again through Tennessee, Alabama, Mississippi, Arkansas, and Texas in search of gold and other treasure. Along the line of march, de Soto practiced his now-perfected methods of muscular diplomacy: kidnapping of senior tribal chiefs for ransom, torture and mutilation, rape, enslavement, and murder. "The governor sent two captives in search of Indians," ran one account of the expedition. "They captured a hundred head, among Indian men and women. Of the latter, the captain selected one or two for the governor and the others were divided among themselves." The native men, prodded along in collars and chains, carried the baggage and performed other menial tasks.

Marching south from the Tennessee River Valley as far as the neighborhood of present Montgomery, Alabama, the Spanish encountered *Choctaw [V]* Indians and, in a fierce and fiery battle at their capital town of Mabila, slaughtered as many as 3,000 warriors at a cost to themselves of 20 dead and 150 wounded, among them de Soto. Here, too, the governor learned that a Spanish fleet awaited him at a rendezvous on the Gulf of Mexico. Still athirst for riches, he withheld the news from his men and, recovered from his injury, veered north again before settling for the winter among the *Chickasaw [V]* Indians along the Yazoo River in northeastern Mississippi.

In June 1541 de Soto's soldiers became the first Europeans to sight the *Mississippi River [V],* which they dubbed the Río del Spirito Santo. On June 15 the expedition crossed the great river in dugout canoes 10 miles below the site of Memphis, Tennessee. The river stretched to 1½ miles wide there—wider, some of the men noted, than the Danube. "If a man stood still on the other side, one could not tell whether he were a man or something else," one awed chronicler recounted. Ranging through northern Arkansas, de Soto's scouts gathered reports of Plains tribes and vast herds of buffalo to the west. One of the governor's scouting parties followed the Arkansas River nearly to the edge of the Great Plains around the same time *Coronado's [II]* army reached the upper Arkansas in central Kansas some 300 miles distant.

Disappointed in his quest for gold, de Soto now wandered with no fixed plan, and briefly considered pushing on west till he reached the Pacific. The Spanish passed the winter of 1541–1542 in camp near the site of Little Rock, Arkansas. De Soto fell ill over the winter and grew increasingly despondent about the expedition's prospects, for it had become clear to him that there were no Inca riches along the Río del Spirito Santo. He died near Natchez, Mississippi, on May 21, 1542—"a failure," historian David B. Quinn remarked, "a Don Quixote not a Cortés." De Soto's soldiers dropped his corpse into the Mississippi River and told the Indians, who remained in awe and dread of him, that he had gone to the sun.

IN THEIR OWN *Words*

(The Mississippi) was of great depth and of very strong current. Its water was always turgid and continually many trees and wood came down it borne along by the force of the water and current. It had abundance of fish of various kinds, and most of them differed from the fresh waters of Spain.

—FROM "A TRUE RELATION OF THE HARD-SHIPS SUFFERED BY DON HERNANDO DE SOTO . . . BY A GENTLEMAN OF ELVAS," 1541

The Spanish remnants under *Luís de Moscoso [II]* made a long detour through east Texas before famine forced them to turn back for the Mississippi in October 1542. Building crude barges, they floated 700 miles downriver to the Gulf of Mexico in the summer of 1543, then sailed southwest along the coast. Some 311 survivors of de Soto's pitiless epic finally reached the Pánuco River near present Tampico, Mexico, in September 1543.

De Soto's reports of a land where the natives lived well but did not amass great wealth dampened Spanish interest in the interior of what is now the southeastern United States. All the same, his foray had a decisive impact on the Native American nations of the region. His soldiers killed thousands; epidemics of European disease claimed thousands more. Spanish depredations sent the southeastern tribes into a long, steady decline from which they never fully recovered.

Velázquez, Antonio   (?–?)

Early in 1541, *Florida* governor *Angel de Villafañe* ordered Antonio Velázquez to sail north with supplies for the Spanish colony of Santa Elena, on the South Carolina coast. After Velázquez set out, probably in late June, from Havana by way of the Bahama Channel and followed the Gulf Stream north, a storm drove his vessel beyond the Carolinas and as far as the mouth of *Chesapeake Bay,* which he in effect rediscovered (*Quejo* had first arrived there in 1521).

Landing at its mouth or within the bay, Velázquez made a brief reconnaissance and encountered two friendly Indians—Paquiquineo (renamed Don Luis de Velasco, or Don Luis, for short) and his follower. The two accompanied Velázquez when he sailed directly across the Atlantic, landing in late August in Lagos, Portugal, from which he traveled overland to Seville to report his discovery to the Spanish authorities. He and Don Luis later spent some three months in Madrid, visiting the royal court. They returned to the New World with the New Spain convoy, landing in Mexico in August 1562.

Reports of these promising fertile lands led to two unexpected consequences. *Lucas Vásquez de Ayllón*'s son revived his father's contract and organized a company to found a small colony of Spanish farmers there. His expedition, which arrived in the Caribbean in late 1563, soon fell apart amid desertions and accusations of fraud against Ayllón the Younger. Nearly a decade after Velázquez's discovery, Don Luis returned with Jesuit Juan de Segura and others to establish a Spanish mission near Chesapeake Bay. Don Luis and other Indians killed the Jesuits in 1571.

Further Spanish voyages to the area, including that of *Vicente González* in 1588, proved inconclusive. The English finally settled the site at *Jamestown* despite prior Spanish claims.

Verrazano, Giovanni da   (1485?–1528)

Little is known about Verrazano's early life; not even the year or place of his birth is known for certain, although he was probably a native of Tuscany, of good birth, possibly a nobleman, with a more extensive education than mariners of his time ordinarily acquired. Verrazano moved to the French Atlantic port of Dieppe about 1506–1507. He may have reached the Gulf of St. Lawrence with Thomas Aubert's expedition of 1508. In any event, Verrazano became an experienced Mediterranean sailor. There is evidence he knew Ferdinand Magellan in Seville before Magellan set out on his attempt to circumnavigate the globe in 1519.

Verrazano petitioned the king of France, *François I,* for a voyage to "the happy shores of Cathay." He obtained the king's patronage, but Italian and French bankers interested in cheap raw silk for the Lyon silk industry supplied most of the financial support for a voyage that would carry him up the Atlantic coast of North America from South Carolina to *Newfoundland* in search of a passage to Asia.

The French navy supplied the ship, the hundred-ton caravel *La Dauphine.* Verrazano sailed with a crew of fifty, including his brother Girolamo da Verrazano, around January 1, 1524. In a letter to François I written after he returned home in July, Verrazano summarized his purpose and what he encountered: "My intention on this voyage was to reach Cathay and the extreme eastern coast of Asia, but I did not expect to find such an obstacle of new land as I have found; and, if for some reason I did expect to find it, I estimated there would be some strait to it through to the Eastern Ocean."

Taking off from the Madeira Islands on January 17 with provisions for an eight-month cruise, Verrazano followed a track four degrees to the north of that of *Columbus [II]* and, surviving a storm "as violent as ever sailing man encountered," made landfall near Cape Fear, North Carolina, at around latitude 34° N on or about March 1, 1524. There, he wrote the king, "appeared a new land which had never been seen before by any man, ancient or modern." Verrazano then struck south along the coast for 150 miles before turning around so as to avoid a meeting with the Spanish. Returning to Cape Fear, he sent a boat ashore to make the acquaintance of a band of natives.

"They fled when they saw us approaching; several times they stopped to turn around and look at us in great wonderment," Verrazano wrote. "We reassured them with various signs, and some of them came up, showing great delight at seeing us and marveling at our clothes, appearance and our whiteness; they showed us by various signs where we could most easily secure the boat, and offered us some of their food."

Verrazano coasted slowly on a north-northeasterly track, landing somewhere on the sandy Outer Banks of North Carolina between Capes Lookout and Hatteras. For a time he believed he had reached his goal: "We found there an isthmus one mile wide and about 200 miles long, in which we could see [the Pacific Ocean] from the ship, halfway between west and north." This was Pamlico Sound, in fact, and even on a clear day the lookouts could not distinguish the main from the ship's masthead. Verrazano named the region Annunziata. "We sailed along this isthmus," he went on, "hoping all the time to find some strait or northern promontory where the land might end to the north, and we could reach those blessed shores of Cathay."

The land stretched on, however. Verrazano landed again in early April, probably at present Kitty Hawk, North Carolina, a place he named Arcadia on account of the beautiful stands of tall trees there. His shore parties abducted an Amerindian boy and caused a native man to "tremble all over with fright" by firing a blank musket shot at him. After lying at anchor for three days, he again pursued a northeasterly course, though so far offshore that he entirely missed the entrances to the *Chesapeake* and Delaware Bays.

La Dauphine reached New York Bay on April 17. He anchored in the Narrows between Staten Island and Long Island now named for him and pushed up the harbor in a small boat for a short distance into a "beautiful lake" (the Upper Bay) whose shores were crowded with people. But the wind began to blow on shore, and he returned to the ship, weighed anchor, and stood out to sea later that day without carrying out a closer examination.

Verrazano sailed east along the coast to a triangular-shaped, heavily wooded island "similar in size to the island of Rhodes." This was present Block Island, Rhode Island (named later for a seventeenth-century Dutch navigator); Verrazano's likening it to Rhodes is the origin of the name of the smallest U.S. state. There were fires burning all along the shore, but unfavorable weather prevented Verrazano from landing. He continued on toward Narragansett Bay and anchored off Point Judith just below the entrance. Natives, probably Narragansetts, approached *La Dauphine* in canoes. As they were friendly, Verrazano decided to proceed up the bay in search of a sheltered anchorage.

He found one in present Newport harbor on Aquidneck Island, remaining at anchor there for fifteen days. The French called it Refugio, and among its five beautiful and fertile islands "any large fleet could ride safely without fear of tempest or other dangers." Verrazano invited two of the Narragansett headmen aboard. "These people are the most beautiful and have the most civil customs that we have found on this voyage," he wrote. "They are taller than we are; they are a bronze color, some tending more toward whiteness, others to a tawny color; the face is clear-cut, the hair is long and black; the eyes are black and alert, and their manner is sweet and gentle, very like the manner of the ancients." They went about naked except for deerskins covering their private parts.

The voyage resumed about May 6. Passing Sakonnet Point, Rhode Island, Verrazano felt his way through Vineyard Sound and the shoal waters of Nantucket Sound before rounding *Cape Cod.* He probably struck the Maine coast at Casco Bay. High mountains—the Whites—were visible to the west. The native *Abenakis* were cold, especially in contrast with the Narragansetts, though they did grudgingly consent to trade, accepting knives, fishhooks, and tools from the French.

"We found no courtesy in them," Verrazano complained, "and when we had nothing more to exchange and left them, the men made all the signs of scorn and shame that any mute creature would make, such as showing their buttocks and laughing."

La Dauphine proceeded eastward along the Maine coast. Within 50 leagues (about 150 miles) Verrazano counted thirty-two principal islands, "small and pleasant in appearance [with] some beautiful ports and channels formed between them." Passing three prominent islands, Verrazano named them for three orphan princesses at the French court—Anne, Isabeau, and Catherine. Like nearly all of the explorers' names, these failed to catch on. The islands today are Monhegan, Isle au Haut, and Mount Desert.

Continuing northeast, Verrazano encountered contrary winds that caused him to miss the entrance to the Bay of Fundy and much of the

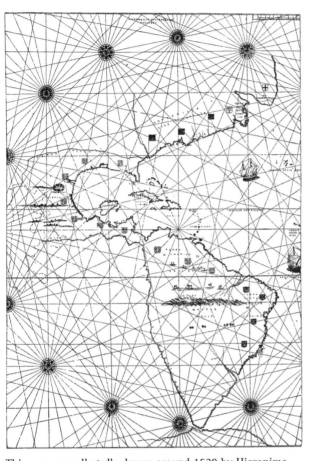

This map was allegedly drawn around 1529 by Hieronimo Verrazano to document the discoveries of his brother Giovanni. Its authenticity has been questioned by many modern scholars, but there is some evidence that it was known in the sixteenth century. This map is taken from J. C. Brevoort, *Verrazano the Navigator,* 1874.

Nova Scotia coast. Landing on the east coast of Newfoundland in early June, he took on wood and water for the homeward voyage. He made his offing from Cape Fogo or *Funk Island* around the middle of June. After a swift passage, *La Dauphine* reached Dieppe in early July.

Verrazano returned to France persuaded that he had discovered a new world, not a promontory of Asia or a mere barrier on the route there. He at once sought financing for a second voyage. War and politics in Europe preoccupied the king, so Verrazano turned to private investors. He sailed from Dieppe in command of a flotilla of four ships in the spring of 1527, reached Brazil, and returned with a cargo of logwood. He then arranged a third voyage, setting out with two or three ships the following spring. After a safe crossing, he made landfall off *Florida* and sailed south to the Lesser Antilles, still evidently in search of a passage that would lead to Cathay. Off Guadeloupe, Verrazano decided to go ashore alone. A party of Carib Indians fell on him, killed him, sliced him up, and ate his still-warm flesh while his brother watched helplessly from a small boat just beyond the surf.

Samuel Eliot Morison calls Verrazano "singularly incurious" for an explorer, since he overlooked Chesapeake Bay and other important places and slighted the Hudson estuary. "His failure to take a good look at the mouth of the Hudson River is perhaps the greatest opportunity missed by any North American explorer," says Morison. Yet he discovered and reported on a coastline extending from the Carolinas to Maine. Because he seemed skeptical about the existence of a passage along that coast, the French turned their attention elsewhere, leaving the Atlantic seaboard of the future United States largely to England to explore, claim, and settle.

> ## IN THEIR OWN *Words*
>
> We often went five or six leagues into the interior, and found the country as pleasant as it is possible to conceive, adapted to cultivation of every kind, whether of corn, wine or oil; there are open plains twenty-five or thirty leagues in extent, entirely free from trees or other hindrances, and of so great fertility, that whatever is sown there will yield an excellent crop.
>
> —GIOVANNI DA VERRAZANO, ON INTERIOR SOUTHERN NEW ENGLAND, 1524

Villafañe, Ángel de   (1505?–?)

In early 1561 Ángel de Villafañe, a veteran of the Pacific explorations of *Cortés [II]*, arrived at *Luna y Arellano*'s troubled Pensacola Bay colony from Mexico to take over as governor of *Florida.* In mid-May, with orders to remove the Florida gulf coast colonists to Santa Elena on the Carolina coast, he set out with four ships by way of the Bahama Channel carrying a diminished group of some one hundred men. With Gonzalo de Gayón as pilot, he reached Punta Santa Elena, reportedly at latitude 33° N, on May 27.

After exploring and taking possession for the crown, Villafañe declared the area unsuitable for settlement and moved on northward to *Cape Fear,* landing to its east on June 3 to explore and again take possession. After next investigating the New River inlet, he reached Cape Lookout on June 14. Stormy weather forced the expedition back to the Caribbean, where he arrived at *Hispaniola [II]* on July 9. He officially reported the Florida (Carolina) coast below 35° as sandy and unsuitable for colonization, and suggested better ports might be found to the north.

An unofficial witness told another story, describing the first landing site as located at Port Royal Sound at above 32° with an excellent harbor. According to this report, the second stop, at the Edisto River, resembled Villafañe's description of Punta Santa Elena. Whether Villafañe deliberately concealed his knowledge of Port Royal in order to support the viceroy's opposition to the king's colonizing plans, or whether the latitudinal readings were incorrect, is controversial. At any rate, his negative recommendations delayed Spanish attempts to colonize the Atlantic coast until later in the decade.

Waymouth, George (fl. 1601–1612)

An experienced English navigator, George Waymouth commanded a voyage in search of the *Northwest Passage [VII]* in 1601 before sailing from England in the ship *Archangel* in March 1605 for Virginia—to the English, the New World mid-Atlantic seaboard—to reconnoiter a site for a settlement. Waymouth made landfall off Nantucket Island in mid-May, then stood north for the Maine coast.

With *Archangel* at anchor off Monhegan Island, Waymouth sent exploring parties up the St. George and Kennebec Rivers to survey the country and make contact with the native inhabitants. The bloom of early Maine summer charmed the explorers; they described a country "whose pleasant fertility bewraieth it selfe to be the garden of nature, wherin she only intended to delight hir selfe." Kidnapping five *Abenaki* Indians to provide firsthand accounts of the region's potential, Waymouth weighed anchor and sailed for England in mid-June.

One of the Abenakis returned in 1607 with a party of one hundred English colonists who established a post, Fort St. George (the Popham Colony) at the mouth of the Kennebec—the first serious attempt to settle in New England. Harsh winter conditions forced the colonists to abandon the settlement.

James Rosier, who sailed in the *Archangel* as chaplain, published an account of the expedition, titled *A True Relation of the most prosperous voyage made by Captaine George Waymouth,* shortly after he reached home in 1605.

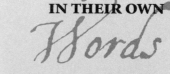

IN THEIR OWN

I will not prefer [the Kennebec] before our river of Thames . . . but . . . then I would boldly affirme it to be the most rich, beautifull, large & secure harbouring river that the world affordeth.

—JAMES ROSIER, *A TRUE RELATION OF THE MOST PROSPEROUS VOYAGE* (1605)

Wood, Abraham (circa 1615–circa 1681)

Abraham Wood reached Virginia from England as an indentured servant in 1620 and eventually acquired a substantial landed estate on the Virginia frontier. In search of an overland route to the Pacific, he organized the first English trans-Appalachian expeditions.

After a series of Indian attacks along the frontier in the early 1640s, the Virginia General Assembly in 1645–1646 authorized the construction and garrisoning of four frontier forts. The assembly appointed Wood to build one of them, Fort Henry at the falls of the Appomattox River on the site of Petersburg. Eventually obtaining trade preferences, he carried on an extensive trade with the Indians from Fort Henry.

In 1650 Wood and Edward Bland carried out an exploration of 180 miles of the wilderness between Fort Henry and present Weldon, North Carolina (see *Bland-Wood expedition*). Continued Indian hostilities put a damper on further forays, and Wood remained quiet at his Fort Henry base for the next two decades. In 1670 he learned from *John Lederer,* just returned from an expedition to the North Carolina Piedmont, that Indians knew of two routes through the Appalachians to the west.

At his own expense, Wood dispatched the *Batts-Fallam expedition* of 1671. Seeking "the ebbing and flowing of [tidal] waters," Batts reached the present Kentucky border before turning back. In 1673 Wood outfitted James Needham and Gabriel Arthur (see *Needham and Arthur expedition*) in 1673. With Indian guides, they explored the Appalachians from present Asheville, North Carolina, to Rome, Georgia.

Expeditions under Wood's sponsorship corrected misapprehensions about the extent of the country beyond the Appalachians—Connecticut's 1662 charter, for example, set the colony's western boundary at the Pacific Ocean—and suggested the vast extent of the North American continent.

Woodward, Henry (1646?–1686?)

A surgeon born probably in Barbados, Henry Woodward arrived at Port Royal Sound in 1666 on *Robert Sandford*'s voyage of discovery to locate a settlement site.

Woodward stayed behind as South Carolina's first English inhabitant and to investigate the country, learn the ways of the Indians, and establish a trade monopoly with them. Soon afterward the Spanish captured and removed him to Saint Augustine, from which he eventually made his way back to become a member of the Albemarle Point colony (later renamed Charles Town, or Charleston).

In 1670 Woodward explored inland between the Savannah and Wateree rivers, an area previously traversed by the Spaniards *de Soto* and *Pardo,* and made a pact with the Indians at Cofitachequi. In 1674 he traveled alone to the Westo villages on the north bank of the upper Savannah to begin the exchange of arms for furs and slaves.

In 1682 Woodward sailed to England to procure a commission to explore west of the *Appalachian Mountains [V]*. In pursuit of this objective he reached western Georgia's middle Chattahoochee River to establish posts at Coweta and Casista and concluded a trading pact with the Lower *Creeks [V],* whom he then incited to attack the Spanish.

The Carolina trading networks initiated by Woodward extended English influence among the Creeks and other Indians southward to the Florida panhandle's Apalachicola River area, where they endangered Spanish missionary efforts. In 1685 a Spanish military force tried to find Woodward, but he escaped. His plans for further westward exploration ended when illness forced his return to Charles Town.

PART IV

Exploring West of the Mississippi, 1635–1800

This part deals with an era—and area—of North American exploration that is undoubtedly the least known to Americans at large: the opening up of lands and shores west of the Mississippi from about 1635 to about 1800. For the most part, the explorers involved in this enterprise were Spanish, but there are several notable exceptions—the English Captain Cook being the best known to Americans, the French Comte de La Pérouse and the Italian Alejandro Malaspina being equally well known to other nationalities.

Much of what is here described as exploration was a continuation of the great enterprise of the Spanish colonial empire based in Mexico. In fact, one of the major motives for the Spaniards' activity was simply their determination to keep other nationalities out of this part of North America. For example, after their truly epic explorations in the 1500s, the Spanish had lost interest in the northwest coast of North America—northern California, Oregon, Washington, Canada, and the coast of Alaska. But as soon as they got wind of the Russian and British presence there, the Spanish renewed their own expeditions in the 1770s—including those of Juan Bautista de Anza, Juan Francisco Bodega y Quadra, Bruno de Hezeta, Esteban Martínez, and Juan José Pérez.

But perhaps the major theme of this era, and the strongest motive for many of these expeditions west of the Mississippi, was Spain's determination to keep the French from intruding in what they regarded as its own territory to the southwest of the Mississippi. Understanding this rivalry calls for some understanding of Spain's and France's tangled relationships, both in this region and internationally. Since 1700, a member of the same Bourbon family that ruled France had been ruling Spain, but the two countries maintained an uneasy relationship. In particular, the Spanish did not accept La Salle's claim in 1682 of the vast Mississippi River valley for France when he named the territory after his king, Louisiana. Then, when in 1685, La Salle appeared on the Texas gulf coast and started a French colony there, the Spanish decided to oust him. To this end, they sent out a series of expeditions in the late 1680s—including those of Barroto and Romero, Alonso de León, Pez and López de Gamarra, and Rivas and Iriarte. Even after the Spanish discovered that La Salle and his colony had come to a disastrous end, they continued throughout the first half of the eighteenth century to send out other expeditions—including those of the Marqués de San Miguel de Aguayo, Domingo del Río, and Terán de los Ríos. Although most of these expeditions were thinly disguised military operations, they contributed considerably to opening up and understanding the remote lands they passed through.

This highlights another theme that distinguishes this era: namely, that it has become more difficult than ever to separate out "pure" explorers from military personnel, seamen, missionaries, colonial administrators, and other government officials. Related to this development is that few of those described here fit the profile of the explorer as a bold, hard-driving, risk-taking individual. These are not the larger-than-life characters that we associate with the conquistadors. That is one reason that most of these names will be unfamiliar to most people—one notable exception being Father Junípero Serra, the Franciscan who founded a string of missions along the coast of California.

That said, many of these individuals are well known to the inhabitants of the regions they explored. And not just to historians or antiquarians—their names appear on all kinds of geographic features and governmental parks, schools, and public buildings, and there are statues and memorial markers dedicated to them. This section should bring these individuals and their achievements to a broader public, and if they are not epic heroes who rank with the great names of exploration, each, in his own way, contributed to increasing the knowledge of North America.

Agreda, María de Jesus ("The Lady in Blue") (1602–1665)

The mysterious story of María de Jesus Agreda cannot be proven, of course, but it remains a fascinating footnote in the history of the exploration of the American Southwest and, more especially, in the reports of early (1620s) Spanish religious activity in East Texas. María de Jesus Agreda was born in the Spanish village of Agreda near the border of Aragon and Navarre in April 1602. In her youth María, baptized María Coronel, demonstrated unusual piety and remarkable memory. At the age of sixteen, she convinced her father that he should convert the family castle to a convent for Franciscan nuns. She took religious vows on February 2, 1620, and accepted the name María de Jesus. The new order of nuns soon expanded beyond the confines of the castle and moved to the convent of the Immaculate Conception in Agreda. The nun's habit was colored Franciscan brown with an outer cloak of coarse blue cloth.

In Spain during the 1620s María de Jesus Agreda was physically present at all times in her convent. But she would repeatedly lapse into deep trances in which she experienced her "transportation" to a distant and unknown land where she taught the Gospel to a pagan people. She claimed to have been in eastern New Mexico and western Texas and that she had contacted several Indian groups, including the Jumanos. These alleged—or to true believers, miraculous—bilocations caused Sister María much distress. When she related her mystical experiences to her superiors, they contacted the archbishop of Mexico, Francisco Manso y Suniga. In May 1628 Father Francisco wrote to the religious superior of New Mexico seeking information concerning the alleged transportation by Sister María. The letter arrived shortly before July 1629.

During the early 1600s, *New Spain [II]* had witnessed the passage of scores of Spaniards from New Mexico along the Río Grande touching upon parts of Texas in their explorations, but there were few expeditions into the interior of Texas until 1680. In July 1629, however, it was claimed that a delegation of some fifty Jumano Indians appeared at the Franciscan convent of Old Isleta, located south of present Albuquerque. They had traveled from New Mexico to request religious instruction for themselves and surrounding tribes in Texas. Mysteriously the Jumanos demonstrated rudimentary knowledge of Christianity and, when asked who had instructed them, replied—"the woman in blue."

An expedition, organized in New Mexico and headed by Father Juan de Salas, set out for the land of the Jumanos. Salas reached a locale in southwest Texas where he was met by a large band of Indians. The Indians claimed that they had been advised by the Lady in Blue of approaching Christian missionaries. Approximately two thousand natives presented themselves for baptism and further religious instruction. Two years later Father Alonso de Benavides traveled from New Mexico to Spain, where he sought more information about the mysterious nun. He interviewed María de Jesus at Agreda. Sister María confessed to some five hundred experiences of bilocations to New Spain and acknowledged that she was indeed the Lady in Blue.

During the last twenty-two years of her life, María de Jesus was an active correspondent with the Spanish king, Philip IV. She died at Agreda on May 24, 1665. Her story was published in Spain several years after her death. Although María de Jesus said her last visitation to the New World was in 1631, the mysterious Lady in Blue was not quickly forgotten in Texas. In 1690 a missionary working with the Tejas Indians heard the legend. In the 1840s a mysterious women in blue reportedly traveled the Sabine River valley aiding malaria victims, and in the twentieth century her apparition was reported as recently as World War II.

Aguayo, Marqués de San Miguel de   (?–1734)

The Spanish-born Marqués de Aguayo is notable for his exploration of East Texas. Appointed governor of Coahuila and Texas in October 1719, Aguayo led a 1721–1722 expedition guided by Fray *Isidro Espinosa* to recover the East Texas missions and presidios seized by the French in 1719. On March 24 Aguayo's eight companies moved north from the Río Grande; each company had 350 horses, 600 cattle, and 800 sheep. From the Hondo River he followed Espinosa's 1709 trail to San Antonio, which then crossed the Colorado River below Austin. Known as Xavier Road, this route was used extensively through the 1730s.

Reaching the Trinity River, he found fields cultivated by friendly Tejas Indians and proceeded to San Pedro Creek to smoke a peace pipe with the Tejas. During the next four weeks, Aguayo established new missions in East Texas, including San Francisco de los Neches, Nuestra Señora de la Concepción, San Joseph de los Nazonis, and Nuestra Señora de Guadalupe de los Nacogdoches. On September 1 some four hundred Adaes Indians welcomed the return of the Spanish. Leaving six cannons and one hundred soldiers, the expedition was back at San Antonio on January 23, 1722.

On March 16, Aguayo set out with forty men for Matagorda Bay and there established a presidio. After his return to San Antonio, he was back in Mexico in late May to recommend that four hundred families be settled between San Antonio and the East Texas missions. On June 13, 1722, he resigned his governorship because of ill health resulting from the hardships encountered on his expedition.

Aguirre, Pedro de (1678–?)

In 1708 Spanish-born soldier Pedro de Aguirre had become commander of Mexico's Presidio del Río Grande del Norte. He was ordered to escort Franciscans *Antonio de Olivares* and *Isidro de Espinosa* to the Colorado River to meet the Tejas Indians. He was also to investigate how far the French had penetrated into Texas. The expedition left San Juan Bautista on April 5, 1709, and reached the Colorado on May 19. The Tejas Indians were uncooperative, and the expedition returned to the Río Grande.

Alarcón, Martín de (?–?)

Little is known of the early years of Martín de Alarcón, the Spanish explorer credited with founding San Antonio, Texas. He had served in the Spanish royal navy and had been to North Africa before moving up through Mexico's military ranks during the 1690s. After service in Guadalajara, Mazapil, and Saltillo, he was appointed commander of the Presidio San Francisco de Coahuila and governor of Texas on December 9, 1716.

In April 1718 he led an expedition of seventy-two soldiers and settlers into Texas with the goal of establishing a mission and presidio on the San Antonio River and then delivering supplies to two East Texas missions. He traced *Espinosa*'s 1709 route, which became known as the Camino Real, from the Río Grande to the San Antonio River, arriving on April 24. By May 5 he had founded the Villa de Béjar and the Presidio de San Antonio at San Pedro Springs, about two miles from the river.

The next day he set out with twenty-five men for Matagorda Bay but got only as far as the confluence of the Guadalupe and San Marcos Rivers four days later. After exploring this region, he turned back and reached San Antonio on May 17. Over the following month Alarcón organized the new presidio. Gardens were planted, but irrigation proved difficult. In mid-June he set out for the Río Grande, arriving June 21. By late August he was back in San Antonio to meet Fray Isidro Espinosa and Captain Domingo Ramón, both of whom joined his second attempt to reach Matagorda Bay, this time by traveling closer to the Texas gulf coast.

On September 8 Alarcón led his party eastward down the Guadalupe's right bank. On September 18 they arrived at the Colorado River below Columbus. From there Alarcón and a smaller group marched toward Matagorda Bay. On this brief tour Alarcón explored several inlets between the Colorado River and Carancahua Bay before heading back to join the rest of his force on the Colorado. On September 29 near Cumins Creek the expedition encountered a large gathering of Indians from the Sana, Emet, Toho, Mayeye, Huyugan, and Curmicai nations.

Then, guided by Ramón and Espinosa, the expedition rapidly moved northeast toward the East Texas missions. From mid-October to the end of November Alarcón met with local Indian leaders and visited the missions, the more distant being San Miguel de los Adaes near Robleine, Louisiana. By early January 1719 Alarcón was back in San Antonio, and he returned to Mexico later that year to be rewarded for his service and relieved of his governorship in November. His later activities are undocumented.

Anza, Juan Bautista de (1736?–1788)

Sometimes called "the last conquistador" because of his role in expanding Spain's possessions in the New World, Juan Bautista de Anza was born at the presidio of Fronteras in Sonora Province of *New Spain [II]*, just south of present-day Douglas, Arizona. Of Basque descent, he was baptized on July 7, 1736. In 1752 he enlisted as a volunteer in the Fronteras presidio army; by 1760 he was a captain and commander of the presidio of Tubac. In this capacity, he was known for heading several successful expeditions into Apache Indian territory.

By 1770 the Spanish were troubled by rumors that Russian expeditions were pushing south from Alaska into Alta California. In 1774 Anza was authorized to lead a land expedition that planned to open a route from Sonora to Alta California, with the goal of establishing Spain's priority in northern California. Anza and some thirty-five men, including Father *Francisco Garcés,* left Tubac on January 8, 1774. They headed north to the Gila River and followed it to its intersection with the Colorado. Anza was instrumental in establishing friendly relations with the Yuma Indians who lived in the area. The expedition then crossed the Colorado and proceeded southward, where they were lost for ten days in the desert. Returning to the Yuma Indians, they took the advice of Sebastian Tarabal, a Cochimi Indian, and followed a new route by heading south-west through the Cocopas Mountains near present-day Signal Mountain (in the area of Imperial Valley, California). A northwest route led them through the San Gabriel Mountains (east of Los Angeles), and they reached the San Gabriel Arcángel mission on March 22. Traveling further north, they arrived in Monterey on May 1. During some three days there, Anza fortified the mission there and, leaving behind some reinforcements, headed back to Tubac.

Upon his return to Sonora Province, Anza was promoted to lieutenant colonel and asked to explore California as far as San Francisco Bay, where he was to establish a colony. On October 23, 1775, Anza left Tubac with a group of 48 soldiers and 240 to 300 colonists. Father Garcés again accompanied the expedition. They proceeded northward to Santa Cruz River Valley; heading west, they followed the Gila River until they met the Colorado River on November 28. They then proceeded across the Yuma desert under adverse winter conditions.

On December 26 they reached the pass into California and straggled into the Mission of San Gabriel Arcángel on January 4, 1776. A further march north brought the large party to Monterey on March 10, 1776.

On March 22 Anza set out with a small group that included a Lieutenant José Joaquín Moraga and a Franciscan priest, Father Pedro Font; five days later they arrived at the northwestern edge of the peninsula that would become San Francisco; they continued to explore the northern tip

> **IN THEIR OWN** *Words*
>
> **Anza Arrives at Site of San Francisco**
>
> *The day broke clear and bright. At seven in the morning we set out from the little creek a short distance north of San Mateo Creek, and at eleven, having marched about six leagues, we pitched camp at a lagoon or spring of clear water close to the mouth of the port of San Francisco. . . . I beheld a prodigy of nature, which is not easy to describe. We saw the spouting of young whales, a line of dolphins or tunas, besides seals and otters. . . . This place and its surrounding country afforded much pasturage, sufficient firewood, and good water, favorable conditions for establishing the presidio or fort contemplated.*
>
> —FATHER PEDRO FONT, JOURNAL ENTRY, MARCH 27, 1776

The San Francisco de Asis Mission was founded in 1776 by priests subordinate to Father Junípero Serra, but the church in this drawing was not completed until 1791. The drawing is by Ludovik Choris, a young Russian artist who accompanied von Kotzebue on his expedition to the northwest Pacific (1815–1818). It remains a major destination for visitors in San Francisco's Mission district (where it is also known as Mission Dolores).

of the peninsula for about a week before returning to Monterey. Having determined that the tip of the peninsula (present-day Fort Point) was suitable for the presidio and mission commissioned by the Spanish viceroy in New Spain, in April Anza set off back to his home province of Sonora in northern Mexico. On June 17, 1776, however, Lieutenant Moraga, with Father Francisco Palou and Father Pedro Cambon, would lead a small group of Spanish soldiers and colonists from the Monterey mission to the peninsula of San Francisco; arriving there on June 27, the priests established the first mission, San Francisco de Asis (also known as the Mission Dolores); because they were Franciscans and *Father Junípero Serra* was their superior at the Monterey mission, he is often credited as the founder of this mission. The priests conducted the first mass there in a rude arbor on June 29. With the settlement of these colonists, the European population of Alta California was virtually doubled.

Upon his return to Sonora, Anza was promoted to colonel, and in August 1777 he was appointed governor of New Mexico. He went on several more exploratory journeys during his ten years in New Mexico, including an expedition into Colorado in 1779 in pursuit of Indians. In 1780 he helped discover a trail from Sante Fe to Arizpe in Sonora Province, Mexico. On October 1, 1788, he was appointed commander of the presidio at Tubac, but he died on December 19, 1788, in Arizpe. Anza's reputation rests on his having established important routes connecting the heart of New Spain with its outposts in California.

Aranda, Miguel de   (?–?)

A San Antonio Franciscan, Fray Miguel de Aranda accompanied the 1753 Juan Galvan expedition to explore Apache territory northwest of San Antonio along the Pedernales and Llano Rivers in order to find a suitable site for Spanish settlement. At the San Saba River they found sufficient water and arable lands, and here Aranda offered mass for the Apaches of the region. A favorable report signed by Galvan, but probably authored by

Aranda, extolled the land as potentially rich in mineral deposits and Apaches willing to be converted. A 1754 survey reinforced Galvan and Aranda's optimistic recommendations for locating a mission at the site of Menard, Texas. Little is known of Aranda's movements thereafter.

Barreiro, Francisco Alvarez (?–?)

Spanish-born Francisco Alvarez Barreiro arrived in Mexico around 1716 and, as a military engineer, joined *Alarcón*'s 1718 expedition to found San Antonio. From 1724 to 1728 he accompanied expeditions led by Brigadier General Pedro de Rivera y Villalón, on which he contributed important work as a surveyor and mapper of the Texas gulf coast, eventually covering nearly seven thousand miles.

On November 21, 1724, the inspection tour began at Zacatecas and proceeded to visit all presidios in northern *New Spain [II]*. From the Presidio de la Bahía, Barreiro spent thirty-five days exploring the coast and the lands that lay between it and the Noches River. His efforts resulted in a comprehensive documentation of the upper Texas coast, although his map, *Plano corográfico y hidrográfico,* contains some errors. For example, the Guadalupe River does not flow into Matagorda Bay. In other respects, its accuracy is remarkable in the depiction of the coast, some river courses, Indian villages, and Spanish settlements. He drafted six maps, five of which are in the Archivo General de Indias. On December 23, 1728, he was back in San Juan Bautista across the Río Grande, and his later activities are unknown.

Barroto, Juan Enríquez (circa 1660–1693)

Juan Enríquez Barroto was most likely born in Mexico and is best known for his expeditions searching for *La Salle*'s *[V]* French colony on the Gulf of Mexico. Barroto studied mathematics and astronomy under the Mexican Carlos de Sigüenza y Góngora. His navigation skills were highly respected by Spanish authorities.

Alarmed by reports of a French presence on the coast of the Gulf of Mexico, the Spanish launched a determined search for La Salle from Florida to Texas, thus initiating intensive exploration of the region. As either chief pilot or commanding officer, Barroto was involved in three of the five Spanish sea voyages of the La Salle quest.

The first of these is sometimes known as the Barroto and Romero expedition, because Barroto was accompanied by Antonio Romero, another experienced pilot of the Armada de Barlovento ("Windward Fleet"). The ships sailed from Havana on January 3, 1686, proceeding to Florida's Apalachee Bay, then rediscovering Pensacola Bay and surveying Mobile Bay. They reached the Mississippi River Delta but failed to recognize the river's mouth, which lay concealed behind silted channels blocked with vegetation and driftwood. They named the delta the Cabo de Lodo ("cape of mud") and named the North Pass the Río de la Palizada, as from the sea the banks resembled palisades of mud.

Barroto's diary of the voyage reports finding wreckage of La Salle's ships at Matagorda Bay. He also tells of the first known exploration of Galveston Bay, the Atchafalaya River, and the Sabine, Calcasieu, and Mississippi Passes. Barroto describes encounters with Coahuiltecan, Karankawan, and Atakapan Indian tribes. He also recorded latitude and longitude determinations that corrected previous readings. Barroto's place names were copied onto European maps.

Both Enríquez Barroto and Romero piloted the 1686 *Rivas and Iriarte expedition,* and Barroto later sailed on the 1687 *Pez and López de Gamarra expedition.* In 1688 Enríquez Barroto sailed as pilot under the command of Andrés de Pez y Malzarraga to explore Chandeleur and Breton Sounds in response to rumors of a French settlement in that Texas area. His maps also served as guide to explore the Soto La Marina River and the mouth of the Río Grande.

In 1691, as captain of a frigate of the Armada de Barlovento, he ferried troops and supplies to Matagorda Bay to support the expedition of Governor *Domingo Terán de Los Ríos.* Terán, on leaving Texas early in 1692, boarded Barroto's ship to seek passage into the Mississippi River as a means of possible access to the Caddoan tribes and the Texas missions. The effort was frustrated by a storm.

Enríquez Barroto's importance as a Spanish explorer continues to be reevaluated. He was overshadowed by his commanders Sigüenza y Góngora and Andrés de Pez. In fact, Pez claimed Barroto's discovery of Pensacola Bay as his own. It was Barroto who provided the information for what is known as the "Pez Memorial," a document describing the merits of Pensacola Bay and advocating its settlement. Pez presented this document to the king of Spain as his own. On September 18, 1693, Enríquez Barroto perished at sea when his ship was lost with all hands in a hurricane off the

Carolina banks. His reputation today rests mainly on his maps and diaries that established coastal features, rivers, and bays in Texas.

Bodega y Quadra, Juan Francisco de la   (1743–1794)

Juan Francisco de la Bodega y Quadra, who played an important role in two early explorations along the northwest coast of North America, was born in Lima, Peru, in 1743, a Creole of mixed Spanish and black heritage. Bodega was a second lieutenant when he was assigned to San Blas on the west coast of *New Spain [II]*, or present-day Mexico. In 1775 a maritime expedition was organized to explore the California north coast under the command of *Bruno de Hezeta.* Hezeta was to be captain of the *Santiago,* and Juan de Ayala would command the schooner *Sonora.* Bodega, as a Creole, was passed over for command but volunteered as second on the *San Carlos* under Captain Mantique. A quirk of fate would change Bodega's life.

The expedition departed northward on March 16, 1775, with instructions to sail as far as 65° N latitude. Three days out of port the *San Carlos* hoisted a distress signal: Captain Mantique was exhibiting signs of insanity. Hezeta named Ayala to command the *San Carlos,* and Bodega replaced Ayala as captain of the *Sonora,* and they continued the voyage north.

In June they discovered a protective bay on the north California coast near present-day Little River. On July 13, halfway up a cove near what now is Point Grenville, Washington, the expedition met Indians and traded with them. The site is now known as Grenville Harbor, but at the time it gained a more sinister name—Martyr's Point: When Bodega sent a crew of six to gather water, they were massacred by three hundred Indian warriors, who also tried to attack the ships. On July 29 Hezeta decided to turn back. Bodega, however, chose to proceed farther north; he was supported in this decision by his pilot, Francisco Antonio Mourelle de la Rúa, a bold young Spaniard; Mourelle's account of the expedition is one of the finest records of Spanish activities in this region and era.

Bodega continued northward, and on August 15 he made landfall at 57° N. This was the coast of present-day Prince of Wales Island, at the southern tip of what is now Alaska. The Spanish named an impressive snow-capped peak San Jacinto (now called Mount Edgecumbe). Three days later Bodega made landfall and again encountered Indians who were friendlier. (A decade later, fur traders would claim that this visit was

Bodega Decides to Push On

*They formulated the daring project of
separating and dying in their craft
rather than return without enlightenment . . .
[they knew] that they would navigate
unmapped seas; perhaps they would find
themselves in an archipelago where it would
not be easy for a small, lone boat to emerge
felicitously; that any illness would put them
in the ultimate risk at such an advanced season; that from the moment of separation they
would have to stretch their rations to last the
rest of the trip; and finally, that if they
returned to port without progress worthy of
consideration, at once there would be leveled
against them accusations of insubordination.
. . . But none of this could overcome the
shameful feeling which they could imagine if
two young men turned back toward San Blas
from that latitude; and hoisting all their sails
at ten that evening, by navigating toward the
west they found themselves in control of
their own destiny by the following day.*

—Francisco Antonio Mourelle, *Journey
of the Sonora in the Second Bucareli Expedition
to Explore the Northwest Coast . . . 1775*

responsible for a smallpox epidemic that ravaged the coast and killed much of the Native
American population. But most likely it was
the Spanish expedition of 1779, hit by an epidemic of unspecified nature at Bucareli
Sound, that was responsible.) Bodega examined every bay and inlet expecting to find the
Strait of Bartholomew de Fonte, or the
Northwest Passage [VII]. They made landfall
on the western side of Prince of Wales Island
at 55°14' N latitude, which now bears the
name Bucareli Sound.

Bodega tacked north again. On August
27 he reached a maximum of 58°30' before
he was turned back by strong winds. Several
of his seamen were injured, and many were
sick with scurvy. On October 3 Bodega discovered Tomales Bay near San Francisco Bay
and a more northerly inlet still called Bodega
Bay. On October 7 the *Sonora* reached Monterey Bay. Hezeta had been waiting there for
him for five weeks. The expedition arrived in
San Blas on November 20.

Bodega's next expedition north took
place in 1779, when he served as second in
command to Ignacio de Arteaga. Arteaga was
instructed to reach a latitude of 70° N. Leaving San Blas on February 11, 1779, the expedition arrived at Bucareli Sound early in May.
After a month of exploration in this area, the
expedition continued north. Near the entrance to what is now Prince
William Sound, a party went ashore to claim possession for Spain. This
was the northernmost territory ever claimed by Spain in North America.
After another possession ceremony near the tip of the present-day Kenai
Peninsula, the expedition sailed as far as Afognak Island (north of Kodiak
Island), where storms and scurvy again forced a return voyage to San Blas.

Bodega continued to serve Spain in North America. In 1792 he was
given command of the Nootka settlement off the coast of present-day

Vancouver Island. Bodega's explorations on behalf of Spain were instrumental in keeping some possessions along the northwest coast for the Spanish until they were gradually forced out, finally withdrawing completely when in 1819 they signed a treaty with the United States limiting their claims to the northern border of California.

Casa Calvo, Sebastián Calvo de la Puerta y O'Farril, Marqués de   (1751–?)

The Marqués de Casa Calvo was born in Havana and rose through the Spanish military ranks; during the American Revolution, he participated in the Spanish campaign against the British along the gulf coast. In 1799 he was sent by the captain general of *Cuba [II]* to assume interim command of *Louisiana [V]*, which he did on September 18. The following June he was succeeded by Juan Manuel de Salcedo. In 1800 Spain secretly ceded the vast territory known as Louisiana back to France, and on April 10, 1803, together with Salcedo, Casa Calvo formally handed Louisiana back to the French, just prior to France's selling the territory to the United States.

But Casa Calvo disputed the French claim that the southwestern boundary of the Louisiana Territory was the Río Grande, and in 1805–1806 he led an expedition with *Nicolas de Finiels* into western Louisiana and Texas to determine what he regarded as the true boundary between the lands of Spain and those of the United States. After consulting the mission and presidio records at Nacogdoches and Los Adaes, he was convinced that Spain had legitimate claim to territory as far east as Arroyo Hondo, which formed the boundary between Louisiana and Texas.

Expelled in 1806 from Louisiana, he sought permission to lead a Spanish military expedition against Louisiana. He regarded this as the only hope of saving Spanish North America. Evidently the request was denied, and Casa Calvo dropped from historical view.

Cook, James   (1728–1779)

Arguably the greatest mariner of his time, Cook commanded two great voyages (1768–1771 and 1772–1775) that revolutionized European knowledge of the geography and hydrography of the Pacific Ocean. But he also made voyages to North America that contributed to knowledge of that continent, too.

Born in Yorkshire, England, and apprenticed to a Whitby shipowner, Cook rose rapidly to command his own merchant vessel. He entered the Royal Navy in 1755. During the French and Indian War, when Canada was held by the French, Cook served as navigator on an exploratory mission to survey the *St. Lawrence River [III];* his charts of the river, the most precise up to then, allowed General James Wolfe to make his way to Quebec, where his victory over the French in 1759 secured English domination of North America. He also carried out a detailed survey of the coast of *Newfoundland [III].*

Between 1768 and 1771, Cook led a Royal Navy expedition to the Pacific, where, among other achievements, he was the first European to visit New Zealand. Between 1772 and 1775, he led a second expedition to the Pacific in search of a reputed southern polar continent; he sailed farther south than any European but was unable to sight what would later become known as Antarctica.

Cook's third major exploring expedition, during 1776–1779 in the ships *Resolution* and *Discovery,* was undertaken for the Royal Navy to search for the western outlet of the *Northwest Passage [VII].* It was also motivated in part by a desire to reassert Britain's claim to the northwest coast of America, based on *Drake's [II]* visit two centuries earlier. After sailing around the South Pacific once more, and becoming the first European to reach the Hawaiian Islands, Cook headed for the northwest Pacific, arriving off the coast of Oregon in March 1778. Moving northward along the coast, he failed to see the mouth of the Columbia River, but he was the first to enter Nootka Sound, the harbor on the coast of Vancouver Island that *Juan Pérez* had only sighted in 1774. Continuing on, Cook explored and surveyed the west coast of Canada and defined the coast of Alaska as he sailed north and west toward what were reputed to be ice-free polar seas. Going along

This engraving of the buildings at Nootka Sound was an illustration in the 1785 edition of Captain James Cook's voyage. It was done by the artist on the 1778 expedition, John Webber. Nootka Sound is on the west coast of Vancouver Island.

the Aleutians, he traversed the Bering Strait and entered the Arctic Sea, reaching latitude 70°41' beyond the northernmost tip of Alaska before towering walls of ice forced his retreat.

Cook then sailed back to Hawaii, where he was killed in a skirmish in November 1778, so he did not live to see the results of his explorations of the northwest coast of North America. But word of Britain's interest in the region had reached Spain even before Cook sailed, and his presence there served only to spur on Spain's own ambitions for the region. Moreover, Cook's journals, published in 1784, reported the fabulous prices the region's high-quality sea otter pelts fetched in China, thus touching off European (and later American) interest in the Pacific fur trade.

 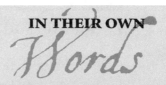
Del Río, Domingo (?–?)

In 1755 Domingo Del Río conducted a Spanish military expedition to the Orcoquiza and Bidai Indians west of the Trinity River in East Texas to investigate reports of French incursion. The next year, while in charge of a temporary presidio east of the Trinity River, he set out in June to investigate the coastal region for a more favorable site for the presidio, as well as locations for a mission and settlement. After visiting the Akokisa tribe to the east, he turned back to survey the Arroyo de Santa Rosa and the San Jacinto River.

By the end of the year Mission Nuestra Señora de la Luz had been built close to the presidio El Orcoquisac near Anahuac, Chambers County, Texas. In 1770 the Spanish withdrew from the area, abandoning the mission and presidio. Del Río later served as interpreter on various Spanish expeditions.

Escalante and Domínguez expedition (1776–1777)

Silvestre Vélez de Escalante was born in Spain about 1750 and was known to be a practicing Franciscan friar at the Laguna pueblo in New Mexico by 1774. Nothing is known of the background of Francisco Domínguez, but he was apparently another Spanish Franciscan who met Escalante in New Mexico. Although Domínguez was put in charge of an expedition to find a route from Santa Fe to Monterey in California and to convert Indians to Christianity, Escalante would become better known because he wrote the account of the expedition. On July 29, 1776, they left Santa Fe, New Mexico, and crossed the Río Grande into Colorado. The men traveled northwest until they met the Dolores River. Escalante and Domínguez found the ancient ruins of a small Indian village, and Escalante made the first written record of a prehistoric Anasazi site in Colorado. Friendly Ute Indians helped them reach as far north as Rangely, Colorado. Turning west they entered what they called "Utah Valley" near the present site of Provo, Utah, and reached the White River. Near Utah Lake they discovered a great salt lake basin. Avoiding the salt desert, they headed south and crossed what is now called the Escalante Desert of southwest Utah. The expedition was almost wiped out because of lack of water.

They then crossed the Paria Plateau in what is now northern Arizona. On October 4, 1776, near Cedar City, Utah, the expedition turned back. Near Toquerville, Utah, they discovered fields of corn and signs of irrigation, indications that the Paiute Indians there had progressed beyond seed gathering and small-game hunting. The expedition crossed the Colorado River at a place near Marble Canyon. After much hardship in the winter weather, the

IN THEIR OWN *Words*

The Spanish Explore into Colorado

[T]he Animas River] flows through a canyon in which there are veins of metal. Although many years ago several persons were sent out to investigate and carry away some ore, it was not learned what metal it was. The Indians and some citizens of this Kingdom said they were silver mines, which caused these mountains to be called Sierra la Plata. . . . The Río de San Buenaventura is the largest river we have yet come to, and is the same which Fray Posada described in his report to the King [in 1686]. According to his record we find it to be the same distance which he places it from Santa Fe.

—SILVESTRE VÉLEZ DE ESCALANTE, JOURNAL OF THE ESCALANTE AND DOMÍNGUEZ EXPEDITION OF 1776 expedition arrived back in Sante Fe on January 2, 1777. Although they had failed to complete their original goal of reaching Monterey, California, Escalante and Domínguez had traveled 1,500 miles throughout the North American Southwest and made many discoveries, including the safest place to ford the Colorado River, later named the Crossing of the Fathers. Father Escalante's account of the expedition chronicled the first European exploration across the Great Basin desert and established part of what would be called the Old Spanish Trail between Santa Fe and California.

Escandón, José de (1700–?)

José de Escandón left Spain at age fifteen and came to the Yucatan Peninsula in Mexico. As a soldier in the Spanish army, Escandón spent the following years pacifying the Indians in the Yucatan and Sierra Gorda areas of Mexico. He was promoted to lieutenant general in 1740. Escandón's explorations during this period helped create what was known as *Colonia de Nuevo Santander.* This area included the steaming rain forests in the south, the rugged mountains of Sierra Madre Oriental in the west, and the semi-arid plains of the Gulf of Mexico up into the southern part of Texas.

In 1746 the viceroy of Mexico chose Escandón to lead an expedition into lower *Seno Mexicano,* the land from Tampico to the mouth of the San Antonio, now known as the lower Río Grande valley around Laredo and Dolores. On January 7, 1747, Escandón left Queretaro in central Mexico with 1,750 soldiers and 3,000 colonists. This expedition proved to be the best conceived and most successful of Spanish explorations and settlements into the borderlands. The plan was to have the expeditionary force leave from seven points and to coincide in an arrival at the mouth of the Río Grande no later than February 24, 1747. Santiago, chief of all the Indian nations in this region, guided Escandón to a campsite on the south bank of the Río Grande. Six of seven columns arrived at the rendezvous point on schedule. Numerous journals were kept, detailing the geographical terrain as well as much information about the nature and size of Indian groups. Escandón returned to Queretaro to make a final report to the viceroy and to present him with a plan for settlement of the area.

Escandón's vision was to divide land along the Río Grande into *porciones,* or portions. They became a special kind of land grant that enabled Escandón to outline a number of towns along the Río Grande between

1748 and 1755. Some 300 of these portions were laid out, with about 170 ultimately granted titles by Spanish authorities. The area settled was intended to establish a bulwark against the hostile Indians of the region. It also provided a firm hold upon territory that Spain considered integral to its New World empire. By virtue of these conquests, Escandón became the most successful Spanish explorer and colonizer of eighteenth-century Texas.

Espinosa, Isidro Félix de   (1679–1755)

Born in Querétaro, Mexico, Isidro Espinosa became a Franciscan priest in 1703 and was assigned to San Juan Bautista mission later that year. On April 5, 1709, Fray Espinosa left San Juan Bautista with an expedition into Texas. After visiting the site of San Antonio, the group journeyed to the Colorado River to contact the Tejas Indians, who resisted colonization.

In 1716 Espinosa accompanied the expedition of Domingo Ramón, which established three missions in East Texas—Nuestro Padre San Francisco de los Tejas, Nuestra Señora de la Purísima Concepción, and San José de los Nazonis. Espinosa's missionary activities in Texas included two more expeditions, those of *Martín de Alarcón* (1718) and of *Marqués de San Miguel de Aguayo* (1721) before he was recalled to Querétaro. His chronicles are still valued as sources of early Texas history.

Espinosa-Olivares-Aguirre expedition   (1709)

Leaving San Juan Bautista on April 5, 1709, Captain *Pedro de Aguirre* led a group of fourteen soldiers, with Fray *Antonio de Olivares* as chaplain and Fray *Isidro Espinosa* as chronicler, into East Texas to the Colorado River. As the first Spanish expedition since 1693 to travel beyond the Frío River, its aim was to convince the Tejas Indians to move from near the Trinity and Neches Rivers to the Colorado some hundred miles to the southwest. Passing the future site of San Antonio, the party moved east toward the Nueces River and camped several miles above the present town of Crystal City. En route they met Payaya and Pompopa Indians and viewed a large encampment of Siupan, Chaularame, and Sigame Indians. On April 17 they camped near the Colorado River about thirty miles downstream from Austin. Negotiations with the Indians proved fruitless as the Tejas chieftain Bernardino resisted the Spanish demands and their religion. Nevertheless, the Spanish had found a more northerly route to the Colorado, one other explorers followed in later expeditions. On April 28, 1709, the group returned to San Juan Bautista.

In his diaries Espinosa had carefully recorded the route and events of each day. His colorful descriptions of the Indians and detailed notes on wildlife and vegetation surpassed those of earlier expeditions. He mentioned deer, bison, wild turkey, bear, and mountain lions. Espinosa later authored one of the most detailed and engaging chronicles of mission life among the Indians of northeastern Mexico and Texas.

Evia (Hevia), José Antonio de   (1740–?)

José Antonio de Evia, an experienced Spanish pilot, completed the most detailed exploration of the Gulf of Mexico coast of the late eighteenth century. After training for the Royal Armada from age thirteen, he first sailed in 1759 to the Americas to visit Veracruz and Puerto Rico. A decade later, as a gulf navigator voyaging between Havana, Veracruz, Mobile, and New Orleans, he drew up a chart of the Mississippi River mouth.

On September 5, 1783, Evia set out from Havana to begin the assignment of remapping the gulf coast from the Florida peninsula to Matagorda Bay. Following further orders to continue the coastal reconnaissance to Mexico's Tampico, he finally finished in September 1786. As governor of *Louisiana [V]* and of West *Florida [III]* and captain-general of *Cuba [II]* (and soon to become viceroy of *New Spain [II]*), Bernardo de Gálvez initiated the project. He instructed Evia to make accurate charts of the entrances to the gulf's rivers and bays, while surveying coastal islands and noting navigational hazards such as shoals and currents.

After arriving at Key West on September 7, Evia began his survey at Cape Romano. During the two weeks charting Charlotte Harbor, he also noted the sources of fresh water, the availability of game animals, and the types of trees suitable for shipbuilding. After working his way up through Tampa and Apalachee Bays, he had to return to Havana in late November to repair his storm-damaged vessel. The next spring, often delayed by storms, he resumed his exploration at West Florida's Cape San Blas and worked westward to the Mississippi River. There, using smaller vessels, he surveyed the delta and entered bayous. After reaching Matagorda Bay, he turned back to study Galveston Bay, which he named and where he ascended six leagues up the Trinity River.

In March 1786 he traveled to Mexico City to present his findings to Viceroy Gálvez, who ordered him to expand his survey to the Mexican coast, with special attention to all rivers, particularly the Río Grande. After assembling vessels and supplies in Veracruz, Evia started north from Tampico on July 14. This time fifty soldiers were along as protection from Indian attacks along the notoriously dangerous Costa Brava. He reached Corpus Christi Bay on August 11 and turned back toward Tampico, to be hampered by a scarcity of fresh water and food along the way. His heroic achievement won him appointment as captain of the port of New Orleans. After the 1803 return of Louisiana to France, Evia retired to Havana, where he spent the rest of his days.

Evia's maps were incorporated into the updated Spanish map of the region, the 1799 *Carta esférica*. On his survey Evia had compared his observations to earlier charts, on which he found various errors that he then corrected. While his latitude readings were fairly accurate, he provided no longitude readings since the chronometer was not yet available to him. Because of time limitations, he had had to concentrate on the major rivers and bays, rather than examine them all. From 1804 to 1821, geographical study of the region intensified as Spain and the United States sought to clarify the boundary between Louisiana and Texas. Thus, observations by later cartographers and pilots refined and adjusted Evia's data. In geopolitical terms Gálvez had intended that Evia's work provide a basis for a possible trade and political network linking Louisiana, West Florida, Havana, Veracruz, the Yucatan, and New Spain's Nuevo Santander, the province that extended from Tampico to Matagorda Bay and was in dire need of settlement and economic development. This ambitious vision ended with the premature death of Gálvez and the disintegration of the Spanish empire in North America.

Fagés, Pedro (?–1796)

Pedro Fagés was born in Catalonia, Spain, and having joined the army as a young man, he was sent as a lieutenant to Mexico in 1767. When the *Portolá* expedition of 1769 set out for Monterey, Fagés was assigned to sail to San Diego on the *San Carlos*. By the time he arrived there, he was weak from scurvy, but he nevertheless joined Portolá on his overland expedition to Monterey. He also accompanied Portolá on the 1770 expedition to Monterey, and when the presidio and mission were established there, Portolá appointed him military governor of Alta California. In November 1770 Fagés made an exploring trip to San Francisco Bay, going as far as the San Leandro Creek near Oakland. In 1772 he made another trip to San Francisco Bay, this time exploring its eastern and southern shores, the San Pablo and Suisan Bays to the north, and the San Joaquin River. In 1774 he was replaced as military commander of Alta California by *Fernando Rivera y Moncada,* and he returned to Mexico. During 1781–1782 he led expeditions to the Colorado River to punish the Yuma (Quechan) Indians, and after the last one he was named governor of Alta California. Don Pedro, as he was popularly known among the early Spanish in California, returned to the capital at Monterey in 1783 as military commander and served there until his retirement in 1791 and return to Mexico.

Finiels, Nicolas de   (1767?–?)

Born in France around 1767, Nicolas de Finiels served as captain of engineers with the French forces in the American Revolution. In 1797 Finiels obtained a passport from Spanish authorities in Philadelphia to travel to *St. Louis [VI]* to help with the fortification of upper *Louisiana [V]* at a time when Spain feared a British attack from Canada. After completing maps of the *Missouri River [VI]* and its environs he was ordered to leave Louisiana and Spanish service in 1798. He then went to New Orleans where Governor General Manuel Gayoso de Lemos hired him as engineer and draftsman to map Baton Rouge and New Orleans. He was reinstated into Spanish service in June 1799.

He became chief surveyor of *Casa Calvo*'s 1805–1806 expedition to western Louisiana and Texas to study the boundary between Spanish and United States territory following the Louisiana Purchase. The party left New Orleans in October and ascended the Bayou de la Fourches de Chetimachas. They then descended the Atchafalaya River and followed the coast toward Texas. Finiels charted the gulf coast, including the Mermentau, Calcasieu, Sabine, and Trinity Rivers. The group explored San Bernardo Bay, and then traveled overland to Atascosito near the Trinity River and to the San Antonio and Natchitoches areas. Finally they explored the region of the Arroyo Hondo, at the boundary between Louisiana and Texas.

Later attached to the Pensacola garrison, Finiels became engineer-in-chief of West *Florida [III]*, a post he held until 1819. He supervised the fortifications of Pensacola, San Carlos de Barrancas, and Mobile. His work as a skilled cartographer and as the inventor of surveying instruments contributed considerably to the geographical knowledge of North America.

Garcés, Francisco Tomás (1741?–1781)

Known for keeping detailed journals of his explorations that helped later explorers and settlers in the American Southwest, Francisco Tomás Garcés was born around 1741 in Aragon, Spain, and came to the New World as a Franciscan friar in 1768. He traveled in northwestern Mexico and southern Arizona and helped rebuild a mission at San Xavier del Bac near present-day Tucson. In 1771 Garcés headed an expedition that left the mission of San Xavier and headed north to the Gila River in Arizona, then west to its juncture with the Colorado River. He befriended the Yuma Indians and learned that another Spanish expedition was nearby. (This would have been one of *Father Junípero Serra*'s missionary expeditions into California.) In searching for these other Spaniards, however, Garcés got lost in the labyrinth of the Colorado River delta. He gave up the search and turned northwest, where he crossed the present-day Mojave Desert. At the foot of the southern ridge of the Sierra Nevada, Garcés halted, then returned to San Xavier del Bac. He had failed to find the other expedition, but he had discovered an important route from the southwest into California.

Three years later, Captain *Juan Bautista de Anza*, commandant of the presidio at Tubac, decided to take Garcés with him on his expedition to cross into California. Anza and Garcés left Tubac on January 8, 1774, with a party of about thirty-five men, a mule train, and cattle to slaughter for food. With the guidance of a Yuma Indian, the Anza expedition reached the San Gabriel Arcángel Mission, east of Los Angeles, on March 22, and then went on to Monterey, arriving there on May 1. Soon thereafter they made their way back to Tubac.

In October 1775 Garcés and Anza again left Tubac for California. They traveled to the Colorado River and erected a building at the site of modern-day Yuma, Arizona. Garcés founded a mission here among the Yuma Indians. When Anza proceeded on to Mission San Gabriel and Monterey, Garcés stayed with the Yuma to carry on his missionary work before returning to the mission at San Xavier del Bac on July 2, 1776. During this time he also explored the countryside, at one point going as far as the San Joaquin Valley. Three years later Garcés helped found two more missions at the mouth of the Gila River. The Indians revolted in 1781, and Garcés and many settlers and soldiers were killed. Francisco Tomás Garcés had helped to discover important desert routes, mountain passes, and rivers in the southwestern United States and California.

Grenier, Chevalier (?–?)

Chevalier Grenier was captain of the French armed merchant vessel *Superbe,* which was wrecked at the mouth of Matagorda Bay in May 1745 while sailing from Veracruz to New Orleans. Confused about their geographical location (they believed themselves to be east of Pensacola Bay), ninety-five of the castaways, Grenier included, began an epic march westward along the gulf coast. Ravaged by heat, thirst, and hunger, and assailed by Indians, who killed fifty-one of them, the survivors eventually reached Mexico's Río Panuco some five hundred miles and forty-three days later on July 5. In Tampico Grenier purchased a ship and on September 22 returned to New Orleans, where he spent several years attempting to recoup his investment. This tragic episode highlighted the problems associated with colonizing the Texas coastal region in the area that became Nuevo Santander and that was first explored by *José de Escandón.*

Guadalajara, Diego de (?–?)

In 1654 the Mexican viceroy asked the New Mexico governor to assess his territory's lands, resources, and people. The governor assigned Sergeant Major Diego de Guadalajara to lead an expedition, and with thirty soldiers and some two hundred Indians, he set out along the route of the 1650 *Martín-Castillo expedition* to the Río Conchos Basin in the Great Plains of southern Texas. There he set up temporary headquarters among the Jumanos, and from there Captain Andrés López explored the surrounding region with a smaller party. East of the Conchos they engaged with, and defeated, a band of Cuitaos, taking some two hundred prisoners and seizing loot of deerskins and buffalo hides. Anticipating reprisals, Guadalajara led the party back to Santa Fe. The expedition brought back a deeper knowledge of the Great Plains and its peoples and helped open up the area southwest of Santa Fe, initiating commercial exchanges between Spanish soldiers and traders and the Jumanos, who bartered buffalo hides.

Hezeta (Heceta), Bruno de (1750?–?)

In 1774 Bruno de Hezeta, a young Spanish naval officer, arrived with five other young officers at San Blas, on the Pacific coast of Mexico. This was the headquarters in *New Spain [II]* for Spanish naval operations in California. The Spanish were fearful that the Russians were expanding their colonies eastward and southward from the Aleutian Islands and wanted to establish a presence on the northwest coast of the continent. To counter this threat, in 1775 the viceroy of New Spain at this time, Antonio María de Bucareli, put Hezeta in charge of a new expedition. He commanded the *Santiago,* with *Juan José Pérez Hernández Pérez* as second-in-command; Juan Manuel de Ayala commanded the schooner *Sonora;* Captain Mantique commanded the *San Carlos.* Hezeta's instructions were to reach a latitude of 65° N, avoid foreign settlements, go ashore, and take possession wherever it was safe to do so. Wherever possible Hezeta was to establish friendly relations with the Indians. The expedition left San Blas on March 16, 1775.

In June Hezeta's expedition put in to Monterey harbor. The *San Carlos,* by now under the command of Ayala, was carrying a letter from the Spanish viceroy in New Spain for *Father Junípero Serra,* instructing Serra

Three Mexicans gaze out over San Francisco from high ground, with the presidio (enclosed with flag) established in 1777 by the expedition led by Juan Bautista de Anza. Beyond is the promontory known today as Fort Point, overlooking the Golden Gate entrance to the bay.

to support the colonization of San Francisco. *Juan Bautista de Anza* would be leading a sizable party of colonizers there overland from Mexico, but on August 4, long before Anza arrived in San Francisco, Ayala sailed the *San Carlos* through the Golden Gate and into the bay of San Francisco, almost certainly the first European navigator to do so. (Most scholars do not believe that *Sir Francis Drake [II]* ever entered this bay.) Ayala spent over a month exploring the waters and coasts around San Francisco before returning to Monterey. Meanwhile, Hezeta, accompanied by two Franciscan priests, Palou and Capa y Cos, also led an expedition that surveyed the peninsula of San Francisco before continuing his journey northward.

In northern California Hezeta stopped in a bay and went ashore to take formal possession. By mid-July, he had reached the coast of what is now Washington and there performed another possession ceremony. By this time most of Hezeta's men were sick from scurvy, and he was already planning to turn back without reaching 65° N. On August 11, after reaching latitude 49° N near present-day Nootka Sound, Hezeta turned back to sail south, while the bolder *Juan Francisco de la Bodega y Quadra* continued north.

Although his instructions obligated him to follow the coast carefully on his return voyage, Hezeta passed the Strait of Juan de Fuca (between present-day Vancouver Island and Washington) without noticing it. A few days later, however, on the evening of August 17, Hezeta sighted a large bay between two promontories. The bay penetrated so far inland that it reached the horizon. Hezeta made several attempts to enter the bay, but the current was so strong that he had to give up. He concluded that it must be the mouth of a river or some major sea passage to the east. Hezeta named it Bay of the Assumption of Our Lady after a feast day celebrated on August 15. Hezeta was almost certainly the first European to observe the mouth of what was later to be called the Columbia River. Hezeta prepared a chart of the estuary on the basis of what he could see from outside the bay, and the bay appeared on maps as *Entrada de Hezeta*

IN THEIR OWN *Words*

Hezeta Takes Possession at Grenville Bay, Washington

*A*t four-thirty in the morning, I landed, accompanied by the Reverend Father Fray Benito de la Sierra, Don Cristóbal Reville, the surgeon Don González, and some armed men. I took possession at six in the morning. . . . Only six Indians presented themselves to me ashore . . . [they] have beautiful faces. Some are fair in color, others dark, and all of them plump and well built. Their clothing consists of sea otter skins with which they cover themselves from the waist up.

—BRUNO HEZETA, *DIARIO*, JULY 14, 1775

("Hezeta's Entryway"). Nonetheless, it was ignored by other explorers until seventeen years later when the American **Robert Gray [V]** managed to sail into the river.

Bruno de Hezeta was a cautious commander who chose to turn back rather than risk unknown seas with an ill crew. Although most of the glory from his expedition would go to the more daring Juan Bodega y Quadra, it was Hezeta who made the most significant discovery of the voyage.

Kino, Eusebio Francisco (1645–1711)

Eusebio Francisco Kino, a German-educated Jesuit missionary born in northern Italy, first arrived in Mexico in 1681. After participating in a failed 1683 attempt to colonize Baja California, he was put in charge of the wilderness of Pimería Alta, the home of the upper Pimas, an area encompassing Mexico's northern Sonora region and southern Arizona. The energetic Kino began his twenty-four-year term of service in March 1687, soon establishing the mission of Nuestra Señora de los Dolores, which became the base for some forty expeditions into Arizona to probe the headwaters of the Río Grande and the Gila and Colorado Rivers, and to survey the lands between the Magdalena and Gila rivers and between the San Pedro and Colorado Rivers. In 1691 he first entered Arizona and traveled as far north as Tumucácori, a Pima town on the Santa Cruz River. In 1692 he entered the San Pedro Valley north of Douglas. He returned to the area eight years later to begin construction near Tucson of the mission San Xavier del Bac. In 1694 he descended the Santa Cruz River to the Casa Grande archaeological ruins on the Gila River and recorded the first European description of the site. By 1702 he had explored the Colorado from the Gila to the Gulf of California, and in 1705 he incorporated his discoveries in a map, the first based on actual exploration of Arizona.

This mission church of San Xavier del Bac, near Tucson, Arizona, was built in the 1790s on the site of a simpler church built in 1700 by the Jesuit missionary Father Eusebio Kino. The church has been greatly restored since this photo and is a popular tourist attraction as well as a parish church of the San Xavier Indian reservation.

He devoted his last decade to proving, at least to himself, that Baja California was indeed a peninsula and not an island, as was still widely believed. Over the years, as an itinerant preacher, he established a number of missions in the Mexican region and three missions in Arizona. To support the missions, he introduced cattle ranching and grain production. Though Kino was one of the greatest explorers of the Southwest, he recorded little ethnographic information, and in the end, his efforts had a limited result. By the end of the Spanish colonial era, the region was sparsely populated by Spanish-Mexicans, and the area north of the Gila remained mostly unexplored. He did, however, open the way for the Spanish colonization of California.

La Pérouse, Jean-François Galaup, Comte de (1741–1788?)

A French aristocrat, the Comte de la Pérouse had served with the French in aid of the American Revolution, after which he accepted the assignment from the French government to lead an expedition to explore the northwest coast of America. With two ships, and accompanied by several scientists (including an astronomer, a physicist, three naturalists, a

IN THEIR OWN Words

A Frenchman Describes the Spanish Mission at Carmel, California, in 1786

The government is a veritable theocracy for the Indians; they believe that their superiors are in immediate and continual communication with God. . . . The friars, more occupied with heavenly than temporal interests, have neglected the introduction of the most common arts. . . . With pain we say it, the resemblance [to slavery] is so perfect that we have seen men and women in irons or in the stocks; and even the sounds of the lash might have struck our ears, that punishment also being admitted, though practiced with little severity. I confess that, friend of the rights of man rather than theologian, I should have desired that to principles of Christianity there might be joined a legislation which little by little would have made citizens of men whose condition hardly differs now from that of the negroes of our most humanely governed colonies.

—JEAN FRANÇOIS GALAUP, COMTE DE LA PÉROUSE, *VOYAGE DE LA PÉROUSE AUTOUR DU MONDE*, 1797 mathematician, and three draftsmen), he left France in August 1785. He first set foot on Alaska soil near Mount St. Elias in June 1786. Arriving at Alaska's Lituya Bay in July 1786, he named it Port des Français and claimed possession of the region for France; however, in his report to the French authorities, he advised against France's making any official efforts to challenge Spain's claims in the region, and France never did. He explored the coastline—and lost twenty-one men when they were taking soundings and their boats were swamped by a sudden storm—and by the time he made his way south to the Spanish port of Monterey, California, he was practically out of food. The Spanish resupplied him, and he set off across the Pacific; after visiting several Asian and Pacific ports, including Botany Bay in Australia, he sailed off and vanished at sea.

León, Alonso de   (1639?–1691)

Alonso de León was born in Cadereyta, Mexico, the son of a soldier-administrator by the same name. He was taken to Spain at age ten; in 1657 he joined the Spanish navy, and by 1660 he was back in Mexico. He prospered through his mining ventures, and in 1687 he was appointed governor of the state of Coahuila, Mexico. The viceroy then assigned León to search for French settlers and, in particular, a colony established by *La Salle [V]* in territory claimed by Spain. (At the same time, the Spanish had sent five naval expeditions to search the gulf coast for traces of La Salle.) Between 1686 and 1690, León led five expeditions, four of them across the Río Grande into Texas.

On his first expedition of June 27, 1686, León followed the San Juan River northeast from near Monterrey, reaching the Río Grande below Matamoros; he turned south from its mouth to Río de las Palmas and was home by July 26. On his second journey, beginning in late February 1687, he forded the Río Grande near Roma, Texas, crossed south Texas to reach the gulf coast on March 20, and ventured north to Baffin Bay (south of Corpus Christi) before turning back. He left on his third expedition in May 1688, fording the Río Grande at Paso de Francia (at Guerrero, Coahuila, southwest of San Antonio). In Kinney County, Texas, among the Coahuiltecans he found fugitive Frenchman Jean Jarry (Jean Géry or Juan Jarri) and took him back to Mexico for interrogation.

On his fourth expedition, with Jarry as guide and joined by Franciscan

Damián Mazanet (Massenet), León crossed into Texas at Paso de Francia on April 2, 1689, and headed toward Matagorda Bay, reaching La Salle's deserted settlement of Fort Saint-Louis on Garcitas Creek on April 22. Indians had massacred most of the French three months earlier. After exploring Lavaca Bay, western Matagorda Bay, and up the Lavaca River, he moved on to find four French survivors among the Tejas Indians along the Colorado River in the Smithville-La Grange area. He traveled east to the prosperous Hasinai settlements before returning to Mexico with two of the Frenchmen (the other two choosing to remain with the Indians).

On April 2, 1690, León, along with Father Mazanet, set out on his fifth exploration, following the same route to Fort Saint-Louis, which Mazanet burned while León checked on artillery pieces he had buried. From the mouth of the Lavaca River he spotted what looked like buoys, but he lacked a boat with which to investigate further. They continued on beyond the Colorado River, where León seized two French youths, survivors of the La Salle colony. They marched on to the Hasinai and, along the Neches River (near the Louisiana border), founded on May 22 San Francisco de los Tejas, the first Spanish mission in East Texas. On the way back, on a side trip to Matagorda Bay, León ransomed three more French children (the siblings of Pierre Talon, one of the youths he had found earlier).

Despite León's notable efforts, the Spanish remained concerned about the French. He was judged harshly for not examining the "buoys" in Lavaca Bay (which a later 1690 expedition led by Francisco de Llanos revealed as harmless logs) and for failing to investigate reports of Frenchmen beyond the Hasinai. Mazanet, who joined the chorus of criticism, returned to Texas with the 1691 *Terán* expedition. León died that same year, and although he hardly ranks as a major explorer, his recorded observations served as a valuable contribution to knowledge of the geography and ethnology of the regions he traveled.

The Unfortunate adventures of Mons.: de la Salle.

This illustration by a Dutch artist, M. Van der Gucht, appeared in a 1697 volume by Louis Hennepin recounting the story of La Salle's disastrous expedition of 1688. It shows LaSalle (foreground) unloading supplies from his ship, *Le Joly,* at Matagorda Bay along the gulf coast of Texas. Although LaSalle's colony would soon collapse, for years the Spanish sent out expeditions determined to keep the French from intruding in what they regarded as their territory.

Malaspina, Alejandro (1754–1810)

Alejandro Malaspina was born into an aristocratic family in Mulazzo, in northern Italy, then under Spanish rule. He enlisted in the Spanish navy and, during the American Revolution, took part in naval battles against the British and was briefly held prisoner. By 1784 he had circumnavigated the earth and had a reputation as a fine navigator. He then conceived of a plan to make a scientific survey of all of Spain's far-flung colonial hold-

ings, and in 1789 he sailed from Spain with the *Descubierta* (*Discovery*) and the *Atrevida* (*Bold*), two specially constructed ships. Motivated in part by a desire to outdo the expeditions of Captain *Cook,* Malaspina had with him a number of leading Spanish astronomers, naturalists, and artists. He was also charged with the usual task of finding the *Northwest Passage [VII].* It was June 1791 before Malaspina's expedition reached the northwest coast of the Pacific, and

This drawing is by José Cardero, who accompanied the Malaspina expedition that sailed along the Pacific northwest coast in 1792. It depicts the so-called praying room of the prominent Natooka Indian chief, Macuina (or Ma-kwee-na). As his people's chief priest, Macuina would get into this box (about six feet long and two feet wide) to observe a fast and enter into a trance; the painted figure presumably represented a mythical spirit.

IN THEIR OWN *Words* — A Serious Scientific Expedition

A plan that we proposed on September 10th last and in which we propose to circumnavigate the world in two corvettes, to work on hydrographic charts of the western coast of America and of the Spanish settlements in Asia, and to reconnoitre New Zealand and various islands of the Pacific Ocean met with approval of [His Majesty]. In emulation of Messrs Cook and Lapérouse, we intend at the same time to carry out as many experiments as possible that can contribute to the progress of geography, navigation, and natural history, for which purpose H.M. will provide appropriate ships, instruments and even personnel expert in those abilities which are unrelated to nautical science.

—ALEJANDRO MALASPINA, LETTER TO THE OFFICERS OF THE SPANISH ROYAL NAVY, NOVEMBER 4, 1788 after sailing up along the Alaskan coast as far as Prince William Sound, he spent some weeks at the Spanish outpost at Nootka Sound. During this voyage the scientists investigated all kinds of geographical features—naming a glacier after Malaspina—and collected native artifacts, recorded the flora and fauna, and came away with many measurements and pictorial records. In August 1791 he sailed back to Mexico, but he sent two smaller ships, the *Sútil and Mexicana,* back to the north coast to seek the Northwest Passage. Malaspina himself continued his expedition by sailing across the Pacific and inspecting Spain's possessions in the Marianas and the Philippines, turning back to South America and making his way to Spain by September 1792. There he issued a highly critical report calling for Spain to establish a true trading empire, not one based on military conquest, but this led only to his being imprisoned for eight years, until finally Napoleon interceded and he was allowed to return to Italy.

Martín-Castillo expedition   (1650)

In 1650 the New Mexico governor sent the two army captains Hernando Martín (Hernando Martín Serrano) and Diego del Castillo with a group of soldiers and christianized Indians to seek a new route across the Great Plains of Texas to Jumano territory. By that time Spanish exploration skills were such that they could cross the arid plains at will, relying on their knowledge of water holes from Indian informants. Along the Río Conchos they discovered pecan trees along the bank and, in the water, shells containing mediocre-quality pearls. From the Conchos of the Jumanos they set out eastward to the humid forests of the Tejas Indians. Returning a different way, they again passed through the Conchos basin and traversed the lower plains back to Santa Fe. Their report added to the knowledge of the region's geography and increased vice-regal interest in further investigation, resulting in the 1654 *Guadalajara* expedition to the Jumano homeland and the 1683–1684 *Mendoza-López expedition* on which Martín served as interpreter of the Jumano language.

Martínez, Esteban José   (1742–1798)

Esteban José Martínez, who was instrumental in providing information for the first Spanish settlement of Nootka in 1789, was born in Seville on

Spain Cedes Rights to Great Britain

*I*t is agreed that the buildings and tracts of land situated on the northwest Coast of the Continent of North America, or on islands adjacent to that continent, of which the subjects of His Britannic Majesty were dispossessed about the month of April 1789 by a Spanish officer [Martínez], shall be restored to the said British subjects. . . . It is agreed that the places which are to be restored to British subjects by virtue of the first article as well as in all other parts of the Northwest Coast of North America or of the islands adjacent, situated to the north of the parts of the said coast already occupied by Spain wherever either of the two powers shall have made settlements since the month of April 1789, or shall hereafter make any, the subjects of the other shall have free access and shall carry on their commerce without disturbance or molestation.*

—THE FIRST NOOTKA CONVENTION, 1790

December 9, 1742. He entered the Spanish naval academy when he was thirteen. He came to the New World at an unspecified date, but in 1773 he was serving as second pilot in the Naval Department of San Blas, Spain's naval headquarters on the Pacific coast of Mexico. In 1774 he was second-in-command to **Juan Pérez** in the first Spanish expedition to the northwest coast of North America. Between 1776 and 1788 Martínez conducted a succession of supply trips from San Blas to Spanish outposts in California.

On March 8, 1788, he undertook an expedition northward from San Blas as captain of the *Princessa;* the other ship on this expedition was the *San Carlos.* By mid-May the two-ship expedition was anchored near the entrance to Prince William Sound, the inlet on the north coast of the Gulf of Alaska. According to reports published after the voyage, it was at this time Martínez began to act irrationally. He quarreled with pilot Antonio Serantes over the *Princessa*'s location, slapped Serantes and knocked him to the deck, and then ordered Serantes arrested and placed on the sister ship *San Carlos.* Martínez continued up the coast. On July 19 he reached Unalaska Island in the Aleutians, where he anchored at Dutch Harbor and met with a Russian trader. On August 5 Martínez quietly performed a brief ceremony of possession for Spain, despite Russia's prior discovery and presence. On the return voyage Martínez arrived in Monterey on September 17 and waited for his companion ship the *San Carlos,* but it had taken a more direct route to San Blas. Martínez finally left Monterey on October 14 and arrived in San Blas on December 5. He filed a report urging the settlement of Nootka before the Russians or English arrived.

Martínez led a second expedition that departed on February 17, 1789. The cruise northward was uneventful except for the outbreak of a mysterious disease. In Nootka Harbor, Martínez met the ship *Ifigenia,* flying the Portuguese flag but with English officers and crew; it was in fact one of two ships that belonged to the English trader John Meares. Martínez planned to seize the *Ifigenia,* and on May he made out an affidavit accusing the *Ifigenia* of violating Spanish sovereignty. He disarmed the *Ifigenia* and placed it under the Spanish flag. Martínez then set his men on land and had them erect a fort. A few days later Martínez changed his mind and released the *Ifigenia* and its crew. Then in July 1789 two more of Meares's ships appeared, and again, Martínez seized them. (One of them, the *Princess Royal,* he renamed the *Princesa Real* and sent to explore the Strait of *Juan de Fuca [II]* under the command of *Manuel Quimper.*) Martínez's aggressive behavior reflected Nootka Sound's role in 1789 as an intersection of rival imperial designs, making it an important crossroads in the early history of the North American continent. In any case, the international uproar resulting from Martínez's actions at Nootka Sound led to the Nootka Convention of 1790, which opened to all nations any territory in the Pacific Northwest that was not settled by Spain as of that year. Martínez's violent and overbearing treatment of sailors and foreign nationals undoubtedly aggravated a difficult situation not of his own making, but his explorations of Northwest territory confirmed Spanish claims to maintain its presence in the Pacific Northwest at least temporarily.

Mendoza-López expedition (1683–1684)

In 1683 delegations from the Jumano Indians arrived in New Mexico with enticing accounts of the great kingdom of Tejas, apparently near Quivira (see *legendary destinations [II]*), and asked for Spanish missionaries to come to their lands. Their real motivation was probably to open trade with the Spanish and obtain aid against Apache attacks. On the orders of the New Mexico governor to survey the Nueces River, collect pearl samples and other items, study the Indian cultures, and to instill respect for the friars, Captain Juan Domínguez de Mendoza led an expedition out from El Paso on December 15, 1683. An experienced soldier from a wealthy family, Mendoza had participated thirty years earlier in the *Guadalajara* expedition to the Jumanos in west central Texas. Mendoza traveled downstream along the Río Grande to the Conchos, adding Fray Nicolás López and two other Franciscans to the party at La Junta. As custodian of the El Paso missions, López was to found missions among the Jumanos. From there the party headed north to the Pecos River, followed it downstream, marched east across the dry plain, and arrived at what was probably the Middle Conchos River, which they followed to the area of the Colorado River of Texas, reaching their eastern limit at the San Clemente River. Along the way they investigated waterways, named rivers, erected crosses on hills, surveyed terrain, noted timberlands and pasture lands, and described plants, fish, and game. They remained in the area for six weeks, receiving delegates from various tribes, baptizing Indians, and killing over four thousand buffalo.

Promising to return in a year and without establishing a mission, they returned to El Paso, claiming the Río Grande's north bank for New Mexico. In 1685 Mendoza and López were in Mexico City, fruitlessly promoting occupation of the Jumano lands with soldiers and missionaries. In the end, the expedition increased Spanish knowledge of west central Texas and its inhabitants and laid the groundwork for future settlement.

Olivares, Antonio de San Buenaventura y   (?–?)

Fray Antonio Olivares spent many years as a Franciscan missionary in the province of Zacatecas in Mexico. In 1699 he was reassigned to San Juan Bautista, then located on the Río de Sabinas. He was present at the founding of the second San Juan Bautista mission, begun on January 1, 1700, at the site of modern Guerrero, Coahuila. Two months later Olivares founded San Francisco Solano mission nearby. In 1709 he served as chaplain to an expedition led by *Pedro de Aguirre* to the site of San Antonio and beyond to the Colorado River in East Texas.

Olivares then traveled to Spain to advocate for the expansion of missions into Texas. On May 1, 1718, Olivares was head of the San Antonio de Valero mission on the San Antonio River. In September 1720 his poor health led to his retirement, probably to San Juan Bautista or the College of Santa Cruz Querétaro.

Ortiz Parrilla, Diego   (1715?–1775)

The influence of Spanish-born Diego Ortiz Parrilla as a soldier, governor, and explorer of the gulf coast region extended from Mexico to *Florida*

[III]. Arriving in *Cuba [II]* in 1734, he rose through the military and administrative ranks of *New Spain [II]*. In 1749 he was appointed governor and captain-general of Sinaloa and Sonora in Mexico. While suppressing an Indian rebellion there, he explored and charted Tiburon Island. In 1756 he went on to head San Xavier presidio in Texas and to move its garrison to a new fort on the San Saba River.

Indians attacked and destroyed San Saba mission on March 16, 1758, while the presidio was understaffed and Ortiz Parrilla was away exploring the region. He then led a punitive military expedition, known as the Red River campaign, to avenge San Saba's loss. Leaving San Antonio in August 1759, he proceeded northward to the Brazos River, where the Spanish forces attacked a Tonkawa camp, killing 55 Indians and taking 140 prisoners. Then followed an October attack on a Taovaya village at the Red River, where the Spanish suffered a humiliating defeat by a Comanche-Wichita coalition.

In 1761 he was called to Florida as Pensacola's military governor in order to suppress an Indian uprising. Later, while serving as Coahuila's interim governor, he was commissioned to survey the Texas gulf coast in response to a rumored English invasion. Beginning on September 13, 1766, he supervised the exploration of the lower Texas coast, including Padre and Brazos Islands and Baffin Bay. The 1767 map of this investigation became part of his official report. Ortiz Parrilla retired to Spain in 1774.

Pérez, Juan José Pérez Hernández   (1750?–1775)

A Spanish naval officer with considerable experience sailing in the Pacific and along the coast of southern California, Juan José Pérez Hernández Pérez was appointed in 1774 to command the frigate *Santiago* on an expedition sailing from San Blas, Mexico, to the northwest coast of North America. The Spanish at this time were greatly concerned about the increasing presence of both the Russians and the English in those waters—the former largely interested in acquiring sea otter pelts, the latter in seeking the *Northwest Passage [VII]*. Pérez was under orders to map the coastline and place the cross and notice declaring Spanish possession at possible sites for settlements, but he was also to stay clear of any other nation's settlements and to avoid antagonizing Native American groups. The *Santiago* sailed with the second officer, *Esteban José Martínez,* and the famed *Fray Junípero Serra,* taking passage to Monterey, California, to rejoin his mission there. Pérez got only as far north as about latitude 55°, the southern tip of the Alaskan panhandle, then turned south and anchored near the entrance to Nootka Sound, along the northwest coast of Vancouver Island. Pérez is credited with making the first documented sighting by a European of this important locale.

Continuing south, he sailed by the entrance to the Strait of *Juan de Fuca [II]* without entering it, and he sighted Mount Olympus in northern Washington before returning to San Blas after his seven-month voyage. His vague descriptions of the terrain and his failure to take possession of any land meant that his expedition actually accomplished very little, but his presence in those waters would be cited later by the Spanish in pressing their claims to the northwest coast. Moreover, the journals of the expedition were filled with valuable ethnographic data concerning the Native Americans Pérez encountered on his voyage, particularly the Haida and the Nootka along the coast of British Columbia. Pérez sailed as second officer on the 1775 expedition under *Bruno de Hezeta* and died on the way back of some illness aggravated by the harsh conditions of voyages in those days.

IN THEIR OWN Words — The Hardships of Explorers

During the whole day the fog did not lift, nor could the sun be seen, it was quite cold and a heavy mist fell. I think the dampness is the cause of the mal de Loanda, *or scurvy; for although during the whole voyage there have been some persons affected with this sickness, these cases have not been as aggravated as they are now, where there are twenty men unfit for duty, in addition to which many others, though able to go about, have sores in their mouths and on their legs; and I believe that if God does not send better weather soon, the greater part of the crew will perish from this disease, judging from the rate at which they are falling sick of it during these days of wet weather.*

—FRAY TOMÁS DE LA PEÑA SARAVIA, *DIARIO,* 1774

Pez and López de Gamarra expedition   (1687)

In two ships captained by Andrés de Pez, a naval hero and cartographer, and by Francisco López de Gamarra, the third Spanish expedition in search of *La Salle [V]* sailed from Veracruz on June 30, 1687, following the route taken by the second 1686 expedition (see *Rivas and Iriarte expedition*) along the Texas coast to the Mississippi Delta before returning on September 4. En route they carefully inspected Mustang and Saint Joseph

Islands, and Corpus Christi, San Antonio, Matagorda, and Galveston Bays. They recorded detailed observations of the delta area, especially the "bird-foot" subdelta, and established reference points in a table of latitudes and longitudes for future expeditions. After making soundings at Mobile Bay and passing Pensacola Bay, they headed back to Mexico.

In the futile fourth expedition (March–April 1688), acting on erroneous information from English pirate Ralph Wilkinson, Pez sailed with *Juan Enríquez Barroto,* veteran of the first and second expeditions, to search Mobile Bay on the assumption that this was the outlet of the still elusive Mississippi River. They did complete the first known explorations of the Breton, Chandeleur, and Mississippi Sounds east of the Delta. Pez, together with Martín de Rivas, also led the fifth and final expedition, which departed Veracruz on August 8, 1688. Concluding that the northern gulf bays weren't large enough to accommodate La Salle's ships, they turned their attention to the Soto la Marina and the Río Grande, becoming the first Europeans to ascend the latter river some one hundred miles upstream to near Roma, Texas. Encountering hostile Indians and no Frenchmen, they returned to making a coastal survey as far as Matagorda Bay. There careful investigation yielded fragments of the French ship *Aimable.* Again they missed the entrance to Lavaca Bay and the remains of La Salle's colony, which was finally found by the 1689 *León* expedition by land from Mexico.

Excited by the possibilities of Pensacola Bay, in March 1693 Pez led Carlos de Sigüenza y Góngora, Mexico's greatest scientist, on its survey: Sigüenza, after making detailed botanical, zoological, and geological observations, declared it the finest in all the Spanish empire. (After a five-year delay, the Spanish finally erected a small fort there.) With their intense focus on Pensacola, they made only a token effort to find the Mississippi's outlet, thus failing to claim for Spain the continent's most important river.

Portolá, Gaspar de (1723?–1784?)

Gaspar de Portolá was born in Balaquer, Spain, into a noble family. After serving in military campaigns in Europe, he was named governor of Baja California in 1767. In that same year King Carlos III of Spain, annoyed at the growing power of the Jesuit Order, ordered that the Jesuits be expelled from Spain and all its possessions, and Portolá became responsible for expelling the Jesuits from their missions in California and replacing them with Franciscans. In 1769 he was named commander-in-chief of an expedition into Alta California that was both to seek out good harbors for Spanish ships and to establish missions among the Indians. The expedition was divided into four units—two to go by ship, two to march overland. Portolá led the larger land party and, accompanied by *Father Junípero Serra,* set forth on May 11, 1769. Portolá's land party reached San Diego on July 1 after traveling overland through country up to then known only to Indians. By the time the four units of the expedition were united at San Diego, so many of the sailors had died of scurvy that Portolá decided to change the composition of the expedition. Of the two ships, the *San Antonio* was sent back to San Blas, and the *San Carlos* remained at San Diego with Father Junípero Serra, while the main body under Portolá set out for Monterey on July 14, 1769. Accompanying him was Captain *Fernando Rivera y Moncada,*

This illustration shows Monterey, California, in 1845, some seventy-five years after it was founded as the site of a mission by Father Junípero Serra. Because of its location on a navigable bay, Monterey was long an important port for the Spanish explorers who made their way north all the way to Alaska. By 1845 Mexico had freed itself from Spanish rule, but within another year, Monterey and California would be taken away by the United States.

the military leader, and Father Juan Crespi, whose detailed diary provides an excellent account of this expedition.

After two and a half months of hardship and difficult travel across valleys that ran from the mountains to the shore, the expedition arrived at Monterey Bay on October 1, 1769, but because the bay did not seem to fit the reports of it as a fine harbor, Portolá's party continued the journey northward. About October 31 men with one of his scouting parties, led by José Francisco Ortega, found themselves looking down on the strait (now the Golden Gate) that joined the Pacific Ocean to San Francisco Bay; Ortega and his men are generally regarded as the first Europeans to see San Francisco Bay. Portolá arrived back in Monterey on November 28, but the expedition ran into trouble after leaving Monterey for San Diego. The men were forced to kill and eat their own mules, but they managed to reach San Diego on January 21, 1770, without losing a single life on the journey.

Persuaded that he had in fact seen Monterey, Portolá led another expedition north in April 1770. Again, Father Junípero Serra went along, but this time he sailed on the *San Antonio.* On May 24 Portolá and his overland unit arrived in the port of Monterey. The area was explored, and they met friendly Indians. On June 3 the possession was solemnized, and the presidio and mission of San Carlos Borromeo de Carmelo were established there, with Father Serra saying mass. Influenced by Portolá's reports of the peninsula and bay at San Francisco, two expeditions would later set out overland from the presidio at Monterey to explore the best routes there and possible sites for missions; the first, in 1772, was led by Captain *Pedro Fagés,* and the second, in 1775, was led by Captain Fernando Rivera y Moncada. Although these expeditions did not settle there or found any missions, their reports led to a third expedition, led in March 1776 by *Juan Bautista de Anza,* and the eventual founding of the presidio and mission at San Francisco in June 1776.

Portolá, meanwhile, had returned to Baja California, and in 1776 he was appointed governor of the city of Puebla, Mexico, where he took office February 23, 1777. Around 1784 Portolá returned to Spain. His date of death is not known.

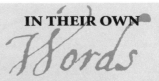

IN THEIR OWN *Words*

A Hard Trek to San Diego

[January 1769] The expedition was composed of 37 soldiers in leather jackets with their captain, Don Fernando de Rivera; this officer was sent in advance with twenty-seven soldiers, and the Governor [Portolá] followed with ten men and a sergeant.

[May 11, 1769] I set out from Santa Maria, the last mission to the north, escorted by four soldiers, in company with Father Junípero Serra, president of the missions, and Father Miguel Campa. This day we proceeded for about four hours with very little water for the animals and without any pasture, which obliged us to go on farther in the afternoon to find some. There was, however no water.

—GASPAR DE PORTOLÁ, *DIARIO,* JANUARY 1769 AND MAY 11, 1769

Posada, Alonso de   (?–?)

Although not himself an explorer, Alonso de Posada made an important contribution to the early knowledge of vast areas of the western United States and so advanced the ability of others to explore. Nothing is known of this Franciscan father until he came from Spain in 1651 to serve the missions in New Mexico, spending much of that time (he would later report) "in the most remote parts of the province." After some ten years there, he was reassigned to Mexico City, and in 1685 the viceroy of *New Spain [II]* commissioned Posada to write a report about the lands and peoples north of the Río Grande. Drawing on many reports now lost, he

IN THEIR OWN **The Spanish Recognize Utah**

Words

*F*rom the Rio San Juan, which runs west
for 70 leagues and is possessed by the
Navajo nation, the trail passes into the land of the Yutahs, a warlike nation.
Crossing this nation for 60 leagues in the same northwest direction one
comes to some hills, and traveling through that country for another 50
leagues more or less, one arrives at the great lake in the land Indians of the
North call Teguayo. The Mexicans call the lake Copalla, according to their
ancient traditions the place where all Indians, even those of Mexico,
Guatemala and Peru originated.

—FRAY ALONSO POSADA, REPORT, 1686

described the travels of numerous obscure Spanish explorers during the
early 1600s, provided valuable information about the different Indian
peoples, accounted for many little-known rivers and other geographic
features, revealed the existence of many remote areas, and indicated possible routes, such as one from Santa Fe to Quivira (now assumed to be in
Kansas). He was the first to inform Europeans of the Great Salt Lake. The
Posada Report, issued in 1686, owes its reputation to the quantity and
quality of new information it provided to Europeans interested in learning more about the New World.

Quimper, Manuel   (?–?)

An otherwise obscure Spanish naval officer, Manuel Quimper was of part
French descent. He appears in the history of exploration only in 1790,
when *Esteban José Martínez* gave him command of the *Princesa Real* (the
former *Princess Royal* seized from John Meares) and commissioned him to
explore the Strait of *Juan de Fuca [II].* Although only an ensign, or sub-
lieutenant, Quimper had an experienced pilot and mapmaker under him,
Gonzalo López de Haro. Leaving Nootka Sound on May 31, they sailed
south and then southeastward into the strait. In the course of his explorations, he put in to various ports along both the north and south shores
of the strait, constantly taking formal possession and assigning Spanish
names to places that would later be renamed by the British. Thus Quimper's Puerto de Córdova has become Esquimault Harbor, his Puerto de

Bodega y Quadra has become Port Discovery. He took numerous sound-ings, was the first European to explore the San Juan Islands, and in numer-ous encounters with the Indians along the coasts traded for many sea otter pelts. When he sailed out of the strait to return to Nootka, he spent six days in dense fog unable to locate its entrance and so had to sail all the way down the coast to the Spanish port of Monterey; from there he made his way to San Blas in Mexico, at which point in time and place Quimper largely vanishes from history. His journal and Haro's detailed charts, how-ever, survive as valuable records of this expedition.

Rivas and Iriarte expedition (1686–1687)

In the second of five Spanish searches for *La Salle [V]* along the gulf coast, Martín de Rivas and Pedro de Iriarte captained two specially built shallow draft vessels (*piraguas*) with sails and oars, with *Enríquez Barroto* and Romero of the first expedition as chief pilots. On December 25, 1686, they left Veracruz, and on March 8 sailed from Tampico to explore the coast to the mouth of the Río Grande, where hostile natives chased them off. They continued along the Padre Island shore of Texas and at Matagorda Bay found the remains of La Salle's ships. There hostile Karankawas prevented further investigation, and thus they missed finding the survivors of La Salle's French colony on Garcitas Creek. Sailing on to Galveston Bay and Sabine Pass, of which they completed the first recorded explorations, they also discovered a series of bays and rivers on the way to the Mississippi Delta, which they reached in mid-May and where they noted the South-west Pass. They reexplored Mobile Bay and continued down the *Florida [III]* peninsula, reaching Havana in mid-June. They arrived back at Vera-cruz on July 3, 1687, having completed the first circumnavigation of the Gulf of Mexico and having designated place names that later appeared on most European maps. Meanwhile the impatient viceroy had sent out a third gulf expedition (*Pez and López de Gamarra*) in June.

Rivera, Juan María de (?–?)

Nothing is known about this Spaniard until he surfaces in the written records as the leader of several expeditions into southern Colorado and Utah between 1761 and 1765. He was apparently based in Santa Fe, and the fact that he was referred to as "Don" suggests he was of high social standing. At least one of his expeditions was commissioned by the then governor of New Mexico, Tomás Vélez Cachupin. On his first expedition at least, he was searching for gold and silver in Colorado. On his second expedition he seems to have led a group of traders and missionaries to Durango, Colorado, suggesting he was prepared to establish a settlement. Setting out from New Mexico, he crossed into the southwestern corner of Colorado. There he went to the San Juan River, crossed a southern spur of the La Plata Mountains, went down the Dolores River, then turned east over the Uncompahgre Plateau and down the Uncompahgre River to its confluence with the Gunnison River. There he carved a cross into a cottonwood tree; the *Escalante and Domínguez expedition* would record seeing this cross when they arrived at this point in 1776. On his third expedition, in 1765, Rivera crossed into southern and central Utah, thus becoming the first European to enter what is today that state; on this expedition, he is credited by some with crossing into northern Utah and Idaho. Rivera would never gain the reputation of other explorers of that era, but in fact he opened up a route from Santa Fe into Utah that future Spanish explorers and traders would follow; later it would become known as the Old Spanish Trail.

Rivera, Pedro de (?–?)

In late 1727 General Pedro de Rivera began an inspection tour of the presidios in the provinces of Coahuila and Texas. Rivera's diary of the expedition is an exceptional contribution to understanding Indian culture and forest and wildlife resources. He was accompanied by *Francisco Alvarez Barreiro*, who contributed to the accuracy of Rivera's diary with his surveying and engineering expertise. Barreiro added his own maps and reports on the expedition.

In November 1724 Rivera began a three-year, seven-thousand-mile inspection tour from Mexico City. By July 1727 the inspection party had done military reviews of presidios in New Mexico and Vizcaya. On August 1 Rivera arrived at the Presidio San Juan Bautista. Barreiro gave a detailed report of the wildlife in the area. The expedition reached San Antonio on August 17 and crossed the Colorado below Austin on August 23. This was the fifth Spanish expedition traveling this route during an eighteen-year span. On the way to Trinity River Rivera passed through woods of oak, walnut, elm, and pine around the lake of San Luis Obispo. On September 5 the expedition met over fifty Necha Indians near the San Pedro Creek area. The Indians were armed with French rifles, gunpowder, and bullets but were not hostile. On September 15 the expedition reached the Presidio de los Adaes. Eight tribes were reported living near the post. By early November the party had completed the East Texas inspection and returned to the San Antonio presidio. On November 8 Rivera visited the ruins of Presidio de la Bahía. He returned to San Juan Bautista by way of San Antonio presidio, arriving on December 18. Shortly after returning to Mexico in 1728, Rivera completed written assessments of the trip and drafted new regulations for the presidios. Rivera's expedition was the last in a very active period of Spanish exploration in Texas between 1709 and 1727.

Rivera y Moncada, Fernando de (1725–1781)

Fernando Javier Rivera y Moncado was born in or near Campostella, Mexico, and in 1742 he began his career as a soldier. Serving alongside the Jesuits in Baja California, he helped them establish several missions between 1752 and 1767. In 1769, now a captain, he was chosen to lead the first overland unit of the *Portolá* expedition to lay the basis for Spanish settlement of Alta California; he led the party across some three hundred miles of unknown territory from Baja California to San Diego. That July he accompanied Portolá's expedition in search of the port of Monterey but ended up going all the way to San Francisco. In 1773 Rivera was appointed military governor of Alta California, with his headquarters at Monterey. In 1774, accompanied by Father Francisco Palou, Rivera led a small party from Monterey that explored the San Francisco area with the goal of finding sites for a presidio and missions. By 1776 Rivera found himself at odds with both *Father Junípero Serra,* who was in charge of the Franciscan missions in California, and also with *Juan Bautista de Anza,* a fellow military man and explorer, and this led to his giving up the governorship of Alta California in 1777. He was then assigned to recruiting soldiers and colonists in Mexico for the new Spanish settlements in Alta California, and it was on one of these expeditions that, while camping near the Colorado River on the edge of California, Rivera and some of his soldiers were killed during a surprise attack by the Yuman (or Quechan) Indians.

Rubí, María Pignatelli Rubí Corbera y San Climent, Marqués de (?–?)

In 1762 France secretly ceded to Spain the territory west of the Mississippi that had been part of French *Louisiana [V],* which included parts of northeast Texas. There had been no expedition from *New Spain [II]* across the province of Texas since that of *Pedro de Rivera* in 1727. The viceroy of New Spain commissioned the Marqués de Rubí to visit the presidios in northern New Spain, from the Gulf of California to Texas. Nicolás de Lafora kept a diary account of Rubí's tour, and José de Urrutia was responsible for preparing maps and plans for the expedition. The expedition left New Mexico and proceeded south and then east, arriving in Saltillo on June 6, 1767. The route that Rubí took to the Sabinas from Monclova followed *Alonso de León*'s road. The trail Rubí followed north from the Sabinas to the Río Grande is easily tracked because most of the rivers still carry the same names today. On July 14 Rubí recorded the presence of Apache Indians in a large encampment on the Río Grande. At the Presidio San Saba the expedition was in constant danger from Comanches who communicated with smoke signals around the encampment. They also recorded taking a bear alive. The expedition continued to San Antonio de Béjar, the largest settlement in Texas at the time.

There were numerous Indian tribes in the area. These included the Payaya, the Sarame, the Chane, the Coco, and the Tecamo. On August 25, 1767, Rubí commenced a journey to the presidio at Los Adaes. The route was along the Camino Real from San Antonio southeast along the left bank of the San Antonio River to Cibolo Creek near Falls City in Karnes County and then east along León's old road to the Guadalupe, crossing at what is now called the Governor's Ford. Diarist Lafora was the first to identify the location of this ford near present-day Cuero, Texas. From the Guadalupe River to the Colorado crossing near La Grange, the Camino Real followed the old Indian trade route used by León in 1689 and again in 1690.

Rubí referred to the Colorado River by its present name, rather than calling it the San Marcos, as had been the practice on earlier expeditions. During the journey near the crossing of the Brazos River, the expedition had to be cautious of the Aranama, a pagan renegade band who had rejected mission life. They reached Trinity on September 3 at a crossing southeast of the present city of Crockett. Near the Angelina River, Rubí saw distinct villages of Tejas Indians living in very large huts divided into room areas by woven grass curtains. On October 7 Rubí found a stone cistern (*aljibe*) near the camp that captured excellent rainwater. After inspecting the Presidio Orcoquisac and the immediate gulf area, Rubí proceeded northwest and on October 23 reached the Colorado River near the present city of Round Top. On the return trip Rubí crossed the Guadalupe at Vado del Pielago. Nearby he passed what was described as a homosexual Karankawa Indian community.

Rubí reached Presidio de la Bahía on October 31. According to Lafora, a cavalry company of fifty men, including three officers, was at the post. The nearby Mission Espíritu Santo contained ninety-three Aranama and Tamique Indians. On November 12 the inspection party completed work at La Bahía and proceeded west toward San Juan Bautista by way of Laredo. The expedition reached Laredo on November 18, reporting that they had passed a prodigious multitude of rattlesnakes that occupied the country. Laredo was a settlement of about sixty huts made of branches and leaves. Once the Río Grande was crossed, Rubí inspected the Presidio San Juan and moved on to Monterrey, the capital of Nuevo León. Rubí's route reflected the changes that had occurred in mid-eighteenth-century Texas, principally the increasingly dominant role played by the Apache and Comanche Indians. The more docile local tribes and the Spaniards were being crowded into an increasingly narrow belt along the Río Grande and the coast. By February 1768 Rubí was back in Mexico City with his report, which strongly protested the practice of disposing of captured Indians by selling them as slaves. At the end of Lafora's diary, a very negative summary description of the province of Texas is given, citing the number of insects as making the place uninhabitable.

Serra, Father Junípero   (1713–1784)

Known as "the Apostle of California" for his extraordinary labors in establishing missions there, Junípero Serra was born at Petra on the Spanish island of Majorca, where he was baptized Miguel José Serra. After entering the Franciscan Order in 1730, he took the name Junípero (from one of the disciples of Saint Francis of Assisi). He was ordained in 1738 and first studied and then taught philosophy at Lullian University in Palma, Majorca. In 1749 Serra requested permission to join a group of Franciscans heading for missionary work in *New Spain [II]*. Arriving in Mexico City in 1750, Serra spent the next seventeen years among the Indians of Sierra Gorda, Mexico City, and south-central Mexico. In 1767 he was appointed president of the former Jesuit missions in Baja California, now assigned to the Franciscans.

At this time, the visitor general to New Spain, José de Galvez, was determined to extend the Spanish empire in America. His plan was to establish a chain of missions at intervals of one day's ride from the border of Baja California to Monterey (which had been discovered by *Sebastián Vizcaíno [II]* in 1602). Galvez reasoned that missions would discourage attempts by Russia or any other foreign power to establish its own colonies in California. The logical choice for presiding over the new system of missions was Father Junípero Serra.

To accomplish this plan, in 1769 the Spanish authorized a major expedition, commanded by *Gaspar de Portolá* but divided into two land and two sea units. Serra was in the larger land unit, led by Portolá, but had a difficult time keeping up with the men because of his asthma and severe pains in one of his legs. The leg swelled to the point where he could barely walk on it, and Portolá threatened to send Serra back. Serra continued with the expedition under tremendous hardship until it reached San Diego. Serra stayed in San Diego tending sick sailors and learning more

The mission San Carlos Borromeo was established at Carmel, California, in 1771 by Father Junípero Serra. San Carlos was Serra's headquarters for his missionary activities, and in 1784 he died and was buried there. In this drawing from the 1790s, the original church is at the left; the still-standing one, completed in 1794, is being erected in the center.

IN THEIR OWN *Words*   **Father Serra Describes a Journey**

My Dear Friend: Thank God I arrived the day before yesterday, the first of the month, at this port of San Diego, truly a fine one, and not without reason called famous. . . . The tract through which we passed is generally very good land, with plenty of water; and there, as well as here, the country is neither rocky nor overrun with brushwood. There are, however, many hills but they are composed of earth. . . . We found vines of a large size, and in some cases quite loaded with grapes; we also found an abundance of roses, which appeared to be like those of Castile. We have seen Indians in immense numbers, and all those on this coast of the Pacific contrive to make a good subsistence on various seeds and by fishing. . . . We found on our journey, as well as in the place where we stopped, that they treated us with as much confidence and good-will as if they had known us all their lives.

—FATHER JUNÍPERO SERRA, LETTER TO HIS COLLEAGUE AND LATER
BIOGRAPHER, FATHER FRANCISCO PALOU, JULY 3, 1769

about the Indians while Portolá went north to Monterey. On July 16, 1769, Serra founded the mission of San Diego de Alcala. This was the first mission established within the present state of California.

In the spring of 1770 Serra took a ship north to Monterey Bay. The mission of San Carlos Borromeo de Carmelo was founded in Monterey on June 3, 1770. Now known as Carmel, this proved to be Serra's main mission and his headquarters for the rest of his life. Over the next fourteen years Serra traveled up and down the California coast under great hardship due to his weak leg and conditions at the time. In 1771 Serra founded San Antonio de Padua, south of Monterey, and San Gabriel Arcángel, near present-day Los Angeles. In 1772 he founded San Luis Obispo and, in quick succession in 1776, the Mission San Francisco de Asis (Mission Dolores) in San Francisco and San Juan Capistrano. Mission Santa Clara de Asis was created in 1777, and San Buenaventura, present-day Ventura, in 1782. In all, he established nine missions between San Diego and San Francisco, which formed the heart of the Spanish settlement of Alta California. Serra died at Mission San Carlos Borromeo (Carmel) and was buried beneath the floor of the mission's church.

Among his other contributions, Serra was instrumental in recording early information about the geography of California as well as detailing the lives of its native population. Serra has traditionally had a reputation as a kind and generous man who opposed prejudice and demanded fair treatment for the Indians. He was also seen as a strong-willed and determined priest who frequently came into conflict with the Spanish civil authorities with whom he had to share the governing of California. Recent historical criticism, however, questions this version of Serra, arguing that he enslaved the natives through religion and helped support an unjust system of colonization. In either case, the records show that by the end of 1783, seven months before Serra's death, 6,000 Indians had been converted to Christianity, nearly 30,000 head of livestock had been introduced to Alta California, and the yearly harvests of the missions produced about 30,000 bushels of grain and vegetables. Indians worked in mission workshops and produced many material goods needed in California. Whatever the views of more recent generations, it is accepted that Serra's explorations and missions were fundamental in establishing a strong Spanish presence in Alta California and a system that would long link Spanish interests along the western edge of California; the route itself became known as *El Camino Real*—"The Royal Highway."

Sútil and *Mexicana* expedition (1792)

After **Alejandro Malaspina** returned from the northwest coast in 1791, he decided to send two ships back to the region to search for the **Northwest Passage [VII]**, now thought to be via the **Strait of Juan de Fuca [II]**. Cayetano Valdés and Dionisio Alcalá Galiano were put in charge of these ships, the *Sútil* and *Mexicana* respectively. In March 1792 they sailed from San Blas, Spain's naval base on the Pacific coast of Mexico. They sailed into the Juan de Fuca Strait in search of the Northwest Passage, but after exploring the waters and coasts around the southern end of Vancouver Island—where they encountered the expedition of **George Vancouver [VI]** himself—they became convinced that there was no such passage, at least by this route. They proceeded north through the Queen Charlotte Strait to the Pacific Ocean again, sailed south to the Spanish outpost at Nootka Bay on the west coast of Vancouver Island, and then continued south to the mouth of the Columbia River. From there they sailed back to Mexico.

Aside from establishing once and for all that the Juan de Fuca Strait did not lead to any Northwest Passage, the expedition had not accomplished all that much, but it owes its fame to the superb report and illustrations made by expedition member José Cardero. Eventually published by the Spanish government in 1802, it was used at that time to reassert Spain's claims to the whole northwestern region of North America.

Terán de los Ríos, Domingo de   (?–?)

On May 16, 1691, Domingo de Terán de los Ríos, the first Spanish governor of the province of Texas, started out from Monclova in northeastern Mexico's Coahuila province. With him was an expeditionary force of fifty soldiers and Franciscan Damián Mazanet (veteran of the 1686–1690 *León* expeditions) leading nine friars and lay brothers. As ordered by the Mexican viceroy, he was to explore Texas, investigate reports of French encroachment, and establish seven more missions among the Tejas and neighboring tribes. On May 28 he arrived at the Río Grande following León's route; by June 13 he reached the San Antonio area; and nearly two weeks later he arrived at the Colorado River below Austin. A detachment sent to Matagorda Bay missed the supply ship. Terán wanted to try again, but Mazanet insisted on hurrying on to the San Francisco mission, reportedly beset by illness, on the Neches River. In late August Terán returned to Matagorda Bay for supplies and received new orders to find a water route to the East Texas missions. On November 6 he set out northeastward from San Francisco mission with a small detachment, along with Mazanet and two other friars. After exploring the Neches River, which he found unnavigable, he trekked to the Sabine River and crossed it near Carthage, Texas, and probably crossed Caddo Lake near Mooringsport, Louisiana. He reached the Sulphur River above its junction (Miller County, Arkansas) with the Red River, which he explored briefly before turning back. During the desperate march to Matagorda Bay through snow, ice, mud, and floods, he lost 800 horses and 165 pack mules. From there on March 24, 1692, he sailed for Veracruz, leaving most of his men to return by land. Beyond the cursory river explorations, the expedition was a failure—no new missions were established, the existing missions remained shaky (and would be abandoned in October 1693), and great quantities of supplies and animals were lost to raiding Indians, with whom relations deteriorated. The grim aspects of East Texas discouraged further Spanish settlement for another twenty years.

Uribarri (Ulibarri), Juan de (1670–?)

Little is known of his background, but in 1692, at the age of twenty-two, Sergeant Major Juan de Uribarri accompanied General *Diego de Vargas* on a punitive expedition from Mexico to New Mexico. The purpose of the expedition was to dislodge the *Pueblo Indians [II]* who had revolted and driven out the Spanish settlers in that region. A year later, in 1693, Juan de Uribarri once again accompanied General de Vargas to New Mexico, only this time with one hundred Spanish soldiers and fifty pioneer families who were returning to their old homes and ranches.

Uribarri apparently remained in New Mexico and rose in rank because on July 13, 1706, he was in charge of an expedition that set out from Santa Fe with forty soldiers and a hundred Pueblo Indian allies, for El Cuartelejo, a locale some twelve miles north of Scott City, Kansas. (One of the Indian scouts was José Naranjo, who had served with distinction under Vargas; he was later to die in the *Villasur* expedition massacre.) During the 1680s the Picuris Pueblo Indians had fled from their pueblo near Santa Fe to the Kansan plains, but there they found themselves enslaved by the Apaches and had petitioned the Spanish for deliverance. Heading for El Cuartelejo, Uribarri's expedition followed the San Fernando Creek and, near the present site of Cimarron, New Mexico, met friendly Indians who warned of hostile groups blocking their way to the east. Uribarri turned northward and climbed the mountains to camp near Trinidad, Colorado. Continuing north, they reached the Arkansas River opposite Pueblo, Colorado. Heading east into Kansas, on July 29 they entered El Cuartelejo and successfully liberated the enslaved Picuris. On August 5 Uribarri dispatched three parties to visit neighboring areas and cemented relationships with the Apache population. With sixty-two freed Picuris Indians, the expedition returned over the same route at a rapid rate. They released the Picuris to their home pueblo near Santa Fe. On September 2, 1706, Uribarri's expedition arrived in Santa Fe, where he reported to Governor Cuerbo. The expedition had succeeded in extending Spanish activities into the northeast of New Mexico, charting out many important rivers and landmarks and learning of French activity near the Rockies.

Valverde y Cosio, Antonio (1671–?)

Antonio Valverde y Cosio was born in Burgos, Spain. The date of his arrival in the New World is not known, but in 1716 Valverde was made governor of Spanish New Mexico. It was while governor that Valverde made his most famous expedition into Indian territory north of Sante Fe.

In July 1719 Comanches and Utes murdered some Spanish inhabitants of Taos and Cochiti pueblos. The hostilities marked an important departure in the traditional friendship between the Spanish and the Utes. After a council of war, Governor Valverde was delegated to head an expedition to attack the Comanches and Utes in northeastern New Mexico. Another goal of this expedition was to explore the territory and to learn the extent of French intrusion into the area. On September 15, 1719, Valverde mustered sixty troops plus Indian allies of over four hundred warriors and traveled to Taos. On September 20 Valverde left Taos and headed east into the mountains to Cimarron, New Mexico, where they met with the Apaches. Valverde's diary and journals outline the life of these Indians, indicating they had a substantial culture at the time. The expedition then proceeded eastward to near Dillon, New Mexico. On September 28 the expedition turned northward toward the Arkansas River in Colorado, where they had to cross mountains in the bitter cold. On October 2 they reached the main stream of the Huerfano River near the Wet Mountains. By October 4 they were southeast of Pueblo, Colorado. The expedition now turned eastward, moving through vast herds of buffalo. They were some distance south of the Arkansas River, about five days from El Cuartelejo (near Scott City, Kansas), when they discovered traces of large bands of Comanches, numbering over a thousand. The camp had been broken, and the Indians were now heading northeast. Apaches in the area told of an attack on Indians by the French and Pawnees some distance from El Cuartelejo. Valverde also learned of other French and Pawnee settlements. On October 14 Valverde convened his troops and decided to return to Sante Fe because of the approaching winter.

There is some speculation about Valverde's return route. From Valverde's report it is inferred that the expedition followed the Arkansas River, passing through the Sangre de Cristo Pass in Colorado down into New Mexico to Taos. The expedition reached Santa Fe some time between the fifteenth and thirtieth of November. Valverde's expedition was instrumental in helping define Spain's control of New Mexico and established the existence of French attempts to take over the area now known as New Mexico.

Vargas, Diego José de (1644–1704)

After the Pueblo Revolt of 1680 (see *Pueblo Indians [II]*) Spain faced the prospect of completely retreating from New Mexico. But it chose not to do so, and during the next twelve years, there was constant friction between the Spanish and the areas' natives. As early as 1683, an exploratory expedition went as far north as Isleta (near Albuquerque) and returned. Finally, in 1690 Diego de Vargas was chosen to lead an expedition north to remove the natives and restore Spanish government in New Mexico. Vargas was a native-born Spaniard of noble lineage, with nearly twenty years' experience in *New Spain [II]* including numerous government posts in northern Mexico.

The Vargas expedition left El Paso on July 13, 1692. On August 16 Vargas, with forty soldiers and fifty Indian allies, crossed the Río Grande and headed north. The expedition arrived at Fray Cristobal on August 27, having crossed the Jornada del Muerto without incident. They arrived in Mejia on September 9, and around September 12 they reached the outskirts of the former Spanish capital of Santa Fe. War seemed inevitable, but the Indians negotiated for peace when Vargas threatened to cut off the city's water supply. Vargas took formal occupation of Santa Fe on September 13, 1692. In the following weeks he conquered other rebel pueblos such as San Juan and San Cristobal. A revolt by the Indians in Taos forced Vargas to use Indian allies to defeat that pueblo in early October 1692. Vargas then went west and took Acoma and Zuni, two of the hardest pueblos to capture. It took several weeks of struggle before Acoma was retaken. With the whole of New Mexico now under Spanish control, Vargas returned to El Paso in late December 1692.

The stage was now set for phase two of Vargas's plan for the recolonization of New Mexico. In July 1693 Vargas led sixty-two volunteer families north from El Paso. These included twenty-seven families of blacks and mestizos from Zacatecas. The trip was slow and rough, food was low, and the weather was cold. Vargas's expedition for the resettlement of New Mexico ended by 1695. In the spring of 1704 Vargas, then governor of New

Mexico, became ill while fighting renegade Apaches near present-day Albuquerque, and he died on April 8, 1704.

Villasur, Pedro de   (?–1720)

By about 1715 the French and Pawnees, approaching from the northeast and east, were invading Spanish territory and attacking Spanish settlements. *Valverde*'s expedition of 1719 had gathered information about a French and Pawnee alliance that further threatened Spanish interests. Antonio Valverde y Cosio was governor of New Mexico and chose Lieutenant Pedro de Villasur to head a new expedition into the area.

Villasur was born in Castile, Spain at an unknown date. He was a lieutenant commander in El Paso before being transferred to Santa Fe. Villasur left Sante Fe in June 1720 with forty-two soldiers and sixty Indian allies, including the famous Indian scout Naranjo as guide. He followed a northeast route from Santa Fe. They crossed the Arkansas River in Colorado on rafts and made their way eastward to El Cuartelejo, Kansas. Traveling north, on August 6 Valverde reached the South Platte River in Nebraska. On August 7 chief scout Naranjo returned to camp with reports of a nearby Pawnee band holding a war dance. On August 10 Villasur and his expedition moved to a camp opposite the Pawnee village, which was on an island in the middle of a river. After preliminary hostilities, Villasur decided to retreat to his original camp near North Platte, Nebraska, on the banks of the San Lorenzo River, now known as the North Platte River. At daybreak on August 14, 1720, the Pawnees and French executed a surprise attack on Villasur's camp. The unarmed Villasur was killed in front of his tent. Twelve Spaniards and forty-eight Indian allies survived the attack, but the expedition came to an abrupt halt. On September 6 the survivors brought the news to Valverde, and Spain's New Mexico settlements now found themselves temporarily weakened by the loss of so many of their best soldiers.

PART V

From the Appalachians to the Mississippi, 1540–1840

De Soto and Champlain had pointed the way. Traders, missionaries, soldiers, and, finally, settlers followed in the two centuries after 1620, opening up the rich lands lying between the Appalachian Mountain barrier and the Mississippi River—and displacing their native inhabitants from their immemorial homelands.

The French advanced westward aggressively along the river and lake systems Samuel de Champlain had explored from 1609 to 1616. Waves of traders and Roman Catholic missionaries—the Indians called them "black robes"—journeyed into the Great Lakes region during the middle decades of the seventeenth century. With the expeditions of Nicollet to Green Bay in the 1630s, Brébeuf and Chaumonot to the Huron and Erie country in 1641, Jogues and Raymbaut to Sault Sainte Marie at the junction of Lakes Huron and Superior in 1641, and Allouez to Lake Superior and the Wisconsin interior in the 1660s, the outlines of the forest, lake, river, and prairie regions of the upper Midwest began to take form on the Europeans' maps.

"A well-cleared country, crossed by streams which empty into the great lake. There is no ugly surface of great rocks and barren mountains," the Brébeuf expedition reported of the region of Ontario province bounded by Lake Huron's Georgian Bay, Lake Ontario, and Lake Erie.

The trader-priest team of Louis Jolliet and Jacques Marquette set out in May 1673 to explore the great river called the "Messi-Sipi," which they believed emptied into a sea of California. By mid-July Jolliet and Marquette had reached their farthest penetration, the junction of the Mississippi and the Arkansas—a ten-day journey from the sea, Quapaw Indian guides told them. This intelligence changed the explorers' way of thinking: "Judging from the direction of the course of the Mississippi, if it continue the same way, we think that it discharges into the Mexican gulf," they wrote.

Another French explorer, Sieur de La Salle, completed the transit of the Mississippi to the sea in 1682,

Some experts consider John Mitchell's map of the British and French possessions in North America to be the greatest map in the history of American cartography. A physician and amateur scientist who lived in Virginia from 1735 to 1746, Mitchell returned to England about 1746 and began working on the map in 1750 for the Lords Commissioners for Trade and Plantations in London. He completed it five years later. The map continues to be admired for its technical and aesthetic qualities. Peace commissioners at the Paris treaty negotiations that concluded the Revolutionary War used a later edition of the map.

unlocking the river's secrets as he followed in the 140-year-old wake of the remnants of Hernando de Soto's expedition. De Soto had sought mineral wealth; La Salle's purposes were frankly commercial—to establish New France's domination of the fur trade from the Great Lakes to the Gulf of Mexico.

During the century's last quarter, the expeditions of Dulhut, Noyon, and Kelsey explored the northern prairies of present Minnesota and the provinces of Manitoba and Saskatchewan. Henry Kelsey in 1690–1691 struck southwest from Hudson's Bay into the Gros Ventre country of northern Saskatchewan and became the first European to sight buffalo on the northern plains.

From farther south, the English advanced from the eastern slopes of the Appalachians. By the mid-eighteenth century, John Howard, John Peter Salley, Thomas Walker, and Christopher Gist had carried the explorations westward beyond the mountains and into the rich Ohio River Valley. Still farther south, English and French traders and soldiers scouted the interior of present South Carolina, Georgia, Florida, and the gulf states. The Englishman Thomas Welch established a trading post in Chickasaw country on the Mississippi as early as 1698.

The Seven Years' War of 1756–1763 ended in a complete British rout of their French rivals for control of eastern North America. Settlement inevitably followed Britain's victory. Walker had reached the Cumberland Gap in 1750. Within fifty years, thousands of migrants would pour through the opening in the mountains into Tennessee, Kentucky, and the Ohio Valley. As a result, the explorers would shift their attention farther west, beyond the great Mississippi.

Albanel, Charles   (1613 or 1616–1696)

A French-born and highly educated Jesuit missionary, Charles Albanel arrived in Quebec in late August 1649 to serve the Lower Algonquians, or Montagnais, at Tadoussac. In 1671 the intendant (or chief administrator) of *New France [III],* Jean Talon, assigned him to find out whether the northern sea (the Arctic Ocean) and Hudson Bay were the same body of water and to investigate the presence of Europeans (the *Grosseilliers and Radisson expeditions,* in British service) on its shores.

On August 6 Albanel left Quebec for the Saguenay River and by September 7 reached the far end of Lac Saint-Jean. After wintering with the Mistassini Indians, he reached Lake Mistassini on June 18, 1672, and Lake Nemiskau on June 25, before voyaging down the Rupert River to its mouth on June 28. There he found a British ship and two deserted houses. After exploring James Bay on lower Hudson Bay, he left a letter for his countryman Radisson and turned back. On July 9 he raised the French royal coat of arms at Lake Nemiskau and was back at Chicoutimi on the *Saguenay [III]* River on August 1. According to his official report, during his difficult journey, with two hundred portages and other hazardous passages, he had identified Hudson Bay, opened relations with the region's Indians, and met with no whites.

On his second expedition north to try to end the Indian trade with the British and to persuade Grosseilliers to return to French service, he left Tadoussac on January 13, 1674, wintered in the Lac Saint-Jean area, and by August 30 reached the Rupert River, where the British seized him and his companions and sent them as prisoners to London. Some two years later, Albanel returned to New France to be assigned as superior at Sault Sainte Marie, where he reportedly sent out expeditions to explore the Wisconsin region.

Allouez, Claude Jean   (1622–1689)

Born in Saint-Didier, France, Allouez arrived in Canada in 1658 and won appointment in 1663 as governor for all the natives and traders of the northwest wilderness, then largely unknown and unmapped. He set out for the Lake Superior region, which he called Lac Tracy, to take up his new post in August 1665.

Following the route of the Indian trader *Jean Nicolet* to Green Bay, Allouez in 1669–1670 pushed southward into the new country of the upper Fox River to establish a mission among the Wisconsin Indian tribes. He found the upper Fox valley "a very attractive place" of plains and open fields and learned from the Indians that it lay only a six-day march from the great "Messi-Sipi" River.

Before Allouez, Lake Superior had been known to the French mainly through reports from Indians, though the fur trader *Étienne Brûlé [III]* may have glimpsed the lake in 1616 and the *Grosseilliers and Radisson expeditions* reached the area in 1659–1660. In 1672 Allouez and Father *Claude Dablon* prepared a map of Lake Superior and environs showing the Jesuit missions and the region's Indian tribes. It remained the most accurate rendering of the world's largest freshwater lake until the nineteenth century.

Appalachian Mountains

A mountain system of eastern North America, the Appalachians extend from Quebec to Alabama and Georgia and are composed of numerous smaller ranges. From the north, the Green Mountains, White Mountains, Adirondacks, Berkshire Hills, Catskills, and Poconos are followed by the Allegheny Mountains, or western Appalachians, which stretch from Pennsylvania to central West Virginia. To the south are the Shenandoah, *Blue Ridge [III]*, Black, and Great Smoky Mountains. For two centuries they imposed a formidable barrier to exploration and settlement westward from the Atlantic seaboard.

From the 1500s to the 1700s, passages through the mountains followed ancient Indian paths. In Canada the *St. Lawrence River [III]* and its tributaries provided a canoe route, with portages, to the Great Lakes. In the United States, Indians, hunters, traders, soldiers, and settlers used three major gateways through the Appalachians. In northern New York State the Mohawk Trail extended from Fort Orange (Albany) on the

Hudson River by way of the Mohawk River through Iroquois lands to Lake Ontario, which offered access to the western Great Lakes.

In the central or Alleghenies region, early Pennsylvania traders approached the upper *Ohio River* on the Kittanning Trail by following the Juniata River, a Susquehanna tributary, to the Connemaugh and Allegheny rivers. In 1752 *Christopher Gist* persuaded Delaware chief Nemacolin to mark another old Indian trail over the Allegheny Mountains, this one from Maryland's upper Potomac River to the Monongahela River near Fort Duquesne (Pittsburgh); General Edward Braddock widened it for military purposes in 1755. Three years later General John Forbes followed the old Indian Highland Trail to travel from Philadelphia by way of Carlisle, establishing Forts Bedford and Ligonier along the way as supply bases, along a new route to Fort Duquesne.

The third and southern gateway, first used by Spanish explorers *Hernando de Soto [III]* in 1539 and *Juan Pardo [III]* in 1567–1568, crossed from southwestern North Carolina by way of the French Broad River into Tennessee. In 1750, to the north of this Spanish passage, *Thomas Walker* named and described *Cumberland Gap,* near the point where Virginia, Kentucky, and Tennessee converge. Only after *Daniel Boone* began to hew out the Wilderness Road in 1775 did this passage begin to be frequently used. The British Proclamation of 1763, which banned settlement to the west of the Alleghenies in order to protect Indian lands, had a limited effect. Colonists advanced the frontier westward at a rate of seventeen miles per year from 1764 to 1774.

The prospect of the Appalachian Mountains as a likely source of gold, silver, and gemstones lured early Spanish explorers into the interior of the Southeast. This quarry proved elusive for the most part, although in the early 1800s northern Georgia settlers found old Spanish mine shafts, and this area was found to have the nation's most important gold deposit until the 1848 discovery in California. In the Alleghenies were found less glittering prizes—iron ore and some of the world's largest coal deposits. Early explorers and settlers bypassed these significant resources in their push to reach the fertile lands of the Ohio, Mississippi, and Tennessee Valleys.

Bartram, John   (1699–1777)

Born near Darby, Pennsylvania, to a Quaker farm family, he broke with the religion of his parents over the issues of Jesus' divinity and pacifism and became a prosperous farmer at Kingsessing, Pennsylvania, in the Schuylkill River Valley, four miles from Philadelphia. Bartram's lack of formal education—he taught himself the classical languages—did not prevent him from making his name as a botanist. He placed many of the rare plants collected in his travels in a famous garden at his estate, regarded as the first botanical garden in the American colonies, and conducted early hybridization experiments there.

In 1738 Bartram completed a thousand-mile journey collecting plant specimens along the James River of Virginia and into the *Blue Ridge Mountains [III]*. Four years later, he collected specimens along the Hudson River to the falls of the Mohawk in upstate New York. In 1761 he explored and collected plant specimens along the *Ohio River.*

In 1765, on his last important trip, Bartram, with his son William, botanized in Georgia and *Florida [III]*, penetrating the 285-mile-long Saint Johns River of east central Florida to its sources near Lake Okeechobee. A gifted amateur endowed with patience, curiosity, and stamina, Bartram added substantially to existing knowledge of America's flora and fauna. The Swedish taxologist Carl Linnaeus, with whom he corresponded, called him "the greatest natural botanist in the world."

Béranger, Jean   (1685–?)

Béranger arrived in the Gulf of Mexico region in 1699 with *Pierre Le Moyne, Sieur d'Iberville* in *Louisiana,* and eventually completed seventeen voyages to and from France over two decades. Ordered in 1716 to sail a brigantine up the *Mississippi* to the *Illinois* country, he was unable to advance because of dangerous flood conditions.

In two 1720–1721 expeditions, Béranger explored the Texas coast in an unsuccessful search for Matagorda Bay (known by the French as Baye Saint-Bernard, previously *La Salle*'s Baye Saint-Louis). After *Sieur de Bienville* ordered him to survey and sound the coast west of the Mississippi, he set out with Valentin Devin as cartographer from the North Pass of the Delta on August 23, 1720. After sounding Terrebonne Bay, he sailed westward to explore St. Joseph Island (near Corpus Christi) and discover Aransas Bay, where he planted a lead plate bearing the French royal coat of arms to claim possession. There he spent some two months investigating the area and observing its flora and fauna (particularly the rattlesnake), noting tar washed up on the sands, and documenting the culture of the Copano (a Karankawa tribe) while compiling a vocabulary of their language. By November 20, 1720, he was back in the Louisiana colony.

On the second expedition, again with Devin as cartographer, to deliver *Bénard de La Harpe [VI]* to establish a fort at Baye Saint-Bernard, Béranger instead arrived at the entrance to Galveston Bay on August 27, 1721. While La Harpe explored, Béranger sounded the bay, noted the natural assets, and made a word list of the Atákapan language. By October 3 they had suspended exploration of the Texas coast and returned to Biloxi.

After 1728 Béranger wrote about his explorations and set down his navigation instructions on a safer way to enter the Bahama Channel, on the best course from westernmost *Cuba*'s *[II]* Cabo San Antón to the Louisiana colony, and on how oceangoing vessels could enter the Mississippi (he had done this three times).

Bienville, Jean-Baptiste Le Moyne, Sieur de (1680–1767)

Montreal-born Jean-Baptiste Le Moyne, Sieur de Bienville, was a central figure in the exploration and colonization of French *Louisiana;* indeed, he is sometimes called the "Father of Louisiana." On his first exploratory voyage in 1697, he accompanied *Iberville,* his older brother, to the Hudson Bay area. In January 1699 he arrived with Iberville on the gulf coast to find the mouth of the *Mississippi,* which they located at North Pass on March 2 and thus became the first Europeans to enter the river from the sea. They also discovered the Mississippi Delta to be a peninsula.

The small party then ascended the river's meandering course some 180 miles before turning back. After this important discovery and the establishment of Fort Maurepas on Biloxi Bay, Iberville returned to France. Bienville stayed in Louisiana to explore Biloxi and Mobile Bays, up the Pearl River, and the coastline eastward toward Pensacola Bay, the site of a Spanish garrison. In late August 1699 he set out to find an alternative route to the Mississippi River by way of Lake Pontchartrain. In 1700 he explored, with *Louis Saint-Denis* along, west of the Mississippi, setting out overland from near the area of Saint Joseph to cross the Ouachita River to the Red River, which he ascended toward the Cadodacho possibly as far

Jean-Baptiste Le Moyne, Sieur de Bienville, was a leading player in the exploration and colonization of French Louisiana. In 1699 Bienville and his older brother, the Sieur d'Iberville, became the first Europeans to enter the Mississippi River from the sea.

upstream as Shreveport before returning down the Red River to the Mississippi. In 1714 he explored the Alabama River.

While serving the Louisiana colony in a series of military and administrative posts, including that of governor at various times, Bienville pursued a policy of expansion by supporting explorations by *Bourgmond [VI]*, *Dutisné,* the *Mallet [VI]* brothers, and others. He was particularly interested in finding a route by way of the Arkansas River to New Mexico. As Louisiana began to falter from economic problems and Indian attacks, Bienville retired in 1743 to Paris.

Blanpain (Blancpain), Joseph (?–1756)

A Flemish-born trader, Joseph Blanpain and his partners explored western *Louisiana* in 1738 while establishing commercial relations with the Atákapa and Opelousa Indians. Later he established a trading post at Natchez on the *Mississippi River.* In 1745 French authorities hired him to search the gulf for the shipwrecked *Superbe* and its survivors. He set off on this futile land expedition along the shore westward toward Matagorda Bay before veering inland to avoid hostile coastal Indians. In late September he reached Fort Saint Jean-Baptiste at Natchitoches on the Red River.

In October 1754 the Spanish arrested Blanpain and others at the French post on Galveston Bay and seized his trade goods. Blanpain was there with an official patent from the Louisiana governor to receive fifty French families from New Orleans who planned to settle between the upper Trinity and San Jacinto rivers, an area he had previously explored. He was taken as prisoner to Mexico City, where he fell ill and died before he could be sent on to Spain for trial. Blanpain's incursions onto Spanish lands in East Texas and along the gulf coast spurred the Mexican viceroy to order renewed exploration and settlement efforts in these areas

Bond, William (?–?)

William Bond sailed from London in October 1698 with two armed vessels to survey the northern coast of the Gulf of Mexico in preparation for its settlement by the Carolina Company. Led by Dr. Daniel Coxe, this group had obtained a royal grant to the lands westward from the Carolinas to the Pacific Ocean, including the gulf coast. Coxe proposed to colonize the region with French Huguenot refugees who had fled to England.

Bond sailed first to South Carolina's Charles Town to spend the winter and agreed to rendezvous with a trading group to be led by Jean Couture to the *Chickasaw* lands along the *Mississippi River.* By June 10, 1699, he had apparently reached Apalachee Bay in the western gulf. For the next twelve days he conducted brief explorations to the east and west along the Florida shore. Then he followed the coast westward, passing and missing the Spanish settlement at Pensacola Bay and the French settlement at Biloxi Bay.

In his search for the Mississippi, guided by *La Salle*'s own account, Bond sailed west of the Mississippi Delta. From Matagorda Bay, Bond's ship sounded the coast eastward while the second ship went to Mexico's Panuco River at Tampico to begin exploring the coast from there. Returning to the Delta, Bond sounded its three passes and sailed through the North Pass on August 29. By the time he had advanced some forty miles upriver, the French official *Sieur de Bienville* arrived to order him to leave on threat of imprisonment. The confrontation at the Mississippi's English Bend ended with Bond's withdrawal, escorted by the French in canoes, despite his assertion of British prior discovery some fifty years earlier.

On his return to England, Bond delivered the charts and journals he had compiled to the Carolina entrepreneurs, who used them to gain only temporary royal support for English settlement of the gulf. In the meantime, Bond's explorations and news of the arrival of the overland expedition from the Carolina coast at the Mississippi intensified Spanish and French efforts to settle the gulf region.

Boone, Daniel (1734–1820)

The archetypal pioneer, Daniel Boone moved as a youth to the western North Carolina frontier along the Yadkin River, where he became a skillful long hunter in search of deer hides. In 1765 he journeyed with other frontiersmen to *Florida [III]* to explore the St. John's River area, attracted by the offer of British land grants. In 1767–1768, following in the steps of other whites, he first crossed the *Appalachian Mountains* to explore eastern Kentucky's mountains.

In May 1769 Boone set out with John Stuart, John Finley, and others on a western hunting expedition, passing through *Cumberland Gap* and exploring the Warriors Path along the way. By December he reached the south fork of the Kentucky River (in today's Daniel Boone National Forest). After a difficult winter and escape from Shawnee captivity, he set out alone in spring 1770 to explore the Kentucky and Licking River valleys and along the *Ohio River* to its falls at Louisville. He headed back to North Carolina in March, only to be robbed of everything by *Cherokees* near Cumberland Gap. By now Boone knew more of Kentucky's terrain than any other white man.

In 1773 he returned to reexplore Kentucky, and in September he led out six settler families, who were turned back by an Indian attack. As a Transylvania Company employee, in March 1775 Boone and some thirty men began to blaze the two-hundred-mile Wilderness Road, also known as Boone's Trace, through Cumberland Gap to the Kentucky River's south bank, where he founded Boonesboro.

Boone took part in several hazardous operations during the Revolutionary War; the government afterward denied him the contract to develop the Wilderness Trail into a wagon route. In the later 1700s, troubled by legal and land claim problems, he operated several Kentucky posts before moving around 1800 to Missouri, where he trapped along the Missouri River and its tributaries.

Cumberland Gap, the main southern pass through the Appalachian Mountains, in a steel engraving by S. V. Hunt published in 1872. Gabriel Arthur may have traversed the gap as early as 1673. With the blazing of Daniel Boone's Wilderness Road in 1775 a century later, Cumberland Gap became a widely used emigrant gateway.

IN THEIR OWN *Words*

After a long fatiguing march, over a mountainous wilderness, in a westward direction, they at length arrived upon its borders; and from the top of an eminence, with joy and wonder, descried the beautiful landscape of Kentucke. Col Boon and John Finley made a tour through the country, which they found far exceeding their expectations: But in spite of this promising beginning, this company, meeting with nothing but hardships and adversity, grew exceedingly disheartened, and was plundered, dispersed, and killed by the Indians, except Col. Boon, who continued as an inhabitant of the wilderness until the year 1771.

—JOHN FILSON, *THE DISCOVERY, SETTLEMENT AND PRESENT STATE OF KENTUCKE* (1784)

Brébeuf, Jean de (1593–1649)

A French-born Jesuit, Jean de Brébeuf arrived in Quebec in 1625 and pushed west in 1626 as a missionary to the land of the *Huron [III]* Indians, valued French allies and middlemen in the lucrative fur trade. He was among the chroniclers of the eight-hundred-mile canoe route west, a twenty- to thirty-day trip with numerous portages from the *St. Lawrence River [III]* up the Ottawa River to Lake Nipissing and along the French River to Lake Huron's Georgian Bay.

The main Huron lands, known as Huronia, lay between Georgian Bay and Lake Ontario. During Brébeuf's three-year sojourn with the Bear tribe, he learned their language and ways, but had little evangelizing success. After a 1629–1633 trip to France, he returned to the Hurons in September 1634 to found the first of several Jesuit missions. During epidemics of European diseases in 1634, 1636, and 1639, some 18,000 of the estimated 30,000 Hurons died, and this aroused the survivors to a campaign of persecution against Jesuits. His 1640–1641 journey through hostile country to the Neutrals, between Lake Ontario and Lake Erie, to start a mission also had little result.

Brébeuf returned to the Hurons in September 1644 at the height of Iroquois warfare and was slain in 1649. Canonized in 1930 as a martyr, he was declared Canada's patron saint in 1940. His writings on the Hurons are a significant contribution to Native American ethnology. He also compiled a Huron dictionary and grammar and translated several Roman Catholic texts into Huron.

IN THEIR OWN *Words*

The Huron country is not large, its greatest extent can be traversed in three or four days. Its situation is fine, the greater part of it consisting of plains. It is surrounded and intersected by a number of very beautiful lakes or rather seas, whence it comes that the one to the North and to the Northwest is called "freshwater sea." There are twenty towns, which indicate about 30,000 souls speaking the same tongue, which is not difficult to one who has a master.

—JEAN DE BRÉBEUF, *THE JESUIT RELATION*, 1635

Cadillac, Antoine de La Mothe (1658–1730)

A French-born adventurer and self-invented aristocrat, Antoine de La Mothe Cadillac landed around 1683 at *Acadia [III]* (Nova Scotia). There he became familiar with the coastline by serving on a privateering ship. In 1692 he completed an exploration, together with cartographer Jean-

Baptiste Franquelin, of the New England coast from Boston to Manhattan. His report to the government of *New France [III]* included a detailed and relatively accurate survey of the North Atlantic seaboard.

Appointed in 1694 to command *Fort Michilimackinac,* he there enriched himself in the fur trade by often resorting to illicit practices. In 1698 he sailed to France to obtain permission for his grand plan to control the western Great Lakes fur trade by establishing (in 1701) Fort Pontchartrain at Detroit, the region's commercial crossroads. Seeking to install himself as the region's despotic ruler, he lost his power struggle with the New France administration by 1710.

In June 1713 he arrived in *Louisiana* as its new governor, appointed by Antoine Crozat, who had obtained a fifteen-year proprietorship over the ten-year-old failing French colony. Assigned to place it on a profitable basis, Cadillac sent out exploratory parties in all directions in a futile effort to find precious metals; in 1716 he reportedly located a copper mine in the *Illinois* country. Rebuffed in his attempt to initiate trade with *New Spain [II]* by sending a ship to Veracruz, he then tried to achieve this by dispatching *Louis Juchereau Saint-Denis* on a 1713–1714 expedition up the Red River and overland across Texas; this was another failure. Cadillac's arrogance and incompetence led to his dismissal in 1717 and return to France.

Cahokia

The first permanent white settlement in Illinois, on the *Mississippi River* across from *St. Louis,* Cahokia was named after a nearby *Illinois* Indian tribe. The explorers *Jolliet* and *Marquette* passed through the region in 1673, and *La Salle* arrived in 1680, leading to strong ties between the Illinois and the French. *Jesuits* from Canada founded a mission there in 1699.

A fur-trading post also attracted settlers, and Cahokia soon became the center of French influence in the middle and upper Mississippi Valley. In 1765 the British occupied Cahokia, and in 1778 George Rogers Clark, brother of *William Clark [VI],* seized it for the United States.

Nearby are the Cahokia Mounds, the largest pre-Columbian site north of Mexico and already in ruins at the time of first European contact. From 700 B.C. to A.D. 1400, this great religious and political metropolis was home to thousands of members of the Temple Mound Culture.

Carver, Jonathan

(1710–1780)

Massachusetts-born Jonathan Carver served as a British colonial soldier in the French and Indian War before setting out from the Great Lakes on his explorations along the upper *Mississippi River.* After *Robert Rogers* commissioned Carver to lead an expedition westward from *Fort Michilimackinac,* he set out, along with a group of French traders, on September 3, 1766, for Green Bay. He then traveled with Winnebago warriors along the upper Fox River with a portage to the Wisconsin River, which he descended to the Mississippi at Prairie du Chien, and crossed on October 19 to the Iowa shore.

After he left his companions at the Yellow River traders' rendezvous, he ventured into territory hitherto unknown to English explorers, journeying northward along the Mississippi to the Falls of Saint Anthony (to the north of present Minneapolis-St. Paul). Nearby on November 10 he met a band of Dakota *Sioux [VI],* whom he accompanied up the Minnesota River to their main camp and there spent the winter of 1766–1767.

The next spring he returned to the Mississippi and by May 6, 1767, was back at Prairie du Chien to meet with a second Rogers expedition led by James Tute, who had been assigned to find an inland northwest passage to the Pacific. Together they ascended the Mississippi to the Chippewa River, which they followed through northwestern Wisconsin to Lac Court Oreilles, and then portaged to the Namekagon River, which they followed to St. Croix Lake. From there they portaged to Bois Brulé River, which took them to westernmost Lake Superior. They followed its northwestern shore to Grand Portage, arriving July 19. Three weeks later, after a message from Rogers informed them that he couldn't provide any more supplies due to a lack of funds, Carver and Tute abandoned their venture.

Carver sailed in February 1769 to London to seek wages Rogers owed him. There he unsuccessfully floated several proposals: to develop the

IN THEIR OWN *Words*

The country of the plains about the river St. Pierre [the Minnesota] exceeds for pleasantness and richness of soil all the places that ever I have seen. On each side of the river which is very full of windings, is large meadows with scarcely any trees. Here grows plenty of wild baum, hopps, angelica, nettles and all sorts of herbs of a most aromatick smell. The banks of the river and many other places covered with vines hanging full of heavy clusters of grapes which I found as late as November. The juice of these grapes was very rich and imagine 'twould make the best of wines.

—JONATHAN CARVER, *JOURNALS,* 1766–1768

lands west of Lake Huron between the Illinois River on the south and Hudson Bay; to send an expedition, together with Rogers, to find the source of the supposed "Ouragon" (Oregon) river, the inland northwest passage; and to journey eastward across Europe and Asia to North America in order to trace the ethnic roots of the Indians. Finally, deep in debt to the moneylenders to whom he pledged his royalties, he published in 1778 the enormously popular *Travels Through the Interior Parts of North America in the Years 1766, 1767, and 1768.* As he probably had no access to his journals, he recreated this account (the first 167 pages) from memory. He also agreed to, or was forced to accept, the inclusion of 340 additional pages of often inaccurate material culled from diverse sources, including *Hennepin, Charlevoix, Lahontan,* and others. Later historians revealed this plagiarism and hence declared Carver's entire expedition a hoax, a view that persisted until his original journals and correspondence finally emerged from British archives. These writings revealed Carver's scientific concerns: Based on his extensive ethnographic observations of the Winnebago and Sioux, he transcribed vocabulary lists of their languages; he tested the most accurate way of measuring distances along winding rivers; and as a cartographer he sought to clarify the different place names used by the Indians, the French, and the British.

Catesby, Mark   (1683?–1749)

English naturalist Mark Catesby spent a bit more than a decade exploring America's southern colonies and Caribbean islands in search of new plants and animals. After his arrival in 1712, he began collecting seeds and specimens as far west as Virginia's mountains for Lieutenant Governor *Spotswood.* In 1714 he made a brief collecting trip to Jamaica and Bermuda.

After he returned to London with his discoveries in 1719, the Royal Society sponsored a second collecting trip to the New World. This time he went in 1722 to Charleston, South Carolina, to spend three years of botanical exploration up the Savannah River and southward into the wilderness of Georgia and north *Florida [III],* capped by a year in the Bahama Islands. Unable to persuade his sponsors to finance an exploration of Mexico, he returned in 1726 to England. There he began work on his two-volume folio *The Natural History of Carolina, Florida, and the Bahama Islands,* issued in 1731 and 1743.

A self-taught artist, Catesby translated his drawings and watercolors into over 200 engravings depicting 171 plants and 113 birds, as well as mammals, reptiles, fish, and insects in the fullest inventory yet of American flora and fauna.

Mark Catesby's engraving of a flamingo on a semi-tropical waterfront was published in his two-volume book *The Natural History of Carolina, Florida, and the Bahama Islands,* 1731 and 1743. Catesby spent more than a decade in North America and on offshore islands in search of plants and animals new to Europeans.

Céloron de Blainville, Pierre-Joseph   (1693–1759)

Montreal-born Céloron de Blainville assumed command of *Fort Michilimackinac* in 1738. After serving in various military expeditions, he received orders for a secret mission to enforce French claims to the Ohio River Valley and to turn back British advances there. He was to map his progress down the *Ohio River* as well; Jesuit chaplain Joseph-Pierre de Bonnecamps accompanied him as cartographer.

He set out from *Montreal* on June 15, 1749, on a three-thousand-mile journey with an expeditionary force of two hundred French and Indians, paddling through a mostly hostile wilderness. Voyaging through Lake Ontario to Lake Erie and by way of the Chatacouin portage near Westfield, New York, he reached the Allegheny River, where he buried the first of six engraved lead plates marking the French claim. Low on supplies in late August, he buried his last plate at the Great Miami River junction near Cincinnati.

En route, Céloron de Blainville unsuccessfully pursued Indian alliances against the British and warned off British traders. He returned to Lake Erie by way of Fort des Miamis (Fort Wayne, Indiana) and arrived in Montreal on November 9. In his report, he advised the French to establish a costly fortified military route from Lake Erie to the upper Ohio in order to avoid loss of the Ohio Valley. His superiors ignored the recommendation, and British traders returned to the area soon after he left. Some of his buried plates were found in the nineteenth century and displayed as curiosities.

Charlevoix, Pierre François Xavier de (1682–1761)

A French historian and explorer of the Great Lakes region, born in Saint-Quentin, France, Charlevoix entered the Society of Jesus in 1608, and in 1705 the order dispatched him to Québec, where he taught in the Jesuit College. Recalled to France in 1709, he joined the faculty of the Collège Louis le Grand (where he had the young Voltaire as a pupil), later becoming prefect.

The French government sent Charlevoix back to *New France [III]* in 1720 with secret orders to reconnoiter an interior route through North America to the Pacific Ocean. He set out in the spring of 1721 on the journey for which he is remembered, using as a pretext a tour of inspection to Jesuit missions in the west.

Traveling by canoe, Charlevoix ascended the *St. Lawrence River [III],* went around the Great Lakes, with stops at Detroit, Mackinac, and Green Bay, and entered the Illinois River by way of the St. Joseph-Kankakee portage. There circumstances forced him to abandon his plan to push on toward the western sea. He turned south instead, voyaging down the *Mississippi River* to New Orleans and Biloxi, where he completed his American explorations in 1722.

Charlevoix returned to France and resumed the life of a scholar. He declined an appointment as missionary at a new post proposed for the Upper Mississippi and never traveled again. His *Journal Historique,* published in 1744, recounts his North American travels, describing the country and the customs of the interior Indian tribes and containing summaries of interviews with Indians and traders.

On an inspection tour of Jesuit missions in 1721–1722, Pierre François Xavier de Charlevoix ascended the St. Lawrence River, crossed the Great Lakes, and floated down the Mississippi River to New Orleans. His *Journal Historique,* published in 1744, recounts his North American travels.

Chaussegros de Léry, Gaspard-Joseph (1721–1797)

A soldier and an engineer of the military forts and defenses of *New France [III],* Gaspard-Joseph Chaussegros de Léry accompanied an expedition against the *Chickasaw* down the *Ohio* and *Mississippi Rivers* to *Louisiana* in 1739. In 1749 he was dispatched to collect geographical, astronomical, and strategic data about the route between Montreal and Detroit. In 1750–1751 he explored the Chignecto Isthmus linking Nova Scotia to the mainland. From 1754 to 1756 he mapped the route between Detroit and Fort Duquesne (later Fort Pitt) while at work on the construction of French forts along the Allegheny River.

Chaussegros documented his travels in a series of nine journals. After France ceded Canada to England in the Treaty of Paris of 1763, he entered British service and was the first Canadian seigneur presented to George III.

Cherokee

The Cherokees were once the largest and most important native group in the American Southeast. Speaking an Iroquoian language, they probably came originally from the North, either from the upper *Ohio River* Valley or the Great Lakes area.

By the time of first European contact, probably with the expeditions of *Hernando de Soto [III]* in 1540 and *Juan Pardo* in 1567, some 29,000 Cherokees occupied from 70 to 100 often palisaded villages in some 40,000 square miles of the southern Appalachians in parts of present-day Alabama, Georgia, Kentucky, the Carolinas, Tennessee, and Virginia.

In the early 1600s, trade with the French and then the English brought the tribe guns and alcohol. From 1730 on, as English allies, the Cherokees often fought the region's other tribes, but they began to lose their lands in treaties, and epidemics halved their number. After the Revolutionary War, they became known as one of the Five Civilized Nations because they adopted white ways of dressing, farming, and government. In 1821 the Cherokee scholar Sequoyah devised a Cherokee alphabet, and the tribe began issuing a Cherokee newspaper. The Cherokee Nation, with its written constitution, dates from 1827.

Although the group known as the Western Cherokees had departed in 1794 for Arkansas and Texas, moving on in 1831 to Indian Territory (Oklahoma), Appalachian gold discoveries led in 1838 to the forced removal west of the others along the Trail of Tears, although some one thousand escaped to the Smoky Mountains to become known as the Eastern Cherokees.

Chickasaw

The estimated five thousand Chickasaw Indians of the American Southeast were the region's fiercest warriors around 1600. Speaking a Muskogean language, they inhabited often palisaded villages in western Tennessee and Kentucky, the *Mississippi River* Valley, northern Alabama, and eastern Arkansas.

The *Hernando de Soto [III]* expedition brutally introduced the Chickasaws to European ways in 1541. In the late 1600s and early 1700s they fought the Choctaws, Caddos, Creeks, Shawnees, and Cherokees in order to enlarge their hunting grounds as they sought more pelts and skins for trade with the English. As English allies they also harassed the French in the Mississippi Valley.

Considered one of the Five Civilized Nations, the Chickasaws adapted to European ways. When game became scarce in the 1800s, they turned to farming, with some even operating cotton plantations with the labor of some one thousand African slaves. In a series of four treaties from 1805 to 1832, many ceded their lands east of the Mississippi and migrated west, with some three thousand forcibly removed after 1837 to Indian Territory (Oklahoma).

Choctaw

The most successful agriculturalists of the American Southeast, the Choctaws were less bellicose than their neighboring tribes. In the mid-1500s, some 15,000 to 20,000 Choctaws inhabited sometimes fortified villages in southern and central Mississippi and in areas of Alabama, Georgia, and *Louisiana.* As probable descendants of the Temple Mound Builders, they may have once been united with the Chickasaws and were culturally similar to the Creeks.

In 1540 the Spanish explorer *Hernando de Soto [III]* burned Choctaw villages as his expedition trekked through their lands. Many Choctaws allied with the French in the late seventeenth century and carried on intertribal warfare with the Chickasaws and Creeks.

Considered one of the Five Civilized Nations, they adopted European ways but were forced from 1801 on to cede their historic lands. From 1831 to 1834, some 12,000 were forcibly removed to Indian Territory (Oklahoma), with 3,000 to 5,000 escaping to the Mississippi and Louisiana back country.

Collot, Georges Henri Victor   (1752?–1805)

In 1796 Frenchman Georges Henri Victor Collot conducted a nine-month, 7,600-mile survey of the *Mississippi River* and its tributaries. After Collot had served with the French forces in the American Revolution and later as a major-general who became chief of staff of the French Army of the North, he was appointed governor of the island of Guadeloupe, where his actions toward an American merchant ship led to his capture and extradition to Philadelphia to face possible legal proceedings. While he was out on bail, the French ambassador to the United States recruited Collot to assemble a detailed report assessing the political, commercial, and military status of the regions west of the *Appalachian Mountains* in order to pursue the possibility of future geopolitical moves by France in North America.

To this end, Collot set out on a secret mission to apply the principles of military topography and hydrology to the areas under American, Spanish, and British control in the Ohio and Mississippi Valleys and along the *Missouri River [VI]*. On March 21, 1796, he left Philadelphia overland for Pittsburgh, together with his assistant Adjutant-General Joseph Warin, whose skills as a draftsman were essential for making precise maps of the rivers and plans of the military installations along them. Working from older maps, Collot found in them a number of serious errors, which he corrected with his considerably more accurate new charts.

On June 6 Collot and his crew set out down the *Ohio River,* making careful measurements of the river and its tributaries, and noting the lands, natural resources, and settlements along its shore. On August 2 he headed up the Mississippi River to *St. Louis [VI]*. To its north he ascended the Illinois River to the Peoria area and then returned to St. Louis to ascend the Missouri River to the Osage River. In his report Collot also included detailed information about the upper Missouri documented by others, including Jean Truteau, who had journeyed there. In mid-September he proceeded down the Mississippi with side trips up the Arkansas and Yazoo Rivers.

On October 27 in New Orleans, Spanish authorities arrested him on suspicion of spying; previously he had been arrested briefly by *Zebulon Pike [VI]* on similar grounds at Fort Massac on the Ohio River. On December 22 his captors allowed him to sail back to Philadelphia and then to France. His report, which included details about meteorology, Indian cultures, wild animals, agriculture, the fur trade, and an inventory of tree species suitable for shipbuilding, assessed the possibility of a northwest passage to the Pacific by way of the upper Missouri River and the strategic defensibility of the continent's natural and artificial boundaries. Collot stated that "it is the situation of the frontiers which makes the safety of empires." His account of this exploration, *A Journey in North America . . . ,* was published in 1826.

In 1800 Napoleon compelled Spain to return *Louisiana* to France (in 1762, the French king had secretly transferred control of the territory to his cousin, Charles III of Spain). In early 1802, as part of his plan to establish a vast empire in the New World, Napoleon appointed Collot to a three-man commission to take possession of Louisiana. The commission never left France. In the end, costly military setbacks forced Napoleon to sell the Louisiana territory to the United States in 1803.

Couture, Jean   (?–?)

Arriving from France to become a Canadian *coureur de bois* (an unlicensed fur trader), Couture traveled to Fort Saint-Louis on the upper Illinois River in 1683 and in 1686 voyaged down the *Mississippi River* with *Henri Tonty* in search of the *La Salle* colony.

At the Mississippi's confluence with the Arkansas River, Tonty left Couture to establish the fur-trading post known as Arkansas Post. While in charge, Couture established trade relations with various tribes and learned their languages. After five survivors of La Salle's colony reached Arkansas Post in 1687, Couture trekked overland to Fort Saint-Louis to inform Tonty of the disaster. Tonty ordered him to East Texas by way of the Mississippi to find other survivors, but he was soon forced to turn back.

In the early 1690s Couture left French employ at Arkansas Post. Reportedly he explored eastward and visited the region's tribes while following the Mississippi up to the *Ohio River* and then the Tennessee River to its headwaters in the *Cherokee* lands. From there he apparently followed an old Indian trading trail to the Spanish posts in *Florida [III]* and then veered northward to the English settlement at Charles Town.

South Carolina traders hired him in 1700 to lead a group from Charles Town to the Mississippi by way of the Savannah, Tennessee, and Ohio Rivers. Their aim was to claim this territory for England and to wrest the Indian fur trade from the French.

Creek Confederacy

Many tribes comprised the so-called Creek, of whom the most powerful group was the Muskogee, itself a group of tribes that migrated to the American Southeast probably from the Great Lakes region.

Sometime before their first European contact, with *Narváez [II]* in 1528 and with the *Hernando de Soto [III]* expedition in 1540, the Creek Confederacy had become a loose alliance of some 20,000 people living in fifty self-governing Creek and non-Creek villages, including those of the Alabama, Apalachicola, Hitchiti, Koasati, Mikasuki, Natchez, Okmulgee, Shawnee, Timucua, Tuskegee, and Yuchi (most of them probably descended from Mississippian Temple Mound Builders).

The Lower Creek lived in eastern Georgia and along its coast. The Upper Creek, settled along Alabama's Coosa and Tallapoosa Rivers, remained more traditional and resistant to change. As English allies in the late 1600s and early 1700s, the Lower Creek fought the Spanish and the Apalachee, *Cherokee,* and *Choctaw,* absorbing some of the tribes they defeated. After turning against the English in the 1715 Yamasee War, many Lower Creek moved to the Chattahoochee River area.

Although they were considered one of the Five Civilized Nations for their assimilation of European ways, in the late 1700s their leader, Alexander McGillivray, was unsuccessful in protecting the confederacy's interests. The Treaty of Horseshoe Bend, ending the 1813–1814 Creek War, deprived the tribe of 23 million acres, and many migrated to *Florida [III]* to form, along with others, the Seminole people. In 1836 further land dispossessions culminated in the forcible relocation of large numbers of Creeks to Indian Territory (Oklahoma).

Cumberland Gap

As the broadest of the region's mountain gaps, Cumberland Gap became the main southern gateway across the *Appalachian Mountains* for explorers, hunters, and settlers pushing westward from the Atlantic seaboard.

Long used by Indians and first known by early European explorers as Cave Gap, this natural passage along a streambed is situated near the point where Virginia, Kentucky, and Tennessee come together. Reportedly the first white man to use it was Gabriel Arthur (see *Needham and Arthur expedition [III]*); he spent a year among the western Indians before returning to Virginia's Fort Henry on June 18, 1674. Later travelers through the gap included *Thomas Walker* in 1750, Henry Scaggs in 1764, Colonel James Smith in 1766, and *Daniel Boone* and John Finley in 1769–1770.

As an explorer for Virginia's Loyal Land Company, Walker named the gap after the English Duke of Cumberland. He was also the earliest scientist to describe its geology in detail. Only after Boone began to blaze the Wilderness Road in 1775 did the gap become widely used. By 1783 some 12,000 people had traversed it, and by 1800 more than 200,000 had passed through in a wave of westward migration to Kentucky, Tennessee, southern Ohio, Indiana, and southern Illinois.

Dablon, Claude   (1618?–1697)

The Jesuit Claude Dablon arrived from France in 1655 as a missionary to the Onondaga Indians in the area near Syracuse, New York. Documenting his journey to the Indian country in his journal, Dablon included a detailed description of the *St. Lawrence River [III]* from *Montreal* to Lake Ontario. On his second voyage in 1656, he compiled information about natural resources and the Onondaga culture. He and nearby French settlers fled to Canada in 1658 to avoid massacre.

In May 1661, on a mission to the Crees, Dablon, together with Gabriel Druillettes, traveled up the *Saguenay [III]* River and crossed Lac Saint-Jean to explore northwestward to determine whether there was any link between the northern sea (Hudson Bay) and the western (Pacific) and southern (Gulf of Mexico) seas. They reached Lake Nekouba (Nikabau) before turning back.

In 1669 the Jesuits sent Dablon, along with Marquette (see *Jolliet and Marquette expedition*) and *Allouez,* to Sault Sainte Marie to head the western missions. With Allouez in the autumn of 1670, he traveled by way of Lake Superior to central Wisconsin, making numerous observations for the *Carte des Jésuites,* a map of Lake Superior and the adjoining areas of Lakes Michigan and Huron. He also noted copper mines in the Lake Superior region.

Appointed in 1670 as superior of the Canadian Jesuit missions, he chose *Charles Albanel* to join a 1671–1672 expedition to Hudson Bay, again in search of the elusive *Northwest Passage [VII].* In his own writings and as editor of his era's volumes of the *Jesuit Relations,*

IN THEIR OWN Words

These regions of the North have their Iroquois. They are a certain people called the Nadouessi [Sioux], who, as they are naturally warlike, have made themselves feared by all their neighbors. . . . They live near and on the banks of that great river called Missisipi, of which further mention will be made.

—CLAUDE DABLON, *JESUIT RELATIONS,* 1670–1671

Dablon introduced new geographic and ethnographic information about the North American interior.

Daumont de Saint-Lusson, Simon François   (?–1677)

The French soldier and explorer Simon François Daumont de Saint-Lusson probably arrived in 1663 in Quebec, where Jean Talon, the intendant of *New France [III]*, assigned him to expand the colony westward beyond the Great Lakes.

In October 1670 Daumont left *Montreal* with Nicolas Perrot as interpreter and traveled by the Ottawa River–Lake Nipissing route to Sault Sainte Marie. There on June 4, 1671, he conducted an impressive ceremony with representatives of fourteen Indian nations to claim the immense territory, discovered and undiscovered, from the seas of the north and west to that of the south. This ritual marked the official start of French explorations toward James Bay in the north, the *Rocky Mountains [VI]*, and the Gulf of Mexico.

Daumont studied the country with reference to the accounts of earlier explorers, sought a *Northwest Passage [VII]* in a northerly direction, and voyaged along the Lake Superior shoreline in a futile search for reported copper mines. By the end of the summer he was back in New France. Then he was sent out to establish a route between Quebec, Castine on Maine's Penobscot Bay, and Nova Scotia's Port Royal on the Bay of Fundy. He explored along the Pemcuit and Kiniliki Rivers and investigated an Acadian copper mine. Little is known of his later activities.

Delaware

The Delaware referred to themselves as the Lenápe or Lenni Lenápe. Possibly migrating from *Labrador [III]* by way of the eastern Great Lakes region and the Ohio Valley, in the 1500s these Algonquian speakers were composed of four groups: the Lenápe of the Delaware River area; the Unami of southeastern Pennsylvania and northern Delaware; the Munsee of northern New Jersey, southern New York, and southeastern Connecticut; and the Unalachtigo, mainly in New Jersey.

Numbering some ten thousand at the time of first European contact—possibly with *Verrazano [III]* in 1524 or *Quejo [III]* in 1525 and certainly with *Hudson [VII]* in 1609—the Delaware soon became active traders of furs with the Dutch, to whom the Manhattan band sold Manhattan Island in 1626. Many then moved inland to the Susquehanna Valley.

The Lenápe chief Tamanend signed a treaty of friendship with William Penn in 1683. After the Delaware were reduced by warfare and disease, the Iroquois Confederacy came to dominate them in the early eighteenth century and sold some of their lands to the English. By mid-century many had retreated to western Pennsylvania and the Ohio Valley.

Various Delaware groups participated in Pontiac's Rebellion of 1763, Little Turtle's War of 1790–1794, and Tecumseh's 1809–1811 rebellion in opposition to the westward pressure of the British and Americans. Some groups migrated to Missouri and Texas, while those remaining in Ohio lost their lands in the 1795 Treaty of Greenville and moved to Indiana, Missouri, and Kansas, where they had to fight the Pawnee and other Plains tribes and where many acted as scouts for the United States Army.

In 1860 most of the western Delaware were forcibly relocated to Indian Territory (Oklahoma), while others had migrated to Wisconsin and Ontario.

Derbanne, François Guyon Des Prés (1671–1734)

Canadian trader François Guyon Des Prés Derbanne searched with *Le Sueur* for minerals along the upper *Mississippi River* in 1698–1699 and voyaged up the *Missouri River [VI]*. He claimed to have ascended the Missouri in 1706 some four hundred leagues farther than any Frenchman to date, to discover that New Mexico was not far off.

Derbanne then moved down to French *Louisiana* to join *Saint-Denis* in a trading partnership. On October 16, 1716, he set out from Mobile on a pioneering expedition to Nuevo León in northeastern *New Spain [II]*. After ascending the Mississippi to the Red River, which he followed to Natchitoches, he transferred his trade goods to a mule train and set out on November 22 to cross East Texas, escorted by Spanish Captain Domingo Ramón, reaching the Texas Colorado River in April 8, 1717. Two weeks later he crossed the Río Grande to San Juan Bautista presidio.

Derbanne left to return to Louisiana on September 1 and was back at Mobile Bay's Dauphin Island on October 26. Along the way, Derbanne compiled a descriptive account of the topography, flora, and fauna of the lands along his route to the Río Grande.

Dollier and Galinée expedition (1669–1670)

French Sulpician missionaries François Dollier de Casson (1636–1701) and René de Bréhant de Galinée (1645?–1678) set out to convert new tribes along the *Ohio River,* but ended up completing a circuit of the three eastern Great Lakes. After he arrived in *New France [III]* in 1666, two years before Galinée, the former soldier Dollier ministered to the Nipissing Indians, from whom he learned of the peoples to the west. Galinée, skilled in astronomy and geography, joined Dollier as a chronicler and cartographer. They were ordered to join *La Salle*'s first attempted expedition and to follow La Salle's more southerly route west.

On July 6, 1669, the combined group left *Montreal* in canoes; Seneca guides led the party up the *St. Lawrence River [III]* to the south shore of Lake Ontario. They followed this to the Niagara River, becoming the first Europeans to enter it, but they were unable to make progress against the powerful current downstream from Niagara Falls. The Indians described the waterfall, and they heard its distant roar. Galinée's narration is probably the first written account of the cataract.

Galinée and La Salle pushed inland to a Seneca village (near present Victor, southeast of Rochester, New York) where they conducted peace negotiations, exchanged gifts, and witnessed the torture of a prisoner. Unsettled by this event and by the delay in awaiting a guide to the Ohio River, they instead followed a passing Iroquois to his village at Lake Ontario's western end, arriving on September 24. There they learned that the Ohio was six weeks away and also encountered explorer Adrien Jolliet on his way back from Lake Superior. Jolliet informed them of a new route west by way of the Grand River to the north shore of Lake Erie and then through the Detroit strait to Lake Huron. At this point La Salle pleaded illness and turned back with his men.

The Sulpicians became the first Europeans to follow this route from east to west through the country of the Ottawas rather than heading directly southward to the Ohio through Iroquois lands. After wintering on Erie's north shore, they lost a canoe and then some baggage containing their essential portable altar to storms on the lake. Deciding to return for a replacement altar by way of a northern route, they traveled to Sault Sainte Marie before setting out back eastward on May 28 along the Georgian Bay–Lake Nipissing–Ottawa River route. They arrived in Montreal on June 18, 1670.

While they failed to reach their planned destination of the Ohio River, they were able to prove definitely that Lakes Ontario, Erie, and Huron were all connected. Based on his observations, Galinée was able to produce the most accurate map to date of the region, which nevertheless depicted Lakes Huron and Michigan as a single body named *Michigane or Mer Douce des Hurons.* Galinée's expedition journal provided one of the first published accounts (including detailed ethnographic notes on the Seneca) of the region. The following year, he sailed back to France, while Dollier remained to become Sulpician superior in 1671 and later the first historian of Montreal.

Druillettes, Gabriel   (1610–1681)

French-born *Jesuit* missionary Gabriel Druillettes arrived in *New France [III]* in 1643 and won eventual fame as a missionary to the *Abenaki [III]* of Maine, who attributed miraculous curative powers to him.

After some years among the Indians north of the *St. Lawrence River [III]* around Tadoussac, with winter journeys through the forested wilderness perhaps as far north as Lac Saint-Jean, Druillettes first journeyed to Maine in the late summer of 1646. After visiting the Abenaki villages of the Kennebec River basin and the nearby English settlements, he voyaged by sea to the Penobscot River. In September 1650 he returned to New England as ambassador in an unsuccessful attempt to seek an English alliance against the Iroquois. On June 22, 1651, he left Quebec on a difficult expedition to approach Maine from the northeast; this time he traveled up the St. John River to reach the Kennebec's headwaters.

Druillettes and *Claude Dablon* set out in 1661 on a northwesterly expedition up the *Saguenay [III]* River toward Hudson Bay, reaching Lake Nikabau before turning back. Sent to the Great Lakes after his 1670 appointment as head of the Sault Sainte Marie mission, Druillettes used Indian information and reports from the *Grosseilliers and Radisson expeditions* to formulate a master plan to establish western missions. Reputedly a remarkable linguist, he inspired Marquette (see *Jolliet and Marquette expedition*), *Albanel,* and other Jesuit explorers of the wilderness.

Dulhut (Duluth or Du Lhut), Daniel Greysolon (1639?–1710)

A one-time soldier from the lesser French nobility, Dulhut immigrated to *Montreal* in 1675 after making two earlier trips to Canada. Cousins of *Henri Tonty,* he and his brother Claude Dulhut probably came to seek their fortunes at a time when Jolliet's return from the *Mississippi* was still exciting news (see *Jolliet and Marquette expedition*).

On September 1, 1678, Dulhut left on a secret mission to seek peace between the *Sioux [VI],* Chippewa, and other tribes at the Mississippi River headwaters west and north of Lake Superior, a region rich with beaver pelts. By winter he reached Sault Sainte Marie and remained there before continuing on in the spring. After a council of the tribes at the site of the future Duluth, he traveled inland to Milles Lac in central Minnesota, where at the village of Nadouesioux he raised the royal coat of arms and claimed the territory for France.

He also sent three men to explore further westward, perhaps as far as the Minnesota-Dakota border region. When they returned with salt that the Indians claimed came from a great body of water twenty days away, this reinforced the mistaken French view that the Pacific Ocean was not far distant (the body of water turned out to be Lake Winnipeg). In a September assembly along Lake Superior, the Sioux, Assiniboine, and other tribes concluded a peace treaty.

Dulhut then explored along Lake Superior's northwest shore to near Thunder Bay and there spent the winter of 1679–1680 at Kaministikwia. In spring he resumed searching for the western sea and followed Lake Superior to its southern shore to enter the Brulé River, which he ascended and then portaged to upper Lake Saint Croix. From there he followed the Saint Croix River to the Mississippi, which he descended almost to the mouth of the Wisconsin River.

Interrupting his journey to rescue three captive Frenchmen from the

IN THEIR OWN Words

A s we had some knowledge of the Sioux language, the Frenchmen begged us to accompany them to the villages. I did so willingly, knowing that the Frenchmen had not received the sacraments in two years. Sieur Dulhut, whom the Indians looked on as chief, noticed that I had to shave the children's heads and bleed the asthmatic old people in order to have a piece of meat. [In other words, the natives made him work for his victuals.] He had the Indians told I was his older brother. This assured my being fed, and I devoted myself entirely to the spiritual comfort of the Indians.

—LOUIS HENNEPIN, JULY 25, 1680

Sioux, among them the priest *Louis Hennepin,* Dulhut afterward voyaged back down the *Mississippi River* and up the Wisconsin River, portaging to the Fox River to reach Lake Michigan's Green Bay in the first recorded passage along this trans-Wisconsin route from west to east. After spending the winter of 1680–1681 at *Fort Michilimackinac,* he returned to find himself declared a renegade and violator of the 1676 edict banning trading beyond the limits of the colony of *New France [III].*

Returning from a 1681–1682 trip to France to defend himself, he received commissions from the new New France governor to continue exploring the western Great Lakes region and the upper Mississippi and to renew his peacemaking efforts. Apparently, however, he never explored beyond the limits of his 1678–1681 expedition.

Dulhut founded two western trading posts in the mid-1680s, one on Ontario's Lake Nipigon and another along western Lake Superior; he later established Fort Saint-Joseph at what is now Detroit. He also assisted various military expeditions against warring tribes. Five years after assuming command of Fort Frontenac in 1690, he retired to Montreal, having opened new lands to other explorers and traders, and having helped to extend French dominion westward.

Dunbar, William (1741–1810)

A prosperous planter, William Dunbar became a key figure in *Thomas Jefferson*'s *[VI]* survey of the lower *Louisiana* Territory following its purchase in 1803. While the *Lewis and Clark expedition [VI]* was in progress to the north, Jefferson moved ahead with plans to explore the Southwest.

Dunbar, a Scottish emigré educated in mathematics and astronomy at Glasgow and London Universities, had arrived in the colonies to become a trader at Fort Pitt in 1771 and then to operate a Baton Rouge plantation. In 1792 he moved to a plantation near Natchez. Appointed Natchez district surveyor in 1789, he made the first meteorological observations of the Mississippi Valley in 1799. Reputedly the region's foremost scientist, he had become a correspondent of Jefferson and a member of the American Philosophical Society.

In early 1804 Dunbar agreed to act as Jefferson's representative in organizing an expedition up Louisiana's Red River. Awaiting the appointment of a leader for this "Grand Excursion," he led a preliminary three-month exploration of the Ouachita River, a lower Red River tributary that started at the Black River. Along with expedition naturalist George Hunter, a Philadelphia pharmacist and chemist, he journeyed up to the Hot Springs area in central Arkansas in the fall and winter of 1804–1805. Later in 1805 Dunbar worked out a new way of figuring longitudes, based on taking lunar altitude meridians. He also designed two flat-bottomed boats for exploring the Red River.

With *Thomas Freeman* designated as its leader and the naturalist Peter Custis replacing Hunter, who had returned to Philadelphia, the Red River expedition finally set off at the end of April 1806 to travel 615 miles upriver before Spanish forces forced it to turn back on July 30. The Dunbar-Hunter and the Freeman-Custis surveys were the first to be led by civilian scientists, who assembled maps of unequaled accuracy of the Ouachita and Red Rivers, as well as copious information on the region's terrain, waterways, natural resources, flora, fauna, and Indian cultures. The surveys failed to clarify the boundaries between American Louisiana and Spanish Texas and indeed added to international tensions.

Dutisné, Claude-Charles (?–1730)

Dutisné left France in 1705 with a colonial military detachment bound for Québec. Assigned in early 1714 to lead a small party to the Wabash River to erect a fort and a trading post, he instead led his men through the Kaskaskia lands of the *Illinois,* where he discovered silver mines.

Dutisné then continued southward to Alabama's Dauphin Island, at the entrance to Mobile Bay, and from there veered west to *Louisiana.* In the fall he helped build Fort Rosalie (later Fort Natchez), and in 1716 he established a post on the island of Natchitoches up the Red River. In 1718 he apparently explored the Galveston Bay area while founding a small fort there. Later that year he set out on foot with only a compass as guide to trek northward through the lower Alabama River region, finally reaching Quebec.

After returning to the Illinois country with his family, he was commissioned a captain of the Louisiana colonial troops in 1719. *Sieur de Bienville* sent him to contact the western Indians between the Missouri and Grand Rivers in northwestern Missouri. He traveled along the *Missouri River [VI]* to near the site of Kansas City, where Missouri Indians barred his advance. Then he retraced his way to the junction of the Osage

River (near Jefferson City) and approached the land of the Osage Indians in western Missouri. Again they tried to bar him, and he veered southward to cross the Arkansas River and pass near the villages of the Wichitas, who also blocked his way. Six days west he came to a Comanche camp and there planted a truce flag on September 27, 1719.

When his odyssey through these unknown lands ended, he had contacted new tribes interested in French trade and had found more silver deposits. He served in various wilderness outposts after 1720 and died of a wound in the Illinois country, where the Fox Indians continued to harass French traders and settlers.

Fort Michilimackinac (Fort Mackinac)

With its strategic location at the head of Lake Michigan and its juncture with Lake Huron, Michilimackinac became a center of French missionary and fur trade activity.

Father Jacques Marquette (see *Jolliet and Marquette expedition*) founded the Saint Ignace *Jesuit missionaries* there in 1671. From the 1680s Michilimackinac was a way station for those exploring westward and southward of the Great Lakes. During the Seven Years' War, the British captured the post in 1761, and two years later, during Pontiac's Rebellion, Chippewa and Sauk warriors seized control; the British crushed the Indians by the end of 1763.

In 1783, following the Revolutionary War, the United States took possession but was forced to surrender the fort to the British in the War of 1812. It remained a center of the British fur trade until it was returned to the United States in 1830.

Freeman, Thomas   (?–1821)

President *Thomas Jefferson [VI]* appointed the Irish-born civil engineer and surveyor Thomas Freeman to explore the Red River in a southern counterpart to the *Lewis and Clark expedition [VI]*. Freeman arrived in America in 1784 and, in the 1790s, surveyed the site of Washington, D.C., and the boundary between the United States and Spanish Florida.

On January 17, 1806, he set out from Philadelphia with his newly hired naturalist Peter Custis for the Natchez plantation of *William*

Dunbar, Jefferson's representative and expedition organizer. Jefferson's instructions, similar to those he issued to *Meriwether Lewis [VI],* directed Freeman to conduct a scientific investigation of the lands surrounding the Red River from its mouth to its headwaters, to try to ascertain the boundaries between American *Louisiana* and Spanish Texas, and to win the loyalty of the region's Indians. Among the scientific tasks were the making of astronomical and meteorological observations, accurately measuring distances, and assembling a detailed inventory of soils, terrains, plants, animals, and minerals. The first government survey led by civilian scientists, the Freeman-Custis venture also was the best-funded and best-equipped expedition of the era.

On April 28, 1806, the party set out from Natchez with a twenty-man military escort and a slave. At Natchitoches, the Red River's last American outpost, Freeman's numbers were augmented by some two dozen more soldiers, Indian guides, and hunter-interpreters. Leaving on June 2, they encountered the hundred-mile-long logjam known as the Great Raft, which forced them to detour through bayous and lakes east of the river. On July 30, north of today's New Boston, Texas, a Spanish military contingent forced them to turn back after a 615-mile journey up the Red River. This made it impossible for Freeman to disprove the widely accepted, but erroneous, theory that the Red River originated in the southern Rocky Mountains. (In 1820 the *Stephen Long [VI]* expedition finally learned that the Canadian River had been mistaken for the upper Red River.)

Freeman was back in Natchitoches by August 23. While he had failed to reach his geographical goal and to clarify the boundary problems, his expedition's scientific achievements were notable. The map produced by Freeman's precise measurements and observations was unequalled in its era and is still remarkably accurate. The inexperienced and overextended Custis catalogued the region's plants and animals with inadequate reference texts and thus missed identifying and naming many of the various new species he found.

Jefferson appointed Freeman to lead an 1807 expedition up the Arkansas River, a plan that had to be abandoned when Congress failed to provide funding. Freeman then surveyed the boundaries of the new *Chickasaw* lands in the Mississippi Territory. In 1809 he retrieved the belongings, including the exploration journal, of Lewis, who died a probable suicide on the Natchez Trace; these he delivered to Jefferson and *William Clark [VI].*

Freeman won appointment in 1811 as surveyor general of the Mississippi Territory; six years later, he moved eastward to map and explore the rivers of the Alabama Territory. He died suddenly, still in his late forties, while marking the boundary between Mississippi and Alabama. His 1806 expedition had opened the Red River as a route for Anglo traders and hunters traveling to the Southwest.

Gist, Christopher   (1706?–1759)

The Virginia-based Ohio Company, with a 1749 royal charter to some 200,000 acres along the upper *Ohio River,* commissioned the Maryland-born Gist to explore and survey this domain, instructing him to document the westward passes through the Alleghenies, note fertile lands suitable for settlement, describe the Indians and their trading patterns, and report on the navigability of the Ohio as far as the Falls of the Ohio at present Louisville, Kentucky.

On October 31, 1750, accompanied initially only by a young black servant and slowed by illness, Gist set out from the upper Potomac River to follow an old trading path along the Juniata River to the forks of the Ohio at Pittsburgh. The end of November found him headed inland in a southwesterly arc through northeast Ohio to the Scioto River. From there Gist made a northwesterly loop to the upper Great Miami River, near its junction with the Loramie, to visit the important Indian town of Pickawillamy. By March 8, 1751, he had returned to the junction of the Ohio and Scioto Rivers.

Gist then crossed the Ohio to Kentucky, following an Indian trail on a southwesterly course to the Kentucky River near present Frankfort. This he ascended, and near Whitesburg in early April he crossed the mountains into Virginia by way of Stony Gap. On May 18, 1751, he reached his home in the Yadkin River Valley of North Carolina.

Two months later, the Ohio Company ordered him to undertake a second expedition, this time to seek the most convenient route across the mountains from the Potomac to the Monongahela River. He was then to descend the Ohio's south bank to the Big Kanawha River in present West Virginia and explore the Kanawha Valley in search of arable lands.

Gist set out on November 4, 1751, and crossed the Alleghenies along the South Fork of the Potomac River on a path unknown to traders; Gist may have been the first white man to use this route. After exploring the rivers and valleys northeastward, he reached the Monongahela and then, hampered by difficult wintry terrain, explored Pennsylvania westward through northern West Virginia to the Big Kanawha before circling back to the Monongahela. He reached the upper Potomac by a shorter and more easterly route and arrived at his western Maryland destination on March 29, 1752.

In his report to the Ohio Company, Gist praised the agricultural assets of western Pennsylvania and eastern Ohio, pointed out the forks of the Ohio River as a strategic location for a frontier fort, and recommended his most recent Monongahela-Potomac passage as a new trading route. In April the Ohio Company hired him to assist in blazing this trans-Allegheny route, a two-year task that he carried out with the expertise of *Delaware* chief Nemacolin. Successively known as Nemacolin's Path, Braddock's Road, and the Cumberland Road, it later became the first leg of the National Road, a highway to the west reaching Vandalia, Illinois, in the 1840s.

The Anglo-French struggle for the Ohio Valley led to more employment for Gist: In late 1753 he guided a young George Washington to warn off the French in western Pennsylvania, and in early 1754 he helped build Fort Prince George at the forks of the Ohio, soon surrendered to the French. During the early phase of the Seven Years' War he acted as guide, scout, Indian emissary, frontier fighter, and commissary for Virginia. Gist died of smallpox while on a mission to the western Carolinas and Georgia to procure *Cherokee* aid against the French.

Grosseilliers and Radisson expeditions (1654–1682)

Brothers-in-law Médard Chouart, Sieur des Grosseilliers (1618?–1696?), and Pierre Esprit Radisson (1636?–1710) helped open the western Great Lakes region and the northern wilderness to the Canadian fur trade, to other explorers, and to European territorial claims.

After arriving in *New France [III]* around 1641, Grosseilliers worked with the *Jesuit missionaries* among the *Huron [III]* before his 1654–1656 westward expedition as a *coureur de bois* (unlicensed fur trader). Voyaging by way of the Ottawa River, Lake Nipissing, the French River, and Georgian Bay, he reached the Detroit strait between Lakes Huron and Erie. From there he may have crossed the Michigan peninsula overland to Lake Michigan and followed its northern shore up to the Straits of Mackinac. He brought back news of the regions south and west of Lake Huron, along with a large haul of furs.

Radisson, who had reached the New World by 1651, joined Grosseilliers in 1659 in an expedition along the Ottawa River trading route to Lake Huron. They followed the north shore to Sault Sainte Marie and portaged around the falls to explore Lake Superior's southern shore to the Chequamegon Bay area. There the brothers veered inland to Wisconsin's Lac Courte Oreilles to winter with refugee Ottawa, Huron, and Chippewa Indians.

Sioux [VI] delegates arrived in the spring to invite Grosseilliers and Radisson for a six-week visit in interior Minnesota, where they were probably the first Europeans to contact the Dakotas. They then traveled to Lake Superior's north shore, where they may have learned of Grand-Portage, the easiest canoe route to the far west, along the Pigeon River and following the United States–Canada border to Lake of the Woods. By the summer of 1660 they were back in *Montreal* with a report of rich fur fields, only to be punished as renegades.

In April or May 1662 the brothers set out for Hudson Bay by way of the Atlantic coast, but difficulties at the Gaspé Peninsula caused them to turn south to *Boston [III],* where they eventually entered the service of the English. In a 1668 expedition sponsored by King Charles II, Grosseilliers reached Hudson Bay's southern area to discover James Bay's Rupert River and to found Fort Charles at its mouth. The value of the furs he obtained there motivated a group of English investors to found, in May 1670, the *Hudson's Bay Company [VI]* to monopolize the northern Canadian fur trade.

Grosseilliers and Radisson completed a series of expeditions for the company, probably becoming the first Europeans to penetrate deep into the Hudson Bay's surrounding woodlands. In 1670 Radisson journeyed to the bay's west coast, to the Nelson River, where he founded a post. England based its claim to Hudson Bay and its tributaries on their explorations.

In 1675 the two shifted their allegiance back to France. The Compagnie du Nord hired them to lead an expedition to Hudson Bay to establish a post on its western shore at the Hayes River. The discontented Radisson returned once more to serve the Hudson's Bay Company in 1684, and he eventually settled in London. His *Voyages* provides a vivid and exaggerated account of his adventures. With their northern explorations, the two opened the most efficient fur trade route yet to Europe, by way of Hudson Bay.

Hennepin, Louis

(1626–1705?)

Flemish-born and French-educated, Louis Hennepin sailed along with other Récollets (reform Franciscans) in 1675 for *New France [III]* with *La Salle,* whom he served as expeditionary chaplain.

Traveling with an advance party, he arrived on December 8, 1678, at Niagara Falls and became the first European to describe this natural wonder in detail—"a vast and prodigious cadence of water" and "the most terrifying waterfall in the universe." He overestimated its height by some four hundred feet and described falls on the western edge that no longer exist. The first illustration of Niagara appeared in his 1697 book and was reprinted in many other eighteenth-century books and maps.

With Indian guides, explorer and missionary Louis Hennepin reached the Falls of St. Anthony on the Mississippi River (at present Minneapolis, Minnesota) in 1680. Some of Hennepin's travels are regarded as apocryphal.

IN THEIR OWN *Words*

*F*ather Gabriel and I went overland to view the great fall, the like whereof is not in the whole world. It is compounded of two great cross streams of water and two falls, with an isle sloping along the middle of it. The waters which fall from this vast height do foam and boil after the most hideous manner imaginable, making an outrageous noise, more terrible than that of thunder, so that when the wind blows from the south their dismal roaring may be heard above fifteen leagues off.

—LOUIS HENNEPIN ON NIAGARA FALLS, *NEW DISCOVERY*

Hennepin rejoined La Salle on August 7, 1679, and with two others pushed on to the *Mississippi River,* which they reached on February 29, 1680. Hennepin claimed to have voyaged to the river's mouth and to have returned by April 10—an impossible three-thousand-mile journey. A *Sioux [VI]* war party captured Hennepin north of the Illinois River mouth on April 11. After nineteen days of paddling upstream and a five-day overland march, they reached their village in Minnesota's Milles Lac area. There he stayed, studying their language and culture, until August, when on a hunting trip to the Wisconsin River he encountered *Dulhut,* who freed him. They spent the winter at *Fort Michilimackinac* before returning to Québec.

Hennepin sailed for France later in 1681 and in 1683 published *Description de La Louisiane,* an exaggerated account of his odyssey that described the exotic Mississippi Valley, its flora and fauna, and its Indian cultures. Issued in numerous editions and translated into various languages, it was followed by two sequels in 1697 and 1698, which enlarged on his alleged Mississippi voyage. Initially the era's most popular writer about North America, he later fell into disrepute and was labeled a plagiarist and a liar. He unsuccessfully tried to return to the New World in 1698–1699.

Iberville, Pierre Le Moyne, Sieur d'   (1661–1706)

Famed for his discovery of the mouth of the *Mississippi River* from the Gulf of Mexico, Canadian-born Pierre Le Moyne, Sieur d'Iberville, became the founder of the *Louisiana* colony fourteen years after the failure of *La Salle*'s enterprise. The French government selected Iberville to head this important venture based on his daring military exploits in King William's War (1689–1697).

Iberville's first Louisiana expedition sailed with four ships from France on October 24, 1698, arriving at Santo Domingo on December 4. There he fruitlessly sought information from pirates and others about the location of the Mississippi—some believed it discharged through Mobile or Pensacola Bay. On December 31 he sailed for the Gulf of Mexico around western *Cuba [II],* and on January 23 he arrived off *Florida*'s *[III]* coast near Saint Andrew Bay. He then began to explore the coast westward, first examining Choctawhatchee Bay, and on January 26, arriving at Pensacola Bay, the site of a Spanish garrison. Concealing his true mission from the Spanish, he tried to sound the entrance to the bay before leaving on January 30. The next day Iberville was at Mobile Bay, where he sounded the channel, investigated Dauphin Island, and landed on its western shore to conduct a brief exploration. A week later he anchored off Ship Island to explore the coast around Biloxi Bay and search for the Pascagoula River.

On February 27 Iberville set off with forty-nine men, including his younger brother *Bienville,* on four smaller boats through Chandeleur Sound to follow the Mississippi Delta coast. On the evening of March 2, 1699, while seeking shelter from a storm, Iberville found the North Pass and thus became the first person of European descent to enter the Mississippi River from the sea. He also proved the Mississippi Delta to be a peninsula. The group explored the Delta and then followed the river's course, meeting along the way with various Indian groups, to a point some 180 miles from its mouth, before turning back on March 22. Two days later Iberville sent Bienville with the two larger vessels back to the river's Delta exit while he voyaged with two canoes by way of the Bayou Manchac (Iberville River) and many difficult portages to Lakes Maurepas and Pontchartrain, reaching the Mississippi Sound on March 30. He then explored the mouths of the Pearl and Pascagoula Rivers before beginning construction of Fort Maurepas on Biloxi Bay, to establish the French claim to Louisiana and as a base for further exploration. After a brief investigation inland from Biloxi Bay, he set sail on May 3 for France to share his remarkable news and to bring back reinforcements.

In early January 1700 he sailed into Biloxi Bay on his second Louisiana expedition. This time he sent out groups to explore the Mississippi Delta more thoroughly, around Lake Pontchartrain, the Pearl River, Florida's Apalachee Bay, and the Red River as a possible passage to Spanish mines and settlements in New Mexico. Iberville met with *Henri Tonty,* La Salle's captain, and then led an expedition up the Mississippi to near Saint Joseph, forging alliances with Indian groups en route. On his return he sought alternate portages from the Mississippi River by way of Lake Pontchartrain to the sea. When he departed for France in May, he left orders that the Mobile River be explored further and that all men leaving the fort seek plants useful for dyes or medicines, look for pearls, and learn about Indian fishing techniques and herbal cures.

He returned on his third and final expedition to Louisiana on December 15, 1701, landing at Pensacola Bay, where he persuaded the Spanish, now allies of France, to assist with the move of his colonists from Biloxi Bay to the Mobile River. On April 27, 1702, he sailed for France, where he developed plans for French expansion in the Mississippi Valley and helped formulate military strategy during Queen Anne's War (1702–1713) between France and England. He died of illness at Havana, Cuba, ending his brief career as one of France's most competent colonizers and most efficient explorers. His discoveries radically changed the maps of the lower Mississippi River and its surrounding lands.

Illinois

In the mid-seventeenth century, the Illinois numbered fewer than ten thousand members of a group of Algonquian-speaking and self-governing tribes, including the Cahokia, the Kaskaskia, the Michigamea, the Moingwena, the Peoria, and the Tamaroa.

First European contact probably occurred with the arrival of the

Jesuit *Claude Allouez* in 1667, followed by the passage of the *Jolliet and Marquette expedition* down the *Mississippi River* in 1673. Warfare with the Iroquois and other tribes forced most of the Illinois to move southward starting around 1700 to seek protection of the French settlements.

The 1769 assassination of Pontiac by a Kaskaskia Indian provoked the Great Lakes Algonquians to a war of extermination against the Illinois. Beginning in the early 1800s, surviving members of the Kaskaskia and Peoria bands, with whom the other Illinois groups had merged, ceded their lands and moved in 1833 to eastern Kansas, which they left in 1867 for northeastern Oklahoma.

Jesuit missionaries

Any early Jesuits traveling into the North American wilderness were, in effect, explorers. Highly educated and often scientifically trained, they recorded valuable information about their own journeys, making note of topography, cartography, natural resources, and flora and fauna, although their focus was on the ethnography of those they sought to convert. Usually the first to become acquainted with individual tribes, they left an account of native cultures before permanent disruption by the white man.

In 1526 the Spanish crown ruled that two priests must accompany each exploring expedition. During the 1566–1572 *Florida [III]* enterprise of *Menéndez de Avilés [III],* Spanish Jesuits operated briefly on the Atlantic seaboard, founding ten missions from southern Florida to Virginia. Juan de Segura's ill-fated *Chesapeake Bay [III]* mission, near *Jamestown's [III]* future site, had as its secondary goal the finding of a route over the *Appalachian Mountains* and onward to China.

Probably the greatest explorer of the American Southwest was Spanish Jesuit *Eusebio Kino [IV],* who from 1687 to 1711 led more than forty expeditions from northern Mexico. The less venturesome Jesuits of Germanic origin who succeeded him in Sonora-Arizona in the 1730s were opposed by a 1751 Pima uprising.

The sojourn of the French Jesuits in Canada became a heroic episode in their history. Ten years after the first missionary efforts of the Récollets (reform Franciscans) who accompanied *Champlain [III]* in 1615, Father *Jean de Brébeuf* arrived with other Jesuits to evangelize the *Huron [III]* south of Georgian Bay. Their journeys—of Brébeuf to Huronia and beyond, of *Isaac Jogues* to Lakes Superior and Michigan, of *Claude*

Dablon to Wisconsin and Hudson Bay, of *Claude Allouez* to the western Great Lakes, of *Gabriel Druillettes* to the Kennebec area of Maine, of *Charles Albanel* to Hudson Bay, and of Jacques *Marquette* down the Mississippi—extended the frontier of *New France [III]* in all directions.

Brébeuf and other Jesuits slain by the Iroquois were canonized as martyrs in 1930. The widely published *Jesuit Relations,* the annual reports compiled from 1632 to 1673 by the Jesuit superior in Quebec from the narratives of the missionaries, became in Europe and elsewhere a popular and essential source of information about the New World.

During the 1699–1702 *Louisiana* colonization, Father Paul Du Ru kept an account of *Iberville*'s explorations and his own notes on the region's Indian cultures. After papal suppression of the Jesuits in 1773 and their reinstatement in 1814, Belgian Jesuits settled near *St. Louis [VI]*. Among them was Pierre de Smet, who blazed the way to Montana, Idaho, Utah, and the Oregon country.

Jogues, Isaac (1607–1646)

The French-born *Jesuit* Isaac Jogues sailed in 1636 for *New France [III]* to become a missionary to the *Huron [III]* south of Georgian Bay. Sainte Marie, his Jesuit mission station in Huronia, became a center of efforts to find new tribes to convert. At the end of September 1641 he and fellow Jesuit Charles Raymbaut were dispatched to visit the Chippewa (whom the French called the Sault) on the upper Great Lakes.

After seventeen days of travel by canoe, they became the first missionaries to reach the strait between Lake Huron and Lake Superior; *Brûlé [III]* in 1615 and *Nicolet* in 1634 had previously explored the region. The Jesuits brought back news of many unknown tribes, particularly the *Sioux [VI],* who lived eighteen days away around the *Mississippi*'s headwaters and westward to the *Missouri River [VI]*. The Chippewa had also described the route to the Sioux by way of Lake Superior, the St. Louis River, and portages to the lakes of the upper Mississippi. The Jesuits lacked the resources to found a western mission at that time; in 1668 Father Marquette finally established the Sault Sainte Marie mission on the upper Michigan peninsula along the strait.

In August 1642, while accompanying a Huron trading group, Jogues and his companions were captured and taken as prisoners south to

Mohawk territory. His hands were mutilated by Iroquois torture before he got away with Dutch help and sailed from New Amsterdam for France. His account of his captivity included the earliest description of northern New York state. By July 1644 he was back in Quebec.

In May 1646 Jogues led a peace mission to the Mohawks by way of the Richelieu River and across Lake Champlain. He was apparently the first white man to see Lake George, which he named Lac du Saint Sacrement. That fall, while on a second peace mission south, he was murdered by the Iroquois, who blamed him for the epidemic, drought, and famine that had followed his previous visit. In 1930 he was canonized as one of the Jesuit martyrs of North America.

Jolliet and Marquette expedition   (1673)

The first North American-born explorer to achieve fame during his lifetime, Louis Jolliet (1645–1700) was hailed as the discoverer of the *Mississippi River.* The Jesuit priest Jacques Marquette (1637–1675) accompanied him as chaplain and interpreter.

Jolliet in 1668 joined his brother Adrien (also an explorer who went with *Jean Peré* to Lake Superior in 1669) in the fur trade after returning from five years in France studying as a religious seminarian and perhaps as a cartographer. In June 1671 he was present at Sault Sainte Marie when *Daumont de Saint-Lusson* ceremoniously took possession of the western Great Lakes region for France. On this trip he evidently first met Marquette, who had founded three missions in the region. The administration of *New France [III]* commissioned him in 1672 to investigate Indian tales of a great river and whether it flowed into the Pacific Ocean (and hence led to China), into the Gulf of California (or Vermilion Sea), or into the Gulf of Mexico.

Jolliet arrived at *Fort Michilimackinac* on December 6, 1672, and delivered a letter assigning Marquette to his small group of voyageurs. He wintered at Saint-Ignace Mission while assembling Indian reports of the unknown lands that lay ahead and reportedly drawing up a map from this

Jacques Marquette and Louis Jolliet examine an Indian dwelling in passing, on the 1673 journey that carried them from the northern reaches of Lake Michigan to the junction of the Mississippi and Arkansas Rivers.

data. His actual route and chronology remain vague because both copies of his expedition logbook and later maps were lost.

Jolliet, Marquette, and five others set out in canoes on May 17, 1673, taking along Jolliet's astrolabe and Marquette's portable altar to assist in the conversion of Indians. After following Lake Michigan's northwest shore down to Green Bay, they crossed present Wisconsin by way of the Fox River and Lake Winnebago. A portage to a tributary of the Wisconsin River led them to the Mississippi on June 17. As they descended the river, they witnessed a new topography, Indian cliff paintings, and strange plants and animals, probably among them catfish, lynx, and bison in large herds.

They encountered the first village of *Illinois* Indians at the mouth of the Iowa River. As the expedition pushed south, the Indians they encountered were less and less friendly, and Marquette, who supposedly knew six Indian languages, could no longer communicate. When the great *Missouri River [VI]* entered the Mississippi, the explorers identified it as a probable route west. They continued at a brisk pace beyond the confluence of the *Ohio River.* Stopping on July 17 at a Quapaw village just north of the Arkansas-Louisiana border just short of Spanish territory, they learned from Indian sources that the river ended in the Gulf of Mexico, apparently fifty leagues, or ten days, away (in reality seven hundred miles south).

Using a shorter and easier route, the expedition returned by way of the Illinois River and Chicago Portage to Lake Michigan. Marquette remained at Michilimackinac and the following year revisited the Kaskaskia Indians on the Illinois River as promised. On his way home he died near the mouth of what is now known as the Père Marquette River. He left behind his *Récit,* an account of the 1673 journey, of which the authorship remains a matter of debate.

Jolliet never returned west, instead attending to his various enterprises as merchant and trader. In 1679 he led an expedition to the Hudson Bay and later took part in an official survey to chart the coast of *Labrador [III]*. During his frequent travels he also completed maps of the *St. Lawrence River [III]* and its gulf, rendering navigation much safer in those parts.

IN THEIR OWN

Words

From time to time, we came upon monstrous fish, one of which struck our Canoe with such violence that I thought it was a great tree, about to break the Canoe to pieces. On another occasion, we saw on the water a monster with the head of a tiger, a sharp nose like that of a wildcat, with whiskers and straight, erect ears; the head was gray and the neck quite black.

—MARQUETTE ON THE MISSISSIPPI, JUNE 1673, *JOURNALS*

Kelsey, Henry   (1667?–1724)

English-born Henry Kelsey, who came to the New World as a *Hudson's Bay Company [VI]* apprentice around 1684, explored the Canadian North and West. In June 1689, on what was probably his first expedition, he sailed from York Factory on Hudson Bay's western shore to explore north of the Churchill River. After ice barred the ship's further progress, he and a guide landed to trek some 235 miles north of the river before turning back.

On his most famous journey, Kelsey left York Factory on June 12, 1690, to establish official trade relations with western Indian groups. Ordered to seek minerals and botanic medicines along the way, he took along trade samples of English guns, Brazilian tobacco, a brass kettle, a lace coat, blankets, hatchets, and beads. After probably traveling up the Hayes and Fox rivers to Moose Lake, he formally took possession on July 10 of the western lands for the Hudson's Bay Company. After wintering near the Saskatchewan River, he set out on July 15, 1691, traveling by an unknown route—he may have canoed up the Saskatchewan to the Carrot River and then proceeded on foot southward to the prairies on the Red Deer River to the Great Salt Plain of central Saskatchewan. There he met with the Assiniboine and wrote the first Canadian description of the grizzly bear and the buffalo (properly, the American bison), distinguishing it from the musk ox, which he had seen in the north. He also may have met with *Sioux [VI]* or *Gros Ventre [VI]* Indians. Known for his linguistic skills, he included detailed ethnographic notes in his journal. After spending the winter of 1691–1692 either south of the Saskatchewan River or back at Derings Point, he returned to York Factory by summer.

During King William's War (1689–1697), Kelsey had to surrender his post twice, in October 1694 and September 1697, to the French under *Iberville.* After the 1714 return to York Factory and his 1717 appointment as overseas governor of all Hudson's Bay Company settlements, he sailed on two expeditions to the north. In the summer of 1719 he reached latitude 62°40' to open trade with the Inuit (Eskimos) in whalebone, oil, and "sea horse teeth," while investigating Hudson Bay's northwest coast. In the summer of 1721 he again journeyed to the Inuit lands. He also sent out two expeditions to the north, one in 1720 and a second in 1722, under John Scroggs, captain of the *Whalebone.* Kelsey's epic 1690–1692 exploration of western Canada was not equaled until the 1750s.

Lahontan, Louis-Armand de Lom d'Arce, Baron de (1666–1713?)

Baron de Lahontan arrived in Quebec with three companies of colonial troops probably in November 1683. After serving for five years in various military expeditions and command postings, he encountered the *La Salle* expedition survivors as they passed through *Fort Michilimackinac* on their way back to *Montreal.*

Lahontan departed Michilimackinac on September 24, 1688, with a detachment of soldiers accompanied by fifty Ottawa hunters on an eight-month exploration for which there is no outside documentation. (On this journey, as on his other North American travels, he kept detailed diaries, even using birch bark to make notes.) Following Lake Michigan to Green Bay and crossing by way of the Fox River to the Wisconsin River, he reached the *Mississippi River* and ascended to a westward-flowing stream he called the Long River.

He claimed to have explored this river for hundreds of miles, along the way encountering various Indian tribes, including possibly the Arikaras in the Dakotas. But most historians consider this Long River episode fictitious. By March 2, 1689, he had returned to the Mississippi, which he descended to the *Ohio River,* from which he reached the Wabash River. He retraced his route to the Illinois River and returned by way of the Chicago Portage to Michilimackinac, arriving on May 22. The authorities never implemented his proposal to secure the western Great Lakes frontier with a chain of three forts linked by patrols of light troop ships.

After his return to France in 1692, Lahontan published three books, starting in 1703 with *Nouveaux Voyages dans l'Amérique Septentrionale.* This volume, with twenty-six maps and plates, was a fanciful account of his voyage up the Long River. The second volume included detailed observations on North American geography, flora, and fauna, with ethnographic notes on the Indians (possibly from secondhand reports) and a glossary and discussion of the Algonquian language. The third volume included five imaginary dialogues with an Indian chief, in an early presentation of the noble savage theme.

Lahontan's controversial and influential works—a mixture of accuracy, hearsay, and exaggeration—attracted a wide audience with such novelties as one of the first descriptions of the Plains Indians on a buffalo hunt. An early exponent of the Age of Enlightenment, he saw the French attempt to eradicate the Iroquois as disastrous, viewed commerce as central to the development of these new lands, and envisioned the continent's future greatness.

La Salle, René Robert Cavelier, Sieur de   (1643–1687)

Famed as the discoverer of the mouth of the *Mississippi River*, René Robert Cavelier, Sieur de La Salle, arrived in *New France [III]* in 1667 to take possession of a *Montreal* land grant. This he later sold to finance explorations initially intended to seek the *Ohio River* and to find a route to the South Sea (the Pacific Ocean) and thence to China.

In July 1669 La Salle set out for the Ohio Valley, accompanied by Sulpicians *Dollier and Galinée.* In October, at the western end of Lake Ontario, La Salle pleaded illness and returned to Montreal while the missionaries went on. La Salle's activities over the next four years are not documented, but he apparently did not explore the Ohio or Mississippi Rivers at this time, as has been presumed. Between 1674 and 1678 he sailed twice to France in order to obtain permission for his ambitious plans, first to establish a series of forts along the Great Lakes, and then to become governor of all lands he might discover and colonize between New France, *Florida [III],* and Mexico.

On August 7, 1679, La Salle set out from Niagara to voyage through Lakes Erie and Huron to *Fort Michilimackinac.* After trading furs at Green Bay, he continued to Lake Michigan's south end and up the Saint-Joseph River with a portage to the Kankakee River, which led to the Illinois River. By January 5, 1680, he was in the Peoria area to begin the construction of Fort Crèvecoeur, where he left his captain, *Henri Tonty,* in charge. At the end of February La Salle sent *Louis Hennepin* with an advance party down the Illinois River to the Mississippi River before he returned to Niagara to find his fort there burned down.

This engraving from Louis Hennepin's *Book of Voyages,* published in 1711, shows La Salle's shipwrights building the *Griffin,* probably on the Niagara River, in 1679. La Salle later abandoned plans to sail an armed vessel down the Mississippi, traveling with Indian guides in canoes instead.

La Salle set out again for the Illinois country on August 10, 1680, this time by a northerly route from Lake Ontario by way of Lake Simcoe to Georgian Bay, arriving at Sault Sainte Marie on September 16. Indians had sacked Fort Crèvecoeur, and La Salle voyaged down the Illinois River to the Mississippi River in search of Tonty before returning to find him at Michilimackinac. After that La Salle returned again to Montreal.

In August 1681 he left Montreal for the Mississippi, reaching it on February 6, 1682. By mid-March he was at the Arkansas River, the southern limit of *Jolliet and Marquette*'s 1673 expedition. Continuing downstream, he reached the Gulf of Mexico on April 6. After a brief exploration of the Mississippi Delta and a ceremony to claim the Mississippi Valley for France, La Salle turned back northward during the second week of April, arriving at Michilimackinac in September.

In December 1683 he was back in France to seek permission to establish a colony in *Louisiana,* named after the French king. Already confused about the precise location of the Mississippi's mouth—his compass had been broken, his astrolabe was inaccurate, and the old Spanish maps he consulted were only conjectural—La Salle presented falsified maps that showed the Mississippi River as being quite close to northern Mexico. At the time, a French faction at court had plans to invade *New Spain [II],* so the location of La Salle's proposed colony at the river's mouth supported this strategy.

In late July 1684 he left France with four ships and 320 passengers, 100 of them soldiers, reaching Santo Domingo in the Caribbean in late September. On January 18, 1685, he arrived on the Texas coast at Matagorda Bay, which he believed to be one of the mouths of the Mississippi. There his colonists erected Fort Saint-Louis along Garcitas Creek. What followed was a string of disasters—the loss of ships, supplies, and people to accidents, desertions, disease, famine, and Indian attacks—due in large part to La Salle's incompetent leadership, exacerbated by his mental instability.

He then made a series of unsuccessful searches for the Mississippi, first by setting out westward to march to the Río Grande, which he ascended possibly to the area of Langtry, Texas. He then

IN THEIR OWN *Words*

We were out of provisions, and found only some dried meat at the mouth [of the Mississippi], which we took to appease our hunger; but soon after perceiving it to be human flesh, we left the rest to our Indians. It was very good and delicate. At last, on the tenth of April [1682], we began to remount the river, living only on potatoes and alligators. The country is so bordered with canes and so low in this part that we could not hunt, without a long halt.

—ZENOBIUS MEMBRÉ, "NARRATIVE OF LA SALLE'S VOYAGE DOWN THE MISSISSIPPI" set out in a northeasterly direction across south-central Texas, perhaps as far as the Trinity River, before returning to Matagorda Bay in March 1686.

La Salle started out with a small party for the Illinois country and Canada in mid-January 1687, only to be murdered by some of his men two months later in East Texas. Aside from some children, his few remaining colonists at Matagorda Bay were massacred by Indians. In the end all that endured of his grandiose scheme was the fact that he was the first European to voyage down the last seven hundred miles of the Mississippi River to its mouth, where he claimed the Mississippi Valley for France.

Le Sueur, Pierre-Charles   (1657–1704)

After Pierre-Charles Le Sueur arrived in Canada as a servant to the Jesuits at their Sault Sainte Marie mission, he became by 1680 a *coureur de bois,* or unlicensed trader, in the Great Lakes region and later among the *Sioux [VI]* of the upper *Mississippi River,* an area of which he developed a considerable geographical knowledge.

Commissioned in 1693 by *New France [III]* to open a route from Lake Superior to the Mississippi River, Le Sueur built a post at La Pointe on Lake Superior's Chequamegon Bay. In 1697 he sailed to France to seek permission to lead an expedition to the Sioux [VI] country to begin copper and lead mining and to set up fur-trading operations. The government of New France opposed the venture; *Iberville,* to whom Le Sueur was related by marriage, supported it, and Le Sueur returned with Iberville's second expedition to *Louisiana.*

At the end of April 1700, Le Sueur and twenty-five men set out in a longboat from Fort Biloxi and began an ascent of the Mississippi with brief side trips up the Yazoo and Arkansas Rivers. His Mississippi voyage ended just below the Falls of Saint Anthony, where he entered the Minnesota River on September 19 and voyaged upstream to the Blue Earth River. There he built Fort l'Huilier and spent the winter. The next April he extracted a large amount of what he believed to be copper ore from a nearby mine and traded with the Sioux for furs. In May 1701 he set out with half his men back to Biloxi.

Le Sueur returned to France in 1702 and died two years later while en route to Louisiana. Although his mineral samples proved worthless and Fort l'Huilier was abandoned after an Indian attack, his hard-won geographical knowledge provided corrections to the era's maps of the North

American interior and of the upper Mississippi region, which he had helped open to French trade.

Louisiana

Spanish explorers with the expedition of *Cabeza de Vaca [II]* in 1528 may have been the first Europeans to see the southern stretches of the vast region of central North America that would later be known as Louisiana. *De Soto's [III]* exploring expedition pushed up the Mississippi as far as present-day Memphis, Tennessee, in 1541.

Reaching the mouth of the *Mississippi River* in 1682, *René-Robert Cavalier, Sieur de La Salle,* claimed the region for France in 1682 and named it for King Louis XIV. The claim roughly encompassed the watersheds of the Mississippi and *Missouri Rivers [VI]*. A French expedition under *Iberville* founded the first European outpost in the territory on the coast of the Gulf of Mexico near present Biloxi, Mississippi, in 1699.

The United States purchased the Louisiana territory from France for $11,250,000 in 1803 (see *Louisiana Purchase [VI]*). The *Lewis and Clark expedition [VI]* of 1804–1806 returned with the first extensive geographical, scientific, and ethnographic information about the territory. Explorers would build on the pathfinding efforts of Lewis and Clark for the next three-quarters of a century.

Mézières, Athanase de (De Mézières y Clugny, Athanase)   (1715?–1779)

A Parisian born to a noble family, Athanase de Mézières reached North America around 1733 as a soldier who eventually became the era's leading emissary to the Indians and the administrator for Spain of the Louisiana-Texas frontier, a region he also explored.

By 1743 Mézières was in Natchitoches, which was to remain his home. In 1756 the colonial government named him to a commission to determine the boundary between *Louisiana* and Texas at the Gulf of Mexico. From 1770 to 1779 he led five expeditions seeking alliances with the Indian nations of Louisiana, Texas, Oklahoma, and Arkansas. In the fall of 1770 he visited the Cadodacho up the Red River. He journeyed in 1771 to Indian villages on the Trinity and Brazos Rivers to foster trade with the

Spanish. In 1772 he again left Natchitoches to cross East Texas on a visit to tribes further up the Trinity River, before heading for the Brazos River, which he ascended some two hundred miles to a Wichita village. He then trekked southward across western Texas to San Antonio. In 1778 he left San Antonio for the upper Brazos and upper Red Rivers. On yet another journey to the nations of the north in 1779, he fell from his horse not long after leaving Natchitoches. After a three-month delay he continued his mission to the upper Brazos River and then to San Antonio, arriving at the end of September. Before he was to be appointed governor of Texas, he died from his injuries.

In his official reports, Mézières provided the first definitive information about the Indian cultures, geography, flora, fauna, and other resources of northern Texas. One of his last recommendations was a thorough exploration of the Texas gulf coast, including its mainland, islands, and hydrological features; he considered the previous Spanish investigations of the area as inadequate. He failed, however, to establish a lasting peace among the region's Indians, or to link Natchitoches and Santa Fe by way of a trade route through Indian territory.

Miami

The Miami nation in the mid-seventeenth century numbered some 4,500 members of the Atchatchakangouen, Kilatika, Mengakonkia, Pepicokia, Piankashaw, and Wea bands living in southern Wisconsin and northern Illinois in the Lake Michigan region.

Originating in part from the Ohio Mound Builders and primarily from seminomadic buffalo hunters, these Algonquian-speaking peoples were first visited by Grosseilliers (see *Grosseilliers and Radisson expeditions*) in 1654 and soon established close trade relations with the French. Miamis guided the *Jolliet and Marquette expedition* down the *Mississippi River* in 1673.

After fighting in Pontiac's Rebellion in 1763, they had to cede most of their traditional lands and move to northern Indiana. In the Miami War the great chief Michikinikwa, also known as Little Turtle, led a coalition of *Delaware, Illinois,* Miami, Ojibwa, Ottawa, Potawatomi, Shawnee, and others, with support from the British in Canada, in opposing the American colonial migration into the Ohio Valley. Their 1794 defeat at Fallen Timbers cost them most of their lands.

Some Miami moved to Missouri around 1814, and in 1846 another group was forcibly relocated to Kansas. Together with the surviving Illinois Indians, with whom they united in 1864 to form the Confederated Peoria Tribe, they were later resettled in Oklahoma.

Michaux, André (1746–1803)

The French-born André Michaux was probably the best-educated and most experienced botanist of his time active in America, where he spent eleven years conducting expeditions south to *Florida [III]*, north to the Hudson Bay region, and west to the *Mississippi River.*

The French government dispatched Michaux to the United States in 1785 to study North American trees that might be useful for French shipbuilding and cabinetmaking. Accompanied by his son François-André Michaux (1770–1855), he set up a nursery in New Jersey and another in Charleston, South Carolina, to ship thousands of trees and seeds back to France. After exploring the Carolina back country and the southern Appalachians, he ventured down to Florida to explore along the St. John's River, followed by a 1789 trip to the Bahamas. Although he covered much of the same area as *John Bartram [III]* and his son, he discovered many new plants that the Bartrams had missed. In 1792 he became the first botanist to explore northward to Hudson Bay in search of the continent's hardiest tree species.

Earlier that year, supported by Secretary of State *Thomas Jefferson [VI]*, Michaux had proposed to the American Philosophical Society a scientific expedition to the Pacific Ocean by way of the *Missouri River [VI]*. Jefferson raised the necessary funds and prepared for Michaux detailed instructions similar to those he would issue to the *Lewis and Clark expedition [VI]* a decade later. Indeed, Lewis sought to accompany the Michaux expedition as a volunteer.

The project was abandoned after Michaux became involved with Edmond Genêt, whose behind-the-scenes maneuvering caused a brief U.S.–France diplomatic crisis. Michaux nevertheless made an unofficial 1,100-mile journey on which he explored the *Illinois* country on his way to the Mississippi River. He probably did not enter the Missouri nor did he descend the Mississippi as far south as Natchez. In 1796 he returned to France to make a final expedition to Madagascar.

Michaux's impressive New World discoveries were documented in his *Flora Boreali-Americana* (1803), issued with the assistance of his son. The younger Michaux explored Ohio, Kentucky, and Tennessee in 1802, and the Atlantic coast in 1806.

Mississippi River

The most important river in North America, the Mississippi rises from streams feeding Lake Itasca in northern Minnesota and flows 2,348 miles to the Gulf of Mexico below New Orleans. Only the *Missouri River [VI],* one of its principal tributaries, is longer; the Mississippi drains 1.2 million square miles in the heart of the continent.

The Spanish explorer *Hernando de Soto [III]* receives credit as the first European to sight the Mississippi. Reaching the site of Memphis, Tennessee, in May 1541, de Soto found an extensive agrarian civilization of Native Americans along its banks. The *Jolliet and Marquette expedition* claimed rediscovery of the river on behalf of France in 1673. The expedition entered the Mississippi from the Wisconsin River and floated downstream to a point just above the junction with the Arkansas. *La Salle* in 1682 explored the Mississippi from the mouth of the Illinois River

This engraving of the 1832 discovery of Lake Itasca in northern Minnesota, the source of the Mississippi River, is based on geologist Henry Rowe Schoolcraft's drawing. Schoolcraft, shown standing near the white tent, portfolio under his arm, led the expedition.

IN THEIR OWN Words

Passed a camp of Sacs, consisting of 3 men, with their families: they were employed in spearing and scaffolding a fish, about 3 feet in length, with a long flat snout; they pointed out the channel, and prevented us from taking the wrong one: I gave them a small quantity of whiskey and biscuit; and they in return presented me with some fish. Sailed on through a continuation of islands, for nearly twenty miles; encamped on an island; caught 1,375 small fish; rained all day.

—ZEBULON PIKE, *SOURCES OF THE MISSISSIPPI,* 1805–1806

to the Mississippi Delta, claimed possession of the entire country for France on August 9, and named the territory *Louisiana* for King Louis XIV of France. French colonial officials founded New Orleans, strategically placed to control the lower river, in 1718.

The American explorer *Zebulon Pike [VI]* approached the Mississippi's headwaters in northern Minnesota in an expedition of 1805–1806. *Henry Rowe Schoolcraft,* in journeys of 1821 and 1832, is credited with actual discovery of the source of the great river.

Montreal

A party of priests and nuns founded the Ville Marie de Montreal in 1642 on an island in the *St. Lawrence River [III]. Jacques Cartier [III]* had visited the stockaded Indian village of *Hochelaga [III]* at the site in 1535, and *Samuel de Champlain [III]* returned in 1603.

Owing to its strategic location near the junction of the Ottawa and Saint Lawrence Rivers, the settlement became an important trading post and outfitting center for explorations of the interior. The westward expeditions of *Jolliet and Marquette, La Salle, Dulhut,* and the *La Vérendrye [VI]* all set out from Montreal. The *North West Company [VI],* a fur-trading enterprise, had its headquarters in the city until 1821.

Nicolet, Jean (Nicollet de Belleborne, Jean)   (1598?–1642)

Reaching Canada in 1618 as an employee of the Company of New France, or Hundred Associates, a fur-trading concern, Jean Nicolet accompanied *Champlain [III]* up the *St. Lawrence River [III]* to the upper Ottawa River's Isle des Allumettes, where he remained for two years to learn the *Huron [III]* and Algonquian languages and ways in preparation for his work as an interpreter and negotiator. In 1620 Nicolet headed west to Lake Nipissing, where he sought to expand the fur trade westward and northward toward Hudson Bay. From 1629 to 1632 he worked among the Hurons south of Georgian Bay.

Nicolet left Quebec in July 1634 on a lengthy expedition to forge a French alliance with the western Indians and find a passage to the China Sea, a route reportedly known to Indians who had traded with a beardless race from the west (assumed by the French to be the Chinese, but actually the *Sioux [VI]*). He voyaged with seven Huron guides by canoe up the Ottawa River and by way of Lake Nipissing and the French River to Lake Huron, and through the Straits of Mackinac to Lake Michigan; this later became the main French trade route to the west.

He apparently thus became the first white man to explore Lake Michigan, and to arrive in what 150 years later was known to the English as the Northwest Territory, or the Old Northwest—the lands northwest of the Ohio River and including the states of Ohio, Indiana, Illinois, Michigan, Wisconsin, and part of Minnesota.

Clad in a floral Chinese ceremonial robe to impress the Winnebago Indians, Nicolet stepped ashore at Green Bay, concluded a peace among the various tribes, and promoted the advantages of trading with the French. He then turned to a search for the *Northwest Passage [VII]*, apparently traveling up the Fox River and across Lake Winnebago to the land of the Mascoutens until he was three days away by portage from the Wisconsin River, a tributary of the "great water" (actually the *Mississippi River* and not the China Sea). This route was later followed by the *Jolliet and Marquette expedition* to the Mississippi.

Nicolet pushed southward to visit the *Illinois* people and then turned northward to visit the Potawatomis near the entrance and islands of Green Bay. He was back in Quebec a year later and was able to add to Champlain's 1632 map of the known west the Straits of Mackinac, Lake Michigan, and Green Bay. He died in October 1642 during a storm in a boating accident on the St. Lawrence River.

Nicollet, Joseph Nicolas (1786–1843)

Following the French revolution of 1830, the accomplished government scientist Joseph Nicolas Nicollet left his homeland to make a tour devoted to North American geography. From his Baltimore base he spent four years traveling the South to visit scientifically inclined gentlemen, determining the precise location of New Orleans based on astronomical observations, and ascending the *Mississippi River* to *St. Louis [VI]*, where he established the river's absolute altitude at low water in relation to the Gulf of Mexico. He later established other absolute altitude stations at Fort Kearny, Council Bluffs, and Fort Snelling near St. Paul, where he first arrived in the summer of 1836.

From there he conducted a fifty-nine-day exploration of the north-central Minnesota wilderness to seek the sources of the Mississippi while studying the documents of those who had preceded him. A detailed investigation of the areas to Lake Itasca's west and south revealed streams *Henry Schoolcraft* had missed on an earlier journey. Nicollet named some twenty of the area's small lakes after leading scientists. He was also the first to journey the Mississippi's entire length while making astronomical observations.

His report and map of the Mississippi's sources, purchased by the Bureau of Topographical Engineers, led to a U.S. government assignment to complete his map and to explore westward to the *Missouri River [VI]*. In April 1838, leading a well-equipped scientific expedition with *John C. Frémont [VI]* as assistant, Nicollet set out from Fort Snelling to follow the Minnesota River, and to explore the headwaters of Iowa's Des Moines River and the lakes west of the Sioux River before returning to Fort Snelling by way of the Cannon River.

On his second expedition in 1839, he ascended the Missouri to Fort Pierre and set off eastward across the Dakota plains to Devil's Lake, which he determined was an isolated saline lake and not a source of the Red River, as was commonly believed. He was the first to make detailed observations of the Coteu watershed between the Missouri and Mississippi Rivers.

Acclaimed for his achievement, Nicollet spent his last years in the Baltimore-Washington area working on his *Map of the Hydrological Basin of the Upper Mississippi* (1842). The first to use barometric pressure readings to determine topographical elevations, he revealed many mapping errors previously accepted as fact. Not only was he the last true explorer of North American rivers, but his interest in documenting place names through time and his extensive ethnographic notes on Chippewa culture also added to the nation's store of knowledge.

IN THEIR OWN
Words

The water of the Minnesota is distinguished from that of the Chippewa by a very tenuous suspension which gives it the appearance of muddled water. As the French of the country say, water slightly troubled, a little whitish, without transparency in the water. It is this condition which the Sioux express by Mini Sotta.

—JOSEPH N. NICOLLET,
"THE EXPEDITIONS OF 1838–39"

Nolan, Philip (1771–1801)

Born in Belfast, Ireland, Philip Nolan migrated to Kentucky and by 1788 had become an agent of the soldier/trader James Wilkinson. From about

1790 he represented Wilkinson's business interests in New Orleans, from where he set off on four trading/exploring expeditions into Spanish Texas in the 1790s.

Nolan's first venture carried him into the country of the Comanches, and he spent the better part of two years trading with, and living among, them before returning to *Louisiana* with a herd of wild horses. A second expedition from 1794 to 1796 carried him as far as San Antonio. In a 1797 journey, Nolan struck south as far as the Río Grande before retracing his route to New Orleans with some 1,700 Texas mustangs.

Nolan carried survey instruments on that 1797 journey, evidently under instruction from the governor of French Louisiana to prepare a map of Texas. (No Nolan map survives, however.) This aroused Spanish suspicions, and the authorities revoked his horse-trading license and issued orders to arrest him should he return.

On this last expedition Nolan penetrated the hill country of central Texas northwest of present Austin. On March 21, 1801, he was killed in a skirmish with Spanish troops sent to arrest him. The Nolan-Wilkinson expeditions proved to be successful business ventures; he also amassed significant information on the Spanish borderlands that he passed on to the French in Louisiana and, through his patron Wilkinson, to the Americans.

Noyon, Jacques de   (1668–1745)

As voyageur and *coureur de bois* (unlicensed trader), de Noyon led the risky life of a wilderness adventurer. Born in Trois-Rivières, Quebec, he made many trips westward.

On the best-known one in 1688, de Noyon apparently pushed farther west than any Frenchman to date when he led a traders' group out from Fort Nipigon in Lake Superior's Thunder Bay area. After following the Kaministikwia River upstream and crossing Dog Lake, he traveled west to Rainy Lake and there spent the winter with the Assiniboine Indians. The meager documentation of his life has yielded little about his other explorations.

Ohio River

A principal tributary of the *Mississippi River,* the Ohio is formed by the junction of the Allegheny and Monongahela Rivers at Pittsburgh and flows 981 miles to its confluence with the Mississippi below Cairo, Illinois.

The French explorer *La Salle* heard about a "great river" from Iroquois Indians and claimed to have reached the Ohio in 1669; the report is disputed. Louis *Jolliet*'s map of 1684 sketched a rough course of the river as far as the falls at present Louisville. Another French explorer, *Gaspard-Joseph Chaussegros de Léry,* traveled downstream to the Mississippi in 1739.

By mid-century, the Ohio had become a focus of British-French rivalry in North America. The English explorer *Christopher Gist* explored the river below Fort Duquesne (present Pittsburgh) in 1750. *Daniel Boone* journeyed as far as the Falls in the spring of 1770.

Working for the Americans, the Frenchman *Georges Henri Victor Collot* carried out a careful survey of the Ohio in a 1796 expedition. By then it had become an important avenue of American westward expansion.

Peré, Jean   (?–?)

Peré arrived in Canada in June 1660 with a group of merchants and, with Adrien Jolliet (brother of Louis Jolliet), won a commission in 1669 to search for copper to the north of Lake Ontario. Also operating as a *coureur de bois* (unlicensed fur trader) on this expedition, Peré found an easier and more southerly route west—from the *St. Lawrence River [III]* along the north shore of Lake Ontario and by way of the Oshawa–Lake Simcoe portage to Georgian Bay, and then along Lake Huron's north shore to Sault Sainte Marie. There he collected pelts from the Ottawa Indians before proceeding to explore Lake Superior and its northern shore, where he discovered a copper mine.

In the late 1670s, while selling furs to the English at Fort Orange (Albany, New York), Peré was taken prisoner and sent to Manate (Manhattan) to meet with Sir Edmund Andros, governor of New York and New England, as the English wanted to establish a trading relationship with the Ottawa Indians.

IN THEIR OWN *Words*

The whole length of [the Lake Superior] coast is enriched with mines of lead in a nearly pure state; with copper of such excellence that pieces as large as one's fist are found, all refined; and with great rocks, having whole veins of turquoise. The people even strive to make us believe that its waters are swollen by various streams which roll along with the sand grains of gold in abundance—the refuse, so to speak, of the neighboring mines.

—JEROME LALEMENT, *THE JESUIT RELATION*, 1659–1660

The English took Peré captive again on a 1684 expedition to Hudson Bay. They eventually sent him back to France by way of England. Once again back in *New France [III]*, he continued fur trading and exploring. The Albany River of northern Ontario, rising in Lake Nipigon and flowing to the southwest end of James Bay, was long named after him. On an early map is the note, "Rivière du Perray, which is the name of the first European to navigate this river as far as Hudson Bay."

Robutel de la Noue, Zacharie (1665–1733)

A native of *Montreal* and by report one of Canada's best white canoeists, de la Noue accompanied Chevalier de Troyes on an expedition to Hudson Bay in 1686. He received a series of promotions in the French colonial army from 1691 to 1725 and participated in various military expeditions.

Assigned in 1717 to discover the northern sea by an overland route through *New France [III]*, he set out in July apparently to retrace *Jacques de Noyon*'s 1688 trip to Lake of the Woods in upper Minnesota, where hostile *Sioux [VI]* ended his search. His orders were also to establish a post on the Kanastigoya River in the northern Lake Superior region. Then he was to proceed toward Lac des Christinaux to erect a second fort, and a third at Lac de Assenipoëlle. He returned to Montreal from Kamanistikwia in 1721.

Rogers, Robert (1731–1795)

Famed during the French and Indian War as the leader of Rogers' Rangers, Robert Rogers later turned to a search for the *Northwest Passage [VII]* and to westward exploration. His interest in this may have been stimulated when he was posted in 1761 to North Carolina. The colony's governor, Arthur Dobbs, had once sent two expeditions to Hudson Bay and had written a 1744 book that led the British admiralty to offer a substantial monetary prize for the discovery of the Northwest Passage.

In 1765 the Massachusetts-born hero sailed to London to obtain permission and financial sponsors for his scheme. While there he published two books—his journal of the recent hostilities and a historical account of North American geography drawn from his travels. The anonymous play *Ponteach* was also attributed to him, but his conflict with the Ottawa Indian leader Pontiac probably only inspired it.

Assigned to the command at *Fort Michilimackinac,* from which he was to advance his project, Rogers arrived there in August 1766 and sent two exploratory parties westward. James Tute, a former ranger, was to find an inland northwest passage or the great River "Ouragon" (the name Oregon in possibly its first written appearance) believed to flow westward at about the latitude of 50° to the Pacific Ocean, which in turn was presumed to connect to Hudson Bay at 59°. Over the next two years Tute was to ascend the *Mississippi* from the Great Lakes and voyage by way of the Saskatchewan River to the "Ouragon." He abandoned the effort at Grand Portage on Lake Superior's northwest shore after hearing from Rogers that no more supplies were forthcoming because of a shortfall in funds. *Jonathan Carver*'s second expedition, which was to rendezvous with Tute, first explored interior Wisconsin and Minnesota before ending at Grand Portage.

In December 1767 Rogers was arrested and charged with high treason as a result of his questionable financial practices and his apparent attempt to establish a personal empire in the West. Acquitted in October 1768, he traveled to London to seek redress. During the American Revolution, he came back to lead Loyalist forces before returning to England.

Roseboom, Johannes (Rooseboom)   (1661?–1745)

Born in Albany, New York, of Dutch parentage, Roseboom made the first push westward of the English fur traders. New York Governor Thomas Dongan in 1685 granted Roseboom a pass to live among the Indians, followed by a license to travel to the Great Lakes region to trade and hunt among the *Huron [III],* Ottawa, and others.

Guided by a French deserter, Roseboom departed in June 1686 at the head of a ten-canoe expedition—the first English flotilla on the upper Great Lakes—to *Fort Michilimackinac.* Offering high prices for furs, he alarmed the French who had been unable to stop his trip.

Believing the French monopoly broken, Roseboom set out west on a second trip in the autumn of 1686. After spending the winter with the Seneca, he continued on in spring 1687 to join with Major Patrick McGregory on his return to Michilimackinac. This time a French military force seized both Roseboom's and McGregory's parties on Lake Erie before they reached the post. Their canoes were plundered and they were taken back as prisoners, first to Niagara, where their French guide was executed, and then on to *Montreal* and Quebec. Governor Dongan eventually negotiated their release.

Roseboom's failure on the second expedition demonstrated that the French, who still dominated the upper Great Lakes region, would not tolerate English incursions. Not until 1760 were English merchants able to begin trading in the area.

Sagean, Mathieu (1655?–1710?)

Mathieu Sagean, a gifted storyteller and apparently a semiliterate enlisted soldier born in *Montreal,* convinced French officials in 1699 that he had discovered Acaaniba, a wealthy primitive civilization in western America. His story unraveled after the French sent him back to America to lead another expedition to Acaaniba; not long after his arrival at Biloxi on the Gulf of Mexico in May 1701, those who had known him in Canada revealed his hoax to the commandant, *Sieur de Bienville.* Chief among his debunkers was the explorer *Pierre-Charles Le Sueur.*

According to Sagean's fantastic tale, he had accompanied *La Salle* on his 1682 voyage down the *Mississippi,* and on the return north he had stopped at Fort Saint-Louis in Illinois to obtain *Henri Tonty*'s permission to undertake an expedition of his own. He supposedly continued up the river beyond the Falls of Saint Anthony and somewhere in central Minnesota encountered a river flowing south-southwest to the Gulf of California. Some 250 leagues downstream he came to Acaaniba, where he remained for five months. The inhabitants of this paradise were descendants of Aztecs who had fled northward to escape the Spanish. They traded riches—gold nuggets lay on the ground like pebbles—with people to the west, possibly the Japanese.

Afterward, Sagean spent fifteen years on a meandering odyssey that started at the *St. Lawrence River [III]* and continued with passages on a series of ships weaving a course from the West Indies along both coasts of Africa, and by way of India to the East Indies, ending in a shipwreck off Formosa, before he sailed back to Europe to report his discovery of Acaaniba.

Sagean's motivation for this elaborate fabrication may have been to gain fame and passage back to the New World. Faced with the expenses involved in the *Iberville* venture to establish the *Louisiana* colony, one that might fail as did the La Salle enterprise, the French officials who believed

Sagean saw in his story a way to avert economic disaster with the discovery of immense amounts of gold and of the long-sought-for transcontinental waterway to the Pacific Ocean.

Saint-Denis, Louis Juchereau de (1676–1744)

The Canadian-born Louis Juchereau de Saint-Denis arrived in 1699 with *Sieur d'Iberville* in *Louisiana,* where he became the foremost trader, Indian diplomat, and explorer on its western frontier. In the spring of 1700 he accompanied *Sieur de Bienville* overland from Lake Saint-Joseph to the Natchitoches villages near the Red River, and in August he led a small party up the Red River first to the Natchitoches and then on to the villages of the Cadodacho. The following year he explored the region between the Red and Ouachita Rivers before assuming command of Fort du Mississippi.

Saint-Denis's numerous forays into Texas led Louisiana administrator *Antoine de La Mothe Cadillac* to commission him to find a trade route to northern Mexico. Thus, in September 1713 Saint-Denis set out with twenty-four men from Mobile for the Red River. There he established a post on the island of Natchitoches before heading across lower East Texas to arrive at, in July 1714, the Spanish frontier outpost of San Juan Bautista across the Río Grande, and some thirty-five miles south of Eagle Pass, Texas. At the time, Spain forbade Mexico to engage in foreign trade; Spanish officials arrested Saint-Denis and confiscated his goods. After a trip to the viceroy in Mexico City to absolve himself of all charges, Saint-Denis returned to participate as a guide on Domingo Ramón's Spanish expedition to settle East Texas. The party left San Juan Bautista on April 27, 1716, and traveled by a more northerly route to found missions among the Indians of the Hasinai confederacy. Saint-Denis continued on to Natchitoches and then to Mobile.

In March 1717 he left on his second trading trip to San Juan Bautista, where his goods were again confiscated and he eventually had to flee. Over the following years, having facilitated the establishment of Spanish settlements close to those of the French, he used his Natchitoches trading post to supply the Spanish of East Texas, albeit illegally. His explorations of the western frontier also contributed to the greater accuracy of the French and Spanish maps of the era.

Schoolcraft, Henry Rowe (1793–1864)

A glassmaker's son, born near Albany, New York, Henry Rowe Schoolcraft is credited with discovery of the source of the *Mississippi River* in 1832. He is also regarded as a pioneer in Native American ethnography.

Trained in geology, Schoolcraft set out in 1818–1819 on a geographical and mineralogical survey of Missouri, then approaching statehood. The results were published as *A View of the Lead Mines of Missouri* in 1819. As a member of the Lewis Cass expedition to the northern Great Lakes in 1820, he approached the sources of the Mississippi, a series of small streams emptying into Lake Itasca in northern Minnesota. His *Travels through the Northwestern Regions of the United States* (1821) is an account of the Cass expedition.

Schoolcraft returned to the upper Mississippi in 1832 to confirm the discovery, coining the name of Lake Itasca out of the Latin phrase *veritas caput*—true source. He recounted the 1832 journey in *Narrative of an Expedition through the Upper Mississippi to Itasca Lake, the Actual Source of the Mississippi*, published in 1834.

Explorer and ethnologist Henry Rowe Schoolcraft in this daguerreotype made in about 1847. In 1832 he discovered and named the source of the Mississippi River, Lake Itasca in northern Minnesota.

IN THEIR OWN *Words*
To have visited both the source and mouth of this celebrated stream, falls to the lot of few, and I believe there is no person living, besides myself, of whom the remark can now be made. On the 10th of July, 1819, I passed out of the mouth of the Mississippi in a brig bound for New York, and little thinking I should soon revisit its waters; yet, on the 21st of July of the following year, I found myself seated in an Indian canoe, upon its source.

—HENRY ROWE SCHOOLCRAFT, *TRAVELS THROUGH THE NORTHWESTERN REGIONS OF THE UNITED STATES* (1821)

Sioux

Groups of Native American nations collectively labeled the Sioux inhabited the northern Great Plains in a broad arc from present eastern Minnesota to the Black Hills of eastern Wyoming. The name, originally *nadoueessioux,* derives from a French-Ojibway word meaning "little snakes," doubtless a pejorative. Regional and dialect divisions are the Dakota, Nakota, and Lakota.

According to tribal legend, the Sioux had their origins beneath the Black Hills, where they dwelled from time immemorial. They came, or were lured, above ground eventually and were unable to return to their subterranean homeland. Left behind at first, the Sioux leader finally emerged in the shape of the buffalo—the life-sustaining creature that would supply food, clothing, shelter, and tools to the people.

The Sioux first encountered Europeans in the form of Spanish explorers along the eastern ranges of the *Rocky Mountains [VI].* The Sioux acquired horses from the Spanish and, by exploiting the many qualities of the animal they dubbed the "holy dog," evolved into an equestrian culture. By the late seventeenth century the Sioux were in regular contact with French traders pushing up the *Mississippi* and *Missouri [VI]* Rivers. The Sioux acquired firearms from the French, somewhat lessening their dependence on buffalo.

One of the *Grosseilliers and Radisson expeditions* made first contact with the Dakota Sioux along the present Minnesota-Dakota border in 1660. A Sioux band captured *Louis Hennepin* on the Mississippi in 1680 and carried him off to the Milles Lac area of Minnesota; the French trader *Dulhut* (Duluth) negotiated his freedom a few months later. The Sioux excited Dulhut with the report of a great lake twenty days' march to the west "whose water is not good to drink"—this may have been the Great Salt Lake, but it was decidedly not the Pacific of Dulhut's dreams.

Pierre Le Sueur ascended the Mississippi as far as the Falls of St. Anthony in the Sioux country of Minnesota in 1702 in search of minerals. The English explorer *Jonathan Carver* encountered Dakota Sioux in November 1766 and wintered with them in their encampment along the Minnesota River. There the Dakota told him of other Indian nations to the west—the Mandan along the Missouri and, beyond, the Cheyenne.

American traders introduced the Sioux to alcohol in the early decades of the nineteenth century. The Americans forced the Fort Laramie Treaty on the Sioux in 1851. It allowed for road building and the establishment of military posts and set territorial boundaries for the Sioux. These were reduced in stages, as the century advanced, to a region of present western South Dakota. Some 100,000 persons are enrolled in the Sioux tribes today.

Spotswood, Alexander (1676–1740)

Alexander Spotswood, while Virginia's lieutenant governor from 1710 to 1722, explored the colony's mountainous areas. An active promoter of westward expansion, he established the Order of the Golden Horseshoe to encourage interest in the wilderness regions. In 1710 he sent a group of rangers to search beyond the *Blue Ridge Mountains [III]* for a route to the Great Lakes in order to support his plan to establish British trade and settlements to block expansion of the French fur trade. In 1714 he conducted a tour of the Virginia frontier and piedmont region to encourage settlers to move westward from the Tidewater region.

Two years later Spotswood organized a leisurely and luxurious expedition for the "knights" of the Golden Horseshoe. In the group of sixty-four were some dozen colonial gentlemen, their servants, and Germanna rangers, whom Indian scouts led on August 30, 1716, from Germanna up the Rapidan River and along its South Branch to Swift Run Gap in the Blue Ridge. They then followed the Iroquois trail down to the Shenandoah River. On September 5 Spotswood claimed possession of the region for England's George I. After a ceremonial toast, the company returned home, leaving some rangers to continue west to the Indian trace known as the Warriors Path.

Back in Williamsburg, Spotswood presented his gentleman adventurers with cravat pins with the inscription *Sic juvat transcendere montes*—it is pleasurable to cross mountains. He later depicted the Shenandoah Valley as an agricultural paradise in an attempt to lure settlers there.

Tonty, Henri (Tonti, Henri de) (1650–1704)

After fighting in seven European naval campaigns and losing his right hand in an explosion, Henri Tonty joined the 1678 enterprise of *La Salle* to explore and colonize the North American wilderness. Known as Iron Hand (the Indians saw his skill with his new gloved hand as a sign of special power), Tonty would emerge as La Salle's most loyal and energetic follower.

Shortly after his arrival in *New France [III]*, Tonty supervised the construction of Fort Niagara and of the ship *Griffin*, which in 1679 became the first sailing vessel to explore the western Great Lakes. From the

Great Lakes, where in October 1680 he had rediscovered *Jolliet*'s Chicago Portage route, Tonty accompanied La Salle on the 1682 voyage down to the Delta of the *Mississippi River*. On their return, at the northern edge of La Salle's planned Mississippi Valley colony on the upper Illinois River, Tonty erected Fort Saint-Louis and began to trade furs with the *Illinois* and *Miami* Indians.

He again descended the Mississippi in 1686 to rejoin La Salle at the river's mouth, arriving in April. Finding no signs of the new French settlement, he sent parties along the gulf coast in a futile search; La Salle had landed at Matagorda Bay instead. On his return up the Mississippi, he established relations with various tribes along the river and founded Arkansas Post, the first French bastion in the lower Mississippi Valley.

Learning of La Salle's murder in 1689, he set off southward in search of surviving colonists, traveling down the Mississippi and up the Red River and westward from Natchitoches. Short on supplies and ammunition, after Indian guides refused to lead him farther and learning of the approach of the Spanish, Tonty finally turned back in East Texas (near the town of Crockett).

In 1695, with permission to trade with the Assiniboine, Tonty left *Fort Michilimackinac* on August 8 on a northwestward expedition, traveling to Manitoba's far north and possibly even reaching Hudson Bay. In 1700 he entered the service of *Iberville*'s *Louisiana* colony as a seasoned explorer and an able Indian negotiator. He reexamined the Red River to Natchitoches and in early 1702 led an expedition to eastern Mississippi between the Chickasawhay and Tombigbee Rivers, which resulted in a preliminary Chickasaw-Choctaw peace. Tonty died in Mobile in 1704, probably of yellow fever.

IN THEIR OWN *Words*

I sent out two canoes, one towards the coast of Mexico, and the other towards Carolina, to see if they could discover anything. They each sailed about 30 leagues, but proceeded no farther for want of fresh water. They reported that where they had been the land began to rise. They brought me a porpoise and some oysters.

—HENRI TONTY, "MEMOIR" (1893)

Viele, Arnold
(Viele, Aernout Cornelissen)   (1640–1704?)

Born in New Amsterdam of Dutch parentage, by 1659 Viele had reached Albany, New York, where he entered the Indian fur trade and learned enough Iroquois to interpret at the 1682 Five Nations conference. On an expedition to expand the English fur trade westward, he led a party into the Ottawa lands of the northern Great Lakes. Captured by the French on Lake Erie as he was en route to *Fort Michilimackinac* in 1687, he later escaped from prison in Quebec.

In the fall of 1692 Viele led a group of Albany traders on a two-year expedition to the Shawnee of the lower *Ohio River* Valley. He probably traveled from the Albany area by way of the Delaware River of northeastern Pennsylvania and then veered inland to the Susquehanna River and from there approached the Allegheny River before its junction with the Ohio. He thus apparently became the first white man to reach the upper Ohio River and to explore some of its tributaries on his way southward.

Walker, Thomas (1715–1794)

A Virginian with a taste for land speculation, Walker was for a time in the 1760s the guardian of his neighbor's son, the young *Thomas Jefferson [VI]*. Although educated at the College of William and Mary as a physician, Walker turned to an investigation of the western wilderness. Together with James Patton, who had obtained a land grant in the Valley of Virginia for Scots-Irish immigrants, Walker in 1748 surveyed the headwaters of the Holston River down to present-day Kingsport, Tennessee.

He returned to the area in 1750 as surveyor for the Loyal Land Company, which had just procured an 800,000-acre land grant in southwestern Virginia and southeastern Kentucky. This official expedition set off on March 6 across southwestern Virginia to cross the Holston, Clinch, and Powell Rivers, and to follow the Warriors Path to Cave Gap, which Walker renamed *Cumberland Gap* in honor of the Duke of Cumberland; he also named the Cumberland River, Valley, and Mountains.

Although Walker was not the first white man at the gap, he was the first to describe its unique geology. After passing through on April 13, he built Kentucky's first log cabin (near Barbourville) as an expeditionary base. He then headed northward in June to discover and name Frederick's River (later known as Licking River). Circling around to explore southeastern Kentucky, he then veered east to the Big Sandy River, unfortunately continuing eastward back into the mountains rather than westward and thus missing the fertile lowlands of central Kentucky. On July 13 he was back in Staunton, Virginia, with a disappointing report of densely forested mountains rich in game but with no lands suitable for settlement. On a 1765 trip to Kentucky he reached the Herrington Lake area (south of Lexington).

On his final major expedition, as part of the 1779–1780 boundary survey continuing the Virginia–North Carolina border to the Cumberland River, and from there westward to the Tennessee River to divide Kentucky and Tennessee, Walker marked an approximate line at latitude 36°30' through difficult terrain with variable accuracy. Barred by hostile Indians, he had to estimate the boundary's final section, which continued to the *Mississippi River.*

A politically active planter, Walker continued after the Revolutionary War to try to expand Virginia's domain, challenging the claims of Indians and of other states.

Welch, Thomas (?–?)

In a bid to open trade with the Indians of the *Mississippi River* Valley, the South Carolinian Welch in 1698 completed a remarkable overland trek from Charles Town to the Arkansas River's junction with the Mississippi.

Welch challenged French control of the region by seeking alliances with the *Chickasaw* and other tribes. He harassed the French by inciting the Chickasaw to attack their main allies, the *Choctaw,* and by selling some 150 Choctaw captives as slaves in Charles Town.

In 1707 he participated in an unsuccessful plan to conquer and unite the Mississippi tribes and incite them to attack the French gulf coast bastion at Mobile. Welch later turned his attention to his Savannah River plantation.

PART VI

Across the North American Continent, 1720–1880

As the eighteenth century advanced, explorers pushed boldly beyond the Mississippi frontier into the Great Plains and on to the Rocky Mountains. Their motives were varied, sometimes personal, frequently commercial, and whether consciously or not, only too often imperial. Fur traders, missionaries, professional soldiers, and the vanguards of settlers opened up the North American continent and stretched the boundaries of the United States and British Canada to the western ocean.

The broad, muddy Missouri River beckoned as a highway into the unknown. In a French expedition of 1714 Etienne Venard de Bourgmond ascended the Missouri as far as the mouth of the Platte River below present Omaha and perhaps beyond. In 1724 he penetrated westward from the Kansas River into the lands of the fierce Comanche—"the most beautiful countries in the world," he marveled.

At mid-century, fur trader Anthony Henday and others approached the Plains country from the north. Henday's journey of 1754–1755 took him south and west from York Factory on Hudson Bay to Blackfoot Indian country in present Alberta. He may have caught a glimpse of the Rockies, though he left no record of a sighting; it is certain, however,

British cartographer Aaron Arrowsmith's 1802 map of North America proved invaluable to Lewis and Clark as they began to plan their famous expedition in 1803. They were especially influenced by its presentation of the upper Missouri basin; this suggested to them that the Missouri provided a direct link to the Columbia River. Although their expedition found no such connection, they did collect the only reliable information then available about the far Northwest. Publication of the Lewis and Clark journals enabled cartographers to begin filling in the blank areas on Arrowsmith's map.

that he observed vast herds of buffalo (American bison) and joined with Indian bands in the hunt.

British trapper Peter Pond struck north to the region of Lake Athabasca in Saskatchewan and beyond to the Great Slave Lake in the 1770s and 1780s. Along with hunting for furs, Pond sought to blaze a trade route to the sea. He underestimated the task, calculating inaccurately, for example, that Great Slave Lake lay "within six days travel of the Grand Pacific Ocean." Pond's successor Alexander Mackenzie corrected his errors and, in two remarkable journeys, reached the Arctic Ocean in 1789 and the Pacific in 1793. With the latter accomplishment, Mackenzie became the first European to cross the entire continent.

The pace of exploration across North America accelerated after 1803, when President Thomas Jefferson acquired the Louisiana Territory, an 800,000-square-mile belt of the continent's midsection lying between the Mississippi and the Rockies, for the newly independent United States. Inspired in part by Mackenzie's account of his 1793 journey, Jefferson detailed the veteran army officers Meriwether Lewis and William Clark to explore the new territory and continue beyond the mountains in search of a water route to the Pacific. Ascending the Missouri to its source in the Montana Rockies, the expedition, with Indian guidance, marched west for the Columbia River and followed it down to the sea. Lewis and Clark sighted the broad Pacific on November 18, 1805.

"Ocian in view," Clark cried. "O! The joy."

The Lewis and Clark expedition returned with a great trove of data on the geography, topography, natural history, and ethnography of the West. For the balance of the nineteenth century, American and Canadian explorers would follow in Lewis and Clark's wake. Trappers such as Jedediah Smith in the 1820s and soldiers such as John Charles Frémont in the 1840s filled in the empty places on the master map Jefferson's pathfinders had created.

By the 1850s settlers making the cross-country trek numbered in the thousands, and the United States, in acquiring the Oregon Country and California, had fulfilled what it saw as its Manifest Destiny to overspread the continent. In the process, migrants and their social and economic systems dispossessed the native peoples and disrupted their traditional ways. Government-sponsored surveys in the 1850s laid out railroad routes that would bind the expanded nation and carry goods and people from the Atlantic to the Pacific.

Exploring expeditions took on an increasingly scientific cast. The great western topographical and geological surveys of the 1870s revealed the last "undiscovered" places in the continental United States, a river and a mountain range in southern Utah. To be sure, there were still adventures to be had—witness John Wesley Powell's thrilling journeys into the Grand Canyon of the Colorado River in 1869 and 1872. By century's end, though, the last unexplored stretches lay in the extreme north, in the polar regions at the far edge of the hyperborean sea.

American Fur Company

John Jacob Astor established the American Fur Company in 1808 to break his dependence on British-Canadian suppliers of furs. His enterprise eventually came to dominate the fur trade in the Old Northwest and the Rocky Mountains.

In 1811 the Pacific Fur Company, an American Fur Company subsidiary, established the *Fort Astoria* trading post on the lower *Columbia River.* Astor's operations in the Pacific Northwest never flourished, but trapping and trading expeditions launched from Astoria added substantially to knowledge of the region.

Trappers and traders working for the American Fur Company, particularly *Robert Stuart,* Ramsay Crooks, and *Thomas Fitzpatrick,* among others, carried out important overland expeditions in pursuit of the company's interests. In 1812 Stuart became the first traveler of European descent to cross the Rockies at South Pass, Wyoming.

In the Rockies, competition with the Rocky Mountain Fur Company had become fierce by the mid-1820s. Within a decade Astor, anticipating a change in fashions and other factors that would cause the collapse of the western fur trade, sold the American Fur Company and sank his fortune into New York City real estate.

Ashley, William Henry (1778–1838)

Born in Virginia, William Henry Ashley resettled in *St. Louis* and became an important early entrepreneur in the fur trade. Ashley developed the brigade system of fur trapping that allowed American firms using small teams of men to challenge the British-Canadians for dominance in the *Rocky Mountains.*

Ashley and his trappers were the first whites to navigate Wyoming's Green River. They also explored the Salt Lake region. A party under Ashley associate *Jedediah Smith* rediscovered South Pass, Wyoming, the key to the overland routes to California and Oregon, in March 1824.

A contemporary, Charles Keemle, remarked in 1826 that Ashley and his trappers had shown the way to the Rockies and beyond to settlers as well as explorers and traders. "It has been proved," Keemle wrote, "that overland expeditions in large bodies may be made to that remote region. General Ashley left St. Louis in March last, and returned in September. The whole route lay through level and open country, better than any turnpike route in the United States."

Ashley sold his fur interests to Smith, *William Sublette,* and Donald Jackson in 1826. He entered politics in Missouri and later served three terms in the U.S. Congress, where he became an important advocate of western interests.

Astor, John Jacob   (1763–1848)

Born in Germany, John Jacob Astor emigrated to the United States in 1783 and amassed a fortune in the fur trade. Seeking to expand his commercial empire and extend U.S. boundaries, he dispatched land and sea expeditions to the Pacific Northwest in 1810 and established a trading post, *Fort Astoria,* near the mouth of the *Columbia River.*

Astor's overland expedition under *Wilson Price Hunt* marched from *St. Louis* to the Columbia in 1811, blazing a new trail to the Pacific and adding substantially to knowledge of the West. The Astorian *Robert Stuart,* returning to New York with dispatches for Astor, in 1812 became the first white to transit South Pass in Wyoming and to travel eastward along what would become the *Oregon Trail.* For explorers and, by the 1840s, westward migrants, the Oregon Trail and South Pass became the most important highway to the Pacific Northwest and California.

Bannock

A branch of the Northern Paiutes, the equestrian Bannocks inhabited lands in what is now southeastern Idaho and ranged into Wyoming and Montana in pursuit of buffalo. Whites called them "the Robbers," and they were also sometimes erroneously referred to as the Snakes, the white name for the Shoshone tribe, a nation with which the Bannocks were closely allied.

The occasion of their first contact with Europeans is difficult to establish. *James Bridger* and other mountain men/explorers probably encountered Bannocks before 1810. They were well known to John Jacob Astor's fur traders of 1811–1814. A Bannock raiding party destroyed an Astor fur-trading post on the Boise River in January 1814 and carried out intermittent raids on trapper and explorer parties thereafter.

Bannock numbers probably never exceeded two thousand. A smallpox epidemic decimated the tribe in 1824; settler migrations damaged the buffalo ranges, drove the game out of the country, and brought disease. By 1840 the Bannock population was probably less than one thousand, and it declined thereafter.

Benton, Thomas Hart (1782–1858)

Born in North Carolina, Benton migrated to Tennessee and then to *St. Louis,* where he practiced law, edited the *Missouri Enquirer,* entered politics as a U.S. senator, and became a champion of western expansion, particularly into Oregon along protected trade routes that would lead across the continent, down the *Columbia River,* and thence to India and China.

Benton's daughter Jessie married the U.S. Army officer *John Charles Frémont* in 1841, and through Benton's influence Frémont won appointments commanding important exploring expeditions into the West. Frémont's reports, particularly of his first two expeditions, to the Wind River Range of Wyoming in 1842 and as far as The Dalles on the Columbia in 1843, publicized what would become the *Oregon Trail* and promoted the westward movement of Americans.

Bent's Fort

Charles Bent and Ceran Saint Vrain completed an adobe fort on the Arkansas River in present Colorado in 1833 as a base for trade with the Cheyenne, Arapaho, and other Indian tribes. The fort's location on the north bank of the Arkansas, then the U.S. boundary with Mexico, made it an important outfitting center too. Bent's traders supplied horses, mules, and supplies to U.S. government exploring and military expeditions.

John C. Frémont set out from Bent's Fort on his third expedition in February 1845. With a handpicked party of mountain men, he marked out a trail through the central *Rocky Mountains* to Great Salt Lake, over the Humboldt Sinks and into California.

When the U.S. government declined Bent's offer to sell the fort in 1849, he blew it up with gunpowder charges and established a new post forty miles downriver.

Bidwell, John (1819–1900)

John Bidwell, along with the obscure Missourian John Bartleson, was the leader of the first California emigrant party. With 34 settlers, Bidwell diverged from the *Oregon Trail* in southeastern Idaho and found his way across the *terra incognita* of the Great Basin to the *Sierra Nevada* in the summer and autumn of 1841. He followed Joseph Reddeford Walker in tracing the outline of the *California Trail.*

Striking south and west from Soda Springs, Bidwell, with advice from friendly Indians, followed the *Humboldt River* to its sink, then the Carson and Walker Rivers to the base of the Sierra Nevada. The party crossed the mountains at or near Sonora Pass in late October and descended into the Sacramento Valley, thus becoming the first Americans to complete the overland journey to Mexican California.

Bidwell stayed on to find work as an agent of the Swiss land baron John Augustus Sutter and eventually to rise to prominence in American California. Twelve of the thirty-four migrants in the Bidwell-Bartleson party, however, returned to the United States in the spring after their arrival.

Blackfoot

The powerful, warlike Blackfoot nation, an Algonquian-speaking Amerindian tribe, were inhabitants of the plains of present Montana when whites first encountered them in the late eighteenth century.

The nomadic Blackfeet, who called themselves "the real people," confederated with the Blood, North Piegan, and other tribes. In 1832 the artist George Catlin estimated the confederacy's population at 16,500. But a smallpox epidemic of 1837 decimated their numbers.

The notorious Blackfoot hostility toward whites dated from 1806, when a member of the *Lewis and Clark expedition* shot and killed a tribesman on a horse-stealing raid on the Marias River. Blackfeet preyed thereafter on explorers, trappers, and early settlers. *Robert Stuart,* for example, marching eastbound from the *Columbia River* in 1812 along what would become the *Oregon Trail,* took long, exhausting detours to avoid contact with Blackfoot bands.

Bonneville, Benjamin Louis Eulalie de   (1796–1878)

Born in Paris, the son of a radical journalist and political opponent of Napoleon, Bonneville came to the United States with his exile family in 1803 and graduated from West Point in 1815. He served in a succession of frontier posts before obtaining a two-year leave from the army to carry out a private trading/exploring venture in the *Rocky Mountains.*

With financial assistance from Alfred Seaton, a former associate of *John Jacob Astor,* Bonneville set out from Fort Osage, Missouri, in May 1832 on what appears to have been a quasi-official expedition. Some historians regard him as a government agent traveling undercover; what is certain is that he promised to provide the War Department with extensive information about the topography, resources, and native population of the Mountain West in return for the leave.

Bonneville's fur-trading enterprises were a failure, as he was no match for the experienced trappers of the *American Fur Company* and its rival, the Rocky Mountain Fur Company. He accounted for more as an explorer, however. Bonneville sent Joseph Reddeford Walker west in 1833–1834 on an important trek that blazed an early trail across the Great Basin of Utah and Nevada to California. He also became the first traveler to take laden wagons across South Pass, Wyoming, the opening in the Rockies that would become the main gateway to Oregon and California. Finally, Bonneville's maps provided the most thorough and accurate geographical information of the West for their time.

Coming down out of the mountains in the summer of 1835, Bonneville found he had been struck off the army rolls for overstaying his leave. He eventually won reinstatement but accomplished nothing out of the routine of garrison duty during the balance of his long army career.

Though a fortune eluded him, Bonneville did achieve fame as the hero of the third of *Washington Irving*'s highly colored, though generally accurate, books about the West, *The Adventures of Captain Bonneville (1837).*

Bourgmond, Etienne Venard de   (circa 1680–circa 1730)

French traders and explorers in the early decades of the eighteenth century sought to push west from the *Mississippi [V]* up the "Pekitanoui" (or muddy) river—the *Missouri.* In pursuit of trade, they were also in search of the elusive route across the continent to the Pacific Ocean. In journeys of 1714 and 1724, French explorer Etienne Venard de Bourgmond penetrated the Missouri as far as its junction with the *Platte River* and established the first French contact with Indian nations of the Central Plains.

Reaching Canada in 1695, possibly as a deportee, Bourgmond served initially as a French colonial soldier. Accused of mishandling an incident with Indians while in command of the French post at *Fort Detroit [V]* in 1706, he deserted to become a *coureur de bois* (unlicensed fur trader) in the wilderness around Lake Erie. In 1712 he journeyed south to Mobile, Alabama, where French authorities accepted his proposal to act as a liaison between the Louisiana French and the Missouri Indians.

Bourgmond set out from the mouth of the Missouri River with a small party on March 29, 1714, becoming the first documented European to travel up the river to its junction with the Cheyenne River in central South Dakota. Along the way, he negotiated successively with the Missouri, Osage, and Pawnee tribes for permission to pass through their lands. The richness of the region astonished him.

"These are the most beautiful countries in the world," Bourgmond wrote of the region where the Kansas River flows into the Missouri. "The prairies are like seas, and are full of wild animals, especially bison and deer, in numbers that stagger the imagination."

But the Pawnees blocked his further progress, denying him permission to push on southwest into the territory of the hostile Padoucas (Comanches). Remaining in the region for four years, he sent back two reports, the first a compilation of topographical data from the Missouri north to the Platte River near present Omaha, and the second describing the region's geography and ethnology as far as the Arikara lands in the Dakotas.

On a trip to France in 1719, Bourgmond received a commission as commandant of the Missouri country and instructions from the Compagnie des Indes to establish an outpost on the Missouri. *Claude-Charles Dutisné [V]* sought to follow up Bourgmond's explorations with a journey along the Osage and Kansas Rivers to the Republican River in present Kansas. Here, too, the Pawnees barred further French progress.

Bourgmond struck west again in 1724, setting out on September 20 from newly established Fort d'Orleans in central Missouri. By late September, through Kansas Indian intermediaries, he had negotiated a passage into Comanche country. In mid-October the expedition reached a large Indian encampment—either Comanches or Plains Apaches—on the Big Bend of the Arkansas River in central Kansas. Talks were cordial, but he failed to negotiate a permanent trading arrangement with the tribes.

The French abandoned Fort d'Orleans in 1726, and Bourgmond returned permanently to France. A decade and a half would pass before the French built on his initial penetration of the Missouri. *La Vérendrye's* expedition of 1738 and his sons' journeys a few years later would reveal the Missouri country to the north and west to Europeans.

Bridger, James (1804–1881)

The quintessential "mountain man," Virginia-born but reared in *St. Louis,* James Bridger served an apprenticeship with a blacksmith before signing on with *William H. Ashley*'s first expedition to the *Rocky Mountains* in 1822.

In late 1824 or early 1825, Bridger became the first white traveler to see the Great Salt Lake. When he tasted salt, he thought he had reached the Pacific. Bridger later worked as a trapper and guide for the Rocky Mountain Fur Company and its rival, the *American Fur Company.*

He served as guide for the 1849–1850 expedition of Captain Howard Stansbury of the U.S. Army *Corps of Topographical Engineers,* which sought railroad passes through the Wasatch and Rocky Mountains. The expedition in 1850 blazed a path over Bridger's Pass in south-central Wyoming and discovered Cheyenne Pass, marking it as suitable for a railroad line through the Rocky Mountain barrier.

Bridger accompanied Captain William F. Raynolds's exploring expedition to the Yellowstone region in 1859–1860 and helped Grenville Dodge survey the route of the Union Pacific Railroad in 1866.

The historian *Bernard De Voto* called Bridger "an atlas of the West." At the time of his death, the exploration of the wild areas he had roamed was virtually complete.

Broughton, Henry (?–?)

An officer in *George Vancouver*'s British exploring expedition along the Pacific Coast of North America of 1792–1794, Broughton completed the first extensive surveys of the lower reaches of the *Columbia River* in the autumn of 1792. Many of the names he bestowed on the natural features of the lower river valley remain in circulation today.

Broughton entered the river in the shallow-draft tender *Chatham* on October 20, 1792, some five months after the American mariner *Robert Gray* discovered the Columbia's mouth. Leaving *Chatham* at anchor in the broad estuary, he set out upstream on October 23 in a small boat provisioned for a journey of seven days.

Correcting Gray's rough charts as he went, Broughton painstakingly surveyed the river for a hundred miles upstream to a point just below the

Cascades. Along the way, he named Mount St. Helens in present Washington State for a British ambassador to Spain and dubbed a lofty snowpeak rising south of the Columbia Mount Hood, after the British naval hero Samuel Hood.

When friendly Indians explained to Broughton that the falls beyond would be impassable to the small sailing vessel, he set out on the return trip. Before pushing downstream on October 30, he "formally took possession of the river, and the country in its vicinity, in his Britannic Majesty's name, having every reason to believe, that the subjects of no other civilized nation or state had ever entered this river before," according to Vancouver. With the current in its favor, Broughton's cutter covered the return journey in three swift days.

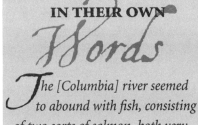

California Trail

Joseph Reddeford Walker's 1833–1834 expedition from the Green River to the Yosemite Valley blazed a rough outline of what would become the California emigrant trail, which would extend from the Great Salt Lake to the *Sierra Nevada*. Walker marched down the *Humboldt River* of Nevada to the marshy Humboldt Sinks and eventually crossed the Sierra Nevada, probably at Mono Pass, and descended into the Yosemite Valley.

In 1841 a small party under *John Bidwell* and John Bartleson left the *Oregon Trail* at Soda Springs, Idaho, followed Walker's route southwest to the Humboldt and its sink, then marched along the Carson River to the Walker River and over the Sierra Nevada between the headwaters of the Walker and the Stanislaus Rivers. Mostly by luck and accident, the party of thirty-three young men, one woman, and a child arrived safely in the Sacramento Valley, the first American settlers to make the overland trip.

In 1844 the Stevens-Murphy party, led by Elisha Stevens and Martin Murphy, with help from an old Indian chief named Truckee, blazed the Truckee River route, which would become the main trail for Gold Rush emigrants as well as the railroad and, eventually, the highway. Stevens led part of the group over Donner Pass in the Sierra Nevada, marking out a path that thousands would follow.

Carson, Kit (Christopher Houston) (1809–1868)

Born in Kentucky, Kit Carson moved to Missouri with his family, found work as a saddler's apprentice, decided he disliked the trade, and ran off at age fourteen with a New Mexico–bound trading caravan. So began Carson's life in the West, an eventful career that assumed legendary proportions as a result of *John Charles Frémont*'s genius for promotion.

Carson worked for the trapper Ewing Young from 1828 to 1831, accompanying Young on his 1829 expedition across the desert Southwest to California. This journey and others served as the foundation for his vast knowledge of the geography and topography of the Rockies and the Great Basin. Carson entered the Rocky Mountain fur trade in 1831. Meeting Frémont on a steamboat in 1842, he signed on as a guide/hunter for Frémont's first expedition up the *Platte River* to the Wind River Range in Wyoming. Carson guided Frémont's important second expedition through the Rockies and on to Oregon and his third expedition to California.

With Frémont, Carson helped establish the short-lived Bear Flag Republic in California in 1846, where, on what he interpreted as orders from Frémont, he oversaw the execution of three Mexican Californians at San Raphael. Later in 1846 he guided Colonel Stephen Kearny's Army of the West from New Mexico to California.

Carson served as a federal Indian agent, campaigned against the Mescalero Apaches and the Navajos (1862–1864), and in 1864 forced the Navajos to make the terrible three-hundred-mile "Long Walk" from their stronghold in the Canyon de Chelley to Forts Canby and Wingate.

Frémont's widely read reports in the 1840s presented Carson as an indomitable American wilderness hero. Carson, who never learned to read and write, dictated his memoirs in the 1850s. Popular dime novelists of the late nineteenth century transformed him into a mythical figure whose fictional exploits far outran his actual achievements. He remains a familiar name in western lore.

Chouteau, Auguste Pierre (1786–1838)

Born in *St. Louis* in the then-Spanish territory of *Louisiana [V]*, a son of the founder of the western gateway city on the *Mississippi River [V]*, Auguste Pierre Chouteau served as an aide to Governor James Wilkinson after the United States acquired the territory in 1803. Under Wilkinson's authority, Chouteau participated in military and trading expeditions to the Mandan and Arikara Indians on the upper *Missouri River.*

In 1815–1816, with a partner, Chouteau blazed a trapper trail into the central *Rocky Mountains.* Before he could complete his journey, however, Spanish authorities arrested him and confiscated $30,000 worth of trade goods.

Chouteau's chief contribution to the exploration of the West lay in his skills in negotiating with Native Americans. He provided guides and interpreters for U.S. expeditions and served as a government envoy to the Kiowa and Comanche tribes. In May 1842 he outfitted *John Charles Frémont*'s first expedition to the Rockies.

Clark, William (1770–1838)

Born in Caroline County, Virginia, Clark grew up on the Kentucky frontier near the *Ohio River [V].* His older brother, the soldier/surveyor George Rogers Clark, played a leading role in opening the Northwest Territory to white settlement. The younger Clark served as an officer in the U.S. Army from 1789 to 1796, resigning to look after his family's business affairs.

In 1803 *Meriwether Lewis* approached Clark, whom he had known in the army, with an offer to become co-commander of a projected transcontinental exploring expedition. In the event, the skills of the two men proved highly complementary on the *Lewis and Clark expedition* (1804–1806) up the *Missouri River,* across the *Rocky Mountains,* and on to the Pacific. Clark served as mapmaker, small boat expert, and leading negotiator with Indian nations encountered along the route. He also produced a set of excellent illustrations of western animals.

Clark settled in *St. Louis* after the expedition returned and later served as superintendent of Indian affairs for the Louisiana Territory and governor of the Missouri Territory. From 1822 until his death, Clark had chief federal government responsibility for dealings with the tribes of the West.

Colter, John (circa 1774–1813)

An important member of the *Lewis and Clark expedition* in 1804–1806, John Colter remained in the West after the expedition returned to the

United States, exploring and trapping in the *Grand Teton Mountains* and the Jackson Hole region of present Wyoming. He almost certainly crossed the area now preserved as Yellowstone National Park.

Colter set out alone in the winter of 1807 to establish trade relations with the Crow Indians for the *St. Louis* entrepreneur *Manuel Lisa.* His route is uncertain, but Crow guides led him to sulfurous geysers and other thermal phenomena in the Rockies, one of which he called "Stinking Water." His contemporaries derisively dubbed the geyser basin he discovered near present Cody, Wyoming, "Colter's Hell." On the return portion of his looping trip, he was probably the first white to see the geysers of Yellowstone Park.

In his travels Colter discovered the sources of the *Missouri,* Snake, and Green Rivers, three of the West's most important watercourses. Historian William Goetzmann calls Colter's journey "the first great exploring trek after Lewis and Clark, and one of the least remembered in history."

Colter narrowly escaped death in the autumn of 1809 when *Blackfoot* raiders attacked him and a companion, John Potts. Colter ran for his life; the Blackfeet caught and killed Potts. He later helped *William Clark* prepare an important though erroneous map of the West based on the Lewis and Clark expedition and published in Nicholas Biddle's edition of the *Journals* in 1814.

Columbia River

The greatest of western rivers, rising in Columbia Lake, British Columbia, the Columbia flows northwest for two hundred miles before bending around the Selkirk Mountains to follow a southward course, arcs west in a great bend just below the mouth of the Spokane, and courses south again to its junction with the Snake, a major tributary, in the southeastern corner of Washington State. From there the Columbia turns westward, cuts through the Cascade Mountains and the coast ranges, and enters the Pacific 1,210 miles from its source. It widens to one and a half miles below the Cascades and to six miles near its mouth. The action of the tides is felt for fully 145 miles upstream.

The Spanish explorer *Bruno de Hezeta [IV]* sighted the opening of "the Great River of the West" on August 17, 1775, but made no effort to enter it. Briton *George Vancouver*'s exploring expedition passed the opening in 1792 without pausing to investigate. The American *Robert Gray,* commanding the ship *Columbia Redivida,* crossed the treacherous bar in May 1792 and became the first person of European descent to enter the river. He named it Columbia after his ship and claimed it for the United States. A few months later *Henry M. Broughton,* of Vancouver's expedition, surveyed the river for one hundred miles inland and claimed the watershed for England.

Meriwether Lewis and *William Clark* were the first whites to reach the Columbia overland (see *Lewis and Clark expedition*). They passed the winter of 1805–1806 at Fort Clatsop near the river's mouth. In 1811 Canadian *David Thompson* became the first white man to travel the river from its source to its junction with the Snake. Beginning with the establishment in 1811 of the Pacific Fur Company post *Fort Astoria,* the lower Columbia became the focal point of American settlement of the Oregon Country. The British *Hudson's Bay Company* developed the trading center of *Fort Vancouver* on the north bank of the river.

Before exploration and settlement, the Columbia teemed with salmon, with as many as 16 million fish returning to upstream destinations to spawn each year. Commercial exploitation and twentieth century damming for irrigation and hydroelectric power depleted the salmon population and pacified the once unruly river, dramatically altering its appearance.

Continental Divide

Known as the backbone of North America, the Continental Divide separates streams flowing east from those that drain west. It runs in a jagged line along the crest of the *Rocky Mountains* from northern Alaska to Mexico.

In their expedition of 1804–1806, *Lewis and Clark* understood when they crossed the divide beyond the *Missouri River* fountain that there could be no all-water route to the Pacific Ocean. Explorer/trapper *Andrew Henry* established the first American post west of the divide on a tributary of the Snake River in 1810.

In 1824, a dozen years after *Robert Stuart* passed through, the *Jedediah Smith* party rediscovered the relatively manageable crossing of the Continental Divide at South Pass, Wyoming, that would carry generations of Oregon- and California-bound explorers, traders, and settlers over the Rockies.

Corps of Topographical Engineers

Established in 1813, the Corps of Topographical Engineers—known as the Topographical Bureau until 1838—explored, surveyed, and mapped vast areas of western North America during its half-century of existence. As early as 1816, the U.S. secretary of war recommended a complete military survey of the American territory, and along with exploration, the corps' duties included prosaic assignments such as laying out canal routes and keeping rivers and harbors clear of obstructions.

Stephen H. Long carried out important Topographical Bureau expeditions into the Great Plains and the *Rocky Mountains* in the 1820s. Two decades later, *John Charles Frémont* led a series of Topographical Corps expeditions to the Rockies, Oregon, and California, carefully mapping the *Oregon Trail* migrant route. John W. Gunnison, *Gouverneur K. Warren*, and others completed the *Pacific Railroad surveys* for the corps in the 1850s.

Altogether, seventy-two officers served in the Topographical Corps from 1838 to 1863. The War Department disbanded the corps in 1863, merging it with the larger Army Corps of Engineers, which continued to carry out surveying duties. The *U.S. Geological Survey* assumed responsibility for surveying and mapping after 1879.

Davis, Jefferson   (1808–1889)

Born in Kentucky, Jefferson Davis moved with his family to the then-frontier country of Mississippi, where his father grew cotton with the enforced labor of slaves. He graduated from West Point in 1828, served in the regular army, and eventually entered politics.

Under Davis's leadership as secretary of war from 1853 to 1857, the War Department carried out wide-ranging surveys and mapping of the West (see *Pacific Railroad surveys*). Four transcontinental railroads eventually used the surveys prepared during his tenure.

Davis reentered the Senate in 1857, resigned when Mississippi seceded from the union in 1861, and served as the only president of the Confederate States of America (1861–1865).

De Voto, Bernard Augustine (1897–1955)

Born in Ogden, Utah, Bernard De Voto came east for schooling and a literary career. In four novels and four works of history, he developed his theme of the importance of the West in the formation of the American character.

After a brief stint as editor of the *Saturday Review,* De Voto produced three studies in succession of the exploration and settlement of the West: *The Year of Decision: 1846* (1943); *Across the Wide Missouri* (1947); and *The Course of Empire* (1952). *Across the Wide Missouri,* an account of the Rocky Mountain fur trade, won a Pulitzer Prize in history for 1948. He published an edited version of the *Journals of Lewis and Clark* in 1953.

De Voto's critical reputation has been mixed, perhaps because—as both a novelist and historian of the West—his place is difficult to define. Literary critics discount his achievement because he was a historian; some historians regard his work as too "literary." In his fiction as well as his historical writing, however, De Voto was a major contributor to an understanding of the American West.

Dutton, Clarence (1841–1912)

An 1860 Yale graduate, the Connecticut-born Dutton joined a Connecticut volunteer infantry regiment during the Civil War, saw hard service in Virginia, and transferred to the regular army in 1864. The tedium of postwar army life left him the leisure to pursue studies in geology with James Hall and others.

Assigned to the Ordnance Bureau in Washington, Dutton met *John Wesley Powell*, and in 1874 Powell offered him a position in his western survey. A series of annually renewed army furloughs would allow Dutton to remain with Powell and the *U.S. Geological Survey* (founded in 1879) until 1890.

During these years Dutton, sometimes in company with his colleague the artist-geologist *William H. Holmes,* carried out extensive explorations of the *Grand Canyon* of the Colorado River. Meticulously observing the canyon country and bestowing romantic names (Vishnu's Temple, Kaibab Plateau) on prominent features, he wrote with unparalleled accuracy of its geological history in three monographs published in the 1880s, the best known of which remains the *Tertiary History of the Grand Cañon Country*

(1882). With his mentor Powell and G. K. Gilbert, he is regarded as a founder of the American school of geology, which focused on the power of erosion, fire, and movement in forming the physical world.

Dutton and Powell fell out in the late 1880s over a question of U.S. Geological Survey funds. He returned to the army in 1890, serving in a succession of routine postings until he retired in 1901. His later geological investigations included important studies of vulcanism and earthquakes.

Dutton's Colorado Plateau monographs are still highly regarded today, according to Grand Canyon scholar Stephen J. Pyne, for "their marvelous prose, esthetic imagination and conceptual grace." Author Wallace Stegner was the first to suggest that Dutton's works defined the meaning of the Grand Canyon for Americans.

"Dutton is almost as much the *genius loci* of the Grand Canyon as *Muir* is of Yosemite," Stegner wrote. "And though it is Powell's monument to which the tourists walk after dinner to watch the sunset from the South Rim, it is with Dutton's eyes, as often as not, that they see."

Emory, William H. (1811–1877)

The Maryland-born son of a planter, Emory graduated from West Point in 1831 and entered the army's *Corps of Topographical Engineers* in 1838. In an early assignment for the corps, he drew an important map of the upper *Mississippi River [V]* basin from *Joseph Nicollet*'s *[V]* explorations of 1836–1840.

At the outbreak of the Mexican War in 1846, Emory won appointment as chief engineer of Colonel Stephen Watts Kearny's rather grandly named Army of the West, whose three hundred dragoons were ordered to capture Santa Fe and then march west through Mexican territory to the Pacific. Emory's task was to extend Nicollet's astronomical and barometric observations and develop the first accurate map of the vast region of the Southwest.

Kearny's dragoons marched from *Bent's Fort* on the Arkansas River on August 2, 1846, took Santa Fe, and after a pause there, set out southward along the Río Grande on September 25. Meeting the scout *Kit Carson* near Valverde, New Mexico, Kearny learned that California had fallen to U.S. forces; he sent two-thirds of the command back to Santa Fe and persuaded Carson to guide the remainder to California.

The column pushed west along the Gila River. Emory, meantime, discovered and carried out important archaeological investigations of the ruins of at least a dozen Native American villages in the Gila Valley, including one at Casa Montezuma, whose four-hundred-year-old sandstone walls still stand. He carefully recorded his astronomical observations, too, fixing, among other achievements, the exact location of the confluence of the Gila and Colorado Rivers.

Suffering from thirst and exposure, Kearny's column trudged through the Arizona deserts and reached Warner's Ranch in California early in December. On the sixth, in a fierce battle with Mexican lancers, Kearny's dragoons lost eighteen men killed, with another thirteen wounded. With reinforcements arriving from San Diego, Kearny broke the Mexican siege and completed his march to the Pacific.

Stephen Watts Kearny leads a U.S. Army column across the Southwest toward California after the outbreak of the Mexican War in 1846. The expedition's chief engineer, William H. Emory, developed the first accurate map of the vast region lying between Texas and California.

As a result of Emory's work, this essentially military expedition yielded important advances in knowledge of the Southwest. Emory published a highly accurate map, titled "Military Reconnaissance of the Arkansas, Rio del Norte [Rio Grande] and Rio Gila," in 1847. His expedition narrative, *Notes of a Military Reconnaissance,* published in 1848, contained significant new information on the natural and geological history of the region. He is credited, too, with introducing the serious study of the archaeology of the Southwest.

Fidler, Peter (1769–1822)

Born in England, Peter Fidler reached Canada in 1788 as a laborer for the *Hudson's Bay Company.* A protégé of surveyor Philip Turnor, he helped establish the location of Lake Athabasca and Great Slave Lake in expeditions of 1791–1792, correcting inaccuracies in the work of a predecessor, fur trader–explorer *Peter Pond.*

Fidler explored the foothills of the *Rocky Mountains* in 1793–1795 and surveyed the northern Manitoba and Assiniboine River country in journeys of 1793–1795 and 1795–1796. A colleague, and later a rival, of *David Thompson,* he succeeded Thompson as the company's chief surveyor and mapmaker when the latter defected to the *North West Company* in 1797.

In later travels Fidler surveyed Lake Winnipeg, the Churchill River, and the Red River, where—in his last assignment before his death—he laid out lots for the Red River Colony. Over three decades in western Canada, Fidler journeyed nearly 50,000 miles and completed some 7,300 miles of surveys. He eventually came to be recognized as Thompson's rough equal in importance as a mapmaker.

Fitzpatrick, Thomas (1799–1854)

Born in County Cavan, Ireland, Thomas Fitzpatrick came to the United States as a young man and gained his first significant experience in the West in 1823 with the trapper/explorer *Jedediah Smith*. The Smith expedition blazed a new overland route that led to the effective discovery of South Pass, Wyoming, which eventually became the main emigrant gateway to California and Oregon.

Fitzpatrick led one of *William Ashley*'s fur brigades and, with mountain man *Jim Bridger* and others, in 1830 formed the Rocky Mountain Fur Company. As a trapper in the 1830s he traversed much of the Mountain West, pushing as far east as Oregon and north into the *Blackfoot* country of Montana.

With the decline of the fur trade in the late 1830s, Fitzpatrick found a second career as a guide. The missionary party of Marcus and Narcissa Whitman traveled as far as the Green River with his trading caravan in 1836. He guided the *Bidwell*-Bartleson California emigrant party in 1841 and the Elijah White Oregon train the following year.

John Charles Frémont employed Fitzpatrick as a guide on his important second expedition of 1843–1844. He assisted Frémont lieutenant James W. Abert in his explorations of the Canadian and Arkansas Rivers in 1845.

By then Fitzpatrick had become one of the best-known and certainly among the most knowledgeable of western trader/explorers. The Indians knew him as White Hair, a condition said to have resulted from a wilderness ordeal with Indians in 1825. Whites called him Broken Hand, alluding to a firearms accident.

Fort Astoria

John Jacob Astor's Pacific Fur Company established this trading depot on Youngs Bay on the south shore of the *Columbia River* estuary in 1811, the first permanent U.S. settlement on the Pacific Coast. The Astorians used the post to trade, trap, and collect information throughout the Columbia Valley. *Robert Stuart*'s important eastbound cross-country expedition set out from Astoria in July 1812.

With the outbreak of the War of 1812, Astor's British trading rival, the *North West Company,* forced the Astorians to sell the post. The United States regained nominal title to the buildings in 1818, but the fort remained an outpost of the Northwesters and, later, the *Hudson's Bay Company,* through the 1830s.

Fort Hall

Trader Nathaniel Wyeth established a crude trading post on the Snake River near the mouth of the Portneuf River in present Idaho in August 1834, after Rocky Mountain Fur Company representatives reneged on an agreement to buy trade goods he had transported to the Green River trapper rendezvous.

Though Wyeth's trading and trapping ventures never flourished, his two transcontinental journeys (1832 and 1834) were important in defining the *Oregon Trail.* He sold Fort Hall to the *Hudson's Bay Company* in 1837. The fort later became an important migrant way station on the road to Oregon and California.

Fort Laramie

Fur traders *William Sublette* and Robert Campbell built an outpost, Fort William, at the junction of the Laramie and North Platte rivers in 1834. The U.S. government bought the post in 1849 and renamed it Fort Laramie.

From the start Fort Laramie was an important way station on the route to Oregon and California. The army used it as a base to protect migrants along the *Oregon Trail* in the 1850s and 1860s. In 1851, the United States and the *Sioux* and Cheyenne nations signed the Treaty of Fort Laramie that divided the Great Plains into tribal spheres of influence and recognized the government's right to establish roads and military posts in Indian territory. In turn, the United States promised the land would belong to the Indians forever.

Laramie declined in importance with the defeat of the Plains tribes and the arrival of the transcontinental railroad. The army abandoned the post in 1890. Restored to its 1880s appearance, it is today a national historic site.

Fort Vancouver

The *Hudson's Bay Company* established this important outpost on the north bank of the *Columbia River* one hundred miles from the Pacific in late 1824. Vancouver became the headquarters of the company's operations in the Columbia Department, which encompassed a vast territory of the Pacific Northwest and British Columbia and served as an outfitting center for trade and exploration expeditions.

Chief Factor John McLoughlin supervised twenty-two interior trading posts from Vancouver. The thriving, orderly settlement of farms, orchards, workshops, and mills produced provisions for the traders, as well as lumber and other products for export. Company officials also resupplied and otherwise aided American exploring expeditions.

Jedediah Smith's important 1827 exploration of California and the Umpqua Country of southern Oregon ended at Vancouver with McLoughlin dispatching a punitive expedition against an Umpqua party that had attacked Smith's camp. McLoughlin proved equally hospitable to Nathaniel Wyeth at the conclusion of Wyeth's cross-country expeditions in 1832 and 1834. Charles Wilkes used Vancouver as a base briefly during his 1842 survey of the Columbia (see *Wilkes exploring expedition*).

The company shifted its base to Vancouver Island, British Columbia, after the Oregon Treaty of 1846 confirmed U.S. control of today's Oregon and Washington.

Fraser, Simon   (1776–1862)

Born near Bennington, Vermont, the son of a British Loyalist, Simon Fraser fled to *Montreal [V]* with his widowed mother during the American Revolution. Educated there, he joined the *North West Company* as a clerk in 1792. By 1801, after service in the Athabasca region of present northern Saskatchewan and Alberta, he had risen to become a partner.

Given responsibility for the company's operations beyond the Rockies in 1805, Fraser established the first settlements in today's central British Columbia, including Fort Fraser in 1806 and Fort George (now Prince George) in 1807, and traveled among Indian tribes that had never before encountered a white man.

Setting out from Fort George in 1808, Fraser followed what he mistakenly believed to be the *Columbia River,* an expedition that marked the first documented penetration of the northern Rockies to the Pacific since *Alexander Mackenzie*'s journey of 1793. "A continual series of cascades, mixt with rocky fragments and bound by precipices and mountains, that seemed at times to have no end," he wrote of a wild and rugged stretch now known as the Fraser River Canyon. "I scarcely ever saw any thing so dreary, and seldom so dangerous in any country." Working his way carefully through this dangerous defile, Fraser followed the river, which he had finally determined could not be the Columbia, down to the Strait of Georgia opposite Vancouver Island. His Northwester colleague *David Thompson* would dub this stream the Fraser River.

Documents recounting Fraser's explorations from 1805 to 1808 were published in 1960 as *The Letters and Journals of Simon Fraser.*

Frémont, Jessie Benton (1824–1902)

The daughter of the expansionist Missouri senator *Thomas Hart Benton,* Jessie Benton mortified her parents and scandalized Washington society in 1841 when she eloped with an obscure young soldier, Lieutenant *John Charles Frémont.* Benton influence, exercised through both father and daughter, brought promotion, preferment, and fame to Frémont, who would become perhaps the best-known American explorer of his time.

Jessie Frémont became her husband's virtually equal partner in writing up the highly regarded government reports of his exploring expeditions of 1842 and 1843. The second published report, which detailed Frémont's journey along the *Oregon Trail* to the Pacific Northwest and then south to California, reached a wide audience and inspired thousands of Americans to venture west. She played a key backstage role in creating Frémont's popular persona as "the Pathfinder."

A prolific writer, Jessie Frémont over five decades produced a steady stream of reminiscences, travel narratives, and stories for children. In the 1880s she collaborated—probably as ghostwriter—on the first volume of her husband's autobiography, *Memoirs of My Life* (1887), which recounts the exploring expeditions that made him famous.

Frémont, John Charles (1813–1890)

Apotheosized as one of the greatest of nineteenth-century American explorers, Frémont was born in Savannah, Georgia, the son of a French dancing master and his Virginian common-law wife. His father died in 1818, leaving a large family in poverty. The marginal circumstances of Frémont's childhood and youth, most of it passed in Charleston, South Carolina, marked him for life. Restless, intelligent, charming, a loner, and something of a misfit, he would, after carrying out a series of acclaimed exploring expeditions in the 1840s, fall victim to his own glittering myth.

From his youth, Frémont played the role of protégé to perfection. A Charleston lawyer sponsored the schooling that prepared him for the College of Charleston, where he excelled in mathematics before being asked to leave owing to his "incorrigible negligence." (He explained later that a love affair had sapped his will to study.) In 1833 the powerful South Carolina politician Joel Poinsett arranged for him to sail as a civilian mathematics instructor on the USS *Natchez* on a two-year cruise to South America.

It was Poinsett, too, who led Frémont to his true vocation, finding him a place on a topographical survey of the projected Charleston, Louisville, and Cincinnati Railroad in 1837–1838. This work, with a companion journey through the Cherokee wilderness country of Tennessee, North Carolina, and Georgia, showed Frémont, as he would remark in his *Memoirs*, "the path which I was destined to walk."

Poinsett by 1838 had risen to be secretary of war, and he arranged for Frémont to join *Joseph N. Nicollet*'s *[V]* scientific and exploring expedition to the upper *Mississippi [V]* region. Poinsett also secured for him a lieutenant's commission in the army's *Corps of Topographical Engineers.* Nicollet's journeys to Minnesota and the Dakotas in 1838 and 1839 completed Frémont's apprenticeship as a scientific explorer.

Nicollet indirectly provided Frémont with the third in a succession of powerful benefactors. Frémont met the expansionist Missouri senator *Thomas Hart Benton* while in Washington to assist in preparing the maps

IN THEIR OWN *Words*

The leader tried every step carefully, and each of us followed in his tracks. Thus we continued, carefully and slowly, and soon we reached the summit. The highest rock was so small that only one after the other could stand on it. Pistols were fired, the flag unfurled, and we shouted "hurrah" several times. Then the barometer was set up, and I observed twice.

—CHARLES PREUSS AT THE SUMMIT OF 13,730-FOOT FRÉMONT PEAK, PREUSS'S DIARY RECORD OF FRÉMONT'S FIRST EXPEDITION, AUGUST 17, 1842 and reports of Nicollet's Mississippi expeditions. He sealed the alliance in 1841 by eloping with Benton's seventeen-year-old daughter, Jessie.

Benton dreamed of a "road to India" leading west from *St. Louis* to the Pacific. In 1842 he pushed through a congressional appropriation for a Topographical Corps expedition to the *Rocky Mountains* and arranged for his son-in-law to command it. Frémont gratefully accepted the assignment. He wrote later, "It would be travel over a part of the world which remained the new—the opening up of unknown lands; the making of unknown countries known; and the study without books—the learning at first hand from nature herself; the drinking first at her unknown springs—became a source of never-ending delight to me."

Frémont reached St. Louis in May 1842, recruited a party of twenty-one men, mostly French *voyageurs,* and traveled by steamboat up the *Missouri River* to Westport, Missouri. With *Kit Carson* as guide, he struck west on his "campaign in the wilderness" on June 10 and reached the line of the *Platte River* ten days later.

Frémont followed the increasingly defined line of the *Oregon Trail* for a week or so, then divided the band at the forks of the Platte. With seven men, he pushed south toward the Rockies, while the others continued due west to *Fort Laramie.* After a pause at St. Vrain's Fort north of present Denver, he marched through a "naked waste" to rejoin the main contingent at Laramie by July 15. There, in the face of news from mountain man *James Bridger* that *Sioux* war parties were abroad in the Sweetwater country, Frémont decided to push on as planned to South Pass. In the event, the expedition avoided conflict with the Sioux. Frémont climbed the gentle slope of South Pass on August 8. "I should compare the elevation which we surmounted at the pass, to the ascent of the Capitol hill from the avenue at Washington," he would write in the expedition *Report.* Clearing the pass without incident, he detoured into the Wind River Mountains, carried out a difficult assault on the summit of what he mistakenly thought to be the tallest peak in the range on August 15, and famously unfurled an eagle flag there.

The expedition then turned back for the United States, reaching St. Louis on October 17. The true significance of Frémont's first expedition lay in the narrative he prepared in collaboration with his wife during the winter of 1842–1843. Their *Report of an Exploration . . . between the Missouri River and the Rocky Mountains* (1843) established Frémont's fame as "the Pathfinder." It also won a place in national legend for Frémont's friend and guide Kit Carson.

On the strength of this first foray, Benton experienced no difficulty in garnering support for a more ambitious second expedition that would take Frémont into the disputed country of Oregon and then into Mexican California—what historian William Goetzmann called "the calculated use of exploring expeditions as diplomatic weapons." Frémont's orders bade him "to connect the reconnaissance of 1842 with the surveys of Commander Wilkes on the coast of the Pacific Ocean, so as to give a connected survey of the interior of our continent." Leaving Westport with thirty-seven men on May 30, 1843, Frémont followed the Kansas and Republican Rivers through present Kansas to Vrain's Fort, veered south to the upper Arkansas, retraced his steps, and crossed the Laramie Plains to the Sweetwater.

Again crossing the **Continental Divide** at South Pass, Frémont explored the area of the Great Salt Lake in early September before turning north to **Fort Hall** and advancing along the Oregon Trail to the **Columbia River,** which he descended as far as the great Indian trading mart of The Dalles. From there in late November he advanced southeast, following the eastern flank of the **Sierra Nevada** along the eastern rim of the Great Basin. This winter march would prove to be an epic of hardship and endurance. In a thirty-day slog through deep drifts of snow and in below-zero temperatures, the band cleared Truckee Pass and descended into the Sacramento Valley and the safety of Sutter's Fort.

John C. Frémont's exploring party pauses at Pyramid Lake in northwestern Nevada early in 1844 during the second expedition. Frémont named the lake for its supposed resemblance to the Pyramid of Cheops. The expedition would go on to make a grueling winter crossing of the Sierra Nevada into California.

Frémont set out for home in late March 1844, working his way south down the San Joaquin Valley before turning eastward to cross the Sierra Nevada at Tehachapi Pass. The expedition then struck northeastward across the Great Basin of Nevada and Utah and on to the mountain and meadow parks of Colorado. Reaching Washington in the autumn, he again collaborated with **Jessie Frémont** on the expedition narrative. This work, "a classic of western exploring literature," according to Goetzmann, appeared in an edition of 10,000 copies as *A Report of an Exploring Expedition to Oregon and California* in March 1845. With its admixture of adventure tale, scientific information, and practical advice to Oregon-bound migrants, it raised Frémont to the height of celebrity.

Frémont's third expedition ended in his temporary undoing. His initial orders called for a mere survey of the Red River. Either they were changed, or he may have simply ignored them; in any case, he returned to the Pacific Coast, reaching Monterey in Mexican California in late 1845. There he encountered difficulties with the Mexicans, who not surprisingly objected to the presence of an organized band of armed foreigners in their precincts. He retired briefly into southern Oregon before marching south again to help touch off the Bear Flag Rebellion. On the outbreak of war with Mexico, Frémont indulged in California political intrigues that led ultimately to his court-martial and ejection from the army. Though a sympathetic President Polk reinstated him, Frémont resigned from the service in a fit of pique, bringing his career as an official explorer to an abrupt end.

Apart from the brief celebrity accorded this charismatic self-promoter and agent of western expansion, Frémont is remembered for substantial achievement as an explorer. The Pathfinder and his men were the first to circumnavigate the American West. Charles Preuss's maps were the most accurate and detailed of their day. Frémont defined the Great Basin, the broad, barren gulf that separates the Rockies and the Sierra Nevada, and debunked the myth of a mighty stream, the "Rio Bonaventura," reputed to flow westward out of the Great Salt Lake to the sea.

In two privately backed expeditions in the late 1840s, Frémont sought to blaze an all-weather railroad route to the Pacific. These efforts were inconsequential in result, though the first rose to the dignity of tragedy, for ten of the Pathfinder's men perished in mountain snows. Frémont temporarily survived the buffetings of his reputation to become the first presidential candidate of the Republican party; he lost to Democrat James Buchanan in 1856. He did not, as it happened, find success as a field commander during the Civil War, and his political ambitions led Lincoln to bring his second military career to a premature end.

Frémont passed the last thirty years of his life in comparative obscurity, beset by failure, disappointment, and debt. A once-adoring public had virtually forgotten him by the time his *Memoirs* were published in 1887, and sales of the book were insufficient to restore his fortunes. He died in a New York City boardinghouse.

IN THEIR OWN *Words*

Today we went through the pass with all the camp, and, after a hard journey of twelve miles, encamped on a high point where the snow had been blown off, and the exposed grass afforded a scanty pasture for the animals. Snow and broken country together made our travel difficult; we were often compelled to make large circuits, and ascend the highest and most exposed ridges, in order to avoid snow, which in other places was banked up to a great depth.

—JOHN CHARLES FRÉMONT, *A REPORT OF AN EXPLORING EXPEDITION TO OREGON AND CALIFORNIA* (1845)

Grand Canyon

The Colorado River cuts a 217-mile, 5,000-foot-deep chasm in the rim rock of northern Arizona as it flows southwesterly toward the Gulf of California. The Grand Canyon of the Colorado has been one of the best-known and most-visited of American landmarks since the end of the nineteenth century.

García López de Cárdenas [II], leading one of *Coronado*'s [II] exploring parties, in 1540 became the first European to view the Grand Canyon. The Spanish Franciscan priest *Francisco Garcés [IV]*, on an expedition in 1775–1776, descended the chasm and spent several days in a Havasupai Indian village.

A portrait of John Wesley Powell. The Civil War veteran Powell, the epitome of the scientific explorer, led a government-sponsored expedition into the Grand Canyon in 1869.

The American fur trader *James Ohio Pattie* traveled along the canyon's South Rim in the 1820s. Joseph Christmas Ives and his party explored the floor of the canyon in 1857; they were perhaps the first whites to enter the chasm. (See *Ives and Macomb surveys.*) In August 1869 *John Wesley Powell*, with nine men, descended the Colorado through the entire length of the Grand Canyon, the first party to traverse the canyon river bottom in a boat. Powell returned with a larger surveying expedition in 1871–1872. The surveys of *Clarence E. Dutton* and *William H. Holmes* in the 1870s created a geological and topographical record of the chasm, published as *The Tertiary History of the Grand Cañon District* in 1882.

The Santa Fe Railroad opened a spur line to the Grand Canyon in 1901, accelerating the region's development as a tourist destination. Parts of the canyon have been preserved since 1908, and in 1919 the U.S. government created the Grand Canyon National Park. The region is one of the world's most popular beauty spots; some 3 million people visit the park each year.

Grand Teton Mountains

Part of the *Rocky Mountain* cordillera, the Grand Tetons rise in sawtoothed abruptness from the floor of Jackson Hole, a broad valley of the Snake River in present northwest Wyoming. At 13,772 feet above sea level, Grand Teton is the highest peak in the range.

The fur trader *John Colter* may have been the first white to see the Tetons and Jackson Hole during his travels with Crow Indians in 1807–1808.

The trapper/explorer *Donald Mackenzie* explored the region a decade later.

Grand Teton National Park, now encompassing 310,000 acres, was established in 1929 in the face of intense opposition from Wyoming ranching and mining interests.

Gray, Robert (1755–1806)

A mariner born in Tiverton, Rhode Island, Robert Gray served in the American navy during the Revolutionary War and later commanded merchant vessels. As captain of the sloop *Lady Washington,* Gray sailed from *Boston [III]* in company with John Kendrick in the *Columbia* in 1787, trading for sea otter furs in the area of Vancouver Island, Canada, continuing on to Canton, China, and proceeding home from China to complete a 40,000-mile circumnavigation of the globe.

After a six-week respite in Boston, Gray set out in September 1790 on a second voyage to the Pacific Northwest, this time in command of the *Columbia.* The expedition wintered on Vancouver Island during 1791–1792 and traded along the coast with the Haida and other native peoples through the spring. For several days in early May 1792, the *Columbia* sailed up and down the coast of present Washington and Oregon, exploring and seeking out otter skins. On May 11 the ship's lookouts spotted two long sandbars, beyond which glimmered what appeared to be a spacious harbor. Clearing the sand barrier, Gray found himself not in a bay but in the fabled Great River of the West, which he named Columbia, for the ship.

Gray's discovery of the **Columbia River**—or rather rediscovery, as the Spanish navigator *Bruno de Hezeta [IV]* had sailed to its mouth in 1775—formed the basis of later U.S. claims to the Oregon Territory. If not the sole discoverers, the officers and crew of the *Columbia* were the first Europeans to enter the river.

Great American Desert

The explorer *Zebulon Pike* likened this semiarid region of the United States between the 100th Meridian and the *Rocky Mountains* to the Sahara of Africa. Both Pike and the soldier/explorer *Stephen Long* regarded the area, which corresponds roughly to the region now known as the Great Plains, as an impediment to American westward expansion.

Pike set out in July 1806 on an expedition with orders to gather intelligence on the trading caravan trail to Spanish Santa Fe. He followed the Santa Fe road through present Kansas and Colorado, then turned toward the Rockies, sighting Pike's Peak and other towering eminences in mid-November. In 1810 Pike filed a detailed report on the area he dubbed "the Great American Desert."

In 1820 Long made a long loop west from Fort Osage, Missouri, along the South Platte River, sent a detachment to climb and measure Pike's Peak, then divided his party into two groups for separate expeditions eastward along the Canadian and Arkansas Rivers. His report and an important map of the region were published in 1823.

With hot summers, bitter winters, and an annual rainfall of less than twenty inches, the plains struck Long as a wasteland. "It is almost wholly unfit for cultivation," he wrote, "and of course, uninhabitable by a people depending upon agriculture for their subsistence." *John Charles Frémont* challenged Long's notions in expeditions of 1838, 1842, and 1843–1844. These were years of higher-than-average rainfall, and Frémont believed that stockraising and subsistence farming were viable. He called the area between the Rockies and the *Sierra Nevada,* which he named the Great Basin, a true desert.

The Homestead Act (1862) and the railroads brought settlers in great numbers. *John Wesley Powell* warned that intensive farming would destroy the fragile plains ecology, and his warnings were borne out with a series of devastating droughts, dust storms, and grasshopper infestations from the 1880s to the 1930s.

Gros Ventre

French traders coined the name *Gros Ventre,* which means "big belly," for the Atsina Indians of the northern Great Plains, an Algonquian-speaking tribe that separated from the Arapaho nation in the seventeenth century. They acquired horses around that time and became buffalo hunters. The Hidatsa of the upper Missouri River, also known as Gros Ventre, were a separate tribe.

European and American traders and explorers regarded the Gros Ventre as a fierce people, who should be given a wide berth. They were often allied with the equally fierce and bellicose *Blackfoot.* Smallpox epidemics in 1781 and 1801 greatly reduced the Gros Ventre population.

Hayden, Ferdinand Vandeveer (1829–1887)

Born in Westfield, Massachusetts, possibly of unwed parents, Ferdinand V. Hayden overcame a troubled childhood and went on to graduate from Oberlin College and earn a medical degree.

An interest in paleontology claimed him early, and Hayden abandoned a medical career for explorations in Kansas, Nebraska, and the Dakotas in the 1850s, participating in *Gouverneur K. Warren*'s plains survey expedition of 1856–1857 and in a failed attempt to penetrate the region of the upper Yellowstone River with William Raynolds in 1859. By the outbreak of the Civil War, he had earned a reputation as America's leading exploring geologist.

After serving as a Union Army surgeon during the war, Hayden became a professor at the University of Pennsylvania. He won appointment in 1867 as geologist in charge of the geological survey of Nebraska, which later expanded into the U.S. Geographical Surveys of the Territories West of the 100th Meridian.

Hayden led the first scientific parties into today's Yellowstone National Park in 1871–1872. The publicity the expedition attracted, together with William Henry Jackson's photographs, built political support for the creation of Yellowstone National Park in 1872. (See *Yellowstone expeditions.*)

Hayden's most influential publication was probably his *Geological and Geographical Atlas of Colorado* (1877 and 1881). His survey merged with the *U.S. Geological Survey* in 1879, leading to a partial eclipse of his influence. His scientific rivals *Clarence King* and *John Wesley Powell,* who regarded him as a popularizer, successively headed the new agency.

Henday, Anthony (*fl.* 1750–1762)

Born in England, Anthony Henday came to Canada as a laborer at the *Hudson's Bay Company*'s post at York and, in the 1750s, penetrated deeper into western Canada than any European up to that time. His journey of 1754 was the first extensive inland excursion since that of *Henry Kelsey [V]* of 1690–1692.

Setting out in canoes from York with a party of Cree Indians in June, Henday reached the Saskatchewan River via the Hayes River and, partly on the water and partly on foot, pushed as far west as present Red Deer, Alberta, where he encountered the great buffalo herds of the Canadian plains and may have caught a glimpse of the *Rocky Mountains.*

After passing the winter with his Cree companions near a large *Blackfoot* Indian camp in the Red Deer area, Henday returned to York laden with furs in June 1755. He made a second trip west in 1759, again passing some weeks or months with a band of Blackfoot Indians. He left the employ of the Hudson's Bay Company and returned to England around 1762.

Henry, Andrew (1775?–1833)

A Pennsylvania-born trapper and miner, Henry's expeditions after 1809 opened up previously unknown areas of the *Rocky Mountains* of Wyoming, Montana, and Idaho to American exploration.

A partner of trader *Manuel Lisa,* Henry in 1810 led the first American trapping expedition to cross the Rockies. Also in that year, he established the first American outpost west of the *Continental Divide,* Henry's Fort on Clark's Fork, a tributary of the Snake River.

In 1822 Henry joined his friend *William H. Ashley* to form the Rocky Mountain Fur Company. Advertising for "Enterprising Young Men to ascend the Missouri to its source," they launched two trading and exploring expeditions in the late summer of 1823. Henry himself led the first, which crossed present Nebraska and the Dakotas and penetrated the central Rockies. *Jedediah Smith* led the second party, which in the spring of 1824 would discover South Pass, Wyoming, the main trade and migrant route through the mountains.

Henry retired from active service in the field in 1825. Smith succeeded him as a senior partner in Ashley's fur-trading enterprise.

Holmes, William H. (1846–1933)

Born in Ohio and trained as an artist, William H. Holmes got his start as an illustrator of paleontological reports for the Smithsonian Institution. In 1872 Holmes won appointment to *Ferdinand V. Hayden*'s survey of the Yellowstone region (see *Yellowstone expeditions*) as geologist-artist in 1871. From his field sketches, he later prepared a series of detailed panoramic views of Yellowstone.

In 1873 Holmes accompanied Hayden to Colorado, where he helped explore and map the Mesa Verde cliff dwellings in Mancos Canyon. He also worked on the text and illustrations for Hayden's *Geological and Geographical Atlas of Colorado.*

In 1878 Holmes participated in a survey of Wyoming and Idaho, and two years later he joined *Clarence E. Dutton*'s expedition to map the *Grand Canyon* under the auspices of the *U.S. Geological Survey.* His topographical drawings were published in Dutton's *Tertiary History of the Grand Canyon District* (1882).

In the later stages of his long career, Holmes served as curator of the Field Museum in Chicago and headed ethnographical and fine arts museums in Washington, D.C.

Ferdinand Hayden's expedition to the Yellowstone region breaks for a meal in camp, 1872. William Holmes, the expedition geologist-artist whose detailed panoramas of the region became famous, is at the far right. William Henry Jackson made the photograph.

Hudson's Bay Company

Established by royal charter on May 2, 1670, the Hudson's Bay Company evolved into a major exploration, trade, and governing institution, controlling a vast region of northern and western Canada. It is the oldest business enterprise in North America.

The original charter granted the "Governor and Company of Adventurers" exclusive economic rights in the watershed of rivers flowing into Hudson Bay and required the company to search out a *Northwest Passage [VII].* By the middle of the seventeenth century, the search had lost momentum and had come nearly to a halt, with nothing but failure on the part of explorers from *Cabot [III]* to, more recently, *Foxe [VII]* and *James [VII].* The latter two had convinced both the merchants and the Admiralty of Britain that no route existed west from Hudson Bay to Asia. If there was a passage, it doubtless began at some point further north, which would present overwhelming difficulties.

In fact, advances in nautical and mechanical knowledge would have to occur to make further progress possible. Not until the middle of the eighteenth century would a pilot be able to correctly gauge his longitude; it would be even longer before captains knew enough about dietary requirements to be able to prevent the attacks of scurvy that had decimated whole expeditions. And the making of charts and maps was so primitively inadequate that records of past voyages were often of little or no use to future ones. These explorers had no way of knowing that ultimately the geographic boundaries of North America, and particularly of the northern Canadian West, would become known only after arduous land expeditions.

In the meantime, the Europeans concentrated on exploitation rather than exploration. North America teemed with riches—including valuable pelts of otter, ermine, marten, muskrat, mink, and Arctic fox, the most luxurious to be found in the world. Above all, there was beaver, with a smooth dense fur, designed to protect it from the icy water and the bitter cold, that had an irresistible appeal to Europeans.

High politics and national rivalries played a role too. With the restoration of Charles II in 1660, Englishmen again began to look outward, and they saw that their substantial resources on the American shore were being preempted by the French, who were moving resolutely westward, sending agents out, establishing posts, and bartering with the Indians for skins that used to go to them. From the *St. Lawrence River [III],* the French had moved westward and then turned north toward Hudson Bay itself.

Ironically, it was two Frenchmen, disgruntled with French taxes, who instigated England's new interest in North America. Seeking backers for their endeavors in the fur trade, Médard des Grosseilliers and Pierre Radisson (see *Grosseilliers and Radisson expeditions [V]*) persuaded King Charles in 1665 that the best entrance to the Canadian wilderness was through Hudson Strait and that there was a lot of money to be made. In 1668 the British built their first post, Fort Charles, at the southern end of James Bay, and a thriving fur trade was established.

Two years later the king granted a charter to "the Company of Adventurers of England Trading into Hudson's Bay." The terms were generous to the "Adventurers," albeit rather free with what was in fact Cree Indian Territory. The charter obligated the company to continue the search for the Northwest Passage, explore and map the unknown regions to the west of Hudson Bay, locate mineral resources, encourage settlements, and build up a market for British products within the indigenous population.

As trading profits mounted, the company lost interest in the search for the Northwest Passage. James Knight in 1718 and the missions of *Middleton [VII]* in 1741 and *William Moor [VII]* in 1746 searched without success for a route to the Pacific. All the same, over the ensuing century and a half, company traders on foot, on horseback, and by canoe explored and surveyed thousands of square miles of "Rupert's Land," as the western wilderness of Canada was then known.

In 1690–1692 *Henry Kelsey [V]* journeyed inland from the company's post at York on Hudson Bay southwest as far as the Great Plains beyond the Saskatchewan River, becoming the first European to see buffalo on the northern plains. In 1754 *Anthony Henday* struck west from York, explored the region of Lake Winnipeg, and penetrated into *Blackfoot* country in present Alberta. Matthew Cocking traced a similar route in 1772–1773. The explorations of *Samuel Hearne [VII],* begun in 1769, charted vast areas of the Northwest Territories previously unknown to Europeans.

In the concluding decades of the eighteenth century, company surveyors *Peter Fidler, David Thompson,* and Philip Turnor explored and mapped the trade routes of Canada's west. *Peter Skene Ogden,* in a series of expeditions from 1824 to 1830, explored the Oregon Country, present Utah, Idaho, and Montana, and Spanish California as far south as the Colorado River.

The company merged with its bitter rival the *North West Company* in 1821. Although the HBC is given credit for supporting the search for the lost *Franklin [VII]* expedition and for sponsoring the *Simpson [VII], Dease [VII],* and *Campbell [VII]* expeditions, it has also been shown to have deliberately withheld much of the information about the far Northwest from competitors in order to maintain its monopoly on the fur trade.

By 1870 the Hudson's Bay Company had sold most of its vast land holdings to the Dominion of Canada. Eventually the company sold its holdings in the western Canadian plains to settlers, yet to this day the company, along with its other massive business enterprises, remains the world's largest fur enterprise.

Humboldt River

The only long-running stream in the Great Basin, the Humboldt rises at the confluence of two creeks in the mountains of northeastern Nevada and flows west-southwest for three hundred miles before entering Humboldt Sink. In drought years parts of the channel are dry.

Hudson's Bay Company trapper *Peter Skene Ogden* discovered the river in 1828, and it went by various names until *John Charles Frémont* named it for the German naturalist and geographer Alexander von Humboldt in the 1840s. By then the river had become part of the *California Trail,* which extended from the Great Salt Lake to the *Sierra Nevada* foothills below Lake Tahoe.

The explorer Joseph Reddeford Walker descended the Humboldt on his way to California in 1833–1834. The first emigrant train to California followed its course in 1841.

Hunt, Wilson Price   (1783–1842)

A New Jersey–born *St. Louis* storekeeper, Hunt became the leader of *John Jacob Astor*'s 1810 overland expedition to the Pacific in spite of his utter lack of wilderness experience.

The Astorian expedition set out from St. Louis on October 21, 1810. After wintering over on the Nodaway River in northwest Missouri, the party set out in earnest in the spring of 1811. Hunt followed the *Missouri River* north to the Arikara villages in present North Dakota; on the advice of Indians, he left the river (and the route of the *Lewis and Clark expedition*) and struck out across the plains to Union Pass, Wyoming.

Hunt is generally regarded to have blundered seriously when he abandoned the expedition's horses at the ruined Henry's Fort in present Idaho and attempted to navigate the tortuous, turbulent Snake River. Forced to divide the party, Hunt pushed on in great hardship along the north bank of the Snake, reaching *Fort Astoria* after a 2,073-mile journey from the Arikara villages on February 15, 1812. "It was a very real pleasure for travelers harassed by fatigue to rest in quiet and be surrounded by friends after so long a journey," he wrote in understatement. Hunt's associate *Donald Mackenzie* had arrived a month earlier with another group of Astorians; a third contingent remained at large until late spring.

Despite his mistakes, Hunt's expedition traced the route between the Snake and *Columbia Rivers* that would eventually form an important segment of the *Oregon Trail*. He returned to St. Louis and the sedentary life of a merchant after the sale of Astoria to the *North West Company* in 1814.

Hunt was a leading figure, treated sympathetically, in Astoria (1836), *Washington Irving*'s account of Astor's imperial mercantile enterprise.

Irving, Washington   (1783–1859)

A New York City–born author, Irving's stories and sketches published between 1808 and 1820 made him perhaps the best-known American man of letters of his time and won him an international reputation. In the 1830s his fascination with the picturesque elements of the American West yielded three volumes that fueled the reading public's fascination with the exploration and development of the region stretching beyond the frontier.

Irving's *A Tour on the Prairies,* an account of his journey to the Great Plains, appeared in 1835. This journey also produced *Astoria* (1836), a highly colored but generally accurate account of **John Jacob Astor**'s ambitious fur-trading venture of 1810–1814, and *The Adventures of Captain Bonneville, U.S.A.* (1837), which recounted **Benjamin Bonneville**'s exploits in the **Rocky Mountains** in the 1830s.

Astoria contains accounts of the important cross-country expeditions of **Wilson Price Hunt** in 1811 and **Robert Stuart** in 1812–1813. Irving based his narrative of Bonneville's explorations on the soldier-trader-explorer's expedition journals, which evidently did not survive.

Ives and Macomb surveys   (1857–1858 and 1859)

In late 1857 the U.S. Army instructed Lieutenant Joseph Christmas Ives to ascend the Colorado River in search of a water route into the Great Basin. Ives, a topographical engineer, sought to survey a supply route for a military expedition the army expected to send to subdue the defiant Mormons in the Salt Lake region of Utah.

Ives and his party assembled the fifty-four-foot-long steamboat *Explorer* at Robinson's Landing near the mouth of the Colorado in November. Ives learned in the third week of December that war with the Mormons had broken out, and on December 29 he pushed upstream in *Explorer.* The

The fifty-four-foot-long steamboat *Explorer* churns up the Colorado River on the U.S. Army Expedition of 1857. The expedition's commanders, Joseph C. Ives and John M. Macomb, were in search of a water route to the Salt Lake region of Utah.

vessel struck a rock in Black Canyon on January 8, 1858, persuading Ives that he had reached the head of navigation on the Colorado. He sent half the party downstream, then continued upriver in a small boat as far as Las Vegas Wash, where he marched overland in search of the Mormon Road.

Returning to the river, Ives followed Hualpai Indian guides to the floor of the **Grand Canyon.** He and his men were perhaps the first whites to enter the canyon itself; in two days of exploration the expedition scientist, John Strong Newberry, carried out the first expert examination of its revelatory geological strata. The party then climbed out of the canyon and marched from the South Rim southeast to the Little Colorado River, whose topographical character Newberry found "more complicated than that of any mountain chain." After a brief detour to the Hopi pueblos in northeastern Arizona, Ives and company reached Fort Defiance, New Mexico, in late May.

In July 1859 Army topographical engineer John M. Macomb set out from Santa Fe along the Old Spanish Trail to survey tributaries of the Colorado. From the headwaters of the San Juan River in northern New Mexico, Captain Macomb's party struck northwest as far as the Indian ruins at Mesa Verde. After a pause to explore these ancient remains, Macomb pushed on in late August to the junction of the Green and Grand Rivers in eastern Utah, where he became the first documented white to survey the area.

Accompanying Macomb as expedition geologist, Newberry produced an important report that sketched the outlines of the Colorado River drainage system. Along the route, Newberry also discovered the first dinosaur bones in the West.

Jefferson, Thomas (1743–1826)

Born in Virginia along what was then the frontier of the eastern slopes of the *Blue Ridge Mountains [III]*, Jefferson had a long and intelligently informed interest in the exploration and eventual settlement of the American West.

As early as 1783, Jefferson discussed with John Ledyard, who had sailed with Captain *James Cook [IV]*, a proposed expedition from the Pacific coast to the *Mississippi River [V]*. Jefferson's two terms as president, 1801–1809, gave him broad latitude to fulfill his expansionist ambitions. His negotiation of the *Louisiana Purchase* from France in 1803 added 800,000 square miles of the land between the Mississippi River and the *Rocky Mountains* to the national domain. He conceived, planned, and—clandestinely, at first—secured funding and other resources for the *Lewis and Clark expedition* of 1804–1806, which collected massive amounts of scientific and ethnographic data on the new lands and established American claims to the Oregon Country on the Pacific.

In July 1803 Jefferson set in motion initial explorations of the Southwest, territory then nominally under the control of Spain. As a result, the expedition of *William Dunbar [V]* explored the Ozark Mountains in 1804, and a party under Thomas Sparks ascended the Red River for some six hundred miles in 1806. Both ventures encountered Indian and Spanish opposition, but Jefferson had set the stage for later and more extensive explorations to the southern and central Rockies.

King, Clarence (1842–1901)

Born in Newport, Rhode Island, the son of a China trader, King graduated from Yale in 1862, studied geology briefly with Louis Agassiz at Harvard, and worked as a volunteer on the Geological Survey of California from 1863 to 1866. With this apprenticeship, he won appointment in 1867 as leader of the government-sponsored U.S. Geological Exploration of the Fortieth Parallel.

In July 1867 King led his team of civilian scientists across the *Sierra Nevada* range of California and commenced what would be a five-year survey of the geology and natural resources of a hundred-mile-wide belt on either side of the transcontinental railroad. The first weeks in the deserts and mountains of western Nevada were nearly a disaster, with malaria striking down most of the party. "This is in every way the most difficult and dangerous country to campaign in I know of on the continent," King wrote his superior, General Andrew A. Humphreys of the Army Corps of Engineers. The men slowly regained their health over the winter, however, and King occupied himself with a geological study of Nevada's Comstock Lode silver mining region.

Expedition photographer Timothy O'Sullivan shows a member of Clarence King's survey of the Fortieth Parallel at work on the edge of Shoshone Falls of the Snake River in the Idaho Territory. King's report on the survey, begun in 1867 and completed in 1872, is regarded as a classic.

King in 1868 explored and surveyed the Great Basin from Humboldt Sink to the Great Salt Lake. In 1869–1870 his teams blanketed the area lying between the Salt Lake and the Green River divide of western Wyoming; King himself, in an expedition to northern California, discovered the first active glacier to be found in the United States, at the foot of Mount Shasta. Battling forest fires and drought, his parties in 1871 surveyed the region between the Green River and the Front Range of the *Rocky Mountains.*

King met the historian and man of letters Henry Adams in the autumn of 1871 at Estes Park, Colorado. Adams would memorialize the industrious and charismatic King as "the most remarkable man of our time" in his classic *The Education of Henry Adams,* published in 1907.

Completing his fieldwork in 1872, King finished his survey ahead of the other three western projects (those of *John Wesley Powell, Ferdinand Hayden,* and *George M. Wheeler*) and published the results in the seven-volume *Report of the Fortieth Parallel Survey* in installments during the 1870s, the last in 1878. Taken together, the volumes were "the first thoroughly professional studies of the Western environment, and they became a model for others to follow," according to historian William Goetzmann.

King won wide acclaim in 1872 for uncovering the fraud known as the Great Diamond Hoax, in which swindlers had salted a northwest Colorado mesa with diamonds and other gems. His fame made him an influential lobbyist for the National Academy of Science, which in 1879 won a decade-long power struggle with the army for control of the western surveys. Thus, when Congress authorized the *U.S. Geological Survey* in March 1879, King received the appointment as its first director. His ally and friend Powell succeeded him in the post in 1881.

La Harpe, Jean-Baptiste Bénard, Sieur de (1683–1765)

Jean-Baptiste Bénard, Sieur de La Harpe set out from New Orleans on December 17, 1718, with fifty men and five vessels loaded with six tons of merchandise, to establish a trading post in the Cadodacho country. He voyaged up the *Mississippi River [V]* and entered the Red River, exploring two of its tributaries (probably the Cane and Little Rivers) on the way up to the French post at Natchitoches.

After claiming the region for France, he reached the Sulphur River on April 1 which, as its first European explorer, he named the Bear River. Back on the Red River, he established Fort Saint-Louis de los Cadodaquious near today's Texarkana, Texas.

In an attempt to find a route to New Mexico, La Harpe explored to the northwest, meeting with Wichita chiefs on the lower South Canadian River and visiting the Tawakoni nation along the Arkansas River in central Oklahoma before returning to his post and then to New Orleans.

Assigned in 1721 to erect a fort at *La Salle*'s *[V]* Baye Saint-Bernarde (Matagorda Bay), he sailed west along the gulf coast and landed on August 27 at Galveston Bay, which he initially believed to be Matagorda Bay. After exploring the bay to the mouth of the Trinity River, he judged the area suitable for settlement but returned to Biloxi after finding the Indians opposed to French settlement.

On December 24, 1721, La Harpe embarked on an exploration of the Arkansas River to determine its navigability and apparently ascended it some 350 miles. By the time he returned to France in 1723, he had erected the furthermost French frontier outpost in the Southwest and opened the region to French traders.

La Vérendrye, Pierre Gaultier Varenne, Sieur de (1685–1749)

After service in the French army in Europe and Canada, Sieur de la Vérendrye entered the fur trade and, as the last of the major French explorers in North America, sought an overland route to the Pacific.

La Vérendrye and his sons, the first Europeans to penetrate the northwest plains of the United States and Canada, explored a vast region from the Saskatchewan to the *Missouri Rivers* from 1738 to 1743 as part of their efforts to expand their fur trade monopoly.

Building a post on the site of present-day Winnipeg as a base for their operations, they pushed into the Black Hills of South Dakota and may have reached as far west as present Wyoming in their search for the Pacific. Among their discoveries were the Mandan Villages and the realization that the broad stream along which they lay must be the Missouri River.

Lewis, Meriwether (1774–1809)

Born in Albemarle County, Virginia, Meriwether Lewis served in the U.S. Army in the 1790s and in 1801 won appointment as private secretary to President *Thomas Jefferson.* The president chose him to lead an overland expedition across the *Rocky Mountains* to the Pacific Ocean in 1803. Lewis suggested a former army colleague, *William Clark,* to accompany him as co-commander of the exploring expedition.

The *Lewis and Clark expedition* of 1804–1806 followed the *Missouri River* to its headwaters, crossed the *Continental Divide* at Lemhi Pass, and proceeded via the Clearwater, Snake and *Columbia Rivers* to the Pacific. The expedition returned by alternate routes after spending the winter of 1805–1806 near the mouth of the Columbia. Lewis and Clark together produced careful observations of plant, animal, and human life in the vast territories of the West. Their official account, compiled and edited by Nicholas Biddle, was published in two volumes in 1814.

Lewis served as governor of the Louisiana Territory from 1806 to

1809. He died under mysterious circumstances—by gunshot, possibly as a suicide—in Tennessee en route to Washington, D.C.

Lewis and Clark expedition (1804–1806)

The most significant of U.S. transcontinental journeys, the Lewis and Clark expedition represents an epic of exploration, a major advance in knowledge, and an event that led ultimately to the settlement and political domination of the American West and the displacement of the aboriginal peoples there.

With the *Louisiana Purchase,* President *Thomas Jefferson* acquired the vast *Louisiana [V]* Territory, some 828,000 square miles (later to comprise thirteen states), in 1803, but even before the successful negotiation with France, he had selected his personal secretary, the Virginian *Meriwether Lewis,* to lead a cross-country exploring party into the Louisiana country, across the *Rocky Mountains* and on to the Pacific. Lewis, only twenty-nine years old, chose a fellow Virginian, the experienced frontiersman *William Clark,* whom he had known briefly in the army in 1795, as his co-commander.

The two explorers joined forces on October 15, 1803, at Clarksville on the *Ohio River [V].* The party, now styled the Corps of Discovery, proceeded down the Ohio to the *Mississippi River [V],* then upstream as far as Wood River, Illinois, opposite the mouth of the *Missouri River.* The corps wintered over there. On May 21, 1804, Lewis, Clark, and the twenty-five fittest recruits, traveling in a keelboat and two pirogues laden with supplies, medicines, scientific instruments, arms, powder, and trade goods, passed the riverside village of Saint Charles, Missouri, marking the formal beginning of the Lewis and Clark expedition.

The route of the Lewis and Clark Expedition, 1804–1806.

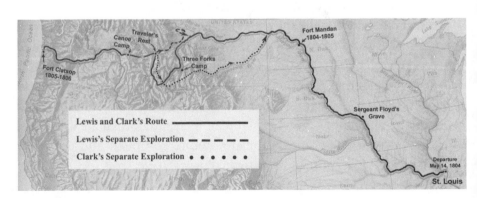

"Set out at half passed three oClock under three Cheers from the gentlemen on the bank," the expedition journal recorded. "Soon after we set out today a hard Wind from the WSW accompanied with a hard rain, which lasted with short Intervales all night."

The corps reached the mouth of the *Platte River* in present Nebraska on July 21, encountering nearby the first of the buffalo that roamed the Great Plains in enormous herds. Two weeks later, at a place called Council Bluffs on the west bank of the Missouri, the Americans met the first of the native peoples, some 250 members of the Otoe and Missouri tribes.

In his instructions, Jefferson had emphasized friendly relations with Native Americans. Lewis and Clark were to approach the Indians cautiously, avoid provocations, and withdraw at once in the face of superior force, even if that meant abandoning the expedition. Jefferson's notions were to teach the natives to farm, to trade with the Americans, and eventually to become useful citizens of the republic. "Make them acquainted with our wish to be neighborly, friendly and useful to them, and of our dispositions to a commercial intercourse with them," the President wrote; "confer with them on points most convenient as mutual emporiums, and the articles of most desirable interchange for them and us."

The Corps of Discovery reached the Mandan and Arikara villages below the Great Bend of the Missouri north of present Bismarck, North Dakota, in late October and went into winter cantonments there. In the spring, when the ice broke up on the river, Lewis and Clark sent the keelboat back downstream to *St. Louis* with the first scientific fruits of the expedition: reports for Jefferson, botanical specimens, skeletons and pelts of Plains creatures, and a menagerie of live animals, including four magpies, a prairie dog, and a prairie grouse.

Lewis and Clark haranguing Indians. The explorers had their first significant encounter with Native Americans—representatives of the Otoe and Missouri tribes—at Council Bluffs on the Missouri River in July 1804. This print was published in 1810 in the expedition journal of Corps of Discovery member Patrick Gass.

The corps set out upriver in six canoes and two pirogues on April 7, 1805. With favorable breezes the corps made rapid progress, covering ninety-three miles over the first four days, and on April 25 they reached the junction of the Missouri and Yellowstone Rivers. On May 26 Lewis climbed a bluff above the Missouri and caught his first view of the shimmering high peaks of the Rockies. They were an awe-inspiring sight, though daunting too.

"When I reflected on the difficulties which this snowey barrier would most probably throw in my way to the Pacific, and the sufferings and hardships of myself and party in them, it in some measure counterbalanced the joy I had felt in the first moment in which I gazed on them," he wrote.

Pausing above the Great Falls of the Missouri in present Montana, the party built a fleet of canoes out of hollowed cottonwoods, then ascended the shallow, boulder-strewn stream into the foothills of the Rockies. The corps entered the mountains in mid-July. Lewis reached the fountain of the Missouri on August 12 and climbed a short distance to the top of a pass, the *Continental Divide.*

Here Lewis had anticipated the sight of the *Columbia River* gleaming in the distance, or at least a broad plain leading gently downslope toward the sea. In the event, a towering mountain rampart loomed before him. This sudden view of the Bitterroot Mountains suggested that Jefferson would be disappointed in his hope of an all-water route across the continent. A party of Shoshone Indians presently confirmed what Lewis and Clark suspected: A hard march of several days separated the headwaters of the Missouri and the Columbia.

The explorers summoned one of the party to translate, the young Shoshone Sacagawea, the wife of a French fur trapper, Toussaint Charbonneau. She had joined the corps as interpreter and guide at the Mandan Villages. Sacagawea explained the expedition's purpose in the Shoshone language, then repeated the replies to her husband in Hidatsa, a Plains Indian language they had in common. Charbonneau passed on what Sacagawea had told him in French to one of the soldiers, who in turn rendered the answers into English for Lewis and Clark.

Lewis was the first to closely describe the Shoshones to whites. The band in the Bitterroot foothills numbered around a hundred warriors and three hundred women. They were a small people, with "thick ankles, crooked legs, thick flat feet." They owned little, but seemed to bear their poverty lightly. "They are not only cheerfull but even gay, fond of gaudy dress and amusements," Lewis wrote in the journal. "They are frank, communicative, fair in dealing, generous with what they possess, extremely honest, and by no means beggarly."

The Shoshones supplied a guide and horses. The Corps of Discovery crossed Lemhi Pass on the present Montana-Idaho border and struck into the Bitterroots. The going was slow and painful for horses and men. On September 16 eight inches of snow fell. "I have been wet and as cold in every part as I ever was in my life," Clark complained. Game became scarce. Some of the horses were killed for meat. With the men near the limit of endurance, the corps reached a friendly Nez Percé Indian village on the Weippe Prairie in present Idaho on September 22, after eleven days and 160 miles of forced marches over the mountains.

Traveling by canoe, Lewis and Clark descended the Clearwater River and then the Snake, reaching the Columbia on October 16. The flotilla passed Beacon Rock, the beginning of tidewater, on November 3. Four days later, Clark caught sight of the Pacific. "Ocian in view," he called out. "O! The joy." That night Clark calculated that the expedition had covered 4,192 miles from the mouth of the Missouri.

The corps spent a wet and miserable winter in an improvised settlement, Fort Clatsop, near present Astoria, Oregon. On March 23, 1806, the expedition broke camp and turned for home, retracing the previous year's route along the Columbia, then moving overland. Nez Percé guides led the party across the snowclad Bitterroots. In early July Lewis and Clark divided the party for explorations north and south of the main route. At dawn on July 27, a party of *Blackfoot* Indians attacked Lewis's camp near the Marias River in present Montana; the warriors were driven off with one dead and one seriously wounded in— remarkably—the only armed clash of the entire eight-thousand-mile enterprise.

The two exploring parties were reunited at the mouth of the Yellowstone on August 12. Reaching the Missouri, the expedition sped downriver on the swift current, covering as much as seventy miles in a day. The men caught sight of cattle grazing along the riverbank on September 20, 1806, and approached the first of the frontier settlements. Three days later the expedition reached St. Louis, journey's end.

Over twenty-eight months and eight thousand miles, the Corps of Discovery had explored a world entirely new to Americans. In all that time, through all the wilderness hardships, the expedition reported only two casualties: one man dead, the other deserted. But Lewis and Clark had not found an all-water route across the continent, nor had they been able to enlist the warlike *Sioux* and Blackfoot nations as allies and trade partners. Those failures were beside the point. "The importance of the Lewis and

IN THEIR OWN Words

My plan is to descend the Ohio in a keeled boat thence up the Mississippi to the mouth of the Missourie, and up that river as far as its navigation is practicable with a keeled boat, there to prepare canoes of bark or raw-hides, and proceed to its source, and if practicable pass over to the waters of the Columbia or Origan River and by descending reach the Western Ocean.

—MERIWETHER LEWIS TO WILLIAM CLARK, JUNE 19, 1803

Clark expedition lay on the level of imagination: it was drama, it was the enactment of a myth that embodied the future," wrote the cultural historian Henry Nash Smith. "It gave tangible substance to what had been merely an idea, and established the image of a highway across the continent so firmly in the minds of Americans that repeated failures could not shake it."

The expedition's successes were substantial and permanent. The explorers brought back detailed knowledge and the first accurate maps of vast, heretofore uncharted, territories. The journey permanently bound up the Louisiana Territory and the Pacific Northwest with the fortunes of the United States. Lewis and Clark returned with the preserved remains of dozens of specimens of flora and fauna. Their journals contained careful descriptions of terrain, weather, and plant and animal life, and documented the customs, practices, and languages of dozens of Indian tribes.

Lewis began work at once on his report to President Jefferson. He had found a "practicable rout" to the Pacific, a means of tapping the enormous potential in the western country in furs and trade. He foretold a great westward surge. A transcontinental land route, he felt certain, would be viable, and sooner rather than later. "If the government will only aid, even in a very limited manner, the enterprize of her Citizens, in the course of ten or twelve years a tour across the Continent by the rout mentioned will be undertaken by individuals with as little concern as a voyage across the Atlantic is at present," Lewis wrote.

Nicholas Biddle edited the official journal, titled *History of the Expedition under the Command of Captains Lewis and Clark.* Appearing in two volumes in 1814, the journal of Lewis and Clark claimed a place as one of the greatest travel accounts of any time.

Lisa, Manuel (1772–1820)

Born in New Orleans, Manuel Lisa became a power in the *St. Louis* fur trade during the first decade of the nineteenth century. With his partner *Andrew Henry,* he established the Missouri Fur Company, which sponsored a series of exploring expeditions that, in the wake of the *Lewis and Clark expedition,* opened much of the upper *Missouri River* country to American trade.

Operating from the outposts of Fort Lisa near present Omaha, Nebraska, and Fort Raymond on the Yellowstone River in Montana, Lisa's exploring and trapping parties traversed the *Rocky Mountain* regions in search of, among other things, a route that followed the western slopes down to the Spanish trading center of Santa Fe.

John Colter's expedition of 1807–1808 took him as far north as, and west of, present Yellowstone National Park, where he became the first known white man to see its spectacular geysers. He later located the source of the Missouri River at Three Forks in Montana. In 1808 George Drouillard followed Colter into the Yellowstone region in search of the western route to Santa Fe, which he believed to be no more than ten days' march to the south. He died at the hands of *Blackfoot* raiders at Three Forks in 1810.

Jean Baptiste Champlain set out from Fort Raymond in 1811 with twenty-three men on a long southeastward march through present Wyoming and Colorado. Dissension and Indian attack greatly reduced his band. Champlain himself vanished among the Arapaho along the upper Arkansas River in central Colorado. Four men eventually reached Santa Fe; a fifth, Ezekiel Williams, was trapped east along the Arkansas and, after many adventures, reached the safety of American territory in the summer of 1813.

Lisa and his Missouri Fur Company operatives gathered vast stores of knowledge about the geography and economic potential of the Rocky Mountain country—details that contributed materially to *William Clark*'s great work in progress, a master map of the western frontier. In 1814 the U.S. government rewarded Lisa for his private exertions on the nation's behalf with an appointment as Indian agent for the upper Missouri tribes. He held the post until his death in 1820.

Long, Stephen H. (1784–1864)

A New Hampshire farmer's son, Long graduated from Dartmouth College in 1809 and, on the strength of his mathematical ability and skills as a surveyor, won a commission in the U.S. Army *Corps of Topographical Engineers* in 1814. Ambitious and determined, he evidently regarded himself as the natural successor to *Lewis* and *Clark;* in the event, his achievements did not achieve the scale of his dreams.

Long's first exploring expeditions led him up the *Mississippi River [V]* to the Falls of St. Anthony, the site of Minneapolis, in 1817 and up the Arkansas River during the winter of 1817–1818, as far as the place he selected for the future Fort Smith. Late in 1818 the War Department chose Long to lead an expedition to the *Rocky Mountains.*

The party, comprised of soldiers, scientists, and artists Samuel

Seymour and Titian Peale, traveled by steamboat up the Mississippi and *Missouri Rivers* to Council Bluffs. After wintering there, Long pushed into the Great Plains in early June 1820, exploring the *Platte,* North Platte, and South Platte Rivers. The party caught its first glimpse of the mountains on June 30. Turning south, Long followed the river's course just east of the Front Range of the Rockies. On July 18 three of his men carried out the first documented ascent of 14,110-foot-high Pike's Peak south of present Denver.

Long then marched south to the Arkansas River, where he divided his party, sending a contingent down the Arkansas while he pressed south in search of the Red River, the boundary between U.S. and Spanish territory. Long mistook the Canadian River in present Oklahoma for the Red and never reached the boundary river. (*Randolph Barnes Marcy* would locate the Red River's headwaters in 1852.)

Stephen J. Long's 1820–1821 expedition to the Great Plains was a disappointment in some ways, but it did yield this important map of the region lying between the Missouri frontier and the Rocky Mountains.

Though a disappointment in some ways, Long's expedition yielded two important results. The map he produced repeated *Zebulon Pike*'s description of the plains as the *"Great American Desert,"* a forbidding designation that discouraged settlement of the region for decades. And artists Seymour and Peale, in the words of historian William Goetzmann, "provided the American public with their first visual impressions of the West."

Louisiana Purchase

In 1803 the administration of *Thomas Jefferson* negotiated the purchase from France of a vast swath of French New World holdings encompassing much of the midsection of the North American continent. For $11.25 million, the United States acquired territory that more than doubled the size of the nation.

Jefferson had made preparations to launch the *Lewis and Clark expedition* to reconnoiter the territory even before the final details of the purchase were settled and the agreement initialed on April 30, 1803. The explorers brought back extensive scientific and ethnographic knowledge of the new lands when they returned from the Pacific in 1806.

For its exacerbation of sectional disputes over slavery, historians now see Jefferson's acquisition as a long-term cause of the Civil War. The United States would eventually carve thirteen states out of the 828,000 square miles of the Louisiana Purchase.

Mackay-Evans expedition (1795)

Working for the Spanish, Scots-born James Mackay and the Welshman John Evans set out from *St. Louis* in May 1795 "to open commerce with the distant and unknown nations in the upper parts of the Missouri and to discover all the unknown parts" as far west as the Pacific Ocean.

In an effort to fulfill this difficult task, Mackay and Evans embarked in four pirogues and paddled up the *Missouri River* as far as the Omaha Indian villages above present Omaha, Nebraska, where Mackay put up a rough outpost he dubbed Fort Charles. He then sent Evans on alone up the Missouri with orders to collect data on latitude, longitude, climate, plant and animal life, and the Indian populations he encountered on the way to the Pacific. Evans had a private agenda too: He intended to pursue his search for a lost tribe of Welsh Indians, the Madoc, that he hoped to find in the Mandan Villages along the Great Bend of the river.

Previously, the Spanish had dispatched the French trader-explorer Jean Baptiste Truteau to the Mandan Villages in 1794, but he encountered strong Indian hostility and could advance no farther than the Arikara Villages near the confluence of the Grand River with the Missouri. Evans reached the Mandan Villages but failed to penetrate any farther.

All the same, Mackay and Evans returned to St. Louis with improved knowledge of the tribes that controlled the upper reaches of the Missouri and of the course of the great river itself. Using information collected from the Mandans, Evans produced a manuscript map in 1787 that included the first mention of the Yellowstone River and the falls of the Missouri.

Mackenzie, Alexander (1764–1820)

Mackenzie and his widowed father emigrated to New York from their native Stornoway, Scotland, to New York in 1774; when the elder Mackenzie joined the Loyalist forces during the Revolutionary War, he sent the boy north to *Montreal [V]*. After a brief period of schooling, Alexander Mackenzie entered the counting house of fur trader John Gregory as a clerk. There he learned the intricacies of the enterprise that would take him west for his two great voyages of exploration.

The firm of Gregory & McLeod sent Mackenzie west to *Fort Detroit [V]* in 1784, offering him a partnership on the understanding that he would penetrate into unknown country and establish trading relations with the Indian nations he encountered. Intense competition in the interior led to a series of mergers and, finally, absorption of the rivals into the *North West Company.* Mackenzie obtained a partnership in the larger enterprise and in 1787 traveled to the Lake Athabasca region of present northeast Alberta as second-in-command to trapper-explorer *Peter Pond.*

Pond's accounts of his explorations touched off an imaginative response in Mackenzie, who now acknowledged that the prospect of crossing the mountains to the Pacific had become "the favorite project of my own ambition." He set out from Fort Chipewyan on Lake Athabasca on his first voyage, one that would carry him "to the northern ocean," on June 3, 1789.

With five *voyageurs* and two Indians, including the Chipewyan leader known as "the English chief," the expedition pushed up the Slave River in three canoes, straining against the rapids and "much troubled with Muskettows and Gnatts," to Great Slave Lake. Crossing the icebound lake, Mackenzie followed the north shore west to the entrance of the river that would bear his name, reaching it on June 29.

The band now made swift progress, traveling for sixteen hours a day through the nightless north (Mackenzie timed the sunset at around 10 P.M., sunrise at 2 A.M.) and covering as many as seventy-five miles in a daily stage. On the morning of July 2, "We perceived a cluster of mountains stretching as far as our view could reach to the Southward and whose tops were lost in the clouds"—the *Rocky Mountains.* Here, too, Mackenzie determined that the eponymous river would not lead him to the Pacific. From coursing mostly west, the Mackenzie now bent north and flowed parallel to the eastern slopes of the mountains.

Three days later, a band of Dogrib Indians passed along grim intelligence: The sea lay many winters distant, the Indians told Mackenzie, monsters roamed the country beyond, and he would be an old man before he saw home again. The news unsettled the *voyageurs,* but Mackenzie pressed on anyway. He encountered tidewater on July 12, an event that contradicted the Dogrib report. Estimating the tidal range at 16–18 inches, Mackenzie on July 15 realized belatedly that he had reached the Arctic Ocean, though today's Langley and Richards Islands blocked a view of the icy expanse.

The expedition set out on the return on July 16. Mackenzie later calculated that he journeyed 1,540 miles on the first voyage. He reached Fort Chipewyan on September 12, 1789, after a round-trip of 112 days. In the view of the North West Company the voyage had been a failure, for Mackenzie had not blazed a practical trade route to the Pacific. "My expedition was hardly spoken of," he wrote, "but that is what I expected." He had, however, filled in vast blank spaces on the map, corrected major errors on Pond's sketch of the country, and added much to existing stocks of knowledge of the Canadian Northwest. In closely questioning Indians he met along the river, who spoke of a river on the other side of the mountains that led down to salt water, he developed the outlines of a possible route to the Pacific, one he was determined to test.

The first voyage exposed the limits of Mackenzie's surveying skills; his calculations were badly in error. He returned to England briefly for training in technique and to acquire more precise surveying instruments in preparation for the second expedition, the journey on which he would realize his "favorite project."

Setting out from Fort Chipewyan on October 10, 1792, in a twenty-five-foot canoe with six *voyageurs* and two Indian guides/interpreters, Mackenzie ascended the Peace River as far as Fort Fork in present west-central Alberta. There, in early November, he decided to winter over among the Beaver Indians—and just in time, for the river had begun to run with ice on October 6 and the southwest wind brought snow on October 11.

As he vaguely formulated it, Mackenzie planned to follow the Peace River and its tributary branches to their headwaters, cross the mountains, and strike a river that would lead to the sea. The band left Fort Fork on May 9, 1793. In the afternoon of the eighth day, he recorded in his journal, "The rocky mountains appeared in sight, their summits covered with snow . . . they formed an agreeable object to every person in the canoe, as

IN THEIR OWN Words

Close by [the Arctic Ocean] the land is high and covered with short Grass and many Plants, which are in Blossom, and has a beautiful appearance, tho' an odd contrast, the Hills covered with Flowers and Verdure, and the Vallies full of Ice and Snow. The Earth is not thawed above 4 Inches from the Surface, below is a solid Body of Ice.

—ALEXANDER MACKENZIE, "JOURNAL OF A VOYAGE FROM FORT CHIPEWYAN TO THE ARCTIC OCEAN IN 1789," IN *VOYAGES* (1801)

we attained them much sooner than we expected." Mackenzie pushed on through a treacherous stretch of river, "a succession of rapids, cascades and falls." He reached the junction of the Finlay and Parsnip Rivers on May 31 and, on the advice of an Indian guide, chose the latter. It led south to a "low ridge of land" that divided the watersheds of the Mackenzie and Fraser Rivers. Crossing this divide, he descended the damp Pacific flanks and struck the Fraser River.

Mackenzie followed the Fraser due south for some distance and, mistaking it for the Columbia, decided to turn back. Abandoning the canoe on July 4, he turned west and marched overland for more than two hundred miles, following a network of small streams to the Bella Coola River. There on July 8 friendly Indians transported the band downstream in canoes. Mackenzie caught his first glimpse of the Pacific on July 17, recording the occasion in his understated way: "I could perceive the termination of the river, and its discharge into a narrow arm of the sea." Four days later he paced the beach facing Dean Channel. *George Vancouver*'s survey parties had explored this stretch of coast a few weeks earlier. Mackenzie left a token of his visit: "I now mixed up some vermilion in melted grease, and inscribed, in large characters, on the South-East face of the rock on which we had slept last night, this brief memorial—'Alexander Mackenzie, from Canada, by land, the twenty-second of July, one thousand seven hundred and ninety three.'"

So Mackenzie and his band became the first whites to cross the North American continent north of Mexico. Following a route chosen on instinct and educated guesswork, he had covered 1,200 miles in seventy-four days, averaging about twenty miles a day. The return voyage, something of an anticlimax, ended at Fort Fork at four in the afternoon of May 9, 1794. "Here," Mackenzie wrote in his journal that day, "my voyages of discovery terminate." After a brief rest, he pushed east to Fort Chipewyan, where he passed an uneventful winter.

Alexander Mackenzie left the Canadian west for good in 1795, served as a senior North West Company partner in Montreal, and returned to

IN THEIR OWN *Words*

We began our journey about twelve noon, the commencement of which was a steep ascent of about a mile; it lay along a well-beaten path, but the country through which it led was rugged and ridgy, and full of wood. When we were in a state of extreme heat, from the toil of our journey, the rain came on, and continued till the evening, and even when it ceased the underwood continued its drippings upon us.

—ALEXANDER MACKENZIE, "JOURNAL OF A VOYAGE FROM FORT CHIPEWYAN TO THE PACIFIC OCEAN IN 1793," IN *VOYAGES* (1801)

Britain in 1799. He published the journals of his two great exploring expeditions as Voyages in 1801. *Thomas Jefferson* read the work as he planned the details of the cross-country journey he would assign *Meriwether Lewis* and *William Clark* in 1803.

Mackenzie, Donald (1783–1851)

A native of the Scots Highlands, Donald Mackenzie emigrated to *Montreal [V]* in 1800 and joined the *North West Company* as a clerk. Mackenzie left the Canadian concern for a partnership in *John Jacob Astor*'s Pacific Fur Company in 1809.

Mackenzie, a massive man who weighed more than three hundred pounds, came west with *Wilson Price Hunt* in 1811 as second-in-command of the Astorians' overland expedition. From March to May 1812, he explored Oregon's Willamette Valley for the Pacific Fur Company. The Mackenzie River of west-central Oregon is named for him.

North West Company operatives besieged *Fort Astoria* during the War of 1812 and Mackenzie, along with Duncan MacDougall, another Scots-Canadian, surrendered the post—actually sold it at less than market value—without a fight. Mackenzie rejoined the North West Company and led its Snake Country trapping expeditions from 1818 to 1822. In April 1819 he became the first European to float through Hell's Canyon of the Snake; he later pronounced the river navigable for trapper brigades. Mackenzie was one of the first whites to follow the Green River to its source in Green Lake.

Mackenzie's explorations revitalized the British fur trade in the Pacific Northwest. When the Northwesters merged with the rival *Hudson's Bay Company* in 1821, he directed company operations in the Red River settlements of present Manitoba.

Mallet expeditions (1739–1742)

Pierre and Paul Mallet set out from New Orleans in 1739 in search of a direct trade route from the Mississippi Valley into what French traders mistakenly believed were the silver-rich precincts of Spanish Santa Fe, New Mexico. The Mallet brothers were thus the first documented Europeans to traverse the Great Plains from the *Missouri River.*

Leading a party of eight Canadians, the brothers pushed up the *Mississippi River [V]* to *Cahokia [V]*, then along the Missouri River to a point north of present Omaha, Nebraska, where on May 29, 1739, Pawnee Indians gently pointed out they had detoured far out of their way. For their trouble, the Mallets had disproved the notion that the best way to Santa Fe lay along the Missouri.

Striking southwest with packhorses, the expedition crossed present Nebraska and much of Kansas before turning due west for Colorado. Successfully negotiating the country of hostile Apache and Comanche Indians, the Mallets reached Taos and Santa Fe in late July and remained there as guests of the Spanish for more than nine months.

On the return, they followed a more direct route, exploring the Arkansas River from the eastern slopes of the *Rocky Mountains* to the Mississippi. The Mallets set out on a second expedition to Santa Fe in 1742, this one waterborne, but low water in the Canadian River of Kansas forced the party to turn back.

Manifest Destiny

The notion that Americans were fated to explore, settle, and dominate the North American continent long predated the 1840s minting of the term Manifest Destiny. *Thomas Jefferson,* whose father had pushed west to settle in the wilderness along the eastern slopes of the *Blue Ridge Mountains [III]* in the 1730s, regarded western expansion as central to his vision of the new nation. With his negotiation of the *Louisiana Purchase* and sponsorship of the *Lewis and Clark expedition* in the first years of the nineteenth century, Jefferson did as much as anyone to make realization of that expansionist destiny possible.

In the 1820s John Quincy Adams predicted that the United States would eventually be "coextensive with the North American continent, destined by God and nature to be the most populous and powerful people ever combined into one social contract." In an essay in 1845, John O'Sullivan, the editor of the *United States Magazine and Democratic Review,* gave a name to this notion of a national mission "to overspread the continent allotted by Providence for the free development of our yearly multiplying millions," calling it Manifest Destiny.

Expansionists cited Manifest Destiny to justify the annexation of Texas and the acquisition of the disputed Oregon Country in the 1840s.

The elaborate government-sponsored exploring expeditions of *Charles Wilkes* (1838–1842) and *John Charles Frémont* (1842–1848) were practical expressions of the national compulsion to push ever westward.

Marcy, Randolph Barnes   (1812–1887)

A native of Greenwich, Massachusetts, Randolph Barnes Marcy graduated from the U.S. Military Academy at West Point in 1832 and served on the Michigan, Wisconsin, and Texas frontiers over the first fifteen years of his army career.

In the spring of 1849, Marcy set out from Fort Smith, Arkansas, on his most important exploring expedition, a wagon road and railroad survey bound for Santa Fe. Leading two companies of infantry and a detachment of cavalry, he followed the Canadian River to the Texas panhandle, then struck south across the Llano Estacado—his "great Zahara of North America." The party reached Santa Fe on June 28, 1849.

Marcy and the topographical engineer on the expedition, James H. Simpson, declared the route superior for a railroad; California-bound goldseekers were using the rough trail along it already in 1849. Amiel W. Whipple's expedition of 1853 (see *Pacific Railroad surveys*) essentially followed Marcy's route. His return journey led along the southern edge of the Llano Estacado through hostile Kiowa and Comanche country to Fort Wachita.

In an 1852 expedition, Marcy reached the sources of the Red River in the Texas panhandle, completing *Stephen Long*'s mission of 1820. After service in Utah in the late 1850s, Marcy wrote a guidebook, *The Prairie Traveler* (1859) with advice for overlanders and specific information about more than thirty cross-country trails.

Missouri River

The longest river of the United States, the Missouri rises in an upland stream in the *Rocky Mountains* near Three Forks in southwestern Montana and flows 2,565 miles to the *Mississippi River [V]* above *St. Louis.* Together with the Mississippi, it forms the third-longest river system in the world. Owing to the heavy freight of silt it carries, the Missouri has long been known as the "Big Muddy."

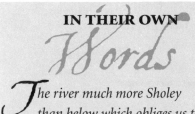
From time immemorial, Native American nations used the Missouri as a highway. The *Jolliet and Marquette expedition [V]* passed the river's mouth on the journey down the Mississippi in 1673 and identified the Missouri as a probable route west. The French trader *Sieur de la Vérendrye* explored the upper reaches in 1738 and discovered the Mandan Villages in present North Dakota. Canadian *David Thompson* explored parts of the upper river in 1797.

The *Lewis and Clark expedition* ascended the Missouri to its source on the way to the Pacific in 1804 and 1805; the explorers' journals provided the most extensive information on the river up to that date. The first steamboat labored upstream against the Missouri's strong current in 1819.

Muir, John

(1838–1914)

Born in Dunbar, Scotland, and educated in a common school there, John Muir immigrated to Wisconsin with his family in 1849. His father worked him brutally on the family farm; Muir found escape in the woods and fields and in extensive reading. He studied at the University of Wisconsin in the early 1860s, but he learned his most important lessons in natural history in the field. His early journeying took him into neighboring midwestern states and Canada, and in 1867 he completed a thousand-mile walk from central Indiana to Cedar Key, Florida.

Far better known as a naturalist and conservationist, Muir carried out important explorations as well. Migrating to California in 1868, he lived for six years in the Yosemite Valley, from which he carried out a series of systematic examinations of the High Sierra. He discovered sixty-five glaciers during his explorations and, more significantly, developed the theory that glaciation rather than cataclysm created the Yosemite Valley. Formally trained geologists such as *Clarence King* ridiculed Muir's theory, but later investigation proved him correct.

In 1879 and 1880 trips to Alaska, Muir explored Glacier Bay near Juneau and discovered the glacier that today bears his name. He campaigned tirelessly during the decade of the 1880s for the preservation of Yosemite Valley; in 1890 Congress established Yosemite National Park.

His lobbying helped lead, too, to the establishment of thirteen forest reserves (today's national forests) in the United States in the 1890s.

A skilled and prolific writer, Muir published many magazine articles and eight books, among them *The Mountains of California* (1894) and *My First Summer in the Sierra* (1911). He died unhappy, however, having lost what he regarded as the great battle of his life, the protection of the Hetch-Hetchy Valley near Yosemite. A 1913 dam created a 240-foot deep reservoir to supply water for San Francisco, drowning the valley.

North West Company

A fur-trading enterprise, based in *Montreal [V],* the North West Company organized in 1779 as a confederation to challenge the *Hudson's Bay Company*'s virtual monopoly on western wilderness trade. As an inseparable element of their trading operations, the Northwesters carried out extensive and important explorations of Canada from the Great Lakes to the Pacific and from the U.S. boundary north to the Arctic.

In the 1780s *Peter Pond* and *Alexander Mackenzie* extended the company's trade to the Lake Athabasca region of present northern Saskatchewan and Alberta. Mackenzie, on North West Company business, completed his epic journeys to the Arctic Ocean in 1789 and across the continent to the Pacific in 1793. *Simon Fraser*'s explorations of 1808 sought to blaze a trade route to the Pacific for the company. Northwester *David Thompson* surveyed and mapped thousands of miles of western Canada and became, in 1811, the first European to descend the *Columbia River* from its source to the sea.

Almost from the start, the Northwesters and their larger trade rival were joined in a fierce and sometimes deadly struggle for supremacy. In 1821, after a bitter contest over the Red River settlements, the North West Company merged with the older firm; the coalition continued operations under the long-established name of Hudson's Bay Company.

Ogden, Peter Skene (1794–1854)

Peter Skene Ogden led a series of *Hudson's Bay Company* trapping expeditions into present Idaho, Nevada, Utah, and California in the 1820s. In 1828 Ogden discovered the *Humboldt River* in the Great Basin and mapped its entire three-hundred-mile length. The river later formed part of the main emigrant route to California (see *California Trail*).

Ogden became one of the first white men to reach the region of the Great Salt Lake. In 1829–1830, he marched from the mouth of the *Columbia River* down the entire length of Mexican California to the head of the Gulf of California. His geographical knowledge informed leading maps of the West of his day, including that of English geographer and cartographer Aaron Arrowsmith.

Ogden later served as chief factor at the HBC's headquarters post at *Fort Vancouver.* Ogden, Utah, is named for him.

Oregon Trail

American trader-explorers venturing to the *Rocky Mountains* and beyond traced what would become a two-thousand-mile transcontinental highway for migrants from 1812 to the mid-1830s. The trail began near Independence, Missouri, followed the *Platte River* west to *Fort Laramie,* cut through the Rockies at South Pass, Wyoming, and ran parallel to the Snake River before veering northward through the Blue Mountains of eastern Oregon to the *Columbia River* and on to the fertile valley of the Willamette.

Robert Stuart led a party of fur traders from *Fort Astoria* eastward along what would become the Oregon Trail in 1812–1813; with advice from Indians, Stuart made the first documented crossing of South Pass, a broad, gentle thoroughfare at 7,500 feet above sea level. Another trapper band under *Jedediah Smith* rediscovered South Pass in 1824. The overland trading and exploring expeditions of Nathaniel Wyeth and *Benjamin*

The emigrant routes to Oregon and California. Trappers blazed the earliest overland routes; formal surveys by Frémont and others helped thousands of migrants to find their way from the Missouri frontier to Utah, Oregon, and California before the era of the railroads.

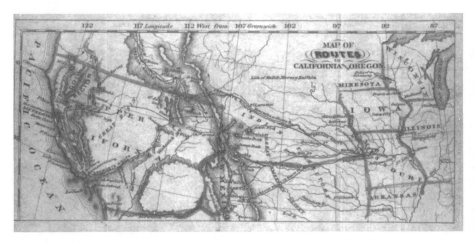

Bonneville further defined the trail in the early 1830s. *John C. Frémont's* expeditions of 1842 and 1843 surveyed the route with greater precision.

The first large-scale settler caravan followed the Oregon Trail to the Willamette Valley in 1843. By the late 1850s some 250,000 Americans had made the six-month trek west along the route. Sections of the trail today still bear deep wagon ruts and other traces of the migrants' passage.

Pacific Railroad surveys   (1853–1855)

In March 1853 the U.S. Congress authorized three government-sponsored exploring and survey expeditions to scout "the most economical and practicable route" for a railroad from the *Mississippi River [V]* to the Pacific Ocean. Caught up in the sectional crisis of the 1850s, the transcontinental route fell victim to the politics of slavery, expansion, and balance of power in the national government.

Jefferson Davis of Mississippi, secretary of war in the administration of Franklin Pierce, favored a southern route that would strike west from Vicksburg, Mississippi, and follow the 32nd parallel to the Pacific. Illinois Democratic senator Stephen Douglas lobbied for a northern route leading out from Chicago. Other interests pressed for a far northern route from St. Paul, Minnesota, to Puget Sound in Washington and for a central route from Springfield, Missouri, that would follow the *Oregon Trail* across the mid-section of the continent. Thus the army expeditions with their cadres of civilian artists, mapmakers, and scientists reconnoitered five possible transcontinental routes.

Starting in June 1853, Isaac Stevens, a former army officer who had won appointment as governor of the newly organized Washington Territory, advanced west from St. Paul, surveying a belt from latitude 47° to the Canadian border at 49°. In his report, Stevens claimed he discovered two feasible northern routes, declaring that the snows of winter "would not present the slightest impediment to the passage of railroad trains." Privately, though, at least one member of the Stevens expedition offered a dissenting opinion. "A road *might* be built over the tops of the Himaleyah mountains—but no reasonable man would undertake it," wrote expedition naturalist George Suckley. "I think the same of the Northern route."

In the third week in June, Lieutenant John W. Gunnison led a party from Fort Leavenworth along the 38th parallel through Kansas and Colorado as far as Sevier Lake in the Ute country of southern Utah, roughly following the route of *John C. Frémont*'s expedition of 1848. A band of Paiutes attacked Gunnison's camp early in the morning of October 26, killing seven men, including Gunnison. Only four of the party escaped.

Lieutenant E. G. Beckwith succeeded Gunnison in command of the expedition and, after wintering in Salt Lake City, marched west across the Great Basin to the eastern flank of the *Sierra Nevada.* Beckwith's teams found two suitable passes through the mountains and into the Sacramento Valley. Between them, the Gunnison-Beckwith survey traced what would ultimately be the route of the first transcontinental railroad.

Lieutenant Amiel Weeks Whipple left from Fort Smith, Arkansas, in July 1853, following the 35th parallel through present Oklahoma, Kansas, and New Mexico to Zuni, then across Arizona to the Colorado River. The expedition then marched northwest to the Needles before advancing due west across the Mojave Desert to San Bernardino. "There is not a doubt remaining that for construction of a railway the route we have passed over is not only practicable but in many respects eminently advantageous," Whipple wrote in his report.

Starting from opposite directions, the expeditions of Lieutenant John G. Parke and Captain John Pope surveyed Davis's favored route along the 32° line. From San Diego, Parke pushed east through Apache country to El Paso, Texas, on the Río Grande. Pope, marching west from Fort Belknap, Texas, traversed the Texas plains, crossed the Guadelupe Mountains, and met Parke near El Paso.

Separate survey parties explored passes through the California mountains and surveyed coastal routes from California to the Pacific Northwest. The Mississippian Davis insisted on the 32° line, and advocates for other routes refused to yield. Though the multivolume *Pacific Railroad Reports,* which began appearing in 1857, showed there were several viable routes across the continent, the issue remained hostage to the sectional dispute until the Civil War broke the political deadlock. The Union government pushed ahead rapidly with the project, and the transcontinental railroad opened in 1867.

Palliser and Hind surveys (1857–1859)

Beginning in June 1857, the British Army officer John Palliser led three survey expeditions into the Canadian Shield between Lake Superior and Lake Winnipeg, the prairie region of present south Saskatchewan, and the passes through the Canadian Rockies that *David Thompson* and others had previously explored. In a separate expedition, the geologist Henry Youle Hind examined the lake and prairie country of south central Canada between Lake Superior and the forks of the Saskatchewan River.

Captain Palliser's party set out from Fort William on Lake Superior in June 1857 and followed a northwesterly course to Lake Winnipeg, then west to Fort Carleton on the North Saskatchewan River. Most of the party wintered over there; Palliser himself rejoined the expedition in June 1858 for a journey through the western prairies to the flanks of the Rockies. The third expedition marched in June 1859 from central Saskatchewan south and west into United States territory. In late October Palliser met the U.S.–Canadian Boundary Survey team on the *Columbia River* in present central Washington and there abandoned his plan to advance all the way to the Pacific.

Over a two-year period, the Palliser surveys mapped extensive new territories and gathered masses of data on Indian nations, plant and animal life, and prospective transportation routes into Canada's midsection. They explored, too, four passes through the Rockies, one of which would ultimately carry Canadian Pacific Railway trains westward to the Pacific.

Hind, a professor at the University of Toronto, sought in his 1859 survey to determine the most efficient emigrant routes into the Saskatchewan country. He completed maps of a vast swath of southern Canada from the western edge of Lake Superior northwest to the forks of the Saskatchewan.

Palliser and Hind, in separate reports on their expeditions, both concluded that despite their rich soils, the Great Plains of Canada would not support large-scale settlement, owing to the unreliability of annual rainfall.

Parker, Samuel (1779–1866)

Born in Ashfield, Massachusetts, Samuel Parker graduated from Williams College and became a Congregational minister. After "home missionary" work in frontier western New York and a stint teaching at a girls' school, he conceived in the early 1830s an ambition to establish a mission station among the Flathead Indians along the western slopes of the *Rocky Mountains.*

The American Board of Commissioners of Foreign Missions demurred at first on account of Parker's age—he was fifty-six years old in 1835—but relented finally and approved a reconnaissance expedition to the Rockies. With fellow missionary Marcus Whitman, Parker set out in the spring of 1835 with an *American Fur Company* caravan bound for the annual trapper fair along the Green River of Wyoming.

They reached the rendezvous safely in August. Whitman turned for home, but Parker continued on to the Pacific with an escort of Nez Percé Indians. He wintered over at the *Hudson's Bay Company* post at *Fort Vancouver* and, in the spring and summer of 1836, explored present eastern Oregon, Washington, and western Idaho in search of mission sites. He sailed for home via the Sandwich Islands in September, leaving to Whitman the task of selecting a location for the mission station. The mission board dispatched the first contingent of missionaries to the Oregon Country in the spring of 1836.

In his book *Journal of an Exploring Tour,* published in 1838, Parker provided generally accurate accounts of the geography and topography of the Pacific Northwest. He wrote that he discovered on his travels that ordinary people could make the journey safely along what would become known as the *Oregon Trail,* and that the Indians of the West would embrace a missionary presence.

Pattie, James Ohio (1804–1850?)

A Kentucky-born trapper, James Ohio Pattie accompanied his father's wagon train to Santa Fe in 1825. From the New Mexico capital, he struck west on two long-range trapping expeditions in which he explored a vast area of the Mexican Southwest, "rediscovered" the *Grand Canyon,* and scouted overland trails to California.

In 1825–1826, Pattie trapped along the Gila River in present Arizona. In September 1826, near the site of Phoenix, a band of Papago Indians attacked the party and killed eleven of the fourteen members; Pattie, with two other survivors, fell in with Ewing Young's trapping expedition. With Young, Pattie crossed the Colorado River and marched along the North Rim of the Grand Canyon, then followed the Grand River to its headwaters in the *Rocky Mountains* of Colorado. They were the first Europeans to see the canyon since *Francisco Garcés [IV]* in 1776. Pattie's later claim to have penetrated as far north as the Yellowstone River in Montana on this expedition has not been substantiated.

In 1829–1830 Pattie and his father, Sylvester Pattie, followed the Gila west to the Colorado, trapping along the route, crossed the latter stream near its mouth, and advanced south and west into Baja California. The Mexican authorities imprisoned the Patties in San Diego in March 1830. The elder Pattie died in jail; his son made his way north to Monterey and San Francisco and eventually returned to the United States by sea.

Pattie dictated the embellished story of his adventures to a Cincinnati clergyman and saw it into print under the title of *Personal Narrative* in 1831. Joining the California Gold Rush in 1849, Pattie disappeared in the *Sierra Nevada* the following year.

Pike, Zebulon (1779–1813)

Born in New Jersey, the son of a soldier, Zebulon Pike enlisted in his father's command at age fifteen and served in a series of outposts on the *Mississippi River* [V] frontier. In 1805 the conspiratorial James Wilkinson, in command of U.S. forces at *St. Louis,* assigned Pike to ascend the Mississippi to its headwaters. He failed to trace the great river to its source in Lake Itasca, but the map and journal of the expedition contained valuable information on the upper Mississippi region.

Wilkinson, whose convoluted imperial intrigues involved a secret relationship with Spain, soon had a second assignment for Pike: a journey to the headwaters of the Arkansas and Red Rivers and a reconnaissance of Spanish New Mexico. Historians believe Wilkinson issued Pike secret instructions to spy on Spanish defenses at Santa Fe and elsewhere in New Mexico province.

Pike set out with twenty-three men from the vicinity of St. Louis on July 15, 1806. The party traveled west through Pawnee country in present Nebraska before turning south for the Arkansas River. From the great bend of the Arkansas in central Kansas, Pike struck due west for the *Rocky Mountains.* The expedition caught its first glimpse of the snowpeaks on November 15. Pike passed the next six weeks exploring the Front Range of the Rockies from the South Platte to the Sangre de Cristo Mountains of southern Colorado. His men failed, however, in their attempt to climb the 14,000-foot-high Colorado peak named for him.

In mid-January 1806 Pike divided the party, sending five men back to St. Louis with dispatches for Wilkinson. With the remainder, Pike struck south across the Sangre de Cristos in bitter winter weather; six of the men were laid low with gangrene. Reaching a branch of the Río Grande (which, in keeping with Wilkinson's instructions, he persisted in referring to as the Red River, the supposed boundary between U.S. and Spanish territory), he

Explorer-soldier Zebulon Montgomery Pike in full-dress uniform. His expedition of 1806–1807 took him deep into the Mexican territory of Texas.

paused to build a log fort. There, on February 26, Spanish cavalry took him prisoner.

The Spanish held Pike in comfortable arrest, allowing him to carefully observe their frontier defenses in New Mexico and Texas. They obligingly escorted him across Texas to the border post of Natchitoches in the *Louisiana [V]* Territory and set him free. He promptly prepared a detailed report for Wilkinson. William Goetzmann has called Pike's three-plus months in captivity the most successful recorded espionage operation in American history.

Pike published a narrative of his travels, *An Account of Expeditions to the Sources of the Mississippi and through the Western Part of Louisiana,* in 1810. It contained the most detailed information to date on the Spanish borderlands. Pike was also the first to describe the Central Plains as a "sandy desert"; *Stephen Long* would dub the plains the *"Great American Desert"* on the map of his 1820 expedition. Taken together, the verdicts of Pike and Long spared the Plains Indian nations from the incursion of American settlement for several decades.

Pike was mortally wounded during the War of 1812 in an assault on the fortified town of York (now Toronto), Canada.

IN THEIR OWN Words

I saw in my route, in various places, tracts of many leagues where the wind had thrown up the sand in all the fanciful form of the ocean's rolling wave; and on which not a speck of vegetable matter existed. . . . Our citizens being so prone to rambling and extending themselves on the frontiers will, through necessity, be constrained to limit their extent on the west to the borders of the Missouri and the Mississippi, while they leave the prairies incapable of cultivation to the wandering and uncivilized aborigines of the country.

—ZEBULON PIKE, *ACCOUNT OF THE EXPEDITIONS* (1810)

Platte River

Formed by the junction of the North and South Platte Rivers at North Platte, Nebraska, the Platte flows eastward for about 310 miles to its confluence with the *Missouri River* at Omaha. Flood-prone in the spring, the river is too shallow and too obstructed with sand for navigation; explorers and early traders had difficulty staying afloat even in canoes.

Etienne Venard de Bourgmond became the first documented European to see the Platte, reaching its mouth in an expedition of 1714. *Robert Stuart* descended the North Platte and then the Platte itself through present Wyoming and Nebraska in his west-to-east transcontinental journey in 1812–1813. From the 1820s, the Platte–North Platte trace became increasingly defined as the *Oregon Trail,* the main migrant route of the 1840s and 1850s to Oregon and California.

The important trader/explorer/migrant way station of *Fort Laramie* lies on the North Platte near its junction with the Laramie River in southeastern Wyoming.

Pond, Peter   (1740–1807)

Born in Milford, Connecticut, Peter Pond served in the French and Indian War and entered the western fur trade at Fort Detroit in 1765. Moving north and west to Fort Mackinac *(Fort Michilimackinac [V]),* he trapped and explored along the upper *Mississippi River [V]* in present Wisconsin and Minnesota from 1773 to 1775.

Aggressive and tough, Pond pushed out beyond the boundaries of the fur trade in 1778. Following Native American trails, he advanced north and west from the western end of Lake Superior to the Athabasca Basin of present Saskatchewan and Alberta to "explore a country hitherto unknown but from an Indian report."

Pond established a fur-trading post near Lake Athabasca and collected information about the country beyond. His Indian informants mentioned a great lake or sea to the northwest—Great Slave Lake. Pond journeyed to *Montreal [V]* in 1784 to raise support for a chain of fur posts from Athabasca to the Pacific, but found no takers for his scheme.

Returning to the Athabasca region in 1785, he pressed his search for routes to the Pacific, probably reaching—and exploring—Great Slave Lake. His own reconnaissances, together with Indian reports, persuaded him that he had advanced to "within six days travel of the grand Pacific Ocean."

Pond lacked training and technical skill as a cartographer, and his maps were more imaginative than accurate. His 1787 map of the country lying between the Great Lakes, Hudson's Bay, and the Rockies showed a large river flowing due west from Great Slave Lake to the Pacific—in fact, the present Mackenzie River, which courses northwest to the Arctic Ocean. Nevertheless, he pointed a route toward the Pacific. Pond's Athabasca associate *Alexander Mackenzie* would follow the eponymous river to the Arctic in 1789 and would find his way to the western ocean in 1793.

Suspected in the murders of at least two fur trade rivals, the violent, impulsive Pond retired as a *North West Company* partner and returned to the United States in 1790. Philip Turnor and his associate surveyors corrected many of Pond's inaccuracies, especially in longitude, in 1791–1792. Narrative accounts of Pond's journeys are reprinted in *Five Fur Traders of the Northwest,* edited by C. M. Gates (1965).

Powell, John Wesley (1834–1902)

Born in Mount Morris, New York, the son of an ecstatically Methodist farmer and part-time tailor, Powell migrated west with his family, eventually settling in Wheaton, Illinois. Intermittently educated, he pursued his real interests—natural history and archaeology—on his own before enlisting in the Twentieth Illinois Infantry Regiment with Lincoln's first call for volunteers upon the outbreak of the Civil War.

Powell soon won a lieutenant's commission. Wounded at the battle of Shiloh, he recovered from the amputation of his right arm to see hard service during the siege of Vicksburg, in the advance to Atlanta, and in the Nashville campaign. He returned to Illinois after the war, taught natural science, and organized his first exploring expedition—to the Colorado Rockies—in 1867. After an ascent of Pike's Peak, he and his wife, Emma Dean Powell, spent two months examining the Grand River region. Resuming his Colorado explorations in 1868, Powell climbed Long's Peak before pushing into the White River country, where he spent the winter in the field.

The Colorado preliminaries readied Powell for his greatest ambition—the exploration of the *Grand Canyon* country. With a combination of private and public backing, he planned a 1,500-mile trip down the Green and Colorado Rivers—the last major unexplored region in the continental United States.

Powell's nine-member team floated out into the Green in four specially constructed boats on May 24, 1869, with Powell in the van in the sixteen-foot pilot boat *Emma Dean*. The men found the upper Green River "deep and calm as a lake," according to expedition member George Bradley. Conditions changed

IN THEIR OWN *Words*

e are now ready to start our way down the unknown. . . . We have but one month's rations remaining. . . . We are three quarters of a mile in the depths of the earth, and the great river shrinks into insignificance as it dashes its angry waves against the walls and cliffs that rise to the world above.

We have an unknown distance yet to run; an unknown river yet to explore.

—JOHN WESLEY POWELL, *EXPLORATION OF THE COLORADO RIVER OF THE WEST AND ITS TRIBUTARIES* (1875) dramatically with the rapids of Flaming Gorge, named for its fiery red sandstone walls. By June 7 the expedition had reached Lodore Canyon. One of the boats pitched over the falls and into the ferocious rapids, struck a boulder, and broke in half. The three men on board were somehow fished out of the boiling stream. "Had they drifted thirty feet further down nothing could have saved them, as the river was turned into a perfect hell of water that nothing could enter or live," wrote Jack Sumner. The boat and its contents were a total loss.

The flotilla cleared Lodore Canyon on June 18, entered Echo Park, and on the thirty-seventh day out, paused for rest and refit in the Uinta Valley. The men sent dispatches home and laid in supplies before resuming the journey on July 6. On July 17, at the junction of the Grand River 538 miles from the start

IN THEIR OWN *Words*

*A*t noon we came to the worst rapid yet seen. The water dashes against the left bank and then is thrown furiously back against the right. The billows are huge and I fear our boats could not ride them if we could keep them off the rocks. . . . This is decidedly the darkest day of the trip but I don't despair yet.

—GEORGE BRADLEY, JOURNAL ENTRY FOR AUGUST 27, 1869

point, Powell halted for a brief exploration of the surrounding country. "Wherever we look there is but a wilderness of rocks," he wrote; "deep gorges, where the rivers are lost below cliffs and towers and pinnacles; and ten thousand strangely carved forms in every direction; and beyond them the mountains blending with the clouds."

The expedition reached the San Juan River on July 31 ("a very rapid tide and quite muddy," Bradley observed), entered Glen Canyon (now inundated) on August 3, and passed the junction of the Little Colorado on August 10. Here before Powell lay the entrance to the Grand Canyon itself. With its rapids, cataracts, and obstructions, the river gave Powell and his men an even rougher and more exhilarating ride—a potentially deadly one too. "Pulled out at 7 o'clock and ran 14 miles, passing 20 rapids many of them bad," Sumner reported with understatement. The three surviving boats sped past Bright Angel Creek on August 16. On August 25, Powell recorded thirty-five miles in the expedition log. "A few days like this and we are out of prison," he wrote. Two days later, the prison almost became a wet grave: a rapids with a twenty-foot fall.

Three of Powell's men declared this rough stretch, today's Separation Rapids, impassable and decided to climb out of the canyon and walk to the Mormon settlements. The others shot the rapids safely the next day. As it happened, they were the last rapids on the river. Powell's band reached journey's end at Callville, where three Mormons were placidly fishing in the river, on August 31. There Powell learned that the three who had walked away were dead, struck down in a hail of Indian arrows on the Shivwits Plateau.

The Grand Canyon expedition attracted wide publicity and made Powell a national hero. He traded off his notoriety to arrange for a second expedition in the summer of 1872, this one a topographical survey of the canyon and plateau country of Colorado, Utah, and Arizona. The river flotilla stopped short of Powell's farthest advance in 1869, but land contingents carried out significant surveys of the country all around. These explorations yielded the last undiscovered river—the Escalante—and the last undiscovered mountain range—the Henry—in the United States.

Powell and his men made the first documented trips down the Colorado, and his topographical surveys produced the first accurate maps of thousands of square miles of virtually unknown country. Powell himself produced two important monographs, *Exploration of the Colorado River of the West* (1875) and *Report on the Geology of the Eastern Portion of the Uinta Mountains* (1876). These works, says William Goetzmann, "formed the basis for the development of an altogether new approach to geology"— the identification of natural processes that created the exotic and terrible canyon and plateau country.

Powell's enterprise and three other western surveys of the period were consolidated in 1879 into the *U.S. Geological Survey.* Powell headed the Washington, D.C.–based agency from 1881 to 1894. Goetzmann judges him "the greatest explorer-hero since the days of Frémont." During Powell's years as head of the Geological Survey, *Clarence Dutton* and others produced definitive studies of the American West. Historian Don D. Fowler thus characterizes Powell as "a prototype of the scientific entrepreneur, an advocate and creator of . . . government agencies devoted to scientific research, to be conducted for the public good."

Teamster turned expedition photographer Jack Hillers works on a self-portrait during John Wesley Powell's second Colorado River exploration in 1871–1872. The expedition yielded a topographical survey of virtually unexplored plateau and canyon country of Colorado, Utah, and Arizona.

Rocky Mountains

The most extensive mountain system of North America, the Rockies run in a jagged southeasterly direction from the Brooks Range of northwest

Alaska to northern New Mexico, forming the *Continental Divide* that separates east- and west-draining rivers. The highest peak in the chain is Mount Elbert, Colorado, at 14,433 feet.

Vásquez de Coronado's *[II]* army traversed southern and central sections of the Rockies in its great march of European discovery in 1540–1542. The *Lewis and Clark expedition* of 1804–1806 crossed the Bitterroot Range of the Rockies at Lolo Pass in Montana, the first American party to penetrate the mountains. The expeditions of *Zebulon Pike* (1806–1807), *Stephen Long* (1819–1820), *Benjamin Bonneville* (1832–1835), and *John Charles Frémont* (1843–1844) explored vast stretches of the American Rockies.

Alexander Mackenzie (1792–1793) marched northward in the lee of the eastern slopes of the Canadian Rockies on his journey to the Arctic Ocean in 1789. Mackenzie and his men became the first documented Europeans to cross the Canadian Rockies from the east on their expedition to the Pacific in 1793. *David Thompson* (1799–1803) and *Simon Fraser* (1803–1807) also carried out important explorations of the Canadian Rockies.

St. Louis

A major U.S. city on the west bank of the *Mississippi River [V]* below the mouth of the *Missouri River,* St. Louis from its founding has been the most important gateway to the North American west. The French trader Pierre Laclède chose the site of the modern city for a fur-trading outpost in 1763 and named it for Louis XI, the namesake of King Louis XV of France.

The French ceded St. Louis to Spain in 1770 and regained the settlement briefly before it came into U.S. possession with the *Louisiana Purchase* of 1803. Many trading and exploring expeditions fitted out in St. Louis and embarked from there. St. Louis merchants established the Company of Explorers of the Upper Missouri in 1793 and sent an expedition under Jean Baptiste Truteau to the Mandan Villages in the Dakotas in 1794. Perhaps the most famous American venture, the *Lewis and Clark expedition,* avoided the gateway town, however. With negotiations for the Louisiana Purchase in the balance, St. Louis remained in French control; the Americans passed the winter of 1803–1804 in camp on the Wood River on the Illinois side of the Mississippi.

St. Louis grew rapidly after the War of 1812 as American settlers flooded into the Mississippi and Missouri River valleys. St. Louis-based fur enterprises—most notably, the Missouri Fur Company and the Rocky Mountain Fur Company—helped open the western mountain country and beyond to U.S. exploration, trade and, eventually, settlement.

Sierra Nevada

A towering mountain range, the Sierra Nevadas stretch for some four hundred miles, mostly in eastern California, from Tehachapi Pass near present Bakersfield northwest to the Feather River near Chico. At 14,494 feet, Mount Whitney in the Sierra Nevadas is the highest peak in the continental United States.

Long a daunting barrier to east-west travel, the range rises steeply from the Great Basin in the east; the western slopes fall gently through foothills to the Central Valley. Donner Pass, at 7,089 feet, is the principal gap in the chain. By the 1840s thousands of migrants followed the *California Trail* through the Donner Pass and down to the rich valleys to the west.

The Spanish navigator *Juan Rodríguez Cabrillo [II]* caught sight of a looming white-topped mountain range from Monterey Bay in 1542. "It seems as if the mountains would fall upon the ships," an expedition chronicler wrote. "They are covered with snow to the summit, and they named them the Sierra Nevadas." The Spanish priest *Francisco Garcés [II]* approached the western slopes in an expedition to the Central Valley in 1776.

The American trapper/explorer *Jedediah Smith* made the first documented west-east crossing of the Sierra Nevadas at Ebbets Pass in May 1827. Joseph Reddeford Walker of *Bonneville*'s exploring expedition penetrated the mountains in 1833–1834, probably crossing at Mono Pass before dropping down into the Yosemite Valley.

Smith, Jedediah (1799–1831)

Born in Bainbridge, New York, Jedediah Smith migrated west in the early 1820s to enter the fur trade via *William H. Ashley*'s Rocky Mountain Fur Company. Smith and two colleagues took over Ashley's mountain operations in the mid-1820s. Ancillary to his business operations, Smith led important exploring forays into Wyoming, the Great Basin, California, and Oregon.

With seven veteran trappers, Smith pierced the *Rocky Mountains* at South Pass, Wyoming, in March 1824. He effectively "rediscovered" what would become the main trader/settler gateway to Oregon and California a dozen years after *Robert Stuart* made the first documented journey over South Pass. Then he pushed on northwestward, trapping industriously through present Montana as far as the Canadian line.

In perhaps his most important expedition, Smith set out from the Salt Lake in present Utah in August 1826 in a trading/exploring venture that sought to fill in some of the empty spaces on American maps of the Great Basin and interior southern California. With sixteen men, he penetrated the barrens of Utah and the Black Mountains of northwestern Arizona to reach the Mojave Indian country of the Colorado River Valley, then pushed on west along an old Indian trade route through the Mojave Desert, across the San Bernardino Mountains, and on to the Pacific, which he reached around the first of December.

Suspicious of the American party, the Mexican authorities detained Smith at San Gabriel through December and part of January before finally granting him permission to travel. Advancing slowly, trapping along the way, Smith pushed north through the San Joaquin Valley, reaching the American River in northern California in early May. He crossed the *Sierra Nevadas* at Ebbets Pass, struck east into the Great Basin and reached the Green River in July, in time for the annual trapper rendezvous there.

With the completion of the circuit, Smith had traced what would become the Old Spanish Trail to California; he and his party made, too, the first documented crossing of the Sierra Nevadas from west to east. After a pause to rest and refit, Smith set out on a second expedition to California. But the Mojaves proved inhospitable this time. A war party attacked Smith's band during a crossing of the Colorado, killing ten men. He reached Mexican territory with eight survivors; after another period of house arrest, the authorities allowed him to continue on north to San Francisco by sea.

By the end of December 1826, Smith had got clear of the Mexicans and was advancing slowly north along the California coast. Calamity struck again in the Umpqua Indian country of southern Oregon in mid-July 1827. With Smith and two others away on a hunting expedition, an Umpqua war party attacked the main camp and killed fourteen of the party—"the worst disaster in the history of the fur trade," according to historian William H. Goetzmann.

Smith escaped with three survivors to the haven of the *Hudson's Bay Company* post at *Fort Vancouver* on the *Columbia River.* Despite his travails, he saw immense potential in the Oregon Country. In an 1830 report to the U.S. secretary of war, he called Oregon a settler's paradise and noted that, based on his own explorations, traders and settlers could take wagons and livestock over South Pass as far as the "Great Falls" of the Columbia. Goetzmann calls Smith's report, together with those of his trapper colleagues Ashley and Joshua Pilcher, collectively "the first emigrant guide to the Far West."

Stuart, Robert   (1785–1848)

Born in Scotland, Robert Stuart emigrated to Canada in 1807 to become a fur trader. With his uncle David Stuart, he joined *John Jacob Astor*'s Pacific Fur Company venture and in 1811 reached the mouth of the *Columbia River* with the shipborne expedition that established the trading post of *Fort Astoria.*

In 1812 the partners at Astoria assigned Stuart the task of carrying dispatches overland to inform Astor in New York of the successful establishment of the Columbia post and other matters. With six men in a canoe, Stuart set out on June 29, 1812, on an epic journey of more than 3,500 miles on which he would make the first documented crossing of the *Rocky Mountains* at South Pass and trace the line of what would become the *Oregon Trail.*

The journey up the Columbia consumed a month. Finally, on July 31, Stuart's band pushed into the trackless foothills and barren landscape southeast of the river and advanced into the Blue Mountains, paused briefly in the delectable valley of the Grande Ronde, and reached the Snake River near present Farewell Bend State Park on August 12. They followed the south bank of the sinuous Snake under a scorching sun, with daytime temperatures soaring into the nineties. Food, water, and firewood were scarce until the Astorians reached the "Salmon Falls" and a village of Shoshone Indians. A brisk trade yielded salmon to fuel the onward journey for several days, but by early September food stocks were short again and the party had to subsist on trout, dried fish, and, from

Shoshone traders, "an excellent sort of cake made of pulverized roots and berries."

Stuart and his band survived a raid in which Crow Indians drove off the expedition's horses, and they proceeded, after a long detour on foot and aboard hastily assembled rafts into the bottomlands of the upper Snake River, toward what friendly Indians had described as an easy passage through the towering Rockies. Rations remained in critically short supply, and Stuart had to quell a near-mutiny when some of the men proposed drawing lots to kill and eat one of their number. By October 22 they had overcome hardship and dissension to reach South Pass, twenty miles wide, a series of hills rising gently to a summit at 7,550 feet above sea level. Beyond stretched a broad dry seemingly endless plain, along which, beginning in the 1840s, long convoys of westward-bound wagons would approach the gateway to the farther West.

The Astorians went into winter camp in early December along the North Platte River in central Wyoming. Buffalo were plentiful there—Stuart's hunters killed more than thirty on the first day. But the presence in the area of raiding Arapaho Indians persuaded Stuart to shift his base two weeks' march to the eastward, to a site near where the Oregon Trail would cross the present Nebraska-Wyoming border.

"We destroyed an immoderate quantity of Buffalo Tongues, Puddings, and the choicest of the meat," Stuart wrote in his journal. "Our stock of Virginia weed being totally exhausted, McLellan's tobacco pouch was cut up and smoked as a substitute, in commemoration of the New Year."

Stuart set out in mid-March 1813 on the final stages of the long march to the *Mississippi River [V]*. The Astorians arrived in *St. Louis* late in the afternoon of April 30 after a circuitous voyage of 3,768 miles and 306 days. Stuart then pushed off for New York City with news for Astor. The fur tycoon regarded the details of Stuart's discoveries as proprietary, although he did offer President *Jefferson* a copy of Stuart's account of his adventures. "You may have seen by the publick papers the arrival of Mr. Stuart & others from the Columbia," he wrote. "He kept a journal of his voyage . . . which he left with the President [James Madison] should you feel a desire to read it." Stuart said nothing, then or later, about Astor's suppression of the journal, leaving the "rediscovery" of the South Pass portal to Oregon and California to the *Jedediah Smith* expedition of 1824.

Sublette, William (1799?–1845)

Born in Kentucky, William Sublette migrated to the Missouri frontier around 1818 and within a few years entered the fur trade as an apprentice employee of *William H. Ashley* and *Andrew Henry.* In 1826 Sublette and two partners, *Jedediah Smith* and Donald Jackson, bought out Ashley's Rocky Mountain Fur Company and went into business for themselves.

On a trapping/exploring expedition with Smith, Sublette participated in the effective discovery of South Pass in March 1824. The long, gradual gap through the *Rocky Mountains* in southwestern Wyoming would become the main trade and migration route to Oregon and California.

In the summer of 1826 Sublette ventured into the Yellowstone region of southwestern Montana, the first documented European since *John Colter* to enter the precincts of today's national park. There he discovered the crystal-clear Yellowstone Lake and reported on the region's geysers and fountains. In 1830 Sublette led the first train of wagons along what would become the *Oregon Trail* through South Pass to the annual trappers' rendezvous in the Green River Valley.

Thompson, David (1770–1857)

Born in London, David Thompson came to Canada in 1784 as a *Hudson's Bay Company* apprentice. From Churchill on Hudson Bay, he explored and trapped as far west as Lake Athabasca in present Alberta and managed, as early as 1790, to undertake a serious study of mapmaking with the company's chief surveyor, Philip Turnor. He would use his skills to provide the first accurate rendering of the western regions of Canada.

Defecting to the rival *North West Company* in 1797, Thompson continued his explorations, mapping connecting routes to the company's chain of posts east of the *Rocky Mountains.* Known as "the astronomer" for the precision of his surveys, he discovered the headwaters of the Saskatchewan River and, beginning in 1806, penetrated the mountain passes west of the Saskatchewan and Athabasca Rivers. These journeys led to the founding of Kootenay House, the first fur-trading post on the *Columbia River,* in 1807.

Exploration and surveys of the upper Columbia and Kootenay Rivers occupied Thompson for three years. In 1807 he discovered the source of the Columbia in Columbia Lake in southeastern British Columbia. Returning east for a furlough in 1810, he received word at Rainy Lake that rival American fur traders were en route to the Columbia. "I was now obliged," he wrote, "to take 4 canoes and to proceed to the mouth of the Columbia to oppose them." Thus he set out to achieve his long-delayed main objective—the descent of the Columbia to its meeting with the sea.

Thompson set out late in 1810 for a difficult winter crossing of the Rockies. With hostile Piegan Indians barring the way to Howse Pass, the most direct route, he struck north for the gorges of the Athabasca River and began the ascent in bitter cold on December 30. The expedition reached Athabasca Pass on January 10, 1811, and wintered on the Wood River, the men taking shelter in a snow hut with split cedar sides.

Thompson's canoe nosed into Clark's Fork River, a tributary of the Columbia, on June 5. Three days later he unloaded for the long portage to Kettle Falls on the present British Columbia–Washington border, arriving there on June 19. Here his people built a canoe large and sturdy enough for the long descent of the Columbia. Starting on July 3, they swept downriver in a rush (a dizzying seventy miles on the first day of the voyage), and passed the mouth of the Snake River on the ninth. Soon Thompson caught sight of "a high mountain, isolated, of a conical form, a mass of pure snow without the appearance of a rock"—Mount Hood.

At The Dalles, the broad river contracted to a width of sixty yards, creating a maelstrom of foam and furious water. "Imagination can hardly form an idea of the working of this immense body of water under such a compression, raging and hissing as if alive," Thompson wrote. Hastily steering for shore, his *voyageurs* carried canoe and contents down the mile-long portage. Below The Dalles, he noted, the country seemed softer in appearance— greener and more fertile.

The expedition glimpsed the shining Pacific on July 15, 1811. Some of the men seemed disappointed with the scene. "Accustomed to the boundless horizons of the Great Lakes of Canada," Thompson wrote, "they expected a more boundless view, a something beyond the power of their senses which they could not describe." Thompson may have felt let-down too. His

IN THEIR OWN
Words

*T*hus I have fully completed the survey of this part of North America from sea to sea, and by almost innumerable astronomical Observations have determined the positions of the Mountains, Lakes and Rivers, and other remarkable places of the northern part of the continent.

—DAVID THOMPSON, *TRAVELS IN WESTERN NORTH AMERICA*

four-year sojourn on the upper Columbia would have fateful political consequences. He reached journey's end a few weeks after the arrival on the Columbia of **John Jacob Astor**'s shipborne party of Americans, who promptly founded the post of **Fort Astoria,** establishing a U.S. foothold in the Northwest. All the same, Thompson dutifully completed the journey, paddling the remaining miles from Astoria to Cape Disappointment.

Thompson later endured criticism for failing to win the "race" to the river mouth; historians now generally agree his orders never explicitly declared that he should arrive there ahead of the Americans.

Retiring from the field in 1812, Thompson settled outside **Montreal [V],** where he completed his master map of western Canada. He also surveyed the official U.S.–Canada boundary from the **St. Lawrence River [III]** to Lake of the Woods near the center of the continent. Altogether, he covered some 50,000 miles of western Canada and the northwestern United States in his explorations, and his exacting methods of observation yielded maps that were the most precise and accurate of their time.

In his last years, blind and ailing, Thompson committed his experiences to paper. Victor G. Hopwood's annotated edition of Thompson's narrative of his explorations, *Travels in Western North America,* appeared in 1971.

U.S. Geological Survey

A survey wagon creeps across sand dunes in the Carson Desert in the Great Basin in 1867, part of Clarence King's Survey of the Fortieth Parallel. The U.S. government sponsored the expedition, which surveyed a hundred-mile swath on either side of the route of the Transcontinental Railroad. Expedition photographer Timothy O'Sullivan made this image.

Established in 1879, with the mission of exploring the geology of the United States, the U.S. Geological Survey superseded the separate surveys of the geologist/explorers **Ferdinand Hayden, Clarence King, John Wesley Powell, George Wheeler,** and others. King won appointment as the new agency's first director.

Part of the Department of the Interior, the survey focused on practical economic issues: geological exploration, preparation of maps, inventories of natural resources, and land use problems. One of King's first projects, for example, involved a survey of the Comstock Lode in Nevada and Leadville, Colorado, silver-mining districts.

Powell replaced King as director and held the post until 1894.

Vancouver, George

(1758?–1798)

Born in King's Lynn, England, George Vancouver served as a seaman on *James Cook*'s *[IV]* second voyage and rose to command a Royal Navy exploring expedition to the coast of the Pacific Northwest in 1792. Vancouver's instructions were to search for the transcontinental water passage that *Juan de Fuca [II]* and other Spanish navigators had hinted about and to reestablish British claims, contested with Spain, to the rich fur-trading district of Nootka Sound along the coast of present British Columbia.

Vancouver reached the coast in his flagship *Discovery* in early in 1792 and explored northward from California. In late April he passed the mouth of the *Columbia River* without noticing it; the American *Robert Gray* would be the first to actually enter the river early in May. Vancouver pushed on to the north, surveying meticulously along the way. His explorations through 1794 revealed a series of islands from Puget Sound northwest to the outer Aleutians. Vancouver circumnavigated and charted the largest of the chain, a 12,408-square-mile island that would eventually be named for him.

Learning from the Spanish at Nootka that Gray had entered the river, Vancouver dispatched *Henry Broughton* in the tender *Chatham* south to confirm the discovery. In October 1792 Broughton explored and surveyed the Columbia for one hundred miles inland. Vancouver, meantime, satisfied himself that no viable water route led across the continent.

Vancouver published an account of the expedition, with charts, as *A Voyage of Discovery to the North Pacific Ocean* in 1798.

IN THEIR OWN *Words*

I trust the precision with which the survey of the coast of North West America has been carried into effect will set aside every opinion of a north-west passage. No small portion of facetious mirth passed among the seamen in consequence of our sailing . . . for the purpose of discovering a north-west passage, by following up the discoveries of De Fuca, De Fonte, and a numerous train of hypothetical navigators.

—GEORGE VANCOUVER, *A VOYAGE OF DISCOVERY TO THE NORTH PACIFIC OCEAN* (1798)

Warren, Gouverneur Kemble

(1830–1882)

A native of New York State and an 1850 graduate of West Point, Gouverneur Warren compiled important maps and reports that went into the exhaustive thirteen-volume *Pacific Railroad surveys* of the mid-1850s.

Warren extensively surveyed and mapped the Dakota and Nebraska territories. As a result, he produced the first accurate and detailed map of the entire trans-Mississippi West, which incorporated knowledge gained from the railroad surveys. The historian William H. Goetzmann called Warren's map a great scientific achievement and one of the most important maps in American history.

Warren later served in the Civil War, commanding a corps in the Union Army of the Potomac.

Wheeler, George M. (1842–1905)

The Massachusetts-born George Wheeler graduated from the U.S. Military Academy in 1866. A strong record at West Point and, perhaps more important, a politically advantageous marriage to a granddaughter of Republican political power Francis P. Blair, led to his assignment in 1869 to "instrumentally explore" desert regions of Utah and Nevada.

This apprenticeship, successfully executed, won for Wheeler command of a far more extensive army exploration and mapping project in 1871 that would evolve into the United States Geological Surveys West of the 100th Meridian, encompassing fully a third of the country beyond a line running from North Dakota south through Texas. The surveys had military, economic, and scientific dimensions. The army sought accurate maps of Paiute and Apache country in the Southwest for operational purposes. In addition, Wheeler's orders bade him to study the country's inhabitants, assess its agricultural and mineral potential, and scout transportation routes.

With soldiers, civilian scientists, photographer Timothy O'Sullivan, and journalist Frederick W. Loring, the first of Wheeler's fourteen exploring and surveying expeditions of the 1870s set out for southwestern Nevada in early May 1871. In his travels, the young soldier-engineer would overlap with the civilian enterprises of *Clarence King, John Wesley Powell,* and *Frederick Hayden.* The presence of a photographer and a writer and the wide distribution of their pictures and stories would—so Wheeler fondly expected—draw attention to his survey and build political and public support for it.

Wheeler divided his expedition into detachments that struck out for different points of the compass, with general instructions to reunite in the region of Death Valley, California. Wheeler's band reached the valley's alkali flats in July. "The stifling heat, great radiation, and constant glare from the sand were almost overpowering," he would write in his report, "and two of the command succumbed near nightfall" in temperatures that approached 120 degrees.

Wheeler struck east and north from Death Valley to explore the Colorado River, which Powell had surveyed before him in expeditions of 1869 and 1871. Pushing upstream in small boats, Wheeler attempted to determine the head of navigation on the Colorado and to survey potential wagon routes. By mid-October, after a hard pull, he had completed this reconnaissance as far as the mouth of Diamond Creek.

So far, Wheeler had carried out a scouting expedition not markedly different from those of *Frémont* and other army predecessors of the 1840s and 1850s. By 1873, however, under pressure from competing civilian expeditions, he concentrated on scientific surveying and mapping, with separate parties advancing eastward from southern California and westward from Denver, Colorado.

Congress took up the issue of duplication in 1874. The War Department sought to assert control over all the competing surveys. Powell, Hayden, and their allies in Congress fought back, using all the political power they could muster on behalf of "Civilian Science." Congress determined that Wheeler had deliberately encroached on territories other surveys were covering. Perhaps unfairly, Powell and Hayden attacked Wheeler's work as inaccurate. The politicians refused to intervene right away, however, and the surveys continued along parallel lines until 1879. By then Wheeler had completed the definitive exploration of eastern Arizona and Nevada, including Death Valley.

Notable achievements of the 100th Meridian Surveys included discovery of ancient rock beds of northern New Mexico with remains of early animal life; the complete survey and mapping of Death Valley; a detailed study of the Comstock Lode and other mining districts; and the remapping of the Lake Tahoe region in the *Sierra Nevadas.* Congress ordered the consolidation of competing surveys in 1879 under the direction of King and the *U.S. Geological Survey.* With the conclusion of Wheeler's project came the effective end of army exploration of the West.

IN THEIR OWN *Words*

The main object of this exploration will be to obtain topographical knowledge of the country, and to prepare accurate maps. It is at the same time intended that you ascertain as far as practicable everything relating to the physical features of the country, the numbers, habits, and disposition of the Indians, the selection of such sites as may be of use for future military operations or occupation, and the facilities offered for making rail or common roads, to meet the wants of those who at some future period may occupy or traverse this part of our territory.

—GENERAL ANDREW A. HUMPHREYS TO GEORGE M. WHEELER, 1871

Wilkes exploring expedition (1838–1842)

A seaborne exploring expedition under Navy Lieutenant Charles Wilkes sailed from Hampton Roads, Virginia, in August 1841 in what would become the most significant and far-ranging reconnaissance the United States government had attempted up to that time. The government organized the venture with the express purpose of aiding American commerce, particularly trade with Asia and the Pacific Ocean whale and seal fisheries.

Wilkes's six-vessel flotilla cruised the Southern Hemisphere from 1838 to 1841, including a hazardous two-month investigation of 1,500 miles of Antarctic coast that established that these frozen wastes in fact formed a new continent. Wilkes and his surveyors also mapped and charted vast stretches of the Pacific—documents American military planners would consult a century later in island operations against the Japanese.

Wilkes's flagship, the sloop USS *Vincennes,* approached the bar of the **Columbia River** in late April 1841; rough waters there led Wilkes prudently to sheer off and bear north to Puget Sound. There he divided his forces, sending one of the vessels north into the Straits of Georgia beyond Vancouver Island while the *Vincennes* explored and surveyed Puget Sound and its hinterland.

Wilkes also dispatched a series of overland exploring expeditions. One struck east and north as far as Kettle Falls on the Columbia, a second pushed due south from Fort Nisqually to the Columbia, and a third marched southwest to Grays Harbor on the coast of present Washington. Despite losing one of his vessels, the sloop *Peacock,* on the ferocious Columbia bar, Wilkes completed a detailed survey of the river, improving upon **Henry Broughton**'s work done in 1792. Overall, Wilkes charted eight hundred miles of Oregon rivers and coastline. And he sent a fourth expedition overland from **Fort Vancouver** through southern Oregon to the Sacramento country of Mexican California.

The expedition returned to the United States in 1842. The venture had political repercussions in hardening American resolve to establish a line through Puget Sound as the boundary between the United States and British Canada. It also yielded masses of data on ethnography, botany, geology, hydrography, and meteorology, eventually published in nineteen volumes, and specimens collected on the expedition formed the basis of the Smithsonian Institution's collection. Wilkes himself eventually published a five-volume *Narrative of the United States Exploring Expedition.*

Charles Wilkes in a photograph made during the Civil War. Shore parties from Wilkes's seaborne exploring expedition surveyed parts of the Oregon Territory in 1841; Wilkes's surveys were later joined with those of the 1843 overland expedition of John Charles Frémont.

Yellowstone expeditions (1869–1871)

Trapper *John Colter* is credited with the discovery in 1808 of the wild and spectacular region now preserved within the boundaries of the Yellowstone National Park. Trapper *William Sublette* was another early visitor. Soldier William Raynolds and mountain man *Jim Bridger* skirted the region in 1859–1860, though they failed to penetrate the area of the park.

Three civilians carried out a prospecting journey into Yellowstone in 1869, prompting the government to organize a formal exploring expedition the next year. In August 1870 Lieutenant Gustavus C. Doane led a combined soldier-civilian party into the area. Doane and his men examined Yellowstone Lake, which Sublette had visited in 1826, as well as thermal springs, lava flows, and geysers; they reached and named the most spectacular steam jet of all Old Faithful.

Separate exploring parties returned to Yellowstone in 1871, one a civilian enterprise under *Ferdinand V. Hayden,* the second an army operation led by Captain J. W. Barlow. Both parties set out from Fort Ellis north of the park within a day or so of one another in mid-July. Barlow followed the route Doane had taken the year before, then struck into new country, discovering Heart Lake south of the much larger Yellowstone Lake. He later produced the first accurate map of the region.

Hayden's party reached Mammoth Hot Springs, then ascended Mount Washburn to the east for extensive views of the Yellowstone Basin and the *Grand Teton Mountains.* In August, Hayden discovered and examined the Upper Geyser Basin north of Old

The Hayden Expedition packs into the Yellowstone area in 1871 in William Henry Jackson's photograph. Ferdinand Hayden led the first scientific expeditions to penetrate what is today Yellowstone National Park.

Faithful. Expedition artist Thomas Moran sketched the Grand Canyon of the Yellowstone, while W. H. Jackson made photographs of Mammoth Hot Springs, the canyon, and the geysers.

The exploring parties were nearly unanimous in recommending that the government preserve the Yellowstone region. It became the first national park in the world in 1872.

PART VII

The Arctic and Northernmost Regions, 1576–1992

For citizens of the United States, the Arctic and sub-Arctic region is the least known and last-to-be-explored territory of North America. Yet it can be argued that European discovery and exploration of many of the geographic features of this part of North America has been essential to the larger story of Europeans' opening up of the continent. In particular, the search for the Northwest Passage—a direct water route from the Atlantic to Asia—played a crucial role in the discovery of many of the other locales and features treated earlier in this volume, so it is only fitting that an overview of this subject has an entry of its own (Northwest Passage), as well as many entries on the individuals and expeditions associated with this search.

Two other major searches also dominate the story of Arctic exploration. One is the search for, or more aptly the race to, the North Pole. Again, this is treated in its own entry (North Pole) as well as in many entries on individuals and expeditions. The third major search is that for the lost expedition of Sir John Franklin; this episode begins with the entry for Franklin himself and then unfolds in several other entries. The stories of these searches, along with many other entries, often overlap in time— or even precede—events detailed in some of the previous sections, but

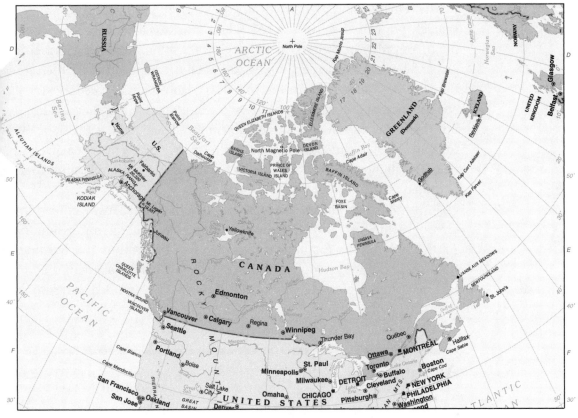

The vast northern tier of North America extends from Canada to the North Pole
and from Alaska to Greenland.

there is a unity that underlies the discovery and exploration of this vast region that justifies grouping all the entries relating to it into one part.

Only in the late nineteenth century did explorers begin to understand the proper way of moving overland on icy terrain. When they realized this, for the first time they began to understand the true nature of the north. Explorer Vilhjalmur Stefansson described the Arctic as a friendly, cozy place, abundant with everything needed for human survival, and when explorers came to see the Arctic as a living place of strange and wonderful beauty, they also began to change the way they related to the Inuit. Only when they could see their guides and helpers as men who had adapted to, and learned to live in harmony with, their fearsome environment, could they in the truest sense be said to have mastered the north.

Something else needs to be pointed out about this part's coverage. Nearly half the total area of the Arctic and sub-Arctic region belongs to

Russia. Furthermore, whereas Canada, Alaska, and Greenland are very sparsely populated above, say, 65° N latitude, Russia actually can point to major population centers in the region such as Murmansk and cities across Siberia. Clearly then, Russia has had more than a passing interest in the Arctic and sub-Arctic realm. Understandably it has devoted most of its energies across the centuries to its own sector and the Eurasian landmass, but there was a period of some two hundred years when Russians also took an active role in exploring in North America. This has been given little notice in most books accessible to English readers but this volume tries to remedy that.

Although not all the explorations described here involved extreme environmental conditions, there is validity to the general impression that Arctic explorations require a special kind of dedication and hardiness (and some would say, foolhardiness!). Perhaps the final element that distinguishes this region is that its "age of discovery" extended well into the twentieth century and indeed may said to be still going on.

Amundsen, Roald (1872–1928)

A new generation of Arctic explorers, from a number of nations, set out in the early twentieth century to conquer the *Northwest Passage* and traverse the deadly, ice-clogged waterway from coast to coast. Although individuals had discovered parts of the route, no one had as yet been able to guide a ship through the tangle of islands, straits, and frequently frozen waterways from Baffin Bay to the Bering Strait. It was the Norwegian explorer Roald Amundsen who in 1906 finally achieved that long-sought goal.

Born in a small village near Oslo, Norway, Amundsen came from a family of prosperous merchant sea captains and ship owners, and from his boyhood he had dreamed of becoming a polar explorer. His mother wanted him to become a doctor, so he began to study medicine, but when both his parents died by the time he was twenty-one, he left school determined to achieve his ambition: to be the first to sail from the Atlantic to the Pacific through the Northwest Passage, as well as to be the first man to reach both the North and South Poles. In preparation for these achievements he first undertook the task of becoming an accomplished seaman. In 1894 he shipped out on a polar seal-hunting vessel, and in 1897 he sailed on a Belgian-financed expedition to Antarctica. By 1899 he had obtained the rank of ship's master and achieved valuable cold-weather sailing experience. Then realizing that he needed a scientific purpose for his explorations, he studied magnetic science; one of his stated objectives was to find the magnetic north pole, which had moved since its initial locating by *James Clark Ross* in 1831, and determine the mechanics of its movement.

By spring 1903 Amundsen had raised sufficient funds to purchase his ship, the *Gjøa,* and five years of provisions. He was now prepared to set off in search of the Northwest Passage. The *Gjøa* left Oslo harbor on June 16, 1903, under cover of darkness, escaping creditors who threatened to seize the ship and stop the voyage. The voyagers passed by *Greenland [I]* and *Baffin Island* before passing into Lancaster Sound. After surviving several nearly fatal storms, in late 1903 Amundsen reached safe harbor at the southern tip of King William Island and prepared to wait out the rapidly approaching winter. In fact, Amundsen and his party were frozen in by the ice at "Gjøa Haven" for the next eighteen months, but the time there was well spent. Amundsen erected a "magnetic observatory" of packing cases held together with copper nails (which would not disturb the delicate recording instruments). Here he fulfilled his scientific obligations and definitively documented the new position of the magnetic north pole. He also collected extensive meteorological data and, with his crew, made an eight-hundred-mile trip by sledge mapping the eastern coastline of Victoria Island as far north as Cape Nansen. The two winters were spent comfortably, despite the −60°F temperature, and food was plentiful, thanks to the herds of caribou nearby. A group of Netsilik Eskimo families settled nearby, and Amundsen learned much about the survival skills necessary for life in the Arctic. The two groups lived in complete harmony, and it was with sadness on both sides that on August 18, 1905, the *Gjøa* pulled out of Gjøa Haven.

The next two weeks were spent navigating the unknown portions of the western passage. They traveled through the rock-studded shallows of Simpson Strait and the twists and turns of the iceberg-riddled channels of Queen Maud Gulf. At times there were only inches of water under the *Gjøa's* keel, and at other times sudden storms threatened to drive them onto the rocky coast. Finally, they sailed into the calm and deep water of Coronation Gulf; at this point they knew they had clear passage through the gulf (eventually to be named after Amundsen) to the Beaufort Sea and they would have completed their voyage through the Northwest Passage.

However, before the *Gjøa* could reach the Bering Strait, thick ice closed in, and the explorers were forced to spend yet another year trapped in the ice. However, determined to announce his achievement, Amundsen set off with dog sleds across the icefields of northern Alaska and traveled over five hundred miles to reach a telegraph station at Eagle City, Alaska, in December 1905. He then returned to his ship, and it was August 31, 1906, before the *Gjøa* arrived at Nome, Alaska, to a wildly cheering, jubilant crowd.

Amundsen's next goal, to be the first to reach the **North Pole,** was achieved by **Peary** (or **Cook**) before he could get his ship, the *Fram* (borrowed from **Nansen**) to the edge of the Arctic, so he simply changed his course and headed for Antarctica. On December 14, 1911, using all the travel techniques he had learned from the Eskimos, Amundsen planted the Norwegian flag at the South Pole, but the recognition he earned as the first man to get there was tarnished by the scorn of the scientific community for his ungraceful treatment of Robert Scott, who arrived at the pole thirty-five days after Amundsen's conquest. Amundsen's personality, fiery and outspoken, had often been the cause of public criticism, and he was never a popular public figure.

His next expedition was postponed because of World War I, and his voyage through the Northeast Passage across the top of Russia in the

IN THEIR OWN *Words*   The Northwest Passage Achieved!

We left our camp on August 13, 1905, and set sail through Simpson Strait. Much of this coast had been mapped by earlier explorers who had traveled to it by land from Hudson Bay, but no vessel had heretofore troubled these waters or charted their shallows. . . .Day after day, for three weeks—the longest three weeks of my life—we crept along, sounding our depth with the lead, trying here, there, and everywhere to nose into a channel. . . . Every nerve was strained to the limit to foresee every danger and to avoid every pitfall. We must succeed!

"A sail! A sail!"

We had succeeded. What a glorious sight that was—the distant outlines of a whaling vessel in the west! It meant the end of years of hope and toil, for that vessel had come from San Francisco through Bering Strait and along the north coast of Alaska. . . . Victory was ours!

—ROALD AMUNDSEN, *MY LIFE AS AN EXPLORER,* 1927

Maud (1918–1920)—Nils Nordenskjöld was the first to have accomplished this (1878–1879), but Amundsen was the first to chart it—brought him little fame but much financial trouble. Bankrupt, slandered by the press, and alienated from his family, Amundsen seemed to be a has-been as he tried to pay off his debts by lecturing to half-empty halls in the United States. His career was revived by a telephone call from an American millionaire sportsman, Lincoln Ellsworth, who proposed a flight over the North Pole; Amundsen enthusiastically agreed to the plan. On May 21, 1925, a first attempt was made in two open-cockpit seaplanes, which reached as close as 160 miles from the pole before engine trouble ended the flight. Amundsen and Ellsworth made a second attempt in the *Norge,* a gas-filled airship piloted by Colonel Umberto Nobile; this time, on May 11, 1926, the airship passed over the North Pole, and Amundsen symbolically dropped a small Norwegian flag onto the crumpled sea of ice below. (**Richard Byrd** and Floyd Bennett had been the first to fly over the pole, only two days before Amundsen—although this claim has since been disputed.)

Amundsen and Nobile became engaged in a feud by the time Nobile attempted a flight to the pole on his own in 1928. But when his airship went down northeast of Spitzbergen and Nobile survived, Amundsen was the first to undertake a rescue mission. He left Tromsø, Norway, for Spitzbergen on June 18, 1928, in a seaplane in the company of Lief Dietrichson, his pilot from his first attempted polar flight, and four other men. The plane was never seen again. Amundsen's stormy career ended fittingly on an ennobling mission of mercy.

Anderson, William (1921–)

William Anderson was born in Tennessee, attended the U.S. Naval Academy, and graduated in 1942 after his class "accelerated" due to the United States' entry into World War II. He joined the submarine branch and saw active duty in World War II and the Korean War. After being recruited by Admiral Hyman Rickover, in 1957 he was given command of the first nuclear submarine, the USS *Nautilus;* with its reactor-powered engine, its range was practically unlimited, and its various life-support systems enabled the sub to stay submerged for more than a month. Anderson made a first try for the **North Pole** in 1957; however, he had to rely on dead

The U.S.S. *Nautilus,* the first nuclear-powered submarine, was commissioned in 1955. Under the command of William Anderson, on August 3, 1958, it became the first submarine to pass under the North Pole.

reckoning and gyroscopic and magnetic compasses for navigation, and at 87° N these instruments failed. Anderson realized that a new system was needed, and in 1958 a new inertial, self-contained navigational system was installed on the *Nautilus* and her sister ship, the *Skate.* In June 1958 the *Nautilus* made two attempts, which failed because of the thickness—more than a hundred feet—of the ice on the continental ice shelf. In July the *Nautilus* set off from Pearl Harbor, made its way through the Bering Strait into the Chukchi Sea, and then found a passage into a deep valley that led to the deep basin of the Arctic Ocean. Two days later Anderson spoke through the public address system of the *Nautilus* to its crew of 115 men: "Stand by . . . Mark! August 3, 1958. For the World, Our Country, and the Navy—the North Pole." He then transmitted a top-secret message to the navy department: "Nautilus 90 North." Anderson was transported off the *Nautilus* by helicopter and then flown to Washington to meet President Eisenhower and Admiral Rickover, then rejoined his crew in England, where the *Nautilus* had docked after emerging from the Arctic Ocean near the Svalbard (Spitzbergen) Islands. After retiring from the navy, Anderson served four terms as a U.S. representative from Tennessee. The *Nautilus*'s successful transpolar voyage was a momentous signal that a new age was upon the world. (On March 17, 1959, its sister submarine, the USS *Skate,* became the first ship to surface at the North Pole.) After years of active service, the *Nautilus* was decommissioned in 1980, and designated as a National Historic Landmark, it was taken in 1985 to its permanent station at Groton, Connecticut.

Back, George   (1795–1878)

George Back was born at Stockport, Cheshire County, England, and joined the Royal Navy in 1808. During Britain's war against Napoleonic France, he was captured and spent five years in a French prison. Returning to naval duty, in 1818 he joined young *John Franklin* on an expedition around Spitzbergen, and the next year, Franklin invited him to join his overland expedition from Hudson Bay to the Coppermine River. During that disastrous expedition, Back became separated from Franklin, and he had to cover over 1,100 miles on snowshoes with the temperature frequently at –40°. Promoted to lieutenant, Back returned to sea, but in 1825 he was invited to accompany Franklin on another expedition to seek out a possible *Northwest Passage.* The expedition did not succeed in this goal, but at least it did not end in a tragedy. In 1833 Back led a search expedition for *John Ross,* who had not been heard from since the summer of 1829; Ross made it back to England on his own, while Back spent two grueling winters in the Arctic. In 1836 he led another survey expedition to the eastern shore of Prince Regent Inlet; his ship, the *Terror,* became trapped in an ice field for nine months, and only superhuman efforts by Back and his crew saved it from destruction. Back returned to England in 1837, but his health had suffered greatly from his Arctic exertions. He was knighted in 1839 and promoted to admiral, but he never again saw active service.

Baffin, William   (1584?–1622)

Little is known of the English seaman William Baffin's early years, but by 1612 he was the navigator on an expedition that surveyed the west coast of *Greenland [I].* In 1615 he sailed as navigator under *Robert Bylot* on the *Discovery* in search of the *Northwest Passage* (and the abandoned *Henry Hudson*). After sailing through the Hudson Strait and into the Foxe Channel and the Frozen Strait, they determined it was not the Northwest Passage. In 1616 Baffin again sailed with Robert Bylot on the *Discovery,* and on this expedition they explored Baffin Bay and Lancaster, Smith, and Jones Sounds. They also surveyed the east coast of *Baffin Island* and were the first known Europeans to reach *Ellesmere Island.* Sailing into the

IN THEIR OWN Words — The Futility of Seeking a Northwest Passage

Therefore briefly thus, and as it were in the forefront, I entend to shew the whole proceeding of the voyage in a word: as namely, there is no passage nor hope of passage in the north of Davis Straights. We having coasted all, or neere all the circumference thereof, and finde it to be no other than a great bay, as the voyage doth truly shew. Wherefore I cannot but much admire the worke of the Almigtie, when I consider how vaine the best and chiefest hopes of men are in thinges uncertaine;. and to speake of no other than the hopeful passage to the North-West. How many of the best sort of men have set their whole endeavoures to prove a passage that wayes? not only in conference but also in writing and publishing to the world. ye, what great summes of money have been spent about that action, as you worship hath costly experience of.

—WILLIAM BAFFIN, LETTER TO SIR JOHN WOLSTENHOLME,
ONE OF CHIEF INVESTORS IN HIS FIFTH VOYAGE, 1616

Smith Sound, between Greenland and Ellesmere Island, they went to 78° north, the farthest north of any known Europeans in the Western Hemisphere until 1853. After 1616 Baffin moved on to expeditions in the Red Sea and Persian Gulf; he was killed in the siege of Hormoz. Publication of Baffin's journals and charts was greatly uneven, so that for some two centuries he went without recognition for his explorations; later, too, some would credit him as the first to determine a degree of longitude by lunar observation.

Baffin Island

At 183,810 square miles (476,068 sq km), Baffin Island is the fifth-largest island in the world. The easternmost island of the Arctic Archipelago, it is separated by the Hudson Strait from *Labrador [III],* of which it is geologically an extension, and from *Greenland [I]* by the Davis Strait and Baffin Bay. Its coastline is deeply indented and has many fjords. Its eastern side is marked by mountains, some rising to over 8,000 feet; its western side is covered with tundra. The Paleoeskimos who first settled there, perhaps as early as 400 B.C., are assigned to the Dorset Culture, which takes its name from Baffin Island's Cape Dorset, where the first remains were found; these people were succeeded by the Thule Culture around A.D. 1100. The *Norse [I]* knew it as *Helluland [I]* and went ashore on several occasions, but the explorer who reintroduced it into the consciousness of Europeans was *Martin Frobisher,* the English navigator. He first explored the region around the bay that bears his name in 1576. He returned in 1577 to search for gold on the Hall Peninsula, which forms the north side of Frobisher Bay; Frobisher, thinking he was on some part of Asia, claimed the entire region for Queen Elizabeth. He made a third voyage to this southwestern corner of Baffin Island and added still more details (many incorrect), but it was another English explorer of the Arctic, *William Baffin,* for whom the island is named. European fishermen of various nationalities, particularly Scottish whalers, visited Baffin Island over the ensuing centuries, and during 1883–1884, Franz Boas, a young German, spent the year living and studying with the native Inuit and drew on his experiences to launch his career as a founder of modern anthropology. Since April 1999 Baffin Island has belonged to the Inuit-controlled Nunavut Territory.

Baranov, Alexander Andreevich (1747–1819)

A successful entrepreneur in Russia and Siberia, Alexander Baranov moved on to Alaska in 1790 and established a series of trading posts in the Kodiak Island region. These activities led to his appointment in 1799 as the first manager of the newly established Russian-American Company, making him, in effect, governor of the Russian settlements in North America. (See *Russians in North America.*) Baranov often abused the indigenous peoples of Alaska, but he proved to be an energetic administrator of Russia's interests in North America, founding shipbuilding, smelting, and coal-mining industries. He should also be given credit for providing schools for the native Alaskans. In the early 1790s he had sailed on several expeditions that explored the coast of Alaska, and as governor he sponsored expeditions that explored the coastal regions of the Pacific. He was removed from his post in Alaska in 1818, and, sailing home by way of the Pacific, he became ill and died off Java. One of the islands of the Alexander Archipelago in the Gulf of Alaska is named after him.

Bartlett, Robert A.

(1875–1946)

Robert Abram Bartlett, "Captain Bob," was born in Brigus, Newfoundland, Canada. His mother enrolled him in a Methodist college to become a minister, but he so loved the life of the sea that he instead embarked on the six-year apprenticeship that would earn him his master's papers. In 1896 Bartlett signed on as mate with his uncle, John Bartlett, who had for some years been sailing for **Robert Peary** on his Arctic expeditions. Bartlett went to the far north with Peary for the first time in 1898, and he impressed Peary with his fortitude, his seamanship, and his aptitude for learning the survival techniques of the Arctic. When Peary's new ship the *Roosevelt* (in which he intended to make his assault on the **North Pole**) was ready in 1905, he asked Bartlett to be the captain. At this time Bartlett was only thirty, but he had proven his worth to Peary. Bartlett was an excellent dog sledge driver and knew the ways and the language of the Eskimo. Physically, he was strong and tireless and seemed almost immune to the bitter cold weather. Captain Bob was an interesting personality, as well. A congenial man, he loved to tell yarns and often held the men spellbound with his tales of seafaring adventures. But the strength of character of Bartlett had a darker side; he was a man of inflexible judgment and sometimes could not be reasoned with. This stubbornness was to bring about tragic results in his captaincy of the *Karluk* at a later time.

When Peary set forth in 1905 in the new *Roosevelt* with Bartlett as skipper, he fully expected to reach the North Pole. The *Roosevelt* was specially designed: It drove up over the ice and then plunged down on it—breaking through from above with the weight of the ship. This maneuver required the greatest skill on the part of the skipper, and Bartlett was up to the task. When the *Roosevelt* was finally frozen in, Bartlett was part of the land expedition that reached the tip of **Greenland [I],** crossed over the Kane Basin and around the northern extremity of **Ellesmere Island** to within sight of Axel Heiberg Island. The party could go no further; retreat was ordered. After dealing with devastating storms, fire, dynamite damage, and a broken rudder in a gale, Bartlett brought the expedition safely back to New York. He had guided the ship to 82°20', farther north than any ship had ever gone before.

In 1908 Bartlett was again captain of the *Roosevelt* for Peary's final and successful attempt at the North Pole. Peary's method was to use a series of advance parties breaking the trail and leaving supplies for an ever-diminishing final assault team. Bartlett was in command of the last support sledge party to turn back, at 87°48', 150 miles from the pole. With frozen face and blackened frostbitten wrists, he reluctantly retreated as Peary, *Henson,* and four Eskimos went on to the great prize. Although he was in despair at the time, he later publicly acknowledged the necessity of Peary's strategy. Bartlett received the Hubbard Medal, the highest award of the National Geographic Society, for his participation in the mission.

In 1913 Bartlett was the captain of the *Karluk* for *Vilhjalmur Stefansson,* on a mission to the Canadian Arctic via the Bering Strait. Disregarding Stefansson's advice, Bartlett sailed too close to shore and was trapped in the ice ten miles off the northern coast of Alaska. A violent storm came up suddenly, and the *Karluk* was carried out to sea, never to be seen again by Stefansson, who had gone ashore to hunt for much-needed caribou. Bartlett and twenty-five crewmen drifted helplessly in the pack ice for more than a thousand miles to the northwest; the *Karluk* was fatally crushed near Wrangel Island and went down. Bartlett stayed on board until the end. He played his phonograph and read the *Rubaiyat.* As the *Karluk* began to settle and waves were washing onto the upper deck, he put on Chopin's *Funeral March* and at the last second leapt to the ice. Eventually, Bartlett was able to leave Wrangel Island to get help for the starving party, and with one Inuit companion, he walked almost seven hundred miles to a Siberian community where he was able to summon help. Half of the crew left on Wrangel Island survived; eleven died from starvation, scurvy, or despair.

In 1917 Bartlett headed a rescue mission to successfully bring back *Donald MacMillan* and the other members of the Croker Land Expedition. MacMillan had been with Bartlett on Peary's second polar attempt. In 1925 Bartlett acquired the schooner *Morrissey,* and until his death, he continued his Arctic explorations, completing twenty voyages into the North on archaeological, geographical, and zoological missions.

Bering, Vitus (1681–1741)

Vitus Bering was born in Denmark in 1681 and was twenty-three when he entered the Russian naval service. During the next twenty years he acquired extensive knowledge of the Far Eastern waters and became a master of navigation. He formed many friendships with men of power and influence in government, and these friendships served him well in his later years of exploration. Bering was a man of great personal strength and integrity; and although he was not a particularly dynamic leader, his command was strengthened by the addition of two assistants, Martin Spanberg and Alexei Chirikov. Following an unsuccessful Russian expedition to Kamchatka Peninsula in 1719, in 1724 Peter the Great gave his orders to Bering and provided him with all the projected required financial backing. Bering was to proceed to Kamchatka and build a boat. He was then to sail the boat north along the northeast coast of Siberia and determine if and where that coast joined the coast of America. Further, he was to contact any settlements and/or sailing ships encountered and obtain detailed information, make charts, and then to return all data and material to St. Petersburg as quickly as possible. Peter the Great died shortly after signing the orders; however, the plans set in motion by him were not only carried forward by successive czars but were eventually considerably extended.

The task set for Bering was formidable: The sea voyage through frozen, uncharted waters was bad enough. But first it was necessary to get to Kamchatka Peninsula and the Pacific Ocean from the Baltic Sea, five thousand miles away, separated by frozen coastline and impenetrable swamps, frozen tundra, unclimbable mountains, and hostile Siberian tribes. Everything that would be needed for the boatbuilding, other than the timber, had to be brought along. Bering left St. Petersburg in late 1724, traveling east from the Baltic Sea, toward the Kara Sea. The expedition was forced inland; the winter of 1725–1726 was spent at Ilimsk. The village of Yakutsk, deep in the interior and surrounded by swamps and high mountains, was reached by June 1726. The final overland stage to Okhotsk, on the shore of the sea of that name, took a great toll of baggage horses (and some men) from cold and starvation. Finally, a small boat was built in Okhotsk, and the explorers sailed to Kamchatka, where they crossed the peninsula on foot and built another boat, the *St. Gabriel*. Bering was now positioned at the southeast edge of Kamchatka, where the voyage was to begin. It was nearly four years since he had left St. Petersburg.

Bering sailed north through what would later be named the Bering Sea and found and named the island of St. Lawrence. An encounter with some Chukchi seagoing tribesmen provided Bering with the information that following the coastline would bring him back eventually to westward and to the mouth of the Kolyma River. If this information was correct,

Bering reasoned, then he would have rounded the northeastern tip of Russia (East Cape) and so proved that there was no land connection between Russia and America. But winter was approaching; the party was at 65°20' latitude, and Bering turned back to Kamchatka. He had in fact been in the strait that would also be named after him, and had it not been for persistent heavy fog, he would have seen Asia to the west and America to the east.

When Bering returned to St. Petersburg, he was chastised for not proving conclusively that Russia and America were not connected, and his pay was withheld. But Bering's many supporters at court came to his aid, and soon after he was put in charge of a grandiose plan to explore and map all the Arctic regions from the Baltic Sea to the East Cape: the Great Northern Expedition.

Bering served this ambitious project as administrator but was not very active in the actual exploration. The work began in 1734 and was essentially completed in 1742. It was conducted in a scientific manner, as a nationally directed, long-sustained project in Arctic exploration; it was largely very successful. Bering made one final journey in 1741, reaching Alaska late in that year; among other discoveries, he was the first European to sight Mount St. Elias, the fourth-highest peak in North America. The return voyage was disastrous; Bering, beset by scurvy, age, and despair, wrecked his ship, the *St. Peter,* at one of the Aleutian Islands (also later named after him). The crew returned to Kamchatka in a boat made from the scavenged remains of the *St. Peter,* but Bering died of scurvy on the island in November 1741.

Bernier, Joseph-Elzéar (1852–1934)

Joseph-Elzéar Bernier, born in L'Islet, Quebec, Canada, did not begin his legendary Arctic voyages until the age of fifty-four. He had, however, by this time spent his entire life at sea. The son of a sea captain, he took command of a merchant ship at age seventeen, and long before he began his Arctic explorations, he had become a master at navigation and seamanship and cold weather survival.

Bernier was a captain of the old school. His experience was with wooden sailing ships augmented with coal-driven low-power steam machinery. The vessels carried extensive sledging apparatus, which was used to extend the range of exploration. The expectation was that, although such ships could not be expected to break through the ice, the vessels would serve as a base, amply stocked with provisions, for sledging forays that would take place when the ship was locked in by ice. It is to be noted that Bernier's travels represent almost the last major Arctic explorations in wooden sailing ships. Such vessels were soon to be replaced by steamers, and eventually by iron-hulled icebreakers, which cut their paths through the frozen wastes of the Canadian Archipelago.

Bernier had long wanted to explore in the Canadian Arctic. He was, however, motivated by more than personal goals. He, like many officers in the Canadian naval establishment, was aware of the scant national presence in the Arctic region; like other Canadians, he felt the need to establish claims of sovereignty in the Canadian Archipelago. Great Britain, Norway, and Russia had historically led the way in Arctic exploration. And those countries had begun to aggressively assert and claim the rights to territories charted by their intrepid explorers. So it was with complete national support that Bernier undertook his Arctic expeditions under the auspices of the Canadian Coast Guard.

In 1904 the *Arctic* was purchased for Bernier from the German government. The *Arctic* was huge, built along the lines of **Nansen**'s *Fram*. She was double-hulled in oak and pitch pine, square-rigged on the foremast with an economical engine capable of producing seven knots. She even had the luxury of a steam-driven generator. Her large capacity meant that she could carry up to five hundred tons of coal, along with immense stores of provisions. The *Arctic* was self-sufficient for at least two years, under full power.

On his first voyage to the Arctic archipelago (1906–1907), Bernier reached the northern tip of Melville Island; along the way, stops were routine, with the building of cairns, the leaving of proclamations of possession, and the planting of the Canadian flag. One such stop was at the Sverdrup Islands, claimed by **Otto Sverdrup** for Norway in 1899. (The Canadian government granted $67,000 to Sverdrup in 1903 to settle ownership.) Bernier returned to **Baffin Island** for the winter of 1906, and in the following year he explored the northeastern regions of the archipelago, particularly Jones Sound, Devon Island, and **Ellesmere Island.** Bernier returned to **Labrador [III]** in 1907 to restock the *Arctic* in preparation for a second voyage to the west.

In 1908 Bernier again traveled to Melville Island, wintering at Winter

Harbour. While the ship was frozen in, Bernier crossed the McClure Strait by sledge and found relics of *McClure*'s search for *Sir John Franklin*. During this voyage, Bernier erected a table proclaiming the annexation by Canada of the entire Arctic Archipelago. Bernier spent much of the winter of 1909 exploring the waterways of the western channels, in the vicinity of Melville, Banks, and Prince Patrick Islands; he concluded that the *Arctic* could indeed force a passage through this northern route of the *Northwest Passage*. Therefore, in 1910, Bernier set forth on his final major expedition. His orders were to "patrol Davis Strait, Baffin Bay, Lancaster Sound, Barrow Strait, Melville Sound, McClure Strait, Beaufort Sea, through Bering Strait to Vancouver, B.C." In short, he was to navigate the Northwest Passage. The route was hopelessly blocked by ice, forcing Bernier to retreat to Baffin Island. Here, in 1910–1911, extended overland trips were made to the Gulf of Boothia and the Fury and Hecla Strait. As always, cairns and proclamations of possession were left along the way, not only as manifestations of Canadian sovereignty, but serving as well as evidence of Bernier's enthusiasm and heroism in his Arctic endeavors.

Between 1906 and 1925, Bernier made twelve trips to the Arctic and enabled Canada to establish sovereignty over some 740,000 square kilometers in the Arctic. Bernier had the advantage of being an explorer at a time when equipment and knowledge were much superior to what they had been in the nineteenth century. But it should be pointed out that Bernier's careful planning and disciplined guidance made his expeditions seem easier than they were. Although his accomplishments were not of the type that gained him the heroic reputation of some explorers, Bernier is now recognized as having made Canadians and their government aware of the future concerns and potential of their Arctic territories.

Boyd, Louise Arner (1887–1972)

This remarkable if little-known American woman conducted a number of significant Arctic expeditions in the first half of the twentieth century. Born into a wealthy California family, she made her first trip to the Arctic in 1926. Using her own money, she hired the ships and scientists for several more expeditions and became an internationally recognized authority on the fjords, glaciers, botany, and magnetic phenomena of the east coast of *Greenland [I]*. In 1955 she was the first woman to fly across the *North Pole*.

Button, Thomas (?–1634)

Thomas Button apparently saw service in Ireland and the West Indies as an English naval officer, but he first came into focus in 1612 when he commanded an expedition to seek the *Northwest Passage.* His ship was the *Resolution* and was accompanied by the *Discovery* under *Robert Bylot.* They explored the coasts of Hudson's Bay for a year, then returned to report that there was no northwest passage from that area. Button was appointed admiral of the royal fleet patrolling Ireland (and knighted in 1616); he held this position to his death, but often saw combat elsewhere, most notably in Algiers in 1620.

Bylot, Robert (*fl.* 1610–1618)

Bylot was an English navigator of whom little is known until he appears as a sailor on *Henry Hudson*'s *Discovery* on the voyage of 1610–1611. Bylot's promotion to first mate apparently contributed to other crewmen's dissatisfaction with Hudson, who was abandoned with seven others in St. James Bay, the southern extension of Hudson Bay. Bylot returned to England in the *Discovery* and seems to have escaped blame for the mutiny because in August 1612 he sailed out on an expedition under the command of *Thomas Button* to seek the *Northwest Passage.* For a year after their departure they explored the coast of Hudson's Bay, then returned to England having concluded that there was no northwest passage from that bay. In 1615 and 1616 he was in command of the *Discovery* on two voyages, both times with *William Baffin* as his navigator. On the first they explored the region around the mouth of Hudson's Bay; on the second, they explored the region between *Ellesmere Island* and *Greenland [I].* What little is known of Bylot is due to Baffin's accounts of these voyages, and Bylot vanishes from history thereafter.

Byrd, Richard Evelyn (1888–1957)

Richard Byrd was born into the prominent Virginia Byrd family, strong-willed successful folk, with deep roots in early American history. At the age of ten he was given the opportunity to visit a family friend, a Judge A. C.

Carson, who was a high-ranking official in the Philippines. The trip was full of exciting events for a boy traveling alone: typhoons, a visit to exotic Japan, and a civil insurrection in Manila, including a battle in which he was allowed to take part. On his own initiative, he decided to return to Virginia by way of the Far East, and so, at age twelve, on his own, he had circumnavigated the world.

Byrd entered the Virginia Military Institute and later the University of Virginia. Byrd's father, Richard Evelyn Byrd I, had hoped that his son would pursue a career in law; but Byrd's interests were in football, mathematics, and engineering. His father, giving in to Byrd's preferences, secured an appointment for him to Annapolis. After graduation in 1912, Byrd spent the next five years as a junior officer on a battleship. From the beginning, his preoccupation with navigation, pilot training, and transatlantic flight showed him to be a young officer of foresight, initiative, and intelligence. Although an injury prevented Byrd from flying in combat in World War I, by 1918 his contributions to the new techniques of flight gained him honors and commendations from three countries, including two from the United States. After World War I, Byrd continued to seek support from naval and political friends for a transatlantic flight. Twice, permission was given to Byrd, and in both instances accidents resulted in the cancellation of the attempt.

> **IN THEIR OWN** *Words*
>
> **Flying over the North Pole**
>
> *M*ay 9, 1926: *We are making good speed. It looks like fog over the polar sea. Send a radio back that we are making fast speed and are about to pass Amsterdam Island. . . . Now we are on the edge of icepack. . . . Send a radio back that we are 85 miles due north Amsterdam Island. . . . Send a radio that we are 240 miles due north Spitzbergen. . . . Send radio that we are 230 miles from the Pole. . . . The starboard motor has an oil-leak. . . . We should be at the Pole now. Make a circle, I will take a picture. . . . Radio that we have reached the pole and are now returning with one motor with bad oil leak.*
>
> —RICHARD BYRD, JOURNAL NOTES TO PILOT, FLOYD BENNETT, MAY 9, 1926

After the aborted Atlantic flights, Byrd spent the next few years in Washington, where he met Captain *Bob Bartlett* (of *Peary's North Pole* party). Bartlett was planning an air survey of one million square miles of unexplored territory in the Arctic Circle, and Byrd happily agreed to join him. *Donald MacMillan* (also of the Peary expedition), and a young flyer, Floyd Bennett, were added to the party; on June 20, 1925, the group traveled to Etah, the northernmost outpost in *Greenland [I]*. Byrd and

Bennett, after flying 2,500 miles in the territory north of Greenland, were convinced that a flight over the North Pole was possible. Two months later, Byrd was back in the United States seeking the necessary financial backing. Much of the required funds came from Edsel Ford, Henry's son; in recognition of that aid, Byrd named his trimotored Fokker the *Josephine Ford,* after the industrialist's three-year old daughter.

On April 5, 1926, Byrd and an expedition of fifty men left New York for Spitzbergen on the *Chantier* with the *Josephine Ford* on board. Time was of the essence; Byrd knew that the Norwegian **Roald Amundsen** had been planning a polar flight and that he was almost ready to leave. In ten days the plane was ready and loaded, and by working night and day, a runway was built and iced to enable the overloaded airplane to take off. At 12:30 A.M., May 9, the triplane, loaded with ten thousand pounds of fuel and emergency supplies, lumbered down the runway and barely lifted into the air, just clearing the jagged ice peaks that encircled the airfield. Byrd and Bennett took turns at the stick; while one flew, the other emptied five-gallon cans of fuel into the tanks. A

On the island of Spitzbergen, Norway, Commander Richard Byrd and his pilot, Floyd Bennett, and some of their staff inspect the *Josephine Ford* just before taking off on their flight over the North Pole on May 9, 1926.

leaking oil tank in one of the engines was ignored: To attempt to land and repair it would have been suicide. At 9:02 A.M. on May 9, 1926, Byrd's calculations showed him to be over the pole. After double-checking the navigational calculations, the *Josephine* headed back to Spitzbergen, arriving safely at 3:30 P.M. Byrd and Bennett had flown to the pole and back, a distance of 1,600 miles in 15 hours and 30 minutes. (Many years later some would challenge Byrd's claim to have reached the North Pole; in particular, there was some doubt as to whether Byrd's plane could have covered the round-trip in the time it took.) As the crew surged around Byrd in celebration of his success, he was gratified to see that one of the first to shake his hand was Roald Amundsen, about to make his own flight over the pole in the airship with Nobile.

Byrd's next great adventure was his pioneering flight over the South Pole with the Norwegian-American pilot Bernt Balchen, on November

28–29, 1929. In the following four decades, Byrd continued his epic expeditions in Antarctica, discovering and surveying more new territory on earth than any other exploring party on record. Although it has since been revealed that Byrd was an often difficult, egocentric individual, it is safe to say that Byrd brought world supremacy to America in modern polar exploration.

Campbell, Robert

(1808–1894)

Robert Campbell was born in Scotland and, as a young man, worked on his father's sheep farm. In 1830 Campbell was hired by the *Hudson's Bay Company [VI]* to help establish an experimental sheep farm in Manitoba, Canada. When the experiment failed, Campbell was transferred to the Mackenzie River District as a clerk. The Hudson's Bay Company was at that time making a concerted effort to move its fur business west from the Mackenzie, to counteract the increasing Russian presence in Alaska and the northern Yukon region. Therefore, Campbell was directed to open a post at Dease Lake, and he was promoted to postmaster there. After two years of troublesome tenure due to Indian hostility and lack of provisions, Campbell was no longer needed, because the company and the Russians came to an agreement as to the division of the territory. Campbell convinced the company that the Yukon area west of the Mackenzie was rich in fur; he was therefore directed to explore the northern reaches of the Laird River, which ran from the Northwest Territory into the north central part of the Yukon. In 1840 he proceeded north to Frances Lake and to the Pelly River (he mistakenly thought he had reached Alaska). He had reached the Yukon River watershed from the east, and was the first European to do so. Campbell returned to Frances Lake, where he built a trading post. Several years passed while he tried unsuccessfully to convince the company that he was in viable trading country. There was also a problem with hostile Indians; Campbell never was able to establish good relationships with the natives and was apparently somewhat timid about confronting the unknown Chilkat tribes. Nonetheless, Campbell pushed forward and reached the confluence of the Pelly and Yukon Rivers, where in 1848 he built Fort Selkirk. Campbell's request to explore further west and reach the Pacific was denied by the company; they feared that their territory might then be opened to competitors from the Pacific coast. Instead they sent Campbell on a wild goose chase: They had him explore the Yukon River from Fort Selkirk to Fort Yukon, in Alaska and map that route—a particularly useless exercise. This voyage was the last of his explorations.

In fact, the company was not happy with Campbell. As an explorer, he was something of an enigma. He had courage and tenacity and had overcome much hardship and personal suffering, but he was overcautious and always drew back when faced with the unknown. He lacked the boldness and the eagerness of the true explorer. He had staked everything on his assessment of the richness of the Mackenzie area. A fellow officer described him as "a zealous, enterprising man, but he is mad when he touches on the prospects of Fort Selkirk." In fact, the region had failed to produce a profit for the company, and they wanted to abandon the whole project. Campbell became despondent about the failure of "his" district. His journals reflect his dislike of the region, his loneliness, and his growing sense of failure. He pleaded time and again for retirement.

In 1852 the Chilkat Indians attacked Fort Selkirk; Campbell's request for the rebuilding of the post was denied, and he was sent to England on forced leave. On his return to Canada, Campbell served at various posts in the Northwest for the next seventeen years. In 1871, after shipping some furs through the United States, which was against the strict rules of the company, he was dismissed. He lived alternately in Scotland and Canada, bitterly resentful of his mistreatment, and died in Manitoba in 1894.

Coats, William (circa 1700–1752)

Little is known of William Coats's origins (although he was probably born in Durham, England), but he was already an officer seaman when he entered the service of the *Hudson's Bay Company [VI]* in 1726. A year later he was given his first command, the *Mary* (named after his wife). His assignment, in general, was to explore the Hudson Bay–James Bay region. Specifically, he was to investigate rumors that there was silver to be found somewhere and that there was an abundance of fur. Also, it was reported that Richmond Gulf (in fact, Lac Guillaume-Delisle) led through the Labrador Peninsula to the Atlantic Ocean. The Hudson's Bay Company was interested in the East Main (the eastern coasts of Hudson and James Bays) as an area to establish settlements and increase their fur trade. A sea passageway through the northern part of *Labrador [III]* would bypass the arduous northern entry to Hudson Bay through the Hudson Strait (above the Arctic Circle and thus frozen over most of the year). It is clear that the company was not primarily interested in geographical exploration.

Despite his experience as a sailor, on his first voyage on the *Mary* in 1727 Coats lost the ship off the coast of *Greenland [I]*. Nine years later his second command met the same fate at Hudson Strait when the ice "crushed our sides in and sunk her in twenty minutes." A few years later, in command of a third voyage, he got into trouble by illegally trading brandy to the garrison at Fort Albany (James Bay) and causing an "oversetting of the reformation" of the crew there. Nevertheless, the company retained their confidence in Coats; they continued to hire him to sail to the region at least once a year, and rewarded him with generous bonuses. That his wife's father was a company committee member might have had something to do with Coats's continued high status within the company.

In spite of his pursuit of his own and the company's profits, Coats became interested in exploration. In 1744 he began to compile a geography of the Hudson Bay region. He claimed that no other person had ever collected so many notes as himself and that few had better experience and opportunity to explain the geography. Coats's private notes, his excellent and accurate manuscript maps, and his reports to the company show that he carefully explored the five hundred miles of coastline from the Hudson Strait to the Richmond Gulf. In the Richmond area he designated an ideal spot for a fort, which would have been the farthest north at that time. That fort was established, and he supervised it and later kept it supplied with necessities until 1751. At that time he was found guilty of engaging in illicit trade and was dismissed. Although his superiors had given him liberal gratuities over the years, he had abused his position in a systematic and cynical way. A few weeks later he was found dead, but no evidence of foul play or suicide was discovered. He left behind a considerable fortune, mostly in real estate. The exploration material given by him to the company was unpublished and forgotten. His own personal writing, which showed his prowess as geographer and explorer, was fortunately discovered by chance in 1852.

Collinson, Richard

(1811–1883)

Richard Collinson, born in Gateshead, England, left school at the age of twelve to enter the Royal Navy as a midshipman. After a number of voyages of survey and exploration, he caught the attention of Captain Francis Beaufort, who praised him for his diligence and the accuracy of his observations. Beaufort's patronage aided his rise to lieutenant in 1835; at the outbreak of the first Anglo-Chinese War in 1840, Beaufort secured for Collinson the position of surveying officer to the fleet. His record during the war was so outstanding that he was promoted to commander in 1841 and to post-captain one year later. Collinson remained in China for four years, completing a major survey of the Chinese coast from Zhoushan to Hong Kong.

In 1849 the British government decided to launch a massive search for the *John Franklin* party. One search party was to approach from the west, through the Bering Strait; Richard Collinson was given command of this mission. In January two ships left the Thames: the *Enterprise,* under the captaincy of the expedition leader Collinson; and the *Investigator,* under *Robert McClure,* the second-in-command. The *Enterprise* was the much faster ship, but Collinson chose to sail westward around the tip of the Aleutian Islands and lost time. McClure, behind at this point, sailed instead through the dangerous Seguam Pass south of the Aleutians. Thus McClure reached the Prince of Wales Strait before the annual freeze-up; when Collinson sailed through the Bering Strait, he found further passage blocked by pack ice and was forced to return to Hong Kong for the winter. At this point a number of Collinson's officers were outraged by his cautious—and slow—progress, so much so that Collinson was forced to place several of them under arrest to restore discipline.

Collinson never made rendezvous with the *Investigator* during the three years of his stay in the Arctic. Everywhere Collinson went, he found evidence of McClure's earlier presence: at Banks Island, Prince of Wales Strait, and Victoria Island. Finally Collinson moved south and passed through the very dangerous Dolphin and Union Strait, Coronation Gulf, and the Dease Strait, into Victoria Strait. He was unaware that he had found the *Northwest Passage* (southern route). He was also unaware that he had passed within thirty miles of the death site of the last surviving members of Franklin's party on King William Island. Shortages of fuel and supplies now forced Collinson to return home, although it was May 1855 before he reached England. Collinson received high praise for his excellent seamanship and his perseverance through an incredibly long expedition. But he was not credited with the discovery of the Northwest Passage; the House of Commons judged that the award of £10,000 be given to Robert McClure for that discovery; Collinson received an honorable mention.

Collinson maintained an active interest in exploration for the rest of his life. He was for many years thereafter an officer in the Royal Geographical Society and an officer in Trinity House (an organization concerned with aids to navigation), and he served in the United Service Institution. The Admiralty gave overdue recognition to his achievements by promoting him to full admiral in 1875. Collinson retired from his work at Trinity House in 1883 and died a few months thereafter.

Cook, Frederick Albert (1865–1940)

After earning his M.D. from New York University, Frederick Cook answered an advertisement for a surgeon to accompany **Robert Peary** on his North Greenland Expedition in 1891. Cook again interrupted his medical practice for Arctic expeditions in 1893 and 1894; on the latter, his ship, *Miranda*, struck an iceberg, and Cook navigated an open boat across ninety miles of Arctic sea to obtain aid. In 1898 he joined the Belgian Antarctic Expedition as a surgeon and again was credited with rescuing the party. In 1902 he joined Peary on an Arctic expedition for the last time because the two men had both personal and professional differences. In 1903 Cook mounted his own expedition to Mount McKinley in Alaska and was the first to make his way around its base; in 1906 he would claim to have ascended it, the first to do so, but this claim has been challenged by some authorities.

In 1908 he embarked on his most famous expedition—an attempt to be the first to reach the **North Pole**. Cook's account of his reaching the pole was simple and direct. He had met a rich American, John R. Bradley, and in June 1907 had gone hunting with him in northwestern *Greenland [I]*. When Cook suggested he might try for the pole, Bradley agreed to finance the venture. In September 1907 Bradley went home, and Cook stayed in Etah, Greenland, and prepared for his expedition. From there on February 19, 1908, he set out with a party of ten men, eleven sledges, and a hundred and five dogs, across *Ellesmere* and Axel Heiberg Islands to the latter's northernmost cape. At that point he set off across the Arctic ice with only two Inuit, two sledges, and twenty-six dogs, reaching what he calculated to be the North Pole on April 21, 1908. The three of them then were forced to spend the entire winter of 1908–1909 in a cave on Devon Island before making their way back to Greenland. Back in Etah, he met Harry Whitney, who was a friend of Robert Peary. Cook left with Whitney a cache of instruments and navigational notes. (Eventually, these items all mysteriously disappeared.) Cook made his way to Copenhagen, but it was September 1, 1909, before he sent a telegram claiming he had reached the pole. Five days later Peary made his first public claim that he had reached the pole on April 6, 1909, thus igniting a controversy that has never been fully resolved.

This picture was taken in April 1908 at the site that Frederick Cook claimed was the North Pole—thus beating Peary by a whole year. It shows two members of the expedition with an American flag stuck in an igloo.

Peary's claim soon became the accepted one, and Cook would spend the rest of his life not only trying to establish priority but refuting charges that he was a pretender. His reputation was further tarnished when he was imprisoned for seven years (1923–1930) for falsely promoting land in Texas as rich in oil. (Later the land turned out to be so, and President Franklin D. Roosevelt pardoned him in 1940.) Cook wrote several books about his explorations, including *My Attainment of the Pole* (1911), and gained the support of some knowledgeable individuals, but he died without dislodging Peary from most accounts as the first to reach the North Pole. At an International Symposium on Cook in 1993, however, most of the explorers and students of this issue endorsed Cook's claim to priority. Aside from such a claim, many scholars believe that Cook has never received proper recognition for his epic explorations in the Arctic.

Davis, John   (1543–1605)

Davis grew up with *Sir Humphrey Gilbert [III]* and his brother Adrian, but he vanishes from history until, at the age of thirty-six, apparently after a career as a seaman, he joined the Gilberts in looking for support to search for the *Northwest Passage.* It was June 1585 before Davis finally set sail from England as commander of the *Sunshine,* accompanied by the *Moonshine.* He sighted the east coast of *Greenland [I],* then sailed around to the west coast (close to one of the original Norse settlements); he named his port there Gilbert's Sound. After some trading with the Eskimos, the ships sailed west across the water that would be named Davis Strait and explored the southern coast of *Baffin Island,* then sailed up into the Cumberland Sound; Davis believed he was finding the Northwest Passage, but the approaching winter and declining provisions forced him to set sail for England in August.

Convinced that he was on the trail of the Northwest Passage, Davis's supporters financed a second expedition, and in May 1586 he set forth on the *Mermaid* with three other ships. He retraced his voyage around Greenland and this time had some unpleasant run-ins with the Eskimos there. Then leaving the *Mermaid* to return home, Davis sailed in the *Moonshine* and made his way southwestward, exploring the coast of *Labrador [III]* down to about 53°50' N (modern Trunmore Bay). After losing two men in a fight with the local inhabitants, he headed back toward England in September. Meanwhile, two of the original four ships had split away before Davis moved on to Greenland and had tried to sail due north between Iceland and Greenland; turned back by the ice, they landed on Iceland, then sailed to eastern Greenland and eventually to its west coast and Gilbert's Sound, where, among other things, they engaged the local Eskimos in a game of "foot-ball." Again, though, relations with the natives deteriorated, and the English ended up killing three Eskimos in a fight. These two ships then set sail for England, but one was lost at sea.

Although little of any value had been accomplished by this second expedition, Davis and his supporters were not deterred, and he set sail on his third expedition in May 1587, this time with the *Sunshine* and two other ships. Drawing on Davis's advanced navigational instruments and knowledge, they sailed straight for the western coast of Greenland and Gilbert's Sound. Two of the ships then left Davis to go seeking the fish they had been promised would repay them for their voyage, but Davis set off in the smallest ship, the *Ellen,* and went up the western coast of Greenland into Baffin Bay, eventually reaching 72°46'. At this point, he headed west over to Baffin Island and—after missing Lancaster Sound, the actual entrance to the Northwest Passage—he made his way south and into Cumberland Sound again. After sailing around it, he headed further south and came first to Frobisher Bay, then to the mouth of Hudson Strait, and then to the coast of Labrador, where he was supposed to rendezvous with the two fishing ships. Failing to find them, Davis set off back to England in August; when he arrived a month later, the two ships had already unloaded their profitable cargo of fish. After this final Arctic expedition, Davis had numerous adventures at sea, including sailing with Thomas Cavendish's second and disastrous attempt to circumnavigate the globe (1591); in 1601 he went off to the East Indies; on a second voyage there in 1605, he was killed by Japanese pirates. Davis had failed in his search for a northwest passage and as a result never gained much of a popular reputation; but experts recognize him as an innovative navigator as well as an intrepid mariner; he invented the backstaff and a quadrant, and his *The Seaman's Secrets* (1594) is regarded as the best book on navigation in the sixteenth century. Despite the many misunderstandings and missed opportunities of his expeditions, his accurate latitude readings and location of many geographic features would ease the way for future explorers.

Dease, Peter Warren (1788–1863)

Peter Dease was born in Michigan, in U.S. territory, but he was raised in *Montreal [V],* Canada, where his father was a superintendent of the Indian Department. At the age of thirteen he was employed by the XY trading company, which soon merged with the *North West Company [VI].* He was posted to the Athabasca Department and later to the Mackenzie River District and Fort Chipewyan. Dease was active in the near warfare between the North West Company and *Hudson's Bay Company [VI],* which ended in their merger; in 1821 Dease was appointed chief trader for the Hudson's Bay Company.

In 1820 Dease provided much useful information to *John Franklin* about the geography and the native peoples of the Arctic; later Franklin requested Dease's help to obtain provisions, the support of Indians and *voyageurs* (French-Canadian woodsmen), and to build a camp on Great Slave Lake. During the winter of 1824–1825, Dease again provided food for Franklin, found Indian support for his party, and supervised the construction of Fort Franklin on Great Bear Lake. In gratitude Franklin named one bay of that lake Dease Arm. In 1831 Dease assumed sole charge of the New Caledonia District (Northern British Columbia).

Under Dease, the region returned huge profits to the Hudson's Bay Company, mostly from the fur trade. Dease's headquarters, Fort St. James, was a happy, well-run place, and his subordinates thought of him as "most amiable, warm-hearted and sociable." The London superiors lauded Dease for "having established a new order of things." They were impressed by his introducing cattle to the fort and by his encouragement of farming in the area. The company thought so highly of Dease that they assigned him the command of a major expedition to fill in the exploration gaps in the *Northwest Passage* search left by Franklin, Frederick William Beechey and *George Back.* These gaps occurred mainly in the region along the Polar Sea from the mouth of the Mackenzie River to King William Island.

Thomas Simpson, who was appointed second-in-command, much to his own dismay, at this point joined Dease. Simpson was in fact the better explorer, being bold and self-reliant; his fierce ambition however drove him to impetuous and dangerous decisions. The two men left Great Slave Lake in 1837 and soon reached the mouth of the Mackenzie River, where they turned west and mapped the coast into Alaska to Return Reef, Franklin's furthest point west. Bad weather forced their retreat and, much to Simpson's chagrin, the travelers returned to Fort Norman for the winter. In 1838 the two men set out on the horrible overland journey from Fort Norman to the mouth of the Coppermine River—the journey that had nearly been the death of Franklin. Simpson was still "sore" at being second-in-command to Dease, whom he described as "worthy, indolent and illiterate." Simpson made a number of side excursions, which in fact often proved to be useful to the assignment. For example, Dease proceeded east from Coppermine as far as Franklin's Point Turnagain but stopped when the ice blocked further passage. But Simpson went on foot a hundred miles further, discovering and naming Victoria Land and Cape Pelly. In early September, facing the rapidly approaching winter, the party retreated to winter quarters, with Simpson complaining that he was "hampered with an old man on my back."

In 1839 Dease returned to the Coppermine River, pressing east past Simpson's Cape Pelly and discovering the Dease and Simpson Strait, which separates King William Island from the mainland. On Montreal Island Dease found a cache left by George Back on his journey of 1819. The missing sections of the extremities of the north Canadian mainland were now filled in. Dease went on to explore part of the western coast of the Boothia Peninsula and the southern part of King William Island. At this point Dease had traced much of Franklin's explorations and had clarified the coastline of the Polar Sea in its entire western segment. Dease and Simpson had explored and charted more than 60 degrees of latitude of the Arctic coast. Dease, although a cautious man, was highly successful in organizing, recruiting, and maintaining discipline among his subordinates; his practical approach to things ensured the safety and success of his missions. Dease went to London in 1840 for medical attention and was granted a pension and permanent furlough. He married his long-time companion, Elizabeth Chouinard, a Métis Indian, and modestly declined the offer of a knighthood. After a long and comfortable retirement, he died in Quebec, Canada, in 1863.

DeLong, George Washington   (?–1881)

Two popular misconceptions about the geography of the Arctic still existed in the latter part of the nineteenth century. One was that the Polar Region was a landmass, corresponding to the landmass of Antarctica; the second was that there existed a branch of the warm Gulf Stream current, which flowed from the northern coast of Siberia eastward to the Polar Region and thus provided an ice-free route to the pole. In 1872 the explorer Karl Weyprecht had failed to find the warm current; but while locked in the pack ice, he had happened upon Franz Josef Land, which he took to be the Arctic Continent.

As a young lieutenant in the United States Navy, George Washington DeLong was intrigued by the theories of Weyprecht. He was convinced that he could find the warm current and drift to at least the vicinity of the pole. It is safe to say that for DeLong, the project was an adventure rather than a scientific project. He had very little Arctic experience and made a first mistake in buying the *Jeannette,* a vessel that naval engineers told him was inadequate for his purposes. Against advice, DeLong hired Indians rather than Eskimos as members of the party; for his crew, DeLong picked inexperienced men who turned out be troublesome and unreliable. The voyage was sponsored by James Gordon Bennett of the *New York Herald* (the backer of Stanley's search for Livingstone), and the endeavor had about it something of a carnival atmosphere.

The ill-fated expedition left California in the summer of 1879 and by September had passed through the Bering Strait, whereupon it became frozen in the pack ice just east of Wrangel Island. A year later, in December 1880, the *Jeannette* was no nearer her goal and still frozen in pack ice at 74°41' N; the temperature stood at 50° below zero. In the summer of 1881, the inadequate supply of coal began to run out; worse, the pressure of the ever-surrounding ice began to crush the hull, and finally the ice tore through the timbers and planks and entered the ship. Strangely, no plans had been made for evacuation; much was lost, including the entire stock of lime juice, without which scurvy was inevitable. The men dragged boats and provisions for six weeks, finally reaching Bennett Island in a desperate state. Here they encountered partly open water and set off by boat for the Siberian mainland. One boat sank with all hands; a second, under the command of Lieutenant Melville, reached an inhabited part of the Lena River delta and all were rescued. DeLong's boat drifted to a part of the delta where there were no settlements. The members of DeLong's party died slowly, one by one, of starvation and cold. DeLong's diary has as a last entry "October 30th, Sunday, Boyd and Goertz died during the night, Mr. Collins dying." His own death is presumed to have occurred on November 1, 1881. Ironically, a few years later, relics from the *Jeannette* were found on the southwest coast of *Greenland [I]*. It was supposed that the relics had drifted across the Polar Sea.

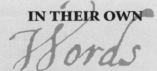

IN THEIR OWN *Words*

The Need for Hope in the Arctic

June 21st, Monday: The advent and departure of another day to record; and except that it is the longest day in the year to some people (though not of course to us, since we have the sun the whole twenty-four hours), it is hardly worth recording. Observations show us that we have drifted, since the 19th, eleven and three-tenths miles to S. 68° E. Discouraging, very. And yet my motto is, "Hope on, hope ever." A very good one it is when one's surroundings are more natural than ours; but situated as we are, it is better in the abstract than in realization.

—GEORGE WASHINGTON DELONG,
THE VOYAGE OF THE JEANNETTE, 1883

Dezhnev, Semen Ivanovich   (1605?–1673)

Little is known of his early years, but by the 1640s Semen Ivanovich Dezhnev was exploring the far northern reaches of Siberia. In 1648, with Feodor Alekseev Popov, he sailed from the mouth of the Kolyma River (up on the East Siberian Sea), over around the Chukchi Peninsula (the northeasternmost point of Siberia), and down into the Bering Sea, thus becoming the first European to discover the Bering Strait. Thereafter he confined his explorations to northern Siberia. The tip of the Chukchi Peninsula and a bay near the Kamchatka Peninsula are named after him.

Ellesmere Island

Lying some fifty miles off *Greenland's [I]* northwest coast, Ellesmere Island's area of 75,767 square miles ranks it as the tenth-largest island in the world (and Canada's third-largest). The first European known to have set foot there was *William Baffin,* during his 1616 voyage. The next European known to have visited the island was the Englishman Edward Inglefield, captain of the ship *Isabel* during a search for *John Franklin* in 1852. As a result of this visit, the British named the island after the First Earl of Ellesmere, president of the Royal Geographic Society. Dr. *Isaac Hayes,* with the expedition of *Elisha Kent Kane* in 1854, was the first white man known to have explored the interior of the island. In 1881 *Adolphus Greely* headed an Arctic observation station on the northeast coast of Ellesmere Island, and in 1899 *Robert Peary* explored parts of it. Although only a few hundred Inuit live there, since April 1999 Ellesmere Island has belonged to the Inuit-controlled Nunavut Territory (which has renamed the island Quttinirpaaq). In the 1970s pieces of a Viking chain armor and fragments of a *Norse [I]* ship were found on the eastern edge; dated to about A.D. 1250, they might be simply remains of a shipwreck, but they may also indicate that the Norse made at least occasional voyages to this part of North America.

Foxe, Luke   (?–?)

In 1616 *William Baffin* returned to London from his explorations of Davis Strait and Baffin Bay with very negative reports as to the viability of Lancaster Sound as the entrance to the *Northwest Passage.* Baffin's assessment dampened English interest in the search for the passage for the next two hundred years. However, two voyages were made to the Arctic in the early seventeenth century that paved the way for the renewed efforts that were to be made later. In 1631 Luke Foxe and Thomas James both departed London to search for the Northwest Passage. Foxe or "Northwest" Foxe, as he preferred to be called, entered Hudson Bay and followed the western shore to the south, where he came upon the remains of a previous expedition—that of Sir **Thomas Button.** Proceeding further south, he reached James Bay, where he claimed all lands and waters in the name of Charles I. Foxe then turned north, passing out of Hudson Bay into the Foxe Basin and reaching 66°47' N, a record not to be exceeded for more than one hundred years. Foxe realized that the area surrounding Hudson Bay was now accurately mapped; he also realized that there was no passage westward from this area. With half the crew sick with scurvy, and with the ice beginning to form, the exploration was finished. Foxe returned to England; he had not discovered the passage, but he had added a sizable chunk to the map of northern Canada.

Franklin, Lady Jane (1791–1875)

The wife of the famed Arctic explorer **John Franklin** earns at least a footnote in the annals of Arctic exploration because of her persistent—and personally costly—efforts to find her missing husband. These efforts, in turn, led to numerous discoveries in the Arctic region of North America. In fact, long before he and his shipmates vanished, Lady Jane had shown a remarkable energy for independent and "unladylike" activities. During her husband's years (1836–1843) as governor of Van Diemen's Land (Tasmania), she traveled widely through Tasmania, Australia, and New Zealand. After Franklin was reported as missing, and when she realized that the British government was no longer committed to continuing the search, she organized five expeditions between 1850 and 1857, using her personal inheritance to pay for the ships and other expenses. It was the last of these, the expedition headed by **Francis McClintock,** that found the evidence of both Franklin's fate and his achievement. Lady Jane continued to travel throughout the world and, in the final year of her life, paid for the yacht *Pandora*'s attempt to break through the ice of the **Northwest Passage,** which she believed her husband deserved credit for discovering.

Franklin, John (1786–1847)

John Franklin's father determined that his twelfth and youngest son should have a career in the church, but a journey to the seaside so strongly affected the young man that he could conceive of no occupation that did not involve going to sea. A voyage to Lisbon on a merchant vessel only whet his appetite further for seagoing, and soon thereafter he entered the Royal Navy as a midshipman. Franklin's rise through the ranks in the Royal Navy was rapid; among other adventures, he fought with distinction aboard the *Bellerophon,* in the battle of Trafalgar. Subsequently he was appointed to the rank of lieutenant and served at the home station until 1814, at which time he was ordered to North America as part of an expedition against New Orleans. One outcome of the North American campaign was that, at its conclusion, Franklin was given command of a brig, *Trent,* with a very different mission. He was to accompany Captain Buchan, the leader, on an exploratory voyage between Spitzbergen and *Greenland [I]* and proceed, if possible, to the **North Pole.** If this were achieved, they were then to proceed directly to the Bering Strait and would thus, in one voyage, have discovered both the North Pole and the **Northwest Passage.** In fact, they were stopped by the quickly forming ice just northwest of Spitzbergen and turned back just in time to prevent utter disaster. This had been Franklin's first taste of Arctic exploration, and it would be only one year before he returned to make the first of his three great historical voyages to the Arctic regions.

Early in 1819 Franklin was appointed the commander of an exploration designed to "amend the very defective geography of the northern part of America." Specifically, he was to determine the boundaries, latitudes, and longitudes of the northern limits of North America from the mouth of the Coppermine River to the easternmost extremities of the continent. This assignment was but a part of a major attempt by the British Admiralty to enter the Arctic region by land and chart the areas in and around the southern portions of the Arctic Sea. Franklin began his odyssey on September 9, 1819, with a small group consisting of two officers, Robert Hood and *George Back* (companions from the *Trent*), six Englishmen, assorted Indians with wives and children, and some Canadian *voyageurs* serving as guides and interpreters. The journey was to be overland, but the group carried portable boats and canoes for travel on the Elk, Saskatchewan, and Coppermine Rivers.

The expedition was ill-fated from the beginning. In March of 1820 Franklin found himself at Fort Chipewyan, separated from his party and desperate for food and ammunition, which had not been left for him, as promised. Saved from starvation by Indians, Franklin wintered in a hut at a place now known as Fort Enterprise and, in June 1821, finally found that the ice on the Coppermine River had lifted, and he was able to proceed to the mouth of that river and thus enter the southern extremity of the Arctic Ocean. From there, he proceeded east by boat until August 1821, when the winter had set in and further passage was blocked by ice. Rapidly diminishing supplies made Franklin realize that he must seek winter haven, and he turned south from the Arctic Ocean, into a river that he named the Hood, after his companion officer. The Hood River turned out to be unnavigable, and after sawing their boats in two and vainly portaging, Franklin desperately struck out overland for Fort Providence. The story of this journey has been called the most terrible account of human suffering on record. The Franklin party was in its final extremities when it was rescued by Indians. Of the original party of twenty-six, there were nine survivors. After resting for some months, those remaining returned to England, having journeyed on land and water some 5,550 miles.

Franklin's second Arctic exploration was conceived in 1823 and was proposed by him to be a cooperative endeavor with *Sir William Parry.* The purpose of this expedition was to explore the region west of the Mackenzie delta, along the southern edge of the Beaufort Sea, all the way past Point Barrow, through the Chukchi Sea to the Kotzebue Sound. At this point at the entrance to the Bering Strait, the entire western part of the Northwest Passage would be determined. It would then remain to map a few regions east of Coronation Gulf (along the northern boundary of North America) and the Northwest Passage would be open—from Davis Strait and the Atlantic Ocean to the Bering Sea.

In preparation for his journey, Franklin persuaded the Admiralty to send supplies and a party of British seamen in advance in early 1825, to be stationed along his intended route. Franklin himself left London in February 1825 for New York. By August 1825 he had reached Fort Norman on the Mackenzie River and soon proceeded down the Mackenzie to the Beaufort Sea, where he planted a Union Jack, made by his just-deceased wife in what he called a moment of "undescribable emotions." Winter was now setting in, and further travel was impossible; Franklin retreated south to winter quarters near Great Bear Lake, which in his absence, his men had named Fort Franklin. The nine-month winter passed pleasantly (unlike that of his first voyage) with an abundance of food and clothing and even the occasional letter from England via the Hudson Bay post. In June 1826 two groups traveled again down the Mackenzie to the Beaufort Sea; one group went east toward the Coppermine River and Coronation Gulf, verifying that that passage was open; the other party, under Franklin, sailed and paddled west, getting as far as Point Beechey, longitude 149°37' W. There was no possibility of their reaching their objective, Kotzebue Bay. It was already August, and the risk of shipwreck by storm increased daily. There was, of course, no question of wintering on the coast.

Once again the explorers retreated to Fort Franklin, where they spent their final winter, again in relative comfort. Franklin left the fort in February 1827 and, by way of *Montreal [V]* and New York, reached Liverpool in September of 1827. This second voyage, not so exciting and tragic as the first, provided much vital geographical information. Honors were heaped upon Franklin: He received the Geographical Society gold medal; he was knighted; and he was given an honorary doctor's degree by Oxford, to name a few.

Franklin spent the next seventeen years in public service, during which time he remarried. For a period of several years he commanded the frigate *Rainbow* on duty in the Mediterranean and received further honors for his service. Subsequently he was appointed lieutenant-governor of Van Diemen's Land (Tasmania), a convict's colony; he brought vast improvements to the administration and reformation of the system there. He came to be greatly beloved by these colonists, for his constant and generous efforts on their behalf. He returned to England in 1844, to a climate of feverish excitement and rekindled interest in polar explorations. *Sir James Clark Ross* had just returned from a remarkable voyage to Antarctica. Various British explorers—*George Back, Peter Warren Dease, Thomas Simpson,* and *John Ross*— had traced the northern coastline of North America almost in its entirety. Suitable vessels were available, and because there was a temporary slowdown in shipping interest, there were seamen clamoring for employment. No reputable

IN THEIR OWN *Words*

An Acceptable Loss of Life

Arctic discovery has been fostered principally by Great Britain; and it is a subject of just pride that it has been prosecuted by her from motives as disinterested as they are enlightened; not from any prospect of immediate benefit to herself, but from a steady view to the acquirement of useful knowledge, and the extension of the bounds of science. Each succeeding attempt has added a step towards the completion of northern geography; and the contributions to natural history and science have excited a general interest throughout the civilized world. It is, moreover, pleasing to reflect that the loss of life which has occurred in the prosecution of these discoveries does not exceed the average number of deaths in the same population at home under circumstances the most favourable.

—JOHN FRANKLIN, *SECOND JOURNEY TO THE SHORES OF THE POLAR SEA,* 1828 men of science now doubted the existence of the Northwest Passage. The only questions now were its practicality and its navigability. Sir John Barrow challenged the Admiralty in 1844 by declaring that if Britain did not move forward now, after all the efforts and sacrifices of the recent past, and if thus the prize of discovering the Northwest Passage passed on to some other country, then England would become the laughingstock of the world.

The Admiralty responded decisively. They decided to dispatch the two ships *Erebus* and *Terror*, just back from Antarctica, to the Arctic. Franklin was by this time fifty-nine, but he was the senior naval officer with Arctic experience, and he demanded to be given command. And so in February 1845 the Admiralty appointed Franklin to command the expedition, with 134 officers and men under him. Captain Francis Crozier was the skipper of the *Terror*, and Commander James Fitzjames was placed in charge of the *Erebus*. The ships were equipped with steam engines (locomotive engines were used) and auxiliary screws, and they had an extra layer of planking on the sides. Iron plates over the bow provided extra strength to the hull. Supplies were provided to last for three years. There were also libraries aboard, containing 2,900 volumes; there were musical instruments carried for musical and dramatic performances. There was every expectation, on the part of the proud Admiralty and the awe-inspired public, that everything necessary had been included and that nothing would go wrong. The two ships weighed anchor and sailed from the Thames on May 19, 1845. In July of that year they entered Baffin Bay and met two whaling ships, one of which hosted the officers of the *Erebus*. The captain of the whaler wrote: "Both ships are all well . . . expecting to finish the operation in good time." The *Erebus* and the *Terror* moved off into the fog of Lancaster Strait and disappeared forever.

As early as the winter of 1846–1847 there was unease in London because no news had been received from the voyagers. And when the following winter passed (1847–1848) without word, the first rescue expeditions began to be organized. Everyone realized that supplies for the Franklin party must now be exhausted and that the explorers, even if still alive, would be in dire circumstances. In the late spring of 1848 there began a series of search expeditions, public and private, that had no parallel in maritime annals; when the British government refused to finance all of these, his widow, *Lady Jane Franklin,* personally organized and paid for several of these expeditions. There were five search expeditions made in 1848, three in 1849, ten in 1850, two in 1851, nine in 1852, five in 1853, two in 1854, one in 1855, and one in 1857. Thus a total of thirty-eight rescue missions over a period of nine years attempted to determine the fate of the Franklin party.

It was, however, fully fourteen years before the complete story of the doomed voyage was pieced together from records, relics, and Indian accounts. In 1850 Captain Erasmus Ommanney discovered the first wintering place of the expedition, Beechey Island; there he discovered vast stacks of meat canisters, all containing putrefied meat—abandoned by the Franklin party. The loss of this large quantity of food would have reduced by at least a year the survival time of the Franklin expedition. In 1854 *John Rae* met some Eskimos at Pelly Bay, at the base of Boothia Peninsula, who provided the first reliable account of how Franklin's men had starved to death—and in some instances, resorted to cannibalism. When Rae reported this back in England, however, he was attacked by Lady Jane Franklin and so the account was discredited. It was not until 1859 that *Francis McClintock* found the first remnants of the actual party: a boat, skeletons, books, and a written record that described the first winter of 1847 and the subsequent move to King William Island. They had reached latitude 69°37'42" N, longitude 98°4' W, but were blocked on all sides by ice and eventually lost both ships to storms and ice. Franklin died here, on King William Island on June 11, 1847, and so was not a part of the slow and terrible decimation of his party—many of whom, according to the Indians, died as they walked. (In 1984 an expedition headed by Owen Beattie, a forensic anthropologist, exhumed the completely frozen and well-preserved bodies of three members of Franklin's expedition; autopsies indicated that they had died from some combination of scurvy and lead poisoning, this latter due to the improperly canned foods they had eaten.)

And so Franklin had gazed upon, but not navigated, Victoria Strait, the body of water that passed between King William Island and the massive Victoria Island. This was a crucial link in the Northwest Passage. To Franklin went the glory of the discovery of the passage, although he died before completing the final few miles that would have put him into known and safe waters. A man of iron resolution and indomitable courage, he was also a man of gentility, uprightness, and simplicity, greatly beloved by all who served with him. Whatever his fate in 1847, John Franklin remains one of England's most honored explorers.

Frobisher, Sir Martin   (1535–1594)

The Welsh father of explorer Martin Frobisher, Bernard Frobisher, died when his son was an infant; Martin was put in the care of a relative, Sir John York. York, observing that the boy had great courage, high spirit, and a hardiness of body, sent him on a commercial voyage to Guinea in 1554. While further employed by his guardian, Martin made ten voyages to Africa and the Levant and acquired a fine knowledge of seamanship. However, by May 1566 a public notice summoned Frobisher to appear on charges of "fitting out a vessel as a pirate"; and later in 1572 he was accused of "providing a boat to convey an Earl away" from some legal difficulties. These early activities give some indication of the degree to which Frobisher's career was part explorer, part soldier of fortune, and part adventurer and pirate. These early adventures brought Frobisher to the attention of Queen Elizabeth, who in 1574 had Frobisher deliver a letter to the Muscovy Company demanding that an expedition be dispatched in search of the *Northwest Passage.* As a consequence Frobisher was granted a license for the search and out of this privilege grew his three attempts to find the passage. On June 7, 1576, Frobisher left the Thames with two barks of twenty-five tons each and a small pinnace of ten tons and sailed into the North Sea. The pinnace was soon lost in a storm, and one ship, the *Michael,* returned to *Bristol [I].* Frobisher continued on, past the southern tip of *Greenland [I]* to the southern end of *Baffin Island,* which he supposed to be Queen Elizabeth's Foreland. He then entered Frobisher Bay, which he thought to be a strait, and made note of the land masses on both sides of his "strait." He concluded that on the right side was "Asia" and on the left was "America." Equally wrong was Frobisher's belief that the bay was a strait. This he would have discovered had he gone further into it than the 150 miles he ventured. After trading some bells, mirrors, and toys for furs and seal coats with the Indians, he returned to England in October 1576 with an Eskimo and a quantity of iron pyrite. The pyrite was declared to be gold, and a second voyage was organized with specific instructions to bring back quantities of the "gold" ore rather than continue any further search for the passage. Thus ended any serious attempts at exploration by Frobisher. The second voyage left England in May of 1577 and basically followed the route of the first, reaching only slightly more southerly, past Frobisher Bay, where vast quantities of the false gold was found. Frobisher returned to England in September 1577 bearing two hundred tons of pyrite and again receiving the accolades of all. Half of the ore was deposited in Bristol Castle and half in the Tower of London, to which Frobisher was given a key.

The third expedition, which occurred in the following year, was noteworthy because of Frobisher's discovery of Hudson Strait (found by accident because of a loss of bearings in a storm). Even vaster quantities of the worthless ore were brought back, despite the fact that no gold had ever been extracted from the pyrite. Frobisher spent the rest of his life as a high-ranking officer in the Royal Navy, distinguishing himself in the battles against the Armada, alongside the likes of *Sir Francis Drake [II]* and Sir John Hawkins. He rose to the rank of vice-admiral and after having received many deserved honors, died of battle wounds in 1594.

Glazunov, Andrei (?–1846)

One of many children of Russian fathers and Aleut mothers, Andrei Glazunov was trained by the Russians to manage trading operations in Alaska and the Yukon with the Aleuts. In 1833 he was assigned to the post at St. Michael, an island in Norton Sound, south of the Seward Peninsula, and in 1834 he was sent into the Alaskan interior to explore its potential as well as to advance trade with the native people. He followed the Anvik River to the Yukon River and crossed to the Kuskokwim River, but failing to find a route to the Kenai Peninsula, he made his way back to St. Michael. In 1834 he returned to the Yukon and selected a site for a trading post, and in 1836 he established the Russian mission of Ikogmiut on the Yukon River. He spent his final years as its manager.

Greely, Adolphus Washington (1844–1935)

After serving as a volunteer in the Civil War, Greely remained in the U.S. Army, joined the Signal Corps, and became proficient at telegraphy and meteorology. In 1881 he volunteered to head an Arctic observation station on the northeast coast of *Ellesmere Island* as part of the first International Polar Year. Sailing on the *Proteus* with twenty-four in his party, he went to Lady Franklin Bay and, in Discovery Harbour, built Fort Conger, where he made meteorological and magnetic observations. He sent Lieutenant

James Lockwood along the coast of *Greenland [I]* to better the record, held by the British, for farthest north in the Western Hemisphere, 83°20'; Lockwood got only some four miles farther, to 83°24'. Greely's party was supposed to be picked up by a ship in the summer of 1882, but it could not get through; when it also failed to arrive by the summer of 1883, Greely led his men on foot and in small boats south to Cape Sabine, about midway down the coast of Ellesmere Island. Although they found caches of supplies left by other parties, these proved insufficient for the winter of 1883–1884 and one by one many men died (although Greely later denied they had resorted to cannibalism). When the party was finally rescued in June, only seven men, including Greely, were alive. Greely was at first blamed for the disaster, but when the full story of the inept rescue expeditions came out, he was exonerated. He published a popular account of his adventure, *Three Years of Arctic Service* (1885). He became the U.S. Army's chief signal corps officer (1887–1906), and as such introduced radio telegraphy into the corps and established both telegraphy and wireless systems in Alaska. Between 1887 and 1891, he also directed the U.S. Weather Service. He was a founder of the National Geographic Society, and Congress awarded him a special Medal of Honor (1935) for his lifetime of public service.

Hall, Charles Francis (1821–1871)

Charles Hall was at the center of one of the most bizarre episodes in the history of Arctic exploration. Born in New Hampshire, Hall had moved to Ohio as a young man and appeared to be settling into an ordinary sort of life. He was at first a manufacturer, and subsequently, an engraver and a newspaper publisher; he married and, with his wife, Mary, had two children. In his capacity as a newspaperman, he became fascinated with the stories of Arctic travel and the mystery still surrounding the failure and the disappearance of the last *Franklin* expedition. By 1860 Hall determined that he would go to the Arctic to search for the men he was convinced had survived that mission. Leaving his family, Hall went to New York City to find financial backing, support, and a way to the Arctic. In July of 1860 a whaler put Hall ashore on *Baffin Island,* and he spent the next two years learning the fundamentals of Arctic life and travel. At this time he met the Eskimo couple, whom he called Joe and Hannah, who were to be by his side until the end of his career. After Hall returned to the United States, he spent several years raising funds and setting up his return to the Arctic, to the almost total neglect of his family. Hall returned to the Arctic in 1864 and lived on Depot Island, at Repulse Bay and King William Island; he traveled and lived with the Inuit, and from them he accumulated much hearsay information about the final days of the Franklin mission. Searchers for the Franklin party had previously been disinclined to pay much attention to the stories and often inconsistent accounts of the tragedy as given by the Eskimos of the region. But the graves and relics found by Hall on King William Island and in the vicinity helped bring about a new attitude toward the reliability of Inuit accounts of the final stages of the disastrous expedition.

This sketch was made by Emil Schumann, a member of the 1871 expedition led by Charles Francis Hall, in his attempt to reach the North Pole. It shows an Inuit family in Greenland— the man making a canoe, the boy holding a spear, and a third person lying in front of an igloo. Hall would die while in Greenland.

Hall returned to the United States in 1869 and was hailed as a hero; on the basis of his fame he was able to secure a substantial U.S. government grant and the necessary backing for a major exploration with the *North Pole* as the destination. So on July 3, 1871, Hall departed New London, Connecticut, aboard the *Polaris* with a crew of fourteen men (and his two Eskimo retainers, Joe and Hannah). Hall took the *Polaris* north into Kennedy and Robeson Channels and into the Kane Sea. On August 30, 1871, the *Polaris* reached 82°11' N, 61° W, 250 miles north of the furthest penetration by *Elisha Kent Kane* in 1853. This was the furthest northern point ever achieved by any Arctic explorer. Here Hall was confronted by the Arctic ice pack and was forced to turn back to find open water on the northwest coast of *Greenland [I]* at a place he called Thank-God Harbor. Hall used the time to explore the surroundings by sledge. On October 24, 1871, he returned to the *Polaris* from such an excursion and was given a cup of coffee, after which he fell deathly ill. After a period of violent seizures, he died; the official cause of death was attributed to apoplexy, but a subsequent exhumation and autopsy revealed that Hall had ingested a massive dose of arsenic.

IN THEIR OWN Words — Saving the Inuits

On July 28th, in the morning, I went over to Whale Island and brought Tookoolito [an Inuit woman] on board to continue the work begun some time previous of getting up a vocabulary of the Innuit of these regions for collation with Parry's, compiled on his second voyage up Hudson's Straits. Tookoolito was very serviceable in this. She gave me valuable explanations of words, and also expeditiously interpreted into her own tongue portions of the Progressive Reader: which I had previously presented to her.

In reference to this really important matter, the following extract from my journal at the time may be here brought forward. I said:

"Oh that such a noble Christianizing work was begun here as is now established in Greenland! What a valuable aid for it could be found in Tookoolito! Will not some society, some people of civilization, see to this matter ere this noble race pass away? . . . It seems to me that the days of the Innuits are numbered. There are very few of them now. Fifty years may find them all passed away, without leaving one to tell that such a people ever lived?"

—CHARLES FRANCIS HALL, *ARCTIC RESEARCHES AND LIFE AMONG THE ESQUIMAUX*, 1865

The circumstances of Hall's death, although not really contributing to the history of exploration, deserve a footnote. There had been dissension and even conflict among those aboard the *Polaris* from the outset because many felt Hall was not qualified to be the leader of such an expedition; all soon realized the ship's master, Sidney Buddington, was a drunkard, and that the scientists aboard were less interested in reaching the North Pole than in obtaining data. Although the main suspicion fell on the ship's doctor, Emil Bessels, who was known to have resented Hall's status, it has never been proved that any individual murdered Hall.

Harriman expedition (1899)

One of the most unusual expeditions into the sub-Arctic region was that sponsored and led by Edward Henry Harriman (1848–1909), the wealthy American financier and railroad executive. Whether to counter his reputation as a ruthless "robber baron" or to demonstrate a serious commitment to scientific understanding, Harriman organized and paid for an expedition that sailed from Seattle on a luxury yacht with 126 passengers and crew. (In fact, he also wanted to hunt for bear.) Along with his own family and some personal friends, Harriman invited some twenty-three scientists, naturalists, and artists, many of them still well known over a century later, such as naturalist *John Muir [VI],* nature writer John Burroughs, ethnologist George Bird Grinnell, ornithologist Louis Agassiz Fuertes, zoologist William Dall, biologist C. Hart Merriam, and photographer Edward Curtis. On the ship, in addition to the luxurious cabins provided for his guests, Harriman brought along a fine chef to prepare the meals. He also provided the scientists with laboratories for their work and space for the preservation of the specimens they would be collecting. (Ornithologist Fuertes shot thousands of birds for his collection.) For two months,

Seen here in Alaskan waters is the luxury yacht *George Elder,* the ship hired by Edward Harriman for his expedition to Alaska in 1899. The photo is by Edward Curtis, who would go on to fame as a photographer of Indians.

the ship sailed along the Pacific coast of Canada and Alaska through the Prince William Sound, down along the Aleutian Islands and into the Bering Sea and past the Pribilof Islands, and across the Bering Strait for a short jaunt to Siberia, all the while putting in to different ports and landfalls. They made several discoveries, including a previously unknown fjord and glacier in Alaska, but their major contribution came from the five thousand photographs and thousands of drawings and the more than one hundred trunkloads of botanical and zoological specimens. After their return, Harriman paid for the publication of the expedition's findings, the fourteen-volume *Harriman Alaska Series* (1902–1914).

Eventually, the expedition and its findings faded into the background of the story of exploration. But in the year 2001, Thomas Litwin, a professor at Smith College, in Northampton, Massachusetts, and director of that school's Clark Science Center, led what was known as the Harriman Expedition Retraced. With twenty-four scientists, naturalists, and artists, the expedition sailed on the 340-foot M/V *Clipper Odyssey* and retraced the 9,000-mile route of the original expedition. This time the goal was not to discover new things but to examine the ecological and cultural changes that had occurred in the region during the century that had passed. Not unexpectedly, they found that the environment and the culture of the Native American in Alaska had suffered considerably from the inroads of such activities as oil drilling and forestry. At the same time, there were some positive changes, such as an increased respect by the Native Americans and this new expedition's scientists for the Native Americans' culture. For instance, they returned six totem poles that had been taken from the Cape Fox Indians and that had been displayed all those years in U.S. museums. If the original Harriman expedition had never quite entered the annals of respectable scientific exploration, the "retraced" expedition validated its usefulness.

Hayes, Isaac (1832–1881)

Isaac Hayes was born in Chester County, Pennsylvania, and went on to become a medical doctor. In 1853 he signed on as ship's surgeon aboard the *Advance,* in the expedition led by *Elisha Kent Kane.* Kane was convinced that the *Franklin* exploration party had gone north after spending the first winter on Prince of Wales Island. Therefore, Kane's voyage was technically a search mission, even though Franklin had disappeared almost eight years before. Kane hired Hayes because he was enthusiastic and because, like Kane, he believed in the idea of an open polar sea. From the beginning, Hayes was jealous and mistrusting of Kane's leadership. In the spring of 1854 he was sent on an ill-advised sledge mission to find the polar sea. Hayes crossed the ice of Kane Basin and was the first non-Eskimo to explore the interior of *Ellesmere Island;* he charted two hundred miles of what he named Grinnell Land. Hayes returned to the *Advance,* snow-blind and with frozen toes. He had survived by eating the tops of his boots, dipped in lamp oil.

As the summer approached, it became clear that the *Advance* would not be freed from the ice; Hayes was the leader of secret meetings that led to open mutiny. Eight of the crew, with Hayes as leader, deserted the expedition and headed for Upernavik and civilization in *Greenland [I].* Kane gave the "rotten pack of ingrates" all the food and supplies they requested;

in four months they were back, emaciated, frozen, and unrepentant. They had survived by the generosity of a band of Eskimos, whom Hayes had subsequently rewarded by making off with their clothes, food, and dogs. Hayes returned to New York, to bask in the reflected praise heaped on Elisha Kane. He later led two unsuccessful voyages to the Arctic, claiming that he had reached further north than Kane. He also professed to have reached the "imaginary" iceless ocean. Both of these claims were subsequently disproved.

Hearne, Samuel   (1745–1792)

Samuel Hearne was born in London and at the early age of eleven became a midshipman for the Royal Navy. After seven years at sea, he entered the service of the *Hudson's Bay Company [VI]*. His first posting was to the company's trading post at Prince of Wales Fort, a settlement on the desolate and forbidding western shore of Hudson Bay.

The Hudson's Bay Company had been given a charter by the British crown in 1670, which gave it a virtual monopoly over the lucrative fur trade in northern Canada. As supplier of fur to the wealthy patrons of England and Europe, the franchise had over the years produced enormous profit for the principals of the charter. But the company had been so preoccupied with reaping their huge financial rewards that they had ignored the terms of the contract. It had been stipulated in the charter that the company was to (1) extend trade; (2) explore the region, including a search for the *Northwest Passage;* (3) map Canada's natural resources; (4) encourage settlements; and (5) develop a market for British products with the indigenous Indian population. The company, of course, had done none of these things; indeed, most of the stipulations were antithetical to serious profit-making from their point of view. Serious criticism against the company was being voiced in England. And pressure came from another direction: Interest was reviving in finding a route to the Atlantic over North America starting from the west.

The company decided to act, most likely to forestall further hostile public opinion. They mandated an exploration to find and follow the far-off Metal River (the Coppermine River) to the polar sea and, if possible, find the Northwest Passage. These orders were passed on to Moses Norton, the governor of Prince of Wales Fort. Norton picked Samuel

Hearne, the young newly arrived navy man, to lead the expedition. Norton probably chose Hearne in order to get rid of him: There was no love lost between the two men. Hearne, though he was courageous and conscientious, had scant navigational experience and less understanding of Native American ways; in addition, he had never traveled in the Arctic nor learned the unique survival skills necessary. Hearne's specific orders were to make a map of the country he traversed, find the Coppermine River's mouth, fix its longitude and latitude, and take possession of the river.

On November 6, 1769, Hearne left Prince of Wales Fort, heading north and west, into territory largely unvisited by Europeans; he carried minimal food, clothes, and equipment, because he had no idea what lay before him. Hearne was back at the fort within thirty days; his Indian guides had deserted him and made off with the ammunition and provisions. A second excursion lasted eight months but was just as unproductive: His quadrant was knocked over by the wind and smashed to pieces. No navigation or mapping was possible without this instrument. In 1771 Hearne set out yet again, with the trusted Indian leader Matonabbee as his guide. Also in the party were Matonabbee's eight wives and a large number of experienced and trustworthy Indians (and their families). No European other than Hearne was included. As the party moved north, other Indians joined, and the entourage swelled to nearly two hundred men, women, and children. Although Hearne was beginning to develop strong characteristics of determined leadership, it was clear that he held little authority over such an unwieldy group; after all, the Indians were nomads and were content to wander around through the wilderness foraging for food and shelter when the weather was bad. Also, it turned out that Matonabbee had a real hatred for Eskimos; often the exploration was detoured or delayed so that a raid could be made on unsuspecting Eskimos, always against Hearne's direct orders.

Nonetheless, the party arrived at the Coppermine River in July 1771, nearly a thousand miles from Prince of Wales Fort. Hearne proceeded to the mouth of the river and "concluded" that the open water visible was salt and therefore the open Polar Sea. The open water, of course, would have been merely the Coronation Gulf, far south of the Beaufort Sea. Hearne took readings at one o'clock A.M. in the fog and rain; he "estimated" his location as 71°55' N and 120°30' W. In fact, he was almost 300 miles south and 130 miles east of where he thought he was. Hearne erected a cairn and took possession of the coast on behalf of the Hudson's Bay Company. He also examined the Coppermine River area for the reputed stores of gold and copper. One four-pound piece of pure copper was found and brought back to the fort. The return to the Prince of Wales Fort was slow and torturous. Hearne was struck with a terrible affliction of the legs and feet and left behind "a thousand miles of bloody footprints." Finally the explorers reached home in June 1772, after nineteen months in the wilderness.

Hearne wrote a full report of his travels, with maps and charts, but in typical fashion, the Hudson's Bay Company suppressed the public circulation of the report. When the French captured the fort in 1782, General *La Pérouse [IV]* allowed Hearne to take the report with him back to England, where it was published. Hearne, while lauded for his adventures, was criticized for the inaccuracy of his latitude and longitude measurements.

Hearne's work was important to the evolving struggle of the search for the Northwest Passage. He was the first European to reach the inland reaches of the Polar Sea by land. He also demonstrated that no waterway to the east crossed the northern Canadian mainland. His journal provided much of what was known about the Canadian Northwest for the next hundred years. His accounts of the habits and ways of the Indians, and his observations of the natural history of the north Canadian region, were useful to the explorers to come. Hearne died of dropsy in London in 1792.

Henson, Matthew (1866–1955)

Matthew Henson was born in an African American sharecropping family in Maryland; at the age of eleven both his parents died. He then spent several years in Washington, D.C., apparently on his own. At thirteen, he signed on to the *Katie Hines* as a cabin boy, rising during the following six years to become an able-bodied seaman. He then obtained a job as a stock clerk in a Washington, D.C. hat shop. Here he was recommended for his hard work and reliability to Lieutenant **Robert E. Peary,** who had just returned from his first Arctic voyage. Peary hired Henson as his personal valet and took the young man on a voyage of survey of canals in Central America. Henson was to accompany Peary on all his succeeding Arctic explorations: two North *Greenland [I]* expeditions, two summer Arctic expeditions to retrieve meteorites, and the three *North Pole* expeditions. In Peary's eyes, Matt Henson was forever his valet only, never his companion or fellow-explorer, even when they stood together on April 6,

1909, at the North Pole. He remained "my colored boy," "my body servant," and "my dark-skinned, kinky haired child of the Equator," as he variously referred to Henson at later times. Henson accepted his lot with equanimity; he never spoke out against Peary, mentioning only, in his writing, his disappointment at Peary's coldness to him after the achievement of the great prize of the North Pole.

In fact, Henson was the most accomplished of all the explorers who accompanied Peary on his polar attempts. He had quickly learned the Eskimo language and had become a master at igloo building and dog handling. The Eskimos called him great "Maktok Kabloona" (black white man) and "Miy Paluk" (dear Matty) and loved him because he had learned their language and, unlike Peary, treated them with affection and respect. Henson had a great thirst for education. He had read widely and carried his Bible and his Dickens wherever he went. Doc John Goodsell of the Polar party called Henson "Othello" and recited Shakespeare to him as they trudged across the ice fields. Henson got *Donald MacMillan* of the party to teach him navigational math as the *Roosevelt* sailed towards the jumping-off point on **Ellesmere Island.** It was MacMillan who later wrote that Henson, with his years of experience and skills, "was of more real value than the combined services of all of us."

Henson served Peary well during the first two polar attempts of 1898 and 1905. Between expeditions he worked at various jobs, sometimes on his own, often for Peary as a messenger or an aide, or in some small capacity. But he was always at Peary's beck and call. In 1908 he organized the expedition's equipment and the fitting out of the *Roosevelt* for the final assault on the pole. As the expedition got underway, Henson served as sledge builder, driver, hunter, carpenter, blacksmith, and cook. And of course he was Peary's personal servant, cooking his meals, tending his Arctic wear, and ministering to the leader when he fell ill or his injured

IN THEIR OWN *Words*

An African American Views the North Pole

The Commander [Peary] gave the word, "We will plant the stars and stripes—at the North Pole!"... Another world's accomplishment was done and finished, and as in the past, from the beginning of history, wherever the world's work was done by a white man, he had been accompanied by a colored man. From the building of the pyramids and the journey to the Cross, to the discovery of the New World and the discovery of the North Pole, the Negro had been the faithful and constant companion of the Caucasian, and I felt that it was possible for me to feel that it was I, a lowly member of my race, who had been chosen by fate to represent it, at this, almost the last of the world's great work.

—MATTHEW HENSON, *A NEGRO EXPLORER AT THE NORTH POLE*, 1912

leg gave way. Henson saved Peary's life a number of times; in every way he was Peary's right-hand man. Later it would also come out that both Peary and Henson had fathered children with Eskimo women, and although neither man publicly recognized these offspring, their descendants eventually did.

On April 1, 1909, Peary reckoned that the explorers were 133 miles from the pole. Peary, Henson, and four Eskimos would complete the final stage. The last Euroamerican accompanying them, Captain *Robert Bartlett,* was sent back, tearfully. Five days later, Henson built an igloo on a spot that was determined by readings then taken to be just beside the pole. A few pictures were taken, and there was a brief ceremony. The return to the *Roosevelt* was, according to Peary, a joyful "hustle" that broke every record of speedy Arctic travel—up to seventy-five miles a day. According to Henson, it was a "horrid nightmare"; the dog team crawling and falling down, the Eskimos with faces of old men, and Peary "a beat figure, shuffling . . . a frightening, walking corpse." Henson recalled that Peary spoke to him only a few times on the return to the ship. And during the return to civilization on the *Roosevelt,* Peary ignored him and never once mentioned the term "North Pole." Henson consoled himself by reading his Bible, in particular the verse in St. Matthew: "Blessed are the meek."

In this photo, taken in 1954, Matthew Henson is showing the location of the North Pole to President Eisenhower. Mrs. Robert Vann, publisher of the *Pittsburgh Courier,* is looking on. The occasion was Eisenhower's awarding of a special citation to Henson after years of neglect.

Peary returned to America and the great accolades awaiting him; Henson received a brusque dismissal and his expedition salary of twenty-five dollars a month. Although Peary later made both disparaging and honorable remarks about Henson, there seemed to be no further contact between the two men; Peary had no further need for Henson and clearly felt uncomfortable having him around. Henson was no longer the "Maktok Kabloona" except to the faraway Eskimos who had said he would be remembered always for his kindness and his strength. The first African American Arctic explorer eked out a living as a Brooklyn car park attendant and subsequently as a seventeen-dollar-a-week messenger boy. (*A Negro Explorer at the North Pole,* published under his name, is believed to have been mainly ghostwritten.) Later his contributions were better recognized: He received a congressional medal in 1944, a citation from President Eisenhower in 1954, and honorary degrees from Morgan State College and Howard University. He had been given a membership to the Explorers Club in 1937, but he seldom, if ever, went there: He could not afford to pay for lunch. Matthew Henson died in 1955; in 1988, he was reburied with military honors in Arlington National Cemetery.

Herbert, Sir (Walter William) Wally (1934–)

After *Peary*'s claim to have reached the *North Pole* on April 6, 1909, many other attempts were made to reach the top of the globe, using a variety of methods and personnel. There were expeditions using icebreakers, submarines, skiplanes, snowmobiles, expeditions with and without dogs, in groups and solo, on skis and on foot. Some attempts refused to allow air support, while some had supplies dropped to them and injured or sick explorers flown out by helicopter. One of the most impressive post-Peary polar journeys was Wally Herbert's trek of sixteen months from Alaska to Spitsbergen via the North Pole. Herbert, of British parentage, was brought up in South Africa and trained at the School of Military Survey. By 1968 he had established himself as a seasoned polar explorer: He had traveled over 25,000 miles by sledge and in open boat, in both the Arctic and the Antarctic. Much of the Antarctic region charted by Herbert had not been visited before by human beings. He had also traced the routes of many of the great polar explorers: Peary, *Sverdrup,* Scott, and *Amundsen,* to name a few. In 1968 Herbert set out to cross the Polar Sea with three companions by way of the North Pole using sledges and forty dogs. The party would be supported by airdrops from planes of the Royal Canadian Air Force. Herbert left Point Barrow, Alaska, in February 1968 and by July had reached only 82°27' N, having encountered impossible ice ridges and uncrossable open water. Accidents and bad ice and weather conditions stalled the expedition; finally in February 1969 they were able to move on, despite the deplorable condition of the ice surface. In April 1969 Herbert reached the Pole and after a brief rest, pressed on toward Svalbard (Spitzbergen), arriving at Table Island, where he was rescued by helicopter in June 1969. Herbert's feat was described as the last truly great adventure in the history of the North Pole. British Prime Minister Harold Wilson called the journey "a

feat of endurance and courage which ranks with any in Polar history."
Herbert received, among other awards, the Polar Medal, the gold medal of
the Geographical Society and the Explorer's medal of the Explorer's Club.
Later he made several attempts to circumnavigate *Greenland [I]*. In 1989
he published a book, *The Noose of Laurels*, in which he argued that neither
Peary nor *Cook* had conclusively established their claims to have reached
the North Pole.

Hudson, Henry (circa 1550–1611?)

Henry Hudson's date of birth and birthplace in England are unknown, but
he must have become a skilled navigator because he was commissioned by
the English Muscovy Company to find a northeast passage across the Arctic regions to China and Asia. This was to be an alternate to the much
sought-after *Northwest Passage* route. In May 1607 he set out in the
Hopewell with a crew of ten and his son, John. On this voyage he reached
the island of Spitzbergen and possibly Jan Mayen Island but had to turn
back. On a second voyage in 1608, he got as far as Novaya Zemlya in the
Barents Sea off the northwest coast of Russia. He had failed to complete a
northeast passage, but he had sailed farther north than any known
explorer.

In 1609 he moved to Holland, and this time under a commission
from the Dutch East India Company, he sailed west to find the Northwest

This imaginative painting by the nineteenth-century American artist Edward Moran depicts
Henry Hudson entering New York bay for the first time on September 11, 1609. An Indian
family watches from the shore in the foreground as Hudson prepares to sail up the river
that will later be named after him.

Passage. His ship was the *Half-Moon* and had a mixed crew of English and Dutch sailors. They set off in April 1609 and headed into the cold northern seas off North America; fearing mutiny, Hudson turned south, sailing down along the coast of Maine, past Cape Cod, and all the way to *Chesapeake Bay [III]*. There he headed back north along the coast of New Jersey until in September he sailed into the harbor where a river met the ocean; he then sailed up the river some 150 miles to what would become the site of Albany, claiming the lands along the river for Holland; the river would eventually be named after him.

On his return Hudson went to England and on April 1610 set out on his fourth major voyage, again seeking the Northwest Passage, this time on behalf of a group of English merchants. His ship was the *Discovery* and in addition to the crew of twenty he had his son John, now twelve years old, with him. Crossing the North Atlantic, the ship sailed into what would become known as the Hudson Strait, the water between *Labrador [III]* and *Baffin Island,* and in August he sailed into the great body of water that he at first believed was the Pacific Ocean; in fact it was the bay also later to be named after him. As the *Discovery* and its crew sailed around the bay, the weather worsened, and by November they were trapped by ice in St. James Bay, the "bulge" at the southern edge of Hudson's Bay. As the crew became cold and ill, they accused Hudson of distributing the dwindling food supplies unfairly. When the ship was finally free to sail, Hudson insisted that they continue on westward, so on June 23 the crew mutinied; they put Hudson, his son, and seven loyal sailors in a small boat and set them adrift. No trace of them was ever found. Of the thirteen sailors who mutinied, only eight made it back to England in the *Discovery,* and for some reason they were never punished—perhaps because their report of their findings allowed England to lay claim to that vast territory. Henry Hudson's reputation as an explorer rests on his willingness to sail into unknown seas, and although he paid for this with his life, his name fittingly lives on with two great bodies of water.

James, Thomas   (1593–1635)

Thomas James left Bristol on May 13, 1631, on the *Henrietta Maria* bound for Hudson Bay and the *Northwest Passage.* His voyage was sponsored by *Bristol [I]* merchants who were fearful of losing out on the lucrative profits of trade, should London interests discover the passage. Thomas James was a gentleman of culture and literary bent, completely unskilled in seamanship, matched by an unruly crew inexperienced in Arctic navigation and survival. Once in the Hudson Bay, the *Maria* sailed to the south, entering the mouth of James Bay in fierce bad weather. The waves were entering the ship, according to the log, from both sides and from the front and the back. Planks and pieces of their own ship drifted past them on one occasion, after they had struck upon the rocky shore. The *Maria* proceeded deeper into James Bay to find winter quarters and found a likely harbor on Charlton Island; there, as the ice was quickly forming, they sank the *Maria* to prevent its being frozen in the ice. Such a decision was apparently typical of James's skill as a seaman. James and his men spent a hard winter, beset by diminishing rations and the inevitable scurvy, which James overcame by feeding the men sorrel. The plan to build a new ship was unsuccessful, so the party began the arduous task of raising the *Maria* from the bottom. Once they had succeeded, on July 1, 1632, James headed north out of James Bay, along the west coastline of Hudson Bay and into the Foxe Basin, and he explored those waters until the threat of ice made him decide to return to England. James reached Bristol in late 1632, on the *Maria*, which was by all accounts falling to pieces. James brought out a well-written romantic account of the voyage and very quickly was acclaimed a public hero. James, like **Luke Foxe,** made it clear that the regions he had explored held no possibility of access to the west.

Kane, Elisha Kent (1820–1857)

Elisha Kent Kane, during his short life span, earned the esteem and respect of the world scientific community and was hailed as one of America's great Arctic explorers. Kane was born into a prominent Philadelphia family and at a very early age was stricken with a severe heart condition. He was not expected to live long, but thanks to the encouragement of his father, he decided to live life to the fullest. He completed a medical degree at an early age and published a brilliant and influential study in regard to pregnancy. In 1844 Kane was a member of the first diplomatic mission to China, and in 1846 he began his duties as surgeon in the U.S. Navy. In the following year President James Polk sent him on a special mission to Mexico, where he was seriously wounded in the struggle occurring there between the Mexican army and political insurgent forces. After his recovery, he had tours of duty in the Mediterranean and in South America. In 1850 Kane, already a popular American hero, joined a mission organized to search for the *Franklin* expedition, missing since its departure in 1845. Kane was designated surgeon and official historian aboard the *Advance.* The searchers found Franklin's first winter camp at Beechey Island, along with a number of graves where members of Franklin's party had been buried. Failing to find further signs of Franklin's whereabouts, the *Advance* returned to the United States in September 1851. Kane was convinced that Franklin had gone north after his first winter in the Arctic, and he determined to undertake another search in the *Greenland [I]* area; in 1853 Kane traveled north along the coast of Greenland, reaching Smith Sound, at the northern extremity of Greenland, south of *Ellesmere Island.* Here the expedition was frozen in the ice. Kane, on the basis of erroneous information, was led to believe that there was open water to the north, which meant that there was an unfrozen polar sea to the *North Pole.* It was this promising prospect that kept Kane from retreating; at any rate, the thaw of 1854 failed to free up the ship. Kane, despite his frail physical condition, dealt with mutiny and desertion, scurvy and starvation. He bartered with the Inuit for some food, and harvested the ship's ample supply of rats as a remedy for scurvy. In the summer of 1855 Kane and his party abandoned the ship to the ice and successfully retreated to Greenland, where they were rescued and returned to the United States as Arctic heroes.

IN THEIR OWN *Words*

The Quest for Franklin

It is the quiet hour at which you and I begin to live; lacking midnight not overmuch, yet in full glare of day.

Now that the thing—the dream—has concentrated itself into a grim, practical reality, it is not egotism, but duty, to talk of myself and my plans; I represent other lives and other interests than my own. The object of my journey is the search after Sir John Franklin: neither science nor the vain glory of attaining an unreached North shall divert me from this one conscientious aim.

—ELISHA KENT KANE, LETTER TO HIS BROTHER THOMAS, AUGUST 1853

In 1856 Kane reluctantly traveled to England to help *Lady Jane Franklin* organize another search mission for her husband. It is ironic that after having survived so many life-threatening adventures previously, Kane should now fall ill in the comfort and security of London. He died early in the next year on February 16, 1857. Kane's travels on five continents resulted in major contributions to medical research, Arctic exploration, and international understanding.

Kashevarov, Alexander Filippovich (1809–1870)

Born on Kodiak Island to an Aleut mother and Russian father, Alexander Filippovich Kashevarov was trained as a mariner in Russia and in 1831 went to work with the Russian-American Company. In 1838 he led an expedition to explore the northwestern coast of Alaska (often using kayaks) from Kotzebue Sound to just east of Point Barrow. He thus became the first to describe much of this coastline. After 1845 he spent most of his time working in the Hydrographic Department of Russia's Ministry of the Navy, and in 1862 he published the *Atlas of the Eastern Ocean*, which described much of the Bering Sea.

Kellett, Sir Henry (1806–1875)

Henry Kellett was born in Tipperary, Ireland, in 1806 and at the age of sixteen joined the Royal Navy. He served with distinction for five years in the West Indies and then on further assignments in the East Indies and Africa. Kellett was promoted to post captain in 1841 and took command of the *Herald* for survey work on the Pacific coast of Central America. From 1848–1850, Kellett was sent to Alaska to help in the search for the lost *Franklin* party. During this assignment Kellett discovered Herald Island and saw but did not land on Wrangel Island. At the end of Kellett's search duty he encountered **Robert McClure** in command of the *Investigator;* Kellett advised McClure to wait for his superior, Captain **Richard Collinson,** from whom he had been separated. McClure, eager for the opportunity to discover the missing link in the **Northwest Passage** (and the £20,000 reward) declined to stop.

Kellett returned to England in 1851 and was immediately given command of the *Resolute,* one of three ships in an expedition led by Sir Edward Belcher to once more search for Franklin. Belcher would continue the search by way of Lancaster Sound, while Kellett, assisted by the *Intrepid* under command of **Francis McClintock,** would concentrate on the Melville Island area. The *Resolute* was also to search for McClure and the *Investigator,* which for many months was unreported and assumed to be in trouble or lost. Kellett, as ordered, passed through the Lancaster Sound and proceeded west to the southern coast of Melville Island, where he dug in for the winter. Expeditions by sledge from the winter base found no trace of the Franklin mission, but a buried message from McClure was found stating that the *Investigator* was frozen solid in the Bay of Mercy on the shore of Banks Island. In the bitter cold of March 1853, a rescue party was sent out and the starving and scurvy-ridden crew of the *Investigator* was brought back to Melville Island. Kellett continued to send out sledging parties, but no evidence was found of the Franklin expedition. However, two new islands were added to the map: Eglinton and Prince Patrick. On the return voyage, the *Resolute* was frozen in the Barrow Strait in the winter of 1853–1854. On Belcher's orders, Kellett very reluctantly abandoned his ship, as Belcher also did his ships; eventually all crews were returned to England via the *North Star*. (The *Resolute* was later found by American whalers, who sailed it to the United States. It was eventually returned to the British, and when they dismantled it, they used some of its wood to make a desk presented to the White House; it was this desk that President John F. Kennedy used in the Oval Office.) Only because Kellett produced Belcher's written order to abandon was he saved from the court-martial that Belcher faced. Kellett was completely cleared and in fact was commended for his extensive service. McClure received the discovery award for finding the Northwest Passage. No credit was given to Kellett by McClure for his rescue, and McClure testified before a parliamentary committee that he could have brought his men out alive.

Kellett subsequently held commands in the West Indies and in China. He spent a long retirement at his place of birth in Ireland and died in 1875. In addition to his rescue of McClure and his survey work in the Arctic, Kellett was credited by Soviet writers with doing the first hydrographic work in the eastern Russian Arctic.

Knight, James   (1640?–1719?)

James Knight was an Arctic explorer who in the early eighteenth century charted some of the territory in the south and southwestern region of Hudson Bay. For many years he was an agent of the *Hudson's Bay Company [VI],* which at that time was interested in finding the *Northwest Passage,* as well as exploiting any other North American riches to be found, such as furs and valuable minerals. In 1693 Knight was the governor of Fort Albany, in James Bay; in 1714 he was the leader of a settlement at Nelson River on the western coast of Hudson Bay. Several years later he established a fort at the mouth of the Churchill River known as Prince of Wales. Knight learned of a mine from the friendly Indians local to that area, which he imagined to be gold, but was probably copper or pyrite. On the strength of the Indian accounts, Knight returned to England and persuaded the Hudson's Bay Company to fit out a search expedition; he returned to Hudson Bay in 1719 with two ships, a crew of fifty and instructions to find the *Strait of Anian [II]* (allegedly leading to the passage westward) and to discover gold or any other valuable commodities. No word was received from the expedition; for a long while it was hoped that the voyagers had found the Northwest Passage and would be returning to England via the Pacific, laden with gold and other valuables from the east. In fact, Knight was never seen nor heard from again; it was 1767 before the remains of the doomed expedition were found on Marble Island. From the Eskimos it was learned that the two ships were disabled at that point, and that the entire party perished slowly and horribly, the last five men dying in 1721. Since Knight was reputed to be almost eighty at the time, it is presumed that he was one of the first to die.

Kotzebue (Kotsebu), Otto von   (1788–1846)

Son of the famous German dramatist August von Kotzebue, who worked for the Russian government, Otto von Kotzebue was a navigator who sailed under Russian Admiral Baron Adam Johann von Krusenstern in the first Russian round-the-world voyage aboard the ship *Nadezhda* (1803–1806). From 1815 to 1818 Kotzebue led his own expedition to the South Pacific and then up through the Bering Strait in search of a northeast passage to the Atlantic. In the course of this voyage, he discovered a sound on the west coast of Alaska that he named after himself. In 1823 Czar Alexander I ordered him to patrol the west coast of North America to fend off foreign smugglers threatening the trade of the Russian-American Company. In 1829 he retired to Estonia with his family.

MacMillan, Donald B.   (1874–1970)

Donald Baxter MacMillan was born in Massachusetts on November 10, 1874. His father was lost at sea when he was nine years old; three years later his mother died. MacMillan lived with family friends a few years before ending up in the care of his married sister in Freeport, Maine. MacMillan excelled in high school, and by dint of hard work and frugal living put himself through Bowdoin College, with a degree in geology. He then went on to teach Latin, physical education, and mathematics in schools in Maine and Massachusetts for a number of years. Along the way he had established a summer camp for boys, specializing in seamanship and navigation. In the operation of this camp, he heroically saved the lives of nine people from shipwreck; it was through this highly publicized event that he came to the attention of **Robert Peary.** Peary asked MacMillan to join his 1905 attempt to reach the **North Pole.** This was not possible for MacMillan, but in 1908 he joined Peary in his third, successful journey to the Pole.

MacMillan was well suited for such an expedition. Although he had no Arctic experience, he was a man of great physical strength and endurance; he was a stable and disciplined person and was able to contribute much to the psychological and mental well being of the polar party. On the voyage north on the *Roosevelt* he taught **Matthew Henson** mathematics, and he instructed the Eskimos in gymnastics; he even had the Eskimos reciting the opening lines of Virgil's *Aeneid* in Latin. During the wintering at Cape Sheridan, **Ellesmere Island,** he orga-

IN THEIR OWN *Words*

Mixed Feelings on Being Rescued

Home! Why, it was like going to another world! Happy? Yes—no! Naturally we wanted to see friends and relatives, but the Great Northland gets a relentless grip on a man. Its drift ice, its towering white bergs, its glittering domes, its receding ice-cap, the stretching trail, the galloping dogs, the happy, laughing, contented Eskimos—all attracting, appealing, and ever calling.

—DONALD MACMILLAN, *FOUR YEARS IN THE WHITE NORTH,* 1925

nized a track meet by pick axing out a smooth track among the ice floes; there at 82°30', at minus 25°F, the Eskimos and crew engaged in sprinting, wrestling, and boxing matches. MacMillan finished off with a display of handsprings and somersaults. At Christmas, to ward off the terrible depression of the long Arctic winter, he organized a splendid feast, followed by the can-can performance of the Floradora Sextet of six Eskimo beauties and the lavish awarding of prizes of cigars or scented soap to all. MacMillan did not reach the pole. At 84°29', on March 14, 1909, he was forced to turn back, with feet so badly frozen that he could no longer walk.

The lure of the Arctic was now firmly in MacMillan's blood. He spent the next years traveling in *Labrador [III],* carrying out ethnological studies among the Inuit. In 1913 he organized and led his own expedition to *Greenland [I],* the Crocker Land Expedition: He was, however, stranded there until 1917, when he was finally rescued by *Robert Bartlett,* his mate from the Peary Polar mission. After a period as a naval officer in World War I, MacMillan turned again to the North, and in 1921, he raised the money for a new type of ship, strong, maneuverable and designed specially for Arctic travel. In the new boat the *Bowdoin* he sailed to *Baffin Island,* the first of many Arctic research explorations. In 1935 MacMillan married Mirian Norton Look, the daughter of a close friend of his. She was twenty-three years his junior and had been for many years his admirer and a follower of his adventures. As his wife, she finally won permission to sail north with him; she proved herself able to withstand the rigors of the Arctic and was able to perform all the duties of an able-bodied seaman. The crew heartily approved of her presence on board. She was the first woman to sail to within 650 miles of the pole; undoubtedly she traveled more Arctic miles than any other woman on record. Mirian MacMillan was to be her husband's travel companion for the rest of his active Arctic exploration. After a second period of service in World War II, MacMillan continued to make voyages of research to the Arctic until 1954. Even after his retirement from active duty MacMillan remained influential in Arctic affairs. MacMillan died at the age of ninety-six in Provincetown, Massachusetts.

McClintock, Francis Leopold (?–1907)

Francis McClintock was a self-made man who entered the upper ranks of the Royal Navy. He was one of fourteen children in a desperately poor Irish family and succeeded by dint of determined self-improvement. He was well educated in engineering and mathematics and a physically powerful man; in addition to his resilient and inquiring intelligence, he was disciplined, fair-minded and compassionate in leadership. McClintock was particularly concerned with the sledge travel methods of the time; in a number of minor Arctic missions, he had seen the folly of men pulling overburdened sledges and in 1854 he had seen two men virtually die in harness. He began to experiment with dog teams, and with some difficulty learned to drive one himself. He accomplished an incredible 470 miles in fifteen days in *Greenland [I]*, a feat that men pulling sledges might have managed in forty-five days. Later in McClintock's career he came to believe that the Royal Navy's methods of Arctic travel were in large part responsible for the tragic conclusion of the *Franklin* mission. McClintock experimented with improvements: a new type of alcohol stove, different kinds of food, a new, lighter-weight sledge, and auxiliary sledge crews to cache food along the intended march line.

McClintock had served in three Franklin search expeditions from 1848 until 1854; none of these missions proved successful. When *Lady Franklin* had raised enough funds for a final attempt to find her husband, Francis McClintock became her logical choice to lead it. In June 1857 *The Fox*, with McClintock as captain, left Aberdeen with instructions to head for King William Island, believed to be the last known wintering site of the Franklin expedition. The first winter was spent frozen in ice off Greenland; the second was spent locked in ice at the eastern entrance to Bellot Strait. In the spring of 1859, at last at King William Island, McClintock set out to explore the island by making a complete circuit of the five-thousand-square mile wasteland. On the northwestern coast Lieutenant William Robert Hobson, McClintock's junior officer, found what the Admiralty and all England had been waiting for: a tin cylinder case containing an official form of the British Admiralty, which stated that Sir John Franklin had died on Friday, June 11, 1847, at the age of sixty-one. Twenty-four officers and men had perished, and the remaining one hundred and five "souls" had deserted the frozen-in ship and set out to march the two hundred miles to the mouth of the Back River, on the Canadian mainland. McClintock followed that route and put together the story of the "death march." It was a colossal tragic military bungle, "rank conscious" and inept. Men died as they pulled sledges overburdened with curtain rods, fine china, silk shirts, and a mahogany writing desk. McClintock tried to soften the report by calling it "noble devotion to naval duty." McClintock returned to England with mixed feelings about his discoveries. But he had discovered eight hundred miles of new coastline. He had, by delineating King William Island, provided the crucial part of the puzzle of the *Northwest Passage.* And most of all, he had resolved, once and for all, the mystery of Franklin's fate. McClintock went on to further achievements in the Royal Navy and in public service.

McClure, Robert John Le Mesurier (1807–1873)

Born in Ireland, Robert McClure was a man driven by a fanatical ambition. Good judgment, good leadership, and regard for his own and his crews' safety were all subjugated to his determination to discover and navigate the long-sought *Northwest Passage.* McClure, who had entered the Royal Navy at seventeen, had long been frustrated by his slow rise through the ranks. By 1850 he had been on two Arctic voyages, but in a subordinate rank. Now, finally, at age forty-three, he was made captain of the *Investigator* under the expedition leadership of Commander *Richard Collinson;* the goal of the mission was to find *John Franklin* and to proceed into the central Canadian Archipelago via the Bering Strait. McClure was able to slip away from Collinson in the Pacific and, by taking a dangerous short cut through the Aleutians, he arrived at the Bering Strait two weeks in advance of his party. He had no intention of waiting; his intention was to find the Passage on his own and to claim full credit. Opposition from his men was met with lashes of the cat-o'-nine-tails and quarrelsome officers were put under arrest. The *Investigator* forced its way into the Prince of Wales Strait, the berg-littered narrow body of water that separates Banks Island from Victoria Island to the south. There, as the ice closed in, McClure could see the tip of Melville Island and he suspected correctly that past Melville lay the route to Lancaster Sound and the eastern end of the Passage. But his discovery was pointless; the *Investigator* was frozen in for the next three winters. Neither blasting, cutting, nor hauling could free the ship; a century later, even the U.S. icebreaker-tanker *Manhattan* (see *Northwest Passage*) could not force its way through the almost eternally frozen Prince of Wales Strait. The party tried desperately to escape, even sledging 160 miles to *Parry*'s Winter Harbor only to find it deserted. The winter of 1852–1853 was the worst. The men were down to half rations; scurvy, insanity, and mutiny were breaking out. McClure devised a plan of setting out overland—one party toward the east, another toward the south. Fortunately, before these suicide treks started out, rescue came from a search ship anchored off of Melville Island; it was the ship with Sir Edward Belcher's expedition. (See *Sir Henry Kellett.*) McClure wanted to stay and attempt to hack the ship out of the ice and continue to the east; with only four exceptions, his men refused to accompany him.

McClure received most of the rewards he had sought upon his return to England; he was given a knighthood, various gold medals, and a parliamentary prize of ten thousand pounds for having discovered the western exit from the Northwest Passage. But despite his claim and honors, the situation was best put in perspective by *Lady Jane Franklin,* John Franklin's widow, when she declared that the discovery of the Northwest Passage and the abandonment of Franklin and his companions must be recorded in "indissoluble association."

Middleton, Christopher   (?–1770)

Christopher Middleton was an employee of the *Hudson's Bay Company [VI]* and later a commander in the British Navy. Early in his career he had a serious interest in the science of navigation and discovered a method for determining true time at sea and for finding longitude. In 1737 Middleton was elected a fellow of the Royal Society. By 1741 Middleton's reputation was such that Arthur Dobbs, a prominent Anglo-Irishman opposed to the Hudson's Bay Company's monopoly, prevailed upon him to leave the employment of the Hudson's Bay Company and undertake a voyage of exploration in search of the *Northwest Passage.* Dobbs was able to secure a commission for Middleton from the Admiralty, and by May of 1741 a hastily organized expedition of two ships departed for Hudson Bay under the captaincy of Middleton. By late summer of that year Middleton had reached the mouth of Churchill River, where winter quarters were established. The party was well dug in, and there was adequate food, fuel, and clothing. The group, however, was immediately afflicted by scurvy, and a number of men died. Middleton also complained that his crew was "a set of rogues, most of whom deserved hanging." In the spring of 1742, the party, still ailing from scurvy, pressed northward, finding what seemed to be a strait to the west, but was actually a large river (the Wager). Further north, between Melville Peninsula and Southampton Island, Middleton found the Frozen Strait, which he thought might be important, but it clearly was not navigable. At this point, with the winter freeze approaching, Middleton knew his sickly crew could not survive another winter in the ice, and so he returned to England, reaching the Thames in October 1742. Dobbs, disappointed no doubt that the passage had not been found, accused Middleton of not ascertaining that the Wager River was not the passage. He brought charges against Middleton with the Admiralty. Although Middleton answered the charges honestly and reasonably, his reputation was put in doubt from that point and his career was essentially over. He lived, unemployed, on a pitiful pension, until his death on February 12, 1770.

Moor, William (?–1765)

William Moor was born in Durham County, England, and went to sea early under the guidance of his cousin *Christopher Middleton*. On annual voyages to the Hudson Bay for the *Hudson's Bay Company [VI]*, Moor rose from ship's boy to first mate. After more than ten years, Moor, with Middleton, left the employ of the Hudson's Bay Company and was given the command of the *Discovery*. With Middleton on the *Furnace* in command of the mission, the two were commissioned by the Admiralty to search for the *Northwest Passage*. The expedition reached Hudson Bay in 1741 and wintered at Prince of Wales Fort. Because of the poor quality of the crew and rampant sickness, Moor was unable to accomplish very much by way of survey and exploration. The two ships left for home in August 1742. Moor noted in his journal that there was "no passage into the other Ocean."

Middleton returned to London to harsh criticism from the main sponsor of the expedition, Arthur Dobbs, and others who maintained that a passage to the west via the Wager River existed on the western coast of Hudson Bay: Either Middleton had simply failed to find it, or it had been found and the Hudson's Bay Company was keeping it secret for fear of commercial competition. Moor at first abstained from the dispute but later joined the attack against his former captain. There was good reason why Moor turned against Middleton and supported Dobbs: Moor was to be in command of a private discovery expedition to Hudson Bay organized by Dobbs and supported by the *North West Company [VI]*. In May 1746 the *Dobbs Galley*, commanded by Moor, and the *California*, under Francis Smith, left for Hudson Bay to determine whether a passageway led from the north Hudson Bay area to the west. The expedition ran into heavy ice in the Hudson Strait and retreated south to winter at the Hudson's Bay Company post at York Factory. The winter was spent dealing with the aftereffects of a fire on board the *Dobbs Galley* and with bitter quarrels between the officers of the two ships. There was hard drinking, a breakdown of discipline, and an outbreak of scurvy, which left one-third of the men incapacitated. The surveying and exploration that were carried out in the summer of 1747 were disorganized and uncertain, no doubt due to the reemergence of scurvy and the constant threat of mutiny by the men. Nevertheless, the party managed to explore a substantial part of the western Bay Shore, from latitude 61° to 65° N and discovered the Chesterfield Inlet but assumed correctly that it led nowhere. They also sailed up the Wager Inlet (which Dobbs was certain was the Northwest Passage) for 150 miles and had the "mortification" to see that huge body of water dwindle down into two little unnavigable streams.

After this disappointment, and stricken with dissension, sickness, and threat of mutiny, the expedition headed for home. Moor's reception by the North West Company was cool, and he was criticized for his conduct and for his refusal to engage in a bit of illegal trade while at York Factory. And certainly the explorers had not found what their backers were looking for—the Northwest Passage. Moor asserted that if there were a passage, then it was further north and was probably unnavigable. This voyage apparently ended the active career of Moor, and there are no further references to him in Hudson's Bay Company records or in the papers of Arthur Dobbs. It is assumed that he retired soon after his return to England, where he died in 1765.

Nansen, Fridtjof (1861–1930)

Fridtjof Nansen, born in Oslo, Norway, was a complex individual, brilliant in so many ways and yet always beset by self-doubt and fears that his many achievements meant nothing. He could be sensitive and outgoing to others, or he could be self-centered, aloof, and impossibly stubborn. He was a man of untiring physical action—he was a champion skier, skater, swimmer, hunter, snowshoer, and ballroom dancer—as well as a philosopher of poetic bent—a painter, a lyrical dreamer, sensitive to human suffering and the healing properties of natural beauty.

Nansen's Arctic career began with his incredible feat of crossing *Greenland*'s [I] polar cap from east coast to west coast. His record of that expedition, from June 1888 until October 1888, was enlivened by his account of eating an extra pair of cherry wood snowshoes—hide, wood, and all. Nansen had long been intrigued by the mystery of the circumpolar ice drift. He believed that the ice current moved slowly around the *North Pole,* and that a ship frozen into the polar pack north of Siberia would drift in the ice over or near the pole. To this end he designed and built a ship, the *Fram,* with a special round bottom, which could sit atop the frozen sea and, while serving as a floating oceanographic laboratory, drift for up to five years to the North Pole. In June 1893 the *Fram* left Oslo and by September, she merged with the ice pack of the New Siberian Islands at 77°44' N. The rudder was hauled up, the engine was removed and packed in oil, and the crew settled down to the extensive marine-life and oceanographic research projects that were Nansen's specialty. Nansen, in a journal, called what followed "a luxury cruise."

When it became apparent that the *Fram* would not pass near enough to the North Pole, Nansen decided to strike out for the pole with one companion, dogs, and 1,400 pounds of supplies. The *Fram,* skippered by *Otto Sverdrup,* was to continue on its frozen journey. Nansen and his companion Hjalmar Johansen failed to reach the pole by 200 miles. At 86°13.6' N, they turned back, heading for the settlement at Franz Josef Land north of Russia, a trek of five hundred miles. It was a journey of great difficulty, but the pair survived and, in August of 1896, were reunited with Sverdrup and the crew of the *Fram* for a triumphant return to Oslo. Nansen did not make his proposed trip to Antarctica and never explored in the Arctic again. He passed the torch, and the *Fram,* to his disciple *Roald Amundsen* and turned to public life.

Nansen's research and his findings from his "floating laboratory"

IN THEIR OWN *Words*

The Rewards of Arctic Travel

Life also had its bright moments. If we had to toil and suffer at times, these nights with northern lights and moonlight made up for a great deal. This part of the world has its beauty too. When the ever changing aurora borealis danced light and fairylike over the southern sky, perhaps in more radiant splendor here than anywhere else in the world, it was possible to forget our trials and tribulations; or when the moon came up and followed its silent course across the star-strewn heavens, played over the tops of ice ridges and bathed the whole of this stark world of ice in its silvery rays, then peace descended all about and life became beauty. I am sure that our nocturnal marches over the Inland Ice of Greenland made an ineradicable impression upon all of us who were on that expedition.

—FRIDTJOF NANSEN,
THE FIRST CROSSING OF GREENLAND, 1892

were invaluable in future studies of the Arctic. Nansen is called the father of modern Arctic oceanography, and the list of his publications (written in five languages) fills four pages. Yet even after he received the Nobel Peace Prize in 1922 for devising the "Nansen passport" for homeless refugees after World War I, he remained unconvinced about his stature and the extent of his service to the international community.

Nares, George Strong (1831–1915)

George Strong Nares, born into a seafaring family from Scotland, entered the Royal Navy in 1845 and served his first tour of duty in the Pacific, and was then called to join the mission (1852–1854) headed by Sir Edward Belcher to search for the missing *Sir John Franklin.* During this expedition, which centered on the area south of Melville Island, Nares undertook a number of extensive sledge journeys, which gave him valuable experience in Arctic travel. For the next eighteen years, Nares performed a successive number of naval duties—in the Mediterranean, in the Crimean War, in Australia, and again in the Mediterranean and the Gulf of Suez, all the time carrying out oceanographic research.

In 1872 Nares was given the captaincy of the *Challenger* and was sent on a voyage of exploration to the Antarctic. He was the first to cross the Antarctic Circle by steamship, reaching a record 66°40' S, 78°21' E. He returned to Hong Kong in 1874, bringing back important geological findings about the southern continent. Nares was then called upon to lead a government Arctic expedition in the vessels *Alert* and *Discovery;* the chief aim of the mission was to reach the *North Pole.* The false report of an 1861 mission by *Isaac Hayes* had convinced the Admiralty that there was an open polar sea all the way to the North Pole, and that the route to that sea lay via Smith Sound, to the north-northwest of *Greenland [I].* The fable of the open sea was soon disproved; nonetheless, the mission was able to proceed to 83°20'26" N, a new record. In addition, much exploration was made in Grantland and Greenland, and new data was supplied for later polar attempts. The severity of the weather, the immense difficulty of sledge travel, and the inevitable outbreak of scurvy brought about much hardship and loss of life. Nares returned to England in 1876 convinced that the Smith Sound route to the pole was neither practical nor possible. Nares carried out a number of naval duties and subsequently entered an extended career as a public servant. He died on January 15, 1915, with the rank of vice-admiral.

North Pole

Any consideration of the North Pole must start with noting that scientists recognize five invisible points on the surface of the earth that go by that name, but only two of them hold the interest of most people—the magnetic North Pole and the geographic North Pole. (The same holds true, of course, for the South Pole.) These two North Poles are not at the same place but are separated by a distance that varies from eight hundred to a thousand miles. Although it is the magnetic North Pole that is of greatest importance to navigators and all who need to plot their journeys, it is the geographic North Pole that has long been a "magnet" for fallible human strivers.

If one stands at any point on the globe holding a compass, the swinging needle will point to the magnetic pole, not to the geographic North Pole. The magnetic North Pole is a location on the surface of the earth where the direction of the earth's magnetic field is vertical. The earth's magnetic field is currently believed to be caused by currents within the liquid core of the earth—flowing iron. Thus the earth's magnetic field is not symmetrical and regular, but varies with the magnetic field at a particular location.

Navigators had become aware of the moving about of the magnetic North Pole not long after they had begun to rely on the magnetic compass—that is, in the decades after about A.D. 1300. But the magnetic North Pole was not "pinned down" until *James Clark Ross* did so in June 1831. It was then on the western coast of the Boothia Peninsula at 70.1° N, 96.8° W. *Roald Amundsen* placed it at 70.5° N, 95.5° W in 1905. In 2001 it was located at 76° N, 100° W. Knowledge of the current position of magnetic north is essential to accurate navigation.

The geographic North Pole, meanwhile, is the point where all the earth's lines of longitude, also known as meridians, meet. It is also the point at which the earth's lines of latitude, counting up from the equator, reach 90°. This North Pole is the point at which a clock or watch has no meaning because all the time zones of the world converge there. This also means that anyone standing at the precise point of this North Pole on

March 21 would see the sun rise and then would wait six months, after a half year of daylight, to see it set.

The discrepancy between the magnetic North Pole and the geographic North Pole—the latter sometimes referred to in this context as "true north"—is measured as an angle called the "declination," and this angle must be known if compass navigation is to be accurate. It is not possible to find the geographic North Pole by using a standard compass; a device called the inertia gyrocompass has been developed which points to the geographic North Pole. This navigation device enabled the *Nautilus* to reach the North Pole under the ice in 1958.

The three other "north poles" are of interest mainly to scientists. One, known as the "instantaneous north pole," is located at the point where the earth's axis—an imaginary line through the center of the earth —breaks the surface. As the earth rotates on this axis in a somewhat wobbly way, it causes the instantaneous north pole to move, too. It takes about fourteen months for this pole to move around an irregular path known as "the Chandler circle." At the center of the Chandler Circle is what is sometimes called "the north pole of balance"—and in fact it is the same as the geographic North Pole. But because it moves along with the movement of the Chandler Circle, this means that the geographic North Pole in fact moves slightly; the result is that there are very small changes in points along both the latitudes and longitudes, too. Finally, there is the geomagnetic north pole, located at the point where the earth's magnetic field, located in the upper atmosphere, is focused; at present this point is located near Thule, *Greenland [I]*.

But it has always been the geographic North Pole that has lured people, and this in turn was the inevitable consequence of the centuries of Arctic exploration. Unlike the search for the *Northwest Passage,* there was no motivation of profit to account for the drive to be the first human there. There were no furs to be traded, no rumors of gold or copper to be found; there was, as the Inuit knew, only more ice and bitter cold. There, at the pole, there was no life: no vegetation, not even the primitive moss; there were no animals or fish to sustain the life of the unfortunate traveler who found himself there. Yet generations of scientists, adventurers, and the boldest of explorers had desired to be the first to stand on top of the world, at that point from which all directions were south.

The region surrounding the North Pole is just as desolate. The area inside the Arctic Circle (66°30' N) is largely occupied by the Arctic Ocean, always called in the early days of exploration the Polar Sea. The Arctic Ocean is roughly circular, in shape, with the pole slightly offset from the center. The Arctic waters are relatively isolated from the deep waters of the world because they are surrounded by a sequence of landmasses. Starting from Greenland and moving clockwise there is *Ellesmere Island,* Devon and *Baffin Island,* the Canadian Archipelago, Northwestern Canada, Alaska, the extensive north coast of Siberia, Franz Josef Land, Svalbard (Spitzbergen), and finally, closing the circle, northern Finland and Norway. A number of seas surround the Arctic Basin as well. They are seen as separate because their ice cover is seasonal and variable, whereas the Arctic Ocean is always frozen.

The landmasses within the Arctic Circle are underlain by permafrost; in parts of Siberia the ground can be frozen to a depth of two thousand feet. Even in the most moderate parts of the Arctic Circle, the earth beneath the surface is frozen, permanently, to a depth of eight hundred feet. At the very top of the land surface (the active layer) there is melting and thaw in the Arctic summer. Because the frozen earth beneath cuts off any drainage, great bogs and shallow lakes are formed by the summer runoff; and these peat-marsh boggy conditions become the home of the legendary swarms of mosquitoes and black flies that have driven both animals and people almost to madness. It is surprising that more than a million people permanently inhabit the Arctic despite the extreme harshness of the climate and the absence of all but the most basic vegetation. In fact, the Arctic is a desert—a cold desert—since all the fresh water is locked up in ice. The annual precipitation averages six to nine inches per year, most of that falling, obviously, in the form of snow.

Running under the Arctic Ocean is the Lomonosov Ridge, which divides the deep water basin of the ocean into two parts: the European Basin and the Canadian Basin in the Western Hemisphere. The existence of this division and the presence of the surrounding seas and a number of warmer water streams all act together to produce a very complex pattern of movement, or drift, to the ice cap that permanently covers the Arctic Ocean. Many an explorer in the nineteenth century had the experience of moving northward toward the Pole at an agonizing rate of two miles a day to find himself further from his goal than the day before. The drift averages about four miles per day and can be as much as six miles. Furthermore, the direction of the drifting ice is not constant; it can, without warning, reverse itself. A number of Arctic explorers, notably *Nansen* and

DeLong, tried to use the drift to float over the pole. This approach was never successful.

For a long time, even into the twentieth century, there was a myth that the Polar Sea was open— free of ice. It is difficult to understand how this myth could be believed. *Elisha Kent Kane,* for instance, until he got to the Arctic, was certain that he could sail his ship right up to the Pole, if he could find the right channel. The ice cover of two different systems sometimes meets under such pressure that gigantic ridges erupt high into the air, forming ice mountains and broken building-sized chunks and temporary patches of open water (leads). And sometimes in the late summer the ice breaks into floes, which in turn break into smaller pieces, which are separated by leads. But the ice, which covers the Polar Sea, is constant, and the occasional open water merely becomes a fatal hazard for explorers traveling by sledge.

There is no precise date on which the search for the North Pole began, but it is known that in 1818 the British Admiralty dispatched two ships under Buchan and *Franklin* from Spitzbergen to search for the pole. That voyage got no further north than did the excursions of the Norwegian whalers. In 1827 a definite attempt was made by *Parry* to reach the pole over the ice starting to the northwest from Spitzbergen. Although the attempt was not successful, Parry found out about the backward Greenland drift, and he did reach 82°45' N, the highest latitude to date. In 1853 Kane made an attempt, using the so-called American route through Smith Sound, and achieved a point farthest north. *Isaac Hayes,* who was a believer in the open polar sea theory, followed Kane's route in 1860, but met with no success. *Charles Hall,* on the third expedition of his *Polaris,* surpassed Kane's mark and reached 82°11' N. A highly organized British attempt under *George Nares* was begun from Ellesmere Island but retreated when the crew was struck down by scurvy. In 1879 DeLong tried for the Pole in the mistaken belief that a land mass existed which went all the way to his objective. His ship was frozen in the ice and the expedition ended in disaster. Fridtjof Nansen deliberately allowed his ship, the *Fram,* to be frozen in the ice with the hope that the drift would carry him over the pole. The unpredictable movement of the ice carried him away from the pole. Finally, *Frederick Cook* may or may not have reached the North Pole in 1908, and *Robert Peary* may or may not have reached it in 1909.

Aerial attempts to reach or fly over the pole began as early as 1897 with Salomon Andrée's failed balloon flight from Spitzbergen. With the development of the airplane, Russian and American pilots were making flights into the Arctic. In 1926 *Byrd* and Bennett flew over the North Pole, followed two days later by *Amundsen* and Nobile in the airship *Norge.* After Peary's claim to have reached the pole, many other successful overland expeditions took place during the rest of the twentieth century. The U.S. nuclear submarine *Nautilus* passed under the pole in 1958 (see *William Anderson*). One of the most impressive post-Peary polar journeys was *Wally Herbert*'s trek of sixteen months (1968–1969) from Alaska to Spitzbergen via the North Pole with three companions and dog sledges. The airplane became a vital support factor in expeditions using the traditional dogs and sledges, as well as mechanized attempts using snowmobiles and Sno-Cats. Now floating research stations are built on Arctic ice, maintained and supplied by helicopter. Yet individuals can still find ways to challenge the North Pole. In 1978 a lone Japanese explorer, Naomi Uemura, traveled all alone to the pole with a dog sled. (He would lose his life while climbing Mount McKinley/Denali in 1984.) In 1992 the American Helen Thayer, pulling her own sledge and accompanied only by a dog pulling its own, walked all alone to the magnetic North Pole.

Although less heralded than its sister ship, the U.S.S. *Skate* followed directly in the wake of the *Nautilus* and, on August 12, 1958, surfaced near the North Pole. The *Skate* returned to the pole itself on March 17,1959, when this picture was taken.

The great quest for what the Inuit came to call "the Big Nail" is over. Generations of explorers have devoted their lives to the search for the cold horizon that lay beyond the nearest ice ridges. Many died in their search, of folly, of vanity, and through ignorance of the awful destructive power of the Arctic. Yet, all had felt the strange and wondrous beauty of the far north and shown to the world that spark of unconquerable will and unquenchable curiosity that is the stuff of heroism in poetry and in life.

Northwest Passage

Just as there is the geographers' North Pole and the explorers' *North Pole,* there is the navigators' northwest passage and the visionaries' Northwest Passage. The quest for the latter—that is, what was assumed to be a direct and short northern sea route to Asia from the Atlantic—engaged, and then possessed, the imaginations of Europeans for almost four hundred years. The quest was at first fueled by greed and commercial interest; but long after that motive was no longer feasible, the search continued—intensified, based on motives that could not be called rational.

The navigators' northwest passage began west of central *Greenland [I]* at the entrance to Lancaster Sound. The latitude is approximately 74° N, far above the Arctic Circle. Once passing through Lancaster Sound, the ship had to be prepared to encounter every meteorological and geographic horror that nature has to offer. Gales often rage, bringing blinding snowstorms; the temperature drops to −40°F. Inviting straits become reef-filled shallows from which there is no return; smooth-looking passageways become traps, which prematurely freeze and stay frozen for two seasons. One wrong turn might mean a winter, or even longer, spent in the ice. Help might arrive in a year, or perhaps two, if the rescuers themselves were fortunate enough to escape the ice. Two-thirds of the water to be passed over would be frozen for ten months of the year.

At the end of Lancaster Sound the route proceeded into Barrow Strait and then turned south, between Somerset and Prince of Wales Islands. After Peel Sound and then Franklin Strait, there was a choice to be made—but the route north through McClure Channel would lead only into thicker ice, so the route lay south. Ahead lay King William Island, where another choice had to be made. To go around the island to the west, through Victoria Strait, seemed logical—although *Sir John Franklin* had chosen that route, and his decision led to his death. *Amundsen* chose a southeast route along the east side, then negotiated the Simpson Strait to enter Queen Maud Gulf. Temporarily there was smooth sailing, but the ship then had to navigate around the tip of the Kent Peninsula, jutting out from the Canadian mainland. Passing through Dease Strait led to Coronation Gulf. Dolphin and Union Strait was next and led to the Amundsen Gulf. This effectively ended the worst of the northwest passage, for ahead lay the open water of the Beaufort Sea north of Alaska. Crossing this led to the Arctic Ocean with the Bering Strait coming up. And one fine morning, many months and possibly years after entering Lancaster Sound, the ship would sail into the Pacific Ocean and be on course to Asia. The route seemed obvious enough once navigated, but scores of men had died trying to navigate it. What had driven them to do so?

By 1507 increasing numbers of Europeans were becoming aware that on the shore of the Atlantic Ocean to the west there was a landmass. Was it Asia or the new continent called America? Perhaps it was a group of islands off the coast of China. Part of the problem was that according to the Ptolemaic system that was current in 1500, for instance, the circumference of the globe was believed to be about eighteen thousand miles, seven thousand miles less than it actually is. So it was reasonable to imagine, at that time, that the continent of Asia lay just on the other side of the great Atlantic. All the maps showed it to be just that.

As early as 1497, long before the full extent of the New World's landmass was known, *John Cabot [III]* was sailing in search of a northern route to Asia. After returning and claiming that he had indeed reached Asia, he went off on his second voyage and was never heard of again. It was an appropriate beginning for the long and often fatal quest for the Northwest Passage.

It was no coincidence that the first expedition was conducted on behalf of English merchants. The motivation was to avoid the long voyage to Asia that required traveling down the coast of Africa, around the Cape of Good Hope and then across the Indian Ocean and the Pacific. (The overland route from Asia to Europe, although in use even from ancient times, was not that appealing to merchants of northwest Europe.) For the English in particular, but also for the French and Dutch, it was the desire to break the monopoly of the Portuguese. British goods would undersell Portuguese goods in the markets of China. Silks, spices, ivory, gold dust, and precious stones would be brought up the Thames and the London merchants would all become as rich as kings.

In the years following John Cabot's voyage, many mariners from various nations sailed in search of the Northwest Passage: the *Corte-Reál [III]* brothers of Portugal in 1500–1502, Thomas Aubert of France in 1508, John Rastell of England in 1516, *Giovanni da Verrazano [III]* in 1524, *Estevão Gómes [III]* of Portugal in 1524–1525, *John Rut [III]* of England in 1527–1528, *Jacques Cartier [III]* of France in 1534 and 1535. Among the best known of these searchers was *Martin Frobisher* of England, who between 1576 and 1578 made three voyages. When on the first he sailed into the bay that would later be named after him, he would exclaim with delight that "America was on one side, and Asia was on the other." Little did he know that a vast continent and another vast ocean still lay between him and the riches of the East.

It would be still three hundred more years before the full vastness of North America would be realized and a possible northwest passage would be located. Just finding the elusive opening to the west out of Hudson Bay took explorers a century from the time *Henry Hudson* first entered that body of water. Every inlet, river, lake, and bog in the tortuous Canadian Archipelago was followed up, always ending in a dead end or an unnavigable tiny stream. And yet seamen and geographers and entrepreneurs were convinced the passage was there and continued to sail forth from Europe.

One of the more extraordinary expeditions was that led by Captain Jens Munck, commissioned by King Christian IV of Denmark and Norway to find the Northwest Passage and also to establish a Danish settlement along the way. With a crew and passengers of 64, Munck sailed into Hudson Bay in 1619 and eventually settled at the mouth of the river and site that later were named Churchill. The Lutheran minister with the group, the Reverend Rasmus Jensen, conducted Lutheran church services but to no avail; as winter settled in, one by one they died off from scurvy and general debilitation; only Munck and two others survived to make it back to Denmark.

Gradually, very slowly, at some point in the eighteenth century, it became clear that, even if there were such a passage, and even if it were not frozen year-round, this was not a viable financial opportunity. But the fervor to find the passage did not abate; instead, it grew. What had first been

IN THEIR OWN Words

A Passage to Death

The 28th of May. During these days there was little of moment to record, save that we seven wretched persons who still remained alive, observed one another with distress and awaited each day that the snow should be thawed and the ice gone. Having regard to the symptomata *and conditions wherewith we were afflicted, it was a strange and remarkable sickness; for all the members and joints were shrunken so sorrowfully, with great spasms in the loins, as were a thousand knives stuck through them, and the body was as blue and brown as a bruised eye, and the whole form was utterly without strength. And the condition of the mouth was ill and wretched, for all the teeth were loose, so that we could not dispatch any* victualis. *During the days when we lay so sick in bed, Peder Nyborg, carpenter, Knud Lauritzen, boatswain, and Jørgen, cook's boy, died, who all remained lying in the poop, for there was no one who could bury their corpses or cast them overboard.*

—JENS MUNCK, JOURNAL OF MONTHS ON HUDSON BAY, 1620

fueled by the promise of riches was now driven by a spirit just as ardent and infinitely purer. The search had become a challenge, a challenge to be answered by skill, courage, and a belief in human intuition.

Robert McClure, approaching from the west, would find what was a final link but he never made the full passage. It would be another fifty years before Amundsen sailed the *Gjöa* into Nome harbor, Alaska, in 1906, having completed the first voyage through the Northwest Passage. Once Amundsen had broken the barrier, all that was left was for others to accomplish variations and refinements. In 1940–1942, the Royal Canadian Mounted Police schooner *St. Roch* completed the first passage west to east. In 1954 U.S. Navy and Coast Guard icebreakers made it through the northern route of McClure Strait. In 1957 the Canadian Navy icebreaker, *Labrador,* led three U.S. Coast Guard cutters through the Bellot Strait between Boothia Peninsula and Somerset Island. In 1960 the U.S. nuclear submarine *Seadragon* made the first underwater crossing of the Northwest Passage. And then in 1969, the U.S. icebreaker-tanker *Manhattan* became the first commercial—and largest—ship to make the passage, entering from Lancaster Sound by keeping to the north of Prince of Wales and Victoria Islands and then coming down through Prince of Wales Strait into Amundsen Gulf. In the years that followed, numerous individual ships have made the passage. In 1977 the Dutchman W. DeRoos made the first single-handed passage in his 42-foot ketch, the *Williwaw*—from east to

This map shows the routes taken by four of the major expeditions seeking a passage from the Atlantic across the top of Canada and over to the Pacific. Only the last two succeeded, but the first two, even though they ended in disaster, have earned the seekers a place in the history of exploration.

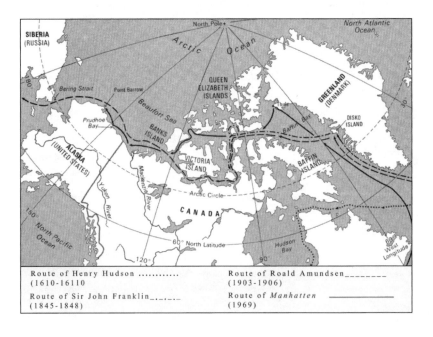

Route of Henry Hudson ....
(1610–16110

Route of Sir John Franklin_._._._
(1845–1848)

Route of Roald Amundsen_____
(1903–1906)

Route of *Manhatten* _____
(1969)

west. In 1984, the *Lindblad Explorer* became the first commercial passenger vessel to make the passage.

These were all noteworthy achievements, but as a route for transporting oil or other goods between the Atlantic and the Pacific, let alone passengers, the Northwest Passage has not proven to be viable. During the sweep of years that the search for the Northwest Passage had gone on, many things had been learned that were not merely geographic or scientific. How rigid and inflexible, for example, the early explorers had been. They had marched to their deaths wearing their good English worsted clothing and their patent leather boots, disdaining the furs and animal skins of the Inuit. When the remains of the *Franklin* party were found, items such as a mahogany writing desk, silver service for ten, and shiny leather dancing shoes were found in the packs of crewmen who dropped dead as they walked. And English seamen stopped dying by the hundreds of scurvy only when they began to pay attention to the Inuit ways.

For some four hundred years the seamen guided their ships into the archipelago. What had the explorers found in their search? They had found seas so cold that they could kill a man in a minute. They had seen floating mountains of ice, which could crush a ship like a tiny matchstick. The searchers had experienced snow and frost so fast and thick that the weight of it could overturn their vessels. All these things and more the explorers had seen—and yet they had returned for more.

Parry, Sir William Edward   (1790–1855)

William Parry, like many of the Arctic explorers of the eighteenth and nineteenth centuries, went to sea at a very early age, as a seaman of the Royal Navy. By the time he was twenty, in 1810, he had already been commissioned a lieutenant. He had early shown an interest in astronomical observation and navigation and had put out a treatise on "nautical astronomy by night," composed while he was stationed in North America. His promising career as a young officer was noticed by his superiors and in 1818 he was given his first command, the *Alexander*. He was to accompany *John Ross* in a search for the *Northwest Passage,* entering the Lancaster Sound (which was known to exist) and passing through it to the Bering Strait and so on to Asia. John Ross, who had command of the mission, was well in advance of Parry in the *Alexander,* and entered the mouth of the

Lancaster Sound and saw before him an immense mass of icy mountains, blocking absolutely any further progress. Ross turned back and, over Parry's objections, ended the mission and returned to England. From the first, there was doubt about what Ross had named "The Croker Mountains." Parry believed at the time (and stated publicly later) that Ross had given up on the probe of Lancaster Sound too early. And Ross's bitter enemy, John Barrow, the secretary of the Admiralty, was convinced that the Northwest Passage existed and that John Ross had simply failed to find it. And so in 1819, a further expedition was organized to follow the exact route of Ross's mission, to verify the existence of the Croker Mountains. The young commander of the mission was William Parry.

Luck was with Parry from the very beginning of the expedition. Favorable winds enabled him to read the mouth of Lancaster Sound by August 1, 1819, and soon his two vessels, the *Hecla* and the *Griper*, reached the flag planted by Ross to mark his farthest progress. On both sides the coast did rise up to jagged white peaks, but ahead there was clear, open water; and thus the myth of the Croker Mountains was abolished for good. Parry was entering waters never sailed upon by European explorers. An unusually extended thaw of the icy waters, and sharp winds blowing from

IN THEIR OWN Words

The Scourge of Arctic Exploration—Scurvy

That a ship's company should begin to evince symptoms of scurvy after twenty-seven months entire dependence upon the resources contained within their ship (an experiment hitherto unknown, perhaps in the annals of navigation, even for one-fourth part of that period) could scarcely, indeed, be subject of wonder, though it was at this particular time a matter of very sincere regret. From the health enjoyed by our people during two successive winters, unassisted as we had been by any supply of fresh anti-scorbutic plants or other vegetables, I had begun to indulge a hope that with a continued attention to their comforts, cleanliness, and exercise, the same degree of vigour might, humanly speaking, be endured at least as long as our present liberal resources should last. Present appearances, however, seemed to indicate differently.

—WILLIAM E. PARRY, *SECOND VOYAGE FOR THE DISCOVERY OF A NORTH-WEST PASSAGE FROM THE ATLANTIC TO THE PACIFIC*, 1824 the east, allowed Parry to make rapid progress. He passed a large body of land (which he named North Somerset) and turned south into a broad strait, which he called Prince Regent Inlet. When blocked by ice, he retreated to the north and turned westward again, following Lancaster Sound. Again Parry had the luck of favorable wind and unusually warm weather, which extended the thaw. The explorers passed islands and inlets on all sides upon which Parry bestowed names: Wellington, Cornwallis, Griffith, Bathurst, Melville, and Barrow. By September the expedition was halfway to the Bering Strait, at the meridian of the mouth of the Copper-mine River (far to the south), and they crossed longitude 110° W (which earned them a Parliamentary prize of £5,000). The crews celebrated that achievement with extra rations and an allotment of beer as they anchored off Melville Island at a point they christened Bounty Cape. The coming of winter ended the progress of this extraordinary mission, and the men pre-pared for the long period of being trapped in the ice. It was not until August of 1820 that the two ships were freed from the ice, and then they were able to ascertain that further progress south or west was impossible. Parry had traversed six hundred miles of open water—a critical segment of the passage—and then had correctly concluded that an unbreachable ram-part of Arctic Ocean ice blocked the further route to the west. Parry returned to England in the autumn of 1820 and was raised to the rank of commander. He received numerous other honors and great public acclaim.

Parry made three other voyages to the Arctic, the final one in 1827 being an attempt to reach the North Pole from Spitzbergen using sledge-boats designed to be hauled over ice, or used as boats on any open water encountered. Although the expedition did not achieve its stated goal, it is to be noted that Parry reached latitude 82°45', farther north than any European had ever gone. When Parry returned to London at the conclu-sion of his final voyage, he settled into a life of public service. He recorded fully his adventures in his memoirs and journals. After a period of severe illness, he died on July 8, 1855.

Peary, Robert Edwin (1856–1920)

Robert Peary was born in Pennsylvania and after the early death of his father, moved with his mother to Maine. As a boy Peary developed a strong interest in the outdoors and in natural history. After graduating from

Bowdoin College, Phi Beta Kappa, Peary became a draftsman for the U.S. Coast and Geodetic Survey. In 1881 he received a commission from the U.S. Navy and spent a few years doing survey work in North and South America. In 1886 Peary made an excursion to the *Greenland [I]* interior and from that point on he was committed to a career in the Arctic.

In the summer of 1891, on leave from the navy, Peary traveled to north Greenland on a voyage, which was obviously an early attempt to map out a polar route. His party included his wife, his valet *Matthew Henson,* and Dr. *Frederick Cook.* Again, Peary made voyages to Greenland and Smith Sound in 1892 and in 1893, and in 1896 and 1897 to Smith Sound. On all of these expeditions he was accompanied by his wife Jo, and in 1892 in Greenland, she gave birth to a daughter, the famous "Snow Baby." He was now sure of his route to the pole, and his intentions were firm and settled. Dr. Cook had parted from the company and was indicating his own plans to make an assault on the *North Pole.* In 1898 Peary requested and received five years' leave from the navy. He was afraid that *Otto Sverdrup* was about to try for the pole, even though Peary had warned him off, claiming that the North Pole was his territory. Without proper preparation Peary rushed to Fort Conger (*Ellesmere Island*) and in the process froze his feet and lost eight toes. Despite this setback, he pressed on into north Greenland and discovered Cape Morris Jesup, the most northerly land in the world. Rough ice soon stopped further progress north. But Peary had reached 84°17' N, a new record, and he returned to the United States determined to find the backing he needed to make his next attempt at the pole successful.

In 1904 a group of influential backers, including Morris Jesup and wealthy banker George Crocker, provided Peary with the specially designed *Roosevelt* and his other requirements, and he departed for Fort Conger and the shores of the Arctic Ocean. His plan was to establish supply caches along his previously charted route, which would sustain the party when traveling over the ice. Timing was critically important because of the existence of the "big lead"—a wide portion of open water at the edge of the Arctic Ocean, which was

IN THEIR OWN *Words*

The Attainment of a Dream

The Pole at last!!! The prize of three centuries, my dreams and ambitions for twenty-three years. Mine at last. I cannot bring myself to realize it. It all seems so simple and commonplace. . . . I wish Jo [his wife] could be here with me to share my feelings. I have drunk her health and that of the kids from the Benedictine flask she sent me.

—ROBERT PEARY, THE NORTH POLE, 1910

passable for a very brief period in the year. The setting up of supply caches did not work; the various parties got separated because of bad weather and lost contact with each other and the *Roosevelt*. The weather was unusually bad: blizzard after blizzard stalled all progress, and an unforeseen easterly current carried the *Roosevelt* off course. The expedition fell into a desperate situation and narrowly escaped starvation before reaching the northern shore of Greenland. Peary returned to New York in 1906, defeated in his second attempt at the Pole. He had, however, reached 87°6' N, breaking his own record. At this point Peary's determination—rather than being diminished by two defeats—reached a new level of intensity. To him his whole life, his whole being and purpose, focused on attaining the North Pole. He would reach his goal on this his third and last attempt or he would die in the trying. He was no longer a young man; he was fifty-two. He had turned his back on any regular career as a naval officer and given up everything for this.

In July 1908, under the sponsorship of the Peary Arctic Club, the National Geographic Society, and a host of powerful and wealthy men, Peary left the United States on the refurbished *Roosevelt* and established his base on the shore of the Arctic Ocean on Ellesmere Island. The party was composed of Peary, Captain **Robert Bartlett,** Professor Ross Marvin, Matthew Henson, Dr. John Goodsell, the young Yale athlete George Borup, and **Donald MacMillan.** Fifty-six Inuit men, women, and children were taken as helpers, and included in the party was Peary's Inuit son, Sammy. Among the Inuit men were experienced dog drivers, and women who were expert at making and repairing clothing and who had served Peary on earlier missions. The plan was that members of the party would drop off and return to the base. The lead group would become smaller and smaller until a final, exclusive assault team would reach the Pole. First Goodsell, MacMillan (with frozen feet), and Borup turned back, along with a number of Inuit and part of the dogs. Then, at 86°38' N Marvin dropped off but mysteriously never returned to Ellesmere Island. Finally at 87°47' N, 133 miles from the pole, Bartlett, on April 1, was tearfully left behind. The final group consisted of Peary, Henson, and four Inuit guides. The six men pressed on, and on April 6, 1909, reached the North Pole. Peary made solar observations, and Henson took 110 photographs. Henson went to Peary to shake his hand—and Peary turned away. Later, Peary confiscated Henson's photographs and Henson's personal diary disappeared. Peary's own diary for the alleged three days at the pole were blank.

On the return, Peary maintained that the group reached Bartlett's last camp—a distance of 133 miles—in two days. The six men reached land in fourteen days, only two days after Bartlett, who would have had a three-hundred-mile head start. While returning from Ellesmere Island, Peary learned that Frederick Cook had claimed the North Pole on April 21, 1908. From *Labrador [III],* in September 1909, Peary denounced Cook's claim with vehemence, and the battle between the two explorers was on.

The battle waged by the supporters of the two explorers goes on to this day. Few comparable events have produced as much debate, so many figures and calculations, and so many charts and diagrams. And never has there been so much hatred generated by the vituperation and slander that passed back and forth. The final consensus, the rational conclusion of rational scholars and scientists, is that neither man obtained the North Pole. The sad thing is that Peary, who some consider the greatest of all American explorers, was forever tarnished by the affair. His iron will and indomitable determination, the stuff without which no man could face the hardship and dangers he took for granted, failed him in the end and made him unable to accept less than what he had given his life to. At the end of his life, still venerated by some, reviled by others, he was haunted by loneliness and tired of the version of himself that came through his lectures. He began to close down at the end; he became dyspeptic and tyrannical and died a sad and lonely death in 1920.

Photographed by Peary himself at the North Pole on April 6, 1909, are the five other members of his expedition holding different flags (left to right, with their flags): Ocqueh, the Navy League Flag; Ootah, Peary's D.K.E. fraternity flag (!); Matthew Henson, a special polar expedition flag; Egingwah, the D.A.R. peace flag; and Seeglo, the Red Cross flag.

Rae, John

(1813–1893)

Born near Stromness, on Mainland Island, largest of the Orkney Islands off the northern coast of Scotland, John Rae studied medicine in Edinburgh and in 1833 sailed to Canada as a ship's surgeon for the *Hudson's Bay Company [VI].* At that time, the company was virtually the ruler of vast areas of Canada, functioning both as the main representative of the British government and as the chief commercial presence. Although he had planned to sail on only that one voyage, Rae found the "wild sort of life" with the Hudson's Bay Company in Canada so appealing that he stayed on in Canada for much of the next thirty years, functioning as a surgeon, trader, and surveyor/mapper. Assigned by the company to explore the Arctic coast and inland regions, he stood out from other Europeans in the region by his willingness to learn from and adopt the ways of the Inuit and the half-caste métis: He used snowshoes, wore fur clothing, made igloos, and drove dog sleds. Marooned on Charlton Island in Hudson Bay one winter, he and his colleagues came down with scurvy, and Rae realized that it was due to a "lack of something" that probably was in vegetables—in effect predicting the role of vitamin C. Possessed of great physical and mental endurance, he is said to have walked some 23,000 miles in the course of his explorations. In 1848 he was with the expedition led by Sir John Richardson that searched for the lost expedition of *Sir John Franklin.* In 1853–1854, he himself led an overland expedition to search for Franklin, and this time he met the Eskimos who gave the first report of the end of Franklin's expedition, including the claim that some of the men had resorted to cannibalism. When Rae returned to England to report

IN THEIR OWN *Words* — Discovery of the Franklin Expedition

From the mutilated state of many of the bodies [of the Franklin expedition] and the contents of the kettles, it is evident that our wretched Countrymen had been driven to the last dread alternative, as a means of sustaining life. A few of the fortunate Men must have survived until the arrival of the wild fowl (say until the end of May) as shots were heard [by the Eskimos], and fresh bones and feathers of geese were noticed near the scene of the sad event. . . . There must have been a number of telescopes, guns (several of them double barrelled), watches, compasses Etc., all of which seem to have been broken up, as I saw pieces of these different articles with the Natives, and I purchased as many as possible, together with some spoons and forks, an order of merit in the form of a Star and a small silver plate engraved Sir John Franklin K.O.H.

—JOHN RAE, LETTER TO HUDSON'S BAY COMPANY IN LONDON, SEPTEMBER 1854 this, *Lady Franklin* orchestrated a campaign to discredit Rae. It succeeded to the point that Rae was the only major British Arctic explorer not knighted, and he was never given full credit for his work. In 1864 he made a land survey to set up a telegraph line from Winnepeg, Canada, over the Rocky Mountains to Canada's west coast.

Rasmussen, Knud Johan Victor (1879–1933)

As much an ethnologist as an explorer, Knud Rasmussen was born in Jakobshavn, *Greenland [I],* son of an Inuit mother and Danish father. As a young man he showed great interest in his Inuit heritage—the language and customs—and became adept at dog-sledding and sea-kayaking. In 1902–1904, he participated in his first major expedition in Greenland. In 1910 he, along with Peter Freuchen, set up a trading station at Thule, Greenland, the profits of which he would use to finance his many expeditions and studies in the Arctic region. His most famous journey was in 1921–1924, when he became the first person to travel overland by dog sled across the entire Arctic—effectively making the *Northwest Passage* from Greenland to Alaska. Over the years, in addition to his careful research notes and sketches, he collected Inuit artifacts; he was also known for being one of the first to compile Inuit folktales, poetry, and songs. Awarded an honorary doctorate from the University of Copenhagen, he continued his travels and studies almost to the end of his life.

IN THEIR OWN *Words* The Life of the Inuit

This, roughly, is the ordinary everyday life of the inland Eskimos, probably the hardiest people in the world. Their country is such as to offer but a bare existence under the hardest possible conditions, and yet they think it the best that could be found. What most impressed us was the constant change from one to another extreme; either they are on the verge of starvation, or wallowing in a luxury of abundance which renders them oblivious of hard times past, and heedless of those that await them in the next winter's dark.

—KNUD RASMUSSEN, *ACROSS ARCTIC AMERICA: NARRATIVE OF THE FIFTH THULE EXPEDITION,* 1927

Roque, Marguerite de la   (?–?)

The niece or cousin of *Sieur de Roberval [III]*, Marguerite de la Roque sailed on his 1542 expedition to Canada. Upon discovering her carrying on an affair with a crewman, the puritanical Roberval marooned Marguerite and her maid, Damienne, on one of the remote Harrington islets in the Gulf of St. Lawrence with some provisions and guns. Her lover swam ashore to join them, but he died over the winter. A child she bore soon died, as did Damienne over the second winter. After twenty-nine months, Marguerite was found by French fishermen and returned to France, where the story of her ordeal came to the attention of Marguerite, Queen of Navarre, who then retold it in her *Heptaméron* as an example of how God sometimes chooses the weak to thwart the mighty (in this instance, Roberval). Although, strictly speaking, she was not an explorer, her incredible tale of survival in North America was told in her day to inspire others to venture there.

Ross, Sir James Clark   (1800–1862)

James Ross was born in 1800, the nephew of the distinguished Arctic explorer *Sir John Ross*. He joined the Royal Navy at the early age of twelve and served with his uncle on two expeditions. He had his first Arctic experience with *William Parry* in 1818, and later with Parry in 1819–1820 on the famous *Hecla*. In 1826 William Parry sought and received permission for an assault on the *North Pole;* this mission was the first directed specifically at the pole. Parry, the commander of the expedition, captained one of the two ships, Ross the other. The party encountered great difficulties at the beginning but managed to reach Spitzbergen, from where they departed on the part water, part overland voyage to the pole. The expedition had brought reindeer to pull the sledges on the overland portions; the sledges were in fact massive boats fitted out with steel runners on the bottoms. Of course, the reindeer proved to be useless and were soon eaten; the converted boats were too heavy to be moved over the uneven, jumbled ice block that constituted the frozen ice fields. In the summer of 1827, a retreat was called. Still, the party had reached 82°45' latitude, further north than anyone had previously achieved. Furthermore, Ross learned a great deal about Arctic travel; and along with Parry he had discovered the polar drift and the terrible effect it could have on progress toward the pole.

Ross returned to the Arctic in 1829 with instructions to find a westward exit from Prince Regent Inlet, a passage vital to a northwest passage. He left England on a ship powered by a steam paddle wheel, the *Victory;* it proved to be utterly useless and the steam engine was soon discarded on the ice. Under sail, Ross went southward and passed by Bellot Strait, which was thought to be a bay. It was in fact the only body of water that led to the west and the continuation of the *Northwest Passage.* Trapped on the east side of the Boothia Peninsula with winter fast approaching, Ross found safe harbor but was frozen in for over two years there. With the help of friendly Eskimos, Ross spent the next three years exploring, by sled, the entire central region: King William, Somerset, and Prince of Wales Islands. It was during these journeys, in June 1831, that Ross became the first person to establish the then exact location of the magnetic North Pole. Eventually, the party made its way in the damaged *Victory* to Lancaster Sound and rescue by whalers.

In 1839 Ross sailed with his uncle, John Ross, to Antarctica. This expedition proceeded to a range of ice mountains, which blocked all further progress. In 1848–1849 he commanded the *Enterprise* on an expedition to the Arctic for the relief of *Sir John Franklin* but failed to make contact. Although he was to see no further active service, he continued until his death to be consulted as the first authority on all matters relating to Arctic exploration.

Ross, Sir John (1777–1856)

It is unfortunate that a large part of John Ross's reputation rests on his discovery of the Croker Mountains—a geographical feature that in fact did not exist. John Ross made important discoveries in the northeastern part of Arctic Canada and helped pave the way for the eventual discovery of the *Northwest Passage.*

Ross went to sea early as a lad and was listed as a crew member of the *Pearl* at age nine. After several years he joined the merchant service in 1790 and made a number of voyages to the West Indies and to the Baltic region. In 1799 Ross joined the Royal Navy and for ten years fought with distinction against the Spanish; he was wounded in battle at least thirteen times, and for this, and because of his heroism, he was honored with a knighthood. After promotion to commander in 1812, he commanded two voyages in the Baltic and North Seas, and was responsible for determining the longitude of the Russian port, Archangel.

It was soon after this, due to the cessation of the naval wars with the French and Americans, that there was a resurgence in the search for a northwest passage and in Arctic exploration generally. Much of the rekindled interest in the search was due to the efforts of Sir John Barrow, the Secretary of the Admiralty. Barrow and Ross did not see eye to eye on Arctic matters at this point, and the hostility between the two men was to intensify greatly over the next few years. Nonetheless, Ross was given the command of an expedition to enter Davis Bay and then find the westward entrance to the passage from that point. The captain of the second ship, the *Alexander,* was **William Edward Parry.** The expedition rediscovered the massive Baffin Bay and affirmed many points and details of the existing Baffin map. The party proceeded north, reaching the crucial water passage, Lancaster Sound, which was in fact the only practical passage to the west. It was here that Ross made the mistake that was to cost him his reputation and undo any of his subsequent Arctic achievements. Well in advance of the *Alexander,* he saw what he thought was a towering mass of Ice Mountains completely blocking Lancaster Sound, barring any possible westward passage. It was sworn later by his crew that only Ross saw the ice, which he named Croker Mountains; in fact, what he saw was an optical illusion. The expedition was ended, and in 1818 the two ships returned to England, where the report was at first accepted as conclusive and Ross was appointed to the rank of vice admiral. But controversy arose almost immediately about the "mountains," and the Admiralty sent a ship under the command of Parry to verify the Ross findings. Parry returned in 1820 with proof of Ross's misjudgment, and there followed a very public disparagement of his work, exacerbated by the enmity between Ross and John Barrow, representing the Admiralty.

John Ross was anxious to return and repair the error, but his services were declined. It was not until 1829 that he was given a ship, the *Victory,* fitted out by Felix Booth and himself, and sent out to find a passage south out of Regent's Inlet. Ross missed Bellot Strait, which led off westward, and proceeding southward found himself stopped by ice. During the following summer, the *Victory* was able to move only a few miles further south, where again the vessel was blocked in by ice; this time the ship was so completely frozen in that it was finally abandoned in 1832. The men were able to make their way on foot to Fury Beach where they built a hut from the wreck of Parry's *Fury* and spent a fourth winter. Eventually, they made their way to Lancaster Sound where a whaler rescued them.

This voyage of Ross was not a complete loss: A record was set for the amount of time locked in the Arctic ice; Ross spent his time in exploration, and a survey was made of the Boothia Peninsula and King William Island. John Ross returned to London to much acclaim late in 1832; in 1835 he published an account of the four years spent in search of a northwest passage.

Ross served as Great Britain's consul to Sweden for the next five years, but when he heard of the proposed Arctic expedition to be headed by *Franklin,* he offered his opinion and assistance but found that neither was wanted. The old antagonism with Barrow, who was still at the Admiralty, had grown even more bitter over the years. A number of public letters appeared, and the feud was intensified when in 1847 Ross urged the Admiralty to begin an immediate search for Franklin. The request was rejected by Barrow. In 1849 John Ross undertook his own rescue mission, but returned having found no trace of Franklin. The sanctioned searches sponsored by the Admiralty that followed pointedly excluded Ross; this slight brought forth another public condemnation of the Admiralty by Ross, blaming Barrow for the failed rescue of Franklin. The Arctic career of John Ross concluded on this acrimonious note. He died in London on August 30, 1856.

Russians in North America (1648–1867)

Not unexpectedly, the Russians concentrated their explorations in the Arctic and sub-Arctic lands and waters to those belonging to Eurasia, but from roughly mid-1600 to the mid-1800s they also undertook a number of expeditions that contributed greatly to the discovery and understanding of the northernmost regions of North America. Not all the claims to priority by the Russians are accepted by all authorities, but there should be recognition of the Russians' role in this area.

Russia had taken over most of Siberia by the end of the sixteenth century, and a hundred years later the Cossacks had established settlements on the northeastern coast of Russia, facing the Pacific Ocean. Meanwhile, five thousand miles of the northern edge of Russia, most of it in Siberia, lay above the Arctic Circle; the few existing maps of the vast region were inconsistent, contradictory, and wildly wrong. An explorer named *Semen Dezhnev* had gone around the East Cape (the farthest northeast tip of the Siberian landmass) in 1648, but this voyage came to light only in the eighteenth century. The lack of interest in empire and exploration might well have continued had it not been for the foresight of Czar Peter the Great (1672–1725).

Peter the Great was concerned with maintaining control of his vast empire; he was well aware of how the English, Spanish, French, and the Dutch were expanding the boundaries of their worlds. But Peter was interested in geography and knowledge as well. In 1719 he mandated an expedition to go to Kamchatka (a peninsula off the northeast coast of Siberia) and determine whether Asia and America were united. Then the explorers were to proceed north and south, and east and west, and put down all that they saw on a chart. This voyage was not successful, but the czar immediately planned another, more ambitious, expedition to be led by *Vitus Bering,* the Danish navigator who served in the Russian navy.

In the Western world, credit for establishing that there is a water strait between North America and Asia is customarily given to Vitus Bering. This discovery is dated to his voyage in 1727–1729. The Russians claim that two Russian explorers, Semen Dezhnev and F. Popov, sailed from the Chukchi Sea south into the Pacific Ocean during their voyage in 1648. In either case, Russia gets credit for discovering what became known as the Bering Strait. Then in 1732 I. Fedorov and Mikhail Gvozdev

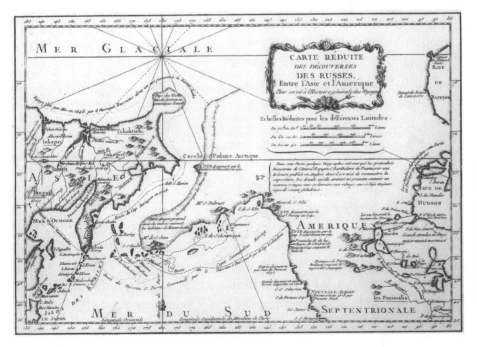

This map, published in a French volume of 1747, shows the lands and locales in the area between Russian Asia and North America claimed as discoveries by the Russians up to that time.

discovered what would eventually become known as the Seward Peninsula, the promontory that forms the eastern side of the Bering Strait. Other Russians also credited with exploring the coast of Alaska in the 1730s include A. Mel'nikov and P. Nagibin.

Between 1759 and 1764 the Russians credit S. Ponomarev, S. Glotov, A. Tolstykh, and others with discovering the Andreanof, Fox Islands, and Rat Islands—groups belonging to the Aleutian chain—and the Alaska Peninsula itself, the narrow body of land that extends from the southwest corner of Alaska. Between 1768 and 1769, P. K. Krenitsyn and M. D. Lavashev discovered most of the rest of the Aleutian Islands. There is no suggestion, though, that any of these Russians did much, if any, exploration of the mainland of Alaska.

In 1784, however, Gregory Shelikof, a Russian fur trader, established a post on Kodiak Island, just off the base of the Alaska Peninsula. This was the first white settlement in Alaska. Between 1784 and 1795, *Alexander A. Baranov,* D. I. Bocharov, G. A. Sarychev, and G. I. Sherlikhov discovered most of the rest of the Alaska Peninsula as well as the Kenai Peninsula, which juts into the Gulf of Alaska from just below Anchorage. In 1790–1791, the Russian ship *Slava Rossii* ("Glory for Russia") charted much of Alaska's coastline from the Bering Strait to St. Lawrence Island; the findings were published by Gavril Sarychev in 1826 as the *Atlas of the Northern Part of the East Ocean.* Sometime in the early 1790s, too, the Lebedev-Lastochkin Company, an early Russian trading company, had gained a foothold on the shores of Iliamna Lake, at the base of the Alaskan Peninsula. The company sent one Vasily Ivanov on an exploratory expedition into the regions north of this lake, and Ivanov evidently traveled as far as the Kuskokwim and Yukon Rivers. Although there has always been some question about Ivanov's travels, he may well deserve to be known as the first European to penetrate the interior of Alaska.

In 1799 Russia chartered the Russian-American Company as a trading monopoly in Alaska, and Alexander Baranov, who had participated in some of the expeditions, became its first manager. Baranov was a harsh man who abused the local Indians and actually enslaved the Aleuts. In 1802 the Tlingit Indians rose up and killed many of the Russian settlers in Sitka and destroyed the town, but the Russians soon regained control, rebuilt Sitka, and made it their headquarters in Alaska. And whatever may be said of Baranov's treatment of the indigenous peoples, he did lead the Russian-American Company to prosper until he was replaced in 1818.

In 1816 the Russians commenced another round of exploratory voyages and expeditions that went on until 1844. During those years, A. K. Etolin, *A. Glazunov, A. Kashevarov,* A. Kilmovskii, P. Kolmakov, Petra Korsakovskiy, O. E. von *Kotzebue,* V. S. Kromchenko, V. Malakhov, G. Shishmaryov, *M. D. Teben'kov, Ivan Vasil'ev, M. N. Vasil'ev,* and L. A. Zagoskin discovered or explored elements of Alaska now known as Kotzebue Sound; Nunivak land; the Copper, Susitna, Nushagak, and Kuskokwim Rivers; the lower and middle reaches of the Yukon River; the Chugach, Wrangell, and Kuskokwim mountains; and parts of the Alaska range.

In 1812 the Russians had established a trading post just north of San Francisco, which became known as Fort Ross. In 1824 Russia signed a treaty with the United States in which it agreed to limit its claims to land north of latitude 54°40'—that is, up in present-day British Columbia—although Russians did not fully abandon northern California until the 1840s. (In fact, the Russians sold Fort Ross in 1841 to John Sutter, the same Swiss entrepreneur on whose land gold was discovered in 1848.) By the 1850s the Russian-American Company had pretty much withdrawn from the fur trade in North America, and Russia was recognizing that its hold on the land was threatened by the encroaching American and British interests. In 1867, after negotiations led by U.S. secretary of state William H. Seward, Russia sold Alaska to the United States for some $7,200,000. This ended the Russians' exploratory activities in North America.

Schwatka, Frederick (1849–1892)

Frederick Schwatka was born in Illinois and lived in the Midwest until his appointment to the United States Military Academy in 1867. After graduation he served garrison duty in the west and made use of the time by studying law and medicine, receiving his credentials in both professions. Schwatka heard of a proposed mission to the Arctic to search for diaries and records of the lost *Franklin* expeditions. There were still tales of survivors of the Franklin party living with Eskimos that needed to be followed up. Schwatka was chosen to lead the expedition, and in 1878 the party landed in *Greenland [I]* and reached King William Island in the summer of 1879. There they found relics and skeletons that neither *Hall* nor *McClintock* had seen, but they discovered no new records or diaries; Schwatka, however, was careful to record Inuit accounts of the white men who had died on King William Island many years before. Schwatka and his party made a round trip of 3,124 miles and established a new record for sledge travel. Although they made only minor geographical discoveries, they collected valuable ethnological data. After Schwatka's voyage, the question of the Franklin records was brought to a conclusion. In 1886 Schwatka led another expedition to Alaska, but made no significant discoveries. By 1889 the public interest in Arctic adventure had waned, and Schwatka turned his attention to other interests. History lists Schwatka as the leader of the "last Franklin search expedition."

Scoresby, William, Jr. (1789–1857)

The activities of Arctic whalers had a strong and positive influence on the renewed interest in Arctic exploration in the first quarter of the 19th century. William Scoresby Jr. and his father were the two most notable English whalers; both men were able to combine their research interests with the successful pursuit of their line of business. William Jr. was born near the English port of Whitby. As well as being a whaling captain, the elder Scoresby was an inventor and an innovator, and the son was university educated (Edinburgh) and in addition profited greatly from his long experience under his father. William Jr. was mate to the father when they set the farthest north record of 83°31'. Five years later, he was the most experienced captain in Arctic waters. By 1823 he had published two books on the Arctic region, and with his father, had mapped nearly a thousand miles of the east coast of *Greenland [I]*. One of his ideas, however—using reindeer to pull sledges—was an absolute failure. Nonetheless, Scoresby was one of the best-informed authorities in England when the new assault on the *Northwest Passage* began. *William Parry* met him in 1819 and was surprised by the extent of his knowledge.

Scoresby had noticed during his voyages of 1816 and 1817 that the ice had withdrawn from the northern Greenland waters. He wrote, "I observed on my last voyage about 18,000 square miles of the surface of Greenland was . . . perfectly devoid of ice." He communicated this information to John Barrow, secretary to the Admiralty, and recommended that this was now the time, if ever, to discover "if or where the passage ran." Scoresby's information must certainly have been a factor in the *John Ross* expedition of 1818. Although Arctic exploration in England was firmly under the control of the Royal Navy, civilians such as William Scoresby must be given a place among those who helped pave the way for the dramatic discoveries soon to be made. Ordained as an Anglican priest in 1825, he continued his interest in scientific matters, and as late as 1856 he went to Australia to investigate terrestrial magnetism.

Simpson, Thomas   (1808–1840)

Thomas Simpson was born in Dingwall, England, where his father was head schoolmaster. Simpson, as a boy, was of delicate health with a tendency to consumption. His parents determined that he should go into the ministry. To this end, he completed a course of study at King's College in Aberdeen with high honors and was awarded an M.A. in 1829. By this time Simpson had developed into a healthy, robust young man; he abandoned a career in the ministry and instead entered the service of the *Hudson's Bay Company [VI]* and was posted to the American Northwest. In 1836 he was appointed to second in command on a mission led by *Peter Warren Dease.* The assignment was "to complete the discovery and survey of the northern shores of America." From beginning to end Simpson resented his subordination to Dease; he thought himself to be much better suited to lead than was Dease. He thought of Dease as an old man, overcautious and fearful. After some time on his own, spent practicing his astronomy and navigation, he joined Dease at Fort Chipewyan, and the two explorers proceeded north on the Mackenzie River, reaching the Arctic Ocean and moving west to 154°23' W. Here, blocked by ice, Simpson journeyed further west on foot to Point Barrow. After an arduous trip up the Mackenzie, the explorers returned to Great Bear Lake, where they spent the winter.

In 1838 Simpson and Dease set out to explore and chart the eastern segment of the northern shore. Bad weather caused the failure of that attempt, but in 1839 Simpson reached the mouth of the Coppermine River and moving east, explored all the way to the Boothia Peninsula, exploring that coast as well as the southern coast of King William Island. Throughout this expedition, Simpson took the initiative and often pressed forward; by himself if necessary, overcoming what he saw as the passivity and timidity of his chief, Dease. Simpson was unable to find a way around the Boothia Peninsula; otherwise he and Dease could have been said to have discovered the *Northwest Passage.*

In the following year Simpson left the northwest to return to England. It is supposed that his Indian guides attacked him; he died with a gunshot wound to the head after killing two Métis Indians. His narrative of his exploration exploits was edited and published by his brother in 1843.

Stefansson, Vilhjalmur (1879–1962)

Vilhjalmur Stefansson has been given the title "The Champion of the North." He raised the standards of Arctic exploration, perhaps more than any other Arctic traveler, from a sport-like competition to break records to a true scientific study of the land and the native people who inhabited it. When asked if he had reached the *North Pole,* he replied, "No, I'm a scientist, not a tourist." Stefansson added about a hundred thousand square miles to the maps of the Canadian far north; and he contributed equally as much to the world's knowledge of the lives and customs of the Eskimo people.

Stefansson was a man of interesting and contradictory character. In New York City he was known to take a cab to go three blocks. Yet in the Arctic he once departed on a jaunt of five hundred miles in −60°F, without companions or dogs, with one day's supply of food in his pack. Stefansson was a scholar who was fluent in ten languages before he easily mastered the Eskimo tongue. He was erudite in all branches of science and had studied thoroughly all the previous Arctic expeditions. He knew the weaknesses of all the earlier explorations and learned from their failings. More than any other polar explorer, modern or earlier, he came to understand the necessity of knowing the land, what it could provide, and how to sustain life from it.

Stefansson was born in Manitoba, Canada, to immigrant Icelandic parents who moved down into North Dakota in 1881. He studied anthropology and archaeology at several U.S. universities. His first expedition (1905) was to Iceland, and in 1906 he joined an Anglo-American Polar Expedition destined for the Mackenzie River delta to investigate native culture in that region. Disdaining to travel by boat around Alaska to the Beaufort area of the Arctic Ocean, he made his own way into the Arctic by means of the Mackenzie River; the main party of the exploration was trapped by ice off the coast of Alaska, so Stefansson happily settled down to spend the winter two hundred miles north of the Arctic circle with a light raincoat, a blue serge suit, a camera, and notebook, and two hundred rounds of ammunition. He spent the next eighteen months living with an Inuit family; there he learned the language and the skills of hunting, fishing, and survival. He learned to eat (and enjoy) half-rotten frozen fish and how, in an emergency, to cook the rawhide lashings of his snowshoes for sustenance. Stefansson claimed later that "fresh rawhide was good eating and reminds one of pigs feet, if well boiled." He learned what kind of clothing to wear, how to deal with the cold, and how to interpret the weather; he learned how to build a snow house and how to stalk a seal. He became a crack shot with the rifle. Most of all, this early time spent with the Eskimos caused him to change his ideas about the so-called hostility of the far north. He came to think of the frozen north as "cozy and comfortable" and not dangerous to the traveler who was prepared and used "sweet logic and intelligence."

Stefansson returned to New York and began to organize an expedition to Victoria Island, where he had heard there was a tribe of blond, blue-eyed Eskimos. These Eskimos were said to be a Stone Age race who had never seen white men; furthermore, they were hostile and supposedly killed their enemies (all strangers) with caribou antlers. In May of 1910, under the sponsorship of the American Museum of Natural History, Stefansson reached the island from the west with the intention of proving that the inhabitants of this forsaken place north of the Arctic circle were descendants of his own *Norse [I]* Viking ancestors who had explored *Greenland [I]* and *Vinland [I]* almost a thousand years before. (And if not Vikings, he thought they might be descended from survivors of the lost *Franklin* expedition.) It was not long before Stefansson and his two Eskimo dog team drivers became the honored guests of the natives, speaking their dialect, sharing their food, and taking part in their hunts. The women mended Stefansson's footwear, and the men showed their prowess with their copper-tipped arrows, for which Stefansson gave them the name, "Copper Indians." The natives were fair-skinned, and one very light maid sang and danced for Stefansson to the rhythms of what he called the ancient Norse scaldic poetry. Nothing conclusive, however, was discovered about the origins of these strange peoples. After returning in 1912, Stefansson wrote an account of his two-year stay on Victoria Island in his book, *My Life with the Eskimos,* in which he maintained that these people might indeed be of Scandinavian origin; at least they were not savages and had standards of honor, family values, and a gentle civility that made them little different from twentieth-century man. Stefansson's opinions, as expressed in his iconoclastic book, were not well received by the scientific community.

Stefansson's final voyage began in 1913; liberally sponsored by the Canadian government, he was to conduct geological, zoological, archaeological and anthropological research on the Arctic mainland south of Victoria Island. Stefansson specifically was to take a northern party into the Arctic Ocean to explore, take depth soundings, look for marine and animal life, and search for new land. The expedition began with a disaster. In September 1913 Stefansson's ship, the *Karluk* (captained by **Robert Bartlett**), was frozen in the ice off the north coast of Alaska. Stefansson and part of the crew remained on shore, but the *Karluk* and its twenty-five-man crew drifted helplessly northward in the pack ice; when the *Karluk* was crushed and sank, all twenty-five got off, but only fourteen of them survived and eventually made their way to safety.

Stefansson, meanwhile, had decided to make his way eastward on foot with dogs, from Point Barrow across the Arctic Ocean to Victoria Island. The remaining crew refused to venture on such an enterprise and a near mutiny resulted. When Stefansson hired two Scandinavian seamen and set off across what was considered the most barren, hostile, and lifeless of all the Arctic territory, the remaining scientific staff scoffed. They described the leaving as "one crazy and two deluded men going north over the sea ice to commit suicide." The party carried on their one two-hundred-pound sled thirty days' worth of pemmican, bacon, malted milk and chocolate for the men and forty days' worth of dried fish for the dogs. Sixty days later, after hacking through the massive jumble of blue ice ridges to very little advantage, the dogs were down to eating sealskin boots and the men were eyeing the dogs. On May 15, 1914, the party managed to shoot a seal, and for the remainder of the journey game was plentiful. As the weather grew warmer, the ice began to break apart, and the troop found themselves marooned on a five-square-mile piece of floating ice. Stefansson took advantage of the situation by conducting his scientific work. He and the crew collected meteorological data; they carried out line soundings through four degrees of latitude and nineteen of longitude; they kept careful records of water and air temperatures, and the related patterns of ice deterioration and flow. They recorded the habits of fish and seal and polar bears and determined the diets of these polar creatures. Amid the spectacle of towering masses of ice, and amid the constant din of the grinding and squealing of colliding ice floes, Stefansson carried out his mission on his floating ice laboratory. He thought of it as a "picnic," though occasionally a bit "monotonous." When he reached the shore of Banks Island on June 25, 1914, the group had traveled seven hundred miles across the Beaufort Sea, living off the land with relative ease. And in so doing, they had mapped and determined the continental shelf off the northern coast of Alaska. They celebrated their arrival on Banks by feasting on caribou steaks.

Stefansson spent the summer exploring and mapping the western coast of Banks Island. *Robert McClure* had dismissed this Arctic Ocean territory as a barren wasteland. In fact, it turned out to be lovely green prairie, sprinkled with clear pristine little lakes, honeycombed with rivers that flowed through lush pastures full of birds and butterflies and bees. In the pastures were the docile musk oxen, fat and tame, to provide variety to the party's diet of seal, caribou, and fish. Stefansson was almost sorry to spot a ship, the *Mary Sachs,* coming into anchor in September 1914. The *Sachs* actually was bearing a handful of Stefansson's loyal followers, who had come in hopes of finding the commander's remains and returning them to civilization for decent burial.

Stefansson stayed and was given up for dead at least four times in the next four years. He traveled over five thousand miles by sledge across the Canadian Arctic, and his furthest north reach was 80° N latitude, where he discovered Meighen Island, opposite what in 1952 would be named Stefansson Point. In 1919 he retired from active exploration. The remainder of his life was spent as lecturer, curator of the polar book collection at Dartmouth College, and writer of more than twenty-four books and hundreds of articles dealing with every phase of the Arctic and its people. He died in August 1962, secure in the realization that he had changed the knowledge of, and the attitudes toward, the Arctic and its inhabitants, for all time.

IN THEIR OWN *Words*

The Independent Explorer

I feel like mentioning here that I cannot understand the psychology of northern travellers who employ Eskimos and Indians to do their hunting for them. I would as soon think of engaging a valet to play my golf or of going to the theatre by proxy. Not that I enjoy the killing of animals as such but I should dislike extremely the feeling of dependence in work or play, of knowing that it hinged on the skill and goodwill of anyone, no matter how competent, whether I should have something to eat tomorrow or whether my plans were to fail for lack of food . . . the open life of him who lives by the hunt keeps indefinitely the thrill of endeavour and achievement, a thing never to be bought or secured by having others carry out for you the most elaborate or ingenious of programmes.

—VILHJALMUR STEFANSSON,
THE FRIENDLY ARCTIC, 1921

Sverdrup, Otto

(?–1930)

Otto Sverdrup left his father's Norwegian farm at the age of seventeen to go to sea; from that time on, the sea was in his blood. He came to be known among seamen as "the king of ice navigators." The Eskimos gave him the name of Akortok, which means "he who steers the ships." As a ship captain he was taciturn and silent but was known as a spellbinding storyteller, drawing upon his countless adventures and harrowing experiences in the Arctic. He was an accomplished hunter, fisherman, and carpenter. In 1888 *Fridtjof Nansen* chose Sverdrup as his right-hand man for his audacious crossing of *Greenland [I]* from the east coast to the west coast. Sverdrup shared with Nansen the romantic adventurous spirit of that seemingly impossible feat. Marooned on the 9,000-foot Greenland glacier, with the blizzard outside raging around the tent at –50°F, Sverdrup told stories of his adventures at sea. It followed that Sverdrup was the choice of Nansen as navigator-captain for the voyage of the *Fram* in 1893. Nansen's intention was to deliberately become frozen in the ice and to use the polar drift to bring the ship to the *North Pole.* When Nansen realized the drift would not go to the pole, he left the *Fram* in an attempt to ski to the pole. Sverdrup was left to complete the expedition and bring the ship safely out of the ice at Spitzbergen, which he did in 1896. Sverdrup had reached 81°57' N, the highest northern latitude ever navigated by a ship. In 1899 Sverdrup returned to the Arctic, in command of the *Fram,* to explore northern Greenland. He was met by heavy ice and the hostility of *Robert E. Peary,* who considered the Greenland area as his private preserve. Sverdrup turned westward and mapped with great accuracy the western coast of *Ellesmere Island;* at this time he discovered the then unknown group of islands known now as Sverdrup Islands. Sverdrup returned to Norway in 1902, never to fulfill his dream of traveling to the South Pole aboard the *Fram* with his lifelong friend Nansen.

Teben'kov, Mikhail Dimitrivich

(1802–1872)

A Russian hydrographer and explorer, from 1825 to 1839 Mikhail Dimitrivich Teben'kov was in command of the Russian-American Company's fleet. During that time, in 1829–1831, he made a hydrographic survey of Norton Sound (south of the Seward Peninsula) and the

Alexander Archipelago (off Alaska's southwesternmost coast). In 1833 Ferdinand Wrangel, governor of the Russian-American Company, sent Teben'kov and Adolph K. Etolin on an expedition to explore the coast of Norton Sound for the purpose of siting a Russian trading post; Teben'kov chose a small island that he named Mikhailovski (St. Michael), and it became an important outpost for Russia. Between 1845 and 1850 Teben'kov served as the governor of Russia's holdings in North America. In 1852 he published an *Atlas of the Northwestern Coast of America.*

Vasil'ev, Ivan Yakovlevich (1797–?)

Ivan Vasil'ev was trained as a navigator and served on vessels in the Baltic Sea until 1821, when he was employed by the Russian-American Company, the dominating Russian trading company and presence in Alaska. Based in Sitka, Alaska, Vasil'ev sailed under several of the company's ships along the Alaska coast and as far south as California. During the summer of 1829 he was sent forth on a sea-land expedition to reach the source of the Nushagak River in southwestern Alaska and to explore the drainage regions of the Kuskokwim and Yukon Rivers. Traveling into the interior often on foot and sometimes in small boats, he did not achieve all these goals, but his expedition was considered enough of a success that he was sent out again in June 1830. This time he reached the Kuskokwim River and visited many of the native settlements in the region, but once again he failed to reach the Yukon River before returning. Vasil'ev was highly honored by the Russians for his work, and then in 1831 and 1832 he made other expeditions along the eastern coast of the Alaska Peninsula. His health, however, had been deteriorating, and in 1834 he requested to leave the company's service. He returned to St. Petersburg, but by 1838 he had vanished from the Russian records. The journal of his first (1829) expedition survived and provides some valuable information about the people and locales of southwestern Alaska in this era.

Vasil'ev, Mikhail Nikolaevich (1770–1847)

A Russian naval officer, Mikhail Nikolaevich Vasil'ev in 1819–1822 was put in command of a round-the-world expedition involving two ships. Their charge was to discover a sea route from the Pacific to the Atlantic, and he first sailed westward to South America and through the Strait of Magellan to Australia. This was of course the only known route. He then headed north and sailed through the Bering Strait, and spent two years fruitlessly trying to find a passage eastward through the Arctic Ocean (a feat that was not accomplished until Henry Larsen did it in 1944). Although he failed in his main goal, Vasil'ev did survey details of the Alaskan coast and discover some islands.

Wilkins, Hubert (1888–1958)

One of the most colorful explorers of the early 20th century was an Australian named Hubert Wilkins. By the time he was a young man, he had had a number of incredible adventures. In 1912 he had faced a Turkish firing squad three times and escaped death. He then worked with *Vilhjalmur Stefansson* for three years in the Canadian Arctic. He returned from the north to fight in World War I and was wounded nine times, receiving numerous awards and medals. As an accomplished pilot, he made many first flights, including a 1928 flight from Alaska to Spitzbergen, for which he was knighted by the British. After two expeditions to Antarctica (1928–1930), during which he discovered new lands from his airplane, in partnership with three colleagues he obtained a surplus World War I submarine from the U.S. Navy for one dollar and proposed to travel to the *North Pole* under the ice. All of Wilkins's attempts failed because his vessel, the *Nautilus,* had to surface every 125 miles, which of course it could not do, and also because it was discovered that not all regular navigation instruments would work under the ice. Wilkins turned his attention to Antarctica and worked there until his death in 1958.

This is the airplane used by Australian explorer Hubert Wilkins in 1926 for one of his several airplane flights across the Arctic regions. As was not uncommon in those days, this particular expedition was sponsored by a newspaper, the *Detroit News.*

Bibliography

General Background

Beck, Warren, and Ynez D. Haase. *Historical Atlas of California*. Norman: University of Oklahoma Press, 1974.

Bricker, Charles. *Landmarks of Mapmaking: An Illustrated Survey of Maps and Mapmakers*. New York: Thomas Crowell, 1976.

Dictionary of Canadian Biography. Toronto: University of Toronto Press, 1966.

Fagan, Brian M. *Ancient North America: The Archaeology of a Continent*. London: Thames and Hudson, 1995.

Garraty, John A., and Mark C. Carnes. *American National Biography*. New York: Oxford University Press, 1999.

Goetzmann, William, ed. *The Atlas of North American Exploration: From the Norse Voyages to the Race to the Pole*. New York: Macmillan, 1992.

Goetzmann, William H., and Glyndwr Williams, eds. *Atlas of North American History*. New York: Prentice Hall, 1992.

Hakluyt, Richard, ed. *The Principall Navigations, voiages and discoveries . . . of the English nation made by sea and over-land . . . 1589*. Facsimile Edition, Cambridge: Cambridge University Press, 1905.

Marsh, James H., ed. *The Canadian Encyclopedia*. 3 vols. Edmonton: Hurtig Publishers, 1985.

Morison, Samuel Eliot. *The European Discovery of America*. 2 vols. New York: Oxford University Press, 1971, 1974.

Phillips, Charles, and Alan Axelrod, eds. *Encyclopedia of the American West*. 4 vols. New York: Macmillan Reference, 1996.

Quinn, David B. *New American World: A Documentary History of North America to 1612*. 5 vols. New York: Arno Press, 1979.

_____. *North America from Earliest Discovery to First Settlements: The Norse Voyages to 1612*. New York: Harper & Row, 1977.

Sauer, Carl O. *The Seventeenth Century*. Berkeley, Calif.: Turtle Island, 1980.

Weber, David J., ed. *New Spain's Far Northern Frontier: Essays on Spain in the American West, 1540–1821*. Dallas: Southern Methodist University Press, 1979.

Weddle, Robert. *The Spanish Sea: The Gulf of Mexico in North American Discovery, 1500–1685*. College Station: Texas A & M University Press, 1985.

Wheat, Carl I. *Mapping the Transmississippi West, 1540–1861*. Vol. 1. San Francisco: Institute of Historical Geography, 1957–61.

Part I: North America before Columbus

Aczel, Amir. *The Riddle of the Compass*. New York: Harcourt Brace, 2001.

Babcock, William H. *Legendary Islands of the Atlantic*. New York: American Geographical Society, 1922.

Burgess, Glyn S., and W. R. J. Barron. *The Voyage of St. Brendan: Themes and Variations*. Exeter, England: University of Exeter Press, 2002.

Enterline, James R. *Erikson, Eskimos & Columbus: Medieval European Knowledge of America.* Baltimore: Johns Hopkins University Press, 2002.

Fell, Barry. *America B.C.: Ancient Settlers in the New World.* New York: Quadrangle Books, 1976.

Fritze, Ronald. *Legend and Lore of the Americas Before 1492.* Santa Barbara, Calif.: ABC-Clio, 1993.

Ingstad, Anne Stine, ed. *The Norse Discovery of America.* Oslo, Norway: Norwegian University Press, 1985.

Magnusson, Magnus, and Hermann Palsson, translators. *The Vinland Sagas: Norse Discovery of America.* New York: Viking Press, 1965.

Needham, Joseph, and Lu Gwei-Djen. *Trans-Pacific Echoes and Resonances: Listening Once Again.* Singapore/Philadelphia: World Scientific, 1985.

Seaver, Kirsten A. *The Frozen Echo: Greenland and the Exploration of North America, ca. A.D. 1000–1500.* Stanford, Calif.: Stanford University Press, 1996.

Sorenson, John L., and Martin H. Raish. *Pre-Columbian Contact with the Americas across the Ocean: An Annotated Bibliography.* 2d ed. rev. Provo, Utah: Research Press, 1996.

Van Sertima, Ivan. *They Came Before Columbus.* New York: Random House, 1976.

Wauchope, Robert. *Lost Tribes & Sunken Continents.* Chicago: University of Chicago Press, 1962.

Williams, Stephen. *Fantastic Archaeology: The Wild Side of North American Prehistory.* Philadelphia: University of Pennsylvania Press, 1991.

Part II: The Spanish Enter the New World, 1492–1635

Alexander, Michael, ed. *Discovering the New World.* New York: Harper & Row, 1975.

Cabeza de Vaca, Alvar Núñez. *Cabeza de Vaca's Adventures in the Unknown Interior of America.* Albuquerque: University of New Mexico Press, 1983.

Chapman, Charles E. *A History of California: The Spanish Period.* New York: Macmillan, 1939.

Columbus, Christopher. *The Journal of Christopher Columbus.* Translated by Cecil Jane. New York: Bramhall House, 1960.

Cook, Warren. *Flood Tide of Empire: Spain and the Pacific Northwest, 1543–1819.* New Haven: Yale University Press, 1973.

Gibson, Charles. *The Spanish in America.* New York: Harper Colophon, 1966.

Kirsch, Robert, and William S. Murphy. *West of the West: The Story of California from the Conquistadors to the Great Earthquake, As Described by the Men and Women Who Were There.* New York: E. P. Dutton, 1967.

Madariaga, Salvador de. *Hernán Cortés, Conquerer of Mexico.* New York: Macmillan, 1941.

Ramenofsky, Ann F. *Vectors of Death: The Archaeology of European Contact.* Albuquerque: University of Mexico Press, 1987.

Raudzens, George, ed. *Technology, Disease and Colonial Conquests, Sixteenth to Eighteenth Centuries; Essays Reappraising the Guns and Germs Theories.* Boston: Brill, 2001.

Part III: The Atlantic Seaboard, 1497–1680

Biggar, H. P. *The Voyages of Jacques Cartier.* Toronto: University of Toronto Press, 1993.

Cartier, Jacques. *Navigations to Newe Fraunce.* Translation by John Florio. Ann Arbor, Mich.: University Microfilms, 1966.

Champlain, Samuel de. *Voyages and Explorations.* 2 vols. Translated by Annie Nettleton Bourne. New York: Allerton Book Co., 1922.

David, Richard, ed. *Hakluyt's Voyages*. Boston: Houghton Mifflin Company, 1981.

Dickason, Olive P. *Canada's First Nations: A History of Founding Peoples from Earliest Times*. Norman: University of Oklahoma Press, 1992.

Quinn, David B. *England and the Discovery of America, 1481–1620*. New York: Alfred A. Knopf, 1974.

————. *The Roanoke Voyages, 1584–1590*. London: Hakluyt Society, 1955.

Rosier, James. *Prosperous Voyage*. Ann Arbor, Mich.: University Microfilms, 1966.

Winship, George Parker, ed. *Sailors' Narratives of Voyages along the New England Coast, 1524–1624*. Boston: Houghton Mifflin Company, 1905.

Wroth, Lawrence C. *The Voyages of Giovanni da Verrazano*. New Haven: Yale University Press, 1970.

Part IV: Exploring West of the Mississippi, 1635–1800

Cook, Warren L. *Flood Tide of Empire: Spain and the Pacific Northwest, 1543–1819*. New Haven: Yale University Press, 1973.

Engstrand, Iris H. W. *Spanish Scientists in the New World: The Eighteenth Century Expeditions*. Seattle: University of Washington Press, 1981.

Foster, William C. *Spanish Expeditions into Texas, 1689–1768*. Austin: University of Texas Press, 1995.

John, Elizabeth. *Storms Brewed in Other Men's Worlds: The Confrontation of Indians, Spanish, and French in the Southwest, 1540–1795*. College Station: Texas A & M University Press, 1975.

Smith, Fay J., et al. *Father Kino in Arizona*. Phoenix: Arizona Historical Society, 1966.

Wagner, Henry. *Spanish Exploration in the Strait of Juan de Fuca*. Reprint. New York: AMS Press, 1971.

————. *The Spanish Southwest, 1542–1794*. Reprint. New York: Arno Press, 1967.

Weddle, Robert S. *The French Thorn: Rival Explorers in the Spanish Sea, 1682–1762*. College Station: Texas A & M University Press, 1991.

————. *Changing Tides: Twilight and Dawn in the Spanish Sea, 1763–1803*. College Station: Texas A & M University Press, 1995.

Part V: From the Appalachians to the Mississippi, 1540–1840

Bailey, Kenneth P. *Christopher Gist*. Hamden, Conn.: Archon Press, 1976.

Briceland, Alan V. *Westward from Virginia: The Exploration of the Virginia-Carolina Frontier 1650–1710*. Charlottesville: University of Virginia Press, 1987.

Caruso, John A. *The Appalachian Frontier: America's First Surge Westward*. Indianapolis: Bobbs-Merrill, 1959.

————. *The Great Lakes Frontier: An Epic of the Old Northwest*. Indianapolis: Bobbs-Merrill, 1961.

————. *The Southern Frontier*. Indianapolis: Bobbs-Merrill, 1963.

————. *The Mississippi Valley Frontier: The Age of French Exploration and Settlement*. Indianapolis: Bobbs-Merrill, 1966.

Chipman, Donald E. *Spanish Texas, 1519–1821*. Austin: University of Texas Press, 1992.

Eccles, William J. *The Canadian Frontier, 1534–1760*. New York: Holt, Rinehart and Winston, 1969.

Flores, Dan L. *Jefferson and Southwestern Exploration: The Freeman and Custis Accounts of the Red River Expedition of 1806*. Norman: University of Oklahoma Press, 1984.

Galloway, Patricia K., ed. *La Salle and His Legacy: Frenchmen and Indians in the Lower Mississippi Valley*. Jackson: University Press of Mississippi, 1982.

Kastner, Joseph. *A Species of Eternity*. New York: E. P. Dutton, 1978.

Kellog, Louise Phelps, ed. *Early Narratives of the Northwest, 1634–1699*. New York: Charles Scribner's Sons, 1917.

_____, ed. *The French Regime in Wisconsin and the Northwest*. New York: Cooper Square Publishers, 1925, 1968.

Kenton, Edna. *The Jesuit Relations and Allied Documents, 1610–1791*. New York: Vanguard Press, 1954.

McDermott, John Francis, ed. *The French in the Mississippi Valley*. Urbana: University of Illinois Press, 1969.

Randolph, J. Ralph. *British Travelers among the Southern Indians, 1660–1763*. Norman: University of Oklahoma Press, 1973.

Van Every, Dale. *Forth to the Wilderness: The First American Frontier, 1754–1774*. New York: William Morrow & Company, 1961.

Weddle, Robert S. *The French Thorn: Rival Explorers in the Spanish Sea, 1682–1782*. College Station: Texas A & M University Press, 1991.

_____, ed. *La Salle, the Mississippi, and the Gulf*. College Station: Texas A & M University Press, 1987.

Winsor, Justin. *Cartier to Frontenac: Geographical Discovery in the Interior of North America, 1530–1700*. New York: Cooper Square Publishers, 1894, 1970.

Part VI: Across the North American Continent, 1740–1880

Ambrose, Stephen. *Undaunted Courage: Meriwether Lewis, Thomas Jefferson, and the Opening of the American West*. New York: Simon & Schuster, 1996.

Bartlett, Richard A. *Great Surveys of the American West*. Norman: University of Oklahoma Press, 1962.

Bergon, Frank, ed. *The Journals of Lewis and Clark*. New York: Viking Penguin, 1989.

Cooley, John, ed. *The Great Unknown: The Journals of the Historic First Expedition Down the Colorado River*. N.p.: Northland Publishing, 1988.

Dolnick, Edward. *Down the Great Unknown: John Wesley Powell's 1869 Journey of Discovery and Tragedy through the Grand Canyon*. New York: HarperCollins, 2001.

Garraty, John A., and Mark C. Carnes. *American National Biography*. New York: Oxford University Press, 1999.

Gates, Charles M. *Five Fur Traders of the Northwest*. St. Paul: Minnesota Historical Society, 1965.

Goetzmann, William H. *Exploration and Empire: The Explorer and Scientist in the Winning of the American West*. New York: Alfred A. Knopf, 1966.

Irving, Washington. *The Adventures of Captain Bonneville*. Edited by Edgely U. Todd. Norman: University of Oklahoma Press, 1961.

Jackson, Donald, ed. *The Journals of Zebulon Montgomery Pike*. 2 vols. Norman: University of Oklahoma Press, 1966.

Jackson, Donald, and Mary Lee Spence. *The Expeditions of John Charles Frémont*. Vol. 1, Travels from 1838 to 1844. Urbana: University of Illinois Press, 1970.

Lamb, W. Kaye, ed. *The Journals and Letters of Sir Alexander Mackenzie*. Cambridge, England: Cambridge University Press, 1970.

Morgan, Dale L. *Jedediah Smith and the Opening of the West*. Lincoln: University of Nebraska Press, 1964.

Preuss, Charles. *Exploring with Frémont: The Private Diaries of Charles Preuss*. Translated and edited by Erwin G. and Elisabeth Gudde. Norman: University of Oklahoma Press, 1958.

Rich, E. E. *The History of the Hudson's Bay Company*. 2 vols. London: Hudson's Bay Record Society, 1958–59.

Stuart, Robert. *On the Oregon Trail: Robert Stuart's Journey of Discovery*. Edited by Kenneth A. Spaulding. Norman: University of Oklahoma Press, 1953.

Thompson, David. *Travels in Western North America*. Edited by Victor G. Hopwood. Toronto: Macmillan of Canada, 1971.

Vancouver, George. *A Voyage of Discovery to the North Pacific Ocean and Round the World*. New York: Da Capo Press, 1967.

Part VII: The Arctic and Northernmost Regions, 1576–1992

Amundsen, Roald. *My Life as an Explorer*. Garden City, N.Y.: Doubleday, 1927.

Anderson, William R., with Clay Blair, Jr. *Nautilus- 90° North*. Cleveland: World Publishing, 1959.

Armstrong, Terence. *The Russians in the Arctic: Aspects of Soviet Exploration and Exploitation of the Far North, 1937–57*. Fair Lawn, N.J.: Essential Books, 1958.

Baird, Patrick D., *The Polar World*. New York: John Wiley, 1964.

Bartlett, Robert. *The Last Voyage of the Karluk*. Boston: Small, Maynard, 1916.

DeLong, George Washington. *The Voyage of the Jeannette*. Boston: Houghton, Mifflin, 1883.

Dodge, Ernest S. *Northwest by Sea*. New York: University of Oxford Press, 1961.

Hall, Charles Francis. *Arctic Researches and Life Among the Esquimaux*. New York: Harper and Brothers, 1865.

Henson, Matthew. *A Negro Explorer at the North Pole*. Reprint of 1912 Edition. New York, Arno Press, 1969.

Holland, Clive. *Farthest North: The Quest for the North Pole*. New York: Carroll & Graf, 1994.

MacMillan, Donald. *Four Years in the White North*. Boston: Medici Society of America, 1925.

Mountfield, David. *A History of Polar Exploration*. New York: Dial Press, 1974.

Nansen, Fridtjof. *The First Crossing of Greenland*. London, New York: Longmans Green, 1890.

Neatby, Leslie H. *Conquest of the Last Frontier*. Athens: Ohio University Press, 1966.

_____. *The Search for Franklin*. New York: Walker, 1970.

Officer, Charles, and Jake Page. *A Fabulous Kingdom: The Exploration of the Arctic*. New York: Oxford University Press, 2001.

Peary, Robert. *The North Pole: Its Discovery in 1909*. New York: Frederick Stokes, 1910.

Rasmussen, Knud. *Across Arctic America: Narrative of the Fifth Thule Expedition*. New York: G. P. Putnam's, 1927.

Stefansson, Vilhjalmur. *The Friendly Arctic*. New York: Macmillan, 1921.

Thomson, George Malcolm. *The Search for the Northwest Passage*. New York: Macmillan, 1975.

VanStone, James W., ed. *Russian Exploration in Southwest Alaska: The Travel Journals of Petr Korsakovskiy (1818) and Ivan Ya. Vasilev (1829)*. Fairbanks: The University of Alaska Press, 1988.

Weems, John Edward. *Peary, The Explorer and the Man*. Boston: Houghton Mifflin Company, 1967.

Wilkinson, Doug. *Arctic Fever: The Search for the Northwest Passage*. Toronto: Clarke, Irwin, 1971.

Index

Note: **Boldface** page numbers indicate extended discussion of topic.

Abenaki Indians, **125–26,** 172, 190, 193, 273
Abert, James W., 332
Acadia, **126,** 146, 165, 172, 258
Acoma pueblo, 58, 87, 112, 122, 246
Adam of Bremen, 50
Adams, Ansel, 112
Adams, Henry, 351
Adams, John Quincy, 366
Africans, **6–7**
Agassiz, Louis, 351
Agreda, María de Jesus, **197–98**
Aguayo, Marqués de San Miguel de, **198–99,** 212
Aguilar, Martín de, 121
Aguirre, Pedro de, **199, 212–13,** 228
Alaminos, Antonio de, 91, 92, 93, **126–27,** 175
Alarcón, Hernando de, 30, **58,** 60, 74, 80
Alarcón, Martín de, **199–200,** 203, 212
Alaska, 205, 222, 225, 226, 230
    Cook's exploration of, 208–9
    Harriman expedition to, 436–37
    Russian explorers in, 403, 432, 448, 450, 481–83, 491, 492
Albanel, Charles, **250,** 269, 273, 286
Albuquerque, N.Mex., 66
Alexander VI, Pope, 109–10, 116–17
Alexander the Great, 19
Algonquin Indians, **127,** 129, 146, 147
Allouez, Claude Jean, **251,** 269, 285, 286
Alta California. *See* California
Alvarado, Hernando de, **58–59,** 74
Alvarado, Pedro de, **59–60,** 65, 77, 78, 79, 91, 102

Alvarez Chico, Pedro, 77
Alvarez de Pineda, Alonso, **128**
Amadas, Philip, **128–29,** 158
American Fur Company, **315–16,** 322, 374
American Revolution, 207, 215, 224
Ameryk, Richard, 120
Amundsen, Roald, **396–99,** 412, 443, 458, 460, 464, 465, 468
Anasazi Indians, 112, 210
Anderson, William, **399–400**
Andrée, Salomon, 463
Andros, Sir Edmund, 302
Anghera, Peter Martyr d', 7
Anglo-Azorean Syndicate, 13
Anian, Strait of, **61,** 62, 65, 67, 85, 86, 88–89, 121, 122, 450
Antarctica, 392, 398, 412–13
Antilia (Antilles), **7**
Antonio de la Ascension, Fray, 31
Anza, Juan Bautista de, 105, 195, **200–202,** 216, 218, 219, 233, 237
Apalachee Indians, 268
Appalachian Mountains, 157, 167, 185, 194, **251–52,** 256, 268, 285. *See also* Blue Ridge Mountains; Cumberland Gap
Aranda, Miguel de, **202–3**
Aransas Bay, 253
Arias de Avila, Pedro, 93, 94, 101
Arizona, 220–21
Arkansas Post, 267, 310
Army Corps of Engineers, 328. *See also* Corps of Topographical Engineers
Arrowsmith, Aaron, 370
Arteaga, Ignacio de, 206

Arthur, Gabriel, **170–71,** 194, 257, 268
Aruba, 106
Ashley, William Henry, **316–17,** 322, 332, 344, 382, 384, 386
Ashley River, 183
Asians, **8–9**
Assiniboine Indians, 83
Astor, John Jacob, 315–16, **317,** 332–33, 348, 349, 365, 384, 385
astrolabes, 42
Aswad, Khashkhash Ibn Saeed Ibn, 32–33
Aubert, Thomas, 188, 466
auks, 153–54
Avila, Alonso, 101
Ayala, Juan Manuel de, 205, 218–19
Ayllón, Lucas Vásquez de, 30, 98, **129–30,** 159, 176, 187
Aztecs, 59, 76–77, 82

Back, George, **401,** 421, 426
Baffin, William, 21, **401–2,** 403, 410, 424, 425
Baffin Bay (Texas), 222
Baffin Island, 10, 21, 52, 53, **402–3,** 408, 433, 452
Baja California. *See* California
Bakari II, 7
Balboa, Vasco Núñez de, **61,** 78, 110, 117
Balchen Bernt, 412–13
Banks Island, 489
Bannock Indians, **317**
Baranov, Alexander Andreevich, **403,** 482
Barcelos, Pedro Maria de, 151
Barkley, Charles William, 89
Barlow, J. W., 393
Barlowe, Arthur, **128–29,** 158
Barreiro, Francisco Alvarez, **203,** 236
Barrio Nuevo, Francisco de, 75
Barroto, Juan Enríquez, **203–5,** 231, 235
Barrow, Sir John, 429, 470, 479, 480
Bartleson, John, 318, 322, 332

Bartlett, John, 404
Bartlett, Robert A., **404–5,** 411, 442, 452, 473, 488
Bartram, John, **252–53,** 296
Bastidas, Rodrigo de, 61, 78
Battista Agnese map, 100
Batts, Thomas, **130,** 194
Beattie, Owen, 430
Beaufort, Francis, 416
Beauvais, Vincent de, 52
Beauvoir, Pierre, 165
Becerra, Diego, 78, 95
Beckwith, E. G., 372
Beechey, Frederick William, 421
Behaim, Martin, 27
Belcher, Sir Edward, 448, 449, 454, 459
Bellot Strait, 478, 479
Beltrán, Fray Bernaldino, **86–87,** 116
Benavides, Alonso de, 198
Bennett, Floyd, 399, 411, 412, 464
Bennett, James Gordon, 422
Bent, Charles, 318
Benton, Thomas Hart, **318,** 335, 336–37, 338
Bent's Fort, **318**
Benzoni, Girolamo, 135
Beothuk Indians, 49, **131–32,** 136, 150, 171
Béranger, Jean, **253–54**
Bering, Vitus, 61, **405–7,** 481
Beringia, 34, 35
Bering Strait, 209, 422–23, 424, 492
Bernardino de Sahagun, Fray, 82, 83
Bernier, Joseph-Elzéar, **407–9**
Bessels, Emil, 435
Best, George, 44
Biddle, Nicholas, 326, 353, 358
Bidwell, John, **318–19,** 323, 332
Bienville, Jean-Baptiste Le Moyne, Sieur de, 253, **254–55,** 256, 276, 283–84, 305, 306
Biscayno, Juan. *See* Cosa, Juan de la
Bjarni Herjolfsson, **10–11,** 24, 49–50
Blackfoot Indians, 83, **319,** 326, 342, 357

Blair, Francis P., 390
Bland, Edward, **132**, 193
Blanpain, Joseph, **255**
Blue Ridge Mountains, 130, **132–33**, 167, 170, 173, 309
Boas, Franz, 403
Bobadilla, Francisco de, 94
Bocharov, D. I., 482
Bodega Bay, 206
Bodega y Quadra, Juan Francisco de la, 195, **205–7**, 219
Bolaños, Francisco de, 60, **62**, 67, 121
Bond, William, **255–56**
Bonnecamps, Joseph-Pierre de, 262
Bonneville, Benjamin Louis Eulalie de, **319–20**, 349, 370–71, 381, 382
Boone, Daniel, 252, **256–57**, 268, 269, 302
Borup, George, 473
Bosque, Fernando del, **62**
Boston, Mass., **133**
Bourgmond, Etienne Venard de, 255, 313, **320–21**, 376
Boyd, Louise Arner, **409**
Braddock, Edward, 252
Bradley, George, 378, 379
Bradley, John R., 417
Brazil, 117, 119
Brébeuf, Jean de, 248, **258**, 285–86
Brendan, Saint, **11–12**, 22
Brereton, John, 158
Bridger, James, 317, **322**, 332, 337, 393
Brion, Philippe Chabot de, 141
Brion Island, 140
Bristol, England, **12–14**, 15, 29, 136
British Columbia, 88–89, 334
Broughton, Henry, **322–23**, 327, 389, 392
Browne, Richard, 164
Brûlé, Étienne, **133–34**, 147, 251
Bry, Théodore de, 119, **134–35**, 178
Bucareli, Antonio María de, 218
Bucareli Sound, 206
Buchanan, James, 339
Buddington, Sidney, 435

Burroughs, John, 436
Button, Thomas, **410**, 425
Bylot, Robert, 401, **410**
Byrd, Richard Evelyn, 399, **410–13**, 464
Byrd, William, II, **135**

Cabeza de Vaca, Alvar Núñez, 56, 60, **62–64**, 73, 87, 88, 97, 103, 112–13, 294
Cabot, John, 13, 28, 29, 79, 120, 123–24, 126, 131, **135–37**, 160, 161, 171, 345, 466
Cabot, Sebastian, 136, **138**, 168
Cabrillo, Juan Rodríguez, 60, **64–65**, 105, 122, 382
Cachupin, Tomás Vélez, 236
Cactus Hill (Virginia), 35
Cadillac, Antoine de La Mothe, **258–59**, 306
Cahokia, **259**
California, 31, 58, 61, 62, 370
  Drake's claims to, 85
  missions in, 216, 231–33, 240–42
  Spanish exploration of, 65, 67, 78, 90, 95, 118–19, 120–22, 200–202, 205–6, 215, 216–17, 218–19, 220–21, 237
  See also Monterey, Calif.
California Trail, 319, **323**, 347, 382
Camino Real, 109, 199, 238, 242
Campbell, Robert, 333, 347, **413–14**
Canada, 125. *See also* Acadia; Bernier, Joseph-Elzéar; Cartier, Jacques; Hochelaga; Labrador; Montreal; Newfoundland; Nova Scotia; Roberval, Jean-François de la Roque, Sieur de; St. Lawrence River
Canary Islands, 12
Cantino, Alberto, 28
Cantino Map of 1502, 28
Canzo, Gonzalo Méndez de, 149, 150
Cape Cod, Mass., **138–39**, 157, 190
Cape Fear, N.C., 188, 192
Carabajal y de la Cueva, Luís de, **66**

Cardero, José, 224, 243

Caribbean Islands. *See* Aruba; Cuba; Dominican Republic; Haiti; Hispaniola; Jamaica; Martinique; Puerto Rico

Carlos III, King, 231

Carmel, Calif., 221

Carson, A. C., 410–11

Carson, Kit, **324,** 330, 337

Cartier, Jacques, 29, 44, 131, **139–45,** 153–54, 163, 166, 171, 180, 181, 466

    Canadian explorations of, 124–25, 139–44, 162, 172, 298

    and search for Saguenay, 143–44, 181–82

Carvajal y de la Cueva, Luís de, **66**

Carver, Jonathan, **260–61,** 304, 308

Casa Calvo, Sebastián Calvo de la Puerta y O'Farril, Marqués de, **207,** 215

Casas, Bartolomé de las, 71–72

Cass, Lewis, 307

Castaño de Sosa, Gaspar, **66**

Castillo, Diego del, 217, **225**

Castillo Maldonado, Alonso del, 63–64, 88

Catesby, Mark, **261–62**

Catlin, George, 54, 319

Cavendish, Thomas, 420

Céloron de Blainville, Pierre-Joseph, **262**

Celts, **14–15,** 22, 53

Cermeño, Sebastián Rodríguez, 62, 65, **66–67,** 105, 121

Champlain, Jean Baptiste, 359

Champlain, Samuel de, 30, 31, 125, 127, 133, **145–48,** 156, 163, 172, 182, 285, 298

Chamuscado, Francisco Sánchez, 113, 115, 116

Chandler Circle, 461

Charbonneau, Toussaint, 356

Charles II, King, 182–83, 281, 346

Charles III, King, 267

Charles V, King, 155

Charleston, S.C., 183, 194

Charlevoix, Pierre François Xavier de, 261, **263**

Charrucos Indians, 63

Chattahoochee River, 194

Chaussegros de Léry, Gaspard-Joseph, **263–64,** 302

Cherokee Indians, 185, **264,** 268, 280

Chesapeake Bay, 31, 86, 129, 134, **148,** 152, 156–57, 164, 166, 170, 176, 178, 184, 187, 285

Cheyenne Indians, 333

Chickasaw Indians, 185, 256, 263, **264–65,** 312

Chicora, 98, 176

China

    Collinson in, 416

    Gray's voyage to, 341

    See also Asians; Northwest Passage

Chirikov, Alexei, 406

Choctaw Indians, 125, 185, **265,** 268, 312

Choris, Ludovik, 202

Chouinard, Elizabeth, 422

Chouteau, Auguste Pierre, **324–25**

Chozas, Pedro Fernández de, **149–50**

Christian I, King, 47

Cibola, 58, 73, 75, 80, 96–97, 98, 100, 112–13, 178

Cienfuegos Bay (Cuba), 106

Clark, George Rogers, 259, 325

Clark, William, 259, 278, 315, **325,** 327, 353, **354–58,** 359. *See also* Lewis and Clark expedition

Clavus, Claudius, 27

Clement VII, Pope, 110

Coats, William, **414–15**

Cocking, Matthew, 347

Cofachiqui, Lady of, 185

Collinson, Richard, **416–17,** 448, 454

Collot, Georges Henri Victor, **265–67,** 302

Colombia, 106

Colorado, 235–36

Colorado River, 30, 58, 74, 80, 210–11, 238, 340, 378–80

Colter, John, **325–26,** 340, 359, 386, 393

Columbia River, 219, 316, 317, 322, **326–27,** 338, 341, 356, 369, 370, 383, 384, 386–87, 392

Columbus, Bartholomew, 68

Columbus, Christopher, 5, 12, 47, 48, **68–72,** 78, 103, 105, 106, 109, 119, 120, 126–27, 128, 174

and Antilia, 8

in Cuba, 79

in Hispaniola, 94

letter from John Day to, 15, 137

maps available to, 27–28, 68

Muslims on voyages of, 33

and Puerto Rico, 114

writings of, 71–72

Columbus, Diego, 79, 106, 114

Columbus, Ferdinand, 68

Comanche Indians, 238, 245, 277, 301

compasses, 41

Confederate States of America, 328

Connecticut River, 173

Contarini, Giovanni Matteo, 28

Continental Divide, **327,** 338, 353, 356, 381

Cook, Frederick Albert, 398, **417–18,** 463, 472, 474

Cook, James, 195, **207–9,** 350, 389

Coosa, 167–68, 169, 174

Copala, 97

Coronado, Francisco Vásquez de, 36, 58, 60, 64, **73–75,** 80, 97, 99, 100, 105, 113, 186, 381

Coronas, Pedro de, 169

Corps of Topographical Engineers, 322, **328,** 330, 336, 337, 359

Corte-Réal, Gaspar, 48, 124, **150,** 151, 466

Corte-Réal, João Vaz, 47, 48

Corte-Réal, Miguel, 124, **150,** 466

Cortés, Francisco, 77

Cortés, Hernán, 65, **76–78,** 79, 82, 93, 95, 99, 103, 104, 105, 107, 110, 114–15, 118, 127, 128, 191

and Pedro de Alvarado, 59–60

Cosa, Juan de la, 28, **78–79,** 106

Couture, Jean, 256, **267**

Coxe, Daniel, 255–56

Cozumel Island (Mexico), 90

Creek Indians, 194, **267–68**

Crespi, Juan, 232

Crocker, George, 472

Croft, Thomas, 13

Crooks, Ramsay, 316

cross staff, 43

Crozat, Antoine, 259

Crozier, Francis, 429

Cuba, 8, 47, 59, 70, 72, 76, **79–80,** 87, 92, 100, 103, 104, 106, 138, 175, 184, 229, 254

Cumberland Gap, 133, 250, 252, 256–57, **268–69,** 311

Cumberland Island (Georgia), 165

Curaçao, 106

Curtis, Edward, 436

Custis, Peter, 276, 277–78

Dablon, Claude, 251, **269–70,** 273, 285–86

Dall, William, 436

The Dalles. *See* Columbia River

Daniel Boone National Forest, 257

Dare, Ananias, 178

Dare, Eleanor White, 178

Dare, Virginia, 179

Daumont de Saint-Lusson, Simon François, **270,** 287

Davenport, Iowa, 18

Davis, Jefferson, **328,** 371

Davis, John, 43, 44, **418–20**

Day, John, 13, **15,** 137

Dease, Peter Warren, 347, **420–22,** 485

Decker, George, 23

Delaware Indians, **270–71**

De l'Isle, Guillaume, 32

DeLong, George Washington, **422–23,** 463

Del Río, Domingo, **209**

Derbanne, François Guyon Des Prés, 271–72

DeRoos, W., 468–69

Devin, Valentin, 253, 254

De Voto, Bernard Augustine, 322, **329**

Dezhnev, Semen Ivanovich, **423–24,** 480–81

Diaz, Bernal, 95

Diaz, Melchior, 73, 74, **80**

Dietrichson, Lief, 399

Dighton Rock (Massachusetts), 45–46

disease, **80–84,** 126, 127, 206, 258, 342

disputed claims for pre-Columbian contacts, 6, **16–17.** *See also* Africans; Asians; Celts; Egyptians; Greeks; Irish; Libyans; Muslims; Norse; Phoenicians; Welsh; Zeno brothers

Doane, Gustavus C., 393

Dobbs, Arthur, 303, 455–56

Dodge, Grenville, 322

Dollier de Casson, François, **272–73,** 291

Domínguez, Francisco, 97, **210–11,** 236

Dominican Republic, 70, 94–95. *See also* Hispaniola

Dongan, Thomas, 304, 305

Donner Pass, 323, 382

Dorantes de Carranza, Andrés, 63–64, 87–88

Dorset Culture, 49, 51–52

Douglas, Stephen, 371

Drake, Sir Francis, 67, **84–86,** 115, 160, 208, 219, 432

Drake's Bay (California), 85, 121

Drouillard, George, 359

Druillettes, Gabriel, 269, **273,** 275

Dulhut, Claude, 274

Dulhut, Daniel Greysolon, **274–75,** 282, 298, 308

Dunbar, William, **275–76,** 277–78, 350

Dutisné, Claude-Charles, 255, **276–77,** 321

Dutton, Clarence, **329–30,** 340, 345, 380

East India Company, 161

Ecuador, 60

Eden, Richard, 168

Edisto River, 192

Egede, Hans, 21

Egyptians, **18,** 26

Eisenhower, Dwight, 442–43

Elizabeth I, Queen, 54, 85, 128, 129, 154, 160, 176–77, 431

Ellesmere Island, 401–2, 404, **424,** 432, 433, 437, 441, 451, 473, 490

Ellsworth, Lincoln, 399

El Paso, Tex., 122

El Turco. *See* the Turk

Emory, William H., **330–31**

England. *See* Bristol, England; Elizabeth I, Queen

Enterline, James Robert, 26

Erik the Red, 10, **18–19,** 20

Eriksson, Leif. *See* Leif Eriksson

Erlandson, Eland, 166

Escalante, Fray Silvestre Vélez de, 97, **210–11,** 236

Escandón, José de, **211–12,** 217

Espejo, Antonio, **86–87,** 98, 105, 113, 116

Espinosa, Fray Isidro Félix de, 198, 199, 200, **212–13**

Esquivel, Juan de, 79

Estevánico, 56, 58, 63–64, **87–88,** 97, 100, 112–13

Etolin, Adolph K., 483, 491

Evans, John, **361**

Evia, José Antonio de, **213–14**

Fabri, Nicolas-Claude de, 146

Fagés, Pedro, **214–15,** 233

Fagundes, João Alvarez, 140, **150–51**

Fallam, Robert, **130,** 194

Farfán, Marcos, 108

Farrukh, Ibn, 33

Fedorov, I., 481–82

Fell, Barry, 14, 17, 18, 26, 46

Fell's Cave (Argentina), 35

Ferdinand, King, 69, 94, 109

Fernandes, João, 28, 32, **151,** 166

Fernandes, Simão, 128–29, 158, 159, 172, 179

Fernández de Écija, Francisco, **151–52,** 165

Ferrelo, Bartolomé, 65

Fidler, Peter, **331–32,** 347

Filson, John, 257

Finiels, Nicolas de, 207, **215–16**

Finley, John, 256, 268

Fischer, Josef, 53

Fitzjames, James, 429

Fitzpatrick, Thomas, 316, **332**

Five Civilized Nations. *See* Cherokee Indians; Chickasaw Indians; Choctaw Indians; Creek Indians

Florida, 30, 86, 103, 105, 127, 134, 149, 151–52, **152–53,** 159, 165, 167, 170, 187, 192, 229, 256

 early map of, 128

 Menéndez de Avilés in, 168–69

 Ponce de León in, 175

 de Soto in, 184–85

Font, Father Pedro, 201

Forbes, John, 252

Ford, Edsel, 412

Fort Astoria, 316, 317, 327, **332–33,** 348, 365, 370, 384, 388

Fort Detroit, 321, 362, 377

Fort Hall, **333,** 338

Fort Henry, 130, 132, 170, 171, 193, 268

Fort Laramie, **333,** 370, 377

Fort Laramie, Treaty of, 308, 333

Fort Michilimackinac, 259, 260, 262, 275, **277,** 282, 287, 290, 291, 292, 304, 377

Fort St. George, 193

Fort Saint-Joseph, 275

Fort Selkirk, 413–14

Fortunate Isles, 12

Fort Vancouver, 327, **334,** 370, 374, 384

Foster, John, 32

Fowler, Don D., 380

Foxe, Luke, 345, **424–25,** 446

France. *See* François I, King; New France; *and names of French explorers*

François I, King, 139, 141, 143, **153,** 180, 188

Franklin, Lady Jane, **425,** 429, 430, 447, 453, 455, 476

Franklin, Sir John, 347, 394, 420, 421, 422, **425–30**

 Arctic expeditions of, 401, 426–28, 463

 search for, 409, 416, 424, 425, 429–30, 433, 434, 437, 447, 448–49, 453, 459, 469, 475, 480, 483–84

Franquelin, Jean-Baptiste, 258–59

Fraser, Simon, **334–35,** 369, 381

Freeman, Thomas, 276, **277–79**

Frémont, Jessie Benton, 318, **335,** 338

Frémont, John Charles, 300, 315, 318, 324, 325, 328, 332, 335, **336–39,** 342, 367, 371, 372, 381, 392

Freuchen, Peter, 476

Frisius, Gemma, 30

Frislanda, 54, 55

Frobisher, Martin, 44, 154, 161, 403, **431–32,** 466

Fuca, Juan de, **88–89,** 389. *See also* Juan de Fuca Strait

Fuertes, Louis Agassiz, 436

Fundy, Bay of, 126, 146, 151

Funk Island, 139, 141, **153–54,** 191

fur trade, 134, 251, 259, 267, 277, 302–3, 315–16, 317, 320, 332–33, 344, 346, 347, 353, 358–59, 362, 369

Fu-Sang, 9

Gali, Francisco, 65, 67, **90,** 105

Galiano, Dionisio Alcalá, 242

Galileo, 38

Galinée, René de Bréhant de, **272–73,** 291

Galvan, Juan, 202–3

Galvez, José de, 240

Gálvez, Berardo de, 213, 214
Garay, Francisco de, 128
Garcés, Father Francisco Tomás, 201, **216–17,** 340, 374, 382
Gass, Patrick, 355
Gastaldi, Giacomo, 29
Gates, C. M., 378
Gayón, Gonzalo, 192
Gayoso de Lemons, Manuel, 215
Genêt, Edmond, 296
George III, King, 264
Georgia, 149
Gibbs, George, 185
Gilbert, Adrian, 418–19
Gilbert, G. K., 330
Gilbert, Humphrey, 128, **154–55,** 161, 171–72, 418–19
Gist, Christopher, 252, **279–80,** 302
Gladwin, Harold S., 19
Glazunov, Andrei, **432,** 483
Glotov, S., 482
Gnupsson, Eirik, 51
Godfrey, Thomas, 43
Goetzmann, William, 326, 338, 352, 376, 380, 384, 390
gold, Spanish explorers' search for, 76, 86–87, 90–91, 96–98, 112–13, 252
Gómes, Estevåo, 30, 130, 140, **155–56,** 159, 466
González, Vicente, 148, **156–57,** 187
González de Avila, Gil, 93
Goodsell, John, 441, 473
Gordillo, Francisco, 130, 175–76
Gosnold, Bartholomew, 139, **157–58**
Grand Canyon, 74, 99, 329, **340,** 345, 349, 374, 378
Grand-Portage, 281
Grand Teton Mountains, **340–41**
Gravé du Pont, François, 145
Gray, Robert, 133, 220, 322, 326–27, **341,** 389
Great American Desert (Great Plains), **341–42,** 360, 365–66, 376
Great Lakes, 134, 147, 248, 263, 269, 273, 280–81, 304–5. *See also* Lake
Erie; Lake Huron; Lake Michigan; Lake Ontario; Lake Superior
Great Salt Lake, 234, 322, 370
Greeks, **19**
Greely, Adolphus, 424, **432–33**
Greenland, 10, 19, **20–21,** 22, 26, 44, 48, 49, 151, 171, 401, 409, 419, 423, 433, 434, 444, 447, 452, 453, 457, 461, 465, 484, 490
  in early maps, 27, 29, 52
  Norse people in, 20–21, 24–25
Green River, 326
Greenville, Treaty of, 271
Gregory, John, 362
Grenier, Chevalier, **217**
Grenville, Richard, **158–60,** 161, 178
Grijalva, Hernando de, 78
Grijalva, Juan de, 59, 76, 79, **90–91,** 93, 101, 127
Grinnell, George Bird, 436
Grosseilliers, Médard Chouart, Sieur des, 250, 251, **280–81,** 295, 308, 346
Gros Ventre Indians, **342**
Guadalajara, Diego de, **217–18,** 225, 227
Guadeloupe, 266
Guatemala, 60, 65
Gulf of Mexico, 95–96, 106, 127, 228–29, 235, 253, 255, 270, 283
  early maps of, 213–14, 215
  See also Cuba
Gulf Stream, 127, 175, 187
Gunnison, John W., 328, 371–72
Gutiérrez de Humaña, Antonio, **91–92**
Guzmán, Nuño de, 77, 78, 95
Gvozdev, Mikhail, 481–82

Hadley, John, 43
Haiti, 94–95
Hakluyt, Richard, 144, **160–61,** 164, 168
Hall, Charles Francis, **433–35,** 463, 483
Hall, James, 329
Hariot, Thomas, 159, **161**

Harriman, Edward Henry, **435–37**
Harrison, John, 43–44
Havana, Cuba, 79–80
Hawikuh pueblo, 58, 88, 97, 99,
    100–101, 113
Hawkins, John, 84, 86, 115, 163, 432
Hayden, Ferdinand Vandeveer, **343,**
    344–45, 388, 390, 391, 393
Hayes, Isaac, 424, **437–38,** 459, 463
Hearne, Samuel, 347, **438–40**
Helluland, **21,** 32, 403
Henday, Anthony, 313–14, **343–44,** 347
Hendricks, Cornelius, 31
Hennepin, Louis, 261, 274, **282–83,** 308
Henry IV, King, 145, 164–65
Henry VII, King, 13–14, 136, 151, 153,
    171, 181
Henry the Navigator, **21–22**
Henry, Andrew, 327, **344,** 358, 386
Henson, Matthew, 405, **440–43,** 451,
    472, 473
Hentry, William, 166
Herbert, Sir Wally, **443–44,** 464
Herjolfsson, Bjarni. *See* Bjarni
    Herjolfsson
Hernández de Córdoba, Francisco
    (explorer of Nicaragua), **93–94**
Hernández de Córdoba, Francisco
    (explorer of Yucatan), 76, 79, 90,
    91, **92–93,** 127
Hetch-Hetchy Valley, 369
Hezeta, Bruno de, 195, 205, 206,
    218–20, 230, 326, 341
Hillers, Jack, 380
Hind, Henry Youle, **372–73**
Hispaniola, 28, 47, 59, 61, 70, 79, 93,
    94–95, 103, 104, 114, 129, 135,
    174, 192
Hobson, William Robert, 453
Hochelaga, 142, 143, 144, **162,** 298. *See
    also* Montreal
Holmes, William (English colonist),
    173
Holmes, William H. (geologist-artist),
    329, 340, **344–45**

Homestead Act (1862), 342
Hood, Robert, 426
Hood, Samuel, 323
Hopi Indians, 87
Hopwood, Victor G., 388
Hore, Richard, **162**
Horseshoe Bend, Treaty of, 268
Hudson, Henry, 31, 271, 401, 410,
    444–45
Hudson, John, 444, 445
Hudson Bay, 138, 250, 281, 410,
    414–15, 445–46, 449–50
Hudson River, 145, 253
Hudson's Bay Company, 166, 331, 333,
    343, 344, **345–47,** 365, 374, 384,
    386, 455, 456, 485
  Campbell's work for, 413–14
  Coats's work for, 414–15
  Dease's work for, 420–21
  and Fort Vancouver, 327, 334
  founding of, 281, 345
  Hearne's work for, 347, 438–40
  Kelsey's work for, 289, 347
  Knight's work for, 449–50
  Ogden's work for, 347, 369–70
  Rae's work for, 474–75
Huguenots, 177, 256
Humboldt, Alexander von, 347
Humboldt River, 323, **347–48,** 369–70
Humphreys, Andrew A., 351, 391
Hunt, S. V., 257
Hunt, Wilson Price, 317, **348,** 349,
    365
Hunter, George, 276
Huron Indians, 133, 134, 146, 147,
    162–63, 298, 299
  Cartier's encounters with, 141, 142,
    143, 144, 163, 181–82
  missionaries to, 258, 285–87
Hurtado de Mendoza, Diego, 78
Hwui Shan, 9

Iberville, Pierre Le Moyne, Sieur d',
    253, **283–84,** 286, 289, 293, 294,
    305–6, 310

Iceland, 53, 68–69. *See also* Norse explorers
Illinois Indians, 259, 276, **284–85,** 288, 296
Incas, conquest of, 110
Indians. *See* Native Americans; Pueblo Indians; *and specific names of tribes*
Inglefield, Edward, 424
Ingram, David, **163–64**
Ingstad, Helge, 23
Inscription Rock (New Mexico), 107
Iriarte, Pedro de, 204, **235**
Irish explorers, **22**
Iroquois Indians, 163, 271, 286, 287
Irving, Washington, 320, **348–49**
Isabella, Queen, 69, 94, 109
Isla Mujeres (Mexico), 90
Ivanov, Vasily, 482
Ives, Joseph Christmas, 340, **349–50**

Jackson, Donald, 316, 386
Jackson, William Henry, 343, 393
Jamaica, 70, 103, 104
James I, King, 31, 177
James, Thomas, 345, 424, **445–46**
Jamestown, Va., 134, 148, 152, 158, 161, **164,** 183, 285
Jaredites, 16
Jarry, Jean, 222–23
Jefferson, Thomas, 32, 275–76, 277, 296, 311, **350,** 353, 354, 355, 358, 360–61, 365, 366, 385
Jensen, Rasmus, 467
Jerome, John, **164–65**
Jesuit missionaries, 259, 263, 269–70, 273, 277, 280, **285–86.** *See also* missions, French; missions, Spanish
Jesup, Morris, 472
Jiménez, Fortún, 78, **95**
Jogues, Isaac, 285–86, **286–87**
Johansen, Hjalmar, 458
John II, King, 69
Jolliet, Adrien, 272, 287, 302
Jolliet, Louis, 249, 259, 274, **287–88**

Jolliet and Marquette expedition, 249, 259, 285, **287–88,** 292, 295, 297, 298, 299, 368
Josselyn, John, 36
Juan de Fuca Strait, 89, 219, 227, 230, 234, 242–43
Julius II, Pope, 110
Jumano Indians, 116, 197, 217, 225, 227–28

Kamchatka Peninsula, 406–7
Kane, Elisha Kent, 424, 434, 437, 438, **446–47,** 463
Karlsveni, Thorfinn, 25, 51
Kashevarov, Alexander Filippovich, **448,** 483
Kaskaskia Indians, 276, 288
Kearny, Stephen Watts, 324, 330, 331
Keemle, Charles, 316
Kellett, Sir Henry, **448–49**
Kelsey, Henry, 249, **289,** 343, 347
Kendrick, John, 341
Kennedy, John F., 449
Kennewick Man, 35
Kensington Stone (Minnesota), 45
Kentucky, 257, 311–12
Kiawah Island, S.C., 183
Kilmovskii, A., 483
King, Clarence, 343, **351–52,** 368, 388, 390
King, Grace Elizabeth, 185
King-Hamy chart, 28
Kingittorsuaq, 51
King William Island, 416, 430, 434, 453, 465, 483–84
Kino, Eusebio Francisco, 105, **220–21,** 285
Kittanning Trail, 252
Knight, James, 346, **449–50**
Kolmakov, P., 483
Korsakovskiy, Petra, 483
Kotzebue, August von, 450
Kotzebue, Otto von, 202, **450,** 483
Krenitsyn, P. K., 482
Kromchenko, V. S., 483

Krusenstern, Adam Johann von, 450
Kyrre, Olaf, 51

Labrador, 10, 28, 32, 138, 139, **165–66,**
    181, 270, 288, 408, 415, 419, 452
Laclède, Pierre, 381
Lady in Blue. See Agreda, María de
    Jesus
Lafora, Nicolás de, 238, 239
La Gran Copala, 98
La Harpe, Jean-Baptiste Bénard, Sieur
    de, 254, **352–53**
Lahontan, Louis-Armand de Lom
    d'Arce, Baron de, 261, **290–91**
Lake Erie, 134, 262, 273
Lake Huron, 127, 133, 134, 145, 182,
    269, 273, 277
Lake Michigan, 269, 273, 299
Lake Ontario, 262, 273
Lake Superior, 134, 147, 260, 269,
    270
Lalement, Jerome, 302
Lane, Ralph, 148, 158–60, **166,** 179
L'Anse aux Meadows, **22–24,** 25, 44, 50,
    52, 171
La Pérouse, Jean-François Galaup,
    Comte de, 195, **221–22,** 440
Lara, Juan de, 149
Larios, Juan, **62**
Larsen, Henry, 492
La Salle, René Robert Cavelier, Sieur
    de, 290, **291–93,** 302
    explorations of, 249, 256, 259, 272,
        282, 294, 298
    search for, 105, 196, 203, 222–23,
        230–31, 235, 267
    and Tonty, 309–10
Laudonnière, René de, 134, **177–78**
Lavazares, Guido de, **95–96,** 105
Lavashev, M. D., 482
La Vérendrye, Pierre Gaultier Varenne,
    Sieur de, 298, 321, **353,** 368
Lederer, John, 130, 132, **167,** 193
Ledyard, John, 350
legendary destinations, 59, 59, **96–98.**

See also Antilia; Cibola; Norum-
    bega; Quivira; Saguenay
Leif Eriksson, 10, 19, 21, 23, **24–25,** 32,
    49, 50, 51, 52
Lenapé Indians. See Delaware Indians
Leo X, Pope, 110
León, Alonso de, 105, **222–23,** 231, 238,
    243
Le Sueur, Pierre-Charles, 271, **293–94,**
    305, 308
Lewis, Meriwether, 278, 296, 315, 325,
    353–58
Lewis and Clark expedition, 32, 36,
    275, 294, 314, 315, 319, 325–26,
    327, 348, 350, **354–58,** 360–61,
    365, 366, 368, 381
Leyva de Bonilla, Francisco, **91–92**
*Liang-shu (Records of the Liang
    Dynasty),* 9
Libyans, **26**
Linnaeus, Carl, 253
Lippershey, Hans, 38
Lisa, Manuel, 326, 344, **358–59**
Litwin, Thomas, 436–37
Llanos, Francisco de, 223
Lloyd, Thomas, 13
Loaysa, Jofre García de, 77
Lockwood, James, 433
Lok, Michael, 89
Long, Stephen H., 278, 328, 341,
    359–60, 367, 376, 381
Look, Miriam Norton, 452
López, Andrés, 217
López, Baltasar, 149
López, Diego, **116**
López, Fray Francisco, 115–16
López, Fray Nicolás, 225, **227–28**
López de Cárdenas, García, 74, **99,**
    340
López de Gamarra, Francisco, 204,
    230–31
López de Haro, Gonzalo, 234
Loring, Frederick, 390
Los Diamantes, 98
Louis XIV, King, 294

Louisiana, 238, 275–76, **294,** 310, 354, 358
  boundary with Texas, 294–95
  French explorers in, 253–55, 259, 263, 266–67, 271, 276, 283–84, 297–98
  Spanish claims to, 207, 215
Louisiana Purchase, 294, 350, 354, **360–61,** 366, 381
Luna y Arellano, Tristán de, 74, 75, 80, **167–68,** 191–92

MacDougall, Duncan, 365
Mackay, James, **361**
Mackenzie, Alexander, 314, 315, 335, **361–65,** 377, 381
Mackenzie, Donald, 341, 348, **365**
MacMillan, Donald B., 405, 411, 441, **450–52,** 473
Macomb, John M., **349–50**
Madeira Islands, 12
Madoc, Prince, 53
Magellan, Ferdinand, 138, 155, 188
magnetic North Pole, 397, 460, 461, 478
Magnus, Olaus, 47
Malakhov, V., 483
Malaspina, Alejandro, 89, 195, **224–25,** 242
Mallet, Paul, 255, **365–66**
Mallet, Pierre, 255, **365–66**
Mandan Indians, 54, 83
Manifest Destiny, **366–67**
Manila galleons, 65, 67, 85, 90, 118, 121
Manoel I, King, 150, 151
Manso y Suniga, Francisco, 197
Manteo, 129
Map Rock (Idaho), 37
maps of North America, early, **26–32,** 37, 68, 119, 128, 156, 213–14, 249. *See also* Corps of Topographical Engineers; Cosa, Juan de la; Piri Reis map; U.S. Geological Survey; Vinland Map

Marcos de Niza, 60, 73, 80, 88, 97, **99–101,** 105, 113
Marcy, Randolph Barnes, 360, **367**
Markland, **32,** 166. *See also* Labrador
Marquette, Jacques, 249, 259, 269, 273, 277, 286, **287–88**
Marston, Thomas A., 52
Martín, Hernando, 217, **225**
Martínez, Esteban José, 195, **225–27,** 229–30, 234
Martinique, 70
Martyr, Peter, 138, 156, **168**
Marvin, Ross, 473
Massachusetts, 133, 138–39
Massachusetts Bay, 30
Massachusetts Bay Colony, 133
Matagorda Bay, 96, 199, 200, 204, 217, 223, 243, 253, 292, 293
Matonabbee, 439
Maya Indians, 90, 92–93
Mazandarani, Shaikh Zayn-eddine Ali ben Fadhel Al-, 33
Mazanet, Damián, 223, 243
McClintock, Francis Leopold, 425, 448, **452–53,** 483
McClure, Robert John Le Mesurier, 409, 416, 417, 448–49, **454–55,** 468, 489
McGillivray, Alexander, 268
McGregory, Patrick, 304
McLean, John, 166
McLoughlin, John, 334
Meadowcroft rock shelter (Pennsylvania), 35
Meares, John, 227, 234
Medici, Lorenzo de', 28, 119
Meldgaard, Jørgen, 23
Mel'nikov, A., 482
Membré, Zenobius, 292
Mendoza, Antonio de, 60, 73, 75, 78, 88, 100, 101, 104, 105
Mendoza, Juan Domínguez de, 225, **227–28**
Menéndez de Avilés, Pedro, 80, 148, 153, **168–70,** 173, 178, 183, 285

Menéndez Marquez, Pedro, 148, 156, 170
Mercator, Gerardus, 30, 31
Merriam, C. Hart, 436
Mexicana, 225, **242–43**
Mexican War, 330–31
Mexico
    early exploration of, 59, 76–78, 79–80, 90–93, 101–2
    possible African contacts with, 7
    See also New Spain
Mexico, Gulf of. *See* Gulf of Mexico
Mézières, Athanase de, **294–95**
Miami Indians, **295–96**
Michaux, André, **296–97**
Michaux, François-André, 296–97
Michikinikwa, 295
Micmac Indians, 131, 136, 140
Middleton, Christopher, 346, **455–56**
Minnesota, 274
Mission Dolores, 202, 241
missions, French, 248, 250, 258, 269–70, 272–73, 285–86
missions, Spanish, 156, 170, 196, 197, 216–17, 233, 285
    in California, 216, 231–33, 240–42
    in Texas, 198–99, 202–3, 209, 212–13, 228
    See also Serra, Father Junípero
Mississippi Delta, 204, 230–31, 254, 283–84
Mississippi Mound culture, 18, 259, 268
Mississippi River, 128, 213, 256, 260, 295, **297–98,** 301–2, 308, 330, 354, 367, 375, 377
    French exploration of 249, 254–55, 263, 265, 267, 271, 275, 282–83, 283–84, 287–88, 290, 299
    La Salle's exploration of, 291–93, 297–98
    Le Sueur's exploration of, 293–94
    de Soto's exploration of, 125, 186, 294
    source of, 297–98, 300, 307

Missouri Fur Company, 358
Missouri River, 215, 266, 271, 276, 294, 296, 297, 300, 308, 315, 320–321, 325, 326, 348, 353, 354, 361, 365–66, **367–68,** 376
Mitchell, John, 249
Mixton War, 58, 60
Mobile Bay (Alabama), 96
Moctezuma, 59, 76, 107
Mohawk Trail, 251–52
Moluccas, 117
Montejo, Francisco, **101–2**
Monterey, Calif., 201–2, 214–15, 216, 222, 230, 232–33
Monterey Bay (California), 121, 122
Monte Verde (Chile), 35
Montreal, Canada, 143, 144, 162, 262, 273, 291, **298,** 303
Monts, Pierre du Gua de, 146
Moor, William, 346, **456–57**
Moraga, José Joaquín, 201, 202
Moran, Edward, 444
Moran, Thomas, 393
Morgues, Jacques le Moyne de, 134
Morison, Samuel Eliot, 13, 72, 126, 136, 138, 141, 150–51, 181, 191
Moscoso Alvarado, Luís de, **102–3,** 186
Mothe, Gillaume de la, 164–65
Mount Hood, 323, 387
Mount McKinley, 417
Mount St. Helens, 323
Mourelle de la Rúa, Francisco Antonio, 205, 206
Moyano, Hernando, 173–74
Muir, John, **368–69,** 436
Munck, Jens, 467
Munn, William A., 23
Murphy, Martin, 323
Muskogee Indians, 267
Muslims, **32–33**
Mystery Hill (New Hampshire), 14, 15

Nagibin, P., 482
Nansen, Fridtjof, 408, **457–59,** 462–63, 490

Napoleon Bonaparte, 225, 267

Naranjo, José, 244, 247

Nares, George Strong, **459–60,** 463

Narragansett Indians, 189–90

Narváez, Pánfilo de, 59, 62, 64–65, 77, 79, 88, **103–4,** 268

National Geographic Society, 433

Native Americans, **33–37**
impact of disease on, 80–84, 126, 127, 206, 258, 342
maps provided by, 29–30, 31–32, 36–37
See also Pueblo Indians; *and specific names of tribes*

Nautilus, USS, 399–400, 461, 464

navigation, **37–44**
challenges of in northern latitudes, 400, 460, 461
instruments used in 41–44
latitude and longitude as determined in early days of, 41–42, 43–44, 345
by Norse explorers, 38–39
units of measure used in, 38–40

Nearchus, Admiral, 19

Needham, James, 132, **170,** 194

Needham and Arthur expedition, 130, **170–71**

Nemacolin (Delaware chief), 252, 280

Newberry, John Strong, 349–50

New England, 133, 138–39, 157–58, 173, 184, 259

Newfoundland, 13–14, 23, 28, 29, **44,** 49, 55, 117, 120, 123, 150, 151, 165, **171–72,** 180, 181, 208
Beothuk Indians in, 131–32
Cabot's exploration of, 136–37, 138, 171
Cartier's exploration of, 139–40
Gilbert's voyage to, 154–55
See also Vinland

New France, 133, **172,** 182, 250, 259, 263, 270, 275, 285–86, 287, 303.
See also Cartier, Jacques; Champlain, Samuel de

New Mexico, 86–87, 115–16, 122, 217–18, 223, 245–47

New Orleans, La., 298, 299

Newport, Christopher, 132, 164

Newport Tower (Rhode Island), 46, 48

New Spain, 62, **104–5,** 149, 197, 200, 229, 259. *See also* Cortés, Hernán; Mexico

New Zealand, 208

Niagara Falls, 272, 282

Nicaragua, 93–94

Nicolet, Jean, 251, **298–99**

Nicollet, Joseph Nicolas, **299–300,** 330, 336–37

Nobile, Umberto, 399, 464

Nolan, Philip, **300–301**

Nootka Convention of 1790, 226, 227

Nootka Sound, 208, 225–27, 230

Nordenskjöld, Nils, 399

Norse explorers, 10–11, 18–19, 26, **45–46,** 403, 424, 487
alleged runic inscriptions of, 45–46
in Greenland, 20–21
at L'Anse aux Meadows, 22–24
in Markland, 32
navigational devices used by, 38–39
See also Bjarni Herjolfsson; Erik the Red; Leif Eriksson; Newfoundland; skraelings; Vinland; Vinland Map

North America
conflict between France and Spain over, 196, 199, 203, 247, 292
as depicted in art, 134–35, 159, 262
disputed claims for pre-Columbian contacts with, 6–7, 8–9, 11–12, 14–15, 16–17, 18, 19, 22, 26, 32–33, 46, 53–55
early maps of, 26–32, 37, 68, 119
first human occupation of, 33–36, 402–3
naturalists in, 252–53, 261–62, 277–78, 296–97, 436–37

North Carolina, 135, 152, 173, 176. *See also* Blue Ridge Mountains; Outer Banks

North Pole, 409, **460–64,** 477–78, 492
  Byrd's flight over, 412, 464
  Cook's expedition to, 417–18, 444,
    463
  Hall's expedition to, 434
  Henson's travels to, 440–43
  Herbert's expedition to, 443–44
  magnetic, 397, 460, 461, 478
  Nansen's expedition to, 458, 463, 490
  Peary's expeditions to, 404–5, 418,
    443, 444, 451, 463, 472–74
  race to, 394, 398, 399–400, 463–64
North West Company, 298, 331, 333,
    334, 347, 348, 362, 363, 365, **369,**
    378, 386, 420, 456–57
Northwest Passage, 13, 30, 61, 139, 161,
    206, 229, 269, 299, 303–4, 345–46,
    416–17, 425, 430, 438, 440, 449,
    453, **464–69,** 476, 484, 485
  Cook's search for, 208–9
  Davis's search for, 418–20
  Foxe's search for, 424–25
  Frobisher's search for, 431–32, 466
  Gilbert's search for, 154, 155
  Hudson's search for, 444–45
  Malaspina's search for, 224–25,
    242–43
  McClure's search for, 417, 448, 454,
    455, 468
  Middleton's search for, 455–56
  Moor's search for, 456–47
  navigators' versus visionaries' con-
    cept of, 464–65
  Parry's search for, 469–71
  Rut's search for, 181, 466
  search for northern route of, 396,
    397–98, 401, 409, 410
  Waymouth's search for, 192–93
  See also Cartier, Jacques
Norton, Moses, 438–39
Norumbega, 98, **172–72**
Nova Scotia, 123, 126, 137, 146, 156,
    171, 263
Noyon, Jacques de, **301,** 303
Nuevo Reyno de León, 66

Ocampo, Sebastián, 79, **105–6**
Ogden, Peter Skene, 347, **369–70**
Ohio Company, 279–80
Ohio River, 163, 253, 257, 262, 263,
    266, 272, 279, 280, 291, **301–2,**
    311, 354
Ojeda, Alonso de, 78, 79, **106,** 110
Oklahoma Territory, Indians relocated
    to, 163, 264, 265, 268, 271, 296
Oldham, John, 133, **173**
Olid, Cristóbal de, 76, 77, 91
Olivares, Fray Antonio de San
    Buenaventura y, 199, **212–13,**
    228
Oliveriana Map, 13, 28
Olmec Indians, 7
Olympic Peninsula (Washington
    State), 88–89
Ommanney, Erasmus, 430
Oñate, Cristóbal, 107
Oñate, Juan de, 87, 92, 98, 105, **107–9,**
    114, 116, 122
Onondaga Indians, 269
Oregon Trail, 317, 318, 319, 328, 333,
    335, 348, **370–71,** 374, 377, 384,
    385, 386
Oregon Treaty of 1846, 334
Orkney Islands, 48
Ortega, José Francisco, 232
Ortega, Pedro de, 116
Ortelius, Abraham, 30–31
Ortiz Parrilla, Diego, **228–29**
Osage Indians, 277
O'Sullivan, John, 366
O'Sullivan, Timothy, 351, 388, 390
Ottawa Indians, 147
Ottawa River, 31, 127, 133
Ouachita River, 276, 306
Outer Banks (North Carolina), 129,
    152, 160, 161, 188–89
Ovando, Nicolás de, 106

Pacific Fur Company, 316, 365, 384
Pacific Ocean, 296
  Balboa's sighting of, 61, 117

Cook's exploration of, 207–8
See also California
Pacific Railroad surveys, 328, **371–72,**
  389–90
Painter, George D., 52
Palliser, John, **372–73**
Palou, Father Francisco, 202, 237
Panama, 61, 71
papal bulls, **109–10**
Paquiquineo, 187
Pardo, Juan, 98, 149, 169, **173–74,** 252,
  264
Pareja, Francisco, 149
Parke, John G., 372
Parker, Samuel, **373–74**
Parry, Sir William Edward, 427, 454,
  463, **469–71,** 477, 478, 479, 480, 484
Pasqualigo, Lorenzo, 136, 137
Passamaquoddy Indians, 125
Pattie, James Ohio, 340, **374–75**
Pattie, Sylvester, 374–75
Patton, James, 311
Peale, Titian, 360
Peary, Robert Edwin, 398, 404–5, 417,
  418, 424, 440–42, 451, 463,
  471–74, 490
Pecos pueblo, 74
Pemisapan, 160
Penn, William, 271
Pennacook Indians, 125
Penobscot Indians, 125
Penobscot River, 165, 172–73
Peré, Jean, 287, **302–3**
Pérez, Juan José Pérez Hernández, 195,
  208, 226, **229–30**
Pérez de Luxán, Diego, 87
Perrot, Nicolas, 270
Peru, exploration of, 110
Peter the Great, 406, 481
Peterborough Stone (Peterborough,
  Ontario), 17
Pez, Andrés de, 204, **230–31**
Philip IV, King, 198
Philippines, 60, 96, 104, 117. *See also*
  Manila galleons

Phoenicians, 14, **46**
Pierce, Franklin, 371
Pike, Zebulon, 266, 297, 298, 341–42,
  360, **375–76,** 381
Pilcher, Joshua, 384
Pineda, Alonso Alvarez de, 128
Pining, Didrik, **46–47**
Pinzon, Martin, 33
Pinzon, Vincente, 33
Piri Reis map, **47,** 72
Pizarro, Francisco, 60, 79, 99, 106, **110,**
  184
Pizarro, Gonzalo, 110
Pizarro, Hernando, 110
Pizarro, Juan, 110
Pizzi Nautical Chart of 1424, 7–8
Platte River, 320, 321, 324, 337, 355,
  360, 370, **376–77**
Pocahontas, 183
Poinsett, Joel, 336
Polk, James, 446
Polo, Marco, 61
Ponce de León, Juan, 80, 92, 93, 114,
  127, 152–53, **174–75**
Pond, Peter, 314, 331, 362, 363, 369,
  377–78
Ponomarev, S., 482
Pontiac, assassination of, 285
Pope, John, 372
popes, 109–10, 116–17
Popov, Feodor Alekseev, 423, 481
Portolá, Gaspar de, 105, 214–15,
  231–33, 237, 240
Port Royal Sound, 177, 192, 194
Portugal
  and papal bulls, 109–110
  and Treaty of Tordesillas, 116–18
Posada, Alonso de, **233–34**
Possession, Spanish Act of, **110–12**
Pothorst, Hans, **46–47**
Potts, John, 326
Powell, Emma Dean, 378
Powell, John Wesley, 315, 329, 330, 340,
  343, 352, **378–80,** 388, 390, 391
Powhatan, 183

Preuss, Charles, 336, 339
Prince Edward Island, 140, 156
Prince William Sound, 225, 226
Ptolemy, 27, 29
Pueblo Indians, 59, 64, 80, 86–87, 92, 107, **112–14,** 115
   and Coronado's men, 74, 75
   rebellions of, 98, 99, 108, 114, 244
Puerto Rico, 104, **114–15,** 127, 128, 152, 159, 174
Pyne, Stephen J., 330

quadrants, 42
Quebec, 142, 172, 208
Queen Charlotte Sound, 89
Quejo, Pedro de, 148, **175–76,** 187, 270
Quimper, Manuel, 227, **234–35**
Quinn, David B., 13, 162, 181, 186
Quirós, Luís de, 148
Quivira, 59, 74–75, 97, 98, 108, 113

Radisson, Pierre Esprit, 250, 251, **280–81,** 308, 346
Rae, John, 430, **474–76**
Rafn, Carl, 23
railroads, 328, 340, 367, 371–72
Raleigh, Sir Walter, 128, 154, 158–59, 160–61, 166, **176–77,** 178, 179
Ramón, Domingo, 200, 212, 306
Rasmussen, Knud Johan Victor, **476**
Rastell, John, 466
Raymbaut, Charles, 286
Raynolds, William F., 322, 343, 393
Red River, 275–76, 277, 278, 279, 306, 352, 360
Rhode Island, 189
Ribaut, Jean, 134, 160, **177–78**
Ribeiro, Diogo, 30
Richardson, Sir John, 475
Richelieu, Cardinal, 148
Richmond, Va., 135
Rickover, Hyman, 399
Río de Paploapán, 59
Río Grande, 58, 62, 66, 75, 122, 197, 211–12, 222, 228, 231

Rivas, Martín de, 204, 231, **235**
Rivera, Juan María de, **235–36**
Rivera, Pedro de, **236–37,** 238
Rivera y Moncada, Fernando de, 215, 232, **237**
Rivera y Villalón, Pedro de, 203
Roanoke Colony, 86, 134, 148, 157, 158, 159–60, 165, 166, 177, **178–80**
Roanoke Indians, 129, 159–60
Roberval, Jean-François de la Roque, Sieur de, 144–45, **180–81,** 477
Robutel de la Noue, Zacharie, **303**
Rocky Mountain Fur Company, 316, 322, 332, 344, 382, 386
Rocky Mountains, 270, 308, 325, 327, 337, 344, 358–59, 375, **380–81,** 383, 384
   Jefferson's interest in, 350, 353, 354, 355
   Long's expedition to, 328, 359–60
   Oregon Trail through, 370–71
Rocque, Bertrand, 152, **164–65**
Rodríguez, Fray Agustín, 86–87, 105, 113, **115–16**
Rogers, Robert, 260–61, **303–4**
Romero, Antonio, 204
Roosevelt, Franklin D., 418
Roque, Marguerite de la, **477**
Roseboom, Johannes, **304–5**
Rosier, James, 193
Ross, Sir James Clark, 397, 428, 460, **477–78**
Ross, Sir John, 401, 469–70, 477, **478–80,** 484
Ru, Paul Du, 286
Rubí, María Pignatelli Rubí Corbera y San Climent, Marqués de, **238–39**
Russian-American Company, 403, 482, 483, 490–91
Russians in North America, 396, 403, 405–7, 423–24, 432, 448, 450, **480–83**
Rut, John, 166, **181,** 466
Ruysch, Johann, 28–29
Ryswick, Treaty of, 94

Saavedra Ceron, Alvaro, 77
Sacagawea, 36, 356
"The Saga of the Greenlanders," 10, 21, 25, 32, 49–50
Sagean, Mathieu, **305–6**
Saguenay, 98, 142, 143–44, 180, **181–82**
Saguenay River, 142
St. Augustine, Fla., 86, 151, 152, 153, 165, 169
Saint-Denis, Louis Juchereau de, 254, 259, 271, **306**
St. John's River (Florida), 164, 178
St. Lawrence River, 25, 31, 125, 133, 139, 140, 142, 145, 162, 172, 177, 180, 181, **182**, 208, 251, 258, 263, 269, 288, 298
St. Lawrence, Gulf of, 141, 181, 188
St. Louis, Mo., 215, 259, 266, 286, 299, 318, **381–82**
Saint Vrain, Ceran, 318
Salas, Gaspar de, **149–50**
Salas, Juan de, **116**, 198
Salcedo, Juan Manuel de, 207
Saldivar, Juan de, 80
San Antonio, Texas, 198, 199, 199–200, 228
Sandford, Robert, **182–83**, 194
San Francisco Bay (California), 122, 219
San Francisco de Asis mission, 202, 241
San Francisco, Calif., 201–2, 219
San Gabriel Arcángel mission, 201, 216
San Juan Islands, 235
San Juan pueblo, 107
San Miguel Island, 65, 67
San Salvador, 69–70
Santa Fe, N.Mex., 109, 218
Santangel, Luís de, 27
Santiago (Indian chief), 211
Saravia, Fray Tomás de la Peña, 230
Sarychev, G. A., 482
Sault Sainte Marie, 250, 270, 286
Savannah River, 182, 183
Scaggs, Henry, 268
Schoolcraft, Henry Rowe, 298, 300, **307**

Schumann, Emil, 434
Schwatka, Frederick, **483–84**
Scolvus (Skolp), Johannes, 47, **48**
Scoresby, William, Jr., **484–85**
Scott, Robert, 398
Scroggs, John, 289
Seaton, Alfred, 320
Seaver, Kirsten, 53
Segura, Juan Baptista de, 148, 285
Seminole Indians, 268
Seneca Indians, 134
Sequoyah, 264
Serra, Father Junípero, 196, 202, 216, 218–19, 230, 232–33, **239–42**
Seven Cities of Cibola. *See* Cibola
Seven Years' War, 250, 280
Seward, William H., 483
sextants, 43
Seymour, Samuel, 359–60
Shan Hai Ching (Classic of the Mountains and Rivers), 9
Shanawdithit, 131–32
Shelikof, Gregory, 482
Sherlikhov, G. I., 482
Shishmaryov, G., 483
Shoshone Indians, 356
Sidney, Sir Henry, 154
Sidney, Sir Philip, 161
Sierra Azul, 98
Sierra Nevada, 318–19, 338, 351, 372, **382**, 383
Sigüenza y Góngora, Carlos, 203, 204, 231
Simpson, James H., 367
Simpson, Thomas, 347, 421, 422, **485–86**
Sinclair, Henry, **48**
Sioux Indians, 260, 281, 282, 286, 293, 298, 303, **307–8**, 333, 337
Skelton, R. A., 52
skraelings, 24, **49**, 51, 131, 132
smallpox, 80–81, 82–83, 126
Smet, Pierre de, 286
Smith, Francis, 456
Smith, Henry Nash, 358

Smith, James, 268
Smith, Jedediah, 315, 316, 327, 332, 334, 344, 370, 382, **382–84**, 385, 386
Smith, John, 31, 125, 148, 156, 164, **183–84**
Snake River, 326, 327
Society of Jesus. *See* Jesuit missionaries
Society of Merchant Venturers (Bristol, England), 14
Sokoki Indians, 125
Soncino, Raimondo de, 137
Soto, Hernando de, 64, 80, 98, 102, 125, 149, 167, **184–86**, 249, 252, 264, 265, 268, 294, 297
South Carolina, 176, 182–83
South Pass, Wyo., 332, 344, 370, 383, 384
South Pole. *See* Antarctica
Spanberg, Martin, 406
Spanish-American War, 115
Sparks, Thomas, 350
Speculum historiale, 52
Spotswood, Alexander, 132–33, 261, **309**
Squanto, 36
Stansbury, Howard, 322
Stefansson, Vilhjalmur, 395, 405, **486–89**, 492
Stegner, Wallace, 330
Stevens, Elisha, 323
Stevens, Isaac, 371
Stine, Anne, 23
Stuart, David, 384
Stuart, John, 256
Stuart, Robert, 316, 319, 327, 333, 349, 376–77, 383, **384–85**
Sublette, William, 316, 333, **386**, 393
Suckley, George, 371
Suleiman the Magnificent, Sultan, 47
Sulpician missionaries, 272–73
Sumner, Jack, 379
surveyors. *See* Corps of Topographical Engineers; King, Clarence; Thompson, David; U.S. Geological Survey

Susquehanna Indians, 133–34
Susquehanna River, 148, 157
Sútil, 225, **242–43**
Sutter, John Augustus, 319, 483
Sverdrup, Otto, 408, 443, 458, 472, **490**
syphilis, 84

Talon, Jean, 250, 270
Talon, Pierre, 223
Tamanend (Delaware chief), 271
Tampico, Mexico, 66
Taos pueblo, 112
Tarabal, Sebastian, 201
Tartars, 36
Teben'kov, Mikhail Dimitrivich, 483, **490–91**
Teguayo, 97, 98
Tejas Indians, 198, 199, 212–13, 225, 239
telescope, invention of, 38
Tenochtitlán, 76
Terán de los Ríos, Domingo de, 204, **243–44**
Texas
  boundary with Louisiana, 294–95
  early maps of, 203
  missions in, 198–99, 202–3, 209, 212–13, 228
  Spanish exploration of, 197–200, 203–4, 209, 211–13, 225, 227–28, 238–39, 243–44
Thayer, Helen, 464
Thompson, David, 327, 331, 335, 347, 368, 369, 381, **386–88**
Thorstein Eriksson, 25, 51
Thorvald Eriksson, 25
Thorvaldsson, Eirik. *See* Erik the Red
Tieve, Diego de, 22
Tiguex settlements, 59, 74–75, 113
tobacco, 143
Tolstykh, A., 482
Tonty, Henri, 268, 274, 284, 291, 292, 305, **309–10**
Tordesillas, Treaty of, 109–10, **116–18**
Toscanelli, Paolo, 8, 27, 69

Továr, Pedro de, 74, 99
traverse board, 43
Trinidad, 70
Troyes, Chevalier de, 303
Truckee River route, 323
Truteau, Jean Baptiste, 361, 381
Tryggvason, King Olaf, 24
the Turk (Indian guide), 36, 74, 97
Turnor, Philip, 331, 347, 378, 386
Tute, James, 260, 304
Twide, Richard, 164

Uemura, Naomi, 464
Ulloa, Francisco de, 78, 105, **118**
Unamuno, Pedro de, 65, 67, 90, 105, **118–19**
U.S. Geological Survey, 328, 329, 343, 345, 350, 380, **388,** 391
Urdaneta, Andrés de, 65, 77
Uribarri, Juan de, **244**
Urrutia, José de, 238
Utah, 97, 210, 235–36. *See also* Great Salt Lake
Ute Indians, 210, 245

Valdés, Cayetano, 242
Valerianos, Apóstolos. *See* Fuca, Juan de
Valle, Juan de, 77
Valverde y Cosio, Antonio, **245–46,** 247
Vancouver, George, 89, 242, 322, 323, 326, 364, **389**
Vancouver Island (British Columbia), 88–89, 208, 242, 341
Van der Gucht, M., 223
Van Sertima, Ivan, 6–7
Vargas, Diego José de, 98, 244, **246–47**
Vasil'ev, Ivan Yakovlevich, 483, **491**
Vasil'ev, Mikhail Nikolaevich, 483, **491–92**
Velasco, Diego de, 170
Velasco, Fray Francisco de, 108
Velasco, Luís de, 105
Velasco, Pedro, 22
Velasco map, 31, 47

Velázquez, Antonio, 148, **187**
Velázquez, Diego, 59, 76–77, 79, 90, 91, 93, 103
Verascola, Francisco de, 149
Verrazano, Giovanni da, 30, 44, 124, 125–26, 128, 139, 153, 155–56, 158, 160, 172, 181, **187–91,** 270, 466
Verrazano, Girolamo, 30, 172
Verrazano, Hieronimo, 190
Vespucci, Amerigo, 28, 78, 106, **119–20**
Viele, Arnold, **310–11**
Villafañe, Angel de, 105, 168, 187, **191–92**
Villasur, Pedro de, 244, **247**
Vinland, 21, 22, 23, 24, 25, 26, 32, **49–52.** *See also* Newfoundland; skraelings
Vinland Map, 26, **52–53**
Virginia, 31, 134, 135, 158–59, 167, 176–77, 183, 193, 309
Vizcaíno, Sebastián, 31, 62, 65, 67, 105, **120–22,** 240
Voltaire, 263

Waldseemüller, Martin, 28, 119
Walker, John, 172
Walker, Joseph Reddeford, 319, 320, 347–48, 382
Walker, Thomas, 133, 252, 268–69, **311–12**
Wanchese, 129
Warin, Joseph, 266
Warren, Gouverneur Kemble, 328, 343, **389–90**
Watts, John, 179
Waymouth, George, **192–93**
Webber, John, 208
Welch, Thomas, **312**
Welsh, **53–54**
Weyprecht, Karl, 422
Wheeler, George, 388, **390–91**
Whipple, Amiel W., 367, 372
White, Elijah, 332
White, John, 134, 159, 178, 179, 180

Whitman, Marcus, 332, 374
Whitman, Narcissa, 332
Whitney, Harry, 418
Wichita Indians, 97, 277
Wichita, Kans., 59
Wilderness Road (Boone's Trace), 257, 269
Wilkes, Charles, 334, 367, **392**
Wilkins, Hubert, **492**
Wilkinson, James, 300–301, 324–25, 375–76
Wilkinson, Ralph, 21
Willard, Simon, 133
Williams, Ezekiel, 359
Wilson, Harold, 443–44
Winnipesaukee, Lake, 32
Winslow, Edward, 173
Witten, Laurence C., 52
Wolfe, James, 208
Wood, Abraham, 130, **132**, 170, **193–94**
Woodward, Henry, 183, **194**
Wrangel, Ferdinand, 491
Wyandot Indians, 163
Wyeth, Nathaniel, 133, 333, 334, 370–71

Xapira, 98

Yamasee War, 268
Yeamans, John, 182
Yellowstone expeditions, 343, 344, 359, **393**
Yellowstone National Park, 326, 343, 344, 359, 386, 393
Yosemite National Park, 368
Yosemite Valley, 368
Young, Ewing, 324, 374
Ysopete, 97
Yucatan peninsula, 90–91, 92–93, 101–2, 127, 211

Zagoskin, L. A., 483
Zaldívar, Juan de, 122
Zaldívar, Vicente de, 107–8, **122**
Zaltierri, 61
Zárate, Ascencio de, 116
Zeno brothers (Antoni and Nicolo), 48, **54–55**
Zeno, Nicolo, 54
Zheng He, 8
Zuni Indians, 88
Zuni pueblo, 58, 87, 96, 100, 112, 113, 246